Austria

Nicholas T. Parsons

D0332716

BLUE GUIDE

A&C Black • London
WW Norton • New York

914. 360453 PAR

4th edition, July 2000
Published by A & C Black (Publishers) Limited
35 Bedford Row, London WC1R 4JH

1st–3rd editions © Ian Robertson
4th edition Nicholas T. Parsons © 2000

Maps drawn by RJS Associates, David Langworth (p 369), © A & C Black
Illustrations © Piotr Turnau

A CIP catalogue record of this work is available from the British Library.

ISBN 0–7136–4831–7

Published in the United States of America by WW Norton and Company Inc.
500 Fifth Avenue, New York NY 10110

Published simultaneously in Canada by Penguin Books Canada Limited,
10 Alcorn Avenue, Toronto, Ontario M4V 3B2

ISBN 0–393–32017–0 USA

Nicholas T. Parsons is the author of numerous guidebooks devoted to the Central European region, including the *Blue Guide Vienna*. He has also written or compiled five books on cultural topics, is a translator, editor and an occasional contributor to the *Hungarian Quarterly*.

Cover picture: House façade, Salzburg by Phil Robinson
Title-page illustration: Romerzeitlicher 'Seelenwagen' ins Jenseits, Maria Saal

Printed in Great Britain by Butler & Tanner Ltd, Frome and London.

Contents

Maps and plans

Introduction

This fourth edition of the *Blue Guide Austria* has undergone a radical transformation, for which some explanation may be helpful. Like other nation states of Europe, modern Austria represents a politically unified and cumulative reality, a reality derived from its component areas with their distinctive historical, economic and cultural traditions. At the same time, it is the surviving German Austrian core of a once great and far-flung polity encompassing many different nationalities. The centralising tendencies of the Habsburgs (most intense from the age of the Enlightenment onwards) were a response to the challenge of keeping a polyglot empire intact, and in some cases they implied an element of imposed Austrian Catholic culture (for example, the Baroque architecture of Prague). The 'Austrian' core territories, however, were German speaking and often divided up amongst the Habsburgs themselves. As former hereditary lands, they have preserved their distinctive roles and cultural profiles, even if their histories and traditions also combine and overlap in many respects.

This individuality has been respected in the constitution of the Austrian Republic (existing since 1920, although under Nazi rule between 1938 and 1945 and allied occupation to 1955), which is that of a Federal State (*Bundesstaat*) with nine Federal Provinces (*Bundesländer*). Each of the *Länder* was a historic component of the Habsburg patrimony except Burgenland, which was part of Hungary (though with a majority of German-speaking inhabitants) until 1919. In most cases, the individual *Länder* also look back to a pre-Habsburg era when they were ruled by local dynasties, or were administered by an Archbishopric, or (even further in the mists of time) were part of the Carolingian order of palatinates. At a time of revival in regional consciousness within the European Union (one thinks of the slogan 'Europe of the Regions'), it seems appropriate that a modern guide should heed and respect the dignity of difference, not least because this approach may hopefully illuminate Austrian history and culture.

With this in mind, the arrangement of the text based on driving routes that largely ignored provincial boundaries has been replaced in this edition with nine different sections dealing respectively with the nine *Bundesländer*. In addition every *Land* is prefaced by a concise analysis of its **topography**, **climate and environment**, **economy** and **history**. The descriptive tour then begins with the provincial capital, and thereafter guides the traveller out into the hinterland along easily identifiable routes. In many cases (typically *Lower Austria* and *Upper Austria*) there are also geographical sub-regions (**Weinviertel**, **Innviertel**, **Salzkammergut**, etc.), which are very much part of an Austrian's mental furniture, and these too have been covered in a way that attempts to evoke their individual character.

In a guide as detailed as this, which covers many out of the way places reached by minor roads, it seems not unreasonable to make driving the basis of route indication. However, all the larger places in Austria are accessible by the very efficient *Österreichische Bundesbahnen* (*ÖBB*, Austrian Federal Railways), while the smaller places between them are well covered by a network of buses (see p 20). Even so, considerable time would be required to travel by bus to the most isolated places described; the motorist enjoys the huge advantage that the *Autobahnen* criss-cross the country from west to east, and from north to south, providing in most cases swift connections to areas of specific interest. The more leisured traveller may be attracted to some of the spectacular stretches of regional railway that Austria offers, for example the **Semmeringbahn**, Europe's oldest mountain railway, the **Mariazellerbahn**, the **Gesäusebahn** in an Upper Styrian valley, through which rushes the foaming River Enns, and various stretches in Tyrol, where steam lives on in the **Achensee** region; also the *Karwendelbahn* running between Innsbruck and Seefeld, and the **Salzkammergut** railway, etc.

For this fourth edition of the guide, a good deal of extra information has been introduced. Opening times for all museums, *Burgen, Schlösser* etc. that are mentioned in the text have been supplied. In some places a museum will only be opened on request, in which case a telephone number has been given. For reasons of security, the keys of a few isolated churches may have to be collected from the addresses supplied. Generally speaking the frescoes, statues, pictures, etc. in churches and secular buildings have been identified in terms not only of style and period, but also of subject matter and location. It is hoped this will make it easier for the reader to find the highlights singled out for attention in (for example) an extremely cluttered Baroque church. In this edition too, rather more space has been given to national parks and conservation areas (e.g. the **Neusiedler See** in Burgenland), as also to bird habitats, *Schloßparks*, and areas with important geo-economic features such as salt- or silver-mines (many of the unworked ones have been turned into museums). Landscape, whether in terms of its fauna and flora, or in terms of its economic exploitation, is clearly a vital ingredient in regional culture broadly defined, and I have therefore tried to indicate its influence where space permitted.

If experienced Austrian travellers discover anything new and stimulating about the country through using this guide, and if newcomers to the country are lured to a perception beyond the clichés of yodelling Tyroleans, prancing Lipizzaners and post-imperial kitsch, then it will have served its purpose.

Nicholas T. Parsons

The three previous editions of this Guide were written by Ian Robertson.

Acknowledgements

I am grateful to Géza and Trixie Hajós and Hannes Stekl for information received and time generously given; also to Marion Telsnig in the Austrian National Tourist Office in London, surely the best ambassador for her country that it would be possible to have. Maria and Karl Pölzl supplied generous hospitality on my travels. The contribution to this book of my wife, Ilona Sármány-Parsons, is virtually impossible to quantify. Suffice it to say that she found time to tour much of Austria with me, despite her own heavy workload, and provided me with the insights of a trained art historian's eye when they were most needed. My greatest debt, however, is to Wolfgang Bahr, writer, local historian and prince of editors in two languages. His sharp-eyed reading of the manuscript saved me from many errors and even more follies. For any of either that remain, however, I must take full responsibility.

How to use the Guide

Blue Guide Austria is divided into nine chapters which correspond to the nine provinces (*Bundesländer*) of Austria. Each provincial section begins with a detailed tour of the capital of the *Land*, followed by various itineraries through the hinterland, these being identified with simple directional references (i.e. road numbers and compass point). It is assumed that motorists will be equipped with an up-to-date road map (see p 20), and the directions have therefore been kept general. The treatment of the provinces themselves takes account of homogeneous geographical areas, although some of these (e.g. the **Salzkammergut**) slightly overlap provincial boundaries. In a very few cases, where it seemed more convenient to deal at a particular point with a sight just outside the border of the province under discussion (examples are **St Wolfgang**, included with Salzburg, or the Lower Austrian sights like **Heiligenkreuz** more easily accommodated with Vienna), I have adopted this pragmatic solution and cross-referenced where necessary.

While some provinces may most naturally be explored in terms of well-defined areas (e.g. the **Waldviertel** or the **Wachau** of Lower Austria), in the mountainous *Länder* of Vorarlberg, Tyrol and Carinthia, the routes inevitably tend to run along the main river valleys, with detours to explore the side-valleys along the way. Obviously the traveller may be following, by choice or necessity, a different route from the one offered in the guide, or the same route in the reverse direction. In this case there should be no difficulty in using the book as a gazetteer by checking the index for each village or town as it is reached. It is hoped, however, that the tours will provide a reasonably logical basis for those who want to cover the ground systematically.

At the front of the book is a substantial section on **Practical information**, which provides essential details to assist in planning a trip, travelling in Austria, dealing with emergencies and much else. Some briefer local information is given just before the text for the capital of each province. This will always include one or two recommended hotels and restaurants (graded according to price). It should be stressed, however, that considerations of space means that no attempt can be made to compete with the numerous guides that deal specifically and in detail with accommodation and restaurants (see also **accommodation and restaurants**, p 22).

Monuments, works of art or **physical features** that are of exceptional importance or otherwise extremely remarkable have been highlighted in bold. The opening times of museums, *Schlösser, Burgen* and so forth are situated at the relevant point in the text.

All measurements are quoted using the metric system. Population figures and most other statistics in the text are taken from the latest edition (1995) of *Österreich Lexikon*. Population data relates to the last census of 1991, and the figures have been rounded up or down to the nearest thousand. German names of cities, towns or regions are cited with their English equivalent (if any) at their first appearance in the text (town maps have been labelled in German). Thereafter the English version is used. For rulers and historical personages, the general rule followed is to cite the name, but not the title, in the original form (so Emperor Karl VI, not Charles VI or Kaiser Karl VI). In the case of saints, I have adopted the English names in every case, since English-speaking readers are naturally more at home with their own versions of these often well-known figures. Likewise, I have generally translated the names of churches and their patrons, if they required mentioning at all; the exceptions are those churches which are so much better known in their concise German form that it seemed better to retain it (examples are Viennese churches such as the **Peterskirche**, the **Karlskirche** and **Maria am Gestade**). Lastly, German adjectives are cited in the inflection they would take were the sentence a German one (the **Kunsthistorische Museum**, in the **Kunsthistorischen Museum**). In all such matters inconsistency undoubtedly occasionally occurs. When in question I have opted for convenience and comprehensibility, rather than rigid rules.

PRACTICAL INFORMATION

 ## Planning your trip

When to go
In Central Europe the summers are decidedly hot and the winters very cold. For the sightseer travelling by car in high summer can be uncomfortably warm and it is not always easy to find parking in the shade. In winter alpine passes are closed (typically from the end of October to the beginning of May), as are a large number of museums, Burgen, Schlösser, seasonal hotels (excepting of course in ski resorts) and other attractions. Probably the best time to visit, therefore, is in the Indian summer that usually stretches into October. The temperature is congenial and the crowds tend to be smaller. The season in Vienna is now almost all year round, although some hotel bargains may be available between Christmas and Easter when beds need to be filled. Museums etc. in the capital are virtually all open all year, although in many cases the opening times may be shorter in winter.

Austrian national tourist offices
- **Australia** 1st Floor, 36 Carrington St, Sydney NSW 2000. ☎ 02 9299 3621, e-mail: oewsyd@world.net fax 02 9299 3808.
- **Canada** 2 Bloor St E., Suite 3330, Toronto ON M4W 1A8. ☎ 416 967 3381, e-mail: anto-tor@sympatico.at fax 416 967 4101.
- **Ireland** Merrion Hall, Strand Rd, Sandy Mount, P.O. Box 2506, Dublin 4. ☎ 00 3531 283 0488, e-mail: ahstdub@indigo.ie fax 283 0531.
- **United Kingdom** 14 Cork Street, London W1. ☎ 020 7629 0461, fax 0207 499 6038, e-mail: info@anto.co.uk.
- **New Zealand Agent** Adventure World, 101 Great South Rd, Remuera, Auckland. ☎ 09 524 5118.
- **USA** P.O. Box 1142, New York NY 10108—1142. ☎ 212 944 6885, e-mail: antonyc@ibm.net, fax 212 730 4568. Website: http://www.anto.com

Websites for Austrian tourist information
- Austrian National Tourist Office: www.anto.com
  www.austria-tourism.at
- Art and music news from Austria: www.austria-info.at/amusa/index.html

Regional tourist boards
- Vienna Tourist Board: www.magwien.gv.at/
- Salzburg Tourist Board: www.salzburginfo.or.at
- Burgenland: www.burgenland-tourism.at
- Carinthia: www.tiscover.com/carinthia
- Lower Austria: www.tiscover.com/noe
- Salzburger Land: www.sagma.co.at/guide
- Styria: www.steiermark.com

- Tyrol: www.tis.co.at/tirol
- Upper Austria: www.tiscover.com/upperaustria
- Vorarlberg: www.vol.at/tourismus

Details of **local tourist information offices** in Austria itself are situated at the beginning of the text for the capital of each *Bundesland*. However, Vienna also has a general information office with useful hotel and events listings for the whole country: **Österreich Werbung/Urlaubsinformation Österreich**, Margarethenstrasse 1, A-1040 Wien (a short walk from the opera or Karlsplatz). ☎ 1 587 20 00, fax: 1 588 66 48. Open Mon–Fri, 10.00–17.00 (to 18.00 on Thurs). **E-mail: oeinfo@oewwien.via at**

Lower Austria (**Niederösterreich**) also has its own tourist information offices. For information and brochures, ☎ 1 536 10 6200. *Reisebüro Intropa*, at First District, Kärntnerstrasse 38, is open (08.30–17.30) for personal visits and provides brochures and a booking service. A useful quarterly overview (in German) of cultural events all over Austria is published by the newspaper *Der Standerd* (*Kultur-Guide*—obtainable on application to the editorial office at Herrengasse 19–21, Wien, ☎ 531-70-0).

For information on Vienna, contact the **Vienna Tourist Board**, A - 1025 Vienna, ☎ 43 1 211 14 222, fax 43 1 216 84 92, e-mail: info@info.wien.at, www.wien.at

Package tours

The range of package tours and holidays available for Austria is extensive and may roughly be divided into the following categories: **winter skiing**, **lakes and mountain holidays** in summer, **city breaks** to Vienna or Salzburg, tours to **arts or cultural festivals** into which category fall the **cultural cruises** on the Danube. Skiing holidays are available from *Air Tours*, *Inghams*, *Thomson* and many others, while *Shearings* ☎ 01942 824 824 and *Wallace Arnold* ☎ 0113 263 4234, based respectively in Wigan and Leeds, have a range of Austrian coach tours. Otherwise the following may be of interest:

Austria Travel, 46 Queen Anne's Gate, London SW1 9AU. ☎ 020 7222 2430, fax 020 7233 0293. City breaks in Salzburg and Vienna. Country holidays and language courses.

Austrian Holidays, 5th Floor, 10 Wardour Street, London W1 4BQ. ☎ 020 7434 7399, fax 020 7434 7393. Austrian Airlines package tour subsidiary. Mostly city breaks.

Danube Travel, 45 Great Cumberland Place, London W1R 7LH. ☎ 020 7724 7577, fax 020 7224 8959. Experts in Central European combination tours.

Habsburg Heritage Cultural Tours, 158 Rosendale Road, London SE21 8LG. ☎ 020 8761 0444, fax 020 8766 6151. Specialises in music festivals and Danube cruises.

Martin Randall Travel, 10 Barley Mow Passage, London W4 4PH. ☎ 020 8742 3355, fax: 020 8742 1066. Cultural tours with academic lecturers.

Disabled travellers

Austria has regulations requiring public buildings to have suitable access for wheelchairs, but public transport and hotels are not guaranteed to offer such facilities. In general, hotels with three stars or more should have elevators (but always check) and the main railway stations and trains now have some facilities for the disabled, the relevant trains being marked with the wheelchair facility symbol in the timetable. However, booking three days in advance is essential to obtain a seat for the disabled, and if you need help getting on to the train, you should register with railway staff at least 30 minutes before departure. Airport assistance is available on request.

In Vienna the public transport system most suitable for the disabled is the U-Bahn, although only the recently completed U3 and U6 lines are fully equipped with lifts and escalators. The newest buses and trams have very low or retractable platforms for boarding and getting off, but the older trams, with their steep entry and exit steps, present difficulties not only for the disabled but for the elderly in general. For detailed information on facilities available in the capital, ask the Austrian tourist office in your country for the leaflet entitled *Vienna for Guests with Handicaps*. A travel agent in Vienna catering for disabled travellers is *Egnatia Tours* at Piaristengasse 60 (☎ 406 97 32).

Elsewhere in Austria the local tourist information office can usually assist with details of parking reserved for the disabled (free in the blue short-term parking zones if your car displays the international disabled sticker), as well as information on toilets and access to the local sights, etc.

The following organisations are worth contacting before you leave for Austria:
Britain *RADAR* (Royal Association for Disability and Rehabilitation): 12 City Forum, 250 City Road, London EC1V 8 AS (☎ 020 7250 3222). This organisation publishes a guide entitled *Holidays and Travel Abroad: A Guide for the Disabled*.
Australia *ACROD* (Australian Council for Rehabilitation of the Disabled): PO Box 60, Curtin, ACT 2605 (☎ 02 6282 4333).
New Zealand *Disabled Persons Assembly*: 173–175 Victoria St, Wellington (☎ 04 801 9100).
Ireland *Irish Wheelchair Association*: Blackheath Drive, Clontarf, Dublin 3 (☎ 01 833 8241).
North America *Directions Unlimited*: 720 N Bedford Rd, Bedford Hills, NY 10507 (☎ 800 533 5343). This is a specialist tour operator. Also *Mobility International USA*: PO Box 10767, Eugene OR 97440 (☎ 503 343 1284). A membership fee is payable to this organisation.

Passports and visas

Visas are not required for citizens of EU states, or of the USA, Canada, Australia and New Zealand. The maximum permitted stay for a tourist without further formality is three consecutive months. Longer stays require registration at the police station nearest to your residence. Citizens of most other countries require a visa, which will be valid for three months and is not normally renewable in Austria itself.

Austria is a party to the Schengen Accord, by the terms of which border controls between EU states were abolished, although it is phasing in full implementation. Since Britain does not accept the provisions of the Accord, UK (and Irish) citizens should always have their passports with them, as they are usually inspected, at least at airports. In addition, Austria has four borders with non-EU countries (the Czech Republic, Slovakia, Hungary and Slovenia—all candidates for EU membership), where border controls are necessarily rigorous and delays may occur. Movement between Austria and the fifth non-EU member,

Switzerland (also Liechtenstein), requires a passport but is practically as non-bureaucratic for EU citizens as it is between EU countries.

Customs

The EU is now theoretically a single internal market, although anomalies still exist in areas such as car pricing, where the market continues to be rigged by the manufacturers with the connivance of governments. However, for the EU tourist there are few restrictions on the import and export of items for personal use and consumption. Exceptions are sporting weapons and firearms generally, the rules for which have been progressively tightened following violent incidents. For the current rules, consult the Austrian embassy or consulate nearest to you (see below). Non-EU citizens over the age of 17 may bring into Austria 200 cigarettes or 50 cigars, 250g of tobacco, plus 2.25 litres of wine and 1 litre of spirits. The import and export of goods in EU states is in practice limited only by what may be deemed to have been purchased for personal consumption. Austria has been accused of being a weak link in the battle against money laundering, so if you are carrying a large sum into the country you may be asked to explain why. It is better to declare it.

Embassies and Consulates abroad

Embassies
Australia: 12 Talbot St Forrest, Canberra, ACT 2603. ☎ 02 6295 1533.
Canada: 445 Wilbrod St, Ottawa, ON KIN 6M7. ☎ 613 789 1444.
Ireland: 15 Ailesbury Court, 93 Ailesbury Road, Dublin 4. ☎ 01 269 4577.
New Zealand: (Consular General): 22 Garrett St, Wellington. ☎ 04 801 9709.
South Africa: 1109 Duncan St, Momentum Office Part, 0011 Brooklyn, Pretoria. ☎ 012 462 483.
United Kingdom: 18 Belgrave Mews West, London SW1 8HU. ☎ 020 7235 3731.
USA: 3524 International Court NW, Washington DC, 20008-3035. ☎ 202 895 6775.

Consulates
Canada: 360 Bay St, Suite 1010 **Toronto** ON M5H 2U6; ☎ 416 863 0649. 1350 Rue Sherbrooke Ouest, Suite 1030, **Montréal** PQ H3G 1J1; ☎ 514 845 8661. 1810 Alberni St, Suite 202, **Vancouver** BC V6G 1B3; ☎ 604 687 3338.
USA: 31 East 69th St, **New York** NY 10021. ☎ 212 737 6400. Wrigley Building, Suite 707, 400 N. Michigan Ave, **Chicago** IL 60611. ☎ 312 222 1515. 11859 Wilshire Blvd, Suite 501, **Los Angeles** CA 90025. ☎ 310 444 9310.

For foreign embassies and consulates in Vienna, see under *Additional Information* (pp 30–31).

Money

Until the year 2002 Austria is retaining the **Austrian Schilling** for day to day use, after which it will be replaced by the Euro. Paper transactions are already possible in **Euros** and in many places double listing of prices in Schilling and Euros may be seen. Schilling prices appear on menu cards against the symbol ÖS, but in official institutions such as banks and in exchange kiosks you will see the abbreviation ATS. Denominations are as follows: 1 ÖS = 100 Groschen, the latter denominated in 10 Gr. and 50 Gr. pieces. Schilling coins are denominated as 1, 5, 10 and 20. Notes are denominated as 20, 50, 100, 500, 1000 and 5000. From the year 2002 all prices will be in Euros.

The amount of money that can be brought in and out of the country is no longer officially limited but the authorities have the right to inquire into the provenance of large sums as part of the government campaign against money laundering. Permission must be obtained to take more than 100,000 ATS out of Austria if that exceeds what you brought in.

The major **credit cards** are now at last accepted in a large number of petrol stations, and have long been acceptable in the middle to upper price shops, restaurants and hotels. Cheaper shops and accommodation will still require to be paid in cash, though some take Eurocheques. In towns, automated teller machines (ATM) are widely available—you will need to know your PIN number. In Vienna and in a few of the larger cities it is possible to change notes through an automatic machine. Travellers' cheques are widely accepted in banks and hotels.

Banks are generally open Mon–Fri, 08.00–12.30 and 13.30–14.00 or 15.00. Banks in the city centres stay open during the lunch hour and most have late opening on Thursday to 17.30. *Wechselstuben* (exchange kiosks) are to be found at airports, railway stations and on major shopping streets.

Health

Medical advice/insurance

EU citizens receive free hospital treatment in Austria **for emergencies only** on production of a passport. For nationals of other countries, treatment is dependent upon reciprocal agreements and the situation should be checked before leaving home. It is nonetheless a good idea to take out extra travel insurance and obligatory to do so if you are going on a skiing holiday (check the terms of the cover provided by your package tour). Non-emergency treatment must be paid for and can be very expensive.

Chemists are usually open Mon–Fri, 08.00–17.00, but in suburbs and smaller towns they may close for lunch. In larger towns there is a 24-hour service rota of chemists on standby, details of which are displayed in the window.

Ticks (Zecken)

The only serious local health hazard is a tick-borne encephalitis to which hikers are at risk. Infection may occur if you find a tick has attached itself to you and you remove its body leaving the head buried in the flesh. The correct procedure is to coax it out by covering the affected area with petroleum jelly or oil. If the tick is malignant, a meningitis type of cerebral inflammation can result and is very occasionally fatal. Lower Austria, Upper Austria, the Wienerwald and parts of Burgenland, Styria and Carinthia are all potentially hazardous in this respect, and in general vaccination is strongly recommended if you are intending to go rambling or hiking in Austria. This should take place two weeks before departure. In case of infection, go at once to the nearest hospital for an injection of antibiotics.

Prospective hikers might also consider a tetanus booster. Otherwise there are no major hazards, although rabies is not entirely absent, and if you are bitten by a dog or other animal a hospital check is advisable.

Getting there

By air
From Britain Both *Austrian Airlines* (AUA) and *British Airways* (BA) fly three or more scheduled flights daily to Vienna. AUA flies out of Heathrow Terminal 2, BA from Terminal 1 and from Gatwick (North Terminal). *Lauda Air* flies daily from Gatwick to Vienna and Salzburg, and also has flights from Manchester to Vienna. In addition there are numerous charter airlines using airports such as the City Airport in London, Luton, Stansted and Gatwick. In 2000 a new ticketless cheap service between Stansted and Vienna was started by *Buzz*, a subsidiary of *KLM*. Bookings are made by telephone or internet.

Airline addresses
Austrian Airlines: 10 Wardour Street, London W1V 4BQ. ☎ 020 7434 7350.
British Airways: 156 Regent Street, London W1R 5TA. ☎ 020 7434 4700, fax 020 7434 4636. Regional office enquiries: 0345 222 111.
Lauda Air: Units 1 and 2, 123 Buckingham Palace Rd, London SW1W 9SH. ☎ 020 7630 5924, fax 020 7828 9611.
Buzz: ☎ 0870 240 7070.

From Ireland Direct flights from Dublin to Vienna on Mondays and Thursdays are operated by *Tyrolean Airways*, but currently booked through *Swissair* in Dublin.

From the USA and Canada *Austrian Airlines* and *Delta* fly direct to Vienna from the USA, while many other airlines have indirect services via European cities, and these flights may sometimes be cheaper. From Canada there are no direct flights, but several one-stop options to Vienna (*Air France*, *Lufthansa*, *KLM*, *Swissair*). *Austrian Airlines* toll-free enquiries for USA and Canada ☎ (1) 800 843 0002. *Delta Airlines* toll-free enquiries for USA and Canada ☎ (1) 800 241 4141.

From Australia and New Zealand The only direct flights are run by *Lauda Air* from Sydney to Vienna. All other airlines involve a transfer or stopover. *Lauda Air Australia* can be contacted on ☎ 02 9251. In New Zealand enquire at the Lufthansa office on ☎ 09 303 1529.

Vienna's airport (Flughafen Wien-Schwechat) lies some 19km east of the city. The *Schnellbahn* (S-Bahn) connects it to the city (S7 to Wien-Mitte) with trains leaving every half hour between 05.00 and 22.00. The journey time is about 30mins and the fare modest. You can buy your season ticket for public transport in the Vienna central zone at the same time.
   Transit buses connect the airport with the City Air Terminal (Information: 08.00–18.00 ☎ 58 00 354) at the Hilton Hotel, which is close to the Wien-Mitte traffic hub. Another bus runs to the Westbahnhof via the Südbahnhof (Western

and Southern railway stations). The fare is currently 70 ATS one way (you can buy a return) and the journey time some 20–30mins depending on traffic and time of day. Buses to the Hilton leave every 20mins from 06.30–23.30, at other times every 30mins. The Westbahnhof bus goes at hourly intervals from 05.40–23.40. These services are constantly being upgraded as passenger numbers at Vienna increase, so check the illuminated bus sign by the terminal exit. In addition there are a number of courtesy pick-up services for the luxury hotels (check if your hotel has one when booking) and a fare-based minibus service is planned. Taxis to the city centre may cost 400–500 ATS, or more to outlying districts, at night, with extra luggage etc.

Salzburg's small airport is some 4km west of the centre at Innsbrucker Bundesstraße 95. Bus no. 77 stops near the main tourist office and runs between 05.30–23.00 to Südtirolerplatz/Hauptbahnhof at 30min. intervals. However, for such a relatively short distance a taxi (costing c 200 ATS) may be preferable.

Airline offices in Vienna

Aer Lingus: Scheibengasse 12. ☎ 369 28 85.
Air Canada: Schubertring 9. ☎ 712 46 08.
Austrian Airlines: Kärntner Ring 18. ☎ 505 5757.
British Airways: Kärntner Ring 10. ☎ 505 7691.
Lauda Air: Opernring 6. ☎ 514 77.
South African Airways: Opernring 1. ☎ 587 1489.
Tyrolean Airways: Opernring 1, Stg. R ☎ 586 36 74.

Domestic flights

Austrian Air Services flies between Vienna and Salzburg, Linz, Graz and Klagenfurt. Bookings may be made through *Austrian Airlines*.
Tyrolean Airways flies between Innsbruck and Vienna (also internationally). ☎ 586 36 74.
Rheintalflug Seewald flies between Vienna and Vorarlberg, but lands just over the border in Switzerland because there is no airport in Vorarlberg. Its Vienna office is in the World Trade Centre. ☎ 7007 6911.

By train from Britain

This is an extremely expensive way of making the journey, although there are concessions for students and pensioners, as well as some apex fares. From June to September there is a direct train from Ostend to Vienna, but this is under threat, so the current situation must be checked with a travel agent or at Victoria Station. A relatively painless way of travelling is to take the *Eurostar* to Brussels and the direct overnight train with couchette or sleeper from Brussels to Vienna. On the most direct route from London the journey takes 22.5hrs, but you can save up to 4.5hrs on this by taking the *Eurostar* option.

Train information: *International Rail Centre*, Victoria Station, London SW1V 1JY. European information on: ☎ 0990 848848. *Eurostar*, EPS House, Waterloo Station, London SE1 8SE. Reservations ☎ 0345 303 030.

By bus from Britain

At about a third of the rail price, buses are the cheapest method of getting to Austria, and of course the least comfortable. *Eurolines* run a thrice-weekly service from Victoria Station in London direct to Vienna (Wien-Mitte, Landstraßer

Hauptstraße). The scheduled time of 22hrs is similar to the train, but obviously there is more potential for delay.

The *Euro Explorer ticket* entitling you to travel on Eurolines services on a circuit comprising London–Budapest–Vienna–Bratislava–London is a bargain, if you think you can endure it physically.

Eurolines: 52 Grosvenor Gardens, London, SW1W OAU (opposite Victoria Station). ☎ 0990 14319.

By car from Britain

The journey from London to Vienna is now motorway for the entire route, whether you land at Calais, Boulogne, Dunkerque or Ostend. Taking a late-night ferry across the channel enables you to start before dawn on the other side, which means that you can reach Bavaria by evening without undue stress. That leaves a relatively easy run through to Vienna the following day. The Hoverspeed service to Ostend eliminates circa 120km of motorway on the French side, while *Le Shuttle* through the Channel Tunnel cuts the ferry time to Calais in half. You could also consider the various Motorail options, taking your car and passengers to a destination on the continent.

The French part of the motorway does not charge a toll, as it is technically not autoroute standard, and there is currently no toll in Belgium and Germany. Austria has introduced a toll, which must be purchased at the border in the form of a *Vignette*. The current cost is 550 ATS (about 40 Euros) for a year, but shorter periods of ten days or two months are available.

Proof of car ownership (or a letter from the owner giving you permission to use the vehicle) should be carried at all times, together with the Green Card insurance certificate indicating that you have third party cover. A red warning triangle (for breakdowns), a spare set of bulbs for the car lights and a first aid kit are obligatory in Austria and on most of the continent. A fire extinguisher is also desirable. The British driving licence is acceptable throughout Europe and you may drive with it in Austria for up to one year, after which residents must take an Austrian driving test. Other European driving licences are likewise acceptable, but non-European drivers should obtain an International Driving Permit (IDP). Drive on the right.

Travelling around

By car

Apart from the items mentioned above, it is worth having a *European Accident Statement* form, with which Austrian motorists are familiar and which can make communication easier in the event of a mishap. British motoring organisations have reciprocal agreements with their Austrian colleagues (for example the *AA* with the *ÖAMTC*, which is the Austrian club with the widest coverage). A European breakdown policy such as the *AA Five Star* or *RAC Eurocover* is worth having; alternatively, if a long stay in Austria is planned, it is well worth joining the *ÖAMTC* (Schubertring 1-3, A-1010 Wien) or the *ARBÖ* (Mariahilferstrasse 180–A-1150, Wien), whose emergency numbers in the event of breakdown are respectively 120 and 123.

The **speed limits** in Austria are 130kph (81mph) on motorways (but 100kph (62mph) for caravans and cars with trailers), 50kph (31mph) in built-up areas, on all other roads 100kph (62mph) unless otherwise indicated. After considerable debate, the permitted alcohol limit in Austria has recently been lowered to 0.5 pro mill and is strictly enforced with random breathalyser tests, heavy on-the-spot fines and even confiscation of driving licences in cases of very excessive drinking. Wearing seatbelts is obligatory (also in the back if fitted); children under 12 should have a special seat or restraint and be seated in the back. All motorcyclists and their passengers must wear crash helmets. An experiment has just ended requiring cars to drive with dipped headlights in daytime outside cities, an over-bureaucratic measure which might yet become law, and is already law in neighbouring Hungary.

Road signs generally conform to continental standards, but drivers should keep an eye open for some local specialities (e.g. a criss-crossed white tyre on a blue circular background, meaning that snow chains are compulsory on the approaching stretch of road). Particular care should be taken in towns with tramways (e.g. Vienna, Graz or Linz), the rule being that cars must give way for passengers boarding or alighting from the tram (unless there is a tram platform), as also for the tram itself at all times. Snow studs are permissible on tyres between 15 November and 4 April, but more importantly, motorists must have the equivalent of Austria's extra-grip 'winter tyres' on their vehicles when driving in winter ('all-weather tyres', despite their manufacturers' claims are usually insufficient).

Warning. Note also that many alpine roads and passes (including the **Großglockner** and the **Loibl Pass** from Carinthia into Slovenia) are closed to cars with caravans.

Austria conforms to the general continental rule whereby motorists must give way to cars coming from the right when both roads are of equal status (also on roundabouts). Otherwise heed the sign indicating an arterial road, whose users have priority even over traffic from the right. STOP, means just that, whatever type of road you are on and however much you think you can see both ways on the road you are joining. There are many automatic railway crossings (a red light means STOP) and various signs indicating potential hazard from suicidal deer or falling rocks, although it is not exactly clear what you are supposed to do about such unforeseen eventualities. Special care should be taken when entering a motorway, above all at night, so that the entry not the exit is taken: the media regularly report cases of *Geisterfahrer* (maniacs) who write off themselves and several others by entering an Autobahn against the traffic.

Basic motoring vocabulary

Tankstelle *petrol station*	Raststätte *service area*
Umleitung *diversion*	Maut *toll*
Unfall *accident*	Strafzettel *parking ticket*

Parking

Most town centres have a short-term parking zone (*Kurzparkzone*, designated with a blue marking line) where parking is allowed up to 1.5 or 3hrs. To use these, a *Parkschein* (parking ticket) must be purchased from a *Tabak/Trafik* and displayed. In some places (including where short-term parking is free) you may require a cardboard clock (also obtainable at the *Tabak/Trafik*) which indicates the time at which you parked. A round blue sign with a red cross means parking is prohibited, while the same sign with a single white diagonal line means pick-up and delivery only (10mins). Beneath the signs, the exact time restrictions on parking are listed (e.g. parking may be allowed outside business or loading hours).

Parking fines are a favourite source of revenue for otherwise tourist-friendly *Gemeinden* (local councils), so it is sensible to obey the rules. If you do have to pay a penalty, this will sometimes be left on your windscreen in the form of an *Erlagschein* (bank pay-slip) and may be paid at any bank or post office (small charge). Otherwise you have to pay the fine at the police station, which is usually not hard to find. Watch out for the unmistakable sign indicating you will be towed if you park in that space—it is very time-consuming and expensive to repossess your car. In particular, any owner of a garage outlet on an urban street has the right to have you towed if you block his exit (such exits are not always very conspicuous).

Car rental

It is usually cheaper to book a car in your home country and pick it up at the airport than to hire one on the spot. Check that the car has a valid *Autobahn Vignette* on the windscreen before driving off. Only drivers who are 21 years of age or over may rent a car in Austria. All the major hire companies have outlets in Vienna and some other cities.

Maps

General maps of Austria (Michelin, Kümmerley und Frey etc.) can be obtained from **Stanfords** at 12–14 Long Acre, London WC2E 9LP (☎ 020 7836 1321, phoned orders taken), but the most complete selection is naturally to be found in Austria itself at **Freytag & Berndt** (Kohlmarkt 9, Vienna, Wilhelm-Greil-Strasse 15, Innsbruck, Sporgasse 29, Graz). Freytag & Berndt's own publications are among the best available and include an *Autokarte Austria* and *Große Straßen Karten* covering the country in four sheets or in atlas form; also good is *Österreich Touring*. The firm produces *Wanderkarten* (hiking maps, see p 33) and other route maps for cyclists, canoeists, etc. Another publisher, **Kompass**, also produce good hiking maps. The **Österreichischer Alpenverein** at Wilhelm-Greil-Strasse 15, A-6010, Innsbruck, produces the *Alpenvereinskarten* (1:25,000), the bible for mountaineers, but also useful for hikers, some showing ski routes as well. The atlas put out by the **ÖAMTC** (*Der Große ÖAMTC–Stadtatlas*) is useful for its town plans, as is the *Kompass-Stadtplan* series. The Austrian equivalent of the Ordnance Survey is the **BEV** (*Bundesamt für Eich-und Vermessungswesen*), Krottenthallergasse 3, A-1080 Vienna (☎ 401 46–0; fax 406 99 92), where there is a sales outlet. Local tourist information offices also provide town plans and regional maps with walking routes etc., sometimes levying a small charge.

Buses

Austria's **Bahnbus** (run by the **Austrian Federal Railways—ÖBB**) and **Postbus** (run by the Post Office) have an extensive network of services between them, but some of the less economic routes are probably under threat from imminent privatisation of the (already partly privatised) post office and the restructuring of the ÖBB. The system is obviously most useful for getting to the outlying areas not reached by the railway, but this may need careful planning. The timetables tend to reflect the needs of schoolchildren and the service is reduced (in some cases suspended) at weekends. Schedules are posted at bus stops (*Bushaltestellen*) or in the booking offices of bus stations (*Busbahnhöfe*) of towns. Tickets are obtainable from the driver or in advance from the booking office and budget-priced 24-hour travelcards (*Tageskarten*) are available. Telephone information for Bundesbahn buses in Vienna on ☎ 711 01; bookings on ☎ 1700. Postbus Tourism Information on ☎ 1582.

Trains

Services The Austrian Federal Railways (*Österreichische Bundesbahnen*, known as *ÖBB*) run an efficient and clean service. InterRail and Eurail passes are valid on the *ÖBB* network.

The *Eurocity* (EC) and *Austrian InterCity* (IC) are the fastest trains, the EC attracting a surcharge on the ticket. Reservations are essential on EC and IC trains at weekends.

Eilzüge (E, fast trains) stop at most intermediate points of importance, but for the smallest stations you must take the *Regionalzug*, which stops everywhere.

Prices and discounts Rail travel is not cheap and some concessions (e.g. the *Bundesnetzkarte* covering unlimited travel anywhere in the country for one month) are arguably too expensive for the use you are likely to make of them. The *Vorteilskarte* involves an initial down-payment and thereafter entitles the bearer to a 50 per cent reduction on rail fares for a year.

Information Schedules of train arrivals (*Ankunft*) and departures (*Abfahrt*) appear in the stations. Telephone information in Vienna, Graz, Linz, Salzburg, Klagenfurt, Innsbruck and Bregenz is available on ☎ 1717. Anywhere else ☎ 1717 prefaced by your nearest city code. The annual *Kursbuch* (timetable) may be purchased at railway stations and includes a section (available separately) showing international connections.

Bicycling

Most regional tourist boards have leaflets on cycling facilities and routes ('Bike Rental' is *Fahrradverleih*). Separate biking paths run parallel to (but sometimes cross!) the pedestrian walkways that are laid out in many towns, Vienna being especially biker friendly, although the cyclists are not always themselves so friendly to Viennese pedestrians. Bicycles can be hired at over 160 railway stations and returned to any other station with a rental office (for a small extra charge). A form of identification is required for hiring. Bicycles may be taken on non-Express trains, on the so-called *Rad Tramper* trains along the Danube, on the *Fahrradbus* that runs along the shore of the Neusiedler See and on the Vienna U-Bahn outside rush hours and all weekend. It is now possible to make a complete circuit of the Neusiedler lake on a bicycle using the special border crossings for cyclists and pedestrians that enable you to pass through Hungarian territory.

River and lake steamers

Travelling by ship in Austria is really only appropriate for tourism and excursions (e.g. the scenic trip on the Danube through the Wachau from Melk to Krems). An exception is the regular hydrofoil service running between Vienna, Bratislava and Budapest. Lake steamers have seasonal timetables and offer an excellent way of seeing the sights in a relaxing way. The celebrated **Donau-Dampfschifffahrts-Gesellschaft** (DDSG) has been in financial difficulty but still operates cruises on five ships from Handelskai 265 (by the Reichsbrücke) in Vienna (☎ 727 10–0 or 727 50–0). A number of specialist British travel agencies (see p 12) offer packaged Danube cruises in the warm months of the year, inclusive of talks by distinguished lecturers.

Accommodation

The *Practical information* section preceding the text on each *Bundesland* capital mentions a few places to stay and one or two restaurants, besides which there are occasional mentions of other hotels or restaurants in the text, where personal experience has prompted a reference. However, these references are suggestions only and the *Blue Guide* does not seek to emulate specialised guides to hotels and restaurants.

Hotel guides

Those looking for a nearly complete listing of hotels arranged by *Bundesland* will find it in the biennial *Hotels in Austria* published by Österreich Werbung and obtainable at Austrian National Tourist Offices or from *Österreich Werbung/ Urlaubsinformation Österreich*, Margarethenstraße 1, A–1040 Wien. ☎ (1) 587 20 00, fax (1) 588 66 48, e-mail: oeinfo@oewwien.via.at. This list uses conventional trade symbols to give full details about the address, telephone, fax, facilities and price range of each establishment, with cross-referencing to a map of Austria. A useful book is *Small and Charming Hotels in Austria*, edited by Paul Wade and Kathy Arnold and published by Duncan Petersen (last update 1997). It lists 250 hotels, many of which are near places of major interest, yet pleasantly off the beaten tourist track. Good food, comfort, friendly service and good taste are the major considerations for inclusion. A book in slightly similar vein but with an itinerary and rather chatty travelogue is Karen Brown's *Austrian Country Inns and Castles*, which includes some 60 hotels, although Lower Austria and Styria are somewhat thinly represented. There are several helpful German publications, all stocked at *Freytag & Berndt* outlets. Particularly useful is *Gut und Preiswert Übernachten*, an alphabetical listing of cheap and cheerful 'bed with bath' hotels, Gasthöfe and pensions.

Restaurant guides

There are a number of restaurant guides for Austria in German, the leading one being the celebrated *Gault-Millau Österreich*. However, although it does list some places in the middle price range, its exacting standards more or less ensure that the restaurants featured are on the expensive side. *À la Carte Österreich* is, like Gault-Millau, updated annually and is another book for German-speaking foodies. An excellent informative listing of every establishment in Vienna is published annually as *Wien, wie es ißt* (the title is a punning reference to a 19C travel book by Charles Sealsfeld entitled 'Austria as it is' and in spoken German could be taken to mean either 'Vienna as it is' or 'Vienna as it eats'). Currently the only detailed guide in English to selected restaurants is Gretel Beer's *Eating Out in Austria*.

Food and drink

Food

In recent years Austrian cuisine has broadened its scope from rather heavy, meat-based traditional meals to incorporate a local version of nouvelle cuisine, as well as 'organic cooking' (*Vollwertküche*) and a wider choice of vegetarian dishes (often described on menus as *Fitnessteller* or 'Fitness Dish'). Nevertheless, the cheaper restaurants will usually have an emphasis on meat dishes (chiefly pork and beef), while the sausage (*Wurst*) in its various forms has not yet been overtaken by McDonald's as the favoured fast food of the urban Austrian, or at any rate of the Viennese. Those with a more or less limitless appetite for girth-expanding ingredients may try the *Bauernschmaus*, a huge dish of mixed meat with sauerkraut and dumplings. There are, in addition, many varieties of pressed and smoked meats in any supermarket delicatessen, including hams, bacons, salamis, mortadellas and the like. These may be combined with cheese to be eaten as a *Jause*, an in-between meal or a rambler's picnic, one of the heaviest ingredients of which is usually the bread. There is an astonishing variety of the latter, the vast majority of it rye bread, often with some form of flavouring such as cumin, onions or sunflower seeds. White breads are mostly limited to rolls (*Semmel*), baguettes, a dreary 'sandwich bread' and a rarely encountered novelty, but the best of them, '*Toskana Laib*'. Another major feature of Austrian cookery is its enormous range of desserts (*Mehlspeisen*) and pastries (*Zuckerbäckerei*), some items of which are world-famous (Sachertorte, Ischler etc.). In the country and alpine regions the traveller can expect to be offered game (mostly venison) while Austria's rivers and lakes contain an abundance of fresh-water fish.

Austrian cuisine owes much to the South German, Central and South-Eastern European influences that made themselves felt over 600 years of the Habsburg Empire. The ubiquitous *Wiener Schnitzel* itself, which is in origin a North Italian veal piccata fried in breadcumbs, was probably introduced in the mid-19C after Marshal Radetzky's Italian campaigns. The almost equally ubiquitous dumplings (*Knödel*) are characteristic of Bohemian cookery, much to the delight of the simple-minded Ferdinand I, who was forcibly retired to Prague after the revolution of 1848, and whose most sensible recorded statement was: 'I am the Emperor and I shall have dumplings.' Other ethnic imports that are frequently encountered all over Austria include the Hungarian goulash (*Gulasch*) or *Paprikahuhn* (paprika chicken), the southern *Slav cevapcici* (small spicy sausages from the grill), and many types of Italian pasta.

Viennese specialities

The ethnic mix and the prosperity of the Habsburg Residenzstadt were factors in the development of a local cuisine ranging from *Wiener Schnitzel* (the genuine one being veal, but now usually pork) and *Tafelspitz* (tender boiled beef said to have been Franz Joseph's daily fare) to a bewildering range of pastries, cakes and puddings. The latter include various *Auflaufe* (steamed or soufflé puddings), *Himbeergrotz* (jellified purée of fresh raspberries or strawberries), *Mohr im Hemd* (steamed pudding with chocolate and nuts), *Zwetschken-* or *Marillenknödel* (plum or apricot dumplings) and *Gugelhupf* (a pound cake that is also the nickname for the 18C cylindrical confinement for the mentally ill in Vienna's General Hospital and a satirical programme on the radio). Almost any *Konditorei* worth the name will have a selection of *Strudel*, *Apfel-* and *Topfenstrudel* (the latter filled with sweet curds) being the most common.

Regional specialities

Of the nine *Bundesländer*, some have very strong individual traditions of cookery representative of the local environment and climate, but also influenced by demographic, ethnic and social factors: for example, different types of noodles and dumplings feature largely in the traditionally peasant economies of Tyrol, Carinthia and Lower Austria, while sophisticated pastries are naturally a product of the aristocratic urban tradition of Salzburg and Vienna. Perhaps the least distinctive regional cookery is to be found in **Burgenland** and **Vorarlberg**. The former has always been a border region, until recently part of Hungary, but with a chiefly German peasant population. Its cuisine is characterised by some Hungarian influence and of course an abundance of freshwater fish from the **Neusiedler See**, while its high quality viticulture is a comparatively recent development. Vorarlberg's outstanding product is cheese, but even local chefs have been known to lament the lack of interesting local dishes.

   Lower Austria is famous for its fruits and wines, and boasts some unusual dishes flavoured with cider must (e.g. *Mostsuppe* and a roast known as *Most Bratl*). There is also a choice of 'Danube' fish (cynics say they are often imported) including *Zander* (Zander), *Barsch* (perch), *Schleie* (tench) and *Wels* (catfish). **Upper Austria**'s proximity to Bohemia has produced a varied range of dumplings, salty or sweet, stuffed or sprinkled, as hors d'oeuvre, main course or side-dish. This being the lake district of Austria, there really is plenty of fish caught locally, specialities being *Reinanke*, *Saibling* (char) and *Hecht* (pike), as well as salmon-trout and trout. A popular way of preparing the fish is to grill it on a charcoal spit (*Steckerlfische*). In the meat department are dishes such as *Steyrer Flößerbraten* (salted meat seasoned with pepper, rosemary, cumin, paprika and juniper) and *Kremstaler Mostbraten* (fatty pork steamed with bacon and must). The best known local confectionery is the *Linzer Torte*, a pastry-topped cake with nuts and redcurrant jam.

   Carinthia, with its proximity to Italy, is strong on pasta such as ravioli, those with a thick cheese sauce (*Kärntner Nudeln* or *Kasnudeln*) being among the most tasty. In **Styria** a best cut of pork steamed with horseradish seasoning (*Steirisches Wurzelfleisch*) is excellent washed down with a local dry white wine. The regional speciality is the black pumpkin oil (*Kürbiskernöl*) which is used with salads and to season several dishes, while the quintessential Styrian dish is *Sterz*, a polenta with several variations. Cholesterollers will go for the greasy sandwich spread with chopped bacon known as *Verhackertes* or *Verhakkerts*, also popular in Carinthia. In Styria, as elsewhere, the asparagus of spring and early summer is an important seasonal offering.

   Tyrol offers a number of trencherman dishes for mountain climbers (e.g. *Tiroler Gröstl*, which is boiled meat with potatoes and egg, or *Tiroler Rindersaftbraten*, which is sliced beef with parmesan cheese, or *Tiroler Knödel*, which are ham dumplings). It also has its variations on the pasta theme (e.g. *Schinkenfleckerl*, which are square pasta shapes with chopped ham, or *Schlutzkrapfen*, which are ravioli filled with spinach and cheese). *Tiroler*

Kirchtagskrapfen are fritters filled with dried pears, prunes and poppy seed, while a first course worth trying is *Tiroler Gerstlsuppe* (barley soup).

Salzburger Land is once again a pasta paradise, with *Kasnock'n* or *Käsespätzle* (homemade cheese pasta) being widespread in the Pongau, Lungau and Pinzgau, while you may also encounter bread dumplings with cheese and onions (*Kaspreßknödel*) or pastries stuffed with meat known as *Bladl* or *Fleischkrapfen*. In the Flachgau the stuffed dumplings (*Klöße*) are a speciality, while in Salzburg itself the souffléd pudding of eggs, sugar, fat and flour known as *Salzburger Nockerln* is itself sufficient for a meal.

A word should be added about the wonderful **soups** of Austria, in the judgement of which all self-respecting Austrians are connoisseurs. Among the best are *Eierschwammelsuppe* made with chanterelle mushrooms, *Leberknödelsuppe* with liver dumplings and *Lungenstrudelsuppe* (which contains pastry bits stuffed with chopped lung). Vegetarians will go for *Lauch-*(leek) or *Knoblauchcremesuppe* (garlic soup), and there are many others.

Popular **meat dishes** that might be encountered anywhere in Austria include *Lungenbraten* (loin of beef) and other beef cuts such as *Beinfleisch* or *Tellerfleisch*, or *Zwiebelrostbraten*, a rib of beef with crispy fried onions. *Naturschnitzel* are pork or veal cutlets that have not been breadcrumbed, *Geselchtes* is smoked meat, *Schöpsernes* is mutton stew, *Beuschel* is offal and *Faschiertes* is minced meat (usually served as meatballs). For the names of basic dishes or ingredients, refer to the list of dishes on p 26.

Wine

Austrian viticulture has a tradition reaching back to the Illyrians and the Celts, while the Roman Emperor Probus put it on a commercial basis with regulations introduced around AD 280. In the Middle Ages it was mostly the prerogative of monasteries and abbeys, but increasing demand gradually led to more independent peasant wine-growing, as well as to substantial production on noble estates and even some that was undertaken by the burghers. The troubles of the Reformation, especially the Thirty Years War, almost destroyed commercial viticulture through military devastation, but it recovered in the Baroque era. In the 19C climatic change and diseases such as phylloxera again laid waste the vineyards, but the vines were gradually re-established, here as elsewhere, by using cuttings from immune Californian vines.

Stricter regulation of the wine trade following the 'glycol scandal' of 1985 (see p 171) has improved both quality and the level of customer information. The label must now indicate whether the wine is *Tafelwein* (table wine) or of better quality (*Qualitätswein* or *Prädikatswein*), the relevant initial letter (T, Q or P) appearing in the band running over the cork or on the label. The label itself must indicate the wine producer or bottler, its alcohol content and the amount of sugar in it; *trocken* (dry), *halbtrocken* (medium dry), or *süss* (sweet). On bottles of *Spätlese* or *Auslese*, which is wine made from late-gathered or selected grapes, the vintage and grape variety must also be indicated.

There are more than 57,000 hectares of vineyards in Austria, the vast majority (85 per cent) producing white wines. About 62 per cent of production is in Lower Austria, 31 per cent in Burgenland, with Styria producing 4.6 per cent, and the area surrounding Vienna under 2 per cent. The best quality wines are produced in the Wachau region along the Danube (Lower Austria), in Eastern and

Menu guide

Soups

Eierschwammerlsuppe chanterelle soup

Frittatensuppe clear broth with crepes

Rollgerstelsuppe pearl barley soup

Meat courses

Backhendl chicken fried in breadcrumbs

Bauernschmaus mixed meats with dumplings and sauerkraut

Beuschel chopped lung in sauce

Blunzen black pudding

Debreziner paprika-spiced sausage

Faschiertes minced meat

Fleischlaberl rissoles

Grammelknödel dumplings stuffed with pork scratchings

Selchfleischknödel dumplings stuffed with smoked pork

Hirschragout venison stew

Jungfernbraten loin of pork

Kalbsvögerl knuckle of veal

Karree shoulder of pork (often smoked)

Kuttelfleck tripe

Lendenbraten roast sirloin

Lungenbraten loin of pork

Krenfleisch boiled pork with grated horseradish

Schöpsernes mutton

Stelze leg of veal or pork, roast, smoked or boiled

Tafelspitz boiled beef, typically with horseradish, chives, apple sauce or other condiments (a Viennese speciality)

Vanillerostbraten garlic-seasoned roast beef

Wiener Schnitzel breaded veal or (usually) pork fillet; (a Viennese favourite, served with cold onion and potato salad)

Zwiebelrostbraten roast or fried beef with crispy onions

Fish

Fogosch pike-perch ('sander')

Forelle trout

Karpfen carp

Lachs salmon

Vegetables and pasta

Blaukraut red cabbage

Bummerlsalat iceberg lettuce

Bohnen beans

Fisolen runner beans

Jägersalat salad of Chinese cabbage

Knödel dumplings (made with flour, potatoes, bread or yeast)

Krautfleckerl square pasta with seasoned cabbage

Nockerl semolina dumplings

Paradeiser tomatoes

Risipisi rice with peas

Schinkenfleckerln ham with square noodles

Semmelknödel bread dumplings with parsley and onion

Serviettenknödel as above, but with different seasoning

Some desserts

Auflauf steamed or soufflé pudding

Buchteln (or *Wuchteln*) yeast dumplings with vanilla sauce or filled with jam

Germknödel yeast dumpling

Gugelhupf pound cake

Himbeergrotz purée of fresh raspberries (also made with other soft fruits; Grütze is the jellified juice)

Kaiserschmarrn pancake with raisins and plum compote

Millirahmstrudel strudel with sweet cheese filling and vanilla sauce, (also Milchrahmstrudel)

Mohr im Hemd steamed pudding with chocolate and nuts

Palatschinken pancakes

Powidl plum sauce

Zwetschkenknödel plum dumplings

Zwetschkenröster plum compote

Southern Styria, around the Neusiedler See and in Central Burgenland. However, there is also very extensive wine production in the Weinviertel of Lower Austria and on the foothills of the Wienerwald and along the periphery of Vienna, particularly at Gumpoldskirchen near Baden bei Wien. The only *Bundesland* completely lacking in commercial wine production is Salzburger Land.

White wine
White wines are the glory of Austrian viticulture, and of these the outstanding one is *Grüner Veltliner*, which constitutes 36 per cent of all production. This is a refreshingly tart white wine that makes an excellent accompaniment to traditional pork dishes (a not untypical Austrian meal might be Wiener Schnitzel with potato salad washed down with *Grüner Veltliner*). The best *Veltliner*, though of extremely high quality, cannot really aspire to the greatness and refinement of a top Burgundy; that distinction is reserved in Austria for the finest *Rhein Riesling* of the Wachau. Other white wines offering solid quality include *Weißburgunder* and *Welschriesling* (particularly those from Burgenland and Styria), as well as *Müller-Thurgau*, *Zierfandler* and *Rotgipfler*, the last two being specialities of Gumpoldskirchen. There are also a large number of *Spätlese* dessert wines that are sought after in Germany, together with the so-called *Eiswein*, which is made from grapes that have been exposed to frost.

Rosé and red wine
The most notable rosé is the often excellent *Schilcher* (see p 216), largely a product of Western Styria, which is a dry wine with a good nose and beautiful colour. The best red wines are generally to be found in Burgenland, including the *Blaufränkisch* typical of Central Burgenland, the *Blauburger* and the fruity *St Laurent*. The most ubiquitous reds are the *Blauer Zweigelt* (6 per cent of production) and the *Blauer Portugieser* (5 per cent). The last-named seems not to travel; in situ it can be superb, having at its best a delightful well-balanced and full bodied character.

Heuriger wine
The wine culture of the Viennese *Heurigen* is a world in itself. Around the periphery of the capital are some 700 small producers, many of them with their own taverns backing on to their vineyards in places such as Grinzing, Heiligenstadt, Stammersdorf, Mauer and elsewhere. The wine here is drunk young and theoretically the taverns should close when the current vintage (*Heuriger*) is exhausted. Most of the wine, which is dryish and slightly petillant, is a mixture of grape varieties (*Gemischter Satz*) and is certainly an acquired taste. Cheap house wine in Heurigen and elsewhere is dispensed in divisions of a litre–*ein Achtel* (one-eighth), *ein Viertel* (a quarter) being equal to small or large glasses; the *Viertel* is usually served in the goblet-like Römer glasses which hold exactly that amount. Wine may be described as *süß* (sweet), *mild* (mild), *resch* or *herb* (dry, but on wine labels the words *trocken* and *halbtrocken* are used). The *G'spritzer* is often resorted to when the weather is hot.

Beer
The most drinkable Austrian beer is on draught (*vom Fass*) and may be ordered in half litres (*Krügel*) or as one-third of a litre (*Seidel*). It is obtainable as malty Lager (or *Märzen*), Pils (strongly hopped) or *Weizen-Bier* (wheat or 'white' beer). There is also a small number of stouts and speciality beers. Austrian beer pro-

duction is concentrated in a few large regional breweries, such as the Schwechater brewery near Vienna or the famous *Gösser brewery* at Göß (Leoben, see p 224) in Styria; also substantial is the production of the *Zipfer* and *Puntigamer breweries* and that of the Salzburg firm of *Stiegl*. In truth Austrian beers are nowhere near as interesting or appealing as those produced just across the border in Bavaria or the Czech Republic.

Fruit juices, mineral waters

Austria is a major producer of **fruit juices** which constitute an important export item, especially to the Arab world. Unfortunately these are almost all from fruit concentrate and are moderately nasty. The vice-like grip of the big producers on this lucrative trade seems to have prevented the mass marketing of chilled fresh juice to the supermarkets. Also drunk by Austrians in the autumn is slightly alcoholic fruit juice (*Most*) and fermenting grape juice (*Sturm*).

Austria has a variety of good **mineral waters**, two of the biggest producers being the *Römerquelle* and *Vöslauer* springs, although there are several others. Almost all exist in carbonated or still form, but they are not necessarily much better than tap water which tends to be of good quality (for example Vienna's supply comes mostly from the Alps).

Coffee

Where Austria differs sharply from Germany is in its sophisticated coffee culture. An entire vocabulary exists to describe the variations of coffee that may be ordered by the habitués of Viennese coffee houses, but the most common are the *Wiener Melange* (coffee with steamed but not frothy milk), *Großer* or *Kleiner Brauner* (small or large white coffees) or Italian-style Espresso often called *Mokka* in Austria.

According to legend, coffee beans were left behind by the besieging Turkish armies in 1683. A certain Georg Franz Kolschitzky, a businessman who had been an interpreter for western commercial interests in Belgrade and was active during the siege, was rewarded with a concession for a coffee house after the victory. However, the **first coffee house** actually opened in Vienna in 1685 was that of a Greek (or possibly Armenian) named Johannes Theodat (Diodato), who had also opened the first European coffee house in Venice in 1645. In 1697 the first of the middle-class coffee houses in Vienna was opened by one Isaak de Luca and from the 18C onwards the coffee house began to acquire its distinctive social features such as free newspapers for the customers and (in some cases) billiards. The heyday of the Viennese coffee house was the turn of the 19C when they were crammed with artists and writers and the *Feuilleton* (a short and witty newspaper essay on some cultural theme) was the ideal catalyst for intellectual discussion, not to say feuding, over the steaming cups. This milieu is well described by Harold B. Segel in *The Vienna Coffeehouse Wits, 1890–1938* (Indiana, 1993), which also offers a good selection of *Feuilletons* by the masters of the genre including Hermann Bahr, Karl Kraus, Peter Altenberg, Felix Salten and others.

Post offices and telephones

Austria is planning to privatise its **post office** having already semi-privatised (1996) its Telecom branch and gradually allowed competition. This has resulted in a steep reduction in hitherto absurdly high telephone charges.

Post offices are open from 08.00–12.00 and 14.00–18.00, Mon–Fri; some in the centres of larger towns do not close for lunch and also open on Sat from 08.00–12.00. Twenty-four-hour post offices exist in Vienna (Westbahnhof, Südbahnhof), Graz (Neutorgasse 46), Salzburg (Hauptbahnhof) and Innsbruck (Maximilianstrasse 2). Poste Restante (*Postlagernd*) letters can be sent to any individual post office. For collection your passport will be required and the letters are held for 30 days. Stamps (*Briefmarken*) are available at *Trafik* shops, which may be found throughout towns and at railway stations etc.

Telephone kiosks and telephone booths in post offices are widespread and preferable to using the hotel phone if you want to avoid an enormous supplement. Phonecards (*Telefonkarten*) can be bought at Tabak/Trafik shops and in post offices in denominations of 50, 100 and 200 ATS. Some phone booths accept major credit cards. Mobile and satellite phone companies now operate in Austria and it is usually cheaper to use the latter for overseas calls if you are a subscriber. In general it is much cheaper to telephone between 18.00 and 08.00 and between 18.00 on Friday and 08.00 on Monday.

Dialling codes to Austria
From Australia and New Zealand ☎ 001143
From the United Kingdom and Ireland ☎ 0043
From North America ☎ 01143
The dialling codes for the provincial capitals are supplied at the relevant place in the text. If dialling from abroad, you should drop the initial 0 of the regional code.

Dialling codes from Austria
Australia ☎ 0061   Ireland ☎ 00353
New Zealand ☎ 0064   United Kingdom ☎ 0044
North America ☎ 001

Emergency telephone numbers
General emergency (Euro-Notruf) number ☎ 112
Ambulance: ☎ 144   Police: ☎ 133   Fire: ☎ 122
Doctor (*Notarzt*): ☎ 141 (for calling a doctor out of hours).

Useful telphone numbers
Inland directory enquiries ☎ 11811
International operator ☎ 11812 (Germany); ☎ 11813 (Europe); ☎ 11814 (others)

Snow reports: Wien, Niederösterreich, Steiermark: ☎ 1583
Salzburg, Oberösterreich, Kärnten: ☎ 1584
Tirol, Vorarlberg: ☎ 1585
Lake temperature reports (May–September): ☎ 1528
Speaking clock: ☎ 1503

Museums and churches

The opening times of all the sights that are not permanently accessible have been given in the main text of the guide. The following additional factors should be borne in mind:

Opening hours are not standardised but in general larger museums are likely to be closed one day in the week, usually Monday. Smaller museums may open only on certain weekdays and are likely to have a long lunch break between 12.00–13.30. Churches in large towns and cities are usually open from about 07.00 or 08.00 until 18.00, sometimes later. In outlying areas churches may be kept locked and instructions for obtaining access have been given in the text.

Admission is charged for access to all museums, although in a few cases there is gratis access on certain days of the year. Admission to *Burgen*, *Schlösser* and monasteries (*Stifte*) is usually only possible with a guided tour, for which payment must be made. Exceptions are the monastery churches which in many cases may be entered free of charge during daylight hours. The same is generally true of major *Schloßparks* like Vienna's *Schönbrunn*.

In the last few years, and indeed since the publication of the previous edition of this guide, many museums have been modernised both in terms of administration and structure. The most striking example is *Schloss Belvedere* in Vienna, which has been restored to its ancient glory after a complete refurbishment lasting several years. Along with modernisation and refurbishment have come better facilities for visitors, usually in the form of cafés and bookshops (e.g. the excellent bookshop in the Upper Belvedere, or the bookshop and somewhat trendy restaurant opened in the Austrian Museum of Applied Art in Vienna).

The descriptions offered of the architectural history and the interiors of the churches mentioned in the guide are necessarily selective, but hopefully not arbitrary. However, supplementary information is usually at hand for German speakers in the form of the detailed *Kirchenführer* which are almost always on sale in the church at a cost of 30–50 ATS. Non-German speakers should also check to see whether there is an English summary, as is sometimes the case for larger and more important churches, or even an English version.

Additional information

Foreign embassies and consulates in Vienna
Australia Mattiellistrasse 2–4. ☎ 512 85 80.
Canada Laurenzerberg 2. ☎ 531 3830 00.
Ireland Landstraßer Hauptstraße 2 (Hilton Centre). ☎ 715 42 46–0.
New Zealand Consulate Springsiedelgasse 28. ☎ 318 85 05, fax: 318 67 17.
South Africa Sandgasse 33. ☎ 320 64 93–0.
United Kingdom Embassy Jaurèsgasse 12. ☎ 716 13–0. Consulate Jaurèsgasse 10. ☎ 716 13–5151, fax: 716 13–59 00.

United States Embassy Boltzmanngasse 16. ☎ 313 39–0. Consulate Gartenbaupromenade 2. ☎ 313 39–0.

Public Holidays in Austria

Many museums and galleries remain open on most Public Holidays (some of them with gratis entry), but there are also a number that close. It is best to check in advance with the place you intend visiting.

1 January (New Year's Day)	*Neues Jahr*
6 January (Epiphany)	*Dreikönigsfest*
Easter Monday	*Ostermontag*
1 May (Labour Day)	*Tag der Arbeit*
Ascension Day (6th Thursday after Easter)	*Christi Himmelfahrt*
Whit Monday (6th Monday after Easter)	*Pfingstmontag*
Corpus Christi (Thursday after Trinity Sunday)	*Fronleichnam*
15 August (Feast of the Assumption)	*Maria Himmelfahrt*
26 October (National Day)	*Nationalfeiertag*
1 November (All Saints' Day)	*Allerheiligen*
8 December (Feast of the Immaculate Conception)	*Maria Empfängnis*
25 December (Christmas Day)	*Weihnachtstag/Christtag*
26 December (Boxing Day)	*Stephanitag/Stefanitag*
On Christmas Eve (an important family ccasion for Austrians) everything closes down from midday.	*Heiliger Abend*

Festivals

For details of festivals see the general introductions to Vienna and the individual *Bundesländer*.

Time

Austria is one hour ahead of GMT, six hours ahead of Eastern Standard Time and nine hours ahead of Pacific Standard Time. Austrian Summer Time lasts from the beginning of April to the end of September.

Tipping

Expensive restaurants tend to present the bill with a service charge (up to 15 per cent) already included. Otherwise the usual ten per cent for *Trinkgeld* is normal for restaurants, cafés, taxis etc., and 50 to 100 *Schillinge* for hotel porters, chamber maids etc. according to the level of service received. When paying the bill state the total you intend to give (i.e. bill plus tip) and the waiter will give you change accordingly.

Newspapers

Despite several attempts, Vienna has never been able to sustain a locally produced English language paper like those, for instance, in Athens, Budapest or Prague. A relatively new venture, *Austria Today*, is shaping up well, and is published weekly. English and American newspapers are widely available in Vienna and Salzburg and at some station bookstalls and kiosks elsewhere during the tourist season. *The Guardian* and *Financial Times* (Frankfurt editions) arrive mid-morning; other papers either late in the afternoon or the next day.

The leading serious paper in Austria is *Die Presse*, a mildly conservative organ with a tendency to pomposity, but many good features, while *Der Standard* is liberal in politics with a strong orientation to business. Some nationwide competition is provided by the *Salzburger Nachrichten*, but in practice these two big Vienna-based papers are the only ones with a wide horizon. The Graz-based *Kleine Zeitung* is a liberal Catholic Styrian paper with a wide distribution in the villages of Styria and Carinthia, so that its circulation is actually higher than some of the nationals. The *Kurier* is middle market and rather anodyne. The gutter press is for the most part virulently conservative, although the *Krohen Zeitung*, perhaps the most influential, can be unpredictable. The feisty *News*, *Profil* and newcomer *Format* are weekly news magazines competing vigorously in the field of exposés.

Ten of Austria's best ski resorts

Austria has several of the best ski resorts in Europe and a relatively long winter season. In a few places skiing is possible at high altitudes even in summer. Below are ten of the country's most favoured resorts catering for differing levels of skiing competence. Websites are included where possible.

Salzburg province

Leogang
Height of resort: 2755ft (839m). Top station 6279ft (1914m).
Nearest airport: Salzburg.
Excellent intermediate skiing pistes, well maintained.

Obertauern
www.salzburg.com/tourismus/obertauern
Height of resort: 5723ft (1744m).
Top station 7872ft (2399m).
Nearest airport: Salzburg.
A resort for skiers of all standards but especially favouring beginners up to a good medium standard.

Tirol

Ischgl
www.ischgl.com
Height of resort: 4600ft (1402m).
Top station: 9394ft (2863m).
Nearest airports: Munich, Zürich.
Suitable for second year to medium skiers, plus ski touring for all grades.
45km of Langlauf trails.

Kitzbühel
www.tiscover.com/kitzbüehel
Height of resort: 2503ft (763m). Top station: 6562ft (2000m).
Nearest airports: Munich, Salzburg.
Skiing for all standards at this internationally famous resort. Four ski schools, recently upgraded lifts, 120km of Nordic ski trails.

Mayrhofen
www.tiscover.com/mayrhofen
Height of resort: 2607ft (795m). Top station: 7283ft (2220m).
Nearest airport: Munich.
Good for beginners and medium grades and offering an excellent children's ski school.

Obergurgl/Hochgurgl
www.obergurgl.com
Height of resort: 6322ft (1927m)/7054ft (2150m). Top stations: 8648ft (2636m)/10,111ft (3082m).
Nearest airport: Munich.
Reliable snow and a long season; skiing for all grades. Quite expensive.

St Anton am Arlberg
www.stantonamarlberg.com
Height of resort: 4210ft (1283m).
Top station: 9222ft (2811m).
Nearest airport: Zürich.

Fashionable international resort ideal for experienced skiers. Expensive.

St Johann in Tirol
www.tiscover.com/st.johann-tirol
Height of resort: 2180ft (664m). Top station: 5578ft (1700m).
Nearest airports: Salzburg, Munich. Suitable for beginners to intermediates. Northerly oriented slopes through wide wooded glades hold the snow well but snow cannons on hand for main runs. 10km from Kitzbühel.

Vorarlberg
Lech am Arlberg
Height of resort: 4712ft (1436m). Top station: 8099ft (2468m).

Nearest airport: Zürich.
A resort well suited for family holidays with many ancillary activities and sports for non-skiers. Expensive.

Zürs am Arlberg
Height of resort: 5590ft (1704m). Top station: 8036ft (2449m).
Nearest airport: Zürich.
Small resort with an international reputation catering for serious skiers.

Detailed descriptions of all Austrian resorts covering terrain, snow conditions, ski facilities, Après Ski etc. are available from Austrian National Tourist Offices.

Walking
For details of hiking maps, see the entry under **maps** (see p 20). Austria is a paradise for hikers offering an enormous choice of walking terrain ranging from the rolling Alpine foothills of Styria, Upper Austria and Lower Austria to the Alps themselves, or the flat land round the Neusiedler See on the edge of the Pannonian plain. Some of the facilities used for winter sports are available for ramblers in summer and there are numerous mountain huts for overnighting in summer. The local tourist office usually has a good selection of **Wanderwege** (walking routes) which are well signposted and for which a map is provided. These are colour-coded, blue for untaxing walks, red for those that are more difficult, black for which fitness is required and ideally should be tackled on a guided tour.

A relevant organisation is the *Österreichischer Alpenverein* Wilhelm-Greil-Straße 15, Innsbruck (☎ 0 51 2 5947, fax: 575 528). This has a UK affiliation: *Austrian Alpine Club*, P.O. Box 43, Welwyn Garden City, Hertfordshire A18 6PQ (☎ 01707 324 835). Membership costs around £30 a year and entitles you to a 50 per cent reduction in all alpine huts run by the *ÖAV*. Included also is worldwide mountain accident rescue cover, but it is also worth checking whether further specific cover might not be desirable. Unless you are an experienced rambler, you should not embark upon a walking tour unless you have familiarised yourself with basic safety precautions, appropriate kit to take, international distress signals and the like. The Cicerone Press publishes some informative titles on walking in Austria. Good ideas for areas to ramble in may also be gleaned from Don Philpott's *Off the Beaten Track–Austria* (Moorland Publishing, 1989).

Golf
There are now a large number of golf courses in Austria, many of them set in idyllic locations around lakes or in the alpine foothills. More and more hotels are offering golf packages with discounted access to a local course and sometimes their own golf ranges, practice holes and professional instruction. For general

information and a list of golf courses in each Bundesland, contact Österreichischer Golf-Verband, Prinz Eugen Straße 12, 1040 Wien, ☎ (00 43 1) 505 32 45, fax (00 43 1) 505 49 62. Another useful organisation is that of the *Vereinigung der Österreichischen Golfhotels und Clubs*, whose catalogue of members may be obtained from Golf in Austria, A-5020 Salzburg, Fürbergstraße 44. ☎ 066 2–827852, fax: 822098. www.golfinfo.at, e-mail: office@golfinfo.at

BACKGROUND INFORMATION

Chronological table of Austrian rulers

House of Babenberg (Margraves)

976–94	Leopold (or Liutpold) I
994–1018	Heinrich I
1018–55	Adalbert
1055–75	Ernst
1075–95	Leopold II
1095–1136	Leopold III (canonised 1485)
1136–41	Leopold IV
	(**Dukes** from 1156)
1141–77	Heinrich II ('Jasomirgott')
1177–94	Leopold V ('the Virtuous')
1195–98	Friedrich I
1198–1230	Leopold VI
1230–46	Friedrich II ('the Valiant')

1246–73	**Interregnum**: Marguerite of Babenberg, widow of Friedrich II, married Premysl Ottakar II of Bohemia in 1251, the latter taking possession of the dukedom, and subsequently losing it to Rudolf of Habsburg after Rudolf was elected German king.

House of Habsburg

1273–91	Rudolf of Habsburg
1291–1308	Albrecht I, elected King of Germany in 1298
1308–30	Friedrich I ('the Handsome'), King of Germany from 1314 as Friedrich III
1330–58	Albrecht II
1358–65	Rudolf IV ('the Founder')
1365–95	Albrecht III, who divided the Habsburg possessions with his brother, Leopold III
1395–1404	Albrecht IV
1404–11	Dynastic struggle between Habsburgs. Tutelary regime with Albrecht V as ward, first of Duke Wilhelm, then of Duke Leopold IV.
1411–39	Albrecht V, from 1438 Emperor Albrecht II of Germany
1439–57	Ladislas ('the Posthumous'), King of Bohemia and Hungary (Ward of Friedrich V of Styria, *see below*, and never ruled)
1457–93	Friedrich of Styria (as Friedrich IV, German King from 1442, as Friedrich III, Holy Roman Emperor from 1452)
1493–1519	Maximilian I
1519–21	Karl V, who in 1521 transferred the German possessions of the Habsburgs to his brother Ferdinand

1521–64	Ferdinand I, Emperor from 1556 on abdication of Karl V
1564–76	Maximilian II
1576–1612	Rudolf II (who ruled from Prague)
1612–19	Matthias
1619–37	Ferdinand II
1637–57	Ferdinand III
1658–1705	Leopold I
1705–11	Joseph I
1711–40	Karl VI
1740–80	Maria Theresia (ruled, until his death in 1765, with her consort, Franz Stephan III of Lorraine, as Franz I Stephan, Holy Roman Emperor from 1745)
1780–90	Joseph II (who had ruled jointly with his mother from 1765)
1790–92	Leopold II
1792–1835	Franz II (from 1804, Emperor Franz I of Austria, anticipating the demise of the Holy Roman Empire in 1806)
1835–48	Ferdinand I (of Austria), known as 'the Benevolent'
1848–1916	Franz Joseph I
1916–18	Karl I

Austrian Chancellors

FIRST REPUBLIC

1918–20	Karl Renner
1920–21	Michael Mayr
1921–22	Johann Schober
1922–24	Ignaz Seipel
1924–26	Rudolf Ramek
1926–29	Ignaz Seipel
1929	Ernst Streeruwitz
1929–30	Johann Schober
1930	Carl Vaugoin
1930–31	Otto Ender
1931–32	Karl Buresch
1933	Introduction of the *Ständestaat* ('corporative state')
1932–34	Engelbert Dollfuß
1934–38	Kurt Schuschnigg
1938	Nazi take-over. *Anschluß* with the Third Reich
1938–45	Nazi regime
1945	Provisional government under Karl Renner

SECOND REPUBLIC

1945–53	Leopold Figl
1953–61	Julius Raab
1961–64	Alfons Gorbach
1964–70	Josef Klaus
1970–83	Bruno Kreisky
1983–86	Fred Sinowatz
1986–97	Franz Vranitzky
1997–2000	Viktor Klima
2000–	Wolfgang Schüssel

Federal Presidents

FIRST REPUBLIC
1920–28	Michael Hainisch
1928–38	Wilhelm Miklas

SECOND REPUBLIC
1945–50	Karl Renner
1951–57	Theodor Körner
1957–65	Adolf Schärf
1965–74	Franz Jonas
1974–86	Rudolf Kirchschläger
1986–92	Kurt Waldheim
1992–	Thomas Klestil

Introduction to Austria: Land and Society

The **Republik Österreich** (Republic of Austria) in Central Europe is bounded by eight countries: Germany to the north-west, the Czech Republic to the north, Slovakia to the north-east, Hungary to the east, Slovenia to the south, Italy to the south-west, Switzerland and Liechtenstein to the west. The **River Danube** flows through the country from **Passau** at the German border in the west to **Bratislava** over the Slovakian border in the east, about 350km (217 miles) of its course being in Austria. Almost two-thirds of Austria is taken up by the Eastern Alps, about a quarter being flat, low-lying or gently rolling terrain, typically along the Danube Valley, in the Vienna Basin and around the eastern foothills of the Alps. A small area constitutes the extension into Austria of the Bohemian tableland, a granitic upland massif which extends at places as far as, and slightly beyond, the Danube.

The Republic of Austria is divided into nine *Bundesländer* (federal provinces), details of whose topography, climate, economy etc. are given under the relevant chapter of this guide. Austria's total area is 83,858 sq km (32,376 sq miles), making it one of the smaller countries of the EU. In 1918 the Austro-Hungarian Empire, just before its demise, encompassed an area of 677,000 sq km, while a century ago the population of the area now constituting the Austrian Republic was approaching 5 million. The present population of Austria was forecast by The Economist Intelligence Unit to reach 8.1 million in 1999, and of this about 1.5 million (18.5 per cent) are resident in Vienna. Population density is around 90 per sq km on average, a figure which masks wide discrepancies between the c 46 per sq km for Tyrol and c 3700 per sq km for Vienna.

Ninety-nine per cent of Austrians speak German as their mother tongue in a version that varies in some small respects (chiefly vocabulary) from *Hochdeutsch*—enough to make a little phrasebook giving German equivalents of Austrian words a bestseller among German tourists. Many of the differences are the result of influences from other languages of the Habsburg Empire, while others are Southern German words or expressions sharing a common provenance with similar or identical words current in Bavaria. In addition each *Bundesland* has its own local form of speech, which in some cases (for example

Vienna, Tyrol and especially Vorarlberg) constitutes a dialect impenetrable to non-Austrians. There are small pockets of ethnic minorities which keep their languages alive and are given some assistance in the educational system to do so. The greatest numbers of these are from the Slovene minority in Carinthia and the Croat minority in Burgenland.

The majority (over 78 per cent) of Austrians are nominal or active members of the Roman Catholic church. Confessing Catholics, like the members of other churches are obliged to pay a 'contribution' to the church which is administered by the state, and thus erroneously often referred to as a tax. It is possible to be excused this 'tax' if a formal declaration is made to the local council that you are leaving the church. Part of the recent crisis in the Austrian church may be attributed to a mass exit provoked by Pope John Paul II's disastrous policy of packing the hierarchy with reactionary clerics, as well as to scandals such as the exposure of the homosexual molestation of minors by a very senior prelate, much exacerbated by the church's initial attempts to cover up the affair. A small group of Old Catholics date their separate status to Pope Pius IX's declaration of the doctrine of papal infallibility in 1870, which a number of contemporary Catholics found unacceptable.

The Protestant faith was legitimised (after nearly two centuries of persecution) by Emperor Joseph II's Tolerance Patent of 1781 and consists of a majority of Lutherans (nearly 340,000) and a minority of Calvinists (1700), together with various other persuasions. Protestantism was often the preferred faith for converted Jews in the 19C, assimilated Jews having a sharply differentiated lifestyle from the later-arriving Orthodox Jews who were congregated in areas such as the Leopoldstadt in Vienna or the ghetto in Eisenstadt. Since the expulsion or murder of the Jews by the Nazis, a post-war Jewish population has grown up in Vienna, having its own religious community, a synagogue (which miraculously survived the Nazi era) and a representative cultural institution in the form of the Austrian Jewish Museum (refounded in 1989 in cooperation with the *Stadt Wien*).

Austria is by any standard a prosperous country, even if it has not been entirely immune to the increasing tide of unemployment caused by the late 20C technological revolution and the triumph of neo-Liberalism. Its GDP per head at $27,347 is greater than that of the UK, and ranks in the EU after the Scandinavian countries and slightly below that of Germany. Projected GDP in 1999 was $222.2 billion, representing a healthy maintained growth of 3.4 per cent, while inflation (traditionally low in Austria, which has memories of the hyper-inflation of the 1920s) is expected to be no higher than 1.5 per cent.

Further reading

Good stocks of guides and travel books on Austria are normally held by *Stanfords*, 12–14 Long Acre, London WC2E 9LP, ☎ 020 7836 1321, *The Travel Bookshop*, 13–15 Blenheim Crescent, London W11 2EE, ☎ 020 7229 5260, and *Daunt Books*, 83 Marylebone High Street, London W1M 3DE, ☎ 020 7224 2295. For some of the more academic titles listed below, you may have to search around, while a few of the others can only be found in a library (if out of print). Bookshops in Vienna having sections of Austriaca with English books include

Freytag & Berndt (see under Maps p 20), **Prachner**, Kärntner Straße 30 (especially good on architecture), *Gerold*, Graben 31, **Shakespeare and Co.**, Sterngasse 2 and the **British Bookshop**, Weihburggasse 24–26 (☎ 512 19 450). The choice below is inevitably a personal one, but the basic criterion has been that of ease of access to information for the interested non-specialist. Publishers' details are in brackets.

General historical background

Alföldy, Geza, *Noricum* (Routledge and Kegan Paul).
Brook-Shepherd, Gordon, *The Austrians* (Harper Collins/Carroll & Graf).
Crankshaw, Edward, *The Fall of the House of Habsburg* (Macmillan).
Evans, R.J.W., *The Making of the Habsburg Monarchy* (Oxford University Press).
Good, D.F., *The Economic Rise of the Habsburg Empire, 1750–1914* (University of California Press).
Heer, Friedrich, *The Holy Roman Empire* (Phoenix).
Jelavich, Barbara, *Modern Austria: Empire to Republic, 1815–1986* (Cambridge University Press).
Kann, Robert A., *History of the Habsburg Empire, 1576–1918* (University of California Press).
Leeper, A.W.A., *History of Medieval Austria* (AMS Press, NY).
Macartney, C.A., *The Habsburg Empire, 1790–1918* (Macmillan).
Rickett, Richard, *A Brief Survey of Austrian History* (Georg Prachner Verlag, Vienna).
Sked, Alan, *The Decline of the Habsburg Empire, 1815–1918* (Longman).
Taylor, A.J.P., *The Habsburg Monarchy, 1809–1918* (Penguin).
Wangermann, Ernst, *The Austrian Achievement* (Harcourt Brace Jovanovich).
Wheatcroft, Andrew, *The Habsburgs* (Penguin).

Books on Republican Austria

Jelavich, Barbara, *Modern Austria: Empire to Republic, 1815–1986* (Cambridge University Press).
Rabinbach, Anson, *The Austrian Socialist Experiments: Social Democracy and Austromarxism, 1918–1934* (Westview Press, Boulder, Colorado).
Stadler, Karl R., *Austria* (Praeger, NY).
Sully, Melanie R., *A Contemporary History of Austria* (Routledge).

Monarchs

Beales, Derek, *Joseph II* (2 vols.) (Cambridge University Press).
Beller, Stephen, *Francis Joseph* (Longman).
Benecke, Gerhard, *Maximilian I* (Routledge and Kegan Paul).
Blanning, T.C.W., *Joseph II* (Longman).
Blanning, T.C.W., *Joseph II and Enlightened Despotism* (Harper & Row).
Crankshaw, Edward, *Maria Theresa* (Constable).
Evans, R.J.W., *Rudolf II and His World* (Thames & Hudson).
Hamann, Brigitte, *Sissy* (on the Empress Elisabeth) (Taschen America).
Palmer, Alan, *Twilight of the Habsburgs* (on Franz Joseph) (Phoenix/Grove-Atlantic).
Spielman, John P., *Leopold I of Austria* (Thames & Hudson).

Cultural and intellectual history

Beller, Stephen, *Vienna and the Jews 1867–1938* (Cambridge University Press).

Brion, Marcel, *Daily Life in the Vienna of Mozart and Schubert* (Weidenfeld and Nicholson).

Gay, Peter, *Freud* (Oxford University Press).

Janik, Allen and Toulmin, Stephen, *Wittgenstein's Vienna* (Simon & Schuster, NY).

Johnston, William M., *The Austrian Mind* (University of California Press).

Luft, David S., *Robert Musil and the Crisis of European Culture, 1880–1942* (University of California Press).

McGrath, William J., *Dionysian Art and Politics in Austria* (New Haven, Conn).

Monk, Ray, *Wittgenstein* (Vintage/Viking Penguin).

Robertson, Ritchie and Timms, Edward (eds.), *Austrian Studies* (Edinburgh University Press).

Schorske, Carl E., *Fin-de-Siècle Vienna* (Cambridge University Press, Knopf).

Shedel, James, *Art and Society: The New Art Movement in Vienna, 1897–1914* (SPOSS, Palo Alto CA).

Timms, Edward, *Karl Kraus: Apocalyptic Satirist. Culture and Catastophe in Habsburg Vienna* (Yale University Press).

Books on Vienna

Barea, Ilsa, *Vienna: Legend and Reality* (Pimlico).

Clare, George, *Last Waltz in Vienna: The Destruction of a Family, 1842–1942* (Holt Rinehart and Winston).

Hofmann, Paul, *The Viennese: Splendour, Twilight and Exile* (Anchor Books, Doubleday).

Lehne, Inge and Johnson, Lonnie, *Vienna: the Past in the Present* (Österreichischer Bundesverlag, Vienna).

Lichtenberger, Elisabeth, *Vienna: Bridge between Two Cultures* (urban history) (Belhaven Press).

Morton, Frederic, *A Nervous Splendour: Vienna 1888/1889* (Penguin).

Zweig, Stefan, *The World of Yesterday* (University of Nebraska Press).

Music

Braunbehrens, Volkmar, *Mozart in Vienna* (Harper Perennial).

Cooke, Deryck, *Gustav Mahler: An Introduction to His Music* (Faber).

Deutsch, Otto Erich, *Schubert: A Documentary Biography* (J.M. Dent).

Deutsch (ed.), Otto Erich, *Schubert: Memoirs by his Friends* (A & C Black).

Gál, Hans, *Johannes Brahms, his Works and Personality* (Alfred Knopf).

Gutman, Robert W., *Mozart: A Cultural Biography* (Secker & Warburg/Harcourt Brace).

Hanson, Alice M., *Musical Life in Biedermeier Vienna* (Cambridge University Press).

Hildesheimer, Wolfgang, *Mozart* (J.M. Dent).

Johnson, Stephen, *Bruckner Remembered* (Faber).

Lebrecht, Norman, *Mahler Remembered* (Faber).

Mahler, Alma, *Gustav Mahler: Memories and Letters* (John Murray).

Mitchell, Donald, *Gustav Mahler* (3 vols.) (Faber/Yale University Press).

Reich Willi, *The Life and Work of Alban Berg* (Thames & Hudson).

Reich, Willi, *Schoenberg: A Critical Biography* (Da Capo Press).

Rickett, Richard, *Music and Musicians in Vienna* (Georg Prachner Verlag, Vienna).

Robbins Landon, H.C. and Wyn Jones, D., *Haydn, his Life and Work* (Thames & Hudson).

Robbins Landon, H.C., *Mozart: The Golden Years* (Thames & Hudson).
Rosen, Charles, *The Classical Style: Haydn, Mozart, Beethoven* (Faber).
Schönzeler, Hans Hubert, *Bruckner* (Marion Boyars).

Art and architecture

Bourke, John, *Baroque Churches of Central Europe* (Faber).
Hempel, E., *Baroque Art and Architecture in Central Europe* (Penguin).
Lustenberger, Robert, *Adolf Loos* (Birkhauser).
Novotny, Fritz, P*ainting and Sculpture in Europe, 1780–1880* (Penguin).
Sármány-Parsons, Ilona, *Gustav Klimt* (Bonfini Press/Crown).
Sármány-Parsons, Ilona, *Viennese Painting at the Turn of the Century* (Corvina, Budapest).
Schezen, Robert, *Adolf Loos: Architecture 1903–32* (Monacelli).
Sitwell, Sacheverell, *German Baroque Art* (Duckworth).
Varnedoe, Kirk, *Vienna 1900: Art, Architecture, Design* (Museum of Modern Art, NY).
Vergo, Peter, *Art in Vienna, 1898–1918* (Phaidon).
Werkner, Patrick, *Austrian Expressionism: The Formative Years* (SPOSS, Palo Alto, CA).
Whitford, Frank, *Egon Schiele* (Thames & Hudson).
Whitford, Frank, *Gustav Klimt* (Thames & Hudson).

19C and 20C Austrian fiction in translation

Bernhard, Thomas: *Wittgenstein's Nephew* (University of Chicago); *Cutting Timber* (Vintage/Quartet); *Extinction* (Penguin/University of Chicago); *Concrete* (Quartet); *The Voice Imitator* (Quartet).
Broch, Hermann: *The Death of Virgil* (Oxford University Press); *The Sleepwalkers* (Vintage).
von Doderer, Heimito: *The Demons* (3 vols) (Quartet).
Jellinek, Elfriede: *Lust*; *The Piano Teacher*; *Wonderful, Wonderful Times* (all published by Serpent's Tail).
Kraus, Karl: *No Compromise: Selected Writings of Karl Kraus*, Ed. Frederick Ungar (Frederick Ungar Publishing, NY).
Musil, Robert: *Young Törless* (Penguin); *Five Women* (Godine, Boston); *The Man Without Qualities* (3 vols translated by Richard and Clara Winston; 2 vols translated by Sophie Wilkins, with the complete material available, however, only in the hardback version of the latter), (Picador/Vintage).
Roth, Joseph: *The Emperor's Tomb* (Chatto & Windus); *Radetzky March* (Penguin/Overlook Press).
Schnitzler, Arthur: *Vienna 1900, games with Love & Death*, (novellas) (Penguin).
Segel, Harold B. (ed. and transl.): *The Vienna Coffeehouse Wits, 1890–1938* (Purdue University Press, Indiana).
Stifter, Adalbert: *Brigitta* (Augel/Dufont).
Zweig, Stefan: *The Burning Secret and Other Stories* (E.P. Dutton).

To read on the journey....

James, Louis, *The Xenophobe's Guide to the Austrians* (Ravette Books/Oval Publications).

THE GUIDE

Wien (Vienna)

Topography

Vienna (*Wien*) is situated in the Wiener Becken (the Vienna Basin) just to the south-east of the outlying north-eastern foothills of the Alps. It owes its rise to its strategic position, already evident even in pre-history, as a trading-post on the 'dustless highway' of the River Danube, as well as its proximity to the ancient

north–south 'amber route'. The latter ran between the Baltic and Aquileia on the Adriatic, crossing the river a little downstream at nearby Carnuntum.

The River Wien (Wienfluss) and the River Danube (Donau)

The old city is bordered to the north by the Danube Canal (**Donaukanal**—part of the 19C regulation of the River Danube), into which flows the small **Wienfluß**, streaming from its source in the hills of the **Wienerwald** (Vienna Woods) to the west. The River Wien (seldom more than a trickle except in the spring thaw) is now covered for part of its course through the city, although it re-emerges in the Stadtpark, before emptying into the Danube via the canal. Regulation of the Danube (1870–75, 1882–1905) was undertaken after a succession of serious floods, to which, however, the area that is now the Second District (Leopoldstadt) and even parts of the Inner City had always been subject. 19C engineers co-ordinated the main arms of the river into the so-called **Große Donau**, over which eleven bridges (three of them for the railway) have subsequently been built. One side-arm to the north is preserved as a recreation and bathing area known as the **Alte Donau** (Old Danube). In the 1980s the **Neue Donau** (New Danube) was isolated and the **Donauinsel** (Danube Island—25km long, up to 250m wide) was created, both serving as recreation areas offering water sports, cycling and various other activities.

The Danube itself, a land and water route taken by settlers, missionaries and crusaders (1098, 1147, 1188), has infused Vienna from earliest times not only with money and the goods of western merchants, but also with culture and religion. The Babenberg Margraves (see p 35) moved their headquarters progressively down the river, finally making Vienna their residence in 1156, while the early missionary, St Severin, spread his gospel (like the earlier St Florian) along both sides of the river, dying in 482 at Favianae (Mautern) and being buried (according to tradition) in Heiligenstadt; the retreating legionaries subsequently took his bones with them to Italy. In the same way, the first monks called to Vienna to found a monastery in the mid-12C travelled downstream from Regensburg to set up their *Schottenstift* (convent of the Scots) which actually consisted of Irish brothers.

Ringstraße

South of the Danube, the ancient core of Vienna is girdled by the Ringstraße, a boulevard created after the defensive bastions built in the mid-16C were demolished by order of Franz Joseph in 1857. Its northern stretch runs parallel to the Danube Canal, beyond which are four districts (Brigittenau, Leopoldstadt, Floridsdorf and Donaustadt) encompassing the UNO-City and two great parks, the Augarten and the Prater. The **Leopoldstadt** in particular has an interesting history, receiving its modern name in 1669 when Leopold I expelled the Jews from the flood area (then known as the **Untere Werd**), which they had occupied since 1625. It again became the Jewish quarter as Jews drifted back to Vienna in the 18C, the trickle becoming a flood in the 19C. Since the Nazi era, which forced into exile or liquidated all but a handful of Vienna's 180,000 Jews, it has become rather a subdued part of town, although efforts have been made to revive it with the opening of a **Crime Museum** (open Tues–Sun, 10.00–17.00) at Große Sperlgasse 24, and the location here of some important institutions such as OPEC. Recently several religious and cultural institutions of the Jewish community have once again begun operating in the district.

Vienna's suburbs

Most of the other suburban districts are south of the Danube Canal and many incorporate ancient settlements that are outside the city's outer Ring Road, known as the **Gürtel**, the latter following the line of the defensive **Linienwall** built between 1704–38 with the compulsory labour of every able-bodied inhabitant between the ages of 18 and 60 and intended to stop the marauding *kuruc* (freedom fighter) armies of the Hungarians. Ottakring, for example, appears in documents of the 12C, and was not incorporated into the city until 1890.

The bulk of Vienna's suburbs stretch to the west and south-west, including attractive wine villages like **Grinzing** and **Heiligenstadt** on the periphery of the city. Fashionable residential areas are **Hietzing** close to Schönbrunn (traditionally favoured by the bourgeoisie and government officials), the **Josefstadt** for the *beau monde*, or the ambassadorial villa territory of Währing and Döbling. **Favoriten** (created 1873) has always been a working-class district, populated during the building booms of the late 19C by Czech construction workers living close to the brickworks of the Wienerberg, and now with a large *Gastarbeiter* population. **Mariahilf** is mixed *bürgerlich* and artisan, containing the shopping emporia of Mariahilfer Straße, Vienna's Oxford Street.

It is said that many families have lived for generations in the same Viennese district, a fact that has accentuated the 'local identities' of the city which counterpoint its 'big city' status, identities also intensified by the infrastructure of small enterprises creating a local self-sufficiency ('*Grätzel-Kultur*' in Viennese dialect).

Climate and environment

In the 16C an aphorism current among the Viennese students stamped an image on the city it has never quite managed to shed: '*Vienna ventosa vel venenosa*' ('in Vienna either the wind or the plague is always raging'—the plague signifying in this case syphilis as much as the recurrent epidemics of the Black Death). It is a nice encapsulation of the relationship between the local climate and the sensual appetites of the natives, the latter being described by the medieval poet Tannhäuser as '*Phaeaces*' after the gluttonous and libidinous race mentioned in the *Odyssey*. The Viennese were, in fact, constantly castigated for their loose ways: the Baroque preacher, Abraham a Sancta Clara, threatened them with hell fire, while Maria Theresia pursued them with a Chastity Commission. On the other hand, the air in the city is actually refreshed by the prevailing west winds, not infrequently also by the *Föhn*, a warm Alpine blow that afflicts the natives with lassitude and migraines.

In general Vienna's climate is subject to Atlantic and Continental influences. Winter can be bitterly cold, although there appears to be some global warming effect, since recent years have been unexpectedly milder and drier. The 1992 statistics show 52 days of frost and a yearly average air temperature of 11.4° C. It is often uncomfortably hot in July and August, when many Viennese leave the city: the general atmosphere of hothouse oppression is brilliantly caught in Franz Grillparzer's portentous lines in *Abschied von Wien* (Leaving Vienna): '*Entnervend weht dein Sommerhauch,/Du Capua der Geister!*' ('Enervating is your summer's breath/You Capua of the mind!'). On the other hand, as is appropriate in a city with a powerful death cult, Reinhold Schneider's unsurpassed evocation of winter in Vienna (written between November 1957 and March 1958) remains a *memento mori* of striking resonance: '... the icy Pannonian wind scattered the barren leaves of the faded year across the paving-stones; they found no more peace here than the poor souls in the storms of hell; no hat was safe on my head ... under a chilling blue sky, in brilliant sunshine, and whipped by the north wind, the street lamps were still burning in the dead streets of a Sunday afternoon ... as if, suddenly, it was midnight'.

Economy

The Viennese economy is dominated by the service sector (around 75 per cent of all employees and 85 per cent of workplaces). Mostly smaller and middle-sized enterprises are active in the city, 46 per cent of them having no more than four employees and 26 per cent being family concerns, while only about 140 concerns employ more than 500 people. Officially some 12 per cent of the workforce are foreigners (Southern Slavs, Turks and Poles), but many more are known to work in the black economy. The population views this with some indulgence (except when unemployment rises in a recession and right-wing politicians make capital out of xenophobic fears): the high cost of services like house renovation and car repairs, with 20 per cent value added tax on official bills, means that '*Pfuscher*' ('unauthorised' workers) are widely used for this sort of work, as also in the construction industry. The government constantly threatens to crack down, but has not yet found an uncontroversial formula for doing so.

Traditionally a substantial portion of Vienna's c 1.5 million inhabitants are engaged in, or dependent on, the state bureaucracy, while another substantial layer of bureaucrats is required for the local administration, Vienna being one of the nine *Bundesländer* (Federal States) since its separation from Niederösterreich (Lower Austria) in 1922. A further boost to the local economy is supplied by the United Nations' organisations and other international bodies holding sessions or located in Vienna (UNIDO, International Atomic Energy Agency, Conference on Security and Co-operation in Europe, OPEC and others); their many relatively well-paid employees swell the takings of restaurateurs and the fashionable shops, not to mention the bank accounts of the city's rapacious real estate agents. Immigration and temporary settlement (a pronounced characteristic of Vienna ever since it existed) thus occurs markedly at both the top and bottom ends of the social and income scales.

Manufacturing or production is primarily in food-processing, brewing, metal-working, chemicals, oil refining and printing. Major income factors are the large industrial fairs held each year, together with substantial tourism. Even in 1883 Vienna had 200,000 visitors, and a century later there were over 6.5 million, 85 per cent of them non-Austrian. Since the fall of the Iron Curtain, there are large numbers of short-stay tourists from the former Communist states, whose spending power is gradually increasing. Indeed the Russians, though not always respectable ones, already match American visitors in per capita expenditure, partly because Vienna may seem a convenient backwater for *sub rosa* Mafia activities.

As the capital of Austria and a Federal State, Vienna also enjoys representative status and is the seat of the Federal Government and Federal President. The headquarters of Austrian TV and radio, together with many other constitutional, administrative, ecclesiastical and commercial bodies are all located here. In addition it is a transport hub with *Autobahn* links to the west, south and east, while three major railway termini serve different points of the compass.

Practical information

Area: 415sq km. Population: 1.5 million. Telephone dialling code: 01

Tourist information
Tourist-Info, 1 Albertinaplatz (open 09.00–19.00), behind the State Opera, offers hotel booking, sightseeing and ticket services. There are other offices at the end of the *West-Autobahn* (Informationspavillon, Wientalstraße-Auhof-Raststätte. Open Apr–Oct 08.00–22.00, 09.00–19.00 in Nov, 10.00–18.00 Dec to Easter), and the end of the *Süd-Autobahn* (Triester Straße 149, open Apr–June and Oct, 09.00–19.00, and July–Sept from 08.00–22.00), as well as at the Donauinsel/Floridsdorfer Brücke Parkplatz and Schwechat Airport.

Maps Various street plans can be obtained from *Freytag & Berndt* at Kohlmarkt 9 in the Inner City.

Getting there
Airport Schwechat (19km east of Vienna). Regular tran-

sit buses to Hilton, Südbahnhof and Westbahnhof. *Schnellbahn* (City Transit Train) to Landstraßer Hauptstraße terminus. Flight information: ☎ 7007 2233. (See p 16 for further details.) The *Schnellbahn* continues to Wien-Nord (Praterstern).

Railway stations *Westbahnhof* (for Western Austria and West Europe, but also some trains to Budapest and beyond), *Südbahnhof* (for Austria east and south of Vienna, Southern and Eastern Europe, but also trains to Prague and Berlin), *Franz-Josefs-Bahnhof* (for north Austria). Information: ☎ 58 00 1717.

Bus station *Autobusbahnhof* Wien-Mitte (Landstraßer Hauptstraße 1B): ☎ 711 07–3850.

Public transport
Tickets may be purchased from *Tabak/Trafik* (newsagent/tobacconist outlets), which can be found at all transport termini and in many other places. It is advisable to buy a three-day or weekly season ticket (photo required), which covers the entire network of

trams, buses, U-Bahn and *Schnellbahn* (single tickets are very expensive). The *Umwelt-Streifennetzkarte* has eight coupons, each for a whole day's travel anywhere on the network: you validate **one coupon for each person** for each day's travel. Machines for validating tickets stand at the entrance to the U-Bahn, and are also located in all trams and most buses (if not, the driver will stamp your ticket). Be sure to validate the coupons starting with no. 1. This ticket is perhaps most convenient for small groups travelling together.
Taxis ☎ 31300, 40100 or 60160.

Hotels

The Vienna Tourist Bureau issues a free list of hotels and pensions with summer and winter rates and there are accommodation bureaux at the airport and main railway stations. For the tourist office's booking service, ☎ (43) 1 211 14 444, fax (43) 1 211 14 445, e-mail: rooms@info.wien.at, www.info.wien.at
Recommended hotels include:
✰✰✰✰ *Hotel Sacher*, Philharmoniker-straße 4. ☎ 514 56; fax 51 456-810. Founded in 1876 by the son of Metternich's pastry-cook, this is the most famous of Vienna's hotels. Its Historicist interiors have been discreetly modernised but the spirit and impeccable taste of the original hotel remains. There is a restaurant, two cafés and two bars, plus, of course, 'Sachertorte'.
✰✰✰✰ *Hotel im Palais Schwarzenberg*, Schwarzenbergplatz 9. ☎ 798 45 15; fax 798 4714. Still owned by a Schwarzenberg, this elegant Fischer von Erlach palace is just the place for a few nights of luxury, no expense spared. The restaurant is one of the best in Vienna.
✰✰✰✰ *ANA Grand Hotel*, Kärntner Ring 9. ☎ 515 80–0; fax 515 13 13. All Nippon Airways claim to have spent a staggering 6 billion ATS on renovating

the long defunct Grand Hotel of the Ringstraßen era, of which only the façade remains. However, the internal decorative effects are elegant rather than brash and the facilities on offer are state of the art. Japanese specialities for weight-watchers at the Unkai Restaurant on the seventh floor.
✰✰✰✰ *Bristol*, Kärntner Ring 1. ☎ 515 16–0; fax 515 16–550. Built in 1894 and a favourite with music stars performing at the adjacent opera, the Bristol has an old-fashioned splendour about it. Regulars tend to stick to their favourite Ringstraßen-palais hotels, and it is hard to choose between them in terms of good taste and quality of service, although each has developed its own ambience.
✰✰✰✰ *Imperial* (Kärntner Ring 16, ☎ 501 10; fax 501 10–410) has a formal grandeur, as befitting the *Staatshotel* where visiting dignitaries are accommodated.
✰✰✰✰ *Radisson SAS Palais Hotel* (Parkring 16, ☎ 51 51 70; fax 51 22 216) has perhaps the happiest combination of style and comfort.
All of these hotels have gourmet restaurants attached, of which the Bristol's *Korso* is considered by many to be the best in the city.
✰✰✰(✰) *Rogner Hotel Biedermeier im Sünnhof*, Landstraßer Hauptstraße 28. ☎ 716 71; fax 716 71–503. Set in a restored Biedermeier (1820s) building of great charm this hotel won the Europa-Nostra prize for architectural conservation when completed. Cherry wood furniture, topographical prints and creamy wallpaper in rooms reached from long corridors completes the period feel. It is conveniently close to the Landstraßer Hauptstraße traffic connections and airport bus.
✰✰✰(✰) *Das Triest*, Wiedner Hauptstraße 12. ☎ 589 18–0; fax 589 18–18. Vienna's newest luxury hotel designed by Sir Terence Conran in a spare, functional style that will please post-modernists and (probably) the ghost of Adolf

Loos. The Vienna Tourist Board, which tends to think the lobbies of five-star hotels should be dripping in gilt and chandeliers, hesitated for a long time over the hotel's official category, but this is academic. If you like this sort of thing, you like it a lot, and the restaurant (as you would expect) is even better. ✿✿✿ *König von Ungarn*, Schulerstraße 10. ☎ 515 84; fax 515 848. Seventeenth-century hostelry built round an open courtyard. Lots of period charm and convenient central location close to St Stephen's.

✿✿✿ *Altstadt Vienna*, Kirchengasse 41. ☎ 526 33 99; fax 523 49 01. Nice views over picturesque Baroque and 19C buildings around St Ulrich's church, family atmosphere. It is situated outside the Ringstraße close to the congenial Josefstadt district.

✿✿✿ *Hotel Römischer Kaiser*, Annagasse 16. ☎ 512 77 51–0; fax 512 77 51–13. The town palace for one of Maria Theresia's officials; a delightful smaller hotel with attractive Rococo interiors. Close to the city centre.

Pensions, small hotels

✿✿✿ *Pension Pertschy*, Habsburgergasse 5. ☎ 534 49; fax 534 49 49. Just off the Graben. Tends to get booked up with faithful regulars.

✿✿ *Pension Nossek*, Graben 17. ☎ 533 70 41; fax 535 36 46. Hard to get more central than the Graben, and some of the bedrooms even overlook it.

✿✿ *Hotel Wandl*, Petersplatz 9. ☎ 534 55; fax 534 55–77. Long-standing hotel of unpretentious charm in a period building.

✿✿ *Pension Landhaus Fuhrgassl-Huber*, Rathstraße 24, Neustift am Walde. ☎ 440 30 33; fax 440 27 14. This very picturesque country-style pension is the rustic option for those preferring a Heuriger wine-village as their base. Its considerable charm makes up for its distance from the centre.

Youth hostels

The large choice of places to stay is supplemented in the summer months (1 July–30 Sept) by student hostels turned into seasonal hotels: ✿ *Academia* (Pfeilgasse 3A, ☎ 401 76 /0; fax 401 76-20), ✿✿ *Atlas* (Lerchenfelder Straße 1–3. ☎ 521 78 /0; fax 401 76–20), ✿ *Avis* (Pfeilgasse 4, ☎ 401 74/0; fax 401 76–20), and a dozen others of varying degrees of comfort. Youth hostel information may be obtained from the **Jugendherbergsverband** at Schottenring 28 (☎ 533 53 53); there are eight hostels in the city.

Restaurants

German speakers might consider investing in Falter's *complete* listing of all categories of eating establishments (currently 4000), updated annually and entitled *Wien, wie es ißt*. Its most useful features are that it includes everything from gourmet restaurants to the local greasy spoon, by area, as well as giving a brief impartial description, a clear price category, telephone numbers and opening hours.

Gourmet restaurants in hotels

Korso bei der Oper (in Hotel Bristol), Mahlerstraße 2.
Restaurant Imperial (in Hotel Imperial), Kärntner Ring 16.
Vier Jahreszeiten (in Inter-Continental Hotel), Johannesgasse 28.
Restaurant im Palais Schwarzenberg (in Hotel im Palais Schwarzenberg), Schwarzenbergplatz 9.
Le Siècle im Ersten (in Radisson SAS Palais-Hotel), Parkring 16.

Fine cooking in elegant surroundings

Drei Husaren, Weihburggasse 4 (noble Austrian cuisine).
Eckel, Sieveringer Straße 46 (Austrian regional dishes and some international cuisine, long and seductive Austrian wine list).
Steirereck, Rasumofskygasse 2 (Styrian

specialities, 'Neue Wiener Küche', shares laurels with **Korso** as gourmets' choice in Vienna, booking required several days ahead).
Kervansaray/Hummerbar, Mahlerstraße 9 (Turkish owned seafood restaurant.

Local cooking–'Wiener Beiseln'
Zu den 3 Hacken, Singerstraße 28.
Figlmüller, Wollzeile 5.
Ofenloch, Kurrentgasse 8.
Pfudl, Bäckerstraße 22.
Zur Tabakspfeife, Goldschmiedgasse 4.

Traditional Wiener cafés
Diglas, Wollzeile 10.
Café Ministerium, Georg-Coch-Platz 4.
Café Landtmann, Dr. Karl-Lueger-Ring 4.
Café Griensteidl, Michaelerplatz 2.

Wine cellars (also serving food)
Augustinerkeller, Augustinerstraße 1.
Esterhazykeller, Haarhof 1.
Melker Stiftskeller, Schottengasse 3.
Urbanikeller, Am Hof 12.

Self-service
Naschmarkt, Schwarzenbergplatz 16, Schottengasse 1.
Nordsee (chain of fish restaurants), Kohlmarkt 6, Kärntner Straße 25 and elsewhere.

Sandwich bars
Trzesniewski, Dorotheergasse 1.
Superimbiss Duran, Rotenturmstraße 11.

Konditoreien
Lehmann, Graben 12.
Heiner, Kärntner Straße 21–23, Wollzeile 9.
Kurcafé Konditorei Oberlaa, Neuer Markt 16, Landstraßer Hauptstraße 1.
Aida, a large chain with cafés at Stock im Eisen-Platz 2 etc. and *Demel*, Kohlmarkt 14.

Main post office
Fleischmarkt 19 (1st District). There is a 24-hour counter here, as also at the Südbahnhof and Westbahnhof. Other post offices are open Mon–Fri 08.00–12.00, 14.00–18.00.

Police
☎ 133

Shopping
There are two main shopping streets in Vienna, although this should not imply that interesting shops do not exist elsewhere (e.g. on the **Graben** and in fashionable streets of the Inner City such as the **Kohlmarkt**). However, **Kärntner Strasse** is the principal location for upmarket shops in the centre, while **Mariahilfer Straße** on the border of the 6th and 7th districts is Vienna's Oxford Street. The big traditional stores such as *Gerngross* or newer ones like the *Virgin Megastore* are situated here, together with shops selling hi-fis, computers, cameras and electrical goods. For items like camera accessories and software, the smaller specialist shops in the streets just off Mariahilfer Straße may offer better value.

Vienna's main market is the **Naschmarkt**, located between the Linke and Rechte Wienzeile in an area just to the south-west of the Secession building. This is the luxury food market (with lots of snack bars), but on Saturdays it becomes a flea market (**Flohmarkt**, open 08.00–13.00) at its western end, where it may still be possible for a knowledgeable collector to pick up smaller antiques that have been overlooked by the traders. However, the staples of the market are recycled goods that have been thrown out of lumber rooms, together with clothes and the usual second-hand books, prints, etc.

Those looking for specifically Austrian artefacts could investigate the **Augarten porcelain**, which is sold from a shop at Stock-im-Eisen-Platz 3–4, and also at Schloss Augarten (Obere Augartenstraße

1). **Gmunden ceramics** from the town of that name in Upper Austria (see p 275) may be purchased at Kärntner Strasse 10, from a shop in the alley known as the Kärntner Durchgang. The firm of *Backhausen* at Kärntner Strasse 33 has inherited the designs of the Wiener Werkstätte and sells a wide range of fabrics and materials. The famous glassware manufacturers of *J. & L. Lobmeyr* have their shop at Kärntner Strasse 26, and above it a small museum that shows off some of their marvellous Historicist creations. Austrian 'ethnic' fashion is hardly likely to appeal to non-Austrians, but the green loden coat made from pressed felt looks good anywhere. You can purchase one at several shops, the most convenient being *Loden-Plankl* at Michaelerplatz 6. For small presents and souvenirs the little shop in the Hofburg Burgpassage (*Maria Stransky*) has some attractive embroidery, while the *Österreichische Werkstätten* at Kärntner Strasse 6 is packed with ornaments, gifts and costume jewellery.

Bookshops The following have a wide selection of books in English, including useful publications on Vienna and Austria: *The British Bookshop* (Weihburggasse 24–26), *Shakespeare and Co.* (Sterngasse 2), *Georg Prachner* (Kärntner Strasse 30, specialists in architectural publications), *Wolfrum* (Augustinerstraße 10, good selection of art books and prints). *Freytag & Berndt* (Kohlmarkt 9) has an enormous selection of travel books and maps (see p 20).

Cultural events

New Year's Day Morning concert by the Wiener Philharmoniker: tickets are hard to come by unless booked a year in advance from the Wiener Philharmoniker, Musikverein, Bösendorferstraße 12, A-1010, Vienna: ☎ 505 81 90, but the concert is shown across the world on television.

February Vienna ball season, the highlight being the *Opernball*.

March–June Spring season of the *Spanish Riding School*. Tickets for 'morning training' (10.00) on the day from the entrance to the Spanish Riding School at Josefsplatz 1. For evening performances (19.00 on weekdays and 10.45 on Sundays) book several months in advance by writing to Spanische Reitschule, Hofburg, A-1010 Vienna. Fax (43 1) 535 01 86. Tickets cost 250–900 ATS, plus at least 22 per cent if bought through ticket or travel agencies.

March–April *Festival Welttöne*: concert programme dedicated each year to a different region of the world. *Osterklang Wien*: Easter Music Festival (founded 1997).

April–mid-May *Frühlingsfestival*: concert series in the Musikverein and Konzerthaus, often dovetailing with anniversary celebrations of a particular composer.

May–June *Wiener Festwochen*: the most important arts festival of the year with opera, dance, theatre, concerts and exhibitions.

Last weekend in June *Donauinselfest*: open air rock, pop and folk festival on the Danube Island.

June–September *Klangbogen Wien*: chamber music and some crossover jazz/classical performances, often in attractive smaller venues such as Baroque palaces.

July *Jazz Festival*: international stars; some performances are in the Staatsoper.

July and August Free showings of opera on screen in front of the Rathaus. *Mozart at Schönbrunn*: Mozart opera performed at Schönbrunn.

October *Viennale Film Festival*.

October–November *Wien Modern*: one of Europe's most distinguished festivals of contemporary music, founded by Claudio Abbado.

November *Schubertiade* held around the anniversary of the composer's death (19 November).

November–December *Mozart and Friends*: Mozart specialists play best-loved works (but also rarities) by the composer in the Konzerthaus. *Christkindlmarkt* in front of the Rathaus and many smaller advent fairs in different parts of the city.

The *Wiener Sängerknaben* (**Vienna Boys' Choir**) hold masses in the Hofburg-kapelle every Sunday at 09.15 from 4 January to 28 June and from 12 September to 27 December. Write at least ten weeks in advance for seat tickets (60–310 ATS) to: Hofmusikkapelle, Hofburg, A-1010, Vienna. Fax: (43 1) 533 99 27–75. Otherwise tickets for standing places (limited to two per per-son) can be purchased at the chapel box office between 15.00 and 17.00 on the Friday preceding the Sunday's perfor-mance. Concert programmes of the Vienna Boys' Choir take place every Friday at 15.30 at the Konzerthaus or at the Lichtentaler Church (Mariahilf District) in May, June, September and October (tickets from hotels or *Reisebüro Mondial*, Faulmanngasse 4, A-1040, Vienna. ☎ (43 1) 588 04–141, fax (43 1) 587 12 68).

Programme of events The indis-pensable monthly *Wien Programm* gives details of each day's events in the month concerned, including opera, con-certs, drama, exhibitions, lectures and walking tours with guides. It is obtain-able from all tourist information offices.

History

From pre-history to the Romans

Settlement in the Vienna area may be traced back to the Neolithic period, while remnants of the La-Tène Celtic culture from the 4C BC have been found on the Leopoldsberg and elsewhere. The Romans arrived at the end of the 1C BC and the region (the province of Pannonia Superior) remained under Roman control until the death of the Emperor Theodosius in AD 395. Their garrison town (named '*Vindobona*' after a local tribe of Vinid Celts) was part of the *Limes* defence system along the Danube and subordinate to nearby *Carnuntum* a few miles downstream. Built on the *urbs quadrata* model, the mil-itary camp occupied the core of the inner city between the Graben and Hoher Markt areas (remains of Roman officers' quarters can still be seen on the lat-ter, while the forum was just to the west of it). The civil town (located around the Rennweg in today's 3rd District of Landstraße) was raised to *municipium* status in AD 212. However, the great migrations eventually overwhelmed the Romans, who withdrew their troops at the end of the 4C.

From the Dark Ages to the Babenbergs

In the confused period of the great migrations between Roman withdrawal and the award of the territory in 976 to the Franconian Margraves of Babenberg by the German Emperor, Otto the Great, the Vienna Basin fell under various hegemonies, latterly that of the Hungarians, until the Magyar horde suffered a crushing defeat at the hands of Otto at the Battle of Lechfeld in 955. In the Babenberg era (976–1246) the burgeoning town called '*Wenia*' from the 9C, eventually '**Wien**', became a glittering centre of medieval cul-ture after Heinrich II, the first Babenberg Duke, moved his residence here in 1156. It was located in today's 1st District in the area still known as '**Am Hof**' (i.e. 'at the court'). The most pious of the dynasty was Margrave (later St)

Leopold III (1073–1136), a ubiquitous figure in Austria's devotional iconography due to his energetic founding of churches and monasteries (Klosterneuburg, Heiligenkreuz, Mariazell). **Duke Leopold VI** (1176–1230), on the other hand, was a patron of the *Minnesänger* (courtly love poets) and a tough crusader who quarrelled with Richard Coeur de Lyon at the siege of Acre in 1191. Richard was captured in 1192 and ransomed, Leopold using his share for building defensive walls in Vienna, Wiener Neustadt and Hainburg. It was Leopold who enriched the Viennese overnight when he instituted the staple right in 1221: foreign merchants were obliged to offer their wares for sale in the city, thus enabling local middlemen to cream off the best of the transit trade.

The Habsburgs

After the Babenbergs died out in 1246, Vienna passed into the control of the Bohemian **King Ottakar II**, who had married the widow of the last Duke. Ottakar was a popular and energetic overlord, giving money for reconstruction after fire seriously damaged the town in 1258 and beginning the construction of the Hofburg. The inhabitants supported him in his struggle with Rudolf of Habsburg, who was elected German King in 1273. Opposition to the new Alemannic dynasty continued after Ottakar's defeat on the Marchfeld north of Vienna in the historic battle of Dürnkrut in 1278 and Rudolf's son, Albrecht I (ruled 1281–1308), was obliged to mollify the Viennese with municipal privileges after an uprising against him in 1287–88.

In the 14C Gothic architecture flourished in Vienna, and in particular the building of St Stephen's proceeded apace; under **Rudolf IV** ('the Founder', ruled 1358–65) its magnificent south tower was begun in 1359 and Rudolf also founded the university in 1365. However, a Theology Faculty at Vienna was refused, without which its university was destined to insignificance until permission was granted in 1384. Successive Habsburgs, like the Babenbergs before them, also strove to have Vienna elevated to a bishopric, but this did not occur until the late 15C. In the early 15C, however, a far more disruptive influence emanated from Bohemia, ripples from the Hussite storm aroused by the corruption of the Catholic Church. As part of **Albrecht IV**'s energetic measures to protect the faith, not only was torture instituted for Hussite converts, but also a pogrom against the Jews (the first **Wiener Geserah**; 1420–21), at which time the Jewish ghetto dating from Babenberg times (today's Judenplatz—see p 77) was razed.

Under the great survivor, **Friedrich III** (1457–93), Habsburg power increased, despite a turbulent start to his reign when he was besieged in the Hofburg (1462) by a rival Habsburg claimant and suffered the indignity of being rescued by the Hussite Bohemian King, George of Podiebrad. Later, the Hungarian King, Matthias Corvinus, was to occupy Vienna from 1485 to 1490, but Friedrich outlived all his enemies. The marriage-bed diplomacy of his son, **Maximilian I**, brought not only Burgundy and the Iberian peninsular with the Spanish New World under Habsburg rule, but also (after his death) Hungary and Bohemia through the marriage (held in St Stephen's, 1515) of his grandchildren to the Jagellonian heirs. In Vienna, Maximilian is remembered for his encouragement of learning at the university, whose teachers included the great humanist scholars, Konrad Celtis and Johannes Cuspinian, as well as his founding of the Vienna Boys' Choir (1498).

By the turn of the 16C, the population of Vienna had reached 20–25,000. This increase was partly due to the city becoming the imperial residence from 1438. Its political situation remained unstable, however, as rival branches of the Habsburgs fought for control of the Austrian patrimony. Three Viennese mayors lost their lives (in 1408, 1463 and 1522) when they ended up on the losing side of these struggles or, like the distinguished humanist Martin Siebenbürger (executed by Ferdinand I in 1522), fought too zealously for municipal autonomy, which was subsequently all but extinguished by Ferdinand in 1526. Three years later came an external shock in the form of the **first Turkish siege**, when the city was ably defended by Count Salm. This narrow escape prompted the building of huge defensive ramparts around the periphery between 1531 and 1566. At the same time there was religious strife, the population at large being increasingly unwilling to accept either the social cost of late-feudal ostentation and dynastic power struggles, or the intellectual muzzle applied by a hopelessly corrupt Church. In 1521 the first Protestant preacher (Paulus Speratus from Salzburg) was heard in St Stephen's and by the 1570s some 50 per cent of the Viennese had turned Protestant. The dynasty remained a staunch defender of orthodoxy, however, only the liberal **Maximilian II** (ruled 1564–76) being suspected of secret Protestant leanings. While Maximilian implemented the Peace of Augsburg in 1568–71, whereby the Protestant nobles could also determine the confession of their subjects, he later used the same settlement to initiate counter-reformatory measures. Meanwhile, his father, **Ferdinand I**, had called the Jesuits to Vienna in 1551, the order gaining control of the most important faculties of the university in the following century (1623). In 1629 the Edict of Restitution restored all ecclesiastical properties appropriated by the Protestants to the Catholic Church, and the last hopes for Protestant resistance were dashed when the Swedes advanced on, but failed to attack, Vienna in 1645 during the Thirty Years War.

The Counter-Reformation and the Baroque Age

Many Catholic orders had been invited to Vienna in the Middle Ages and the Counter-Reformation saw nine more settling in the city with a mission to consolidate the true faith. Inspired by the catechism and teaching of Peter Canisius, the Jesuit Rector of the Am Hof Church and briefly Dean of the Theological Faculty of the university, their activities were designed to counteract the Protestant influence in education, which in turn was partly rooted in the Renaissance, and partly in the expressive power of Protestant translations of the Bible. The didactic preaching of the Counter-Reformation, combined with aesthetic sensuality in the art and architecture it promoted, was well attuned to the Viennese mentality. Music, drama and the fine arts flourished, while the face of the city was transformed by the dramatic and monumental Baroque architecture of churches and aristocrats' palaces. Spectacles in the Hofburg reached a high point under the spendthrift **Leopold I** (1657–1705), but it was also Leopold who invited the anti-Semitic preacher, **Abraham a Sancta Clara**, to Vienna, where he lashed the Viennese with his fire and brimstone rhetoric in the terrible plague year of 1679. On this occasion it was more difficult to blame the Jews directly for the population's afflictions, since Leopold (influenced by his bigoted wife, who held the Jews responsible for her miscarriage, and the ruthless Cardinal Kollonitsch) had expelled the entire community from the Unteren Werd in 1670 (the second **Wiener Geserah**), renaming the area the Leopoldstadt. The plague epidemic was soon followed by the **second Turkish siege** of 1683, which very nearly succeeded, Vienna being rescued at the eleventh hour by an imperial army under the titular leadership of the Polish king, Jan Sobieski. The Emperor had removed himself to Linz for the duration of hostilities, leaving the city in the hands of Count Starhemberg, whose look-out post for observing Turkish manoeuvres can still be visited halfway up the south tower of St Stephen's.

Under Leopold, the Hofburg's existing Renaissance and pre-Renaissance core was extended by Italian architects (the Leopoldinische Trakt; 1681) to which the Renaissance Amalienburg was connected early in the following century. Between 1723–30 a new wing containing the offices of the Holy Roman Empire (Reichskanzleitrakt) closed the square to the north-east. These additions were planned by Lukas von Hildebrandt (the building) and Fischer von Erlach the Elder (the noble façade), the latter also building (with his son, Joseph Emanuel) the Court Library, while the Spanish Riding School is entirely a work of Fischer von Erlach the Younger. Together with the Karlskirche (built between 1716 and 1739) these buildings represent the summit of Habsburg-inspired Baroque architecture in Vienna under Joseph I and Karl VI. Not to be outdone, the aristocrats were building palaces which rivalled those of the dynasty in grandeur, the greatest being the Belvedere Palace, built between 1714–22 by Hildebrandt for Prince Eugene of Savoy. Prince Eugene (like the Liechtensteins) required a winter palace within the city walls as well as his gracious summer palace with a park and this was built for him in the Himmelpfortgasse, while the Schwarzenbergs, Lobkowitzes, Harrachs and many others also built city residences of astonishing magnificence.

Maria Theresia, Joseph II and Enlightened Absolutism

Despite Karl VI's efforts to ensure the succession in the female line by means of the Pragmatic Sanction (1713)—there were no male heirs—his daughter **Maria Theresia** had to fight to defend her inheritance against the opportunist Frederick the Great of Prussia (**Seven Years War**, 1756–63). During her reign the empire's ramshackle administration and finances were rationalised, while the incompetent army was reformed, together with the legal code and education. The first census was taken and houses in the city were numbered to facilitate conscription (1770). Maria Theresia's reforming zeal was taken much further by her son, **Joseph II** (co-ruler from his father's death in 1765 until that of his mother in 1780). In the spirit of benevolent autocracy, Joseph tried to improve the lot of his people. Some of his measures (like opening the parks of Schönbrunn, the Augarten and the Prater to the public) were popular, others (like introducing re-usable bottomless coffins) were not. An opponent of ecclesiastical obscurantism, he closed many monasteries which he believed served no useful purpose, preserving only those engaged in what he regarded as socially valuable work. His Edict of Tolerance (1781) granted freedom of worship to non-Catholics and alleviated the lot of the Jews, although there were strings attached to both concessions. In Vienna he founded the General Hospital (1784) and a school for training military surgeons (Josephinum, 1785). The Theresian and Josephine era also saw the liberation of opera from Italian precepts in the work of Christoph Willibald Gluck (1714–87) and of Wolfgang Amadeus Mozart (1756–91). In the works of the latter and of his mentor, Joseph Haydn (1732–1809), the Viennese Classic reached its apotheosis, even if Joseph seemed insufficiently to appreciate Mozart's genius.

The Biedermeier era (Vormärz) 1814–48

After the brief interlude of Leopold II, an enlightened ruler in his brother's mould, the heavy-handed **Franz II** ruled from 1792–1835, a period that saw Vienna twice occupied by Napoleonic troops (1805 and 1809) and the Emperor obliged to marry his daughter, Marie Louise, to the Corsican upstart. Vienna lost prestige in these years: Franz was obliged to give up the title of Holy Roman Emperor in 1806, contenting himself thereafter with the title Franz I of Austria; and in 1811 the pressures of war drove the state into bankruptcy with serious consequences for Vienna's finances and trade.

In 1814–15 the post-war settlement was decided at the Vienna Congress, a triumph of diplomacy for a malign reactionary genius from the Rhineland, Prince Clemens Wenzel Lothar Metternich, who had become Chancellor in 1810 and was to remain in harness until the outbreak of revolution in March 1848. The 'Pre-March' (*Vormärz*) years were characterised by a displacement of public activity into the private sphere, a culture of domesticity, intimacy and the cultivation of small, private virtues. *Der Nachsommer* (*Indian Summer*) by **Adalbert Stifter** (1805–68) is generally taken to be the classic expression of the Biedermeier ethos in literature, although only in retrospect, since it was not published until 1857. In music it is **Franz Schubert** (1797–1828) whose genius (again retrospectively, since his music had little public performance in his lifetime) evokes a combination of private passion and Romantic idealism. He was greatly influenced by his hero Beethoven, who had lived in Vienna from 1792 to his death only a year before Schubert, and whose *Fidelio* (ironically) had been given its first performance under the French occupation. Despite the repressive regime, Vienna experienced a first wave of industrialisation in the *Vormärz*, helped by the building of the first railways (1837) and the founding of the Danube Steamship Company (1829), as well as the Polytechnic (1815). The population rose from 231,000 in 1800 to 431,000 in 1850.

The Gründerzeit (Founders' Period)

Ferdinand I, Franz's simple-minded son, was replaced by the 18-year-old **Franz Joseph I** after the outbreak of revolution in 1848, although not before he had made important constitutional concessions on which his successor brutally reneged. One of the most influential figures in Franz Joseph's initially neo-absolutist regime from 1849 was **Alexander Freiherr von Bach**, who had begun his career with liberal views. It was the now extremely conservative Bach who was the moving spirit behind the regressive Concordat with the Holy See (1855), which handed back the regulation of marriage, education and the clergy to the Catholic Church, and which was not abrogated until

1874. On the other hand, Bach was a man of considerable vision and it was he who encouraged the Emperor to order the demolition of the bastions round the old city of Vienna in 1857, perhaps the most economically liberating moment in the city's history.

Between 1869 and 1888 the great public buildings of emergent Liberalism and modern capitalism (the parliament, city hall, stock exchange, Burgtheater, opera, university, Kunsthistorisches Museum) arose along the new boulevard (**Ringstraße**), where formerly there had been only ramparts and military exercise grounds. The new style for the architecture and decoration of the Ringstraßen palaces was Historicism, which drew on the symbolism of the past (for instance, Athenian democracy for the parliament, Renaissance humanism for the university) to express the aspirations of the present.

The confident statement of belief in progress epitomised by the Ringstraße was in contrast to the increasingly rickety nature of the Empire, Franz Joseph having been forced into the *Ausgleich* (compromise) with Hungary that created the Dual Monarchy after setbacks in Italy and his disastrous defeat by the Prussians at Sadowa in 1866. The failure of the 1873 World Exhibition held in Vienna to celebrate the Empire's achievements, also seemed a portent: just after it opened the stock market crashed and there was a serious outbreak of cholera. Yet the glittering lifestyle of the well-to-do continued, the champagne song from Johann Strauss's *Die Fledermaus* (1874; 'Happy is he who forgets all about/What anyway cannot be changed...') often being regarded as emblematic of the city's heedlessly expensive tastes.

Turn of the century Vienna

Throughout the 19C immigration to Vienna increased: Czech and Friulian labourers came to work on the construction sites, Slovak girls took jobs in domestic service and other nationalities arrived from all over the Empire. By the turn of the century there was a large population of **Jews**, divided into the long assimilated (like the families of Freud, Schnitzler or Wittgenstein), who were extremely successful as entrepreneurs and financiers, or in the free professions, and the orthodox community in the Leopoldstadt.

Towards the turn of the century an extension of the franchise brought the anti-Semitic **Karl Lueger** to power (1897–1910) in the city hall, a protagonist of the petit bourgeoisie who resented the corrupt hold of the wealthy Liberal regime on the city's affairs and feared the influx of poor migrants. Lueger's Christian Social party municipalised the electricity and gas supply in Vienna, set up a cheap funeral service to combat rapacious private concerns and also instituted a savings bank. With Lueger begins the building of a political constituency from the creation of municipal jobs that has continued ever since under Socialist regimes. Meanwhile the working-class was beginning to flex its muscles, following the founding of the Social Democratic Party under the leadership of Viktor Adler in 1889.

From World War I to the present day

Following the assassination of the heir to the throne, Archduke Franz Ferdinand, on 28 June 1914, Austria-Hungary was plunged into a war that ended with her defeat and the break-up of the 600-year-old Habsburg

Empire. Vienna, from 1918 the capital of the diminutive Austrian Republic and disparagingly referred to as a *Wasserkopf* (hydrocephalus), lost nearly half a million inhabitants who returned to their newly independent states, and was also flooded with unemployable officials returning from the Empire. The Social Democrats won the 1919 elections, while the constitutional separation of Vienna from conservative-dominated Lower Austria in 1922 ushered in the era of **Rotes Wien** ('Red Vienna'), the Socialists having subsequently won a majority in every free vote for the City Council up to the present. Red Vienna's housing programme (63,736 dwellings built between 1919–34), together with its educational and social measures, were achieved by a steeply progressive tax on the well-to-do, while the hegemony of the Social Democrats was consolidated by the conscious promotion of 'worker culture' and party dependence. The country as a whole, however, turned to the right under the government of the priest Ignaz Seipel (in power 1922–24 and 1926–29) and underlying political tensions erupted in 1927, when the Palace of Justice in Vienna was burned down by a furious mob after a miscarriage of justice by the conservative judiciary.

In 1934 there was a brief civil war, in which the outgunned Socialists were easily overwhelmed; the Parliament (1933) and autonomy of the Vienna municipality (1934) were suspended and a Catholic-Fascist authoritarian regime was set up under **Engelbert Dollfuß** in May 1934. Only two months later Dollfuß was murdered in an attempted Nazi putsch and **Kurt Schuschnigg** became Chancellor and leader of the only permitted political association, the Fatherland Front. In an attempt to tackle the high unemployment at this time, the winding Höhenstraße was built up to the Wienerwald, and the Reichsbrücke (formerly named after Crown Prince Rudolph) was reconstructed.

After Schuschnigg's humiliation by **Adolf Hitler** at Berchtesgaden in February 1938, the *Anschluss* followed on 13 March, anticipating a plebiscite called in desperation by the Chancellor to demonstrate support for Austrian independence. On 15 March Hitler was hysterically applauded as he addressed the masses (estimated at 250,000) on the Heldenplatz and a rigged referendum in April to approve the *Anschluss* produced the result of 99.6 per cent in favour. On 9 November a pogrom swept through Vienna and the rest of the German Reich (the **Reichskristallnacht**), destroying 42 synagogues and Jewish sanctuaries. Some prominent figures were able to buy their freedom (Sigmund Freud among them), but about a third of Vienna's 180,000 Jews were shipped to the concentration camps and liquidated. In 1942 Adolf Eichmann chillingly reported the city to be 'free of Jews'. The Nazis degraded Vienna (which Hitler had described as a 'pearl' to be given its appropriate 'setting' in the Reich) to the *Reichsgau Groß-Wien*, incorporating 97 municipal districts of Lower Austria.

The final struggle for Vienna at the end of the war left the city with some 30 per cent of its building stock destroyed or damaged. Allied occupation lasted ten years (Vienna being divided into four sectors, with the Inner City under joint control, until the *Staatsvertrag*, signed in the Belvedere in 1955, liberated Austria. The post-war Marshall Plan then greatly helped to put the economy on its feet. Learning from the past, the main political parties worked closely together and a system of '**Sozialpartnerschaft**' aimed to secure a just distribution of the fruits of peace and economic growth. Money began flowing into the Vienna economy with the establishment of the International Atomic Energy Agency in the city in 1957, a trend intensified under the Socialist government (1970–83) of Bruno Kreisky, when Vienna became the third seat of the United Nations. In 1968 work began on the U-Bahn network, some of which incorporated earlier elements of the transport infrastructure planned by Otto Wagner (*Stadtbahn*). A rolling programme of renovation has made Vienna one of the most elegant cities in the world, and greening measures have made it one of the cleanest. The population (in 1910 over 2 million and sinking almost uninterruptedly from the end of World War I to 1971) has grown faster since the collapse of the Iron Curtain and a city that 15 years ago could still be accused of being a historical museum piece inhabited by pensioner curators, is now a modern metropolis with style and vigour.

Architecture

In architecture, Vienna has a rich tradition of Gothic, Baroque, Historicist and Secessionist buildings, the Inner City being a cornucopia of all these styles. The **Gothic** masters (some from the Prague workshop of St Vitus Cathedral) who built the Stephansdom and Maria am Gestade (see p 67 and 77) are known to us, but others are lost in the mists of time. The **Renaissance** produced only a limited number of major works, perhaps because so much money and effort flowed into the building of the great *tracé italien* fortifications against the Turks (1531–66). However, the Stallburg wing of the Hofburg was built with its storeyed arcades in Renaissance style and there are some other relics of the period, such as the fine portal of the Salvatorkapelle of the old city hall. The great architects of the early **Baroque** are nearly all Italian (Tencala, Burnacini, Martinelli and others), but from the late 17C Vienna had its own (albeit Italian-trained) superlatively original masters: **Johann Bernhard Fischer von Erlach** (1656–1723), his son **Joseph Emanuel** (1693–1742), and **Lukas von Hildebrandt** (1668–1745). All of them worked on great imperial projects, as well as on palaces for private patrons such as Prince Eugene of Savoy, Count Schönborn or Prince Schwarzenberg.

Vienna's most celebrated example of the Rococo is Maria Theresia's summer palace at Schönbrunn, for which the principal architect was **Nikolaus Pacassi** (1716–90), a man of only moderate gifts who was nevertheless kept busy with the endless alterations and extensions required by the court in Vienna, Prague and elsewhere. The reign of her son, Joseph II, already heralded the age of **neo-classicism**, the most notable architect of which was **Josef Kornhäusel** (1782–1860; see pp 76 and 112). After Joseph's Tolerance Patent in 1781, Kornhäusel was able to build a new synagogue in Vienna and he also built extensively in Franz I's favourite spa of Baden bei Wien.

The **Ringstraßen era** (1860–90; see p 55) produced a crop of outstanding architects of **Historicism** (notably **Theophil Hansen**, **Friedrich Schmidt** and **Heinrich Ferstel**), while the Secession's subsequent rebellion against an increasingly stale repetition of historical forms was epitomised by the striking functional architecture of **Otto Wagner**. Elegant Jugendstil villas were built in the Vienna suburbs at the turn of the century by Wagner, **Josef Hoffmann** and **Joseph Maria Olbrich** (the architect of the Secession building), while **Adolf Loos** (influenced by certain aspects of American and English architecture) was to strike out on his own with a more puritan concept of functionalism. His house designed for the bespoke tailors, Goldman and Salatsch on the Michaelerplatz and facing the Hofburg (see p 81), caused an uproar on completion in 1911. The last really controversial building to be erected in the Inner City is the post-modern Haas House (1990) opposite the Stephansdom, designed by the Vienna-born **Hans Hollein**.

Music

'*In Vienna, even the stone angels sing.*' Dr Charles Burney, *Musical Tours in Europe, 1772.*

Vienna's music scene is arguably the richest in the world with the **Staatsoper**, the **Musikverein** and the **Konzerthaus**, as well as a host of smaller venues, keeping alive a unique tradition. Musical performance runs uninterruptedly through the city's history from its beginnings with the *Minnesänger* at the Babenberg court (the most famous were Walther von der Vogelweide, Neidhart von Reuental, Tannhäuser) and liturgical chant developed to a high level of refinement in the medieval churches. Even during the Reformation, humanist scholars kept Vienna's music traditions alive, most notably **Wolfgang Schmeltzl** (c 1500–c 1561) who himself was raised as a Protestant, yet became a teacher at the *Schottenstift* and a writer of vernacular didactic dramas with religious themes. He published a collection of popular Viennese songs for four voices in 1544, and his famous verse celebration of Vienna (1547) also stressed its status as a city of music and musicians.

The Habsburgs, a number of whom were also composers, were enthusiastic musical patrons: Maximilian I founded the **Hofsängerknaben** (today the Vienna Boys' Choir) in 1498, to which Haydn and Schubert belonged in their youth. Court patronage in the early Baroque age, when lavish musical spectacles as well as religious music were constantly required, went to Italian composers like Giovanni Battista Bononcini and Antonio Caldara. In the mid-18C, the increasingly rigid Italian operatic tradition was epitomised by the works of the court poet Pietro Metastasio set to very dull music; the static alternation of recitative and highly embellished arias, was first challenged by **Christoph Willibald Gluck** (1714–87; *Iphigenie in Aulide, Orfeo ed Eurydice*), who introduced a more naturalistic and dramatically convincing approach to opera. Gluck quite frequently resorted to traditional musical recipes, however, and many of his contemporaries were also content to churn out respectable but uninventive works, both sacred and secular. An exception was **Karl Ditters von Dittersdorf** (1739–99), the son of a Viennese lacemaker and a violin virtuoso whose excellent concertos have been rediscovered. His contemporary success with comic opera and *Singspiel* may be gauged from his elevation to the nobility in 1773. However, the most influential theoretician of the age was **Johann Joseph Fux** (1660–1741), the son of Styrian peasants who was organist in Vienna's Schottenstift and Kapellmeister at St Stephen's before he was appointed Hofkapellmeister in 1715.

Fux has been called the 'Austrian Palestrina' and his instructional work, *Gradus ad Parnassum* (1725), was admired and studied by the founder

(**Joseph Haydn**, 1732–1809) of the Vienna Classic (the style dominant from c 1770–1830) and its greatest master, **Wolfgang Amadeus Mozart** (1756–91). Mozart, often regarded as the supreme Austrian composer, nevertheless had mixed fortunes in Vienna and was generally more appreciated in Prague, where *Le Nozze di Figaro* (1786) was performed and *Don Giovanni* (1787) premiered to great acclaim. On the other hand, his collaboration with the actor and impresario, Emanuel Schikaneder (1751–1812) produced the best-loved opera of the Viennese, *Die Zauberflöte*. In Mozart's work the influence of folk music becomes apparent, an influence that runs through the work of the Romantic composers who were active in Vienna the following century (Ludwig van Beethoven, Franz Schubert, Anton Bruckner and Johannes Brahms). Of these, two were Germans, one a native of Upper Austria and one (Schubert) quintessentially Viennese in spirit, though born just outside the city. **Beethoven** lived in Vienna from 1792, and from 1809 was guaranteed 4000 florins a year by his aristocratic patrons, the most important being the Archduke Rudolph, to whom his famous Trio is dedicated.

Song, both as the popular *Wienerlied* and as 'art song' achieved the greatest heights of perfection in 19C Vienna. The genre is above all associated with **Schubert**—in one year alone (1815) he wrote 145 songs, including two of his most famous, *Heideröslein* and *Erlkönig*. Another composer, **Hugo Wolf** (1860–1903), is almost exclusively known for his *Lieder*, which include sophisticated settings of Goethe, as well as the famous 'Spanish' and 'Italian' songbooks. Meanwhile, in the taverns on the edge of the Wienerwald, the quartet founded (1878) by **Johann** (1850–93) and **Josef Schrammel** (1852–95), played melodies in the popular idiom, many of them their own compositions. The Schrammel brothers have given their name to this distinctive Viennese form of sentimental light music (*Schrammelmusik*), which had its roots in the folk music sung by their mother, Aloisia, and played by their clarinettist father, Kaspar. However, both studied at the Vienna Conservatoire under the violinist Joseph Hellmesberger, thus bringing a degree of sophistication to their playing and composition that was admired by Brahms and Strauss, as well as by many other local musicians.

The cross-fertilisation between 'classical' composition and the popular or folk idiom perhaps lies behind the appeal of much music that has been written in Vienna. Its most remarkable instance, whereby the vernacular entertainment of the peasant became astonishingly triumphant in higher social stratas, is the Upper Austrian *Ländler* (see p 247). It developed eventually into the immortal *Wiener Walzer* as perfected and refined by **Josef Lanner** (1801–43) and the **Strauss dynasty**. The Lanner-Strauss ensemble had so much work they had to create two orchestras, while Johann Strauss the Elder carried the fame of the Viennese waltz abroad (playing, for instance at Buckingham Palace in 1838 as part of Queen Victoria's wedding celebrations). His son wrote the most famous operetta of all time (*Die Fledermaus*), and was the first modern 'pop star', at the height of his fame receiving almost daily requests from fans (mostly female) for locks of his hair or other souvenirs. (As he needed his hair, he occasionally sent tufts clipped from his dog instead.)

The late 19C saw a bitter feud in Vienna between the adherents of Brahms' more conventional style of Romantic music (particularly Eduard Hanslick) and the Wagnerians, who adopted the saintly **Anton Bruckner** as their totemic figure (see p 248). However, Bruckner has endured better than Hanslick, his immortal symphonies (above all the 4th and 7th) attracting passionate allegiance from later generations and his wonderful Masses being joyfully rediscovered by modern audiences. Controversy also flared during **Gustav Mahler**'s tenure as director of the Hofoper (1898–1907), due to his strict regime and impatience with the second rate: 'What you call tradition is merely *Schlamperei* (sloppiness)', he once told an enraged orchestra. There was considerable prejudice against Mahler's own work in Vienna and in fact none of his symphonies was premiered in the city.

Mahler himself gallantly championed the even more controversial Modernism of **Arnold Schönberg**'s 12-tone system and the work of his followers of the Second Viennese School (**Alban Berg** and **Anton von Webern**), which met with such resistance from conservatives that one concert consisting entirely of their works, held in the Musikverein on 31 March 1913, ended in a riot. As so often, Vienna has retrospectively taken Schönberg to its heart and in 1998 the Schönberg foundation, together with its archives, was attracted back to the city.

The above represents only the highlights of Viennese musical achievement: the list of great masters alone is so distinguished and multifarious that names of the second rank have tended to be obscured, but are now being rediscovered, for example, Antonio Salieri, once the 'musical pope' of Vienna and unfairly accused of poisoning Mozart; the fine late Romantic, Franz Schreker (1878–1934) and the Schönberg follower, Egon Wellesz (1884–1974); not to mention the versatile Erich Wolfgang Korngold, whose recently revived opera *Die tote Stadt* first took Vienna by storm in 1920.

The performance history of Vienna is no less distinguished, even if it is some years since it produced a voice to take on the superstars (always excepting **José Carreras**, who is a sort of honorary Viennese). In the past the city has nurtured the artistry of Elisabeth Schwarzkopf, Irmgard Seefried, Christa Ludwig, Leo Slezak and many other star singers. The record with conductors is no less distinguished, and includes Wilhelm Furtwängler, Clemens Krauss, Karl Böhm and Herbert von Karajan. Today, the flow of brilliant conductors shows no sign of abating, the torch currently being held by men like **Nikolaus Harnoncourt**, one of the pioneers of performance on original instruments strictly true to the score, and **Franz Welser-Möst**, a star of the new generation. Lastly, the **Wiener Philharmoniker** (founded by Otto Nicolai in 1842) remains one of the most distinguished orchestras in the world, a lofty status that enabled it to ignore until 1997 the mounting criticism of its prohibition on women members; by then, increasingly desperate justifications for the ban (e.g. the claim that female violinists lacked the right muscular configuration for the most taxing cadenzas) were in danger of making the orchestra a laughing stock. While the Philharmoniker is an independent private association, the less well-known but also distinguished **Wiener Symphoniker** receives a subsidy from the city council. The **Wiener Sängerknaben** (Vienna Boys' Choir) has also been exposed to the winds of change (here too female membership has been mooted by the new managers), and to some tough commercial competition from mixed youth choirs such as the delightfully named Gumpoldskirchner Spatzen ('The Sparrows of Gumpoldskirchen'—a wine village on the southern edge of Vienna).

Theatre

The theatres of Vienna (all except one subsidised by the city council) are still regarded as among the finest in the German-speaking world, despite the celebrated Burgtheater having recently lost some good actors opposed to the politically and artistically provocative direction (between 1986 and 1999) of the German, **Claus Peymann** (although he also attracted talent). It was the Peymann productions of Thomas Bernhard's corrosive deconstruction of the Austrian mentality, not least the ambivalent attitude to the country's collaboration with the Nazis (*Heldenplatz*, in 1988, produced at the height of the Waldheim affair) which provoked ill-tempered debate in the 1980s. Less controversially, Peymann has also staged some remarkable versions of the classics (for example memorable productions of Kleist and Brecht), that may well come to be regarded as milestones in theatrical history.

Controversy and audience participation in theatrical life is in any case nothing new in Viennese cultural history: at the turn of the century, **Arthur Schnitzler**'s *Reigen (La Ronde)*, a sexually candid exploration of turn of the century decadence, was banned after publication in book form; under the Nazis, the famous 'in praise of Austria' from Franz Grillparzer's patriotic masterpiece '*König Ottakars Glück und Ende*' (1825) was cheered so enthusiastically that the production was immediately suppressed; and under the heavy-handed absolutism of Metternich, **Johann Nestroy** (1801–62) infuriated the censor by ad libbing his satirical sallies against the authorities and their manifold absurdities. Nestroy's own work grew out of a vernacular tradition of mildly subversive comedy with slapstick elements incorporated in the semi-clown figure of the Wienerischen Hanswurst, created around 1710 by **Josef Anton Stranitzky** (1676–1726). Stranitzky was a jack-of-all-trades who splendidly combined the professions of dentistry and acting, and who was the first director of the (long demolished) Kärntnertortheater, which stood on the site now occupied by Hotel Sacher. This preceded the Burgtheater, founded under Maria Theresia and originally situated on the Michaelerplatz until the opening of the modern house on the Ringstraße in 1888. In 1781 the theatre in the Leopoldstadt was opened, the beginning of a long tradition of comic genius culminating with Raimund and (as the Carltheater) Nestroy, although the building survived until 1944. In 1787 the Theater auf der Wieden was opened by Christian Rossbach, later to become famous when (1789) it was taken over by **Emanuel Schikaneder**, a bustling entrepreneur, actor (famous as Hamlet), librettist (for Mozart's *Die Zauberflöte*), dramatist and composer. Schikaneder subsequently opened the still existing Theater an der Wien in 1801, where Beethoven's *Fidelio* was premiered, but which is also associated with a string of successful operettas and now musicals. Another famous venue still going strong is the Theater in der Josefstadt, built in 1788, but now perhaps best known for **Max Reinhardt**'s directorship of it after World War I.

If theatre has provided a sometimes strident, sometimes muffled opposition to the powers that be, it has also traditionally supplied the Viennese with an alternative world of sentimental illusion, as in the fairytale-like musical plays of **Ferdinand Raimund** (1790–1836), or the vast flood of operettas from the mid-19C by Strauss, Lehár, Kálmán and many others. Theatre is in the Viennese blood—in the 19C life even imitated art, as the population took their cue from the tics of the fashionable actor of the day, Alexander Girardi (1850–1918); 'We Viennese are always playing a role,' warned Schnitzler, 'the wise man remembers that'.

With the exception of operetta, which went on to conquer the world, the popular Viennese theatrical tradition is also to a large extent a private, even introverted affair, not least due to the nuances of the local dialect that exploits the comic potential of the warring elements in the Viennese character. But even Austria's greatest formal dramatist, **Franz Grillparzer** (1791–1872), is also quintessentially Viennese, writing of himself that he was constituted of 'two completely separate beings: ... a poet whose fancy teems with images tumbling one upon another, and a dogged, coldly rational thinker'. These contradictory elements are evident in Grillparzer's great Historicist dramas set at crucial moments in Habsburg history (or in one case Bohemian history, *Libussa*; 1851), although he also treated themes from antiquity. In the context of the great passions of Romantic drama, Grillparzer examined the nature of power, its use and abuse, a fact not unnoticed by the censor, with whom he frequently had difficulties. It was perhaps the 'coldly rational' (and disappointed, patriotic, liberal) Grillparzer who prophetically spoke of the end results to be expected from the nationalist and populist political tendencies that he experienced in his lifetime: '...*von der Humanität durch die Nationalität zur Bestialität*' (from humanity via nationality to atrocity).

Literature

Vienna has had its poets and writers of eulogies at least from the time of **Jans Enikel** (c 1230–c 1290), whose *Book of Princes* celebrated the Babenberg court and is a source for contemporary Viennese history. **Enea Silvio Piccolomini** (1405–64, from 1458 Pope Pius II) was a counsellor to Friedrich III whose detailed and highly laudatory description of Vienna sent to a friend in Basle in the spring of 1438 has survived, together with remarks in his *Historia Australis* (1458). The humanist and rector of Vienna University, **Wolfgang Lazius** (1514–65), wrote *Vienna Austriae* (published in Basle, 1546), the first scientific history of the city: his local patriotism was such that he financed out of his own pocket the restoration of the Peterskirche (predecessor of the present church); and in 1547 Wolfgang Schmeltzl, a former schoolmaster in the Schottenkloster published 'In Praise of Vienna' (*Lobspruch der Stadt Wien*), 1600 verses of flattering doggerel that supplies many interesting insights into the city of his time.

The ideological counter-attack of the counter-reformatory Baroque era was concentrated more on the 'culture of the senses' than the 'culture of the word' (hence the importance of the Viennese tradition of theatre, shows and spectacles of every kind), but nevertheless produced a great description of Vienna in the plague year of 1679 by the preacher **Abraham a Sancta Clara**. His bloodcurdling call to repentance *Merck's Wien* (Take Heed, Vienna!) uses Viennese street-names to great literary effect ('In the street of the lords, death is the lord of all, in the Singerstraße, Death has sung many a requiem, on the Graben Death does nothing but bury the corpses ...'). The preacher tapped a vein of popular sensationalism, cunningly introducing a typically Viennese figure into his sermons, the drunken bagpiper Augustin (see p 70).

The capacity for the Viennese to reinvent themselves, usually as a way of making fun of their oppressors, was exploited in the *Volkstheater* (popular theatre) of the early 18C, which flourished with **Josef Anton Stranitzky** (see p 62). If Augustin was the great survivor, Stranitzky's 'Hanswurst' (originally 'Hans Wurst') was the first incarnation of the parody of local types that was to develop with La Roche's 'Kasperl', Hasenhut's 'Thaddädl' ('a weak-willed man, an idiot' in the local patois) and Bäuerle's engaging umbrella-maker called 'Staberl', all of them at once identification figures and mouthpieces for the commonalty. Their largely improvised texts were sufficiently irreverent for Maria Theresia's censor, Joseph von Sonnenfels, to clamp down on the popular theatre, albeit with limited success.

The most distinctive prose writer of the Biedermeier age (1814–48) was **Adalbert Stifter** (see p 246), while the poet **Franz Grillparzer** (1791–1872) romantically evoked the dynastic myth of the Habsburgs and Austrian history in his great dramas, which he managed to write despite a full-time job as director of the court archives. A number of other bureaucrats were also writers and poets, a state job giving them the security and leisure needed for writing, as well as an acute sense of what the censor would tolerate. Towards the end of the 19C, there was a great literary flowering in Vienna, based on coffee-house coteries and the *Jung Wien* movement led by the critic Hermann Bahr. His circle included the poet and later librettist for Richard Strauss, Hugo von Hofmannsthal, and the unofficial laureate of Vienna, Peter Altenberg, whose impressionistic sketches vividly evoked the atmosphere of life in the city.

In 1900, **Sigmund Freud** published his *Interpretation of Dreams*, like much of his work now regarded as more of a literary than a scientific achievement, although Freud himself praised the playwright **Arthur Schnitzler** (1862–1931) for exhibiting the same imaginative insights into human nature (and Viennese society) that he had painfully acquired from his 'researches'. An unflagging opponent of Freud, Bahr, and of the Secession, was the satirist **Karl Kraus**, who edited and almost entirely wrote his own magazine, *Die Fackel* (The Torch), for 37 years from the time of its foundation in 1899. His public readings of the great Austrian dramatists and Shakespeare were packed out and his merciless exposure of charlatanism, the dubious basis of Freud's 'scientific' claims, the government's malevolent incompetence in the conduct of World War I, the corruption of Viennese journalism and much else, made him admired, feared and hated.

A very different character from Kraus was the writer **Robert Musil**, who emigrated in 1938 to Switzerland and died in poverty in Geneva in 1939. In the 1930s his massive unfinished novel, set in Vienna and chronicling the spiritual exhaustion of the Habsburg monarchy, first began appearing (vols 1 and 2), but only after his death did *Der Mann ohne Eigenschaften* (*The Man without Qualities*) become recognised as one of the masterpieces of the 20C. Its picture of a crumbling, directionless state and a sophisticated people acting out absurdist roles in a claustrophobic, nihilistic environment has become the dominant image of the later days of the Habsburg monarchy. However, this picture is contradicted by the enormous intellectual vitality of Vienna at that time, which produced geniuses in fields ranging from science and medicine to philosophy, law, literature and the arts. It is noteworthy that of 12 Austrian Nobel prize-winners to date, seven were born in Vienna and most of the others worked in Vienna's academe. Lastly, one of the finest intellectual and spiritual chroniclers of the city in 20C fiction is **Heimito von Doderer** (1896–1966), whose classic novel *Die Strudlhofstiege* (1951; after the famous art nouveau flight of steps in the city) is a superbly insightful evocation of Viennese society in the troubled early part of the century.

The Fine Arts

Apart from the astonishing Romanesque Verdun altar in Klosterneuburg (see p 114), the earliest treasures of Vienna's fine arts patrimony are to be seen in the **Museum of Austrian Medieval Art** in the Orangery of the Belvedere Palace (see p 105) and in the **Cathedral Museum** on Stephansplatz (see p 70). The unknown masters who created the *Man of Sorrows*, the *Servant Girl Madonna* and several fine tombs in St Stephen's Cathedral are indicative of the astonishingly high quality of Viennese Gothic and the generous patronage available. A notable painter of the mid-15C 'international style' of Gothic is the so-called '**Schottenmeister**', whose altar displayed in the Schottenstift Museum shows the earliest known view of the Inner City. Painters in this soft and graceful style were succeeded by those of the naturalistic and sometimes brutal Danube School, of which **Lucas Cranach the Elder** (1472–1553), who was working in Vienna for several years, is a leading exponent. Other fine Danubian masters whose work may be seen in the Belvedere include Albrecht Altdorfer, Rueland Frueauf and Wolf Huber.

After much destruction of this Gothic heritage during the Reformation (it is said that Protestant nobles rode their horses round the interior of St Stephen's slashing at works of art with their swords), the Counter-Reformation produced a flowering of **Baroque** art, typical examples of which can be seen in the Austrian Baroque Museum of the Lower Belvedere, the Schottenstift Museum on Freyung (see p 79), and of course in many Viennese churches. The great masters of this period (the sculptors, Lorenzo Mattielli, Peter and Paul Strudel and Georg Raphael Donner; the painters Johann Michael Rottmayr, Daniel Gran, Paul Troger and Franz Anton Maulbertsch, to name only the most distinguished) were extraordinarily prolific and never short of a commission. New churches were built or converted from Gothic, requiring hundreds of Baroque altars, altarpieces and statues, while every self-respecting noble required frescoes, sculptures and lavish ornamentation for his palaces.

In the **Biedermeier period** (1815–48) when neo-classicism still reigned in architecture, soothing landscapes and domestic portraiture were the favoured genre (see p 55), brought to a high degree of refinement in the works of Friedrich Amerling, Ferdinand Waldmüller, Josef Danhauser and others exhibited in the Austrian Gallery of the Upper Belvedere. The leading painter of Historicism in the **Founders' Period** (*Gründerzeit*, 1850–1900) was **Hans Makart** (1840–84) who had studied under Karl von Piloty in Munich and whose vast tableaux with historical themes showed strong

French and Venetian influence. His atelier was frequented by the *beau monde*, and it was he who organised the great pageant on the Ringstraße to celebrate the Silver Wedding of Franz Joseph and Elizabeth (1879). There were also a number of gifted sculptors working on the imperial and private commissions in the second half of the 19C (Anton Fernkorn, Viktor Tilgner, Carl Kundmann and others), mostly on monuments to honour great figures in Austrian history. In this period also, Vienna's celebrated dynasty of topographical painters was at work, the most gifted being **Rudolf von Alt** (1812–1905) whose innumerable watercolours of Vienna have left an unparalleled historical and artistically refined record of the changing face of the 19C city.

The **Vienna Secession**, not as rich in sculpture as in applied art (the province of the Wiener Werkstätte) and painting, is dominated by the figure of **Gustav Klimt** (1862–1918), but there were several other fine painters among his fellow Secessionists, including **Carl Moll** and **Kolo Moser**. Klimt's work spans the transition from fine naturalism (for example his celebrated portrait of the *Burghers of Vienna* at a performance in the Burgtheater) to a decorative Symbolism which combined erotic sensuality (*The Kiss*) with turn of the century pessimism (the notorious Law and Philosophy faculty pictures turned down by the University for their rejection of the prevailing positivist ethos). The post-Secessionist generation produced three great protagonists of Austrian **Expressionism**, who were active synchronically with Schönberg's new departure in music, all of whom began their careers in Vienna: the young **Egon Schiele** died in the Asian influenza epidemic at the end of World War I, **Richard Gerstl** committed suicide and **Oskar Kokoschka** (1886–1980) went abroad, but not before he had stirred up controversy with his Expressionist drama *Murderer, Hope of Women* (1909) and had a somewhat scandalous affair with Gustav Mahler's widow. Kokoschka's earliest work is influenced by the Secession (the coloured lithographs of *Die träumenden Knaben*), but he soon developed his style of cruelly revealing portraiture and Expressionist landscapes (Prague, London) for which he is better known.

The turbulent first half of the 20C has not been beneficial for artistic production, but since the 1950s Vienna has had a lively modern art scene, sometimes provocative, as, for example, the Actionism of **Hermann Nitsch**, which involves Dionysian 'happenings' where participants and canvases are smeared with animal blood. Magical Realism, with its symbolic and surrealistic, often pseudo-religious content, has found an able exponent in **Ernst Fuchs**, while **Friedensreich Hundertwasser** has built on the ornamental and sensual exuberance of the Baroque and *Jugendstil* to develop his highly idiosyncratic style in painting and architecture (see p 109). Of modern sculptors, **Fritz Wotruba** (1907–75) stands out, not least for his astonishing Wotrubakirche (23 district; see p 112), an experiment in volume and mass using concrete blocks, while the ever-controversial and militant left-winger, **Alfred Hrdlicka**, has produced a powerful *Monument against War and Fascism* (1988) situated on the Albertinaplatz (see p 92). Some of the passions for and against this work and its location were evident in the prolonged controversy concerning the *Holocaust Memorial* by **Rachel Whiteread**, which has been erected on the Judenplatz, the site of the medieval Jewish ghetto.

Vienna's Bezirke (districts)

The city's 414.97 sq km are divided into the 23 *Bezirke* (districts), as listed below. The main ones of interest to the tourist have been highlighted.

1 · **Innere Stadt (Inner City)**
2 · Leopoldstadt
3 · **Landstraße (Schloß Belvedere)**
4 · **Wieden (the Karlskirche)**
5 · Margareten
6 · Mariahilf
7 · Neubau
8 · **Josefstadt (the Piaristenkirche)**
9 · **Alsergrund (the Liechtenstein Summer Palace, the Servite Church, Sigmund Freud Museum)**
10 · Favoriten
11 · Simmering
12 · Meidling
13 · **Hietzing (Schloß Schönbrunn)**
14 · Penzing
15 · Rudolfsheim-Fünfhaus
16 · Ottakring
17 · Hernals
18 · Währing
19 · **Döbling (the wine villages of Grinzing and Heiligenstadt)**
20 · Brigittenau
21 · Floridsdorf
22 · Donaustadt
23 · Liesing

Sights of Vienna

Most of Vienna's historic monuments are in the 1st District (Inner City), which is dominated by the spiritual focus of the city (**Stephansdom**) and the dynastic focal point of the **Hofburg** residence of the Habsburgs. These two great edifices may also be thought of as symbolising the powerful alliance between throne and altar, which was the lynchpin of Habsburg power and which determined much of Vienna's history. The **Inner City** has remained a domaine of conservatism, an area where the Socialists have never obtained a majority in municipal elections, and therefore (claim many of its businessmen and women) the perennial target of petty restrictions and subtle discrimination. Its most illustrious streets (**Kärntner Straße, Graben, Kohlmarkt**) have been turned into pedestrian precincts and the car is slowly but inexorably being driven out of the city centre (or at least underground) by parking restrictions and greening measures.

Stephansdom (St Stephen's Cathedral)

The U1 (Stephansplatz) delivers you to Stephansdom (St Stephen's Cathedral), the marvellous Gothic South Tower ('*Steffl*') of which is the city's greatest landmark. According to the art historian Ludwig Hevesi, Rudolf von Alt (see p 66) drew or painted St Stephen's more than 100 times, while the writer Adalbert Stifter has left us an unforgettable description (1844) of the dawn breaking over the sleeping city, as he watches from his eyrie high up in the tower (*Vom Sankt Stephansturme: Aus dem alten Wien*).

The cathedral had modest beginnings as a new parish church (consecrated 1147) for the expanding Viennese population, placed under the jurisdiction of the Passau bishops by the terms of an agreement between them and Leopold IV of Babenberg in 1137 (the so-called Mautern Contract). The first buildings on the site suffered extensive fire damage (1193 and 1258) but two Romanesque features, the '*Heidentürme*' ('Heathen Towers') and the *Riesentor* (great western portal) survive from the early 13C, having been restored by the Bohemian King Ottakar (1251–76) after a second fire.

Tours of St Stephen's take place Mon–Sat, 10.30 and 15.00, Sun and PH 15.00, June–Sept; evening tours on Sat at 19.00; also Fri in July and Aug at 19.00.

Exterior The glory of the exterior is the **south tower** (137m—you can climb to 96m) begun in 1359 under Rudolf the Founder and completed in 1433 by Hans von Prachatitz. The north tower was never finished and capped with a Renaissance cupola in 1566. Fine Gothic work on the southern façade (chosen as the representative one because of the building's situation) includes the tomb of the *Minnesänger*, Neidhart von Reuental (to the left of the Singertor with its sculpted tympanum of the Conversion of St Paul), and a Man of Sorrows (to the right). On the east façade is a pulpit (possibly original) on the site where the Franciscan Giovanni da Capistrano preached against the Turkish menace in 1454–55; it is surmounted by a dramatic Baroque sculpture showing the preacher trampling a Turk beneath his feet. The tiled roof of the cathedral is a post-war reconstruction following the original pattern of black and yellow chevrons: on the north pitch of the roof over the Albertine Choir, the ceramics are patterned into two double-eagles, one bearing the shield of Austria, the other that of Vienna. This is a reference to the fact that Friedrich III granted Vienna the right to use the double eagle in its coat of arms in 1461, a reward for its loyalty in the power struggle with his brother and rival, Albrecht VI.

Interior Inside St Stephen's the eye is drawn to the lofty vaulting of the **nave**, built 1359–1446 by a number of hands, but certainly including the Prague architects Peter and Hans von Prachatitz (d. respectively 1429 and 1439), while Hans Puchsbaum (alternatively known as Hanns Puchspaum) completed the work. Prague masons of the St Vitus lodge had been crucial to the early construction of St Stephen's, and had supplied advice on necessary corrections to the South Tower in 1407; by 1459, however, the Vienna lodge had emerged as the leading workshop in the region, a position confirmed after a long conference in Regensburg. The middle section of the cathedral, for which it had been responsible, represented a sophisticated achievement of late Gothic, having been constructed over and around the smaller Romanesque predecessor, which was only demolished in 1426. Even more graceful, however, is the earlier High Gothic **Albertine Choir** (1304–40) east of the transept, named after Duke Albrecht II (1326–58), although it began as a civic endowment. The Viennese attachment to their cathedral has always been evident: they also gave money for the building of the South Tower, later endowed many altars of the interior and finally joined other Austrians after 1945 in contributing to the restoration of the cathedral. Fire had destroyed the roof, the Gothic choirstalls, and the great bell ('*Pummerin*'), originally made from cannons abandoned by Turkish besiegers in 1683. A poetic inscription composed by the writer Max Mell may be seen on the north-east column of the transept and records the parts of the restoration financed by contributions from individual provinces of Austria (Vienna financed the roof).

Close to the west door is the **late Gothic pulpit** (c 1500) by Anton Pilgram, the panels of which show the church fathers depicted as the four humours, a balance of which was thought to constitute the man of good judgement. At the foot of the pulpit is the portrait of Pilgram himself, shown as if leaning out of a window, this cameo being repeated (1513) under the delicate ribs of the small organ loft on the north wall of the cathedral.

From here you continue east past the entrance to the **catacombs** (guided tours 10.00–11.30, 14.00–16.00. ☎ 515 52/560), where the embalmed entrails of 56 Habsburgs are preserved in the Herzogsgruft (Ducal crypt).

At the end of the north nave is the **Wiener Neustädter Altar** (1447, but in fact a combination of various earlier altars) with its painted panels of saints which open up to reveal scenes from the life of Christ and the Virgin. The inner wings are closed on Sundays, while on feastdays the relief figures of the shrine are displayed. The device of Friedrich III (AEIOU—over 300 Latin and German interpretations of it were already current in the 16C, but it is generally believed to be an assertion of dynastic power and honour) may be seen on the predella.

On the east wall of the choir is the **tomb of Rudolf IV** (1339–65) and his wife, Katharine, daughter of the great Karl IV of Bohemia, Holy Roman Emperor; their features are vividly etched in sandstone, but the original gilding and gemstones decorating the clothing have been lost. The Baroque high altar has an altarpiece (the *Stoning of St Stephen*, 1640) by Tobias Pock and is flanked by marble figures sculpted by his brother, Johann Jakob. The choice of subjects (Sts Sebastian, Leopold, Florian and Rochus) combines reverence for local patron saints with protective ones (both Sebastian and Rochus were invoked against the plague), but the full programme of the patrons of each Austrian *Land* was never carried out.

At the end of the south nave is the magnificent **tomb of Emperor Friedrich III** designed by Niclaes Gerhaert van Leyden in 1467 and completed by Michael Tichter and Max Valmet early the following century (access to this and the Wiener Neustädter Altar is by guided tour only).

The pillars of the naves all have small Baroque altars attached, most of them the work of Matthias Steinl, which replaced 34 original Gothic ones. On the front pier of the south transept is the so-called *Servant Girl Madonna* (c 1320), which is supposed to have intervened miraculously on behalf of a servant wrongly accused. Across the nave under the north tower is another object of popular devotion, the *Christ with Toothache* (1420), whose nickname recalls a legend that students once irreverently likened this 'Man of Sorrows' to a man with toothache and were duly humbled for their blasphemous jest.

Continuing our clockwise tour, the 14C **St Katharine's Chapel** on the eastern edge of the south tower has a graceful stellar vault with a pendant boss showing a bust of *St Katharine of Alexandria*, the design of the chapel again illustrating the influence of the builders of St Vitus in Prague. Note the ornate 15C **font** with figures of the Four Evangelists on the base and reliefs of Christ, the Twelve Apostles and St Stephen on the 14 panels of its polygon. Across the south transept is a **Gothic baldachin** (1434) by Hans Puchsbaum, while towards the south-west end of the church is a late Gothic canopy over an icon supposed to have helped Prince Eugene to victory at the Battle of Zenta (1697). The Prince's sepulchral monument is to be found in the Tirna Chapel (not accessible) to the left of the main entrance.

Twelve metres below street level in the U-Bahn concourse to the south-west of the cathedral is the 14C **Virgilkapelle**, probably the crypt of an earlier burial chapel for the cemetery that lay around St Stephen's until its closure under Joseph II.

The **Dom und Diözesan Museum** (Cathedral Museum, Stephansplatz 6, open Tues–Sat 10.00–17.00) has a fine treasury (including the St Leopold Reliquary, 1592, a 17C monstrance in the form of the Tree of Life), a rich collection of Gothic altarpieces and statuary (including Veit Stoss of Nürnberg's *St Anne with Mary and the Child Jesus*, 1505) and Baroque religious painting by the Czech Karel Škréta, as well as Austrian masters (Franz Anton Maulbertsch, 'Kremser' Schmidt, J.M. Rottmayr and others). The historic *portrait of Rudolf IV*, who donated many of the items in the Treasury, dates to 1360–65 and is by an unknown Bohemian master.

East of Stephansdom

The Rotenturmstraße runs north-east of St Stephen's towards the Danube Canal. The third turning to the right is the **Fleischmarkt**, originally a meat market, whose existence is recorded as early as 1220. The narrow Griechengasse (first left) leads down to **St George's Church** (no. 5), which was reserved for visiting or resident Greek subjects of the Sultan by Maria Theresia: the Holy Trinity (Orthodox) Church for the Viennese community of Greeks is further along the Fleischmarkt at no. 15. The façade and lobby are sumptuous neo-Byzantine works by Theophil Hansen commissioned by the banker, Simon Georg Sina, whose family was of Greek (Aromunian) origin. On the way to it, you pass the *Griechenbeisl* restaurant, dating to 1453, and a favourite with literati and composers in the 19C. The bagpiper Augustin, mentioned in the sermons of Abraham a Sancta Clara, is said to have dined here all too well in 1679, as a result falling into a pit filled with the corpses of plague victims as he made his way home. The song *Oh! Du lieber Augustin* (which first became popular over a century later) celebrates his remarkable capacity for survival, and by implication that of the Viennese themselves.

Passing the main post office (no. 19) and the diminutive **Uniat Church of St Barbara** (Postgasse 10) mainly for the Ruthenian (Ukrainian) subjects of the Empire (who followed the Byzantine rite, but were in communion with Rome following settlements imposed on them by the powers to which they were subject at Brest-Litovsk), you reach the Baroque **Dominican Church** at Postgasse 4. Built in 1674, it was made a Basilica minor in 1927 and from then on also bore the name Rosenkranz Basilica ad S. Mariam Rotundam, a reference to the cult of the Rosary prayer allegedly formulated by St Dominic to combat the Albigensian dualist heresy and propagated by the Dominican 'rosary confraternity'. The main altarpiece inside shows the *Virgin as Queen of the Rosary* (1839, Leopold Kupelwieser), while the altar to the left has a vivid depiction of the *Adoration of the Shepherds* by Johann Spillenberger, a gifted painter whose career was cut short by the plague in 1679. In the Dominikus Chapel Claudia Felicitas of Tyrol is buried, Leopold I's second wife, who died (1676) aged only 23; above her last resting-place is an altarpiece by Tobias Pock showing *St Dominic praying before the Holy Trinity*. Note also the pulpit by Matthias Steinl and the imposing statue of *St Dominic with a dog* to the left of the high altar: this representation refers to the vision of St Dominic's mother, who saw her son as a dog with a torch in its mouth, by implication a man who would set the world on fire with his preaching. The Dominicans were known as *canes domini*, the Hounds of the Lord. Next to the high altar, Baroque frescoes allude to the victories for which the Order had so tirelessly worked, over the Albigensians (**Battle of Muret**, 1215) and over the Turks (**Lepanto**, 1571).

Towards the end of Postgasse, a right turn (Bäckerstraße) brings you into Dr. Ignaz-Seipel-Platz, named after the priest and Christian Social Chancellor in the 1920s. The square is flanked to the north-east by the Old University, facing which is the **Academy of Sciences** (1755), originally the University hall with the Law Faculty and an astronomical observatory on the top floor. Jean Nicolas Jadot de Ville-Issey's elegant late Baroque building has housed the Academy since 1857, the latter having been founded despite the misgivings of Metternich in 1847. His view that free enquiry by intellectuals only stirs up trouble for their rulers, was of course entirely correct. The ceremonial hall inside has frescoes showing allegories of the teaching faculties, repainted from the originals of Guglielmo Guglielmi destroyed by fire in 1961, while the Theological Hall has the fine original frescoes by Franz Anton Maulbertsch. To the north is the **Jesuit Church** (1631), built after the order had obtained control of the university and subsequently extended with late Baroque alterations, including impressive trompe l'oeil effects to the interior (1703) by Andrea Pozzo. Its most striking feature is the red and green barley sugar columns, imitating Bernini's solomonic columns for St Peter's in Rome.

If you go down the Jesuitengasse to the left of the church and turn left at the end into Schönlaterngasse, you come shortly to **Heiligenkreuzerhof**, which belongs to the ancient Cistercian abbey of Heiligenkreuz (see p 116) and was much expanded in the 17C. Its St Bernard Chapel is named after the greatest Cistercian, St Bernard of Clairvaux, known as '*Doctor mellifluus*' on account of his speaking powers; a fierce ascetic, he was yet a man of temperate judgement and a rare clerical opponent of the medieval church's persecution of the Jews. The chapel (1729) was designed by Giuliano Giuliani while the altarpiece (*St Bernard and the Virgin Mary*) by Martino Altomonte, is flanked by Giuliani's sculptures of Sts Leopold and Florian. (If the chapel is closed, enquire at the *Hauswart* [caretaker] for the key.)

Leaving the Hof by the north-east corner (Grashofgasse), you reach the Wollzeile via Köllnerhofgasse and beyond it an alley in which is situated *Figlmüller*, a Viennese institution where the biggest and best *Wiener Schnitzel* are served by waiters who would have little problem being re-employed on the stage should the establishment ever go out of business. The Wollzeile, as the name suggests, was occupied by wool traders in the Middle Ages, while the 'Köllnerhof' refers to the settlement here of Cologne merchants, first mentioned in documents of 1394.

West of Stephansdom

Overlooking the west façade of St Stephen's is Hans Hollein's impressive **Haas Haus** (1990, Stock-im-Eisen-Platz 6), the interior of which is a five-storey atrium housing a number of elegant shops and topped by a first-class restaurant (*Do & Co*) and a café with fine views of the cathedral. However the original concept of pricey boutiques has not been very successful and changes are planned.

GENERAL HOSPITAL

Votivkirche

ROOSEVELTPLATZ

Börse

BÖRSEG.

WERDERTO

UNIVERSITÄTS STRASSE

SCHOTTENRING

WIPPLINGERSTRASSE

BÖRSEPLATZ

Landesgericht

LIEBIGGASSE

SCHOTTENBASTEI

HOHENSTAUFENGASSE

HELFERSTORFERGASSE

CONCORD PLATZ

GRILLPARZERSTRASSE

SCHOTTEN GASSE

Maria a Gestad

WIPPLINGERSTRA

Schottenstift

RENNGASSE

Universität

TEINFALTSTRASSE

FREYUNG

TIEFER GRABEN

JUDEN PLATZ

STRASSE

Rathauspark

Harrach Palais

Am Hof

Bohemi Chancell

LANDESGERICHTS STRASSE

Rathaus

LÖWEL-

Ferstel Palais

HEERENGASSE

Kirche am Hof

Obi Pala

DR. KARL LUEGER RING

BANKGASSE

WALLNERSTRASSE

KOHLMARKT

RATHAUS

REICHSRATS-

STRASSE

Burgtheater

Peters-kirche

STADIONGASSE

Minoriten-kirche

AUERSPERGSTRASSE

DR. KARL RENNER RING

Volksgarten

BALLHAUS-PLATZ

SCHAUFLERG.

Michaeler-kirche

HABSBURGERGASSE

GRA.

Parlament

Alte Hofburg

LERCHENFELDERSTR.

Justiz-Palast

JOSEFSPLATZ

DOROTHEERG.

Palais Trautson (Ministry of Justice)

BELLARIASTRASSE

Burgtor

Neue Hofburg

Augustiner-kirche

AUGUS

PLANKE

NEUSTIFTGASSE

BURGRING

AUGUSTINERBASTEI

SPIEGEL

Volkstheater

Naturhistorisches museum

Kapuzinerkirch Kaisergruft

TINERSTR.

BURGGASSE

MESSEPLATZ

Maria-Theresien-Platz

Burggarten

ALBERTINA-PLATZ

VEGETTHOFSTR.

BREITEGASSE

Kunsthistorisches museum

Hotel Sacher

Messepalast

BABENBERG-STRASSE

OPERNRING

Staatsoper

SIEBENSTERNGASSE

ESCHENBACHGASSE

ELISABETHSTRASSE

KÄRNTNER

STIFTGASSE

SCHWEIGHOFERG.

SCHILLER PLATZ

NIBELUNGENGASSE

OPERN-

MARIAHILFER STRASSE

GETREIDEMARKT

Akademie der Bildenden Kunste

FRIEDRICHSTRASSE

WINDMÜHLGASSE

FILLGRADERGASSE

LEHARGASSE

Secession

KARLSPL

Ressel-p

GUMPENDORFER STRASSE

Naschmarkt

WIEDNER HAUPTSTRASSE

0   200 yards

0   200 metres

LINKE WIENZEILE

RECHTE WIENZEILE

OPERNGASSE

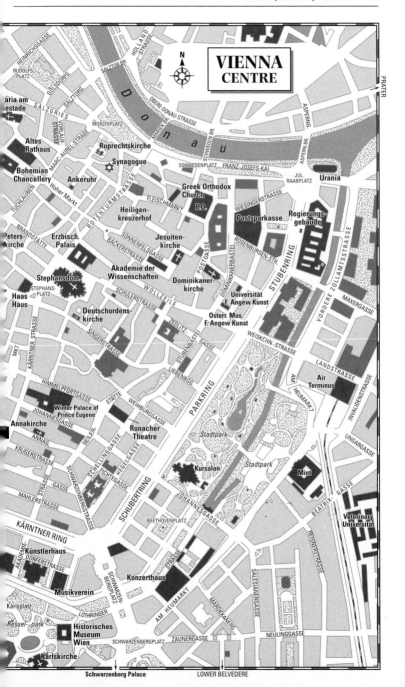

VIENNA CENTRE

N

Donau

PRATER

HEINRICHSGASSE

RUDOLFS PLATZ

GÖLSDORFG.

SALZTORG.

SALZTOR BR.

HOLLAND. STRASSE

OBERE-DONAU-STRASSE

SCHWEDEN BR.

ASPERNG.

aria am estade

SALZGRIES

VORLAUF STRASSE

MARC-AUREL-STRASSE

MORZINPLATZ

SCHWEDEN BR.

ASPERN BR.

Altes Rathaus

Ruprechtskirche

SCHWEDENPLATZ FRANZ-JOSEFS-KAI

JUL. RAABPLATZ

Urania

Bohemian Chancellery

Ankeruhr

Synagogue

Hoher Markt

ROTENTURMSTRASSE

FLEISCHMARKT

Greek Orthodox Church

P.O.

WIESINGERSTRASSE

Regierungs-gebäude

TUCHLAUBEN

Heiligen-kreuzerhof

Postsparkasse

ROSENBURSEN-STR.

STUBENRING

Peters-kirche

BRANDSTÄTTE

Erzbisch. Palais

SONNENFELSGASSE

BÄCKERSTRASSE

Jesuiten-kirche

POSTGASSE

Akademie der Wissenschaften

DOMINIKANERBASTEI

VORDERE ZOLLAMTSSTRASSE

Stephansdom

STEPHANS-PLATZ

Dominikaner-kirche

Universität F. Angew Kunst

MAXERGASSE

Haas Haus

SCHULERSTRASSE

WOLLZEILE

Deutschordens-kirche

ZEDLITZ

Österr. Mus. F. Angew Kunst

WEISKICHN.-STRASSE

LANDSTRASSE

INVALIDENSTRASSE

SINGERSTRASSE

STUBENBASTEI GASSE

LIEBENBGG

PARKRING

AM HEUMARKT

Air Terminus

UNGARGASSE

HIMMELPFORTGASSE

STÄTTE

WEIHBURGGASSE

Winter Palace of Prince Eugene

JOHANNESGASSE

Annakirche

SEILER-

SCHELLINGGASSE

HEGELGASSE

Ronacher Theatre

Stadtpark

ANNAG.

KRUGERSTRASSE

FICHTEGASSE

Kursalon

Stadtpark

Mint

STRASSE

SCHWARZENBERGSTRASSE

SCHUBERTRING

JOHANNESGASSE

BEATRIX- GASSE

FEISTNERSTRASSE

MAHLERSTRASSE

BEETHOVENPLATZ

Veterinary Universität

KÄRNTNER RING

AKADEMIE

Künstlerhaus

DORFERSTRASSE

STRASSE

Konzerthaus

SALESIANERGASSE

Musikverein

SCHWARZEN-BERGPLATZ

LOTHRINGER

AM HEUMARKT

MAROKANERG.

NEULINGGASSE

Karlsplatz

Ressel- park

Historisches Museum Wien

SCHWARZENBERGPLATZ ZAUNERGASSE

Karlskirche

Schwarzenberg Palace

LOWER BELVEDERE

The Graben

The Graben (once the defensive ditch for the southern periphery of the Roman camp) is an elegant promenade and shopping area running between Stock-im-Eisen-Platz and the junction with Naglergasse/Kohlmarkt. Walking from east to west, the buildings of note include the late Historicist (1891) **Equitable Palais** (Stock-im-Eisen-Platz 3–4) with a superb stairway of variegated marble and Zsolnay ceramics, the **Bartolotti-Partenfeld** Palais at no. 11 Graben, possibly designed by Lukas von Hildebrandt, the clothing shop *Knize* at no. 13 with an interior by Adolf Loos, the august **Grabenhof** (nos 14–15) built (1876) by Otto Wagner to a design by Otto Thienemann and the graceful neo-classical **Erste Österreichische Spar-Casse** (no. 21, now Erste Bank) designed by Alois Pichl in 1840. At the Graben's east end is the **Leopold Fountain** (1804) by J.M. Fischer, who also made its counterpart at the west end, the Joseph Fountain. Although these show the figures of the medieval St Leopold and the father of Christ, they were dedicated by their commissioner, Franz I, to the memory of his predecessors, likewise a Joseph (II) and a Leopold (II). However their impact is dwarfed by the great **Pestsäule** (Plague Column, correctly Trinity Column), commissioned by Leopold I in thanksgiving for the end of the 1679 plague. Its symbolism represents both the Holy Trinity and (at the base) the three pillars of Habsburg *Hausmacht*, as shown by the three coats of arms of Bohemia, Hungary and the Crown Lands. Ludovico Burnacini and J.B. Fischer von Erlach were involved in the planning and design of the column, while Paul Strudel carried out much of the work, including the vivid representation of Leopold I at prayer on the south side.

The **Peterskirche** (1703–1708), built on a graceful oval ground plan, is just to the north of the central Graben. It is one of the finest works attributed to Lukas von Hildebrandt, although original plans were drawn up by Gabriele Montani in 1702 and some modifications were made by Franz Jänggl in 1733. The relief in the gable of the portico (by Andrea Altomonte, 1751) shows the *Calling of Peter by Christ* and allegorical statues of *Faith, Hope* and *Charity* may be seen above. The most striking feature of the interior is Lorenzo Mattielli's sculptured scene (to the right of the choir) of *John of Nepomuk being thrown into the Moldau* from Charles Bridge (20 March 1393). According to legend he had refused to reveal the Queen's confessional secrets to Wenceslas IV; however, the more probable cause of the King's displeasure was that John (who was Vicar-General of Prague) had resisted Wenceslas's attempts to create a new see for one of his favourites. Mattielli's work dates to 1729, the year of John's canonisation. Other furnishings of note include the Baroque pulpit (Matthias Steindl, 1716), the altar designed by Antonio Galli-Bibiena and executed by his father-in-law, Santino Bussi, with an altarpiece by Martino Altomonte (the *Healing of the Lame by Peter and John*), and (over the tabernacle) a *Maria Immaculata* (1836) by Leopold Kupelwieser. The altar is flanked by monumental statues of the Emperors Constantine and Charlemagne, protectors respectively of the Eastern and Western Churches: a (spurious) tradition that Charlemagne was the founder of the original Peterskirche is remembered in a relief (1906) by Rudolf Weyr on the eastern exterior wall. Other attractive ornamentation by Galli-Bibiena includes illusionist architectural effects and a fresco under the organ loft of *Christ ordering Peter to walk on the Water*. The cupola fresco of the *Assumption of Mary* is by J.M. Rottmayr (1714).

The **Kohlmarkt**, originally the link between the Porta Decumana of the Roman camp and a recreation area (*canabae*) for the legionaries, runs south to the Michaelerplatz from the west end of the Graben. The name of the street dates to 1314 and refers to medieval charcoal sellers. There are several interesting buildings, including the *Jugendstil* façades of the travel book and map specialists *Freytag & Berndt* (Max Fabiani, 1901) at no. 9, the portal (1912) of the bookshop *Manz* (no. 16), designed by Adolf Loos, and Hans Hollein's shop fronts at nos 7, 8–10.

At no. 14 is *Demel*, Vienna's most famous *konditorei* which was originally situated (1786) on the Michaelerplatz and remained in the hands of the founding family up to 1972. The Große Michaelerhaus at no. 11 had a number of distinguished inhabitants, mostly musicians who lodged here to be close to their patrons at court and to the Hoftheater that stood before the Burg. Pietro Metastasio, who was court poet from 1729 and wrote numerous opera libretti, died in the Michaelerhaus in 1782 and was buried in the crypt of the adjacent Michaelerkirche. The 16-year-old Joseph Haydn found refuge in one of its garrets after his voice broke and he was dismissed from the Hofkapellen choir; he earned money by teaching music to the daughter of Metastasio, who lived in splendour on the third floor.

A turn in the opposite direction from the end of the Graben, to the north, brings you into the Tuchlauben. At no. 19 you can see the **Neidhart Frescoes** (open: Tues–Sun 09.00–12.00), discovered in 1976. They feature scenes from the poetry of the 13C Minnesänger (German courtly love poets), Neidhart von Reuental (d. before 1246), and are one of the very few visual records of life at the Babenberg court. (Neidhart, whose assumed name meant 'the envious man', probably intended humorously, satirised the contrast between the over-sophisticated court and the unsophisticated life of the peasants in his *Summer and Winter Songs*.) Round the corner at Brandstätte 6 is the **Zacherlhaus** (named after its owner), designed by the distinguished Slovene architect, Josef Plecnik, a pupil of Otto Wagner.

The Bauernmarkt leads north-east from Brandstätte to the south-eastern end of the **Hoher Markt** (once the main market and the city's first recorded one). The square lies at the heart of Vienna's history, being the site of the pre-medieval *Berghof* as explained by a plaque on a building at the west end: the attested existence of this overlord's residence, where justice was also dispensed, provides vital evidence of the continuity of civilisation in Vienna during the Dark Ages. At no. 3 are the remains of Roman officers' quarters (open Tues–Sun 09.00–12.15, 13.00–16.30), while the rectangular market space is dominated by the **Wedding Fountain**, (1732), designed by Fischer von Erlach the Younger and successor to a monument originally dedicated to Joseph I by his father, Leopold I, in thanksgiving for his son's return from the defence (1702) of Landau during the War of the Spanish Succession. Antonio Corradini sculpted the wedding group of Joseph and Mary under the bronze baldachin, below which are biblical reliefs. At the east end of the Hoher Markt is the *Jugendstil* **Anker Clock** (Franz Matsch, 1913), situated on a gallery running between two wings of the Anker Insurance building. Each hour an important figure from Viennese history appears on the clock-face and at noon all 12 revolve across it.

A walk under the clock and down the Bauernmarkt will bring you via the western end of Fleischmarkt and up some steps to **Ruprechtsplatz**. Here stands the **Ruprechtskirche**, originating perhaps in the 8C, the oldest surviving parts being 11C, and thus the oldest extant church in the city. St Ruprecht's was under the jurisdiction of the Salzburg bishops, St Peter's under those of Passau; these two dioceses not only competed with each other for secular power in Vienna through their landed possessions and local administrators, but for long prevented the Babenbergs from fully establishing their writ.

The Seitenstettengasse leads down from the church towards the Danube Canal; at no. 4 is the fine neo-classical **Synagogue** (*Stadttempel*) (1826) by Josef Kornhäusel (1782–1860), which is just beyond the Kornhäusel-Turm, part of an imposing Biedermeier house (now in possession of the Jewish religious community) where the architect had a studio. It was from this tower that Adalbert Stifter, as described in *Aus dem alten Wien* (From Old Vienna), watched a full eclipse of the sun in 1842. The inconspicuous façade of the synagogue

The Ruprechtskirche, Vienna

(Joseph II's Edict of Tolerance stipulated that non-Catholic sanctuaries should not be identifiable as such from the outside in order not to offend the sensibilities of *bien pensant* Catholics) is thought to have preserved it from destruction in the *Reichskristallnacht* of 1938. The interior has a domed ceiling studded with gold stars and supported by Ionic columns, behind which are two tiers of galleries. You need to bring a form of identification with you if you wish to visit the synagogue.

Returning to Ruprechtsplatz, take the Sterngasse to the west (at no. 2 is *Shakespeare and Company*, one of Vienna's best English language bookshops) and descend the steps, turning left up Marc-Aurel-Straße, then right into Wipplinger Straße. Shortly on your right is the **Alte Rathaus**, the City Hall until 1885, now housing the Museum of Vienna's 1st District (open Wed and Fri 15.00–17.00) and the Archive of the Austrian Resistance in World War II (open: 09.00–17.00, Mon–Thur).

In the courtyard of the Alten Rathaus is Georg Raphael Donner's **Perseus and Andromeda Fountain** (1741), a work of kinetic bravura showing Andromeda being rescued from the monster, above which is a wrought-iron balcony borne by energetic-looking putti on consoles. On the main (southern) portal of the house are to be seen allegories of *Justice and Benevolence*, together with *Piety* and *fides publica* by J.M. Fischer, while on the north side of the building is the superb Renaissance **portal of the Salvatorkapelle**, Viennese centre of the Old Catholic Church, which rejected Pius IX's declaration of papal infallibility in 1870 (p 38) (the chapel is open Mon, Wed, Sat 09.00–11.00, Sun 10.00–12.00). The portal bears a 14C inscription to the chapel's founder, Otto Haimo, whose property (which included the whole Rathaus building) was confiscated following an unsuccessful plot against Friedrich the Handsome in 1309, the latter donating the house to the city in 1316.

The Austrian Resistance in World War II

The *Österreich Lexikon* (1995) states that 'in contrast to other occupied countries, Austrian resistance fighters had to operate in an environment bristling with fanatical supporters of the regime and informers ready to denounce' all those regarded as suspect. Two main groupings (Catholic-Monarchist and Communist- or Socialist-inclined workers) made up the resistance movement, whose exact numbers are hard to estimate, but were probably at least 30,000 with more joining towards the end of the war as the allies closed in. Some 2700 Austrians were executed for resistance activities and many more imprisoned as potential subversives, a significant number of these dying in the camps. Beginning with the distribution of flyers to counteract Nazi news monopoly and propaganda, the movement gradually broadened its activities, graduating even to armed intervention, mostly organised by the Communists. A widely based 'Group 05' took the leading role in Vienna towards the end of the war. The contribution of the resistance, though modest, was of considerable political importance following the Allies' Moscow Declaration of 1943, which stated that the post-war settlement for Austria would be significantly affected by the degree to which the country assisted in its own liberation.

At the west end of Salvatorgasse is the lovely Gothic church of **Maria am Gestade** (completed c 1414, its beautiful filigree spire c 1440). The main architect was Michael Knab, whose choir is reminiscent of similar work by him on the Stephansdom, while another cathedral architect, Peter von Prachatitz, has left his mark on the narrow and soaring western façade which is only 9.7m wide but 33m high. This slenderness and the kink in the church's axis were dictated by the somewhat precarious site on the Danube bank (hence also the church's name). Maria am Gestade was one of the last parishes to remain in the patrimony (until 1805) of the Passau bishopric, which had been so decisive an influence in the early history of the city and whose administrative centre was situated at no. 6 of the emcompassing square (Passauer Platz). Not only the struggle for precedence with the secular rulers of Vienna was conducted from here: during the Reformation it was also used as a prison for Protestants and Anabaptists.

The interior of the church is mostly neo-Gothic but contains in the north chapel a rare Renaissance **altar** donated by Johann Perger in 1520, while near the crossing is a carved *Annunciation* group dating from 1380. In 1820 the Redemptorists took over the church, thus fulfilling a wish of their recently deceased leader, the charismatic Moravian preacher, Clemens Maria Hofbauer (since 1914 patron saint of Vienna), whose remains were moved here in 1862. Some services are still held in the Czech language.

Returning east along the Wipplingerstraße (reached via Schwertgasse from the church) you will see the former **Bohemian Chancellery** (1714, partly by J.B. Fischer von Erlach) opposite the Alten Rathaus, and beside it a turning to the right into the **Judenplatz**, the site of the ghetto, which was originally built against the walls of the Babenberg court and demolished in the savage pogrom of 1421. Archaeological excavations prior to the construction of a **Holocaust Memorial** in a form resembling stacked books and entitled *The Nameless Library* by Rachel

Whiteread have revealed extensive remains of the medieval settlement; there was much controversy concerning the fate of these remains and the possible relocation of the memorial (resisted by Whiteread). Great Jordan's House (no. 2) to the south-east has a relief on the wall showing the *Baptism of Christ in the River Jordan* with an anti-semitic Latin inscription applauding the 1421 pogrom. Siegfried Charoux's modern statue of *Gotthold Ephraim Lessing* (1729–81, author of the philosemitic *Nathan the Wise*) stands in the middle of the square, a counter-weight to the sentiments expressed on the relief.

Clemens Maria Hofbauer (1751–1820)

In the first half of the 19C the Congregation of the Most Holy Redeemer (founded by the Italian, Alfonso di Liguori in 1732 and generally known as the Redemptorist movement) spearheaded a religious revival that reflected the contemporary ethos of idealistic Romanticism. The organisation therefore concentrated on missionary work and charitable activities, refusing attempts of the Popes to side-track it into a conventional educational role. The spirit of Hofbauer's reform-oriented preaching and the stress on individual conscience was not in keeping either with the paternalistic anti-clericalism of Joseph II or the suspicious conservatism of Franz I, with the result that the Redemptorists could not officially be established in Vienna until just after Hofbauer's death. Unofficially, Hofbauer was influential in the city from 1808, while his admirers included leading German writers such as the Schlegels and the poet, Joseph von Eichendorff.

The Kurrentgasse towards the south-west of the square runs down to the Schulhof (so-called because of the medieval Jewish school here) where the attractive 17C Obizzi Palace houses an interesting **Uhrenmuseum** (Clock Museum, open Tues–Sun 09.00–16.30). The collection contains over 3000 items gathered by Rudolf Kaftan (its first curator) and the writer, Marie von Ebner-Eschenbach, ranging from mechanisms for early tower clocks to astronomical timepieces and novelty clocks. At Schulhof 4 is the **Puppenmuseum** (Doll and Toy Museum) which is open Tues–Sun 10.00–18.00.

A narrow street running north-west brings you into the large space known as **Am Hof** since the Babenbergs established their residence here in 1156. In the centre is a **Marian Column**, a replacement (1667) for an original (1645) set up on the initiative of Ferdinand III as thanksgiving for the delivery of the town from the danger of Swedish invasion at the end of the Thirty Years War. The armoured angels on the plinth defend themselves from the snakes and dragons of Protestant heresy, while at the top of the column a crowned Immaculata sits on a snake-entwined globe.

To the east is the **Church of the Nine Choirs of Angels** (occupying the former site of the Babenberg residence), from the balcony of which a herald announced the dissolution of the Holy Roman Empire in 1806. From the same balcony, Pope Pius IV delivered his blessing to a vast crowd in 1782 at the end of a visit that was notably unsuccessful in its aim of discouraging Joseph II's administrative assault on ecclesiastical drones. This former Carmelite church was the first home of the Jesuits after they were summoned to Vienna in 1551 by Ferdinand I and its first Rector was the combative theologian, Peter Canisius

(1521–97), compiler of the *Catechismus Major* (1554), of which over 130 editions have subsequently appeared. Canisius was the main intellectual force behind the success of the Counter-Reformation in southern Germany and parts of Central Europe.

The later (1662) façade of the church shows Italian influence (possibly the work of Carlo Carlone) and features sculptures of the nine angels of the Celestial Hierarchy (angels, seraphim, cherubim). The interior of the church can usually only be visited at times of mass and is not of great interest, with the possible exception of F.A. Maulbertsch's *Glorification of St Franz de Regis* in the second side-chapel on the left.

At the north-west of Am Hof is the **former Bürgerliches Zeughaus** (Citizens' Armoury, now the fire station) which was the headquarters of the hastily formed National Guard during the Revolution of 1848. Anton Ospel's façade (1732) is topped by the Habsburg coat of arms and attic statuary by Lorenzo Mattielli, with allegories of *Strength and Fortitude* (the motto of Karl VI) holding up a globe. A Roman sewer runs through the cellar.

Freyung

North-west of Am Hof (reached via Heidenschuss) is the area known as Freyung, an historic part of town that takes its name from the right of asylum granted to fugitives from justice, if they were able to reach the area under the jurisdiction of the Schottenkirche to the north. Adjacent to the church are lodgings known as the **Schubladkastenhaus** ('Chest of Drawers House', 1774) originally built to accommodate the guests of the Prior of the Schottenstift and the Stift school, now one of the most desirable addresses for wealthy Viennese. In front of it stands Ludwig Schwanthaler's *Austria Fountain* (1846) with an allegory of 'Austria' presiding over figures representing rivers of the Empire.

On the southern wall of the **Schottenkirche** is the monumental statue (1893) of Heinrich II of Babenberg (1114–77), who first invited the Irish monks here in 1155. He is buried in the crypt, together with other distinguished figures, notably Count Ernst Rüdiger Starhemberg, the defender of Vienna in 1683. The interior of the church is enhanced by a noble high altar (1883) in neo-Renaissance style by the Ringstrassen architect, Heinrich von Ferstel, as well as the Baroque funerary monument (1725) of Count Starhemberg by Fischer von Erlach the Younger.

Adjacent to the church entrance is the neo-classical Schottenhof (1832) by Josef Kornhäusel, in the courtyard of which is the entrance to the new **Museum im Schottenstift** (open Thur, Fri, Sat 10.00–17.00, Sun 12.00–17.00). Besides many high quality artworks of the 17C and 18C, the star item of the collection is the famous **Schottenaltar** (room 5), a winged altarpiece by an anonymous master or masters painted in the 1470s; of its 21 surviving panels, two show contemporary views of Vienna, incorporated into the main themes of *The Life of Mary* (shown on weekdays) and *The Passion* (shown Sun, PH and during Lent). In the Prelacy Hall is Joachim von Sandrart's huge altarpiece (1671) of the *Heavenly Gloriole*, originally in the Schottenkirche.

On the west side of Herrengasse (no. 4) is Lukas von Hildebrandt's **Kinsky Palais** (1716), while the south side of Freyung is dominated by the monumental **Harrach Palais** (Domenico Martinelli, 1702), in whose gracious first and second floor rooms exhibitions are held, many of them themed extensions of the collection in the Kunsthistorisches Museum (see p 100). The elaborately decorative **Oratorium** (1720) by Antonio Beduzzi is a feature of the interior, as is the great double stairway.

Beside the palace is the Freyung entrance to the arcade of the so-called **Ferstel-Palais** with elegant shops, a Danube Fountain and a remarkable double-return stairway leading to the colourful neo-Gothic upper chamber, originally the Stock Exchange. On the ground floor is the lovingly restored *Café Central*, once the haunt of Hermann Bahr and the *Jung Wien* group of literati, who moved here after the nearby *Griensteidl* closed in 1897; that event was memorialised in Karl Kraus's malicious article entitled 'The Demolished Literature' in which he mocked the affectations of *Jung Wien*, especially the writing of Bahr ('... he did not as yet possess the mellow composure of Goethe, it was ... difficult for beginners to follow him through the thicket of his oddly ornate and elaborately branched Un-German'). The humorist Alfred Polgar wrote a *Theory of the Café Central* containing a memorable evocation of it lying 'on the Viennese latitude at the meridian of loneliness', its habitués, 'for the most part, people whose hatred of their fellow human beings is as fierce as their longing for them, who want to be alone but need companionship for it.'

A brief detour from Freyung via the Schottengasse, turning left towards the end of it, brings you to the Mölker Bastei. At no. 8 is the **Pasqualatihaus** (1798, named after its owner, a distinguished professor of chemistry), who let rooms to Beethoven in 1804–05. Beethoven's apartment may be visited and it contains several relics including a five-pedal piano of 1821. In the same building is a collection of drawings and paintings by the writer Adalbert Stifter (1805–68): both memorial rooms are open Tues–Sun 09.00–12.15 and 13.00–16.30. Nearby at Schreyvogelgasse 10 is the **Dreimäderlhaus** (1803), a town house in neo-classical style spuriously associated with Schubert's courtship of a '*Mädel*' (Viennese for an enticing young woman with complaisant morals).

The Herrengasse ('Street of the Lords', so-called because of its association with the Lower Austrian Diet that was formerly here) leads to the south. A detour to your right (via Leopold-Figl-Gasse) brings you to the **Minoriten Platz** flanked by elegant Baroque palaces once or still belonging to noble Austrian families (Liechtensteins, Dietrichsteins, Starhembergs). The ancient **Minoritenkirche** has officially been the National Italian Church ('Maria Schnee') since 1784, although its Italian associations go back much further to the arrival in Vienna of the Franciscan Friars Minor in the mid-13C. Later its fine west portal was built by Jakobus Parisiensis, a member of the Order and confessor to Albrecht II, who supported the building of a new church for the friars in 1339; its tympanum relief of the *Crucifixion* (1350) shows a distinctive French influence. The church's spire was knocked away by a Turkish cannon ball in 1683, leaving the present truncation, which determines the less than graceful effect of the whole building. Furthermore the interior was 're-Gothicised' by Ferdinand von Hohenberg between 1784–89 and is frankly rather bleak. Its most conspicuous, but certainly not its most attractive, feature is G. Raffaelli's huge mosaic copy of Leonardo's *Last Supper*, originally made for Napoleon, who was thus dissuaded from detaching the original from the refectory wall of Santa Maria delle Grazie in Milan. More pleasing is Vincenzo Luccardi's funerary monument (1854) for Pietro Metastasio, with a rather touching relief on the plinth of the poet receiving the blessing of Pope Pius VI via the Papal Nuncio: Salieri carries a cushion for him to kneel on and Mozart can be seen wiping away a tear. In the Minorites' first church on this site, the embalmed body of Ottakar II (see p 35) was exposed for (it is claimed) 30 weeks after his defeat by Rudolf of Habsburg, having been brought here in a great procession of 'all the secular and profane orders, with complete interdiction of any chant, or sounding bell, of obsequies of any kind, or even the reading of the Mass'.

The Herrengasse leads into the **Michaelerplatz**, in the centre of which archaeological remains of Roman baths and some Baroque foundations and drainage pertaining to the Hofburg may be seen. On your right as you enter the square is the *Café Griensteidl*, re-opened (1992) nearly a century after its closure. Founded in 1847, it was strongly associated with the revolutionary cause in 1848 and nicknamed 'Café National', while *Café Daum*, a stone's throw away at Kohlmarkt 6, was packed with purple-faced officers and reactionary aristocrats.

To the east stands the **Michaelerkirche** with its Gothic spire and a fine portal (1725) by Antonio Beduzzi; above the portal is Lorenzo Mattielli's sculpture of *St Michael casting out the rebellious angels*, which greatly enhances Ferdinand von Hohenberg's neo-classical façade (1792). The oldest part of the church, which was originally in the possession of the Barnabite Order, dates to the 13C, while the choir was built between 1327 and 1340. In the **interior**, the eye is caught by Karl Georg Merville's dramatic stucco, which repeats the theme of St Michael casting out the angels; it is poised above a theatrical high altar (J.B. d'Avrange, 1781). There are some lead reliefs of high quality, also by Merville, in the Priest's Choir (accessible only on a guided tour, except during periodic exhibitions laid on by the Salvatorian owners of the church who took it over from the dwindling number of Barnabites in 1923).

As the parish church of the Court, the Michaelerkirche was also the burial-place of many court retainers, while the side-chapel in the south choir was endowed (1350) by an imperial cook (Stiborius Chrezzel) who had been wrongly accused of poisoning Duke Albrecht II. After his innocence was established, his accuser (a Swabian priest) was displayed in a bird cage on the Hoher Markt for two weeks and then buried (just) alive in St Stephen's cemetery. For the most part it is the ultra-loyal nobility (Trautsons, Herbersteins, Mollards) who are laid to rest here on the basis that those who were most faithful to the Habsburgs in life should be placed near to them in death. The church interior is rather dark but there are several works of art worth seeking out, including a bronze *Crucifixion* (1646) made in Augsburg in the north chancel and two altarpieces by Tobias Pock against the triumphal arch (*Pentecost* and the *Fourteen Healing Saints*). Near the south entrance is a 15C *Man of Sorrows* and on the exterior south wall (in the Michaeler Durchgang) a fine polychrome limestone relief of *Christ on the Mount of Olives* (c 1494).

On the north side of the square is the **Loos-Haus**, built in 1912 by Adolf Loos for the tailors Goldman and Salatsch. The plainness of its façade caused an uproar in the contemporary press, and Loos felt obliged to add the window boxes as a concession to the 'ornament' he had so bitingly condemned in his pamphlet *Ornament and Crime* (1908). The exterior indeed gives little intimation of the discreetly luxurious elegance of the interior with its variegated marble and mahogany furnishings. The house is now owned by a bank which holds periodic exhibitions on the first floor. It is also open during business hours 08.00–15.00.

The Hofburg

The south-west rim of the Michaelerplatz is entirely occupied by the north-east frontage of the Hofburg (the Habsburg Residenz), in the middle of which is the **Michaelertor** with its gleaming green and gilded dome. The neo-Baroque sculptures on the lateral wings represent Habsburg power on land and at sea, while a plaque to the left of the arch recalls the old Burgtheater that stood here. The latter was built under Maria Theresia, who allowed the tenant of the Kärntnertortheater to alter an existing ballroom and a neighbouring building at his own cost. It was here that Gluck, Salieri and (on occasion) Mozart saw their works performed. Joseph II made it the National Theatre in 1776, when its mostly French and Italian repertoire was largely superseded by works in German. As you walk through the archway and under the cupola, you will notice allegorical representations of the mottoes of Karl VI, his daughter Maria Theresia, her son Joseph II and finally (skipping three generations) Franz Joseph I. On the other side you find yourself in the residence's inner courtyard ('*In der Burg*'), once the site of executions, then of Baroque spectacles and a daily changing of the guard which (typically for the Habsburgs) was more of an excuse for a short concert. The whole complex of the Burg grew out of an original fortress (1275) built by Premysl Ottakar of Bohemia during his occupation of Vienna. His successful opponent, Rudolf of Habsburg, enlarged this building, as did many of his successors over the centuries up to 1913, when the architecturally vacuous Neue Burg was completed, itself the counterpart to a planned matching wing on the other side of the Heldenplatz which was never embarked on.

In the centre of the courtyard is a statue of *Franz I* (1792–1835), represented by Pompeo Marchesi as a Roman emperor. To the south-west is the **Leopoldinische Trakt** (wing), completed by an Italian architect (Domenico Carlone) for Leopold I in 1681 after a fire (1668) destroyed a previous commission for the same site. It was altered under Maria Theresia to make it harmonise with the **Reichskanzleitrakt** to the north-east, planned (1723) under Karl VI by Lukas von Hildebrandt and continued (1726–30) by Joseph Emanuel Fischer von Erlach. It was intended to house the officials of the Holy Roman Empire in suitable dignity (its two main doors are appropriately adorned with Lorenzo Mattielli's sculptures of the *Labours of Hercules*), but the cupola remained unfinished until the completion of the Michaelertrakt extension and Michaelertor by Ferdinand Kirschner in 1893.

Between these two lateral wings stands (to the north-west) the **Amalienburg**, built in the Renaissance (1575), but also modified under Maria Theresia at a cost of 26,000 Gulden to house her favourite daughter, Maria Christina, at the time of the latter's marriage to Albert of Sachsen-Teschen. These comfortable lodgings were used by Tsar Alexander I during the Congress of Vienna (see below). To the south-east is the **Schweizertor** and **Schweizerhof**, the oldest part of the Burg, resting on the site of Ottakar's early fortress.

Access to the **Silberkammer** (Imperial Tableware and Silver Museum) and the **Kaiserappartements** (Imperial Apartments of Franz Joseph and Elisabeth and the Apartments of Tsar Alexander I) is via the Reichskanzleitor to the north-east (both museums are open daily, 09.00–17.00). With the possible exception of imperial portraits by Winterhalter and the historical paintings of Johann Peter Krafft, the apartments contain little of aesthetic interest, although the dressing-room of Empress Elisabeth with its exercise equipment is a curiosity. The penultimate room of the tour contains a magnificent long table laid for an imperial banquet. You descend into the Ballhausplatz (Viennese nomenclature with the same associations as 'Foggy Bottom' or 'Carlton House Terrace'), and must retrace your steps to the Michaelertor to continue with the more interesting part of the Hofburg visit. The Federal Chancellery is opposite the exit.

The marvellous **Weltliche und Geistliche Schatzkammer** (Sacred and Profane Treasuries, open Wed–Mon 10.00–18.00) are reached through the Schweizerhof to the south-east. On your way you pass under the Schweizertor, surmounted by an inscription to Ferdinand I dated 1552 and listing his many titles. Swiss guards were quartered in this part of the Burg under Maria Theresia (hence the name Schweizertor), while in the 19C the Schweizerhof accommodated Franz I and later the ill-fated Crown Prince Rudolph. Highlights of the **Profane Treasury** include an agate bowl, once thought to be the Holy Grail, the equally exotic and implausible 'horn of a unicorn' (room 8), the Insignia of the Holy Roman Empire with its Crown, the Austrian Imperial Crown, the so-called Sabre of Charlemagne and an 11C Imperial Cross, together with the Carolingian gospel on which Charlemagne's successors swore their oaths (rooms 9–12). In the **Sacred Treasury** is a magnificent gilt replica of the Marian Column Am Hof (room 1, see p 78), the so-called Purse of St Stephen of Hungary (room 11) and in the same room the penitential scourges of the Empress Anna, besides monstrances, reliquary crosses, chalices and crucifixes, all of astonishingly refined workmanship. It is here that one can best appreciate how the pronounced piety of the Habsburgs fed their insatiable desire for collecting, as also how aesthetic symbol reinforced dynastic and apostolic pretensions.

Above the entrance to the Treasuries, Jadot de Ville-Issey's 18C 'Ambassador's Stairway' ascends to the **Burgkapelle**, whose west wall dates to the 13C, but which mostly acquired its present form in the 15C under Friedrich III; the latter is thought to have built the chapel for the use of his ward, the unfortunate Ladislas Posthumus of Hungary (1440–57). Under the baldachin the two founders of chapels on this site, Friedrich and Albrecht I (ruled 1282–1308), are honoured with statues. The refined wooden statuary of the interior may be from the workshop of Niclaes Gerhaert van Leyden, the creator of Friedrich's tomb in the Stephansdom. The figures appear to represent the 14 healing saints, while another figure with a ducal cap is probably St Leopold III of Babenberg, who was canonised (1485) during Friedrich's reign. The Baroque bronze cross (1719) hanging above the high altar is by Johann Baptist Känischbauer. (**Sunday mass** is sung here at 09.15 by the Vienna Boys' Choir from Sept–June: for details of seat tickets, see p 51).

From the Schweizerhof an archway at the south-west corner used to lead into the **Josefsplatz**, but has been closed for security reasons. You must retrace your steps through the Michaelertor and turn right to reach the square, which is enclosed on three sides by stunning Baroque façades. In the centre is Anton Zauner's *Equestrian Statue* (1807) *of Joseph II*, a Habsburg again being represented as a Roman emperor; this time it is Marcus Aurelius who was (erroneously) believed at the time to have died in Vienna in AD 180, and whose monument on Capitol Hill in Rome was the model used.

At Josefsplatz I is the old entrance to the **Hofbibliothek** (forerunner of, and now incorporated in the Nationalbibliothek, open May–Oct, Mon–Wed, Fri–Sat 10.00–16.00, Thur 10.00–19.00, Sun PH 10.00–14.00, Nov–April Mon–Sat 10.00–14.00), built for Karl VI by the Fischer von Erlachs, father (the design) and son (completion in 1726). The building was subsequently extended to the south by Maria Theresia's court architect, Nikolaus Pacassi. The **Prunksaal**

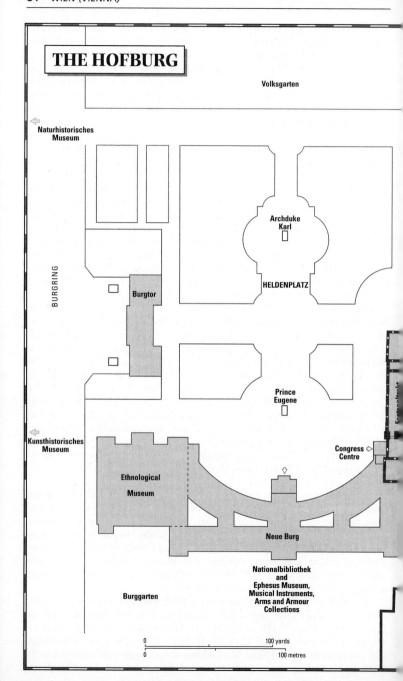

THE HOFBURG

Volksgarten

← Naturhistorisches
Museum

BURGRING

Burgtor

Archduke
Karl

HELDENPLATZ

Prince
Eugene

← Kunsthistorisches
Museum

Congress ◁
Centre

Ethnological
Museum

Neue Burg

Burggarten

Nationalbibliothek
and
Ephesus Museum,
Musical Instruments,
Arms and Armour
Collections

| 0 | | 100 yards |
| 0 | | 100 metres |

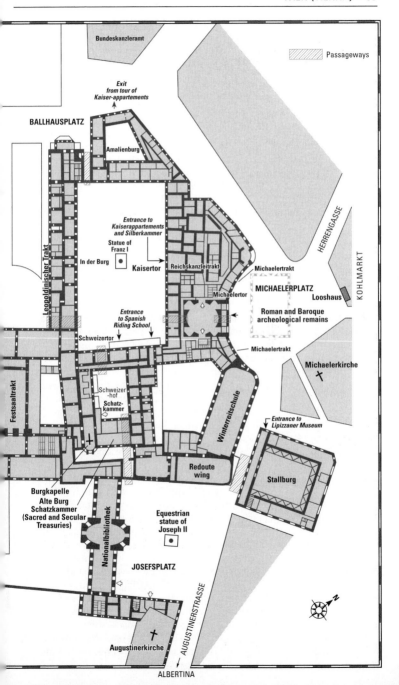

Passageways

Bundeskanzleramt

Exit
from tour of
Kaiser-appartements

BALLHAUSPLATZ

Amalienburg

HERRENGASSE

Entrance to
Kaiserappartements
and Silberkammer

Statue of
Franz I

In der Burg

Kaisertor

Reichskanzleitrakt

Michaelertrakt

MICHAELERPLATZ

Looshaus

KOHLMARKT

Michaelertor

**Roman and Baroque
archeological remains**

Leopoldinischer Trakt

Entrance
to Spanish
Riding School

Schweizertor

Michaelertrakt

Michaelerkirche

Schweizer-
hof

Schatz-
kammer

Festsaaltrakt

Winterreitschule

Entrance to
Lipizzaner Museum

Redoute
wing

Stallburg

**Burgkapelle
Alte Burg
Schatzkammer
(Sacred and Secular
Treasuries)**

Nationalbibliothek

Equestrian
statue of
Joseph II

JOSEFSPLATZ

AUGUSTINERSTRASSE

N

Augustinerkirche

ALBERTINA

(Ceremonial Hall) has a fresco in the dome by Daniel Gran (the *Apotheosis of Karl VI*); a life-size statue of the Emperor (together with those of other Habsburgs) in the hall is by Paul and Peter Strudel. Some indication of the no-expense-spared approach is given by the fact that Daniel Gran demanded and received no less than 17,000 Gulden for his frescoes in the cupola and on the walls. There are regular exhibitions of the library's treasures, while in the adjoining Old Reading Room of the Augustinertrakt is the **Cartographical Collection** including the remarkable **Globenmuseum** (open Mon–Wed & Fri, 11.00–12.00, Thur 14.00–15.00), which possesses a globe (1541) made by Mercator for the Emperor Karl V in 1541, no doubt so that he could study more precisely the extent of the Habsburg dominions 'on which the sun never set'.

The north-west side of the Josefsplatz once accommodated the court theatre, but was remodelled in 1744 by Jadot de Ville-Issey to create a concert hall in which Beethoven performed (1795–96) and a ballroom where, as the Prince de Ligne famously remarked during the peace negotiations in 1814 after the Napoleonic War, '*Le congrès danse beaucoup, mais il ne marche pas.*' De Ligne, who was known as 'the rose-pink prince' (even his house on the Mölker Bastei was painted this colour) died in the same year, 'Vienna's last cavalier of the Rococo'. The Redoutensaal (ballroom/concert hall) has recently been repaired after a serious fire and is used for international congresses.

The Congress of Vienna: 18 September 1814–9 June 1815

Called to reconstruct the conservative order in Europe after the defeat of Napoleon, the Congress was also a brilliant public relations exercise by Metternich to mask the incipient weakness of Franz I's Empire and secure for Austria a key role in the European concert of powers. The hospitality of the hosts was unbelievably lavish and, as the Viennese soon bitterly discovered, to be paid for by them in higher prices and taxes. A contemporary satirical flyer proclaimed: 'Alexander of Russia makes love for them all, Friedrich Wilhelm of Prussia thinks for them all, Friedrich of Denmark speaks for them all, Maximilian of Bavaria drinks for them all, Friedrich of Württemberg eats for them all and Kaiser Franz pays for them all.' At the same time each and every one of the visiting crown heads, as well as their retainers, wives and lovers, were reported on round the clock by Metternich's spies. Napoleon's escape from Elba brought the festivities to an abrupt halt on the 5 March ('The congress is dissolved' he remarked matter-of factly as he stepped ashore at Cannes six days later). 'Vienna', wrote Comte de la Garde Chambonas 'resembled an individual who, having been lulled to sleep by dreams of love and ambitions, suddenly found himself violently awakened by the rattle of the nightwatchman or the clanging of the belfry warning him that his house was on fire.' The ex-Emperor's arrival in France had an electrifying effect on the hitherto procrastinatory and often devious proceedings (Austria, England and France were secretly in alliance against Russia and Prussia). The hastily reached final settlement (signed on 9 June) was extremely favourable to Austria, to whom extensive territories in Italy, Istria, Dalmatia and Galicia were restored: far more, in fact than she soon proved able to defend and hold. The unbelievably bloody Battle of Waterloo (45,000 dead or wounded) followed on 18 June.

Emperor Karl VI was also the initiator of another historic building on the north side of Josefsplatz, the **Winter Riding School** (*Winterreitschule*), again to plans by Fischer von Erlach and completed in 1734. The performances of the famous Spanish Riding School that take place here are part of a long imperial tradition of spectacle involving horses, music and symbolic triumph, the uniqueness of the Lipizzaner performances lying in the ultimate refinement of *haute école*, originally based on manoeuvres in battle. But the school was also used for the famous '*carrousels*' in the 18C and 19C. These were spectacles for large numbers of participants who trained for long periods before the big occasion, which was also a fancy dress gala and pageant. The most famous such show was led off by Maria Theresia herself in 1743, to celebrate the reconquest of Prague. Her High Chamberlain, Khevenhüller, noted disapprovingly in his diary that the monarch spent a long time each day in the riding school, while her doctors were appalled at her exertions in the *carrousel* (followed by an all-night ball), since they knew she was pregnant.

The riding school has been put to other uses over the years: it housed the first industrial fair in 1830, the stock exchange briefly thereafter, the first Burghers' Assembly in 1848, followed by the first Austrian Parliament. The galleried interior is functional rather than beautiful, an aesthetic touch being the portrait of Karl VI by Johann Georg Hamilton, to which the riders lift their caps as they ride in. (For details of tickets for performances of the Spanish Riding School and the morning training of the Lipizzaners, see p 50.)

Across the street to the north-west of the Winterreitschule is the Renaissance **Stallburg**, whose lovely tiered loggias were laid bare in 1956 after several centuries as blind windows. Note the attractive wrought-iron well in the courtyard (1675, formerly in the Amalienhof). Originally planned as lodgings for the future Maximilian II, the Stallburg was modified in 1565 after Maximilian took over the reins of power and moved to the Hofburg proper; thereafter it was used partly as stables and partly as accommodation for court officials. By 1700 the building was known as the 'Stallburg of the Spanish horses', an allusion to the original Spanish breeding stock of the Lipizzaners, which was crossed with the sturdy Karst horses from the Lipizza stud near Trieste (now in Slovenia). Founded in 1580 by Maximilian's brother, the Archduke Karl, the stud was enthusiastically promoted by subsequent emperors, especially Leopold I, who needed a supply of excellent horses for his Baroque spectacles.

An interesting new **Lipizzaner Museum** (Reitschulgasse 2, open daily 09.00–17.00) has been opened in the former Hofapotheke, a site which was threatened with a fast food take-over. The museum documents the history of the Lipizzaners and the Spanish Riding School (aided by seductive videos), but the high point is the view through a picture window of the fabulous white beasts in their stalls.

The most recently built part of the Hofburg is the **Neue Hofburg** (more often referred to as the '**Neue Burg**'), to reach which you must walk back under the Michaelertor and through 'In der Burg', emerging through an arch into the **Heldenplatz**. The two equestrian statues here are both by Anton Fernkorn (*Prince Eugene of Savoy*, 1865, and *Archduke Carl*, 1860), the latter being the victor over Napoleon at the Battle of Aspern (1809), then a village to the east of Vienna, now part of the 22nd District. The neo-Renaissance Neue Burg was constructed between 1881 and 1913 and contains the main part of the Austrian National Library, as well as the *Hofjagd-und Rüstkammer* (Imperial Arms and Armour Collection, open Mon, Wed–Sun 10.00–18.00); the **Collection of Historical Musical Instruments** (same opening times); the **Museum für Völkerkunde** (Ethnology Museum; Mon, Wed–Sun 10.00–16.00) and the **Ephesos Museum** (display of artefacts from the Austrian excavations in Ephesus and Samothrace, open Mon, Wed–Sun, 10.00–16.00).

To the south-west, the Ringstraße is approached through the beautifully restored **Äußere Burgtor** (Outer Gate of the Burg) built between 1821 and 1824 on the orders of Franz I to celebrate the victory over Napoleon at the Battle of the Nations (Leipzig, 1813), and designed by Peter Nobile and Luigi Cagnola. The Latin inscription on the inside cornice reads: 'Justice is the Foundation of Governance' and the arch was also subsequently (1933) adopted as a memorial to the Austrian dead of World War I (see the further inscription on the Ringstraße side: 'Glory to the Soldiers who are Worthy of Glory' dating to 1916). Unfortunately it was later discovered that Wilhelm Frass, who had made the sculpture of the dead soldier for the memorial hall inside, was also a closet National Socialist and had slipped a Nazi manifesto under it. The crypt-like hall is accessible only on public holidays and contains rolls of honour of those who fell between 1914 and 1918, and a further list of the dead of World War II. In 1965 it was decided to add a memorial chamber for members of the Resistance in Austria (see p 77).

The **Burggarten** to the east of the Burgtor was laid out by Louis von Remy in 1818 and contains Friedrich Ohmann's Jugendstil glasshouse (1907). Monuments in the garden include an equestrian statue (1780) by Balthasar Moll of *Emperor Franz I. Stefan*, the husband of Maria Theresia; a statue (1957) of Franz Joseph I in military uniform after an original (1904) by Johann Benk; and the popular *Mozart Monument* (Viktor Tilgner, 1896). The relief on the front of the last named shows scenes from the opera *Don Giovanni*.

South and south-east of Stephansdom

A stone's throw from St Stephen's to the east is a cluster of streets that have retained their somewhat rambling Baroque and neo-classical character, a notable house being Domgasse 5, also known as the **Figarohaus** (open Tues–Sun 09.00–18.00). Mozart lived on the first floor between 1784 and 1787, writing here not only the *Marriage of Figaro*, but also three piano concertos. Further south at the rear of a large department store which is always going bust, a plaque marks the site (Rauhensteingasse 8) of the house in which the composer died on 5 December, 1791.

At Singerstraße 7, to the south, is the **Deutschordenskirche** dating to the 14C but with a few Baroque touches by Anton Martinelli dating to the 1720s, and belonging to the Teutonic Order whose coats of arms and tombstones line the walls of the interior. Note to the right of the entrance the so-called Cuspinian Altar (1515, actually a small votive shrine), endowed by the distinguished humanist scholar and diplomat, Johannes Cuspinian (1473–1529) as a memorial for himself and his wife, and showing a late Gothic relief of St Anne, Christ and Mary. To the left is an equally fine Renaissance epitaph. The main theme of the exquisite Flemish altar (1520) is the *Passion* and the *Resurrection*, while Tobias Pock's altarpiece (1667) shows *Mary and Jesus blessing St Elisabeth*, together with other patrons of the Order.

The treasures of the Knights may be seen in their adjacent **Schatzkammer** (Treasury, open May–Oct, Mon, Thur–Sun 10.00–12.00, Wed, Fri, Sat also 15.00–17.00; Nov–April, Mon, Thur and Sat 10.00–12.00, Wed, Fri and Sat also 15.00–17.00). It contains documents pertaining to the history of the Teutonic Knights, ecclesiastical and profane treasures and portraits of Grand Masters. A curiosity is the 'viper's tongue credence' used for testing food for poison. The Knights were founded during the siege of Acre in 1190 with a remit to look after the sick and the poor, and were invited to Vienna in 1205 by Duke Leopold VI of Babenberg. Thereafter they became increasingly militant, converting the Prussians and the Lithuanians and colonising their territories. After the Lithuanians turned Catholic and united with the Polish throne in 1386, the Knights' ostensible *raison d'etre* was increasingly exposed as a cover for secular aggrandisement. They suffered a disastrous defeat at Tannenberg (1410) at the hands of a Polish-Lithuanian army (a turning-point in Polish history) and a century later their Grand Master (Albert of Prussia) converted to Lutheranism (1525), the Order's territory being subsequently incorporated into the Prussian kingdom. From 1780 to 1923 the Grand Master of the now primarily charitable body of Knights was a Habsburg, although the Archduke Maximilian (son of Emperor Maximilian II) had been titular head of the Order between 1590 and 1618.

Further east along Singerstraße, the **Franziskanerplatz** opens to your right, in the centre of which is the *Moses Fountain* (J.M. Fischer, 1798). The **Franciscan Church** stands on the east side of the square, next to its cloister which is on the site of a medieval house for reformed prostitutes. The penitents' small chapel was replaced with a somewhat idiosyncratic church (1611), perhaps designed by a Franciscan monk, Father Bonaventura Daum. The Renaissance gable is framed with volutes broken by interspersed obelisks and figures, the Holy Trinity being represented at the top. The portal, surmounted by a sculpture of *St Jerome with the lion* and wearing his cardinal's hat, dates to 1742. Traces of Gothic vaulting from the previous church may be seen inside, but its most striking aspect are the *trompe l'oeil* effects of Andrea Pozzo's altarpiece (1707) and of the stucco drapery on the north wall. The organ (1642) built by Johann Wöckerl is the oldest still in service in the city and is beautifully carved and painted with figures of St Cecilia (patron of music) and (on the inside) St Anthony and St Francis with the Stigmata.

If you walk down Weihburggasse to the south of the square and turn right into Seilerstätte (just before the well-stocked *British Bookshop*), you will see across the street the **Ronacher Etablissement** (Seilerstätte 9), built (1888) as a variety theatre incorporating a hotel by the ubiquitous theatre architects of the Dual Monarchy, Ferdinand Fellner and Hermann Helmer. Threatened with decay in the 1970s, it was restored by Luigi Blau and subsequently became a venue for musicals.

A right turn opposite the theatre into the Himmelpfortgasse brings you at no. 8 to the superb **Winter Palace of Prince Eugene of Savoy** (now the Finance Ministry), designed (1696–8) by J.B. Fischer von Erlach and enlarged (following

Fischer's plans) in 1702 by Lukas von Hildebrandt. The stairway with Atlas figures by Giovanni Giuliani is impressively heroic, as are the classical groups and allegories of *War* and *Peace* on the façade by Lorenzo Mattielli. The interior (not normally accessible except for occasional exhibitions, concerts, or by special appointment: ☎ 514 33) is decorated with murals depicting the exploits of Hercules and Apollo, a reference to Prince Eugene's twin roles as general and patron of the arts repeated in the ornamentation of his Belvedere park. From the vestibule a dolphin fountain and Triton figure can be seen in the courtyard, the work of Santino Bussi.

On the corner of Seilerstätte and Johannesgasse to the south is the **Academy of Music**, housed in the former Ursuline Convent (Johannesgasse 8) and retaining a small collection of **Religious Folk Art** (open Wed 09.00–16.00, Sun 09.00–13.00).

One street further south is the Annagasse with the charming **Annakirche** (no. 3B), since 1897 also the church of the Oblates of St Francis de Sales, the patron of writers. (As Bishop of Geneva, he so impressed his Calvinist adversaries that one of them said he (Francis) would qualify as a saint if it was proper to have saints.) Earlier the church belonged to the Brotherhood of St Anne, an Order founded by the pious Leopold I in 1694, which based its work on the Christian humility practised by St Francis. Originally the building had been part of a complex housing (until 1530) pilgrims and the homeless, with strict rules regarding the allowed lengths of stay (e.g. two weeks for sick beggars, four weeks for priests without office). The Gothic church was barockised in 1634, and again remodelled by Andrea Pozzo in 1715. The altarpiece by Daniel Gran shows the *Holy Family* and the same artist painted the ceiling fresco of the *Immaculate Conception* (both c 1748). The Order possesses a reliquary of St Anne (her mummified right hand) displayed yearly on St Anne's Feast Day (26 July), and a valuable sculpture (c 1510) in the side-chapel attributed to Veit Stoss of Nürnberg (*St Anne with Mary and Jesus*).

Kärntner Straße

If you leave the Annagasse by the western end, you find yourself in the fashionable shopping precinct of the Kärntner Straße. Just to the south is the **Esterházy Palais** (no. 41) built in the mid-17C with a later façade (1785), and now housing a casino. Nearby at no. 37 is the diminutive **Malteser Kirche** belonging to the Knights of St John, originally a chapel to offer hospitality to pilgrims arriving in the city on the Carinthian road. The Gothic church was remodelled in neoclassical style from 1808 on the orders of the head of the Vienna Knights at that time, Count Colloredo. It was then that the elegant pulpit was installed, together with a vivid relief, flanked by the figures of two Turks in chains, which shows the harbour at La Valletta, where the Knights made their famous stand against the Turks in 1558, under their leader Jean de la Valette-Paresot.

At no. 26 Kärntner Straße is the glass shop of *J.& L. Lobmeyr* with a museum (open Mon–Fri 10.00–18.30, Sat 10.00–16.00) on the upper floor. The firm was founded in 1823 and includes among its distinguished designers Josef Hoffmann, Kolo Moser, Alfred Roller and Adolf Loos, although it is perhaps its elaborate Historicist works that best display the mixture of craftsmanship and technical sophistication for which Lobmeyr is justly celebrated. Not far beyond the shop in the Kärntner Durchgang to the left is Adolf Loos's **Kärntner Bar**

(American Bar), the architect's tribute to the American way of life. Its mixture of sumptuous marble and brash lettering on the façade, and its clever illusion of space created by a wall mirror in the diminutive interior, does indeed suggest a marriage of unashamed but transient wealth with the enduring human ingenuity that makes it. Between 1985 and 1989 the bar was lovingly reconstructed according to Loos's plans by Hermann Czech and Burkhardt Rukschcio.

The junction of Kärntner Straße and the Graben to the north is formed by the now redundant 'Stock-im-Eisen-Platz', only retaining its name (*Stock* means stick) because of the nail-studded stump which can still be seen on the corner, and into which journeymen blacksmiths hammered a nail for good luck before leaving the city. It has been there at least since the 16C.

Neuer Markt and Kapuzinerkirche

Just to the west of Stock-im-Eisen-Platz, the Seilergasse runs south from the Graben entering shortly the **Neuer Markt** (formerly, but unofficially **Mehlmarkt**), in the centre of which is Georg Raphael Donner's beautiful **Providentia Fountain**; the originals of its sculpted figures (1739) are, however, in the Austrian Baroque Museum of the Belvedere (see p 105), the present copies dating to 1873. The figure of *Providentia* presides over personifications of the main rivers of Upper and Lower Austria: a bearded figure for the Enns, a river goddess in a shell for the March, a fisherman with harpoon for the Traun and a river nymph with a vase of flowers for the Ybbs. Maria Theresia apparently considered the two attractive nude ladies as too risqué for the public and had them removed in 1773, but the sculptor J.M. Fischer won a lengthy battle to have them re-instated in 1801. The commission for the fountain actually came from the Vienna Council, hence the figure of Providentia herself represents the 'providential' care of the city government.

Towards the south-west is the **Kapuzinerkirche** (Capuchin Church, 1632) with its celebrated **Kapuzinergruft** (Capuchin, or Imperial Crypt, open daily 09.30–16.00, the church 09.30–12.00, 14.00–16.00).

The Capuchin monastery was founded in 1617 by the Empress Anna, who, with her husband Emperor Matthias, was the first Habsburg to be buried here (1633) in the reign of Ferdinand II. The crypt was subsequently enlarged several times and now contains the remains of 145 Habsburgs, of which 12 were emperors and 17 empresses, plus one non-imperial person, the Countess Fuchs, who was Maria Theresia's governess. There are numerous powerful examples of Baroque funerary sculpture, notably Balthasar Moll's *tomb for Karl VI*, showing a macabre skull with a gilded crown, and the graceful **sarcophagus** for Maria Theresia and her husband Franz I (Franz Stephan): the loving pair are portrayed on the lid in the hour of resurrection, gazing fixedly into each others' eyes while a putto hovers between them raising aloft a crown of stars. The marble base is supported by mourning female figures respectively bearing the four Habsburg crowns (that of the Holy Roman Empire, the Hungarian Crown of St Stephen, the Bohemian Wenceslas Crown and the Crown of the King of Jerusalem: the last-named title referred to the Crusader State defunct since 1291). The reliefs on the left side show Franz Stephan's entry into Florence as Grand Duke of Tuscany (1739) and his coronation as Holy Roman Emperor in Frankfurt (1745). These scenes are complemented on the other side by the coronation of Maria Theresia as Queen of the Hungarians in Pozsony (Pressburg/Bratislava) in 1741 and her subsequent coronation as Bohemian queen in Prague's St Vitus Cathedral (1743). The last Habsburg to be buried in the modern vault (1962), with its fanned concrete ceiling by Karl Schwanzer, was the ex-Empress Zita in 1989.

The Capuchin Church above the crypt has an ugly façade dominated by a huge cross and Hans Fischer's fresco (1936) of *St Francis with angels*. In a niche to the left is the figure of Marco d' Aviano, who accompanied the imperial army that liberated Vienna in 1683, and whose death (1699) in the Capuchin monastery was attended by his friend and admirer, Leopold I (d'Aviano was his confessor). In the Kaiserkapelle to the left are the wooden statues of three Emperors (Matthias, his successor Ferdinand II and the latter's son Ferdinand III) as well as Ferdinand IV, who was crowned as 'Roman King' but died (1654) before coming into his inheritance. His younger brother Leopold I, intended for holy orders as his life-long promulgation of '*Pietas Austriaca*' suggests, thus unexpectedly inherited the throne. Across the church in the confessor's chapel is one of the few major art works in the Capuchins' generally rather spartan church, a superb *Pietà* (1712?) by Peter and Paul Strudel.

The Albertinaplatz

Tegetthoffstraße leaves the Neuer Markt to the south-west, bringing you into the Albertinaplatz, of which the northern part merges into Lobkowitzplatz. The **Tirolerhof café**, to your right as you enter, was the first to admit women in the 19C, while the **Café Mozart** on your left was made famous from scenes in Carol Reed's film of *The Third Man*. It adjoins to the east the celebrated **Hotel Sacher**, founded (1876) by the son of Metternich's pastry cook and retaining to this day its reputation as a haven of good taste and traditional service. It was built on the site of the Kärntnertortheater (see p 62), which was demolished in 1868 when the Oper was built. Eduard Sacher had to give an undertaking that no concerts or operas would be given in his establishment in competition with the latter. After Eduard died, the hotel was managed with idiosyncratic flair by his cigar-smoking widow, Anna Sacher, until her death in 1930. It became a meeting-point of the aristocracy and diplomats, many of whom enjoyed discreet *rendez-vous* in the hotel's elegant *chambres séparées*. At the same time the city's poor were being fed with left over food at the back door.

On the south-west edge of the Albertinaplatz is the **Albertina** itself, housing the great collection of 44,000 drawings and 1.5 million graphics spanning a period from the beginning of the 15C to the present. Outstanding are the Dürers, some 145 drawings and watercolours including the celebrated *Hare* and *Praying Hands*. The Albertina was founded by Duke Albert of Sachsen-Teschen (1738–1822), the husband of Maria Theresia's fifth child (of 16), Marie Christine. The building (1745, originally the Tarouca-Palais) became the couple's residence after their marriage, being altered in neo-classical style and enlarged (1801–04) on the orders of Albert by Louis Montoyer. The Albertina has been closed to the public for some time for urgently needed restoration works, but in the meantime temporary exhibitions of its contents are being shown in the **Akademiehof**, Makartgasse 3, ☎ 581 3060/21; open Tues–Sun, 10.00–17.00. In theory the main building is due to re-open by the end of 2000, although access is still possible to the **Austrian Film Museum** (a club for film buffs) on the ground floor.

The balustraded ramp in front of the Albertina to the south boasts an

equestrian statue of **Archduke Albrecht**, (Caspar von Zumbusch, 1898) the victor at Custozza in 1866, while an earlier (1869) fountain adorns the rampart façade. This somewhat clumsy *Danubius-Brunnen* is by Johann Meixner and shows allegorical figures of *Danubius* and *Vindobona* at the centre flanked by the *Sava* and *Tisza*; in niches to the right, the *Rivers Raab*, *Enns* and *Traun*; to the left, the *Mur*, *Salzach* and *March*.

In the middle of the Albertinaplatz is Alfred Hrdlicka's controversial **Monument against War and Fascism**, unveiled in 1988 on the 50th Anniversary of the *Anschluss*. The four components of this striking work bear the titles The *Gate of Violence*, The *Jews washing the Streets* (as they were compelled to do in 1938 to eradicate the slogans of the Fatherland Front, after the latter's independence referendum was forestalled by Hitler), *Orpheus entering Hades* and *The Stone of the Republic* on which the Austrian declaration of self-govern-ment (27 April 1945) is engraved.

To the north-west (moving into Lobkowitzplatz) is the **Lobkowitz-Palais** (1687) by Giovanni Tencala with a façade (1710) by J.B. Fischer von Erlach. The palace houses the Theatre Museum (open Tues–Sun, 10.00–17.00). Another branch of the museum, consisting of memorials to individual performers, is nearby at Hanuschgasse 3, next to the Bundestheaterkassen (Box Office for State Theatres) open Tues–Fri 10.00–12.00, 13.00–16.00, Sat, Sun 13.00–16.00. The Lobkowitz-Palais latterly belonged to one of the principal patrons of Beethoven, Franz Joseph Maximilian of Lobkowitz (himself an accomplished singer and violinist) and it was here that the composer conducted the first per-formance of his Third Symphony.

To the south-west, adjoining the Albertina at Augustinerstraße 3 (but entered from Josefsplatz) is the Gothic **Augustinerkirche**, built for a monastery founded in 1327, later barockised, the Baroque furnishings in turn being removed by Ferdinand von Hohenberg in 1783. Its clock-tower dates from 1652. The high-light of the interior is Antonio Canova's neo-classical (1805) **Cenotaph for Marie Christine of Habsburg**, showing allegorical figures of *Virtus* and *Caritas* entering a pyramidal burial chamber watched from the right by a genius resting on a lion. In the **Loreto Chapel** the hearts of the Habsburgs are pre-served in silver urns. The church has a strong musical tradition and sung mass on Sunday at 11.00 is well worth attending (performance details are given in the Wien Programm, see p 51).

A walk to the north along the Dorotheergasse (the first street to be furnished with street lanterns by Leopold I in 1698) brings you to the two Protestant churches of the Inner City, the **Lutheran** at no. 18 and the **Calvinist** at no. 16. The Calvinist ('Reformed') community, though small, has had many influential members, including one of only three non-Catholics to marry into the Habsburg line and retain their religion, the Archduchess Henriette of Nassau-Weilburg (1797–1829). She was married to the Archduke Carl, the victorious general over Napoleon at Aspern, and is credited with introducing the Christmas tree to Vienna. The marriage was extremely happy, which was perhaps why Emperor Franz intervened after her death, when the Capuchins at first refused to bury a Protestant in the Imperial Crypt. ('She was with us in life,' he explained, 'so should she also be with us in death.')

Habsburg necrology

The cult of obsequies in Vienna had its roots in the Counter-Reformation, was promoted by the Catholic church and Habsburg rulers of the Baroque period (especially those connected with the Spanish line), and was still evident among ordinary people at the turn of the century when Mayor Lueger set up municipal undertakers to make a decent funeral more affordable. The Augustinian monks from the monastery adjacent to the Court had long been associated with death rites, in that they were responsible for removing the corpses of executed criminals to the common burial-ground outside the city walls.

The Habsburgs introduced a ritual involving the dispersal of imperial corpses to selected sites, partly as a way of honouring churches or religious orders particularly associated with the dynasty. Imperial hearts were placed in the Augustinerkirche (the parish church of the Court), the bodies were placed in the imperial crypt attended by the favoured Capuchin Order (see p 91), and the embalmed entrails in the catacombs of St Stephen's Cathedral. These churches became dynastic shrines, focal points of loyalty to the Habsburgs expressed through Catholic piety. The tradition began in the 17C, following the wish expressed in the will of Ferdinand IV (see p 92) that his heart should be 'laid at the feet of Our Dear Lady of Loreto', in the Augustinerkirche. While the Capuchins had overall charge of the imperial obsequies, the court doctors had the task of dissecting the corpses of the deceased, removing the heart and entrails, often also the brain, tongue and eyes. What remained was embalmed with herbs, oil and beeswax for the public lying in state (*Paradebett*) that lasted several days. The custom of dispersal lapsed after the death of Franz Joseph's father, Archduke Franz Karl, who was the last Habsburg to be given the full works in 1878.

At no. 17 is the state auction house of the **Dorotheum**, founded by Joseph I as an honest and cheaper alternative to rapacious pawn-brokers. The site had formerly been that of a cloister dedicated to St Dorothy the Martyr, hence the name of both street and auction house. At Dorotheergasse 11 is the **Jewish Museum of the City of Vienna** (inaugurated in 1993 and open Sun–Fri 10.00–18.00, Thur 10.00–20.00), located in an 18C palace belonging in the 19C to the Jewish bankers Arnstein and Eskeles. Both of their wives presided over famous salons in Vienna, Jewish women taking the lead in bourgeois female emancipation at that time. The museum contains a permanent exhibition of Austrian Jewish history (2nd floor) and an important collection of Judaica, incorporating that of Max Berger and the treasures formerly in the Stadttempel (ground floor, central hall and 4th floor); in addition there are frequent temporary exhibitions, and both the café and bookshop can be recommended.

The Dorotheergasse leads back to the Graben and St Stephen's via the famous literary café of *Hawelka* at no. 6 and the equally celebrated sandwich bar with the unpronounceable name of *Trzesniewski* at no. 1.

Around the Ringstraße

The Ringstraße can be travelled by tram (no. 1 clockwise, no. 2 anti-clockwise), although it is better to go on foot if time permits. The following descriptions proceed clockwise from **Schwedenplatz**, which is reached by U-Bahn 1 or 4. The square is named in honour of the Swedes in gratitude for their assistance to Austria after World War I.

As the tram turns south from the Franz-Josefs-Kai, note on your left the ship-like **Urania** building, an adult education centre built by Max Fabiani in 1910. The freshly painted **Regierungsgebäude** (formerly the War Ministry, completed in 1913 and designed by Ludwig Baumann) looms up to the east. In front of this bombastic edifice is Caspar von Zumbusch's **equestrian statue of Field Marshal Radetzky** (1766–1858), honouring the greatest Austrian general of the 19C. Radetzky drew up the battle plan for the decisive encounter with Napoleon in 1813 and distinguished himself in the Italian theatre during the 1848–49 revolution (at Custozza and Novara). A heroic quotation from Grillparzer is inscribed on the plinth ('In your camp is Austria!'), but the general's name has also become immortal for many who could not tell a musket from a mortar on account of Johann Strauss Senior's irresistible *Radetzky March*, traditionally the closing number of the Wiener Philharmoniker's New Year's Concert. Radetzky gazes proudly across the Ring towards the Georg-Coch-Platz, named after the anti-semitic founder of the Post Office Savings Movement (1883), whose bust (Johann Scherpes, 1913) stands before the movement's bank, the **Postsparkassenamt**, one of Otto Wagner's most innovative works. The building was constructed in two phases, 1904–06, and 1910–12 and memorably integrates function (materials) with aesthetics (ornament). The façade is clad in panels of marble secured by some 17,000 conspicuous metal pins, while the rusticated walls of the base are faced with granite slabs fixed with countersunk aluminium-headed bolts. 'The effect of this cladding,' writes M.P.A Sheaffer in her booklet on Otto Wagner, 'as well as the rustication, suggests the idea of a gigantic strongbox, the studding a familiar decorative and structural device used in the construction of Medieval and Renaissance treasure chests.' Functional elegance is also evident in the interior, whose glass roof gives a light and airy effect, while everywhere the furnishings combine the practical requirement of ease of cleaning with the aesthetic requirement of harmonious simplicity.

Across the Ring to the south-west is the High School of Applied Arts and beyond it the **Museum für Angewandte Kunst–MAK** (Museum of Applied Arts; open Tues–Wed, Fri–Sun, 10.00–18.00, Thur 10.00–21.00), a neo-Renaissance building (1871) by Heinrich Ferstel. Representative items of the collection are now displayed in a series of interiors designed by leading contemporary artists, while more densely arranged materials (textiles, furniture, ceramics and glass) entice students and specialists to the basement area. The objects range chronologically from the Romanesque period to the present and geographically from Europe to the Orient. Those interested in Austrian artefacts will be drawn to the Empire style and Biedermeier furniture (first floor), the Historicism and Jugendstil displays, and especially to the material from the Wiener Werkstätte (see p 66).

Adjoining the museum is the **Stadtpark**, laid out on the initiative of Mayor Andreas Zelinka in 1862–3 by Rudolf Siebeck and Josef Selleny. This is perhaps Vienna's most intimate and attractive park, with paths that wind through verdant shrubbery between ornamental pools and graceful monuments. The **Schubert Monument** (Carl Kundmann, 1872) was financed by Wiener Männergesangverein and shows the composer sitting with staves and pencil in hand; that for *Bruckner* is a bronze bust (1899) by Viktor Tilgner, while another celebrates *Johann Strauss Junior* (Edmund Hellmer, 1921); it shows a gilded figure of the composer leading his *Kapelle* in the *Blue Danube Waltz* against a background of figures in thrall to his music. There are also monuments to *Emil Jakob Schindler* (Edmund Hellmer, 1895), who was a leading 19C landscape painter, and to the painter *Hans Makart* (Viktor Tilgner, Fritz Zernitsch, 1898), showing him in the Renaissance costume he wore at the pageant he organised for the Silver Wedding (1879) of Franz Joseph and Elisabeth.

The **Kursalon** at the west end of the park was designed by Johann Garben (1867), its ground floor imitating the Rundbogen architecture of Munich. It was once a fashionable health café, where mineral water and fresh goat's milk were dispensed, but nowadays it has diverse functions, none of which seem quite to succeed in making the place very appealing.

Facing the Stadtpark on the other side of the Ring is the **Karl Lueger Monument** (Josef Müller, 1916), followed to the south-west by the Marriott and Radisson SAS hotels, the last named a superb conversion of two Ringstraßen palaces.

The Schwarzenbergplatz

Continuing south-west of the Stadtpark you reach the extensive **Schwarzenbergplatz**, in the middle of which is E.J. Hähnel's *Equestrian Statue* (1867) *of Field Marshal Karl Philipp, Prince Schwarzenberg*; this particular scion of a line that supplied the Habsburgs with everything from archbishops to prime ministers was a successful general against Napoleon. Invisible beyond the far end of the rectangular square is the Schwarzenberg-Palais (now a hotel, another part housing the Swiss Embassy), designed by Hildebrandt, the interiors and the park being completed by the Fischer von Erlachs, father and son. It is concealed by the **Russian Liberation Monument**, put up by the Soviets shortly after their arrival in 1945. Cynical locals referred to the monument's central figure of a heroically presented Soviet soldier as 'the unknown plunderer', since the Russians immediately removed everything that was not screwed down, together with everything that was.

The **Hochstrahlbrunnen** (literally 'high jet fountain') in front of the monument was built by Anton Gabrielli and opened in 1873, when the city's first long distance water supply from the area of the Schneeberg and Rax Mountains was instituted. The **Imperial Hotel** (1865; formerly the Duke of Württemberg's Vienna seat, but turned into a hotel for the World Exhibition of 1873) is at the north-west end of the square, which is lined with other 19C palaces: at no. 1 the experimental stage of the Burgtheater is now ensconced, while in the former Palais Fanto (no. 6 Zaunergasse 1) the **Arnold Schönberg Centre** was instituted in 1998, and inaugurated by his daughter, the wife of Italian composer, Luigi Nono. From the southern end of the square, across Lothringerstraße to your left, the **Akademietheater** and **Konzerthaus** (Fellner and Helmer, 1912) are reached, the latter with an exhortatory inscription from Die Meistersinger von Nürnberg (but originally Goethe) on the façade: 'Honour your German masters, for thus will you conjure the benevolent spirits.'

A turn to the right along Lothringerstraße brings you to Theophil Hansen's **Musikvereinsgebäude** (1869), while on your right and just beyond it is August Weber's **Künstlerhaus** (1868), incorporating a cinema in the extended left wing and a theatre in the right wing. To guarantee the income needed to maintain the building and the conservative Austrian Artists' Association that owned it, the triennial official exhibition of Austrian art could only be held here. It was against this stranglehold of academicism on the art scene that Gustav Klimt and the Secessionists rebelled in 1897.

The **Musikverein**, home of the Wiener Philharmoniker, could be described as the world's most illustrious concert hall and certainly is among those with the best acoustics. Instrumental in building it was Franz Matzinger, a former *Sängerknabe* (boy singer) who had become President of the Imperial Building Council and had formulated the text of Franz Joseph's 1857 ordinance abolishing the bastions round the old city. The Musikverein's main hall ('Goldener Saal'), with its coffered ceiling and galleries supported by gilded caryatids, is regarded as Hansen's masterpiece. The ceiling painting of *Apollo with the Nine Muses* is the work of August Eisenmenger. The Society of the Friends of Music, for whom the hall was built at the enormous cost of 801,000 Gulden, has its important archive and library here.

By walking through the underpass to the south, you emerge by Otto Wagner's splendid green and gilded **pavilions** built for the Stadtbahn, part of his plans for the urban transit railway commissioned by the City Council in the 1890s.

Karlskirche

The view to the south-east takes in Henry Moore's sculpture of **Hill Arches** (1978), set in a pool reflecting the façade of the glorious Karlskirche beyond, the greatest Baroque church in Central Europe, which was founded by Karl VI as thanksgiving for the ending of the plague epidemic of 1713. Money was raised from all over the Empire to build an edifice designed to represent the spiritual and secular claims of the Habsburgs. The architects, Fischer von Erlach father and son, succeeded in producing (1716–39) a uniquely beautiful combination of didactic symbolism and architectural grace, their most brilliant touch being the two Trajanesque columns (in part these were a reminder of the 'pillars of Hercules' at the western end of the Mediterranean, on the borders of the ancient known world therefore, but also a sidelong glance at the now thwarted Habsburg claim to Spain). The columns were also a memorial of the recently departed plague, like many such *Pestsäule* in the Habsburg lands, as well as representing the twin bulwarks of Karl VI's personal rule expressed in his motto *'constantia et fortitudine'*, the one a spiritual, the other a military virtue. Their frieze, however, records the life of St Carlo Borromeo, the church's dedicatee, who was heroically associated with plague relief as Bishop of Milan in 1576. The columns are topped with the imperial crown and eagle, although these symbols of earthly powers are still lower than the cross over the monumental dome. The relief in the gable by Giovanni Stanetti shows an angel withdrawing the sword from the city, an allusion to the end of the plague, while allegories and symbols on the façade show the *Four Virtues* (above the tympanum), *Faith* and *Hope* (over the gateway towers), *Charity* (over the main portal) and (flanking the steps) the *Old* and *New Testaments*. The effect of the interior is entirely governed by the vast dome, frescoed with a dramatic representation of *St Carlo* (supported by the Virgin Mary) interceding with God to end the plague (Johann Michael Rottmayr, 1730).

Just to the north of the Karlskirche is the **Historische Museum der Stadt Wien** (open Tues–Sun, 09.00–18.00), the display of which is chronologically arranged from the ground floor upwards, beginning with archeological remains of the Hallstatt culture and Roman Vindobona. The various models and illustrations of Vienna at different periods repay detailed study (especially Augustin Hirschvogel's city plan of 1548) and there is an informative section on the Turkish siege of 1683.

The second floor has important artefacts, Biedermeier paintings (by Fendi, Danhauser, Amerling and topographical works of the Alt painter dynasty) and some interiors from the same period (1814–48), also from the turn of the century (Vienna Secession). There are major paintings by Gustav Klimt (*Portrait of Emilie Flöge*, *Pallas Athene*), Richard Gerstl, Egon Schiele, as well as Oskar Kokoschka's *View of Vienna from the Wilhelminenberg*.

Retracing your steps westwards past the Technical University (Karlsplatz 13) and the **Lutheran School** (Karlsplatz 14, a work by Theophil Hansen) you pass into the Resselpark with monuments to Joseph Madersperger (1768–1850), who invented a sewing machine (1814), and Josef Ressel (1793–1857), the first person to develop a workable form of ship's screw (1827). Both men suffered what local masochists gleefully describe as the 'fate of Austrian inventors'—Madersperger died in poverty and his invention was never exploited by his contemporaries, while Ressel saw his discovery appropriated (without acknowledgement or reward) by the British. Nearby, between the Friedrichstraße and the Rechte Wienzeile, is the monument (1929) to the actor, Alexander Girardi (1850–1918; see p 63) by Otto Hofner.

The Secession building

To the west, across the road at Friedrichstraße 12, is the Secession building (1898) by Joseph Maria Olbrich open Tues–Sat 10.00–18.00, Sun PH 10.00–16.00. Financed by the industrialist Karl Wittgenstein (father of the philosopher), the exhibition hall was designed for the annual shows of the Secessionist artists who broke with the official Society of Fine Artists in 1897. The striking stereometric form of the building is sparsely decorated with a pattern of gilded

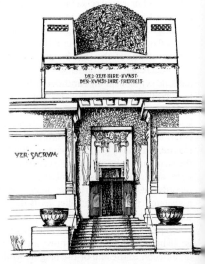

The Secession building, Vienna

leaves on the wall and the words *Ver Sacrum* (Sacred Spring, the title of the Secession's journal) to the left of the entrance. Above it is the movement's motto devised by the critic, Ludwig Hevesi, 'To the age its art, to art its freedom'. The building is crowned with a globe formed from intertwined gilded laurel leaves, known as the 'Golden Cabbage' by the Viennese, a reminder that the Secession stands at the north-east end of the Naschmarkt, Vienna's equivalent to the old Covent Garden Market. Inside the Secession may be seen Gustav Klimt's **Beethoven Frieze**, a symbolic work realising in visual form the themes of the composer's 9th Symphony, and created for the Beethoven Memorial Exhibition held by the Secession in 1902. Just to the north is Arthur Strasser's bronze (1900) of **Mark Antony in a Panther-drawn Chariot**.

A short walk south-west along the Linke Wienzeile brings you at no. 6 to the *Theater an der Wien* (1801), once managed by Mozart's librettist, Emanuel Schikaneder, and boasting a long tradition of operetta and *Volksstücke* (folk plays). It now stages musicals (*Cats* ran for five years, 1983–88), a slight come-down from Beethoven's *Fidelio*, which was premiered here in 1805 before an audience packed with officers of the French Occupation. The attractive houses (1898), nos 38 and 40 further along the same street, are by Otto Wagner. Both show an exuberant form of decorative Jugendstil: Kolo Moser designed the medallions on the façade of no. 38, while the **Majolikahaus** (no. 40) is so-called from its majolica tiles adorned with floral motifs.

The Staatsoper

Returning north-east past the Secession building you reach via the busy Operngasse the Staatsoper, passing on the way the **Café Museum** (1899), designed by Adolf Loos and a famous watering-hole for turn of the century intel-lectuals, by whom it was dubbed 'Café Nihilismus'.

The neo-Renaissance **Staatsoper** (Opernring 2) was built by August von Siccardsburg and Eduard van der Nüll and opened in 1869. In World War II it suffered serious bomb damage—appropriately the last performance before clo-sure had been *Götterdämmerung* and it reopened in 1955 with *Fidelio* conducted by Karl Böhm. Much ornamentation was destroyed, but Moritz von Schwind's frescoes of *Die Zauberflöte* in the loggia of the Ringstraßen façade have survived. A Rodin bronze of **Gustav Mahler** has long been in place in the interior and in 1997, 100 years after Mahler began his great reform of operatic production, the Mahler Hall was inaugurated in the Upper Interval Lobby. Its focal point is R.B. Kitaj's huge (1.5m) pastel portrait of the composer, depicted against a back-ground of the Salzkammergut that had provided him with so much elemental inspiration. The work was commissioned by Gilbert Kaplan, the American busi-nessman and Mahler fanatic, and ownership reverts to him, should it ever be removed from its place. Mahler himself was eventually driven from his post by intrigue and press attacks, a fate suffered by many of his successors.

The opera building itself had controversial beginnings; the cruel and mani-festly unjust attacks on it in the press (inadvertently substantiated by Franz Joseph) drove Van der Nüll to suicide and Siccardsburg to an early death. For tours of the interior (35mins at 14.00 and 15.00 hours, and only if no rehearsal), consult the board in the east arcade.

Not far to the west on the Ring is Edmund Hellmer's Olympian **Goethe**

Monument (1900), counterpointed across the street by the **Schiller Monument** (Johannes Schilling, 1876), the latter being regarded by contemporaries as a classic expression of ambivalent Liberal aspirations: Schiller is depicted as an apostle of freedom, but also embodies the *Großdeutsch* (Greater German) idea. Honouring great Germans was part and parcel of *Großdeutsch* enthusiasm at that time.

At the back of the Schillerplatz is the neo-Renaissance **Academy of Fine Arts** (1876) by Theophil Hansen, the aula of which boasts a fine ceiling fresco of *The Fall of the Titans* (1880) by Anselm Feuerbach. The Academy was founded as a private institution in 1692 and gained imperial status in 1705. Its small, but rewarding collection of paintings (the original purpose of which was to provide models for academy students), is open Tues–Sun & PH 10.00–16.00. There are works by Cranach, Murillo, Guardi, Tiepolo and Boeckl, but the *pièce de résistance* is the astonishing *Last Judgement* by Hieronymus Bosch (room 1), a triptych (possibly commissioned by Philip the Fair in 1504) with scenes from the *Garden of Eden*, *Christ Sitting in Judgement on the World*, and *Hell*. Also worth visiting is the Academy's etching collection at Makartgasse 3 (open Mon–Thur 09.00–12.00, 14.00–16.00, Fri 09.00–13.00).

Across Babenbergerstraße to the west is the noble Maria-Theresien-Platz flanked by two great edifices, the Kunsthistorische Museum (to the east) and the Naturhistorische Museum (to the west). In the centre is Caspar von Zumbusch's **Maria Theresia Monument** (1888) showing the ruler on her throne holding the Pragmatic Sanction of 1713, a document whereby her probably homosexual father, Karl VI, who gave up the struggle to produce male heirs after two daughters were born, hoped to ensure the Habsburg succession in the female line. The figures on horseback round the base portray four of Maria Theresia's generals (Daun, Laudon, Traun and Khevenhüller), while the reliefs on the plinth show her advisers and administrators, as well as outstanding figures of science and the arts during her reign (including Haydn and Mozart). The four allegorical figures at the corners of the platform stand for *Strength*, *Wisdom*, *Justice* and *Mercy*, all of which virtues Maria Theresia possessed in abundance.

Kunsthistorisches Museum

The Kunsthistorische Museum (open Tues, Wed, Fri–Sun 10.00–18.00, Thur 10.00–21.00) was built by Gottfried Semper and Karl von Hasenauer between 1871 and 1891 to house the imperial collections of antiquities, decorative arts, coins and pictures, and is one of the world's richest museums. Originally this and its counterpart across the square (the Naturhistorische Museum) were to be part of a huge *Kaiserforum* devised by Semper, which would have stretched across the Ring from the Neue Burg and have symbolically reconciled dynastic glory with the institutions of an aspirant bourgeoisie. Some of the best artists of the day worked on the internal decoration: the Hungarian Mihály Munkácsy painted the ceiling of the stairwell (The *Apotheosis of the Renaissance*), while Hans Makart painted twelve lunettes depicting great painters of the past. The brothers Gustav and Ernst Klimt worked on the spandrels and arches, symbolic representations of artistic golden ages. In the Hall of Fame under the dome are medallions by Johann Benk of the Habsburgs on whose collections the museum is based, including Maximilian I, Karl V, Rudolf II and Karl VI. On the landing half way up the stairs is Antonio Canova's sculpture of *Theseus fighting the Minotaur*, originally in the Theseus temple of the Volksgarten.

The **Egyptian Collection** (rooms I–VIII) is in the mezzanine floor's west wing and follows on into the **Collection of Greek and Roman Antiquities** (rooms IX–XVIII), which contains the remarkable **Gemma Augustea** and a **Theseus mosaic** discovered in the remains of a Roman villa near Salzburg. Crossing the central axis of the museum rectangle at the rear, you proceed to the **Sculpture and Decorative Arts** collection (rooms XIX–XXXVII), much of the contents of which come from the *Kunst- und Wunderkammer* (Cabinet of Art and Marvels of Nature) of Renaissance rulers, in the Habsburg case from those of the Archduke Ferdinand II in Tyrol and Rudolf II in Prague.

The **Picture Gallery**, which alone could occupy a whole day, is on the first floor. In the West Wing (rooms 1–VIII) are Italian and Spanish works; in the East (rooms IX–XV) are the German, Flemish and Dutch collections. The choice of pictures reflects the conservative imperial and canonical taste of the dynasty, geographically determined by areas where it ruled (Venice, Northern Italy, the Netherlands, Spain). Highlights are the Breughels (the largest single accumulation of them under one roof), the Giorgiones (of whom so few works are extant) and the Velázquez (the celebrated portraits of the *Infanta Margarita Theresa* sent to her prospective bridegroom, the future *Leopold I*, and of her brother, *Philip Prosper*). An interesting example of Habsburg (especially Rudolf II's) taste for the bizarre are the works of Giuseppe Arcimboldo (1527–93), whose paintings consist of human portraits made out of inanimate objects such as animals, fruit and objects of various kinds.

Naturhistorisches Museum

Opposite the Kunsthistorischen Museum is the Naturhistorische Museum (open Wed–Mon, 09.00–18.00), opened in 1889. It is less decorative than its counterpart, but Hans Canon's fresco of *The Circle of Life* above the stairway provides a welcome touch of visual flair (he also painted the lunettes). Carl Kundmann's seated figures on the balustrade by the main entrance symbolise America, Australia and Europe; on the other side of the building, Africa and Asia. The collection contains minerals, fossils, 25,000 skulls, artefacts of Hallstatt culture and from the Iron Age, and a zoological section on the top floor. Its most celebrated object is the *Venus of Willendorf*, a fertility symbol which dates to 25,000 BC. A children's room has been introduced, and more recently an ecologically aware section devoted to the rainforests; but the problems engendered by so many objects remain somewhat intractable. The meteorite collection (1000 items) and those of fossils (3 million) or insects (6 million) are the largest in the world. Franz I Stephan, Maria Theresia's husband, founded the **Naturalien-Cabinet** on which the museum is based in 1748 by purchasing the c 30,000 objects of J. von Baillou's collection in Florence, and subsequently (in keeping with the spirit of the Enlightenment) arranged it according to a scientific system and made it publicly accessible. Maria Theresia, approving this exercise in popular education, added the gift of a remarkable 'Bouquet of Gemstones'.

South-west of the two museums is the vast complex of the **Messepalast**, formerly the court stables (1723) built by the Fischer von Erlachs, and since 1921 the venue for trade fairs. In 1990 the architect Laurids Ortner won the competition to convert the Messepalast to an ambitious 'Museum Quarter', his plans unleashing the usual backbiting and hostility. Particularly controversial was the plan for a library situated in a 56-metre tower, which has, however, been abandoned in the face of general derision. After many delays, work started on this mega-project in spring 1998, and completion is expected in the year 2000.

To the north-west is the **Volkstheater**, which has reached new peaks under the energetic direction (since 1988) of Emmy Werner, the first woman to conquer the hitherto male chauvinist bastions of Vienna's mainstream theatre administration, in an era when Vienna also had its first female head of the *Wiener Festwochen* (Vienna Festival weeks), Ursula Pasterk.

Behind the Volkstheater is the **Trautson-Palais**, built by J.B. Fischer von Erlach for Joseph I's Comptroller of the Royal Household, later (from 1760) headquarters of Maria Theresia's Hungarian Lifeguards and now the Ministry of Justice. Opposite it to the east is the **Palace of Justice** (1881), burned down by the mob on 15 July 1927 (see p 57), at which time valuable cultural archives stored here were lost. Returning north-east to the Ringstraße from the Palace, you pass the **Monument to the Republic** (Schmerlingplatz, Dr Karl-Renner-Ring), consisting of busts of Jakob Reumann (the first Social Democratic Mayor of Vienna, 1919–25), Viktor Adler (founder of the Austrian Social Democratic Party in 1889), and Ferdinand Hanusch (the principal founder of Austria's welfare state after World War I).

North of the monument is Theophil Hansen's neo-classical **Parliament** (1883); until 1918 it was the **Reichsratsgebäude**, i.e. the Imperial Council for the Cisleithanien (Austrian–Bohemian–Ruthenian–Polish–Italian–Slovenian) part of the Dual Monarchy, a perennially fractious body with limited powers (tours of the Parliament, when not in session, start from Dr Karl-Renner-Platz 3, Mon–Fri, 11.00 and 15.00). It is now home to the legislative *Nationalrat* (elected by proportional representation) and the *Bundesrat* (an Upper House where representatives of the nine *Bundesländer* sit). The portico with its freshly restored mosaics is surmounted by a tympanum with a relief (by Edmund Hellmer) of Franz Joseph granting a constitution to the diverse recognised peoples of his Empire in 1861. At either end of the approach ramp stand sculptures (by Josef Lax) representing horse-breaking, a rather far-fetched way of symbolising the calming of the passions. The sitting figures flanking the ramp are the historians of antiquity (Herodotus, Thucydides, etc), while at the corners of the roof are triumphal chariots sculpted by Vinzenz Pilz.

The **Pallas Athene Fountain** (Carl Kundmann, 1902) in front of the building has figures representing the main rivers of Cisleithania and flanking allegories of *Legislative* and *Executive Powers*.

Directly across the Ring is the **Volksgarten**, laid out by Ludwig Remy in 1823 and incorporating an imitation Theseus temple (by Pietro di Nobile) of the same date. At the southern end is Carl Kundmann's **Monument to Franz Grillparzer** (1875), Austria's greatest playwright, while at the other end is the **Monument to Empress Elizabeth** (Hans Bitterlich, Friedrich Ohmann, 1907).

North of the Volksgarten is the **Burgtheater** (afternoon tours of the interior on Mon, Wed and Fri at 13.00, 14.00 and 15.00. ☎ 514 44 2613), a joint work (1888) of Gottfried Semper with Karl von Hasenauer. The design resembles that of Semper's Dresden opera house, but Hasenauer's influence is visible on the decorative façade, with its busts of the great playwrights and the muses. The highlight of the elegant interior is the decoration of the lateral stairways by the Company of Artists (Gustav and Ernst Klimt with Franz Matsch). Gustav Klimt's *Apollo Altar* and *Thespis Chariot* are in the left-hand wing, together with an *Antique Theatre* by Matsch and the *Globe Theatre* (Gustav Klimt). Ernst Klimt painted the Hanswurst figure and Molière's *Le Malade imaginaire*.

Facing the theatre to the west is Friedrich Schmidt's neo-Gothic **Rathaus** (City Hall, 1883), one of the masterpieces of Ringstraßen Historicism, albeit an over-ambitious transformation to a larger scale from Flemish medieval models. The central tower (98m) is topped by the *Rathausmann*, a figure modelled on the armour of Maximilian I in the weapons collection of the Neue Burg. The **Festsaal** is adorned with statuary of figures from Vienna's past and is the venue for the *Wiener Vorlesungen*, an ongoing lecture series that has attracted illustrious personalities from Gombrich to Gorbachov. The **Council Chamber** is frescoed with scenes from Viennese history by Ludwig Mayer. The Rathaus has a useful library and valuable archive which contains original protocols of rights granted to Vienna by the Habsburgs, autographs of important local artists and the manuscript of Johann Strauss's *Die Fledermaus*. Tours of the Rathaus take place on Mon, Wed and Fri at 13.00, if the Council is not in session. The starting-point is the information office in the Schmidthalle at the rear, where also much interesting material regarding hiking and cyclist routes, as well as facilities and events for which the Council is responsible, can be obtained. (☎ 525 50).

In the Rathausplatz and park in front of the building are statues of Babenberg and Habsburg rulers (lining the *allée*), together with those of the defenders of the city in the two Turkish sieges, Bishop Kollonitsch (honoured here for his humanitarian activities in the plague years), Joseph von Sonnenfels (Maria Theresia's liberal-minded minister) and J.B. Fischer von Erlach. There are also monuments to the great popularisers of the Viennese waltz, Josef Lanner and Johann Strauss Senior and a modern bust of the Socialist Karl Renner (Alfred Hrdlicka, 1967), Chancellor of both the First and Second Austrian Republic (and subsequently President in the Second Republic).

Further north the **University** (Heinrich Ferstel, 1884) stands on the corner where the Ringstraße turns north-east. The gilded monument across the Ring opposite is in honour of Andreas Liebenberg, mayor of the city during the Turkish siege of 1683. The **Votivkirche** (1854–79) north of the university is one of Ferstel's most ambitious works, but the rigidly neo-Gothic exterior is intimidating and the deserts of space inside only relieved by extensive over-painting in warm colours. It was built as thanksgiving for Franz Joseph's escape from an assassination attempt in 1853, but the protracted construction was due partly to lack of funds from a less than enthusiastic public that was supposed to contribute from all over the Empire, as well as to Ferstel's obsessive perfectionism. Its main object of interest is the **Renaissance tomb of Count Salm** (1533) in the baptistery, a suitably splendid memorial to the defender of the city during the first Turkish attack of 1529.

The last stretch of the Ringstraße, the Schottenring, runs north-east past two of

Vienna's best hotels (*De France* and *Vienna Plaza*), the police headquarters and (just to the north) the extraordinary **Roßauer Kaserne**. This Disneyland-like 'Windsor-style' fortress was created by military architects as part of a ring of similar strongholds that were originally planned to contain potential civil disorder following the 1848 Revolution. It now houses police offices and living quarters. By contrast the **Börse** (stock exchange) (1877) on the south side of the Ring at no. 16, is one of the most pleasing neo-Renaissance works by Theophil Hansen. From here it is a few minutes' walk to the original starting-point of this tour at Schwedenplatz on the Donaukanal.

The Augarten and the Prater

In Vienna's 2nd District (Leopoldstadt) are two great parks, the Augarten and the Prater. The Augarten was laid out in 1650, ravaged by the Turks in 1683 and restored by Jean Trehet in 1712. It was opened to the public by Joseph II in 1775, whose gracious, if mildly disingenuous, dedication to the populace may be read above the main gateway on Obere Augartenstraße. Although disfigured by two of the *Flaktürme* (anti-aircraft batteries) dating from World War II, the park retains some of its former charm.

The **Gustinus Ambrosi Museum** (open Tues–Sun, 10.00–17.00) to the east is devoted to the Rodin-influenced sculptor (1893–1975) of the same name. Joseph II also erected a pavilion (1781) in the park, which is known as the **Joseph-Stöckl** and was designed by Isidore Canevale, who also built the triumphal arch at the entrance mentioned above. The former Augarten-Palais is home to the Wiener Sängerknaben (Vienna Boys' Choir), while the **Saalgebäude** to the west houses the manufactory of the Augarten porcelain, founded in 1718, just eight years after Meißen.

If you head south-east from the Augarten along Heine Straße, you reach the junction of **Praterstern**, at the centre of which is a monument (1886, Karl von Hasenauer, Carl Kundmann) commemorating Vice-Admiral Wilhelm von Tegetthoff's victory over the Italians at Lissa in 1866, which was some small consolation for the Empire's catastrophic defeat by the Prussians at Sadowa in the same year.

The **Prater** (Tram N from Schwedenplatz) is Vienna's oldest park. Maximilian II appropriated most of it from the church in the 1560s for use as a hunting-ground, while Ferdinand I had already planted its great chestnut *allée* in 1537. It was opened to the public by Joseph II in 1766. The Prater's destiny as an amusement park may be traced to the first firework display here in 1773, while in the 19C the **Wurstelprater** (**Volksprater**) with its inns and luna park attractions gradually developed into the Viennese cliché of popular entertainment it is today. The Prater was nonetheless big enough to accommodate all classes and walks of life, whether it was those who attended the springtime *Blumenkorso*, a middle-class fashion parade instituted in 1886 by Princess Pauline Metternich, or those who marched with the workers each year on the 1 May, starting in 1890. Apart from the **Ferris Wheel** built by Walter Bassett in 1897, the Prater also offers a fun-fair, pubs and restaurants, a planetarium, a football stadium and (at the eastern end) race-courses for trotting (*Krieau*) and conventional racing (*Freudenau*).

Schloss Belvedere and Arsenal

• Entrance to the Belvedere palaces and park are at Rennweg 6A (Lower Belvedere); Landstraßer Gürtel or Prinz-Eugen-Straße 27 (Upper Belvedere). Both palaces and their attached museums have the same opening times: Tues–Sun, 10.00–17.00).

The greatest work of Lukas von Hildebrandt in Vienna is the magnificent palace built for Prince Eugene of Savoy and consisting of two parts: **Unteres Belvedere** (Lower Belvedere, completed 1716) and **Oberes Belvedere** (Upper Belvedere, completed 1722).

The Lower Belvedere was the administrative area and usual living quarters for the prince, and now houses the **Austrian Baroque Museum** with works by J.M. Rottmayr, Daniel Gran, Paul Troger, Franz Anton Maulbertsch and the sculptor, Georg Raphael Donner. Unique are the extraordinary busts with grimacing faces by Franz Xaver Messerschmidt, based on Lavater's ideas of physiognomy that explained personality in terms of facial characteristics. The spectacular **marble hall** has a fresco by Martino Altomonte showing the *Apotheosis of Prince Eugene*, a glorification of the palace's owner that was repeated elsewhere, notably in a sculptured apotheosis (1721) by Balthasar Permoser in the **cabinet doré**. The park, laid out (1717–19) by Dominique Girard, also boasted a scheme of statuary that alluded to the Prince's cultural patronage (Apollonian themes) and his successful generalship (Herculean themes). The southern park, beyond the Upper Palace, has a substantial *pièce d'eau* on the Versailles model and an extremely fine wrought-iron gateway topped by the Prince's coat of arms.

In the **Orangery** adjacent to the Lower Belvedere is the **Museum of Austrian Medieval Art** with masterpieces primarily from the great flowering of Gothic art in Austria in the 15C; it includes works by the Master of Großlobming, Conrad Laib and Michael Pacher.

To the east of the park are the **Alpine Garden** (open April–July, 10.00–18.00) and the university-run **Botanical Gardens** (open from Easter–Oct daily from 09.00 to one hour before sunset).

The **Obere Belvedere** (Upper Belvedere) rivals any building erected by the Habsburgs themselves. It is divided into seven harmoniously integrated architectural components, with a ceremonial portal at the centre and four domed corner-pavilions on the Renaissance model. From the **Sala Terrena** with its Atlas figures and Santino Bussi's sophisticated stucco ornamentation in the vaulting, you climb the stairs to the **Festsaal**. The latter is richly clad in marble with a ceiling fresco showing an allegory of *Fame and Glory* by Carlo Carlone. It was in this chamber that the *Staatsvertrag*, liberating Austria from post-war occupation by the four allied powers, was signed in 1955. The palace passed into Habsburg ownership after Prince Eugene's death, and later (from 1904) became the residence of the ill-fated heir to the throne, Archduke Franz Ferdinand. Since the First Republic, it has been home to the **Austrian Gallery**, which houses Austrian works of the 19C (Biedermeier, Realism, Historicism), the turn of the century (Secession) and 20C (Expressionism, and the art of the 1920s and 1930s). There is one section of non-Austrian works of the 19C (formerly the *Neue Galerie* moved here from the Stallburg in the 1980s). It is worth spending a long afternoon in the various Belvedere galleries, but currently the biggest draw is the collection of works by Gustav Klimt (the best anywhere, especially the landscapes) and the Expressionist Egon Schiele. Less well-known Secessionists (especially Carl Moll) should also not be ignored, nor the topographical paintings by the Alt dynasty, the highly individual works of Anton Romako, a handful of masterly Kokoschkas and finally Oskar Laske's powerful modern rendering of the medieval theme of the *Ship of Fools* (1923).

Prince Eugene of Savoy (1663–1736)

The grand-nephew of Cardinal Mazarin, Prince Eugene became the most successful general of his age, as well as being a patron of the arts and collector of some 15,000 books, 237 MSS and innumerable prints and paintings, which eventually found their way into the National Library and the Albertina. Even as he laid siege to Belgrade, the prince was corresponding with his artistic adviser with a view to acquiring some pictures in Bologna that had come on the market. An enigmatic figure (rumoured to be homosexual), Eugene was a master tactician both on the battlefield and off it. The slightly hunchbacked *kleiner Kapuziner* (so-called because of his preference for a plain black smock) knew how to inspire affection among his troops and did not forget 1500 veterans of his wars who found jobs as gardeners on his estates after demobilisation. When Louis XIV refused him a commission, he signed up for the Habsburg cause, distinguished himself at the siege of Vienna in 1683 as a junior commander, then rose to prominence in the Italian and French campaigns. He became Commander-in-Chief in 1697, after which he joined with Marlborough in the spectacularly successful conduct of the War of the Spanish Succession. He was Governor of Milan (1707–16) and of the Netherlands (1716–24), besides leading the expulsion of the Turks from Central Europe, the crowning success of which was the re-taking of Belgrade in 1717. Prince Eugene was always his own man, a loner who could not write correct German and would not speak it, yet demonstrated his perception of himself as an essentially European prince in the service of Christendom and the 'Roman' Emperor by signing himself trilingually 'Eugenio von Savoye'.

After leaving the Upper Belvedere by the Landstraßer Gürtel exit and crossing the busy ring-road in a south-easterly direction, you reach the **Schweizer Garten** (so-called in memory of Swiss aid to Austria after World War I) coming shortly to the **Museum des 20 Jahrhunderts**. The building is a permanent version of Karl Schwanzer's Austria Pavilion made for the 1958 Brussels World Fair and is used as an exhibition hall for modern art shows.

Some way further south-east (follow the signs) is the huge **Arsenal** (1854), a complex built by five leading Ringstraßen architects to house military barracks and a depot after the 1848 revolution. The part of interest to the tourist is **Objekt 18,** the **Heeresgeschichtliches Museum** (War Museum) built by Theophil Hansen (open Mon–Thur, Sat, Sun 10.00–16.00). To follow the display chronologically, begin with the **Hall of Fame** on the first floor, the walls of which are hung with heroic pictures of Austrian victories. The various halls give an overview of the Thirty Years War, the Turkish Wars, the Napoleonic War and World War I. Notable is the car in which Archduke Franz Ferdinand was riding when he was assassinated in Sarajevo on 28 June 1914, and his bloodstained uniform displayed nearby (ground floor, west wing). Although most of the paintings are in the heroic vein, an interesting exception is the Tyrolean Albin Egger Lienz's (1868–1926) Expressionistic depiction of the masses marching to slaughter with the title *To the Unknown Soldier*.

Josephinum and Liechtenstein Garten-Palais

The **Josephinum** (1785) at Währinger Straße 25 was founded by Joseph II for military surgeons and designed by Isidore Canevale. Of interest is its **Museum of the History of Medicine** (open Mon–Fri, 09.00–15.00) which contains unusual anatomical wax models made by Felice Fontana of Florence. Their purpose was the systematic exhibition of the internal organs and muscular structure of the human body for the instruction of apprentice surgeons at a time when dissection was not commonly practised. Those who have a taste for such things will be intrigued by the museum in the nearby **Narrenturm** (Fools' Tower) in the old Allgemeinen Krankenhaus (the nearest point of entry is from Spitalgasse 2, and follow the signs to Hof 6).

The Narrenturm was likewise built on the orders of Joseph II to house the mentally disturbed in a cylindrical building (1784), designed with maximum control in mind. It is now the remarkable **Museum for Pathological Anatomy** (open Wed 15.00–18.00, Thur 08.00–11.00, first Sat in the month 10.00–13.00), exhibiting all manner of medical curiosities from human deformities to gall stones. Returning to Währinger Straße from Spitalgasse, you come shortly on your left to Strudlhofgasse leading to the attractive art nouveau steps (Strudlhofstiege, Theodor Jäger, 1910), named after the Baroque court painter, Peter von Strudel, whose residence was in the area.

The Strudlhofstiege leads down towards the **Liechtenstein Garten-Palais** (entrance at Fürstengasse 1) which is the home of the **Museum of Modern Art** (open Tues–Sun, 10.00–18.00) at least until the year 2000. Eventually the contents will be moved to the Museum Quarter under construction on the site of the Messepalast, but meanwhile the collection (which includes works by Fritz Wotruba, Max Oppenheimer, Oskar Kokoschka, Ben Nicholson, René Magritte, Max Ernst and Pablo Picasso) may be viewed in the gracious surroundings of the palace. The latter was built (1691–1706) by Domenico Egidio Rossi and Domenico Martinelli and has a **Ceremonial Hall** frescoed (1708) by Andrea Pozzo (the *Apotheosis of Hercules*).

Servitenkirche and Freud Museum

By following the Fürstengasse east and turning right into Porzellangasse, then left down Grünentorgasse, you come to the **Servitenkirche** (1677) by Carlo Canevale, the first in Vienna to be built with an oval nave. It contains impressive stucco scenes under the towers at the entrance (the *Death of Juliana Falconieri*, a Servite saint, and the *Martyrdom of St John Nepomuk*, the latter by Santino Bussi). The pulpit (1739) is by Balthasar Moll and Franz Joseph Hilber, and shows the *Four Evangelists*. The adjoining St Peregrine Chapel is richly decorated and has a copy of Pontormo's *Annunciation* in Santissima Annunziata, Florence. Servitengasse runs south and the first turn right brings you into Berggasse, at no. 19 of which is the **Sigmund Freud Museum** (open daily July–Sept 09.00–18.00, other months 09.00–16.00), situated in the lodgings where Freud had his consulting rooms from 1891 until his enforced departure for England on 3 June, 1938.

Central Cemetery (Zentralfriedhof)

Vienna's Zentralfriedhof was founded in 1870, when the rapid expansion of the city and the saturation of St Marx's Cemetery and others precipitated an urgent need for new burial space. It was laid out by Frankfurt architects (Karl Mylius and Friedrich Bluntschli) on land purchased by the *Gemeinde Wien* in Simmering and covers an area of one square mile, encompassing 300,000 graves and mausoleums divided according to faith (Russian Orthodox, Jewish, Protestant and Catholic, as well as some Soviet war graves and memorial grounds for the Austrian dead of two world wars). The visitor will perhaps be most interested in the Ehrengräber (Graves of Honour); while many celebrities (Mozart, Beethoven and Schubert among them) having been transferred here from elsewhere, the most distinguished Austrian artists, writers, scientists, actors and politicians who have died since 1870 were customarily given a magnificent send-off in the Zentralfriedhof. One of the latest to receive this honour is the opera singer Leonie Rysanek, who died in 1998. A map of the graves is available at the main gate (Tor 2).

The **Dr-Karl-Lueger-Church** (1911), built by Max Hegele, a pupil of Otto Wagner, and containing the tomb of the populist mayor after whom it is named, stands to the north of the Ehrengräber. Its glass windows are by Kolo Moser, while Hans Zatka painted the *Last Judgement* over the high altar. Austrian Presidents are buried in front of the church. Opposite the cemetery's main gate in the grounds of Maximilian II's **Neugebäude**, destroyed (1704) in the Hungarian War of Independence, is Clemens Holzmeister's Crematorium (1923).

Geymüller-Schlößl

Reached by Tram 41 (the end-stop, 18th District), this late-Empire palace (1808) was built for the banker, Baron Johann Geymüller (1754–1824), one of the founders of the Austrian National Bank and a man who played a vital role in raising the tribute monies demanded by Napoleon from the defeated Austrians in 1809: a secret provision of the Treaty of Schönbrunn (14 October 1809) required Austria to pay the French 85 million francs in 'war reparations'. The **Museum of the Geymüller-Schlößl**, Pötzleinsdorfer Straße 102 contains the Sobek Collection of clocks and Biedermeier furniture (open March–Oct, Mon–Wed 10.30–15.00, Thur–Sun, by appointment ☎ 71 136/232).

Kahlenberg (484m), Leopoldsberg (425m)

The two spurs of the Alpine foothills north-west of Vienna (from which there are fine views) are reached via the scenic **Höhenstraße**, built in the 1930s, or on public transport (Bus 38A from U-Bahn (4) station Heiligenstadt). The **Leopoldkirche**, built on the site of a Babenberg fortress, is a Baroque church (1730) by Antonio Beduzzi and contains documentation relating to the 1683 siege of Vienna. Both church and hill are named after St Leopold III of Babenberg. According to tradition, but disputed by many, it was in the **Church of St Joseph** on the neighbouring Kahlenberg that Marco d'Aviano held the dawn mass for King Jan Sobieski of Poland, on the day the liberating armies swept down to overwhelm the besieging armies of Kara Mustafa on 12 September 1683.

Hundertwasserhaus

This council block is either a self-indulgent folly or the architecture of the future, according to taste. The brightly coloured walls and designed-in greenery reflect Friedensreich Hundertwasser's post-modernist ecological preoccupations. A whole museum dedicated to the artist's vision is the **Kunsthaus Wien** nearby at Untere Weißgerberstrasse 13 (open daily 10.00–19.00). The Hundertwasserhaus itself is on the corner of Löwengasse and Kegelgasse.

- Tram N from Schwedenplatz to Hertzgasse.

Hundertwasserhaus (1983–85), Vienna

Karl-Marx-Hof

The most spectacular achievement of Red Vienna's housing programme was built (1927–34) by Karl Ehn, yet another pupil of Otto Wagner. The 1km long building contains 1325 flats with accompanying services and facilities, creating thereby a self-contained workers' colony. It was bombarded by Clerico-Fascist forces during the Civil War of 1934, forcing the surrender of members of the Socialist *Schutzbund*, who were holed up inside.

- Heiligenstädter Straße 82–92. Reached via tram D from Schottentor or U-Bahn (U4 or U6) to Heiligenstadt.

Kirche am Steinhof

Built for Lower Austria's Psychiatric Hospital, this is one of Otto Wagner's most exciting and exuberant works. The architect's functional preoccupations were given full scope in the structuring of the church interior with its hygiene and safety factors (running water in the stoop, ease of access to the smoothly rounded pews). Kolo Moser designed the blue mosaic windows (over the entrance, *The Fall*, in the middle, *God the Father*, on the right, *Adam and Eve*). The complicated iconography of the church's ornamentation stresses the co-extensive imperatives of Christian brotherliness in its practical and emotional manifestations, as expressed in stained-glass work and mosaics by Remigius Geyling and Rudolf Jettmar. The two monumental figures on the western façade (Sts Leopold and Severin, patrons of Lower Austria) are by Richard Luksch.

- The church is situated in the 14th District; buses 47A, 48A to Baumgartner Höhe 1. Open only with a guided tour on Sat at 15.00–16.30. ☎ 910 60-200 31.

Lainzer Tiergarten and Hermes Villa

On the western outskirts of Vienna is the **Lainzer Tiergarten**, a former imperial hunting-ground, now a park and animal reserve which also offers summer grazing for the Lipizzaners from the Spanish Riding School. The **Hermes Villa**, situated in the park, was a gift from Franz Joseph to Elizabeth and was built by

Karl von Hasenauer in 1882. Its main interest is the bedroom of the Empress, decorated by Hans Makart with a fresco of *Midsummer Night's Dream*, Elisabeth's favourite Shakespeare play. Temporary exhibitions are held in the villa by the Historischen Museum der Stadt Wien.

• Trams 60/61 from Hietzing U-Bahn to Hofwiesengasse, then bus 60B along Hermesstraße. The Lainzer Tor (entrance to the park) is open daily 08.00 till dusk. The Hermes Villa is open Wed–Sun and PH, 09.00–16.30, daily during exhibitions.

Piaristenkirche (Maria Treu) and Schönborn-Palais

Lukas von Hildebrandt and the Prague architect, Kilian Ignaz Dientzenhofer, were the principal designers of the elegant, late Baroque **Maria Treu Church** (1751), which was built for the Piarist order, whose school is adjacent. The superb ceiling frescoes (1733) by Franz Anton Maulbertsch show biblical scenes: *Adam and Eve*, the *Crowning of the Virgin*, the *Fall of the Angels*, the *Assumption* and the *Four Evangelists*; in the side-chapels: the *Parable of the Good Shepherd* (to the right) and *Jacob at the Well* (to the left). The *Pietà* in the Chapel of the Crucifix is early 15C. The church is in the 8th District on Jodok-Fink-Platz and reached via tram J to Lederergasse. Nearby at Laudongasse 15–19 is the Schönborn-Palais (Lukas von Hildebrandt, 1714), altered by Isidore Canevale in the 1760s. It now houses the **Austrian Museum of Folklore** (open Tues–Fri, 09.00–17.00, Sat, 09.00–12.00, Sun 09.00–13.00).

Schloss Schönbrunn and Technisches Museum

Schloß Schönbrunn (13th District) is reached via the U4 to Hietzing or Schönbrunn (open Apr–Oct daily, 08.30–17.00; Nov–Mar 08.30–16.00). The present palace is chiefly the work of Nikolaus Pacassi, begun in 1743 after J.B. Fischer von Erlach's ambitious original plans (which envisaged a site for the building on the hill where the Gloriette now stands) had been abandoned as too expensive. In the western part of the entrance courtyard are the **Schlosstheater**, with a Rococo interior by Ferdinand von Hohenberg (1767), and the **Carriage Museum** (Wagenburg), with an interesting display of mainly imperial carriages. There is limited access to the Fischer von Erlach designed **chapel** (open on Sun), which has a fresco of *Faith, Hope and Charity* by Daniel Gran and an altarpiece by Paul Troger (The *Betrothal of the Virgin*); likewise to the **Bergl-Zimmer** (1777) overpainted with landscapes by the Bohemian artist, Johann Wenzel Bergl.

The rooms of the palace can be visited on the **Grand Tour** (40 rooms out of 1441), or the **Imperial Tour** (22 rooms), the saving on the latter being scarcely worth making, since some of the more interesting rooms are excluded and you may have to wait anyway (in summer, perhaps more than an hour) before being allowed in with a timed ticket. Both tours supply some insights into the domestic life of Maria Theresia and her vast family, also (to a lesser extent) into that of Franz Joseph and others of the dynasty. Several individual rooms have important historical connotations: Franz Joseph was born in his parents' apartments here and died in his Schönbrunn bedroom on 21 November 1916; his demise marked the end of an era and practically-speaking the end of the Austro-Hungarian Empire, which was already staring defeat in the face. His successor, Karl I, struggled on for two years, finally announcing his withdrawal from government (not quite a full abdication) in the palace's Blue Chinese Salon on 11 November 1918. The Duc de Reichstadt (1811–32), Napoleon's son by the daughter of Franz I, lived in Schönbrunn, part guest, part prisoner, and died here of tuberculosis at the age of 21. The child prodigy, Wolfgang Amadeus Mozart, played for Maria Theresia in the Mirror Gallery of Schönbrunn in 1762.

Highlights of the tour include the **Rosa Room** with panel landscapes by Joseph Rosa; the **Round** and **Oval Chinese Rooms** with their decorative mirrors, oriental porcelain and gilt panelling inset with Chinese landscapes; and the **Great Gallery** with Guglielmo Guglielmi's ceiling frescoes (1761) showing the *Territories of the Empire Paying Homage to Maria Theresia and Franz I Stephan*, flanked by the *Glories of War* (a copy after the original was, ironically, destroyed by a bomb in World War II) and the *Blessings of Peace*. In the **Small Gallery** the same artist painted the *Union of the House of Habsburg-Lorraine with the Holy Roman Empire*. The Grand Tour continues with the **Blue Chinese Salon**; the **Vieux-Lacque Zimmer** with black lacquer wall-panels featuring Japanese landscapes; the **Porcelain Room** and finally the **Millionenzimmer**, built at huge cost with rosewood panelling inset with Indian and Persian miniatures.

Schönbrunn Park, altered from Jean Trehet's original (1706) Versailles-inspired design to Rococo style in the 1750s, contains artificial Roman ruins (its stones brought here from Maximilian II's destroyed Neugebäude in Simmering). To the north-east is the original **Schöner Brunnen** ('beautiful spring') from which the palace takes its name, marked by Wilhelm Beyer's fountain of the nymph Egeria dispensing water from a pitcher. Above the **Neptune Fountain** (Anton Zauner, 1781) at the end of the central gravel walk is Ferdinand von Hohenberg's **Gloriette** (1775), built to celebrate Maria Theresia's triumph over her enemies, more especially, the victory at Kolin over her arch-foe, Frederick the Great. There is a pleasant view over the western purlieus of the city from here and recently a café has been opened in the arcade.

To the west is the **Palm House** (1882), a glass and iron construction modelled on those of Kew Gardens, and nearby the **Botanical** (or **Dutch**) **Garden** (1754). Furthest to the west is the **Tiergarten** (zoo) in which Jadot de Ville Issey constructed an octagonal **viewing pavilion** (1759) from where the members of the imperial family could watch the animals. Menageries had been a feature of imperial display since the Renaissance and the reign of Maximilian II, while Prince Eugene of Savoy also kept wild animals at the Belvedere, including a lion and several more exotic beasts. Maximilian had brought the first elephant to Vienna, when he returned to the city with his Spanish bride in 1552; it was trotted through the streets in a grand procession, causing panic among the populace whenever it trumpeted. Unfortunately the climate did not agree with it and it died a year later, its bones being made into a curio chair now kept at Kremsmünster. The Schönbrunner zoo was the first zoo in Europe in the modern sense, built by Franz I Stephan with a view to the scientific study and preservation of animal species.

The **Technische Museum** (Museum of Technology) is a short walk from Schönbrunn at Mariahilfer Straße 212. It contains a superb display of Austrian inventions and gives an overview of the development of industry and technology in Austria through the ages. It reopened after seven years of renovation in 1999 with new 20th century exhibits and a section on energy (open Mon–Sat 09.00–18.00, Thur 09.00–20.00, Sun 10.00–17.00).

Gustav Klimt's garden studio near Schloß Schönbrunn was rediscovered in 1999. Klimt lived and worked here from 1912–18. The studio and villa are to be restored and a cultural centre established there in the next few years.

Wotrubakirche

The most remarkable example of modern ecclesiastical architecture in Vienna is surely the **Church of the Holy Trinity** (1976) in Mauer, an asymmetric creation of 152 rectangular concrete blocks and glass panels. The architect was the sculptor, Fritz Wotruba, whose symbolism was based on the idea that the apparent chaos of asymmetry leads nevertheless to a harmonious whole, in other words, a plea for pluralistic tolerance expressed in aesthetic and religious terms.

• The Wotrubakirche is in Mauer (23rd District) at the junction of Georgsgasse and Rysergasse, and can be reached via bus 60A. It is open Thur, Fri 14.00–16.00, Sat 14.00–20.00, Sun 09.00–17.00; from Mar–Oct also Tues and Wed, 14.00–16.00.

Heurigen villages

Favourite excursions for the Viennese are to the taverns (*Heurigen*) in villages at the edge of the city where the previous year's vintage of white wine is drunk on summer evenings in the gardens and terraces that adjoin the taverns. Simple food is also often served. The most famous of these villages (and therefore the most over-run with tourists) are **Grinzing** and **Heiligenstadt**, with strong competition from **Neustift am Walde**. All of these do indeed retain a certain rustic charm, while Heiligenstadt is worth visiting on its own account for the **Beethoven-Haus** at Probusgasse 6; it was here that the composer wrote his tragic *Heiligenstädter Testament* when he realised that he was becoming permanently deaf. The museum is open Tues–Sun 09.00–12.15, 13.00–16.30. Bus 38A to Armbrustergasse from U-Bahn Heiligenstadt. Other less touristy Heurigen villages include **Mauer** in the south-west and villages north of the Danube such as **Jedlersdorf** and **Stammersdorf**. To the west, the village of **Gumpoldskirchen**, close to Baden bei Wien (see below), is famed for its local white wine varieties (*Zierfandler* and *Rotgipfler*).

Sights around Vienna

Baden bei Wien

A *Lokalbahn* runs from the Staatsoper all the way (25km) to Baden bei Wien, a favoured resort for officials in the Biedermeier period when Kaiser Franz made the spa fashionable (although there had been a spa here since Roman times). After a serious fire in 1812, much of the town was rebuilt under the direction of the leading architect of neo-classicism, Josef Kornhäusel. His works include the **Rathaus** on the main square, the **Theresienschlößl** and **Metternichhof** in the Theresiengasse, as well as the **Sauerhof**, a fashionable spa. Franz I's summer residence was the likewise neo-classical **Kaiserhaus** at no. 17 on the east side of the Hauptplatz, opposite Giovanni Stanetti's Baroque **Plague Column** (1718).

A long list of well-known people took the waters here, including Mozart's wife Constanze and Beethoven. The **Beethoven Memorial Rooms**, Rathausgasse 10 (open Tues–Fri 16.00–18.00, Sat, Sun & PH 09.00–11.00, 16.00–18.00) include mementoes of the great theatrical producer, Max Reinhardt, and Franz Joseph's platonic companion in later life, the actress Katharina Schratt (both were born in Baden).

Mozart stayed for a while at Renngasse 4 where he dashed off the immortal *Ave verum Corpus* (1791) at the request of Anton Stoll, the local schoolmaster and director of the choir in the Baden parish church. In the latter is an altarpiece (1750) by Paul Troger showing the *Stoning of St Stephen*. The Helenenstraße leads out to the western districts past the **church of St Helen** with its massive sandstone relief (1500) showing the Holy Trinity in human figures. A curiosity is the **Rollett-Museum** (open Wed–Mon 15.00–18.00) on Weikersdorfer Platz to the south, with a display of skulls, brains and death masks that belonged to the founder of the 'science' of phrenology, Franz-Josef Gall (1758–1828). Baden is also the setting for *Venus in Furs*, an erotic novel based on personal experience and written by Leopold Sacher-Masoch; it gave birth to the term 'sado-masochism' (popularised by the psychiatrist Krafft-Ebing), the 'sado' bit referring to the equally exotic tastes of the Marquis de Sade.

Hinterbrühl and sights to the south

Hinterbrühl (reached by bus from Südtiroler Platz) is notable for its **Seegrotte**, actually a former gypsum mine used as an aircraft factory in World War II and subsequently flooded to create Europe's largest underground lake. Boat trips on the lake are possible (warm clothing required). On the edge of the village is the picturesque **Höldrichsmühle** (Gaadner Straße 34), a hotel with a good restaurant, supposedly the spot where Franz Schubert composed *Die schöne Müllerin* (1823). There had been a water-mill here at least a century before Schubert, the name of the place being derived from its mid-18C owner, Anton Hiltrich. The restaurant part was opened in 1786 and became a favourite haunt of city-dwellers in the Biedermeier period.

Southwards out of Vienna, those not taking the bus may pass two places of interest. The first is the Gothic **Spinnerin am Kreuz** monument (much restored) near the summit of the arterial Triester Strasse, erected in 1452 and replacing an earlier column (destroyed by Hunyadi's Hungarian army) that marked the southern limit of the city, following a division of territories between Duke Leopold III and his brother Albrecht III in 1375. This new work was designed by Hans Puchsbaum, who worked on the Stephansdom, replacing that by Michael Knab, the architect of Maria am Gestade church in the old city. Just beyond it stood the public scaffold from 1311 to 1747 and again from 1805 until the last public execution in 1868.

Nearby, in Windtenstrasse to the east is the **Favoriten water tower** (in use between 1899 and 1910) now accessible for periodic exhibitions. Equally of interest is **Perchtoldsdorf**, reached from the second exit of the southern Autobahn (A21), an ancient settlement where the scholar Thomas Ebendorfer (1435–64) secretary to Emperor Friedrich III was once the priest. A bloodbath occurred here as the advance guard of the Turkish army reached Perchtoldsdorf in 1683. The people took refuge in the church and negotiated a ransom payment: although the ransom was paid, all 500 were massacred as they left their retreat. The turreted keep of 1465 (extended from fortifications begun under Albrecht II in 1340) and the lofty Gothic parish church of 1340 are worth visiting. Close to the 15C Rathaus on the market square stands a **plague column** (1713) with a relief on the plinth by J.B. Fischer von Erlach. On the Kalenderberg overlooking nearby **Brunn am Gebirge** from the west is the impressive **Burg Liechtenstein**, a neo-Gothic reconstruction undertaken in the 1870s of a partly ruined castle dating to 1165. The surrounding woodland park shows the same romantic spirit, being dotted with follies and artistic 'ruins'. The castle and grounds are open April–Oct, Tues–Sun 09.30–17.00.

Klosterneuburg

The peripheral town (and now fashionable commuter dormitory) of Klosterneuburg is reached from Vienna (13km) on the Schnellbahn (line S40 from the Franz-Josefs-Bahnhof; trains run every 30mins during the day).

On leaving the station, you will see the **Augustinian abbey** on the heights above you, reached in a few minutes on foot. The abbey can be visited with guided groups only, and the commentary is in German. (**Museum** open May–Nov, Tues–Sun 10.00–17.00. Stift tours 09.00–12.00, 13.30–16.30, Sun from 10.00.) The monastery has a long history that begins with a Romanesque foundation (1114) by Leopold III of Babenberg, who moved his residence here from Tulln, and built a **Neue Burg** over the ruins of a Roman garrison, possibly that of *Asturis*. Leopold's original plan was to erect a bishopric for his new residence, with his son Otto as the Bishop; but Otto decided to enter a Cistercian cloister in France. Instead, the Augustinians were invited to settle in the abbey (1133), their church being completed in 1136. Klosterneuburg became a place of pilgrimage after Leopold's canonisation in 1485. The existing Romanesque and Gothic building was to be extended under Karl VI by his Milanese architect, Donato Felice d'Allio, working (from 1730) to plans by Fischer von Erlach. Karl's ambitious attempts to create an Austrian version of the Spanish Habsburgs' Escorial were cut short, however, with the Emperor's death in 1740, although Josef Kornhäusel did complete two of the projected nine cupolas in the 19C. The incomplete building has been taken as emblematic of the Habsburgs' endlessly ambitious but eternally unrealised secular and spiritual aspirations, what Robert Musil ironically referred to as 'provisional arrangements that lasted for ever'.

The abbey's greatest treasure is in the 12C burial chapel of St Leopold to the east, a superb Romanesque **winged altarpiece** by Nicolas of Verdun (1181), (the remains of St Leopold are buried under the altar) made of gilded copper with 51 plaques of champlevé enamel. Six of these were added to the central part after a fire in 1330 nearly threatened to destroy what was regarded as the greatest existing pre-Gothic artefact in Europe (the monks saved it by dousing it in wine). The plaques show the Bible story from the Creation to the end of the New Testament, whereby the latter is didactically presented as a theological and historical continuum with the Old Testament, a deliberate attempt to combat the contemporary heresy of Cathars, who accepted only the prophetic elements of the Old Testament. The three horizontal rows of panels represent the three ages in the history of mankind's salvation: that prior to the establishment of the law by God through Moses (*ante legem*), that under the law of Moses (*sub lege*) and that of salvation through Christ (*sub gratia*). The last six panels on the right represent the Last Judgement.

The tour proceeds through the **Well-House** (c 1300) with a seven-armed **bronze candelabra** made in Verona in the first half of the 12C, the whole being symbolic of the Tree of Jesse, while the seven candles represent the Seven Gifts of the Holy Spirit (Wisdom, Understanding, Counsel, Fortitude, Knowledge, Piety and Fear of the Lord). The mostly Baroque **Residenztrakt** (residence wing) to the east contains the impressive **Marmorsaal** (marble hall) with a ceiling fresco (1749) by Daniel Gran of the *Apotheosis of the House of Habsburg*. The neighbouring *Kaiserzimmer* has rich stucco decoration by Santino Bussi, while in the **Gobelinsaal** are 18C Brussels tapestries depicting the story of Telemachus.

In the **Stift Museum** (part of the tour) is the *Klosterneuburger Madonna* (1310) and a *genealogical tree of the Babenbergs* (1492, by Hans Part), as well as panels originally on the back of the Verdun altar, a cycle (1505) by Rueland Frueauf the Younger showing the foundation legend of the monastery. According to this legend, the wind blew away St Leopold's wife's veil as she and the Margrave stood one day on the Kahlenberg. Nine years later, Leopold found the undamaged veil on an elderberry bush while out hunting. This he took to be a sign from God that a church should be built on the spot where it was found.

The **church** is the oldest part of the complex with basic elements from the 1136 Romanesque structure surviving, although the two western towers were much altered by the Ringstraßen architect, Friedrich Schmidt in 1879, not with entirely happy results. The Baroque decoration of the interior includes J.G. Greiner's frescoes of the *Virgin Crowned*, the *Virgin with Angels* and the *Virgin as Protector against the Turks* in the nave, and one by J.M. Rottmayr (the *Assumption*), in the apse, below which is the altarpiece (1728) by Johann Georg Schmidt (the *Birth of the Virgin*). The finely carved choirstalls (1723) showing 24 coats of arms of the Austrian Crown Lands are by Matthias Steinl. The exceptionally ornate Baroque **organ** (1642) was built by Johann Freundt of Passau. In a building to the west of the church is to be found the famous '**Thousand-Bucket-Wine-Barrel**' (made in 1704 and reputedly holding 56,000 litres), in which the public get a chance to slide every year on St Leopold's Day (15 November).

The monastery is famous for its white wine and red St Laurent, which can be enjoyed in the Stiftskeller.

In the centre of the Stiftsplatz is a Gothic column (1381) attributed to Michael Knab and decorated with reliefs of the Passion, while across the square is the Sebastianikapelle containing the celebrated **Albrechtsaltar** (1439). It consists of 24 panels painted with remarkable realism, and including one (*Joachim and Anna*) with an early view of Vienna showing the Stephansdom. In the town, the 14C parish church of St Martin is worth a visit, not least for the 16 Baroque over-life-size wooden statues by Franz Caspar. These representations of Christ, Mary, the Evangelists and Apostles were brought here from the Camaldolensian Hermitage on the Kahlenberg. There is rather less to see for those who make a pilgrimage to the **Franz Kafka Memorial Room** in the Kierling region of the town (Kierlinger Hauptstraße 187, open Mon–Sat 08.00–12.00, 13.00–17.00), which is in fact the room in the former Hofmann Sanatorium where the writer (1883–1924) died of tuberculosis aged 40.

Enthusiasts for modern art should not miss the **Sammlung Essl** (Schömer-Haus, Aufeldstrasse 17–23, ☎ 02243/410), a gallery of contemporary Austrian work assembled by the owner of a DIY chain, Karlheinz Essl, of which various aspects are regularly shown in special exhibitions, another part being permanently displayed. A new building was opened in November 1999.

Heiligenkreuz and Mayerling

The historic Cistercian abbey (1133) of **Heiligenkreuz** is reached by bus 265 from Südtiroler Platz and was another foundation of St Leopold III of Babenberg. It is named after the relic of the True Cross brought back here (1187) by Leopold V from the Third Crusade. The **chapter house** is also the burial-place of 13 Babenbergs, although the only tomb to be seen is that of the last one, Friedrich der Streitbare ('the Valiant'), the last of the line who died in 1246. Babenberg portraits can also be seen in the glass panels of the enneagonal **well-house**, parts of which date to 1290. The **Joseph's fountain** (1739) and **Plague column** (1737) in the courtyard are by Giovanni Giuliani, who lived in the abbey for much of his life and died here. The originally Romanesque church (1187) has a fine **Gothic choir** added in 1295. The Baroque choirstalls are by Mattäus Rueff and are topped with vivid carvings by Giuliani of popes, cardinals, bishops and other important figures from church history.

• Heiligenkreuz is open daily April–Oct, 09.00–11.30, 13.30–17.00; Nov–Mar, 13.30–16.00. Guided tours five times daily in April–Oct.

Bus 265 continues to nearby **Mayerling**, nestling in a fold of the Wienerwald, and now notorious as the hunting lodge where the 29-year-old Crown Prince Rudolf shot himself and his 17-year-old lover, Marie Vetsera on the night of 29 January 1889. After the suicide, the lodge was mostly demolished and a Carmelite convent erected in its stead on the orders of Franz Joseph. The chapel may be visited, as also may the room in which the tragedy took place, which has been preserved as part of the memorial (ring the bell for admission. Closed 12.30–13.30).

Laxenburg

Seventeen kilometres south of Vienna is the imperial pleasure palace and park at Laxenburg, reached by Triester Straße (B17), via the *Süd-Autobahn*, or by bus from Landstraße/Wien Mitte. Laxenburg's **Neue Schloß** (or 'Blauer Hof', 1752) was built by Nikolaus Pacassi, while the Alte Schloß is a 14C edifice remodelled by Ludovico Burnacini in the late 17C. The latter houses the Austrian Film Archives. In the English-style **park** (open all year) is the moated **Franzensburg**, a medieval folly built for Franz I between 1796–1836 by Michael Riedl and Franz Jäger (guided tours are available only in the summer months; open daily 10.00–12.00, 14.00–17.00, (museum) Sun 10.00–12.00, unless there is a special exhibition). In many ways it expresses the Biedermeier desire for retreat from the turmoil of the world (the Emperor hoped the French would 'at least let me keep Laxenburg' when it seemed he would lose everything else) as well as a sentimental re-creation of a 'German' past (in contrast to the threatening, enlightened modernism of the French). Franz collected any number of artefacts from churches and cloisters and other bits and pieces of interiors, including the superb Gothic **Capella speciosa** (1220) from Klosterneuburg.

Niederösterreich (Lower Austria)

Area: 19,173sq km. Population: 1.47 million.

Topography, climate and environment

The largest Austrian province in terms of territory, **Niederösterreich** (Lower Austria) also has the second largest population (18.9 per cent of the total). It lies on both sides of the Danube and between the confluence of the latter with the River Enns in the west, and that of the **Danube** and the **March** at Devîn (Slav, 'Theben') in the east. The March itself forms a long border between the province and the Slovak Republic. Lower Austria has several distinctive regions, the most important located as follows (relative to Vienna): the **Marchfeld** (to the east); the **Wiener Becken** and **Bucklige Welt** (to the south); the **Wienerwald**, **Mostviertel** and **Eisenwurzen** (to the west, south of the Danube); the **Wachau** and **Tullner Becken** (along the Danube Valley to the west); the **Waldviertel** (to the north-west); and the **Weinviertel** (to the north). The province borders in the east and north-east with the Slovak Republic, in the south-east with Burgenland, in the south with Steiermark, in the west with Oberösterreich and in the north with the Czech Republic. It also encircles Vienna which, until 1922, was part of its territory.

The climate is variable, continental in the Danube Valley and Pannonian in the plain to the north and east, while towards the Alpine foothills the Atlantic-influenced weather produces higher rainfall than elsewhere. In the south of the region the Alpine influence is noticeable in rapid and pronounced changes in temperature. The mixed woodland in the south and in the Waldviertel (forest district) is also of climatic significance, while in the flat lands to the west and in the Weinviertel, the perspective of arable fields is broken characteristically by groves of hornbeam and oak. In the Wienerwald are extensive plantations of beech.

Economy

About 11 per cent of the population is directly employed in agriculture, a marked decline since World War II, but still a higher proportion than elsewhere in Austria. Thirty per cent of Austria's pigmeat is produced here, besides a substantial share of the country's wheat, cooking oil and wine (75 per cent). Logging is an important industry and the area just to the north of the Marchfeld contains most of Austria's modest reserves of oil and natural gas. After suffering severely from plunder by the Soviet occupation forces at the end of World War II, Lower Austria has recovered well, partly through developing innovative light industries south of Vienna and at St Pölten. Tourism was hitherto of less significance in the local economy than elsewhere, but is growing, especially in the beautiful Wachau region along the Danube between Melk and Dürnstein. Resorts fashionable in the 19C (Alpine Semmering and the spa at Baden) are doing what they can to re-establish themselves in a highly competitive environment, yet it is often their slightly faded air of gentility that makes them attractive in a world multiplying with Disneylands and worse.

NIEDERÖSTERREICH

C Z E C H
R E P U B L I C

Karlstein

Drosendorf

Hard

Raabs an
der Thaya

Riegersburg

Waidhofen
an der Thaya

Gr.-Siegharts

Geras

Gmünd

Horn — Maria
Dreieich

Weitra

Greillenstein
Röhrenbach

Altenburg

Eggenb
Rosenburg

Schloss Rosenau

Zwettl

Gars am
Kamp

Schiltern

Rappottenstein

Langenlois

Grafenegg

Schönbach

Krems

Dürnstein

Grafenwört

Weißenkirchen i.d.W.

Mautern a.d.D.

St. Michael

Rossatz

Nuß
a.d.

W A L D V I E R T E L

K A M P T A L

W A C H A U

Weiten

Spitz

Furth b.
Göttweig

JAUERLING
960

O B E R Ö S T E R R E I C H

Pöggstall

Maria
Laach

Maria
Langegg

St. Andrä

Waldhausen i. Strud.

Emmersdorf a.d.D.

Aggsbach Dorf

Herzogent

Mauthausen

Perg

Artstetten

Schönbühel a.d.D.

ST. PÖLT

Grein

Säusenstein

Mauer bei Melk

Enns

Persenbeug

Melk

Loosdorf

Donau

STRUDENGAU

Ybbs a.d.D.

Pöchlarn

Schallaburg

A1

Erlauf

A1   E60

Ybbs

Amstetten

Steyr

Neuhofen
an der Ybbs

Hainfe

Seitenstetten
Markt

SONNTAGBERG

Lilienfeld

Waidhofen
a.d. Ybbs

Frankenfels

SCHNEEBL

E I S E N W U R Z E N

Gaming

Ötscher-
Tormäuer
Nature
Reserve

S T E I E R M A R K

Mariazell

RA

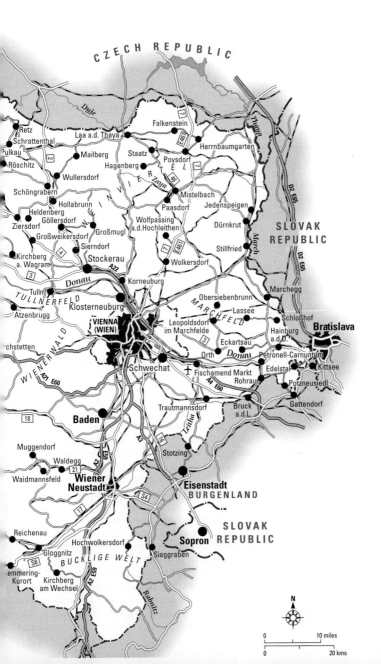

History

Lower Austria has been inhabited from prehistoric times and some of the earliest archaeological discoveries of Central Europe have been made in the region (the most celebrated is the 25,000-year-old Willendorf *Venus* in Vienna's Natural History Museum). The **Romans** built border fortifications (*limes*) along the Danube in the area that later became Lower Austria, with forts at strategic places such as Ybbs, Melk, Mautern, Zwentendorf, Vindobona (Vienna) and (the biggest) Carnuntum. Subsequently the Danube Valley was also the cradle of Austrian Christianity, the faith being kept alive by St Severin as the great migrations swept over the area and Roman power weakened. He died at Favianae (Mautern) in 482 and it was at Mautern too that he founded a monastery, from where he attempted to protect his vulnerable flock and maintain a semblance of order and civilisation. St Severin's cloister was the first of the four magnificent monasteries to be established along the Danube (the two greatest under Leopold III of Babenberg), all of which were subsequently transformed into sumptuous Baroque edifices in the 17C and 18C. In the Middle Ages and the Counter-Reformation they were thriving centres of culture, learning and artistic excellence, a tradition not entirely extinguished, despite greatly depleted numbers of monks.

The events of the next 400 years of the **Dark Ages** are not easily verifiable, but it seems clear that Christianity survived in the area, even if in isolated outposts and frequently under siege. Under **Charlemagne** the two Carolingian Marks were established (799), the southern one ('Karantine') stretching down to Istria, the northern one ('Avarian') encompassing what later became Lower Austria. The Ottonian Mark superseded the Avarian and extended its territory to the Thaya (Czech: *Dyje*), March and Leitha rivers, which to this day constitute the north, east and south-east borders of Lower Austria. After the defeat of the Hungarians on the Lechfeld (955) at the hands of **King Otto I**, Lower Austria came gradually (after 976) under Babenberg suzerainty, but it was not until 1254 that its territory was definitively delineated, when the border with Styria was fixed. From 1278 it fell under Habsburg rule after **Rudolf of Habsburg** had defeated **Ottakar II of Bohemia** on the Marchfeld and most of what is now Austria became the Habsburg 'Hereditary Lands'. In a settlement of 1282, Rudolf was granted '*das Land unter der Enns*', although the nomenclature 'Archduchy of Austria below the Enns' by which Lower Austria (*Niederösterreich*) came to be known (as opposed to the Archduchy 'above the Enns', i.e. Upper Austria, *Oberösterreich*) did not become current until the 16C.

In the 15C Lower Austria was subject to feuding between the local magnates (Kuenringer, Puchheimer, Pottendorfer and others), but even more destruction was caused by the devastating attacks of the Bohemian Hussites (1427–30), evidence of whose marauding may still be encountered in the Waldviertel and Weinviertel. In the 16C however, Lower Austria followed a somewhat similar pattern to that of its northern neighbour and in the course of several peasant rebellions became largely Protestant. As a consequence, the **Counter-Reformation** was subsequently pursued here with a thoroughness (and ruthlessness) that has left its mark in the enduring conservative piety of the population, as also in the lavishness of Baroque ornamentation in churches and monasteries. In general the history of Lower Austria follows closely that of Vienna from the 16C, with the ravages of the Turks, and then of the Swedish armies of the **Thirty Years War**, being far more damaging in the countryside than in the now heavily protected Residenzstadt, which never succumbed to either.

A significant milestone here as elsewhere was the **1848 revolution**, which ended the semi-feudal status of the peasantry and abolished the rule of the nobility who mainly constituted the Lower Austrian Diet. The latter was subsequently replaced (in the February Patent of 1861) by a *Landtag* (Provincial Parliament), albeit one elected on a very limited and manipulated franchise, the seat of which remained in Vienna even after the elevation of the capital to the status of *Land* (Province or Federal State) in 1920–22. Under the **Nazi regime**, Lower Austria was called *Niederdonau*, gaining parts of former Czechoslovakia and Burgenland and being reunited with an enlarged Vienna. During the post-war occupation, the area was under Russian control and subsequently suffered (notwithstanding the settlement of 1955 that liberated Austria) from its proximity to the Iron Curtain in the north and the east.

In 1986 St Pölten was chosen to be the new provincial capital and as soon as a modern government quarter could be built, its parliament, administrative offices and museum were all moved there from Vienna.

ST PÖLTEN

Practical information

Population: 50,000. Telephone dialling code: 02742.

Tourist information

The main tourist information bureau is inside the Rathaus on Rathausplatz (☎ 02742 53 3 54. Open Mon–Fri 08.00–18.00 from Easter to 31 Oct, Sat from 09.30–18.00 and Sun from 13.30–18.30). There is also a smaller office outside the station. The *St Pölten In-Guide* available here is a plan of the city with listings of sights and facilities. For Lower Austria generally the *Kulturkarte Niederösterreich* (pub. Hölzel, Wien) provides a detailed listing of sites that are highlighted on a road map of the province. The Lower Austrian tourist office in Vienna

(Niederösterreich Information) is at Heidenschuss 2, ☎ 01 533 3114, Fax 53 110 6060.

Getting there

St Pölten is on the main east–west railway line and there are regular trains from Vienna (journey time 40mins). Buses serve most of the main sights in the area, and leave from outside the main station.

Hotels

The choice in St Pölten is somewhat limited, though it should improve as the city gets into its stride as a provincial capital.

☆☆☆ *Austria Trend Hotel Metropol* (Schillerplatz 1. ☎ 70 700; fax 70 700 133).

☆☆ **Stadthotel Hauser** Eck (Schulgasse 2.
☎ 733 36; fax 783 86).

Restaurants

Galerie (Fuhrmanngasse 1)
Gasthaus Bamberger (Kremser
Gasse 22).

Cultural events

From **mid-June to early July** St Pölten
stages the *Niederösterreichisches
Donaufestival* an arts festival in conjunction with neighbouring towns which
includes ballet, drama and concerts,
with the emphasis on contemporary
works. Information from the
Festspielhaus, Franz Schubert Platz 2.
☎ 0 2742 2010.

History of St Pölten

St Pölten was built round and over a Roman settlement (*Aelium Cetium*) that
was raised to a *municipium* by Hadrian in AD 122. The Carolingian monastery
of Sanct Hippolytus gave the successor town its name and the latter prospered sufficiently to have claimed market rights by 1050, then the first
municipal rights granted by an Austrian dynasty in 1159. In the following
century the town was surrounded by walls which later proved strong enough
to resist two Turkish sieges.

The old town of St Pölten is noted for its Baroque architecture and indeed
one of the greatest Austrian Baroque architects, **Jakob Prandtauer**
(1660–1726) lived here from 1690 until his death. He surrounded himself
with fellow architects and artists, some of them his relations (Joseph
Munggenast, his nephew, the sculptor Peter Widerin, his son-in-law, as well
as Antonio Beduzzi, Matthias Steinl and others).

Sights of St Pölten

In the south-east of the city, overlooking the River Traisen, rises the dramatic
modern architecture of the new **Provincial Government Quarter**
(*Regierungsviertel*). The project cost 4 billion ATS to realise and some of the most
distinguished contemporary Austrian architects were commissioned for specific
parts of it: Hans Hollein for the Landesmuseum, Gustav Peichl for the ORF studio, Klaus Kada for the Festspielhaus, Paul Katzberger for the library and archive,
Ernst Beneder for the Media House and Boris Podrecca for the ceremonial
entrance to the *Landtag*). The three storeys of the 65m belfry by Ernst Hoffmann
are open to visitors, a feature being its ingeniously varied combinations of bell
peals.

The two central squares of the old town are the **Rathausplatz** and the nearby
Domplatz. The **Rathaus** on the south side has an octagonal tower dating to the
time when two Gothic buildings were given a common façade in the late 16C, the
latter altered by Joseph Munggenast in 1727. The **Mayor's Chamber** inside may
be visited on request and has a ceiling with portraits of 12 Habsburg Emperors
(1722). Passing the **Trinity Column** (1782) in the middle of the square, you
reach the **Franciscan** (formerly Carmelite) **church** (c 1779) at the north-east
corner, with its pink convex façade; its architect is not known, but the Rococo
high altar inside may be by Andreas Gruber, who also designed the Trinity
Column on the square. The side-altars have altarpieces by Kremser Schmidt (on
the left, *Mary of Mount Carmel*, *Judas Thaddeus*, on the right, *St Theresa* and

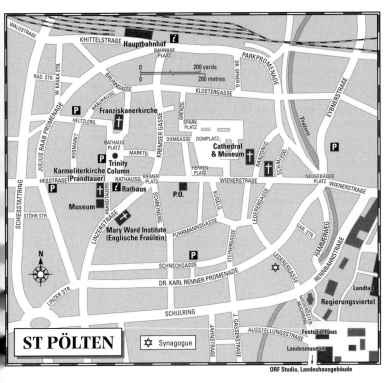

ORF Studio, Landeshausgebäude

St John of Nepomuk). Diagonally opposite the Franciscan Church is the **Carmelite church** (1712), known, however, as the Prandtauer church, although in fact Martin Witwer was the principal architect. The high altar is attributed to Lukas von Hildebrandt. Its dependencies house the **Municipal Museum** (Prandtauer Strasse 2, open Tues–Sat 10.00–17.00, Sun 09.00–12.00).

Behind the church on Linzer Strasse nos 7–9 is the **Church and School of the Englischen Fräulein**, an order founded on Jesuit lines by Mary Ward (1585–1645) for the education of aristocrats' daughters. She ran into opposition from the church hierarchy, partly because she wanted her order to be exempt from episcopal control, and in 1631 Ward was actually interned in the Convent of the Poor Clares in Munich. However, the schools mostly survived and a number are still to be found in Central Europe. The building's Baroque façade is the most notable in St Pölten, although the left-hand section was built to harmonise with the existing parts as late as 1900. The statues (from left to right) show *St Catherine below Ignatius Loyola, a guardian angel and an Immacolata*; then *St Anne* and *St Joseph*. The oldest part of the fabric (1715) in the centre may be by Prandtauer. In the church, the cupola fresco (*Christ Incarnate*, 1729) is by Paul Troger, whose work is to be found in cloisters and churches all over Lower Austria. Bartolomeo Altomonte painted the frescoes of the *Life of Mary*.

From here the **Domplatz** may be reached via Riemerplatz and Herrenplatz. It is dominated by the mid-13C **Cathedral of the Assumption** with an extremely plain façade. The effect of the elaborate interior by Prandtauer (1722–30) is therefore all the greater, a lush confection of red marble and gold, its frescoed nave sweeping impressively up to the altarpiece of the *Assumption* (Tobias Pock, 1658) surmounted by a representation of the Trinity. The rich decoration includes frescoes (1739) by Thomas Gedon in the nave (*Angels Interceding with God the Father*, the *Fall of Satan*, the *Transfiguration of St Hippolytus*, the *Triumph of the Church over False Teaching*, *Jesus with Angels*, the *Last Judgement* and the *Resurrection of the Dead*). The references to St Hippolytus are a reminder that the cathedral was originally the church of the Augustinian monastery of St Hippolytus founded here in the 11C, itself the successor to the original Carolingian foundation from which the town took its name.The erstwhile anti-pope St Hippolytus (c 170–235) was a conveniently combative figure to be celebrated by the now triumphant counter-reformatory spirit of the late Baroque. Other points of interest in the cathedral include its fine organ with the figure of *King David* (1722), and the side-walls of the nave showing scenes from the *Life of Christ* by Thomas Gedon, although his work is thought to have been the execution of a plan supplied by Daniel Gran; to the latter is attributed the *Veneration of St Hippolytus* (1746) in a left-hand side-chapel and in another, the *Flight to Egypt* (1746). Notable is the **Rosary Chapel** (to the right of the choir) with grisaille representations of the 15 secrets of the rosary (1660).

The **Diocesan Museum** (open April–Oct, Tues–Fri 10.00–12.00, 14.00–17.00, Sat 10.00–13.00, Sun 10.00–12.00) is reached through a door in the north aisle and has a collection of ecclesiastical art of some interest, beyond it being the **former convent library** with frescoes by Gran and Troger. The convent's fine Baroque stairway is by Joseph Munggenast. Before leaving the city it is worth visiting the restored **Jugendstil Synagogue** (1913) at Dr Karl Renner Promenade 22, now a centre for research into the history of the Jews in Austria (open Mon–Fri 09.00–16.00 or ring the bell at Lederergasse 12). Of somewhat earlier date is the remarkable and once controversial Stöhr-Haus at Kremser Gasse 41 (near the station) designed (1899) by Joseph Maria Olbrich, builder of the Secession in Vienna. Notable is the relief on the façade (an allegory of medicine) supplied by the Secession artist Ernst Stöhr, brother of the doctor who had commissioned the house.

Around St Pölten

East of St Pölten

Kirchstetten (reached via the St Christophen/Neulengbach exit of the A1 *Autobahn*) is some 13km east of St Pölten and was the summer home from 1957 of W.H. Auden (1907–73), who is buried in the churchyard. The **Audenhaus** is at Hinterholz 6. ☎ 027 42 200/31 04 for opening times. The village also has memorial rooms to an Austrian poet, Josef Weinheber (1892–1945), whose politics, to say the least, were rather different from Auden's (☎ 02743/89 89 to visit the Weinheber house containing the furniture he made himself). Weinheber was a devout believer in the German cultural mission and also a vernacular poet whose *Wien wörtlich* (1935), written in Viennese dialect, established his popularity. An unrepentant Nazi, he took refuge in alcohol as the fortunes of the Third Reich declined and committed suicide when the Russian army was approaching Kirchstetten in 1945. His grave is in the garden of his house.

South of St Pölten

Road 20 leads south (20km) to the **Cistercian Abbey of Lilienfeld** (open weekdays 08.00–11.00, 14.00–17.00, Sun & PH 10.00–11.00 and 14.00–17.00). Its name is taken from the biblical text concerning the 'lilies of the field' and it was founded in 1202 by Leopold VI of Babenberg, who is buried in the fine late-Romanesque abbey church. Also buried here is his daughter, Margaret of Bohemia, and the Polish mother of Friedrich III, Zimburga of Masovia. The abbey has a long and distinguished history as a centre of learning. In the early 19C one of its abbots, the Hungarian Ladislaus Pyrker (1772–1847), an admirer and promoter of Schubert and Franz Grillparzer, was himself a considerable dramatist and poet in the patriotic (*Rudolph von Habsburg, An Heroic Poem*) and lyrically introverted (*Nostalgic Songs of the Alps*) Biedermeier mode.

The monastery buildings chart the transition from Romanesque to Gothic and exhibit the lofty and spare Cistercian style which has been little disturbed by later barockisation. A beautiful 16-columned Gothic **portal** leads into the church, completed in 1263; it is the largest in Lower Austria as also the latter's first hall church, with soaring reticulated vaulting and seven vast pairs of columns dividing the main and side aisles. The side-altars are also distinctive with their pink and black cladding of Türnitz marble. The main altarpiece of the *Assumption* and those of the two lateral altars (*St Benedict* and *St Bernhard*) are by Daniel Gran (1746). The beautiful neighbouring **cloister** (1260) has stained-glass from the early 14C and a graceful well-house. To the west is the **larder** and the **dormitory of the lay brothers**, where documents relating to the Babenberg dynasty may be seen. Lilienfeld's foundation document shows the earliest seal with the characteristic 'red-white-red' arms of Austria, the origin of which lies with the crusading Babenberg margraves and dukes.

In the south wing of the monastery is a small **picture gallery** including etchings by Dürer and Rembrandt and a **library** with fine stucco, frescoes and intarsia-work (1700) by lay brothers.

In the town of Lilienfeld is a **museum** (open Thur 17.00–19.00, Sat 15.00–17.00, Sun 09.30–11.30, or by appointment: ☎ 02762 524 78) with rooms devoted to Matthias Zdarsky (1856–1940), a pioneer of alpine skiing techniques.

South-east of St Pölten

East of Lilienfeld on Road 18 is the town of **Hainfeld**. At a congress held here at the turn of the years 1888–89 the divided Austrian workers' movement was united by the efforts of Viktor Adler, and the Social Democratic Party was born.

Viktor Adler (1852–1918)

Trained as a doctor of medicine, Adler was a middle-class Jew who became increasingly dismayed by the gap between rich and poor in the Liberal Austria of the **Gründerzeit** (Founders' Period; see *History*, p 55). In his professional capacity, he witnessed at first hand the often appalling effects of rapid industrialisation on the health and life-expectancy of workers. His political orientation, which he shared with a broad spectrum of right- and left-wing opinion in Austria, was initially 'Greater German' and he was one of the signatories of the so-called **Linzer Programm** of 1882, a pan-German manifesto opposed to the cosmopolitan policy of Taaffe government and its conspicuous refusal to favour the Germans as 'the people of State' in the Empire. The manifesto was, however, cleverly exploited by a co-signatory, Georg von Schönerer, who added a specifically anti-semitic clause to an otherwise purely 'German nationalist' document, to which the subsequently eminent historian Heinrich Friedjung had also appended his signature.

Ten years later, Adler's views had matured and he was active at the Social Democrats' Brno Congress of 1899, at which demands were put forward for the transformation of the Monarchy into a democratic federal state with equal rights for all nationalities. Adler campaigned for universal suffrage as a Parliamentary Deputy from 1905 and was Secretary of State for Foreign Affairs in the provisional government set up on the collapse of the Dual Monarchy in 1918. In this position he campaigned for the incorporation of Austria in a single German state until his death in November 1918. However, his views were now more Socialist International than German National: for Social Democrats like Adler, union with Germany seemed to open the way for greater collective Socialist influence and solidarity in Europe.

His son, Friedrich Adler (1879–1960), likewise 'Greater German' and Socialist, was more radical than his father and was to become Secretary of the Second Socialist International. In 1916 he assassinated the Prime Minister, Count Stürgkh, in protest at the government's prosecution of a war of mass slaughter and the continuing suspension of civil rights due to the war emergency.

South-west of St Pölten

South-west of St Pölten at **Frankenfels** (Road 39) is a **Bergbauernmuseum** devoted to hill farming (open by appointment; ☎ 027 25 5218) and nearby the so-called **Nixhöhle**, a cave where the now disused sinter and chalk mines can be viewed on Sundays and PH between May and October. At **Puchenstuben**, just to the south in the Ötscher-Tormäuer nature reserve, is the **Treffling Waterfall** with a 300m drop, reached from the village on foot in half an hour. The **Charterhouse of Gaming** is further west on Road 25 (south of Scheibbs) and has the remains of 16C walls and a 15C church. Gaming was founded in 1330 by Duke Albrecht II (of Habsburg), who is buried here, in fulfilment of a vow following the release of his brother, Friedrich the Handsome, from imprisonment by the Bavarian Duke. It remained in Carthusian hands until its dissolution by Joseph II in 1782. Today it houses a private Catholic university seminar and a

Chopin festival is held on the premises every August. Impressive is the **Prälatensaal** with its Renaissance decoration and the library with Wenzel Rainer's frescoes of the *Seven Free Arts* (in the cupola), the *Four Evangelists* and *Fathers of the Church* (in the lunettes) and the *Four Continents* (in the pendentives). The **museum** documents the history of the period of Albrecht II , known as 'the Wise', but also as 'the Lame' (when his remains were exhumed in 1985, he was found to have suffered from advanced polyarthritis). In 1993 Karl Habsburg, grandson of the last Emperor, held his wedding reception in Gaming after his marriage to Francesca Thyssen. (Guided tours at 11.00 and 15.00 by arrangement. ☎ 07485 97290).

North and north-east of St Pölten

Some 12km north of St Pölten (S33) is the Augustinian abbey of **Herzogenburg** (open 1 April–31 Oct daily 09.00–11.00, 13.00–17.00, obligatory tours on the hour). It was built here in 1244 after the monastery's original site was endangered by the River Traisen changing its course. The buildings were barockised by Joseph Munggenast to plans by Jakob Prandtauer after 1714.

The impressive **Festsaal** and **Inner Court** were designed by J.B. Fischer von Erlach, while the frescoes above the stairway showing the *Removal of the Augustinians to their New Cloister in 1244* and the *Honouring of the Passau Bishopric* are by Bartolomeo Altomonte. The same artist was responsible for frescoes in the church: the *Martyrdom of St Stephen*, the *Apotheosis of St Augustine* and the *Martyrdom of St George*, while the marvellous *Glorification of the Church through the Holy Spirit* (1749) in the choir is by Daniel Gran. The latter also painted the main altarpiece (the *Virgin with St Stephen and St George*). Joseph Henke made the organ (1750), which bears an illusionist representation of King David.

The monastery's **art collection** contains some fine paintings including a wing-altar (1501) by Jörg Breu the Elder with depictions of the *Calvary* and scenes from the *Life of Mary*. In the **Kunst- und Wunderkammer** is a remarkable bronze Roman helmet in the shape of a facial mask (c AD 150) discovered during building work in 1972. It was probably used for ceremonial purposes and bears the stylised features of Alexander the Great, as was still customary at the time it was made.

Close to Herzogenburg is **St Andrä**, whose parish church has ceiling frescoes and an altarpiece by Paul Troger, showing *King David, St Augustine, Christ with Andrew and Peter*, the *Resurrection* and the *Holy Spirit*. At **Heiligenkreuz-Gutenbrunn** is a Baroque Schloss and a church with works by F.A. Maulbertsch at his most accomplished, including altarpieces and superb ceiling frescoes (1758: the *Virgin Mary*, the *Healing of the Sick*, the *Guardian Angel*, the *Discovery of the True Cross* and the *Assumption*). In the **Schloss** (open April–Oct, Tues–Sun, 10.00–17.00) is a Baroque picture collection including works by Troger, Maulbertsch, Wutky, Platzer, Schmidt and others.

A few kilometres to the east is **Schloss Atzenbrugg** (open Easter–26 Oct; Sat, Sun, PH 14.00–17.00) where *Schubertiads* were held by the composer's friends, the poets Schober and von Bauernfeld and the painters Kupelwieser and von Schwind.

Mostviertel and Alpenvorland

South-west of the town of Amstetten, Roads 121/122 lead to **Seitenstetten** whose **Benedictine Monastery** (guided tours daily, Easter to All Saints Day at 10.00 and 15.00, on Sun at 10.30 and 15.00) is no less charming for being off the beaten track. It has survived fires in the Middle Ages, then the Reformation (when two of the abbots turned Lutheran, the second even marrying in 1572), then Josephinism, and even the attentions of the Nazis.

The high points of the Baroque complex on which both Prandtauer and Munggenast worked is the north staircase with its ceiling fresco of the *Triumph of St Benedict* (1744) by Bartolomeo Altomonte, the **Marmorsaal** (also in the north wing) with Paul Troger's *Harmony of Faith and Virtue with the Sciences and the Arts*, and the same painter's *Revelations of St John* on the library ceiling. The church retains Gothic features despite a luxurious and occasionally clumsy barockisation between 1670 and 1706.

The **cloister** (1354) is in the northern part, as is the former **Chapter House** with a Gothic (1360) tympanum over the door showing St Peter and St Catherine, from which the Romanesque Knights' Chapel (*Ritterkapelle*) is reached, its altar possessing a late Gothic so-called *Madonna in the Mussel Shell* (1440), the iconography of which is obscure.

The **picture collection** (☎ for guided tours: 07477 42300-0) contains Gothic and Baroque works of high quality, including Paul Troger's celebrated *Mater Dolorosa* and works by Peter Breughel, Georg Raphael Donner, Francesco Solimena, F.A. Maulbertsch, and Alessandro Magnasco. Efforts have been made to re-establish the monastery garden in its original Baroque form. In 1620, under Abbot Plantz, the monks planted potatoes here for the first time in Austria (although Maximilian II's court botanist, Carolus Clusius, had obtained two tubers from America as curiosities for the Botanical Gardens in Vienna as early as 1588).

At **Schloss Ulmerfeld** south of Amstetten is an interesting collection of weapons, the earliest of which date to the Iron Age (open April, May, June, Oct, Sun and PH 14.00–17.00, July, Aug, Sept, Mon–Thur 09.00–12.00, 13.00–16.30, Fri 09.00–12.00, Sat, Sun 14.00–17.00).

Not far to the south-east is **Neuhofen an der Ybbs**, where the **Ostarrichi-Kulturhof** (open April–Nov, Tues–Fri 10.00–12.00, 14.00–16.00, Sat, Sun, PH 09.00–12.00 and 13.00–16.00), built for the millennium exhibition of Austria in 1996, has changing programmes of historical exhibitions. In a document designating territories granted to Bishop Gottschalk of Freising signed by Emperor Otto III and dated 1 November 996, the land around Neuhofen is referred to as being in *Ostarrichi*, the first recorded occurrence of the nomenclature for Austria.

Further upstream overlooking Ybbs rises the **Sonntagberg**, on whose summit (700m) the Abbott of Seitenstetten first erected a chapel in 1440, a rock on the hill having been associated with miracles since pagan times, from which its name 'Mons Salvatorius' comes. The present pilgrimage church was begun by Jakob Prandtauer and completed (1733) by Joseph Munggenast. The frescoes in the vault by Daniel Gran follow the theme of the Trinity as Divine

Revelation, beginning in the choir with *Creation* and *Paradise* scenes, in the cupola the *Glorification of the Trinity*, continuing in the nave with the *Archangel Michael joining with the Fathers of the Church and the Evangelists in the Church's Struggle against Heresy*; in the crossing may be seen the *Birth of Christ* opposite the *Holy Spirit*. Over the organ loft is *Jacob's Dream*, also by Gran. The choice of theme goes back to the relief representing the Trinity placed over the original wonder-working stone in 1614. The high altar and fine pulpit with a relief of the *Conversion of St Paul* are by Melchior Hefele of Tyrol.

Six kilometres further up the Ybbstal is **Waidhofen an der Ybbs** at the con-fluence of the rivers Ybbs and Schwarzbach and at the heart of the Eisenwurzen region, which lies between the Erlauf and Enns rivers. Its name refers to its net-work of *Eisenstraßen*, by which iron ore from the Styrian mountains was trans-ported to the Danube, and to numerous smithies that exploited local water power and deposits of coal and wood to produce weapons, tools and artefacts. The smiths (*Hammerherren*) themselves became so prosperous that they were known as the Black Counts, and a roaring barter trade of iron against necessities for the hundreds of Styrian miners flourished until the 19C. At **Ybbsitz**, east of Waidhofen, a typical former smithy may be visited (**Fahrngruber Hammer** located in the market called 'An der Noth', visits by arrangement ☎ 074 43 863 40, or 866 01-0).

Picturesque **Waidhofen** itself was celebrated by the Minnesänger Neidhart von Reuental for the high quality of its blades and it is no wonder that its motto inscribed over the Ybbstor giving on to the river reads: *ferrum chalybsque urbis nutrimenta* ('Iron and steel nourish the city'). The town has a somewhat turbu-lent past on account of its competition with Styria for imperial favour, its acri-monious divisions during the Reformation and the Turkish attacks of 1532. Thereafter the impressive **Stadtturm** of the Rathaus on the **Obere Stadtplatz** was built, the hands of its clock set permanently at 12.45, the time of the final victory over the Osman raiders. The Burg beyond the north-west end of the square dates to 1407, but was neo-Gothicised by the Ringstraßen architect Friedrich Schmidt between 1885–87 for its then Rothschild owners. The nearby **parish church** (rebuilt by 1510 with a later Baroque tower) has fine Gothic reticulated and star vaulting and a 15C wing-altar in the choir, while on the exte-rior is a noble Renaissance epitaph for the Zeysl family. The **Freisinger Berg** joins the Obere and Untere Stadtplätze; at its north-east end is a Marian Column of 1665, while on the Untere Stadtplatz are numerous attractive burgher houses of the 16C and 17C. At no. 39 the *Konditorei Piaty* has a **museum** of local peas-ant artefacts on the upper floor (accessible, by prior appointment ☎ 074 42 53 110), while the **Heimatmuseum** is on the Obere Stadtplatz at no 32 (open Easter to 15 Oct, Tues–Sat 09.30–12.00, 14.00–17.00, Sun 09.00–12.00) and documents all aspects of the region. Also worth a glance is the former **Bürgerspitalkirche** (1271) on the southern periphery of the town, with a 17C crucifixion group in the south aisle.

WIENER NEUSTADT

The influential centre of Wiener Neustadt 50km from Vienna does not seem especially welcoming and parking in the old town is difficult, but it is worth persevering. Its foundation by Leopold V of Babenberg in 1194 was partly financed by ransom money paid for the release of Richard Coeur de Lion (see p 52). It became important as an alternative Habsburg seat to Vienna, particularly under Friedrich III (1457–93), whose motto AEIOU (perhaps '*Alles Erdreich Ist Österreich Untertan*'—'The whole world is subject to Austria', but over 300 interpretations have been suggested) is encountered in various places in the city. It was in Wiener Neustadt that Ferdinand I had the Viennese mayor, Martin Siebenbürger, executed in 1522; and under Leopold I the Hungarian rebel nobles Péter Zrínyi and Franz Frangepán suffered the same fate here in 1671. The military tradition of the city is strong and in 1752 its Burg became an academy for Maria Theresia's officers (the academy, Austria's Sandhurst, still exists). In the 18C and 19C, Wiener Neustadt's industry expanded from its textiles base, its economic importance making it a prime target for Allied bombing at the end of World War II.

At the south-east of the inner city stands the former Burg, largely a post-war reconstruction, which can be visited (apply for a soldier guide at the main gate). It was in this building that the unfortunate General Benedek was court-martialled after the devastating defeat of the Austrian army by the Prussians at Königgrätz (1866). The most interesting feature is the huge **Wappenwand** (1453) on the eastern façade of St George's Church, which is incorporated into the Burg complex, a decorative relief of coats of arms, 107 in all, but only 19 of them (the hereditary lands of Friedrich III) genuine. The invented ones are a fantasy genealogy of the Habsburgs, probably taken from Leopold Stainreuter's *Austrian Chronicle of 97 Rulers*, made for Duke Albrecht III c 1385. The statue in the bottom niche represents Friedrich III. In the church, objects of interest include the bronze *St George* on the high altar (reconstructed after a thief broke it into 14 parts in 1948), the *Cherry Madonna* of 1470 on the right-hand sidealtar, the only column (with frescoes of biblical scenes) to survive the war, and a reliquary shrine (1480); also the important manneristic stained glass behind the St George altar showing the *Baptism of Christ* and (below) *Philip the Handsome*, the first Habsburg King of Spain, together with his father *Maximilian I* (who is buried under the altar), the latter's second wife *Bianca Sforza* and his first wife, *Maria of Burgundy*.

From the Burgplatz the Kesslergasse leads to the Hauptplatz with a **Marian Column**, a Renaissance **Rathaus** and a group of likewise Renaissance houses known as the **Grätzl**. To the north-west is the mostly Gothic **Cathedral of St Stephen**. The southern **Brauttor** is an interesting survival of decorative Romanesque work. On the triumphal arch inside the cathedral is a fresco of the *Last Judgement* (1300) and an altarpiece of the *Assumption* by Domenico Cignaroli. The remarkable tomb (1630) of Cardinal Khlesl, one of the more brutal protagonists of the Counter-Reformation in Austria, is the work of a follower of Bernini. The busts of apostles and prophets along the nave and the *Annunciation* (c 1500) at the crossing are attributed to Lorenz Luchsberger.

Returning to the Hauptplatz and leaving it to the east towards the Ungargasse, you reach (just to the south) the **Neukloster**, in the church of which Mozart's *Requiem* (commissioned by Count Walsegg-Stuppach as a memorial to his wife) was first performed on 14 December 1793. Martin Winter barockised most of the originally Gothic church in 1736, but there is earlier Baroque decoration in the interior, such as the pulpit (1699) surmounted by the figure of *St Bernard* and the high altar (1693) by Jakob Lindner, with its over-life-size figures of *St Peter and St Paul* and gilded statuary by Andreas Schellauf. Of the Baroque side-altars, notable is the one in honour of the plague saints by the Tyrolean, Michael Angelo Unterberger (left-hand aisle); in the right-hand aisle is a John of Nepomuk altarpiece by Paul Troger, showing saints interceding for widows and orphans. In this aisle also the **Guardian Angel Altar** shows an angel leading a child up to heaven (by Martino Altomonte), and the same artist's representation of *St Benedict presenting his order's rule to St Robert of Citeaux*. Through the prelacy door access is gained to the monastery garden with its Renaissance well, while to the left is the entrance to the area behind the high altar where the lovely **Tomb of the Empress Eleonore** (the Portuguese wife of Friedrich III) is to be found. It was made in the 1470's by the same master (Niclaes Gerhaert van Leyden) who created Friedrich's superb tomb in St Stephen's Cathedral in Vienna.

The **Wiener Neustadt Museum** (open Tues, Wed, 10.00–17.00, Thur 10.00–20.00, Fri 10.00–12.00, Sun & PH 10.00–16.00) contains a celebrated **Corvinus-Becher**, a fine example of medieval goldsmith's work, and some 14C gospels.

Around Wiener Neustadt to the south (Bucklige Welt)

The south-east corner of Lower Austria bordering on Burgenland is known picturesquely as the '*Bucklige Welt*', a delightful landscape of Alpine foothills much favoured by Austrians for their summer holidays, but less visited by tourists. The rather isolated village of **Hochwolkersdorf** is well to the east of the main Road 54 leading down to the hills, but the historically inclined might make the detour to see its **1945 Memorial Room** (open daily 09.00–12.00 and 14.00–16.00), documenting the negotiations with the Soviet Army over the peaceful surrender of Vienna at the end of World War II. Dr Karl Renner, first Chancellor of the First Republic, was brought here to negotiate Austria's future from his retreat in Gloggnitz, where he had passed the war unmolested (surprisingly, considering he was a Social Democrat, but perhaps because, as a long-standing *Großdeutscher*, he had so warmly welcomed the *Anschluß*). Further south at **Aspang am Wechsel** an enterprising local has founded an **Automobile Museum** of 120 cars made between 1888–1960, which is open Sat, Sun & PH 09.00–17.00 or by appointment ☎ 02642 52329.

To the south-west at **Kirchberg am Wechsel** is a permanent exhibition concerned with the philosopher Ludwig Wittgenstein (open by appointment ☎ 02641 2460). Between 1920–26 Wittgenstein was an elementary school teacher in this part of Lower Austria, with mixed results for his pupils and unfortunate consequences for himself. On the one hand he inspired excellence in the brighter boys, on the other his exasperation with the slower ones sometimes got the better of him. One day he struck a sickly child on the head, causing the victim dramatically to collapse. Although he was exonerated in the subsequent enquiry (the authorities apparently taking a relaxed view about hitting recalcitrant pupils and no doubt mindful of Emperor Franz I's famous dictum: 'I don't need scholars, I need obedient citizens'), Wittgenstein never returned to teaching and his initial enthusiasm for bringing education to the rural public seemed to have dissipated. Of the people of nearby Trattenbach, for instance, he wrote that they 'are not human *at all*, but loathsome worms'.

The less philosophically minded may prefer to visit the nearby stalactite cave of the **Hermannshöhle** (open April, Oct at weekends, May–Sept 09.30–16.30), which is host to 15 different species of bat.

A little to the north of Kirchberg at **Enzenreith** is a **Mining Museum** (open 23 March–1 Nov, Sat, Sun, PH 09.00–12.00, 13.30–17.00), documenting the extraction of brown coal in nearby Hart, whose mining traditions reach back to the Bronze Age. **Gloggnitz**, just to the west, is overlooked by an impressive Baroque Schloss—its ecclesiastical aspect does not deceive, it was originally a Benedictine cloister. In the town centre the **Christkönigskirche** (*Kardinal-Piffl-Pfarrkirche*), built in the 1930s, is an interesting attempt by Clemens Holzmeister to harness concrete to the cause of Christian imagery. In the **Renner Villa** (open weekends and PH 09.00–17.00, or by arrangement: ☎ 02662 42498), where the former Chancellor spent World War II (see above) is a documentation of Renner's place in contemporary Austrian history.

To the north-west of Gloggnitz is **Reichenau**, a favourite summer resort for well-to-do Viennese artists and writers at the turn of the 19C, as also for members of the imperial family. It lies in the Höllental, which separates to the northwest the two Alpine peaks nearest to Vienna, the Rax and the Schneeberg. The **Alpengarten Rax** at Reichenau (open June–Sept daily 09.00–17.00) covers 4000sq m and is home to some 200 species of alpine plant. Not far to the northwest at **Kaiserbrunn** is the interesting **Wasserleitungsmuseum** (Water Supply Museum; open May–26 Oct, Sun and PH 10.00–12.00 or by arrangement, ☎ 02666 52548). The spring here was discovered in the 16C by Emperor Karl V while out hunting; in the 19C the first long-distance water supply (1870–73) for Vienna was sourced here, the Kaiserbrunn spring being public-spiritedly donated by Franz Joseph (who owned the land around), while a similar gesture was made by the other affected landowner, Count Hoyos-Sprinzenstein.

The main road south-west from Gloggnitz leads up to the popular alpine resort of **Semmering**, the 'healthy lungs of Vienna' according to a 19C advertising slogan. The **Semmering Railway** (*Semmeringbahn*, 41km long between Gloggnitz, Lower Austria, and Mürzzuschlag, Styria) was completed in 1854, the first great feat of railway construction in the Alps. The works were directed by Karl von Ghega and provided a vital transport link between Vienna and Trieste beneath a 1000m pass in use from earliest times. A planned new tunnel below it (**Semmering Basis-Tunnel**) is controversial and has pitted two Provincial Governors (of Lower Austria and Styria), ironically also of the same political party (*Volkspartei*), against each other, Styria being strongly for the project, Lower Austria doggedly against. A ride on the old Semmeringbahn, with its mountainous curves, viaducts and tunnels, is recommended for railway buffs.

A turning off to the left just below Semmering brings you shortly to the pilgrimage church of **Maria Schutz** built on the site of a miraculous spring (now to be found trickling out of a pipe behind the high altar, where it is enthusiastically sampled by the laity). After the chapel proved inadequate to cope with the flood of pilgrims, Count Leopold von Walsegg financed a new Baroque church in 1740. The Baroque high altar framing the icon of *Madonna and Child* (dating to c 1400 but with added Baroque trappings), is the focus of the otherwise unremarkable interior.

West and north-west of Wiener Neustadt

Passing by **Miesenbach** (Road 21, then left beyond Waldegg), where a small museum is devoted to the Biedermeier painter **Friedrich Gauermann**(open Easter–26 Oct, Sat, Sun, PH 10.00–17.00), you reach the ruins of **Schloss Gutenstein**, built by the Babenbergs and the place where Friedrich the Handsome died in 1330. Matthias Corvinus, later the ambitious Renaissance King of Hungary, is supposed to have been imprisoned here in his youth (1456). At **Muggendorf**, somewhat to the north by Pernitz, the picturesque **Myrafälle** waterfall is worth the detour, at least when in full flood.

At **Berndorf** (Road 17, then left on Road 18) the iron magnate Hermann Krupp and Alexander Schoeller founded a cutlery factory in the mid-19C, and Arthur Krupp subsequently financed the building of school rooms in 12 different styles ranging from Egyptian and Byzantine to Empire and Classical. These can be visited between 13.30 and 17.00 hours on teaching days; on non-teaching days, 08.30–12.00 and 13.00–17.00. Berndorf was an early example of a modern worker settlement, the Krupps' paternalist project being similar in spirit to Lord Leverhulme's Port Sunlight. The town also has mini-arts festivals in June–July and August–September, performances being in the **Kaiserjubiläumstheater** built by the ubiquitous architect duo of the Dual Monarchy, **Hermann Helmer** and **Ferdinand Fellner**.

At nearby **Pottenstein** the parish churchyard boasts a twin-towered Romanesque charnel house. In the inn *Zum Goldenen Hirsch*, the actor playwright **Ferdinand Raimund** (1790–1836), one of the greatest figures of Viennese theatrical tradition, committed suicide in the (mistaken) belief that the dog which had just bitten him was rabid.

MARCH-DONAULAND
• • • • • • • • • • • • • • • • • • • •

South of the Danube from Vienna to Hainburg

The A4 *Autobahn* runs east from Vienna past the huge ÖMV oil refinery at Schwechat and Vienna International Airport, crossing eventually into Burgenland at Bruck an der Leitha (the boundary with Hungary until 1919), and continuing on partly newly-built *Autobahn* all the way to Budapest. Just beyond Schwechat is the ancient Danubian crossing at **Fischamend**, whose parish church has a *Last Supper* by F.A. Maulbertsch. The fortified town of **Bruck an der Leitha** is also bypassed by the motorway and contains Renaissance buildings in the centre with a town museum, as well as Schloss Prugg, a medieval castle barockised by Hildebrandt with neo-Gothic alterations in the 19C. It belongs to the once powerful Harrach family, on whose estates **Joseph Haydn** (1732–1809) was born at **Rohrau**, a few kilometres to the north-east of Bruck, where the Renaissance **Schloss Harrach** with a neo-classical façade (1777) (open Easter–Oct, Tues–Sun 10.00–17.00) may be visited. It houses the family picture collection, which reflects the average taste of the Austrian 18C nobility and includes Spanish, Neapolitan, Flemish, Dutch and French works, besides family portraits. **Haydn's birthplace** (open Tues–Sun, 10.00–17.00 all year) is in the village and contains a few objects of interest.

Joseph Haydn (1732–1809)

Joseph Haydn and his brother Michael (1737–1806, see p 289, who made a musical career in Salzburg), were descendants of a peasant and craftsman line (their father was a wheelwright). Both brothers received musical training as St Stephen's Choristers, who were the forerunners of the Vienna Boys' Choir. Joseph Haydn's training in composition continued under the influence of Johann Joseph Fux (see p 60), Johann Christian Bach and Antonio Caldara. After a period as assistant to the celebrated singing teacher, Niccolò Porpora, his career blossomed as *Kapellmeister* to the Esterházys at Eisenstadt (then *'Kismarton'*) and at their summer palace at Esterháza (now *Fertőd*) in Hungary. His visits to England in 1791–92 and 1794–95 were commercial and artistic triumphs, the composer receiving an Honorary Doctorate of Music at Oxford. Haydn also happily acknowledged the profound impression made on him by Handel's music, his great generosity of spirit in artistic matters being typically combined with commercial acumen and a quiet confidence in his genius. When Mozart tried to dissuade him from going to England on account of his ignorance of the English language, he replied serenely: 'But all the world understands my language!'

Haydn is regarded as the Nestor of the immortal triumvirate of the *'Wiener Klassik'*, which developed from his contribution through the work of Mozart and Beethoven. His output was enormous, covering every genre, including the new one of string quartets. He also composed the melody for the imperial anthem, *'Gott erhalte Franz der Kaiser'* ('God Preserve the Emperor Franz', 1797), a tune which was unfortunately later appropriated by the Germans, who turned it into their own *'Rule Britannia'* with a vulgar text (*Deutschland über alles*). Its popular setting as an English hymn is singable even by the musically illiterate.

Haydn's career spans a revolutionary period in politics as in music. He was treated as a servant by his Esterházy patrons, but as a hero by the revolutionary French occupiers of Vienna, who posted a guard of honour outside his house at Windmühle 73 (now Haydngasse 19) as he lay dying, and who buried him with full honours after a funeral in the Gumpendorfer Pfarrkirche. His phlegmatic temperament enabled him to endure with equanimity the fact that his students sold his works without telling him (he merely raised his teaching fees) and many other indignities. The only thing he could not endure was his nagging, bigoted slut of a wife, from whom he separated, and of whom he wrote with uncharacteristic venom: 'That woman was a devilish beast.'

From Rohrau it is only a few kilometres north-east to **Petronell** and the nearby Roman ruins of **Carnuntum**. The function and exact date of the impressively cyclopean **Heidentor** at Petronell (to the south of the Vienna road) remain a puzzle, but it has been suggested that it was a Roman triumphal arch or part of a ceremonial mega-tomb, erected perhaps in the 4C. Nearby is a Roman amphitheatre and to the south-east of it a circular Romanesque chapel. Carnuntum was an important *limes* garrison (larger than Vienna) and the capital of Pannonia. It was here that the successful general, Septimius Severus, was proclaimed Emperor by the legionaries in 193 (he was to die in Eburacum, i.e. York); in gratitude he subsequently raised Carnuntum to a colony. Other remains include a **Temple of Diana** and a **Burial Museum**, the so-called **Palace of Ruins**, as well as a stretch of the famous *limes* highway still showing the wheelmarks of Roman vehicles. (The **Archaeological Park** at Carnuntum is open April–Oct, daily 09.00–17.00, Sun 09.00–18.00). **Schloss Petronell** (built by Domenico Carlone in the 17C) stands perhaps where the forum was situated.

Further to the north-east towards **Bad Deutsch-Altenburg** was the legionaries' camp and there is another amphitheatre on the outskirts of the village. On the northern periphery is a Romanesque church and charnel house, together with the **Carnuntum Archaeological Museum** (open Tues–Sun, 10.00–17.00). It is located in a villa built by Friedrich Ohmann and August Kirstein after 1900, but in the style of antiquity. Its most precious exhibit is a Mithraic shrine, this religion being particularly favoured by the Roman soldiers. There is also a bust of *Julia Domina*, wife of Septimius Severus.

A short distance to the east is **Hainburg**, which retains its impressive 13C **Vienna Gate** (with knightly figures on the inner side), and sections of the old town walls. A tobacco museum is housed inside the huge gate. At Wiener Straße 9 a **Gothic synagogue** has survived, while in the adjacent main square is a Rococo **Marian column** (1749) and the **parish church of St Philip and St James** (1714). Its 57m tower (1756) was built by the noted Vienna architect, Matthias Gerl. The fountain on the square is dedicated to Joseph Haydn, who spent some of his schooldays here (1737–40). His grandfather, Thomas Haydn, was a native of Hainburg and one of those to survive the massacre of the inhabitants near the riverside **Fischertor** by the incursive Turks in 1683. Above the city is a ruined 10C castle where musical/theatrical programmes are held from June to August. From Hainburg it is a short hop across the Slovak border to Pressburg/Pozsony/Bratislava (the nomenclature depending upon whether you are a German, a Hungarian or a Slav).

North of the Danube

(*Note: These sights can also be reached by crossing the Danube at Bad Deutsch-Altenburg*). Road 3 runs east from Vienna and north of the Danube, passing through the suburb of **Aspern**, where the Habsburg Archduke Karl inflicted a significant, if costly, defeat on Napoleon's troops in 1809 (**Deutsch-Wagram** to the north was the site of a battle in the same year when Napoleon avenged the defeat at Aspern). Beyond is **Groß-Enzersdorf**, whose ruined castle was owned by the Knights Templar in the Middle Ages. **Schloß Sachsengang** a little further east stands in a park with Avar remains and a mound from which treasures were recovered, giving rise to the theory (now discredited) that it was Attila's grave. You continue eastwards past the castles at **Orth** and **Eckartsau** on the edge of the Donau-Auen National Park, set up to preserve the fauna and flora of the

Danubian flood region. Orth has a bee-keeping and Danubian fishing museum (open 15 March–15 Nov, Tues–Sat 09.00–12.00, 13.00–17.00, Sun and PH 09.00–17.00), while at Eckartsau Karl I resigned his governing powers over Hungary (having previusly done so with regard to Austria) and left for Swiss exile in 1919 (open Apr–Oct, weekends and PH; tours at 11.00 and 13.00). The Schloss was altered by J.B. Fischer von Erlach and there is a ceiling fresco by Daniel Gran (the *Gods on Olympus*).

Some kilometres north of Eckartsau is **Obersiebenbrunn** with a Schloss that belonged to Prince Eugene of Savoy converted in Baroque style (1725) by Lukas von Hildebrandt, who added a charming garden pavilion containing scenes of hunting and court life by Jonas Drentwett. Returning south to Leopoldsdorf, the minor road leads east via Lassee to another of Prince Eugene's country residences, this one (**Schlosshof**) being close to the Slovak border. Hildebrandt was at work here too, creating a magnificent hunting lodge (1729) for his patron with an equally magnificent (but now decayed) garden laid out by Dominique Girard, who worked on the garden of the Belvedere in Vienna. The Schloss passed to Maria Theresia who enlarged it (1755) and it underwent further alteration in the Josephin era. It was here that Maria Theresia first heard an opera by Christoph Willibald Gluck and was so impressed that she invited him to become her *Kapellmeister*, a decision that proved to be the beginning of the end for the rigid and by then moribund Italian opera style that had hitherto held sway at court. The restored interiors of the Schloss with rich stucco by Alberto Camesina and Santino Bussi, together with Carlo Carlone's *Holy Trinity* in the cupola of the chapel, a *Deposition from the Cross* by Francesco Solimena and other luxurious ornamentation, may be visited (open 22 March–2 Nov, daily 10.00–17.00).

A little to the south is another of Prince Eugene's properties, **Schloss Niederweiden** (open 22 March–1 Nov daily 10.00–17.00), which was built by J.B. Fischer von Erlach in 1694, originally for Count Ernst Rüdiger von Starhemberg, the defender of Vienna in the Turkish siege of 1683. In the domed rooms are illusionistic Chinoiserie frescoes by Jean Pillement. At **Marchegg** to the north of Schlosshof is a handsome ochre-coloured Schloss whose origins lie in the time of Ottakar of Bohemia (1253–78), its barockisation dating to 1733. It contains a **Hunting Museum** and an **African collection** of some repute (open 15 March–Nov, Tues–Sun 09.00–12.00, 13.00–17.00).

All these castles stand on the southern **Marchfeld**, a fertile plain intensely cultivated from earliest times. At **Dürnkrut**, on its north-eastern edge, the decisive battle establishing Habsburg hegemony in the region took place on 26 August 1278 (p 52), fought between Rudolf of Habsburg and Ottakar II of Bohemia. A small display (open May–Oct weekends and PH, 10.00–17.00) in the nearby Schloss at **Jedenspeigen** documents this portentous event. On the road between the two villages is a memorial to the battle. Eight kilometres to the south lies **Stillfried**, an area of archaeological interest since late Bronze Age. Some of the finds made here are exhibited in the local museum. In the Roman period this was the base of Marbod, chief of the warlike Germanic tribe of Marcomanni, who gave the legions endless trouble.

THE WEINVIERTEL

The area between the March-Donauland and the Waldviertel (see below) is known as the Weinviertel with good reason, since it is Austria's largest wine-producing region. Its Pannonian climate is the chief factor influencing its dry white wine, 60 per cent of which is Grüner Veltliner, but there is also increasingly Weissburgunder and Welschriesling, as well as the very palatable reds of Zweigelt and Blauer Portugieser. It is also an area where much of the country's oil and natural gas is extracted between Matzen and Gänserndorf.

Road 7 leads north-east from Vienna through pleasant rolling landscape and eventually heads into Moravia, a long-standing direct route (*Brünner Straße*) from Vienna to Brno. There are, however, few sights of major interest along the way. In the main square of **Wolkersdorf** is a provincial Trinity Column, and there is also a 13C castle where Napoleon stayed before and after the battle of Wagram (1809). Just off the main road are the villages of **Wolfpassing**, with a Baroque church of 1744, and **Pellendorf**, where the parish church has a painting by Kremser Schmidt of the *Martyrdom of St Catherine*. At **Niedersulz** (turn off the main road to the east at Schrick) is the **Weinviertler Museumsdorf** (open Palm Sunday–Nov, Mon–Fri 10.00–16.00, weekends and PH 10.00–18.00) where a reconstructed Moravian peasant house and other domestic or utilitarian buildings of the region may be seen. The **Pilgrimage Church of Maria Moos** at **Zistersdorf** has two works by Paul Troger, an altarpiece of the *Assumption* and another work for a side-altar dedicated to St Anne. In the parish church of Zistersdorf are two works by Bartolomeo Altomonte (the *Death of St Joseph* and *St Anne Teaching Mary to Read*).

Around **Prinzendorf an der Thaya**, north-east of Wilfersdorf, potatoes (then still a rarity, despite the efforts of Maria Theresia and her son Joseph to overcome the mistrust of the conservative peasantry), were planted in 1761 on the initiative of one Johann Jungblut, who had brought them from his native Holland. A small 'Potato Monument' may be seen against the wall of the parish church. In the Schloss at Prinzendorf the 'action painter' (or charlatan, according to taste) Hermann Nitsch stages his '*Orgy and Mystery Theatre*', although his use of smeared blood for artistic or quasi-religious effect has become rather passé, familiarity having dulled the capacity for official or officious indignation. **Poysdorf** is a centre of viticulture with a wine museum (open Mon, Wed–Sun, 09.00–12.00, 13.00–17.00) and a 'wine panorama route' through the vineyards makes a pleasant programme.

A minor road to the north-east from Poysdorf leads to **Herrnbaumgarten**, where there is an amusing **Nonsense Museum** (*Nonseum*—open March–Oct, weekends and PH, 13.00–18.00). The display is of 'useless inventions' or (which is not the same at all) of inventions that are no longer of use. Inventions are a sensitive subject with Austrians who talk of the *österreichische Erfinderschicksal*, meaning the fate of having their inventions ignored so often suffered by their most gifted fellow-countrymen. Good ideas were frequently considered politically dangerous by the absolutist Habsburg regime, especially under Franz I and Metternich, on the grounds that technological advance tended also to extend the freedoms of the people. At **Falkenstein** (north-west of Poysdorf) are ruins of an 11C castle which may be visited.

A turn to the south-west onto road 40 at Wilfersdorf (before you reach Poysdorf on road 7) brings you to **Mistelbach**, where a Romanesque charnel house with a sculpted frieze over the portal may be seen next to the parish church. The frieze shows two fabulous beasts fighting for the soul of mankind. The library of the **Pfarrhof** nearby, formerly part of a Barnabite cloister, contains ceiling frescoes by Franz Anton Maulbertsch assisted by Johann Bergl, an allegory of *Progress and the Fruits of Science*.

At **Asparn an der Zaya** is a **Museum of Pre-History** (open April–Nov, Tues–Sun 09.00–17.00) in the Schloss and a wine museum in the nearby Minorite cloister (open April–Oct, Sat 13.00–17.00, Sun & PH 10.00–17.00). At **Michelstetten**, 4km further west, the church has 13C frescoes in the apse (*Christ with the Four Evangelists and the Twelve Apostles*). The village also has an unusual historical exhibition of education, featuring classrooms from the 18C and 19C **Altes Schulhaus** (open April–Oct, daily 09.00–17.00). In front of the Schloss at **Loosdorf** to the north-west is an impressive Renaissance monument (1574) and the small museum has a celebrated collection of toy soldiers (14,000 in all) displayed in battle dioramas (open May–Oct, ☎ 02524 8222).

At **Hagenberg**, to the south, the church of St Giles (Aegidius) has an altarpiece by Franz Anton Maulbertsch. Returning to the main road (46), you pass the ruins of the castle at **Staatz** before reaching **Laa an der Thaya**, a town that was exposed to regular flooding of the Thaya and Pulkau rivers until their regulation in 1830. It has suffered for half a century from its proximity to the 'dead border' with Communist Czechoslovakia, but is now pulling itself up by its bootlaces. The tourist information office is in the **Alten Rathaus**, on the Stadtplatz; on the latter a medieval Roland figure that was formerly part of the pillory may also be seen. The Gothic **parish church of St Vitus** has a notable Baroque high altar (1745) by Ignaz Lengelacher showing the *Martyrdom of St Vitus*, while the church's west portal is thought to have been designed by J.B. Fischer von Erlach. There is a **Beer Museum** (open May–Oct, weekends, PH 14.00–16.00) in the **Wasserburg** (the oldest brewery in Austria commenced operations here in 1454), and another museum devoted to the South Moravian Germans who were driven from their homeland at the end of the last war (Altes Rathaus, Hauptplatz 17 April–Oct, Sun, PH 14.00–17.00).

Korneuburg, Burg Kreuzenstein, Stockerau

About 17km north-west of Vienna on road 3 (or off the A22) is the historic town of **Korneuburg**. However, its conspicuous **Rathaus** is actually a neo-Gothic edifice (1894), although the tower (which can be climbed) is original (1450). The **Augustinerkirche** (1773) has works by Maulbertsch, including the main altarpiece of *The Last Supper* (1770). Eight kilometres to the north is the 12C hilltop fortress of **Kreuzenstein**, which was destroyed on the orders of the Swedish General Torstenson in 1645. The present building is a neo-Romanesque and neo-Gothic folly (1874–1906) built by Count Johann Nepomuk Wilczek. Its **museum** is a serendipity of c 11,000 objects, including medieval works of art, paintings, furniture, musical instruments and more (open mid-March–mid-Nov, Tues–Sun 09.00–16.00).

Stockerau to the west is not now as interesting as its past. It was here that the subsequently canonised Koloman was killed in 1012. The son of a Celtic prince (possibly a Scottish King) the pilgrim Koloman was taken to be a Hungarian (some say Moravian) spy by the locals at a time when the Babenbergs were fighting to consolidate the borders of their recently acquired territories. He was tortured to extract a confession and then put to death; yet miracles kept occurring at his grave, which suggested that an unfortunate mistake had been made. His body was transferred to Melk two years later and Koloman became the patron saint of Austria until replaced in that role by Leopold of Babenberg in 1663.

West and north-west of Stockerau

Due west of Stockerau the minor road continues to **Kirchberg am Wagram**, where the workshop of a 16C alchemist may be visited in the **Alten Rathaus** (open Sat 14.00–17.00 or by arrangement. ☎ 022 79 2332). This is a unique collection of over 1000 objects discovered in the 1980s in the chapel of the neighbouring Renaissance **Oberstockstall** (now a good restaurant).

Ten kilometres before Krems is **Schloss Grafenegg**, a delightful hotel and restaurant, more especially a Romantic-style castle bearing some resemblance to Tudor Gothic. The then existing building was altered in this manner by Leopold Ernst between 1845–72, ravaged by Soviet troops after 1945, but lovingly restored subsequently. It is usually accessible between April and November and regularly hosts major exhibitions, concerts etc. The artist Johann Fischbach (1787–1871) was born at Grafenegg, which now belongs to the Metternich-Sándor family (the name however is an adopted one of the Prince von Ratibor and Corvey, a German and Polish line). North-west of Grafenegg is **Langenlois** (see p 144), the centre of the Lower Austrian wine trade, whose old squares (Holzplatz, Kornplatz) have Renaissance and Baroque houses. Two kilometres south-east is the Baroque **Schloss Gobelsburg** (open May–Oct daily 11.00–18.00, Nov–April Mon–Sat 11.00–18.00).

From Stockerau Road 4 heads north-west in the direction of Horn. At **Großweikersdorf** the parish church (1740) was built to plans by Johann

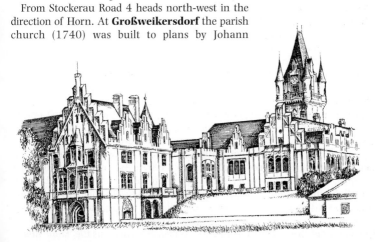

Schloss Grafenegg

Bernhard Fischer von Erlach and has an altarpiece (1734) by Martino Altomonte (the *Martyrdom of St George*).

Just before reaching Ziersdorf, a bizarre example of Austrian necrolatry is encountered at Schloss Wetzdorf by the village of **Kleinwetzdorf**. This is the extraordinary **Heldenberg** (open May–14 Sept, 10.00–18.00), a bizarre necropolis, with the busts of 142 Austrian generals arranged along a ceremonial allée. It was the brainchild of Josef Pargfrieder (a military contractor rumoured to be an illegitimate son of Joseph II) who blackmailed Field Marshals Radetzky and Wimpffen into being buried here by paying off their debts. Poor Franz Joseph, who had wanted Radetzky to be buried in the Vienna Kapuzinerkirche with the Habsburgs, was subsequently even more dismayed to receive the war profiteer's pantheon as a patriotic gift. The bottom line was that Pargfrieder's self-less donation to the nation was to be underpinned by a modest demand for 500,000 Gulden in recognition of his patriotic enterprise. The court officials were furious, but it appears that he was indeed paid a considerable sum, although the Franz Joseph Order, which he had hoped would be included in the package, was indignantly refused. However, his wishes regarding his own burial in the place of honour below the crypt of the Field Marshals were respected: steps lead down to an iron door, behind which Pargfrieder's embalmed body has been placed in a sitting position and wearing an ornate suit of armour, as befitted a man who had never seen military service. The Austrian sense of irony has been much stimulated by the Heldenberg, and has given rise to the following doggerel: '*Here lie three heroes who have paid their dues;/Two fought battles and one supplied shoes.*'

The road from Stockerau to Hollabrunn traverses the village of **Sierndorf**, in whose Renaissance and Baroque Schloss there is a chapel (recently restored) with a superb sandstone altar (1518) showing *The Annunciation*, and on the predella the *Adoration of the Magi* and *Mary with the Christ Child*, together with portraits of the founders of the chapel, Wilhelm von Zelking and his wife Margareta von Sandizell. The polychrome portraits (1516) recur on the left-hand part of the oratory above the choir, possibly the work of the great Anton Pilgram, who made the pulpit of the Stephansdom in Vienna. There are also fragments of another late Gothic altar and font (c 1520). Further on Road 303 and to the east is **Schloss Schönborn**, the present building (1717) being the work of Lukas von Hildebrandt, house architect to Friedrich Karl von Schönborn, Prince Bishop of Bamberg and Würzburg and Vice-Chancellor of the Holy Roman Empire, for whom Hildebrandt also built a palace in Vienna. The decorated **Sala Terrena** is accessible as it houses a restaurant pertaining to the golf club here, the golf course itself in the Schlosspark having been designed by an English golf professional. At the north-western edge of the park is a shrine (1733) to St John Nepomuk, also by Hildebrandt. The same master designed the Schloss and plague column at the village of **Göllersdorf** to the north. The tumulus 10km east of Göllersdorf at **Großmugl** dates to the Iron Age and (like many such tumuli in the region) has been claimed to contain the remains of Attila the Hun.

Hollabrunn, the largest town of the area, is bypassed by road S3 (E84). Four kilometres to the north of it on road 2 the village of **Schöngrabern** is reached, notable for its Romanesque sandstone parish church set in an apple orchard. On the exterior of the apse are relief figures known collectively as the '*Stone Bible*'. Low down on the south side, *The Fall* is depicted with great pathos, above the window is the visage of *God the Father* (or possibly Christ) with the *Holy Spirit* in the form of a dove, perched bizarrely above the six wine vessels of the *Marriage Feast at Cana*; to the right, a *Madonna and Child* on a lion's throne; on the left, the *Last Judgement* and *St Michael* weighing souls, *Damnation and Pride*; to the east, the *Offerings of Cain and Abel*, *God enthroned on a dragon* with (above) nuns and monks fighting evil, *Samson and the Lion*, the *fable of the wolf and a crane* (perhaps symbolising innocence); to the north the *Struggle of David* (representing mankind) *with the lion* (perhaps symbolising evil), and above it *Steadfast men and a bear-fight* (perhaps symbolising temptation). These somewhat mysterious reliefs have been the subject of numerous theories, including one which suggests that they represent gnostic beliefs, or were placed here to demonstrate repentance by the local Kuenringer Lord for the imprisonment of Richard Coeur de Lion in one of his castles. The church also has Gothic frescoes of Saints Barbara and Catherine, and one of the *Virgin Sheltering Supplicants* (on the south wall of the choir), further a monumental *St Christopher* on the north wall of the nave.

Three kilometres to the east of Wullersdorf is the **pilgrimage church of Maria Roggendorf** (Carlo Carlone, 1696), which possesses a wonder-working icon of the *Madonna* painted on leather and paintings by Kremser Schmidt of the *Crucifixion* and the *Death of St Benedict*.

To the north-east of Wullersdorf minor roads lead to **Mailberg**, with its **Malteserschloss**, since 1145 the (oldest) base of the Knights of St John in Austria, with a museum that can be visited by arrangement (☎ 02943 22 51). Near Wullersdorf was the castle where a number of Klimt paintings were stored during the war, only to be destroyed by fire shortly before its end.

Heading west from Schöngrabern, however, you shortly reach **Röschitz**, where the vintner owners of the **Ludwig-Weber-Keller** have a display of locally made reliefs of figures ranging from those of Greek mythology to Leonardo da Vinci and Kurt Waldheim (for access, ☎ 029 84 2723).

Six kilometres to the north is **Pulkau** with its celebrated **Church of the Precious Blood of Christ** (*Kirche zum kostbaren Blut Christi*), built where the Eucharistic Host is said to have bled in 1338 following desecration by the Jews, who were the victims of a pogrom here at about this time (it was not until 1988 that this 'wonder' was proclaimed an invention). The church contains a fine wing altar of 1515 by a master of the Danube School (perhaps Niklas Breu). The wings show *Christ's Calvary*, together with the *Deposition from the Cross* and *Entombment*, while the over-life-size carved figures of the shrine represent *Sts Bartholomew and Sebastian with Christ as Man of Sorrows*. On the south side of the choir is a likewise Gothic relief of the *Death of Mary*.

Standing nearby in a hilltop cemetery studded with cypresses is the **parish church of St Michael** with its Romanesque tower. Likewise Romanesque are the columns with cubiform capitals of the triumphal arch of the interior, and the columns in the sacristy, whose capitals are decorated with reliefs of fabled beasts. The church's Baroque organ by Martin Jeßwanger is impressive, as also is the Renaissance tabernacle. In the cemetery is an imposing Romanesque charnel house surrounded by cypress trees. Above the Romanesque base rise Gothic gables with water-spouts; on the points of the arches are statues including (perhaps) those of the commissioners, Count Dewin of Hardegg and his wife Wilbirgis. In the interior is a ribbed vault, on the keystone of which is a relief figure of Christ.

South of Pulkau is **Eggenburg** whose **Krahuletz-Museum** (open April–Dec 09.00–17.00) documents the pre-history of the region through fossils found on the territory of the Eggenburg Sea that existed 22 million years ago. They include a crocodile and large aquatic mammals. The white stone of Eggenburg is renowned in the area and was used extensively by the builders of the Baroque age for Melk, St Florian, the Belvedere in Vienna and elsewhere. The patrician houses of the main square are impressive, especially the **Gemalte Haus** (Painted House) on the corner with Kremser Straße with sgraffiti of antique and biblical subjects. The **parish church of St Stephen** (apply to the Pfarrhof at Pfarrgasse 6 or Frau Kugler at Kirchengasse 6, Mon–Fri 08.00–12.00, Fri only 15.00–18.00) has a superb stone pulpit (1515) featuring relief portraits of the church fathers, as well as a Gothic fresco in the side-aisle of *The Last Judgement* (1520) and a wing-altar (1521) showing *Sts Elizabeth and Mary Magdalene* below a *Coronation of the Virgin*, on the predella *Pope Urban* and *St Goar,* the Rhineland patron of the vintners.

The way north-east of Pulkau to **Retz** (ravaged by the Hussites in 1425 but recovering to become a prosperous market town) passes through Schrattenthal with its fortified castle and chapel of 1453. The attractive **main square** of Retz has a tourist information office, from which start the tours of its great wine cellar (daily May–Oct 10.30, 14.00 and 16.00, March, April, Nov, Dec Mon–Sat 14.00, Sun, PH 10.30, 14.00). Three levels of wine cellar stretching over 20km, of which 1km are visited, are enlivened with pictures and objects illustrating the history of local viticulture. In the late 18C some 5.5 million litres of wine were stored here. Note also the **Sgraffitohaus** (1576) on the main square, whose façade is entirely covered with scenes from Greek mythology and the Old Testament, as well as the 'Ages of Man' symbolised by animals. On the north side of the square is the **Verderberhaus** (1580) with a turreted parapet giving it a look of the Venetian Renaissance. Also on the square is a pillory of 1561, a plague column of 1680 and a Trinity Column of 1774 (by Jakob Barth) and two fountains that spouted wine at Harvest Festival. In the western central part of the square is the towered (1572) and galleried (1617) former **Rathaus**, which houses the City Museum (open Easter to All Saints day, Sun and PH, 10.00–12.00).

Windmill, Retz

On the north-eastern edge of the old town is the **parish church of St Stephen**, barockised by Jakob Prandtauer in 1728, whose high altarpiece depicts the martyrdom of the church's patron (a work by Leopold Kupelwieser, 1852), and which also has a painting of *St Augustine* by Martino Altomonte in the crossing. The **Dominican Church** is at the opposite side of town to the south-west, and has a Gothic tympanum relief over the main entrance that shows Mary as Queen of Heaven with the church's founders kneeling at her feet. The interior contains little of note, other than Kremser Schmidt's left-hand side-altarpiece of *St John of Nepomuk*. On the calvary hill outside the town stands a picturesque windmill (1772), disused since 1927, but with machinery pre-served (☎ 02942 2700).

North-west of Retz road 30 leads to the Baroque Schloss of **Riegersburg**, built in the 1730s for Sigmund Friedrich von Khevenhüller by Franz Anton Pilgram (a pupil of Hildebrandt), to whom it owes its graceful façade. The interior is not especially remarkable, except for the kitchens preserved with working systems of some ingenuity and the permanent exhibition of European furniture arranged by the Museum of Applied Art in Vienna. A dog cemetery in the adjoining park is another peculiarity.

The Schloss is open daily from April–Nov, 09.00–17.00, in July and Aug on Wed until 19.00. You can buy a combined ticket to include nearby **Burg Hardegg** on the Czech border. Like Riegersburg, Hardegg is technically in the Waldviertel region, a finger of which extends here. The partially accessible fortress is dramatically situated on a crag overlooking the hamlet of Hardegg and the sunken, wooded valley of the swift-flowing River Thaya at the confluence with its tributary, the River Fugnitz.

Burg Hardegg

The castle has been owned by many different families since its construction in the 12C. The chief interest of the interior lies in the permanent (and rather dusty) exhibition concerning the tragic Maximilian of Mexico (1832–67), Franz Joseph's ill-fated brother who was installed on the Mexican throne by Napoleon III and executed in the subsequent revolution. The 19C owner of the Schloss (again a Khevenhüller) had been Maximilian's adjutant throughout the unfor-tunate Emperor's three-year rule. In the village church below is a cross carved from the wooden fittings of the *Novara*, in which Maximilian sailed to Mexico and in which his remains were brought back. The Gothic frescoes in the church show the *Last Judgement* and the altarpiece (1785, by Joseph Winterhalter) depicts the *Apotheosis of St Vitus*, to whom the church is dedicated.

Stift Geras

While you are in the area, it makes sense to include the Premonstratensian Monastery of Geras in your itinerary (road 30, south-west of Riegersburg). Geras is open May–Oct. Guided tours Tues–Sat at 10.00, 11.00, 14.00, 15.00, 16.00; Sun at 11.00, 14.00, 15.00, 16.00. The monastery dates to the 12C but was completely rebuilt in 1625 after the Protestant Bohemian army had destroyed it five years earlier (it had already suffered repeated Hussite attacks). Between 1736 and 1740 Joseph Munggenast rebuilt it in Baroque style, the so-called **Neugebäude**. In the **Marmorsaal** are frescoes by Paul Troger of the *Marriage Feast at Cana*, the *Meal with the Pharisees* and the *Feeding of the Five Thousand* (a reminder that this was the summer refectory). In the Prelacy is the **Paul-Zimmer** with paintings (1770) by a Troger pupil (J.N. Steiner) celebrating the *Life of St Paul* and adjacent is the so-called **Weiße Zimmer** with elaborate stucco and reliefs showing, among other things, the victory of Christendom over the Turks. The frescoes in the library are by Josef Winterhalter, a collaborator of Maulbertsch. In the vault of the **Stiftskirche** are frescoes by Troger's pupil, Franz Zoller, illustrating the *Loretan Litany* (encomia of the Virgin Mary in her various manifestations).

The colourful Rococo decoration of the church overlays Romanesque and Gothic features. On the high altar is a late-Gothic icon (1520) with an altarpiece of *St Norbert* (the Order's founder), perhaps by Bartolomeo Altomonte. The church's fine Baroque portal (1655) is flanked by statues of *St Norbert* and *St Augustine*. A feature of the monastery are its famous fishponds established in 1664 (the oldest of their kind in Europe) and consisting of 32ha of stone basins pullulating with carp. Opposite the main entrance to the monastery buildings is a charming herb garden laid out by a Premonstratensian monk who had lived for a number of years in China and whose herbal expertise earned him the affectionate sobriquet of *Kräuterpfarrer* ('Herb-Priest').

Ten kilometres to the south is Pernegg, once a convent, then a dependency of Geras, until its dissolution under Joseph II. Its Gothic church has fine stellar vaulting (1520) with painted fields showing angels with musical instruments.

THE WALDVIERTEL

The Lower Austrian plateau 'above the Manhartsberg', described in ancient documents as *silvia nortica* or 'Northern Forest', suffered a faltering economy, emigration, and unemployment during the years of the Cold War owing to its relatively long 'dead' border with the Czech Republic. Even its promising name is a legacy of forests which are now diminished, and what remains has been badly affected by former Eastern Bloc air pollution and acid rain. Through the northwest of the area runs the watershed for the Elbe and the Danube, dividing the rivers of Central Europe flowing north from those that flow east and south.

The **Waldviertel** can be approached via the picturesque and winding **Kamptal** from **Langenlois** (north of Krems an der Donau, see p 164), a centre of the wine trade providing a living for 800 vintners. There is a museum (open May–Oct, Tue–Sun 10.00–12.00) in the Rathausstraße at no. 9 whose display deals with the stone-age hunter-gatherers of the Kamptal, and the central market squares (named after their principal trades of wood and corn) have some fine Renaissance and Baroque houses. The late-Romanesque parish church has an altar dating to 1500 showing *Sts Barbara, Catherine and Dorothea*. The missing side-panels have been supplied (1964) by a contemporary artist, Helmut Kies, and show scenes from the *Life of St Lawrence*. Good views may be had from the ruined 13C castle at **Kronsegg** 7km to the north-west, while gardeners may be interested in the **Arche Noah garden** at nearby **Schiltern** (open June–Sept, Sat, Sun 14.00–18.00), which has 1000 different plant species.

Passing by the 12C **Schloss Buchberg**, owned by the well-known historian of modern art, Dieter Bogner (whose collection of Constructivist works is accessible only to serious students in summer on application) you reach the market town of **Gars**. It is overlooked by the ruins of a formidable castle associated with the Babenbergs, where open air performances attract opera fans in summer. The 13C–15C **Gertrudskirche** has interesting features, including a *pietà* from 1420, fine net vaulting in the Johanneskapelle and three Gothic windows in the choir showing scenes from the *Life of John the Baptist* and of the church's patron, *St Gertrud of Nivelles* (only accessible with a tour). Gars was a summer resort for the Viennese during the Dual Monarchy, attracting among others Franz von Suppé, who composed his *Boccaccio* here. The Secession architect Josef Hoffmann was a co-designer of a house at Weisengasse no. 179 in the villa quarter.

Around Horn

Rosenburg

The two most significant sights of the Waldviertel region are close to Horn. The stunning Schloss Rosenburg was first mentioned in documents of 1175 and in the mid-16C was the base of the local Lutherans, when owned by Sebastian Grabner and his brother Leopold. The latter's chaplain, Christoph Reuter, and the theologian David Chyträus, who was a follower of Melanchthon, put the organisation of the Lutheran church in Austria on a statutory basis which was recognised by Maximilian II, although this was largely because the Emperor needed money from the Protestant nobility to prosecute the Turkish war. Under Leopold's son, Sebastian, Rosenburg was extended (1593–97) to become a great Renaissance Schloss, much of which survives. Between 1604 and 1611 the castle was the base for the Protestant 'Horner Bund' in its resistance to the Viennese court. The storming of Rosenburg by the Protestants in 1619, after it had fallen to imperial forces, and

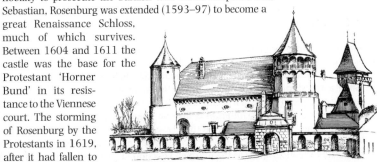

Schloss Rosenburg with the Turnierhof

its reconquest the following year by Count Bouquoy, were particularly bloody incidents which are recalled in a famous folksong '*Es liegt ein Schloss in Österreich*'. After the Thirty Years War, however, Rosenburg became a centre of the Counter-Reformation under Joachim Freiherr von and zu Windhag, who toured the Waldviertel villages (1652–54) with Abbot Benedikt of Altenburg 'persuading' some 40,000 peasants to return to Catholicism.

The castle (visits with an obligatory tour are possible between April–Nov, daily from 09.00–17.00) has been in the possession of the present owners, the Hoyos-Sprinzensteins, since 1681, the Hoyos being nobles of Spanish origin. Count Ernst lavishly restored the castle in the 1860s and 1870s. Highlights include the great **Turnierhof** flanked by columned arcades and the **library** with a superb coffered ceiling and painted panels of mythological scenes, the **conference room** with a fine Renaissance fireplace and pine panelling, the **oratorium** with a *Coronation of the Virgin* (1493) by the Viennese master of the Schottenstift (but much restored), the **lecture room** with busts of Roman emperors and the **Prehistoric Collection** of artefacts that have been found in the Horn area. A special attraction is the fascinating **falconry display** that takes place daily at 11.00 and 15.00 (also featuring fanfares and medieval costumes) during the summer.

Stift Altenburg

Close to Rosenburg is the Benedictine Altenburg, one of the loveliest abbeys in Austria and particularly notable for the paintings of Paul Troger, who lived and worked here for many years. The monastery is open from Easter Sunday to All Saints Day with obligatory guided tours at 10.30, 14.00 and 15.00; Sun and PH at 11.00 and 14.00.

The Baroque buildings that rise on the Romanesque and Gothic remains of a cloister destroyed by the Swedish armies in 1645 is mostly the work (1730–43) of Prandtauer's pupil and nephew, Josef Munggenast. Notable is the **crypt**, painted by pupils of Troger with grotesqueries representing the vanity of life and the inevitability of death, the salutary effect of which is by no means diminished by the weeping caryatids around the entrance. The **library** above has marbled columns, whose surfaces seem to reproduce the appearance and texture of bubbling blue waters. The frescoes are by Troger: in the first and third cupolas *Theology, Justice, Philosophy* and *Medicine* are allegorically represented, while in the main cupola is a depiction of the *Queen of Sheba before Solomon*. The library's lobby has representations (presided over by Chronos) of the four continents, the four seasons, the four periods of the day (indicated by putti with diverse coloured drapery), the four elements and the four characteristics of man (Johann Zeiller, 1742). The oval church is uniquely rich in Baroque ornament with pink and grey pilasters, blue pendentives and gilt capitals. Its crowning glory is Troger's cupola fresco, cunningly lit by oval windows at the side and a lantern at the centre, which represents the *Revelation of St John the Divine*. It is full of astonishingly vivid details, such as (at the western end) a dragon (representing evil) spewing fire at a fleeing angel (representing the persecuted church). The altarpiece of the *Assumption* is also by Troger. A grand marble staircase (**Kaiserstiege**) climbs beneath another Troger fresco (1738) of the *Harmony between Religion and Science* (which could stand as the leitmotif of the whole monastery's iconography) to the marbled **Festsaal** (1730) with a ceiling fresco, again by Troger, of *Apollo as Sun-God*.

A few kilometres to the west near Röhrenbach is the Renaissance **Schloss Greillenstein** (1590), which may be visited between April and Oct daily, 09.30–17.00 (to 18.00 in July, Aug), the seat of the Kuefstein family since the 16C. In the 18C it was barockised and given its imposing entrance flanked by obelisks. The unusually interesting tour includes the room where the local court of justice sat and a Renaissance bath.

The important town of **Horn** to the east was known as the 'Protestant Rome of the Waldviertel' during the Reformation and the base for a Protestant League (1608) of 166 nobles in opposition to the Habsburg overlord, Archduke (later Emperor) Matthias. It returned to Catholicism and experienced a cultural and economic boom between 1628 and 1659 under Count Ferdinand Sigmund Kurz. The **Höbarth- und Madermuseum** (open Palm Sunday to All Saints, daily 09.00–12.00, 13.00–17.00) has a display of pre-historical artefacts and curiosities including a mammoth's tusk, while the **Mader** section deals with the history of local agriculture. The **Piarist Church** (1660) has an altarpiece by Kremser Schmidt (1777, *St Anthony of Padua*) and fine decorative carpentry of scrollwork and acanthus (1723) in the choir by Matthias Fries of Colmar. The late Gothic **Church of St George** (1593) has a four-turreted tower strongly reminiscent of the tower of the Týn Church in Prague's Staroměstské Náměstí, and was in fact added in imitation of the latter in 1880. Like the Týn Church, which was long in the hands of the Utraquists, moderate Hussites (as opposed to the more radical Taborites), St George was a Protestant church for some time after its consecration. The **parish church of St Stephen** on the edge of town possesses a decorative pulpit of 1500 and attractive 14C cross-vaulting, as well as 17C epitaphs. Next to the Schloss in the south-east corner is the **Landgericht** (1591) with two tiers of arcaded galleries. On the main square, the **District Court** at no. 3 has sgraffiti dating to 1583.

Situated prominently on the Molderberg a few kilometres south-east of Horn on road 303 is the **pilgrimage church of Maria Dreieichen**, built after 1744 by a pupil of Munggenast at the instigation of Abbot Placidus of Altenburg and the local grandee, Count Hoyos. It boasts a superb cupola fresco (1752, *The Trinity, Church Fathers and Saints*) by Paul Troger. The 'Three Oaks' which gave the church its name, and marked the spot where a wax icon of the Virgin had stood, are depicted above the *pietà* (1680) by Matthias Sturmberger on the main altar.

Road 4 leads north of Horn to the Abbey of Geras (see p 144), from which Schloss Riegersburg and Burg Hardegg can be reached (p 143). North-west of Geras (road 4) is **Drosendorf**, the upper part of the village strikingly situated on an outcrop overlooking the (here meandering) River Thaya.

From here, leaving to the south the dramatic ruins of the border fortress of **Kollmitzgraben** containing a display about the topographer G.M. Vischer (1628–96), you approach **Raabs an der Thaya** some 3km to the west. Its rambling castle (originally 11C, rebuilt in the 16C), was the scene of violent clashes between Protestants and Catholics during the Counter-Reformation. The **Rittersaal** has early 17C frescoes and in the courtyard is a well plunging to a depth of 70m. The castle may be visited March–Nov, daily 10.00–18.00.

West of Raabs is **Waidhofen an der Thaya**, a centre of the textile industry reached via **Karlstein**, in the castle of which the entire general staff of the Montenegran army was interned during World War I. A subsequent involuntary guest was the Communist leader of Hungary's short-lived Republic of Councils, Béla Kun. Waidhofen's **parish church of the Assumption** has an ornate interior, the high point of which are the ceiling frescoes by J.M. Daysinger which show the *Life of the Virgin Mary*. The statues of the high altar are of *St Carlo Borromeo and St Leopold*, while in the choir are two further works by Daysinger, the *Mission of the Apostles* and the *Last Supper*. The carved group of *Mary and the Christ Child* on a side-altar dates to 1510 and the icon with the same theme in the Marienkapelle to a century earlier.

At **Groß Siegharts** south-east of Waidhofen is a castle dating to the 12C, whose chapel contains Baroque frescoes by Carlo Carlone. It is possible to visit, despite the fact that it is now the seat of the local council (open Mon–Fri 15.00–16.00, Sun, PH 10.00–12.00 and 14.00–16.00). Also of interest is the **Textile Museum** (open May–Nov, Sun and PH 10.00–12.00 and 14.00–16.00), showing the rise of the local industry on the initiative of Count Ferdinand von Mallenthein, who became the lord of Groß Siegharts in 1681. His ambitious and socially engaged plans (he even set up social housing for his workers) eventually came to nothing because Emperor Karl VI buckled to English mercantilist pressure and fatally agreed to dissolve the Empire's Ostend Trading Company, a vital channel for exporting the town's textiles; (in return the Emperor got entirely worthless 'recognition' of his famous Pragmatic Sanction, supposedly assuring the Habsburg succession in the female line). However, the outlines of Count Mallenthein's great enterprise survived and in the 19C Groß Siegharts' now automated textiles industry had some success. Mallenthein called on the Milanese Donato Felice d'Allio (who worked on Klosterneuburg for Karl VI) to build the generously proportioned **parish church**, which also has ceiling frescoes (1727, including a fine *Assumption*) by Carlo Carlone.

The Renaissance **Schloss Schwarzenau** (open May–Oct with daily guided tours), a few kilometres south of Waidhofen off road 303, is noted for its superb stuccoed interiors by Giovanni Battista d'Allio. Among the themes of the ornamentation are the *Four Seasons*, the *Cardinal Virtues* and the *Triumph of Light over Darkness*, besides freemasonry symbols. In the sumptuous chapel, which is also filled with Counter-Reformatory imagery, d'Allio's life-sized representations of the apostles occupy the side-wall niches. The west wing of the castle (1592) is inspired by Michelangelo's façade for the Palazzo Farnese in Rome.

Gmünd and surroundings

The attractive border town of Gmünd makes a good base for exploring the central and western Waldviertel. The town takes its name from the confluence (*am Gemünde*) of the Lainsitz and Braunau rivers and was established as a border point between Bohemia and Austria by Friedrich Barbarossa in 1179. It has a discouraging past, having been overrun at different times by Hungarians, Hussites and others, as well as suffering the usual natural disasters of fire and plague, and even managing to be struck by a meteorite in 1403. In 1919 it lost its western districts, and with them the railway terminus and workshops, to Czechoslovakia.

In the main square is the free-standing **Rathaus**, and at Stadtplatz 34 is the **Town Museum**, also devoted to glassmaking and quarrying, (open May–Sept, Mon–Fri 09.00–12.00, 13.00–17.00, weekends 09.00–12.00) which documents the history of settlement in the Waldviertel. Around the square are characteristic Renaissance houses with sgraffito decoration (especially attractive is no. 33 with mythological scenes). The **parish church** has frescoes from the 14C and 15C (*Madonna and Child, Sts Lawrence and Stephen*) and was extended in the 1980s following plans made just before his death by Clemens Holzmeister. The much altered Schloss at the western end of the town belongs to a branch of the Habsburgs.

North-east of Gmünd is the conservation area of the **Blockheide-Eibenstein**, an 'ur-landscape' featuring so-called *Wackelsteinen* (literally: 'wobbling stones'). Further north-east on Road 30 is the massive **Burg Heidenreichstein** (open April–Oct, guided tours Tues–Sun at 09.00, 10.00, 11.00, 14.00, 15.00 and 16.00) with walls 4m thick in places, originally the property of the Counts of Raabs-Litschau, but with many subsequent owners, including the Habsburgs in the 13C and 14C. Unlike neighbouring castles it was never attacked, its conical towers and battlements evidently presenting a sufficiently visible deterrent to would-be besiegers. On the outskirts of the settlement is an interesting **Moor and Peat Museum** (open 26 April–Oct, Fri, Sat Sun and PH 14.00–16.00, July–Aug also Wed) which is devoted to the ecology, fauna and flora of the Upper Waldviertel.

South-west of Gmünd is **Weitra**, formerly a stronghold of the Kuenringer, later of the Habsburgs, and passing to the family of the current owners of Schloss Weitra (Fürstenberg-Heilgenberg) in 1605. The town has been a centre of brewing since a 1321 privilege was received from Friedrich the Handsome, at one time having 36 breweries within the town walls, and now boasting Austria's smallest, the **Brauhotel** on the north-east corner of the main square. To the left of the latter is a Renaissance sgraffito house (no. 4) with scenes from Livy's Roman history on the upper storey, beneath which are the 'Ten (*sic*) Ages of Man', each symbolised by an animal. Off the street just to the west of the Rathaus is a curiosity in the form of a Gothic **cistern** embedded in the rock-face and fed from the well of the house above (if not open, obtain a key from the Tourist Information Bureau). It is supposed that this was one of many similar refuges hacked into the hillsides at the time of the 15C Hussite raids.

To visit the **Holy Ghost Church** (*Spitalskirche*) on the other side of the river, the key must be obtained from Gasthof Stenzel—an inconvenience that is worth the effort—to see the 14C frescoes of the *Adoration of the Magi*, the *Vision of the Shepherds*, *Sts Christopher and Catherine*, and the *Legend of St Elisabeth*, as well as unusual didactic verses in Gothic script. Further along the river to the north is the **Textile Museum** (in der Brühl 12. Open May–Oct, Tues–Sun and PH, 10.00–12.00, 14.00–17.00). Returning to the city centre, you enter the **parish church of St Peter and St Paul** to the north of the main square; it contains an unusual **Holy Cross Chapel** with a Baroque altar consisting of a baldachin and volutes resting on gnarled oaken supports. The Renaissance **Schloss** (1606) (open May–Oct, Wed–Sun and PH 09.30–17.30) to the south of the square is attributed to Pietro Ferrabosco, one of the Hofburg architects in Vienna, and has beautiful tiered arcades around the central courtyard, as well as idiosyncratic Baroque chimneys. The neo-Rococo **Schlosstheater** (1885) is ornamented with gilded papier mâché. The small **museum** is also of interest and there are fine views from the tower.

Four kilometres to the south is to be found a Gothic hall church at **St Wolfgang** with a finely carved retable (1694) by a local master, Balthasar Dreyer, among several unique features of which are the hollowed columns consisting of interwoven acanthus decoration. Remarkably, this graceful Baroque framework has been placed at the service of the three late-Gothic polychrome figures (1490) in the central niches with gilded acanthus frames, *St Wolfgang* (centre), *St Erasmus* (left) and *St Nicholas* (right), thus creating a rare harmony between the style languages of the Gothic and Baroque ages. The main Road 41 continues south-west over the border to Freistadt in Upper Austria (see p 284).

From Weitra a secondary road leads south-east to **Zwettl** at the south-west tip of the massive **Truppenübungsplatz Allensteig** (15,000ha), a legacy of Hitler whose grandmother was born here. In 1938 he declared that the former Döllersheimer Ländchen should henceforth be a military exercise area and 6800 inhabitants of 42 settlements were summarily removed. Although the exercise ground was reduced after the war, the Second Republic has not seen fit to reverse Hitler's edict; former inhabitants and their families must content themselves with a yearly wake in the renovated Gothic church at Döllersheim on All Saints' Day (1 November).

Central Waldviertel

The town of **Zwettl** lies in a basin where the River Zwettl joins the Kamp and was another stronghold of the Kuenringer, who built a fortress overlooking the 'bright valley' (Slav *svetlá dolina*, the origin of the place name), where a settlement grew up and prospered, receiving a town charter from the Babenbergs in 1200. Despite destruction of the Burg by Friedrich the Valiant in revenge for a revolt in which the Kuenringer were involved, and despite attacks by Hussites (1427), Hungarians (1486), revolting peasants (1595), Swedish troops in the Thirty Years War and finally Napoleonic troops, Zwettl (with its defensive walls and towers) remained an important trading and administrative town, which included producing a popular beer.

On the north side of the main square the **Alte Rathaus** has 16C sgraffiti with scenes from the Old Testament and The Revelations, and a **museum** on the first floor (open May–Oct Fri 14.00–17.00, Sat, Sun, PH 10.00–12.00, 14.00–17.00 in summer also Tues–Thur 14.00–17.00). It includes material on a political forerunner of Hitler, Georg Ritter von Schönerer of Rosenau (see p 152). A greater contrast to the arid *Weltanschauung* of Schönerer could hardly be found than that of the playful post-modernist Friedensreich Hundertwasser, who designed the colourful well-head on the main square. A feature of the adjacent **Dreifaltigkeitsplatz** is the plague column erected in 1727. The Landstraße contains fine Baroque houses and leads down to the 16C **Pernerstorferhof** (a tower) at no. 65. The Hamerlingstrasse leads from the centre towards a Renaissance **Gasthof**, '*Zum goldenen Stern*' (1590) beyond the city walls. Of the town's three churches, that to the south on the Propsteiberg dedicated to St John the Evangelist is the most interesting with its adjacent Romanesque charnel house.

Stift Zwettl

The Cistercian monastery of Stift Zwettl (tours of the monastery take place May–Nov, Mon–Sat at 10.00, 11.00, 14.00, 15.00; Sun 11.00, 14.00, 15.00, also 16.00 from July–Sept) in the Kamp Valley nearby (3km north-east) was founded by Hadmar von Kuenring. Its graceful 90m church tower (Josef

Munggenast/Matthias Steinl, 1727), made of grey gran-ite from the Waldviertel and decorated with Baroque statuary, is the first thing that strikes the visitor. It sits like a candle in a centrally convex façade, which in turn rises harmoniously from three portals at the base, those to the left and right supplying a concave counterpoint to the main door at the centre. Perched over the clock on the elegant lantern is a gilded statue of *Christ the Redeemer* with a cross (Johann d'Ambrosy, 1727). Below it are obelisks and trophies, located just above the Archangels Michael and Gabriel placed on the lateral volutes. A statue of *St Bernard of Clairvaux* occupies the niche above the central portal, and below him are *Hadmar I* and *Hadmar II* of Kuenring, founders of the monastery. The richly decorated **interior** of the church con-tains Baroque altarpieces by several leading mas-ters, including Martino Altomonte (the *Holy Family*), Paul Troger (*Mary Magdalene, St Peter and the three Archangels*), Kremser Schmidt (*St John* and *St Paul*), Matthäus Jacob Pink of Prague (*Sts Erasmus and Blasius*) and Johann Bergmüller (a mysti-cal depiction of the *Adoration of the Three Kings*). Munggenast designed the beautiful high altar executed and elaborated by Josef Matthias Götz of Passau, which combines the foundation legend of the monastery (in the green oak setting for the crucifix) with an ecstatic rendering of the *Assumption of the Virgin Mary*, together with Götz's lime-wood carvings of the Twelve Apostles.

The church tower at Zwettl

This Baroque lushness is miraculously integrated into a Gothic framework of which the ambulatory by Master Johannes (c 1348) is the most impressive aspect. Gothic treasures feature also in the side-altars, the oldest being the **Bernhardi altar** (1500) in the southern side-chapel of the crossing, showing the *Virgin flanked by St Bernard and St Benedict*. Its panels were painted by Jörg Breu the Elder of the Danube School and show scenes from the life of St Bernard. Other notable aspects of the church include the walnut choir-stalls with marquetry, the dramatic representation of St Alberich receiving the Cistercian cloak from the Virgin Mary, and a magnificent Baroque organ (1731) by Johann Egedacher. Adjacent is a beautiful transitional **cloister** (1204–17) with an adjoining Baroque lavabo (1706), and a **chapter-house** (c 1180) having a remarkable Romanesque column at its centre, from which spring four ribs that divide the room harmoniously into four parts. The column is usually interpreted as a symbol of Christ as the Tree of Life.

Unfortunately the tours do not always include the **library** with frescoes by Paul Troger, and the **refectory**; but they do include the **dormitorium** with its **necessarium** utilising the rushing stream below, which is claimed to be the old-est surviving latrine in Europe.

The ancient **Dürnhof**, formerly an agricultural dependency of the Stift, has an interesting **museum** devoted to the relationship between bodily health and environmental or meteorological conditions (open May–Oct, Tues–Sun 10.00–17.00).

Nine kilometres west of Zwettl is the attractive **Schloss Rosenau** (open daily 09.00–17.00, including the Freemasonry Museum) whose present aspect dates to 1736–47, when the existing Renaissance castle was barockised by Count Leopold Christoph von Schallenberg with advice from Joseph Munggenast. The walls of the Salettl (a sort of miniature belvedere or tower) above the main entrance (and reached by a graceful stairway) are covered with illusionist architectural motifs (classical, medieval and imaginary), the work of an Italian painter, Giovanni Rincolin. In the other rooms are frescoes (1746) by Daniel Gran, who also decorated the cupola of the elegantly stuccoed Schlosskapelle (1740). Rincolin's frescoes mentioned above have also been interpreted in masonic terms, Rosenau having hosted a freemasons' lodge at the time of the Enlightenment. On the first floor of the south wing is a **Freemasonry Museum**, of considerable interest. In 1868 the Rosenau was acquired by Matthias von Schönerer, the newly ennobled builder of the pioneering Vienna-Gloggnitz railway (1840), and earlier of the horse-drawn railways between Linz and Budweis (1832) and between Linz and Gmunden (1835). More famous, or notorious, was his disagreeable son, Georg Ritter von Schönerer (1842–1921), from 1879 the (Protestant convert) leader of the *Großdeutsch* faction in Austrian politics and an indiscriminate hater of Habsburgs and Austrian patriots, as also of Catholicism and Liberalism. His anti-semitism (an inspiration for Hitler) began close to home with a campaign to keep the Rothschilds out of railway financing in Austria, but soon grew into a generalised racial campaign. Jewish journalists were a particular bugbear. When the *Neues Wiener Tagblatt* prematurely reported the death of Emperor Wilhelm I of Germany in 1888, an enraged Schönerer and his thugs invaded the editorial offices. He was subsequently sentenced to prison for assault.

Fifteen kilometres south-west of Zwettl is the romantically situated **Burg Rappottenstein** (open May–Sept and over Easter, Tues–Sun, guided tours at 10.00, 11.00, 14.00, 15.00, 16.00 and 17.00). Overlooking the Lesser Kamp River, it was originally (1176) a Romanesque Kuenring castle named after one Rapoto von Kuenring, but was subsequently altered in Gothic and Renaissance styles. Notable are its well-preserved **Gothic frescoes** in the Banqueting Hall,

The cloister, Stift Zwettl

the **Drinking Hall** and especially the so-called '**Archive**' (*Floral decoration with grenadine apples*, in an adjacent room *Noble ladies and gentlemen at leisure*). The **chapel** (1378) has fine reticulated and star vaulting and possesses a late Gothic winged altar dedicated to *Sts George and Pankraz* (the supposed child-martyr; St Pancras is more celebrated as a railway terminus than as a saint, since nothing is known of his life). The side-panels (when open) show *Sts Vitus and Sebastian*, when closed *Sts Christopher, Wolfgang and Florian*. Other notable features are the sgraffitoed Renaissancehof and the suitably chilling dungeons. The castle was so well designed that it was never successfully besieged.

Just south of Rappottenstein a minor road leads south to **Schönbach**, whose Gothic parish church has life-sized figures in a winged altar (c 1500) of *John the Baptist, St Anne with Jesus and Mary, the Virgin and Child Jesus, St Catherine and St Barbara*. The inside panels show scenes from the *Life of Mary*, the outside ones have not survived. The two winged altars to the left and right of the choir date to 1520, the one on the left showing *Sts Catherine, Barbara and Mary Magdalene*, that on the right *St Anne with Mary and Jesus* and *God the Father*. The Altar of the Cross has a **Gothic crucifix** (1380) with real human hair and thorns on the head of the Christ figure. Elsewhere there are works by Kremser Schmidt (the *Holy Family, St Jerome*). The **Maria Rast** icon on the north arch of the choir was and is an object of devotion for pilgrims, but had to be hidden in the 16C when the Starhembergs (at that time the owners of Schönbach) converted to Protestantism and Lutheran preachers forbade the worship of images. It was reinstated in 1629.

East of Zwettl (reached via Rastenfeld on road 38) is **Burg Ottenstein** (open April–Oct, Wed–Sun by appointment, ☎ 0 28 26 8251), which overlooks the artificial lake for the hydroelectric dam of the Kamptal. Its most interesting features are the **Romanesque frescoes** (1200) in the chapel, while the '*Popes' Room*' shows 241 stucco portraits of popes from Peter to Innocent XI created by Maurizio Andorra in the 17C. The stucco of the chapel by Lorenzo Alipardi is from the same period.

THE DANUBE VALLEY: NIBELUNGENGAU TO TULLNER FELD

Ybbs to Melk: the south bank of the Danube eastwards

Ybbs an der Donau (Roman *Adiuvense*, from 837 Bavarian *Yparesburg*) is situated where the river of the same name joins the Danube and was always of strategic significance. Its first mention in documents (1317) refers to already existing toll and staple rights and the town was also an entrepôt on the salt and iron trading-routes and a centre of wine commerce. Since 1959 there has been a hydro-electric dam (Ybbs-Persenbeug) just to the west of it, one of nine on the Danube run by the para-statal *Österreichische Donaukraftwerke A.G.* Ybbs retains part of its medieval city walls and a number of patrician houses from the Renaissance.

The **parish church of St Lawrence** has fine reticulated vaulting and a raised choir (to accommodate a passage to the river beneath it). The organ loft and other Baroque features date to 1716, but more notable is the **tomb of the**

Knight Hans von Ybbs (1368), whose very exact and realistic representation has been a source for details of contemporary costume. Also notable is the *Christ on the Mount of Olives* (1480) in an external niche of the tower.

Following the meander of the Danube to the north and west on the south bank you come shortly to **Säusenstein**, where the plain façade of the Baroque church (1775) belies its lush interior of white, green and pink ornament. The ceiling frescoes (1767) by Johann Bergl show the *Apostles John and Paul*, while the *Apotheosis of St Donatus* (1746) on the high altar is by Paul Troger. Notable is the richly carved **Renaissance pulpit** of 1600.

At **Erlauf** on the main road to the south two monuments (by Jenny Holzer and Oleg Komov) mark the place where American and Soviet (mostly Ukrainian) troops met for the first time on 8 May 1945 as they liberated Austria. **Pöchlarn**, a few kilometres to the east was once part of the Roman *limes* fortification bearing the name *Arelape*. It also appears in the German sagas, as a monument on the side of the Danube recalls. In the previous century the town thrived on its saw mills, which were fed by wood floated down the River Erlauf on rafts to its confluence with the Danube at Pöchlarn. The parish church is of ancient origin, perhaps resting on a pagan shrine, but received its Baroque aspect in the 18C. It boasts three paintings by Kremser Schmidt: in side-altars, the *Sts Sebastian* (left) and a *John of Nepomuk* (right), in the choir an *Assumption*. **Oskar Kokoschka** was born in March 1886 in the house at Regensburger Strasse 29, where temporary exhibitions concerning his life and work are staged. The Kokoschka Archive has recently been placed in the care of the Universität (formerly Hochschule) für Angewandte Kunst (University for Applied Art) in Vienna.

Stift Melk

From Pöchlarn it is a short distance to the great Benedictine Monastery of Melk on its Danubian promontory. Its huge but graceful Baroque proportions enclosing a domed and twin-towered church have made it one of the Danube's most beautiful landmarks, ideally viewed from the river.

Melk's origins lie with the Babenbergs (1089) and it rapidly became a spiritual and cultural centre of great importance. The Baroque transformation between 1702–36 is the masterwork of the Tyrolean Jakob Prandtauer, who pressed into service the best artists of his day (Troger, Rottmayr, Beduzzi, Mattielli, Bergl) in the realisation of his great project, although he himself died ten years before its completion (the work was carried on by his nephew, Josef Munggenast).

Melk lies on the heartbeat of Austrian history: it was here that the first *residenz* of the rulers was erected after Leopold I of Babenberg acquired a local Burg in 976, with which went the responsibilities devolved upon him by Emperor Otto II as Margrave of the Ostmark. Continuity of Christian civilisation was stressed by the removal to Melk of the remains of the Irish Saint Koloman, who was murdered near Stockerau (see p 138), following which Leopold II founded the cloister and invited Benedictines from Lambach to occupy it. After the monks became independent of the secular rulers (who moved to Klosterneuburg and finally to Vienna), their influence in the organisation of the Austrian church increased, reaching a high point in the 15C with Abbot Nikolaus Seyringer's **Melk Reform** aimed at counteracting the decline of the monastic ideal.

The great wealth of the monastery, material as well as spiritual, found an outlet in the ambitions of Berthold Dietmayr, elected Abbot in 1700 aged only 30. It was he who transformed a repair job on the medieval buildings into a mega-project of rebuilding, the resulting southern façade of which alone is 362m long and which boasts a total of 1353 windows. The sceptic philosopher David Hume, visiting in 1748, spoke of 'a set of lazy rascals of Monks [living] in the most splendid Misery of the World.'

• The monastery is open from Palm Sunday to All Saints' Day, daily 09.00–17.00, May–Sept 09.00–18.00, last entrance one hour before closure. Hourly tours available. During the rest of the year visits are only possible with guided tours daily at 11.00 and 14.00.

After entering through portals flanked by Lorenzo Mattielli's statues (1716) of *Sts Leopold and Koloman*, you pass through a **Vorhof** (outer courtyard) with a second portal flanked by statues of *Sts Peter and Paul*. The Benedict corridor follows, with a ceiling fresco of the saint's apotheosis, and thereafter the huge **Prälatenhof** is reached, with its modern frescoes of the *Cardinal Virtues* (1988, Peter Bischof and Helmut Krumpel). The well in the middle of the courtyard is 17C. The pink **Kaiserstiege** with statuary by Mattielli leads up to the **Kaisertrakt**, the splendid imperial quarters that all monasteries had to keep available for possible visits by the Habsburgs, although some were never used. Most conspicuously in the case of Melk they represent a sealing of the alliance between throne and altar so characteristic of Habsburg rule, and occupy nearly a third of the whole building. In a flanking passageway are the portraits of Austrian rulers. The quarters were used by Karl VI, his daughter Maria Theresia, and also by Napoleon, who somewhat pointedly installed himself in the grandest imperial residences, here as at Schönbrunn. The **museum** has much of interest about the history and activities of Melk and its Benedictines, as well as many beautiful objects, among them Jörg Breu the Elder's altarpiece of 1502.

The most valuable treasures are locked away in the Treasury and are not normally on view. The most famous of these is the **Melker Kreuz**, a fantasia of gold and emeralds (made in 1363 on the orders of Rudolf IV) encasing an earlier artefact said to contain splinters of the True Cross brought back from the Holy Land by Margrave Adalbert (1018–1055). The **Marmorsaal** to the west contains Paul Troger's ceiling fresco (1731) of the *Triumph of Wisdom* (metaphorically represented as Hercules and Pallas Athene—strength and wisdom—leading mankind out of chaos and sin to the light of knowledge) and illusionist architectural painting by Gaetano Fanti. At the west end is the magnificent **Altane**, or terrace, with breathtaking views over the Danube Valley, as also of the church façade, the latter a triumph of rhythmic grace by Prandtauer. From the terrace you enter the **Library** which includes 1900 MSS and 750 incunabula. The illusionist decoration is once again by Fanti and the ceiling fresco (1732) is by Paul Troger (*Hercules christianus, the Cardinal Virtues* and *Wisdom*, whereby the civilising moral perspective of antiquity is again combined with Christian teaching). Note the globes by Vincenzo Coronelli (1688 and 1692).

The general design of the superb and theatrically didactic monastery **Church of St Peter and St Paul**, with its warm radiance of gold and honey-coloured marble is by Antonio Beduzzi and includes works by numerous Baroque masters. The effect of the symmetrical three chapels on each side topped by inward and outward curving cornices has been likened to that of waves urging the eye repeatedly towards the monumental eastern focus of the church.

The ceiling frescoes by J.M. Rottmayr represent (in the cupola) a *Vision of Ecclesia Triumphans with the Holy Trinity, the Blessed Virgin Mary, the Apostles and the Heavenly Host* (in the spandrels of the crossing the *Evangelists* and *Fathers of the Church*, continuing a motif of Prandtauer's façade for the church, where Christ the Redeemer is flanked by humbled angels).

In the nave the frescoes show the *Triumphal Assumption of St Benedict* as experienced by two monks in a vision. The imposing marble high altar is by Antonio Galli-Bibiena with a central scene of Peter taking leave of Paul, flanked by gesticulating Old Testament prophets (1735) by Peter Widerin (Prandtauer's son-in-law), who also was responsible for the elegant pulpit. Above this scene is an inscription in a cartouche: *Non coronabitur, nisi legitime certaverit* ('Without a just fight there is no victory'—which does of course beg the question of the criteria used for the definition of 'just'). Above it hangs an enormous tiara, emblematic of the Counter-Reformatory church's struggle that has been crowned with success, as also of Christ's kingship and St Peter's leadership of the church. The altarpieces in the side-chapels are of high quality and include representations of *Sts Sebastian and Nicholas* (1746, Paul Troger), of *John the Baptist* (1727) and *St Michael* (1723) and the *Three Kings* (1723) by J.M. Rottmayr.

The town of **Melk** has a 17C **Koloman Fountain** on the Rathausplatz and a number of 17C and 18C buildings, including the **Stiftstaverne** (*Gasthof zum goldenen Stern*) by Franz Munggenast. The Gothic parish church has an interesting calvary from the early 16C. In the villa quarter of the town is Josef Plecnik's **Kachelvilla** (tiled villa), a minor work by one of the most gifted pupils of Otto Wagner, who went on to do great things in Prague.

Five kilometres south of Melk is the imposing castle of **Schallaburg**, with an eye-catching Renaissance tower rising from within its formidable outer walls (open April–Oct, daily 09.00–17.00). Each year a different temporary exhibition is held here. The Burg's most impressive feature is the great courtyard surrounded by tiered arcades. The supporting columns of the upper tier are decorated with unique **terracotta reliefs** (Jakob Bernecker, 1573), showing masks, gods, mythological figures, and fabulous beings all related to the *Labours of Hercules*. There are also allegories of the *Free Arts* and the *Cardinal Virtues*.

The village of **Loosdorf** is on the main Road A1 on the north-east side of the *Autobahn* and has a church with an altarpiece by Paul Troger (the *Martyrdom of St Lawrence*). In **Mauer bei Melk** north-east of Loosdorf the **church of the 'Name of Mary'** (*Mariae Namen*) has a superb lime-wood **winged altar** (c 1515), showing the transition between Gothic and Renaissance. Its central focus is a powerful relief representing the *Madonna and Child* surrounded both by adoring saints and a vividly evoked populace beseeching her protection, while ecstatic angels place a crown on her head. The *Life of the Virgin* (following the typology of Dürer) is the theme of the side-panels.

The north bank of the Danube:
Persenbeug to Weitenegg

A hydro-electric dam binds Ybbs to Persenbeug on the Danube's north bank, its name derived from the medieval Persinpiugun castle. It is recorded that a reception at the castle for Emperor Heinrich III in 1045 ended in disaster when the floor of the banqueting hall gave way, injuring or killing several high-ranking guests but not the Emperor himself. Despite this mishap, the Burg was favoured by successive rulers and indeed the last Austrian Emperor, Karl I, was born here on 17 August 1887. It remains a Habsburg possession. The parish church (in front of which stands a lime tree reputed to be 700 years old) has a Gothic choir and late Gothic statues (the **Madonna Enthroned**, the **Man of Sorrows** and *St Catherine*). A few kilometres further east is the pilgrimage church of **Maria Taferl** (1711), partly the work of Prandtauer, in a pleasing setting overlooking the Danube Valley. Its most striking features are the gilt **pulpit** (1727) by Matthäus Tempe of St Pölten with sculptures by Peter Widerin and a monumental high altar (enclosing the miraculous icon of the *pietà* by Josef Matthias Götz, 1736), flanked by the portentous figures of the prophets *Isaiah* and *Jeremiah*. The frescoes (under the organ loft the *Foundation Legend of the Church*; in the choir, the *Victory of the Holy Cross*; in the illusionist cupola, the *Life of Mary*; and in the nave the *Life of St Joseph*) were carried out by Antonio Beduzzi between 1714 and 1718.

A minor road leads north-east to **Schloss Artstetten**, the country residence (from 1889) of the heir to the throne, Archduke Franz Ferdinand. The Schloss dates to the 16C but was still being extended and modernised up to 1914 by its doomed owner. In the crypt rest the bodies of the two victims of the Sarajevo assassination, brought here by train and water ferry, the last lap of a mournful journey across the southern part of the empire Franz Ferdinand had hoped to save by a settlement with the Slavs. His morganatic wife could not be buried in the Imperial Crypt in Vienna, so her husband, showing a human side of his character not otherwise conspicuous, had already arranged that they should both be buried at Artstetten. The interior has an extensive exhibition on the Archduke's life and contemporary Habsburg history (open April–Nov daily 09.00–17.30).

A few kilometres to the east is **Schloss Leiben** (open April–Nov, Sun, PH 10.00–17.00, Oct, Nov, also Sat 13.00–17.00) built between 1575–1625 and standing at the mouth of the Weitental. It possesses a fine coffered ceiling in a first floor room, with astrological signs and mythological scenes painted in the panels. There is also an **agricultural museum**.

Schloss Luberegg, 8km to the south-east and facing Melk across the river, is an interesting neo-classical **Landhaus** dating to 1780 and acquired by Franz I for summer holidays in 1795. The decidedly bourgeois and rustic-looking Schloss contains a permanent exhibition on Franz I (open daily April–Nov 09.00–17.30). Right on the Danube with a fine view of Melk to the south are the ruins of **Weitenegg**.

To the north on road 216 **Schloss Rogendorf** at **Pöggstall** is soon reached, with an impressive **barbican** (supposedly inspired by designs of Albrecht Dürer in his work on fortifications) set to the south of it. From its north side the Burg itself is accessed through a towered gateway into the inner courtyard, from where the partly Gothic, partly Renaissance aspects of the building may be admired. In the southern **Arkadenhof** Renaissance frescoes have survived. In the castle dungeons is the torture chamber, with various instruments of the torturer's art on display. A pendant to this is provided by the **Museum for the History of Law** (open April–Oct, Tues–Sun, 09.00–17.00) in the barbican, where we are reminded that only in 1776 was Maria Theresia (against her better judgement) persuaded by her adviser, Sonnenfels, to abolish the torture of suspects as a means of interrogation. Other displays concern apiculture and the work of a local artist, Franz Traunfellner. The adjacent **parish church** (formerly the **Burgkapelle**) has attractive star vaulting, a 15C winged altar and carved pews (1492) in the choir, as well as paintings by the followers of Kremser Schmidt.

THE WACHAU

The beautiful region of terraced vineyards, rolling forests and shoreline, April-blossoming orchards along the winding Danube from Melk to Krems (30km) is known as the Wachau. It is here that the river breaks through the south-east corner of the Bohemian Massif, cutting it off from the Dunkelsteiner Wald to the south. It is perhaps the oldest inhabited region of Austria, Stone Age settlements having been located in its caves and narrow valleys (the so-called 'Venus of Willendorf' was discovered in the neighbourhood, see pp 101 and 161). The Wachau (originally '*Wahowa*') was from earliest times a military and commercial transit area, as its many fortified settlements and wayside churches and the now mostly ruined castles testify. Viticulture flourishes here on the fertile loess soil and benefits from the relatively mild climate, spring arriving up to one and a half months earlier than in the north of Lower Austria and the winters being less harsh. The best quality wines produced in the region are white, above all the excellent Riesling and Grüner Veltliner, but also Neuburger and Müller-Thurgau. Fruit-growing, especially apricots ('*Marillen*' in Austrian speech) is a speciality and the excellent *Marillenknödel* (apricot dumplings) are on offer everywhere during the picking season in early summer.

South Danube shore: Schönbühel to Mautern

Five kilometres downstream from Melk is **Schloss Schönbühel** on a fortified crag at the water's edge, its neo-classical façade dating to 1821, but the tower (with a later onion dome) and the rugged walls betraying an origin in the 12C. The castle is not accessible but the **parish church** has a crypt replicating the Holy Grave in Jerusalem and a chapel dedicated to St Peregrine with a Rococo fresco (1767) in the cupola by Johann Bergl.

Turn off at **Aggsbach-Dorf** for the **Marienpforte Charterhouse**, which was dissolved by Joseph II in 1782, and now houses a museum relating to the Carthusians (visits by arrangement: ☎ 0 27 53 393). Its **Church of the Assumption** has a single narrow nave and graceful Gothic vaulting, the keystones of which are decorated with depictions of creatures with fabled attributes such as phoenixes, unicorns and pelicans. The altarpiece (1673) is by Tobias Pock and the 16C tombs are those of the church's founding family of Heidenreich von Maissau.

Passing the dramatic ruins of **Burg Aggstein** (open daily March–Nov, 08.00–18.00) 300m above the Danube, from which there are marvellous views, you reach **Maria Langegg** with its **Servite parish church** (1775) built by Michael Ehmann. The ceiling frescoes and altarpieces are by Josef von Mölk and his workshop: in the choir is the *Birth of the Virgin Mary*, adjacent to the *Annunciation* and a *Visitation*. The cupola spandrels show the *Evangelists* below a depiction of *Mary as Healer of the Sick*.

The riverbank road runs through **St Johann im Mauertale**, whose church has a large 16C *St Christopher* depicted on the external wall, and **Hofarnsdorf**, where the church has a finely carved stone pulpit and works by Kremser Schmidt in the side-chapels, to **Rossatz** with its Gothic and Renaissance houses.

Last stop on the Wachau opposite Krems is **Mautern**, an important Roman military camp (*Favianis*) from the 1C. According to the hagiography of St Severin (d. 482) by his pupil Eugippius, he settled here in 453, founded a cloister nearby and organised the local population to defend themselves against the barbarian attacks. The town appears in the *Fulda Annals* (899) as '*civitas Mutarensis*' and in the Nibelunglenlied as a staging-post ('*Mutaren*') in Kriemhild's bridal journey. In Viennese history it is significant due to the **Treaty of Mautern** (1137), whereby the Babenbergs and the Passau bishopric agreed that a new church of St Peter (the forerunner of the Stefansdom) should be built just outside the city boundary; Vienna is first referred to as *civitas* in this document. Mautern's Gothic parish church, likewise dedicated to St Stephen, has a fine Baroque calvary cycle by Kremser Schmidt, the artist's father, Johann, being buried in the church. The former **Margarethen Kapelle** (built on the Roman walls) is now a museum with Roman fragments (*Römermuseum Favianis*, open April–Oct, Wed–Sun 09.00–12.00). Also of interest are the Renaissance Bürger houses (some with sgraffiti) and the barockised **Geierhof** on the Göttweig road.

Stift Göttweig

Göttweig itself, dubbed the Austrian Montecassino due to its 260m hilltop location (Celtic '*Kettwein*' or small hill) commanding the surrounding countryside, is only a few kilometres to the south and was founded in the 11C for Augustinian canons by Bishop Altmann of Passau, a supporter of the Pope in the investiture controversy with Emperor Heinrich IV. The monastery was subsequently taken over by the Benedictines and developed into a cultural centre, its sister convent nurturing the celebrated Ava, the first recorded poetess of the German language. The monastery complex was steadily expanded and rebuilt, surviving both the Turkish attacks and the turmoil of the Reformation, but suffering major fires in 1580 and 1718. Parts of the present buildings have survived from the 17C plans of Cypriano Biasino and Domenico Sciassia, but very substantial Baroque rebuilding took place under Abbot Gottfried Bessel after the 1718 fire and is the work of Lukas von Hildebrandt. Shortage of money meant that Hildebrandt's plans were not completely realised.

From the entrance (open from 21 April–Oct, daily 10.00–17.00, June–Sept, 09.00–18.00, with guided tours daily at 10.00, 11.00, 14.00, 15.00, 16.00 and 17.00), the pink and cream classical façade of the **church** is seen diagonally across a huge expanse of courtyard. The colourful light blue and morello tones of the nave are offset by a raised high altar (1639, Hermann Schmidt) with its massive and gleaming Salomonic columns. The altarpiece of the *Assumption* (1694) is by Andrea Wold. Schmidt was also responsible for the pulpit, while the finely carved choir pews with marquetry (1766) are by a local man, Franz Staudinger.

The interior of the church with its four closed off side-chapels is mostly the work of Cypriano Biasino (1634) and is richly decorated with stucco, partly in the form of vegetation motifs. In the side-chapels are pictures (1675) by Johann Spillenberger (the *Summoning of St Peter*) and Tobias Pock (*Crucifixion*). In the crypt is the tomb of St Altmann with its splendid late Gothic portrait in stone (1540).

To the west is the main entrance to the monastery, via the spectacular **Kaiserstiege** (1738) by Franz Anton Pilgram with sculptured allegories of the months and seasons by Johann Schmidt and *trompe l'oeil* architectural painting by Johann Rudolf Byss. The ceiling fresco (1739) by Paul Troger shows the *Apotheosis of Karl VI* (the latter depicted as the sun-god Apollo, in his train allegorical figures representing the free arts, of which '*Architecture*' bears the features of Maria Theresia). The top landing has a model of the Stift before its Baroque conversion, while in the Benedictine room adjacent are paintings (1728) of the life of St Benedict by J.S. Hötzendorfer.

The **Fürstenzimmer** has tapestries again by the Swiss J.B. Byss and his brother, and is used for exhibitions of treasures from the monastery's library of 320,000 volumes, also from its print cabinet and picture collection. The **Altmannisaal** or refectory is decorated with views of the monastery and its dependencies, again by Hötzendorfer, together with a portrait of Maria Theresia and Franz Stephan I painted after their visit in 1746. The ceiling fresco by the Byss brothers shows the *Marriage Feast at Cana*. Also accessible are the **Kaiserzimmer** (Imperial Apartments) with period furniture.

North Danube shore: Emmersdorf to Krems

Facing Melk across the river is the picturesque village of **Emmersdorf** with attractive burgher and vintner houses and a **Magdalena Chapel** (1516) on the main square, together with a late Gothic basilica serving as the parish church.

Church of Maria Laach
To the north and east rises the **Jauerling** (1000m), on which is situated the 15C pilgrimage church of **Maria Laach** at 644m, for a while the burial church of the Kuefstein barons and also the haunt of apostate priests during the Reformation. It acquired its Baroque aspect in the late 17C. An interesting feature of the interior is the splendid late Renaissance tomb (1607) of Johann Georg II von Kuefstein, attributed to Alexander Colin, who worked on Emperor Maximilian I's sarcophagus in the Innsbruck Hofkirche. The knight is depicted in full armour, kneeling in prayer on a cushion, and facing towards the altar, his visored and plumed helmet before him. Equally fine is the Gothic winged altar (1480) in the choir featuring the *Madonna with the Christ Child* in the shrine flanked by angels; above is an *Ecce Homo with Sts John and Paul*, on the predella *Sts Mary Magdalene and Ursula*. The panels show the *Life of the Virgin Mary* and *The Passion*. A curiosity is the votive icon on the left-hand side-altar, a *Rosary Madonna and Child*, the Madonna's right hand having a sixth finger. Elsewhere is a late Gothic *Crucifixion* of great pathos and realism.

Further east along the Danube Valley is the village of **Willendorf**, where a c 25,000-year-old fertility statue was discovered when the railway was being built in 1908, later also a '*Venus II*' figure carved from the ivory of a mammoth tusk.

The road runs along the river to the idyllic **Spitz**, whose 16C **parish church** on the pleasant main square has a choir built at a 20-degree angle northwards to the nave. It is notable also for its irregular vaulting and the marvellous wooden statues of *Christ and the Twelve Apostles* on the western gallery, masterworks of the soft Gothic style made perhaps between 1380 and 1400. The high altar dates to 1630, the altarpiece by Kremser Schmidt of the *Martyrdom of St Maurice* (patron of the church) to 1799. A crucifix of the Danube School may be seen in the Antonius Chapel. St Maurice, also the patron of the Niederaltaich cloister to which Spitz belonged, is one of the more obscure saints, supposedly the 3C commander of a Roman legion in the Swiss Valais (*Agaunum*, now St Maurice en Valais) that refused to punish local Christians, the soldiers of his Theban legion being themselves Christian. The entire legion was butchered for insubordination, according to the legend.

The town of Spitz is full of houses built between the 15C and 18C and is overlooked by the ruins of Hinterhaus castle. The Erlhof in the northern part of the town houses the extremely evocative **Schiffahrtsmuseum** (open April–Oct daily 10.00–12.00, 14.00–16.00, Sun and PH 10.00–12.00, 13.00–17.00) which documents the history of the Danube shipmen.

Road 217 leads up the Spitzerbach valley to Mühldorf and the imposing Ottonian **Burg Oberranna** (open May–Oct. Guided tours Sat 15.00–17.00, Sun and PH 14.00–18.00. The Burg is also a hotel). The castle had assumed its present Renaissance form by 1560 and contains an unusual and spectacular Romanesque chapel dating to the 12C. There are remnants of 15C frescoes and fine trapezoid capitals on the four columns of the half-sunken crypt, showing animal motifs, human heads, wind instruments and foliage.

Back on the Danube bank, **St Michael** to the east of Spitz has a fortified church (1500 on an earlier Romanesque base), partly restored by Cypriano Biasino, who supplied the vaulting (1634) after a partial collapse. The side-altars contain works by Kremser Schmidt (the *Holy Family*, *St Florian*, *St Bartholomew*) and there are unusual terracotta representations, apparently of deer and horses in headlong flight (but popularly dismissed as 'the seven hares') on the ridge of the roof above the choir. The Gothic charnel house with its huge fresco of *St Christopher* contains mummified remains from 1150–1300, reusable coffins from the time of Joseph II and skulls heaped up in the form of an altar.

Three kilometres further east is **Weißenkirchen** whose likewise fortified church is approached via a shingle-roofed stairway from the town. Gothic features of the interior include a polygonal font and a crucifix. One of the arcaded Renaissance vintner houses (the **Teisenhoferhof**) contains the **Wachaumuseum**; open April–Oct, Tues–Sun 10.00–17.00), which includes turn of the century painting from the '*Wachaumaler*' colony and landscapes by Jacob Alt, Rudolf von Alt and Emil Schindler.

After negotiating a wide bend in the river, the road reaches **Dürnstein** 6km to the east. Parking is available at either end of the tunnel that runs beneath the town, high above which towers its castle, ruined by the Swedes in 1645. According to legend, it was through a window of this castle that the song of the faithful Blondel was heard by Richard Coeur de Lion (1157–99), who had been incarcerated (1193) by the Kuenringer, acting on behalf of the Babenberg Duke, Leopold V. Blondel's wanderings are the stuff of myth and have now suffered the ultimate degradation of being turned into a banal musical, but the fate of the disastrous King Richard is well documented. The ransom (25 tons of silver or 150,000 German marks, perhaps 1.5 billion pounds at today's prices) obtained by the German Emperor Heinrich VI, and shared with Duke Leopold, required the melting of church silver all over England and virtually bankrupted the country. The Babenberg share was enough to found Wiener Neustadt and extend the defences of Vienna, Enns and Hainburg.

Richard Coeur de Lion's quarrel with the Babenberg Duke

Richard was accused by Leopold of the murder of Conrad of Montferrat, the Emperor's appointee as the future King of Jerusalem, which (it was confidently expected) would be taken during the Third Crusade. Richard is also supposed to have insulted his nominal ally by pulling down the Babenberg flag placed on a tower after the successful siege of Acre, and to have refused to share the booty. The English king clearly knew that he was a wanted man in Central Europe: after his shipwreck north-west of Trieste at Aquileia, he decided to make a detour via Vienna in order to throw his pursuers off the scent (he would have been expected to take a more direct route across Austria to reach the territory of his brother-in-law, Heinrich of Saxony). In fact he was monitored almost as soon as he reached Austrian soil: Meinhard of Gorizia followed his movements in Friuli and the Lord of Friesach in Carinthia even arrested some of his followers.

Stift Dürnstein

The former Augustinian Monastery (1733; open April–Oct, daily 09.00–18.00, guided tours every hour on the hour) in Dürnstein was built by Joseph Munggenast, perhaps from plans drawn up by Jakob Prandtauer and Matthias Steinl, but with the active involvement of the epicurean Prior, Hieronymus Übelbacher (1710–40). Steinl was probably responsible for the southern portal (1718) with its decorated figures representing *Strength* and *Vigilance*, and in the pediment *Faith*, *Hope* and *Charity*. This gateway leads into the elegant courtyard, where the grandiose coat of arms of Übelbacher presides over the monastery entrance. The monastery building, with its curving supraport windows and portals decorated with allegorical figures, suggests the inspiration of Prandtauer, while the statuary was executed by Johann Schmidt, the father of the painter, 'Kremser' Schmidt. The overall decorative scheme is a quaternion: on the north façade, the *Four Seasons* and *Four Parts of the Day*, on the south façade the *Four Elements* and *Four Continents*. The glory of Dürnstein, however, is the beautiful **church tower** (1733), since 1987 shimmering in the vivid blue of its stylish Baroque form contrapuntally decorated with icing-sugar stucco and statuary. Its lower section has four vast volute-like corner columns dividing the field of statuary and rising from a terrace overlooking the Danube. The programme of the statuary follows Christological and Marian themes (see below), with (at the bottom, and appropriately closest to the river) allusions also to St John of Nepomuk.

The **entrance to the church** is via a triumphal arch (probably by Steinl), the doorway itself being flanked by powerfully animated statues of the *Fathers of the Church* perched on decorative volutes. Adjacent to these are columns with pedestal reliefs that again play on the number four—this time the eschatology of *Death and Judgement, Heaven* and *Hell*. Over the arch is the figure of *Christ the Redeemer* with a huge cross, while above are obelisks (emblems of eternity) and another relief that symbolises redemption through Christ. On the cartouche in the middle is a quotation from the Psalms: '*I was glad when they said unto me: let us go into the house of the Lord.*' The vestibule has richly ornamented confessionals decorated with themes that summon the faithful to repent of their sins.

The **interior** of the church is breathtakingly sumptuous, a dazzling display of white stucco (by Santino Bussi) and gilded statuary mingling with the dark, mellow tones of the wooden furnishings and umber marble, the whole scene framed by the wave-like movement of concave and convex architectural elements, again probably the concept of Steinl. The main altarpiece shows the *Assumption* (Carl Haringer, 1723) in front of a tabernacle by Johann Schmidt featuring a gilded globe with biblical reliefs. Flanking the altar are the figures of *St Augustine* and *St Possidius* (c 370–c 440), the latter a co-protagonist with St Augustine in his struggles against the Donatist schismatics and Pelagiac heretics (he was also the saint's biographer). The highly decorative **pulpit** (Johann Schmidt) is counterpointed (as in the Vienna Peterskirche) by the vivid Nepomuk statue on the other side of the crossing, the saint being formally represented here, however, without the descriptive elements of his martyrdom. The side-altars are rich in high quality works by Kremser Schmidt (1767; *Sts Jerome, Joseph, Monica and Catherine*), and there are other works (*Sts Augustine and John*) by Haringer (Schmidt's teacher). The delightful **cloister** (1724) to the south of the church is also delicately stuccoed and contains a theatrical *Holy Sepulchre* by Francesco Galli di Bibiena.

Steinl's sublime **steeple** is ideally viewed from the river itself, but a good impression of its powder blue limbs encrusted with stucco ornamentation may nevertheless be gained by looking back at it from the viewing terrace. The quaternion theme of Johann Schmidt's sculpture is continued with the *Four Evangelists* at the corners of the lantern, these being surmounted only by angels holding the cross, emphasising thus the crowning sacrifice of the crucifixion and pointing also heavenwards to the after-life and redemption. Below is the main trunk of the clock-tower with stucco reliefs of *The Passion* divided by four obelisks. The base of the tower is formed by massive volutes with statues of *St Nicholas* and *St Augustine* on the balcony corners, while above the door is the *Mater Dolorosa* with the sword in her heart. The view of the river from the balcony is unforgettable.

The Clarissan Cloister in the town (which did not survive the Reformation) is now a hotel, but preserves remnants of 14C frescoes showing *St Francis* and *St John with Mary, Mother of Jesus* beneath the Cross. Also a hotel is the *Schloss Dürnstein* (built by Christoph Wilhelm von Zelking in 1622) on the Danube shore, with attractive terraces overlooking the river. The **Kellerschlössl** (1714, perhaps built by Prandtauer for Prior Übelbacher) to the east of the town is ornamented with stucco and frescoes and is adjacent to wine cellars where the Wachau wines may be tasted. It is possible to wander round the ruins of the old castle (**Burg Dürnstein**) and the arduous climb up to it is worth it for the view.

Between Dürnstein and Stein, **Loiben** was the site of a battle (11 November 1809, described in Tolstoy's *War and Peace*) between an Austro-Russian army under Kutusov and the French under Mortier. The east end of the Wachau finishes with the virtually twin cities of Stein and Krems, separated only by a suburb appropriately called '*Und*' as the inhabitants like to jest.

The natives of **Stein** built a wooden bridge across the river to Mautern in the 15C, only the second Danubian bridge in Austria after that of Vienna, and the town consequently became rich as a nodal point of salt transportation. The walled city has delightful 16C mansions and squares such as **Schürerplatz** and **Rathausplatz** (Mozart's cataloguer, Ludwig von Köchel was born on the latter in 1800. The 15C **parish church of St Nicholas** has a number of paintings by Kremser Schmidt (who nevertheless lived latterly in Stein). The decorative tombstones dating to the turn of the 15C–16C, including one (1519) showing the *Mocking of Christ*, are interesting transitional works between the Gothic and Renaissance styles.

A steep climb brings you to the **Frauenbergkirche** (1380), from which Göttweig can be seen distantly across the river. The former **Minoritenkirche** (1264), off the Landstrasse to the east, is now an exhibition hall, but was for a long time a tobacco warehouse after the monastery was dissolved in 1796. This fine example of early Gothic has majestic grace and simplicity, the heavenward surge of its internal columns being enhanced by the stars painted on the keystone bosses of the vaulting. Adjacent to the **Kremsertor** of the old city wall is the **Göttweigerhof**, formerly the administrative centre of the monastery of the same name, and containing a chapel with rare Gothic frescoes from the 14C (a key to the chapel may be obtained from the tourist information office in Und). The frescoes are by an itinerant Italian master and include a *Crucifixion* and a *Man of Sorrows*.

Krems

Krems, first mentioned as a town in the 10C, and still larger than Vienna in the 12C, is situated close to the confluence of the Krems and Danube rivers and is bisected by the long pedestrianised (**Obere** and **Untere**) **Landstraße**. It was a Babenberg stronghold, which is perhaps why the first mint in Austria was set up here. It grew rich from trade in corn, wine, salt and iron, as well as from market privileges and tolls; 20 per cent of the inhabitants still make their living from viticulture. It is entered from the west by the **Steinertor**, built (like the other three that have now disappeared) as a defence against the troops of Matthias Corvinus in 1480 and bearing the motto of Friedrich III, AEIOU (see p 130). Its clocktower is a late Baroque addition (1754).

The **Schwedengasse** to the right is an allusion to the events of 1645/46 when the Swedish General Torstenson made Krems his headquarters preparatory to an assault on Vienna that never materialised. On the **Körnermarkt** is a Marian column, while to the north-east is the former Dominican Church and monastery at Körnermarkt 14 (now the municipal and viticulture **museum**, open Tues 09.00–18.00, Wed–Sun 13.00–18.00), the cloister of which has been reconstructed.

A narrow street leads east to the **parish church of St Vitus**, an early Baroque (1630) work by Cypriano Biasino which partly retains its former Gothic tower. The interior has a number of works of note: the marble high altar (1733) is by Josef Matthias Götz, while the altarpiece (the **Martyrdom of St Vitus**, 1734) is by Johann Georg ('Wiener') Schmidt. Götz was also responsible for the pulpit and the choir-stalls with gilded reliefs of St Vitus's martyrdom, while 'Kremser' Schmidt frescoed the ceiling. Other frescoes were supplied by Martino Altomonte and Franz Anton Maulbertsch. The Baroque **Altar of the Cross** in the south apse is the work of Matthias Steinl, while the small *Madonna* on the **Marian Altar** is a Bohemian work dating to 1420. Note also on the exterior chapel wall a sculpture of *St Anne blessing Mary*, dated to 1320, while on the west façade are Baroque statues of *Sts Leopold and Vitus*.

North of the church you ascend covered steps to the late Gothic **Piarist Church** (1457–1502), also known as the **Frauenbergkirche**, which was used by Protestants during the Reformation and taken over by the Jesuits in 1616, then transferred to Piarist possession when the Jesuit Order was dissolved under Maria Theresia. Its lofty and spacious interior and clustered columns recalls the nave of St Stephen's in Vienna, as also does the fine star vaulting in the choir. J.M. Götz is again the creator of the Baroque high altar (1756), while Kremser Schmidt supplied its altarpiece and those for the side-altars.

A stroll through the town reveals innumerable historic houses of interest. They include the **Gozzoburg** off the Margarethengasse, named after a rich 13C burgher who turned it into a substantial fortified mansion with Gothic arcades, its chapel having remnants of Gothic frescoes. Also of interest are the **Gattermannhaus** (1559) at Untere Landstrasse 52, the **Göglhaus** on the Täglichen Markt of the Untere Stadt (medieval and Renaissance with neo-Gothic additions) and the **Alte Post** at Obere Landstrasse 32, a 16C inn with an arcaded courtyard. Lastly it is worth looking at the 15C **Rathaus** with its elegant Renaissance columns in the entrance hall, its groined vaulting in the **Ratsstube**, and the oriel window on the street corner, below which is a sculpture of *Samson and the Lion*, a reminder of Krems's struggle against its enemies. Lying between Krems and Stein in the former **Capuchin Monastery** (Undstrasse 6) is a wine college with regular tastings of Wachau wines (open daily, 13.00–19.00). An unusual **Motorcycle Museum** is at Ziegelofengasse 1, Krems-Egelsee (open March–Oct daily 09.00–17.00). In June and July Krems participates in the Lower Austrian Donaufestival with various cultural events.

THE TULLNER BECKEN

The north bank of the Danube

This stretch of the Danube north shore has comparatively little to interest the tourist, although there are sights a little further north, such as **Grafenegg** (see p 139) and **Kirchberg am Wagram** (see p 139). The otherwise unremarkable Grafenwörth was the birthplace of the artist Martin Johann Schmidt ('Kremser' Schmidt) on 25 September 1718, who died in Stein in 1801. After Franz Anton Maulbertsch, he was perhaps the most successful Baroque painter of his day and astonishingly prolific (more than 1100 works are attributed to him, although many of them were substantially the work of his collaborators). His father, Johann Schmidt, was a gifted sculptor (see Dürnstein, pp 162–3).

From Grafenwörth the main road runs east along the edge of the **Binderau**, formerly flood lands of the Danube, to Stockerau (see p 138) and on to Korneuburg (see p 138).

The south bank of the Danube

The south bank is reached across the Krems bridge on a main road that leads to St Pölten (S33; see p 121). Leaving Göttweig to the west, you come by minor roads to **Nussdorf ob der Traisen**, where the **Pre-History Museum** in **Schloss Nussdorf** (open April–Oct, Tues–Sun, 09.00–17.00), with finds from the Bronze Ages from the Traisental, is worth visiting. **Traismauer** itself, situated on the Traisen river, was a Roman settlement called *Augustianis*, part of the *limes* fortified border. It also has a **Museum of Early History** (open April–Oct, Tues–Sun, 09.00–17.00) in the Schloss and a somewhat Spielberg-like **Saurierpark** north of the town with 35 reconstructions of sauria, ammonites, birds and other extinct creatures (open April–Oct, daily 09.00–1800).

Further north and close to the Danube is Austria's most celebrated white elephant, the unused nuclear power station at **Zwentendorf**, the only such to be built in the country. Its commissioning was, however, narrowly rejected in a referendum held in 1978, after Chancellor Bruno Kreisky realised he would probably lose the upcoming elections if he did not allow the people to decide the issue. The building of the power station had itself been a response to the energy crisis of 1973, and was also part of the job-creation schemes and deficit financing by which the government had hoped to ward off recession.

Tulln

Somewhat to the south is Schloss Atzenbrugg (see p 127), but the minor road runs east along the Danube shore before veering inland to meet the main road (19) just below Tulln, an important river crossing from earliest times. The Romans kept a Danube fleet here and named the place *Comagena* after the Syrian base of the resident legion; from the 9C. it reverted to *Tullina*, a corruption of the Illyrian-Celtic nomenclature meaning, perhaps, a patch of scrub. It was at *Tulne* that Attila came to meet his bride Kriemhild according to the Nibelungenlied. The settlement increased in importance under Carolingian and Babenberg hegemony as an entrepôt and a town with staple rights, then also under the Habsburgs when it acquired its city charter and the right to levy a toll.

The Gothic **parish church of St Stephen** on the eastern edge of the old city is evidence of the wealth and importance that Tulln enjoyed, its extension and rebuilding being continuous from Romanesque to Baroque times. The west portal is Romanesque and has an unusual decoration in the form of supposed **busts of the 12 apostles** in the arched niches of the lateral gateposts. The interior, however, was largely destroyed by fire in 1752 and the present furnishings are therefore late Baroque. The high altar was brought here from the Carmelite Church in St Pölten and supplied with Joseph Steiner's altarpiece (the *Stoning of St Stephen*) above it is the same artist's *Holy Trinity*. To the existing flanking figures of *Sts Camillus and Leopold* were added (1788) those of *Mary Magdalene* and *St Rosalia* by Matthias Klöbl. The superb Rococo choir-stalls came from the Charterhouse at Gaming after it was dissolved in 1790. The altarpieces of the altars on either side of the triumphal arch show respectively a contemporary copy of Maulbertsch's *Annunciation* and a *St Lucia* by a Maulbertsch follower. The moving and expressive altarpiece for the **Thomas Altar** in the right-hand aisle (showing Jesus reaching out to the doubter) is by Franz Anton Maulbertsch himself. The ornate pulpit, with allegories of the church as ruler and teacher of the secular world and a relief of *Christ handing Peter the Keys of the Kingdom of Heaven*, is also attributed to Matthias Klöbl. The oil paintings in the nave (*St Peter* and the *Evangelists*) are by Steiner.

Adjacent is the Romanesque charnel house or **Three Kings Burial Chapel** with an impressive five-banked portal, its columns separated by notched ornamentation, and with a foliage frieze above the capitals and an original door, the finest Romanesque portal to survive locally apart from those of the Stephansdom in Vienna and Ják in western Hungary. It was in fact a Hungarian (Franz Storno of Sopron) who heavily over-restored the church's 13C frescoes in 1873 (they show the *Last Judgement* in the apse, the *Archangel Michael Fighting the Dragon* on the arch, with depictions of the *Wise and Foolish Virgins*, the *Adoration of the Kings*, and the *Transfiguration of St Catherine*).

Egon Schiele (1890–1918)

Interest in the Austrian Expressionist painter Egon Schiele has grown in the past few years and he now ranks with Gustav Klimt and Oskar Kokoschka as one of the boldest spirits of Austrian art since the beginnings of Modernism. The tortured nature of his early phase suggested a combination of cultural pessimism and sexual turmoil for which the art-loving public was ill-prepared. His childhood had been troubled, his father having been pensioned off from his job as station master due to incipient general paralysis of the insane resulting from poorly treated syphilis. Schiele produced a steady supply of erotica for private patrons, which assured him a living, although they also involved some risk, as his arrest in 1912 demonstrated. However, even his work designed for public consumption was too strong for conventional taste: when Franz Joseph encountered one of Schiele's typically provocative female nudes at an exhibition in 1910, he hastily turned away, muttering 'This is really quite awful!'

During the 1914–18 war Schiele was able to continue painting due to the civilised leniency of a senior officer and by the end of it he began to be regarded as a major artist. His work may be seen in the Belvedere in Vienna and includes a number of superb brooding landscapes, most famously those of Český Krumlov (Krumau) in Bohemia, where his family had roots. Even more powerful are the angst-ridden portraits, often featuring the artist himself as a protagonist. Above all, his drawings (many in the Albertina and the Leopold Collection in Vienna) were equalled only by Klimt in the spontaneity and sureness of line when treating the human body. Schiele died in 1918 (along with Otto Wagner and Gustav Klimt), a victim of the Asian flu of that year, which killed more people in Europe than the war itself.

The **Minorite Church** in the north-west of the old town has fine stuccolustro in the apse of its extremely elegant interior, and ceiling frescoes of the *Life of St John of Nepomuk* by an unknown hand, probably a Minorite monk. The theme is continued with the altarpiece of the *Apotheosis of John of Nepomuk*. The adjacent Minorite cloister is now a **museum** with sections dealing with archaeology, local history, etc. (open Wed–Fri, 15.00–18.00, Sat 14.00–18.00, Sun and PH 10.00–18.00). The Expressionist painter Egon Schiele (a native of Tulln, born in 1890–his father was the station master) was briefly incarcerated in the town following accusations of the exploitation of under-age girls for pornographic pictures during his stay at nearby Neulengbach. In a truly Austrian gesture of *Wiedergutmachung* ('making up for it'), the gaol in which he languished (at Donaulände 28) periodically puts on shows of his works.

Burgenland (Burgenland)

Area: 3,966sq km. Population: 271,000

Topography, climate and environment

Burgenland (Burgenland) is the easternmost of the Federal Provinces of Austria, bordering in the west with Lower Austria and Styria, in the east with Hungary and (briefly) with Slovakia, in the south with Slovenia. It has always been a border territory, as testified by its substantial fortified cities (from four of which it derives its name) and its many churches with medieval defensive walls. As a buffer zone under the control of powerful lords with unpredictable allegiances, it was sporadically disputed between Hungary and Austria for centuries, and today is only 4km wide at its narrowest point (**Sieggraben**). Millions of years ago, it formed another border, that with the Great Pannonian Sea, which eventually retreated south, leaving a landscape of limestone, basalt and serpentine, beneath which bubbled hundreds of thermal springs.

The landscape of Burgenland is characterised by alpine foothills that peter out in the western periphery of the Pannonian Plain (Hungarian *kisalföld*), the central part of the territory being a cradle strung between the **Wiener Becken** (Vienna Basin) in the north and the **Grazer Becken** (Graz Basin) in the south. Two distinctive hill formations obtrude into this area: the continuation of the Buckligen Welt runs from Lower Austria into Central Burgenland, while the East Styrian Highlands unfold into South Burgenland. The area is drained eastwards by a number of rivers, the most important being the **Leitha** (until 1919 the border between Hungary and Austria), the **Raab**, the **Rabnitz** and the **Pinka**. Burgenland also includes most of the **Neusiedler See (Lake Neusiedl)** (see *climate and environment* below), of whose total area of 320sq km only a small southern part (88 sq km, *Fertő-tó*) remains in Hungary. The lake is 33.5km long from north to south, has a width east to west of some 12km, and is only 1.8m deep at the deepest points. The westernmost steppe-lake in Europe, it also has the largest surface area of any Austrian lake.

The northern part of Burgenland, with its Pannonian micro-climate, regularly records some of the highest figures for annual sunshine in Central Europe. The effect of the large expanse of the **Neusiedler See** ensures, however, that there is always a relatively high humidity. The waters of the lake itself, which are nourished primarily by rainfall (162 million hectolitres), together with some river feed (65 million hectolitres) from the Wulka and subterranean springs (8 million hectolitres), are kept at a relatively stable level by regulation through the Einser-Kanal on the Hungarian side. This has forestalled the danger of the lake drying out altogether, as nearly happened in 1740, 1773, 1811–13 and 1864–70; or on the other hand suddenly expanding, as happened in 1741–2, 1786, 1797–1801, 1838 and 1941. A prominent feature of the Neusiedler See is its thick girdle of reeds, which has increased greatly in the 20C. About 15 per cent of the reeds are harvested annually and put to commercial use, but their

greatest value is as shelter for more than 250 species of birds, some of them rare. The lake is also home to more than 30 species of fish. The area on the east bank was incorporated in 1996 into the **Nationalpark Neusiedler See-Seewinkel**, which straddles Austrian and Hungarian territory, a model example of cross-border cooperation. Of the park's 20,000 ha, 8000 are on Austrian soil (see p 185 for more information).

The Burgenland climate with its late-arriving spring and lingering autumn is a stimulus for orchard blossoms and productive vineyards (see *Economy* below). From the humid warmth of the north, with its low rainfall, to the central and southern areas with a temperate micro-climate and the pure air of the alpine foothills, Burgenland offers an agreeable weather pattern and is a highly favoured holiday resort, especially for the Viennese. Its often romantic landscape retains features of the Hungarian steppe, the traveller occasionally coming upon draw wells (*Ziehbrunnen*) set against a backdrop of Pannonian vastness, or sociable pairs of storks perching on village rooftops. The birds leave for their Southern African winter quarters with uncanny calendrical punctuality in the last few days of August. The white storks (*ciconia ciconia*) arrive in March, and are accompanied by a smaller number of black storks (*ciconia nigra*). During the summer months the birds may often be seen looking for delicacies in the fields, but their numbers are declining due to the use of pesticides which has diminished their food supply.

Economy

Agriculture plays a relatively important role in the Burgenland economy, particularly in the fields of market gardening and viticulture. This is despite the fact that only 6.4 per cent of land under cultivation is actually vineyards (47.3 per cent is arable, with forestry accounting for 32 per cent). The high returns from the Burgenland viticulture, however, are an indication both of its productivity and quality, the most significant wine-growing regions being the rolling hills west of the Neusiedler See. The highest quality is achieved with the white wines (**Welschriesling**, **Muskat-Ottonel**, **Weißburgunder**), although good red wines such as **Zweigelt**, **Blaufränkisch** and **Sankt Laurent** are also grown, together with a local speciality of sweet **Prädikatsweine** from Illmitz and Rust. The great wine scandal of 1985 (in which Burgenland wines were found to be spiked with glycol, an ingredient of automobile anti-freeze) proved to be a long-term blessing in disguise, insofar as the total collapse of the market for Austrian wines actually allowed wine-growers to improve the quality of their (unspiked) product in the post-scandal regime of strict controls.

Although Burgenland is relatively rich in mineral resources, these are only exploited on a fairly modest scale, typical being the limestone quarrying on the periphery of the Leitha Mountains and at St Margarethen near Rust, the lignite mining at Tauchen, and chalk quarrying around Müllendorf; elsewhere small quantities are mined of copper pyrites, antimonial ore, and precious serpentine (*Edelserpentin*), a local speciality found near Bernstein. There are, in addition, natural or thermal springs at Bad Tatzmannsdorf, Bad Sauerbrunn, Deutschkreutz and Sulz bei Güssing, some of which produce mineral water in marketable quantities or feed health spas.

Partly due to historical factors (see *History* below), Burgenland has a relatively backward industrial sector and this is reflected in a below-average contribution to the Austrian per capita GDP. Industries such as clothing manufacture, electronics and foodstuffs account for most of the industrial activity. More important is the tourist industry, although this tends to be concentrated on the Neusiedler See, with nearly 70 per cent of the overnight stays in Burgenland being recorded in its resorts. Health tourism at the spas (especially Bad Tatzmannsdorf) is also a significant income producer. Most tourism is concentrated in the months between May and October, but exotic experiences such as ice-sailing on the Neusiedler See in winter are also on offer. In view of its regional gross product lying below 75 per cent of the EU average, Burgenland has received development area subsidies from the European Union continuously since Austria joined in 1995.

History

Burgenland is the youngest of the Austrian Federal Provinces, having been incorporated into the Republic only in 1919 as a result of the Treaty of St-Germain-en-Laye at the end of World War I. Its name (the original suggestion was '*Vierburgenland*') is derived from the four Hungarian administrative districts in which the territory lay up to that time, namely **Pressburg** (Hungarian *Pozsony*, Slovakian *Bratislava*), **Wieselburg** (Hungarian *Mosonmagyaróvár*), **Ödenburg** (Hungarian *Sopron*) and **Eisenburg** (Hungarian *Vasvár*). In Hungarian, this area is called the **Őrvidék** which means 'Land of the Sentinels', a reference to its former role as a guarded border. The town of Sopron itself was intended to have been included in the new Austrian province, but a plebiscite held there on 14 December 1921 resulted in a majority of 64 per cent opting to stay with truncated Hungary (the plebiscite was held under Italian auspices and may have been subject to manipulation). In consequence, Burgenland lost what would have been its natural political centre, and the new capital (from 1925) became **Eisenstadt** (Hungarian *Kismarton*).

The earliest settlement of the Burgenland area dates to the Mesolithic era (10,000–5000 BC). From about 5000 BC the flatlands around the Neusiedler See and the Pullendorf Basin were quite densely populated with farming communities. **Mining** of antimonial ore and copper began in the Bronze Age in the Rechnitz and Bernstein hills, while **viticulture** existed from about 700 BC. Illyrian settlements formed a defensive ring of settlements between 800 and 400 BC against the incursions of the Scythians from the east (their habitation is confirmed by relics of so-called Urn Burial). From about BC 450 the area was settled by **Celts**, as witnessed by an important find of 180 Celtic silver coins near Güssing; subsequently (in 15 BC) it was absorbed into the **Roman province of Pannonia** at the time of the Emperor Augustus. The important **amber trade route** that had run from earliest times between the Baltic and the Adriatic, now passed from Roman *Carnuntum* through Burgenland via Ödenburg (*Scarabantia*), and on to *Aquileia* via *Emona* (*Ljubljana*, in German, Laibach).

Overrun by Huns, Goths and Avars in the era of the **Great Migrations**, the Burgenland area fell under Carolingian hegemony (the *Ostmark* of which extended as far as Lake Balaton) after Charlemagne defeated the Avars in AD 800. In the 10C, the westward-pressing Hungarians (Magyars), who had entered the Carpathian Basin in 896, defeated the Bavarians at the **Battle of**

Pressburg (907), and thereafter the Rivers Leitha and Lafnitz (now the province's borders with Lower Austria and Styria) became the border between Hungarian and Austrian territory. However, the region was always settled both with Magyars and Austrian Germans, the former living in fortified border villages with a defensive function, the latter living in the countryside as peasants, miners or handworkers. After the marriage of King Stephen of Hungary to Gisela, the daughter of the Bavarian Duke, there was an influx of German knights and nobility, from which time the population was in majority German.

These local knightly dynasties (in particular the Counts of Mattersdorf and Güssing) were powerful enough to be quasi-independent of their liege-lords. After the last of the Bavarian/Austrian Babenberg dynasty (Friedrich II) was killed fighting the Hungarians at the **Battle of the Leitha** (1246), they became even more autonomous, until subdued by Albrecht I of Habsburg in 1289–90, the Hungarians subsequently crushing some lingering resistance in a campaign of 1327. In the 14C and 15C, the Habsburgs and Hungarians struggled for the upper hand in this disputed border territory, although trade between east and west continued unabated. Cloth and luxuries travelled from Vienna to Hungary, and bullocks on the hoof (the beginning of a long tradition) passed through Burgenland in the opposite direction. However, the Magyar habit of arresting and ransoming Viennese merchants led to military action in Burgenland from 1440 by Friedrich V (the later Emperor Friedrich III). The **Treaty of Ödenburg** (1463) and later agreements brought about a considerable increase in Habsburg possessions in the region, possessions which were not to return to Hungarian control until the Counter-Reformation. In 1459 Friedrich III even had himself crowned King of Hungary by disaffected Magyar magnates in Güssing, but despite (or because of) this *démarche* a protracted war ensued, which culminated in the occupation of Vienna by the Hungarian King Matthias Corvinus from 1485 until his death (possibly by poison) in 1490. His demise provided the opportunity for Friedrich's son, Maximilian I, to impose the **Peace of Pressburg** (1491) on the Hungarians.

After the catastrophic Hungarian defeat by the Turks in 1526 at Mohács in southern Hungary, the border region of later Burgenland was fully exposed to Osman depredations. These were so devastating that the landlords were already inviting new settlers in the following decade; it was at this time that substantial numbers of **Croats** arrived in the area, fleeing from the Turkish onslaught on their homeland. From 1520 **Protestantism** was also spreading through the territory, above all among the German-speaking majority of the population, who adopted Lutheranism, while the Hungarian aristocracy were to opt for Calvinism. The Mohács' defeat also meant that the crown of Hungary had legally passed to the Habsburgs through Maximilian I's inheritance contract; however, this was to be repeatedly challenged in the following centuries, both on the basis that the Hungarian throne was traditionally elective and (more particularly) on the basis that the Habsburgs frequently did not hold themselves to their coronation oath to defend the country from all its enemies. A further ground for strife was religion, so that Protestantism often (but not exclusively) came to be associated with patriotic resistance to the Habsburgs and their policy of religious intolerance. Incursions into

Burgenland from the Protestant armies of István Bocskai (1557–1606), then Gábor Bethlen (1580–1629) were followed in the late 17C by the rebellion of the so-called *kuruc* Hungarians (in contradistinction to the *labanc*, who were loyal to the Habsburg dynasty). Originally raised against the Turks in Transylvania, this loosely organised army of peasants was later turned against the Habsburg territories (1678) under the generalship of Imre Thököly (1657–1705). The major *kuruc* war of liberation took place, however, between 1703–11 under the leadership of the Prince of Transylvania, Ferenc Rákóczi II (1676–1735).

As if this continuous devastation was not enough, Burgenland was threatened by the advance of the Turks, who were defeated in a closely fought battle at **Mogersdorf** in 1664 (see p 198). Nineteen years later another larger Turkish army under Kara Mustapha made a final ill-fated attempt to conquer Vienna in 1683; on this occasion Hungarian generals (including Thököly) allied themselves with the Turks and negotiated the peaceful submission of the most important Burgenland strongholds of the Batthyánys in south Burgenland, as the Osman horde swept on towards its goal. The other great Hungarian landowner of Burgenland, **Prince Pál Esterházy**, was the Palatine of Hungary and fought on the imperial side; this was in the Esterházy tradition of loyalty and generalship, his father, Count Miklós Esterházy, having defeated an insurgent Hungarian army under Gábor Bethlen at Lackenbach (see p 192) at the beginning of the Thirty Years War in 1618. The Esterházys were well rewarded for their loyalty, not only being elevated to the rank of Prince and (in two cases) Palatine of Hungary, but emerging in the early 18C as the lords of the whole of central and northern Burgenland. Until the hegemony of lords loyal to the Habsburgs was established in a territory finally free of the Turkish menace, Burgenland remained a potential battlefield. The ordinary people, if they survived at all, took refuge in the Burgen—and in piety: the many medieval and Baroque wayside shrines (*Bildstöcke*) placed around the edges of villages, especially to the east of the Neusiedler See, are emblematic of the way in which the Catholic population clung to their faith through repeated eras of devastation.

Following the expulsion of the Turks from Central Europe and the compromise reached at the Treaty of Szatmár (1711), which ended the Hungarian War of Independence, Burgenland entered a period of peace and consolidation. The new atmosphere was reflected in the boom of Baroque and Rococo architecture and the flowering of the arts under local nobles and princes, above all under the patronage of the *labanc* Esterházys. At their palaces in **Kismarton/Eisenstadt** and later at the 'Hungarian Versailles' of **Esterháza** (built in the 1760s for Prince Miklós Esterházy), they employed Joseph Haydn to write and direct music for their great festivities at which Maria Theresia herself participated. From the early 19C Burgenland was discovered by travellers and intellectuals who (like the dramatist Franz Grillparzer later) came to take the waters at Bad Tatzmannsdorf, or who wrote about the landscape (like Nikolaus Lenau) or performed for the local nobility (like Ludwig van Beethoven).

A further impulse for opening up the region was the inauguration of the Wiener Neustadt—Sopron (Ödenburg) railway in 1847. Despite the revolution of 1848, when the Hungarian independent government abolished serfdom and the privileges of the nobility, the aristocratic owners of the Burgenland *Burgen* and *Schlösser* were not dislodged and continue, in many cases, to keep their estates. Industrially, commercially and culturally Burgenland was oriented towards Wiener Neustadt and Vienna, both towns being only a short distance away, and this fact (together with the predominance of the German-speaking inhabitants) was decisive in the majority's desire to join Austria after 1919. On the other hand there were some sons of Burgenland, like **Franz Liszt**, (1811–86, born at Raiding, see p 192), whose emotional and cultural orientation was entirely Hungarian. 'Liszt Ferenc', the intensely patriotic Magyar, could not speak the Magyar tongue, and his Hungarian rhapsodies were not based on Hungarian folk originals as he thought. Nevertheless, he remains a classic example of the magyarised German ('*hungarus*'), with a stronger Hungarian identity even than the assimilated Jewish composer, **Károly Goldmark** (1830–1915, see p 192), who settled in Vienna and whose music is Viennese in inspiration.

Following World War I, the **Peace of St-Germain-en-Laye** of 10 September 1919 provided that an area of 4300 sq km with 341,000 inhabitants should be detached from the Hungarian part of the defunct Austro-Hungarian Monarchy and awarded to the Republic of Austria. This was subsequently carried through, with the exception that Sopron/Ödenburg remained Hungarian after a plebiscite (see above). Under the Nazi regime Burgenland was divided between the **Reichsgau Niederdonau** (in the north), and the **Reichsgau Steiermark** (in the south). In 1945 the *status quo ante* was restored. Thereafter, until 1989 Burgenland suffered from its proximity to the Iron Curtain, remaining one of the more backward economic areas of the country. However, in the last two decades, investment in tourism and infrastructure (e.g. the building of the motorway from Vienna to the Hungarian border) has brought economic benefits and a new vitality to the province. Burgenland was under conservative (Christian Social) rule from 1924 to the beginning of World War II, but from 1945 has been predominantly Social Democratic, with only two periods of *Volkspartei* (People's Party) governance between 1956–64. There are local arrangements to cater for the province's small ethnic minorities: 28 schools are dual-language (Croat and German), while two elementary schools teach in Hungarian and German, and there are possibilities for dual-language instruction at higher levels of education.

EISENSTADT

Practical information

Population: 10,300. Telephone dialling code: 02682.

Tourist information
Schloss Esterházy (see p 179), A-7000 Eisenstadt. ☎ 02682/33 84 or

67390. Fax: 02682 338420. A useful map is *Schubert & Franzke's Kulturausflug Burgenland*. Sights of historical or cultural interest are numbered on the map against brief descriptions with opening times etc. on the reverse. *Eisenstadt Tourismus* (☎ 02682/67390) organises guided tours of the city, some with themes such as '*In Haydn's Footsteps*' etc.

Neusiedler See (for general information)

Nationalpark Neusiedler See-Seewinkel, A-7142 Illmitz. ☎ 02175/3442; fax 02175/3444.

Hotels

✰✰✰ *Hotel Burgenland* (Schubertplatz 1, 7000 Eisenstadt. ☎ 696. Fax: 65531. Closed July). This is generally considered to be the best hotel in town and has a good restaurant ('*G'würzstöckl*').

✰✰ *Gasthof der Familie Ohr* (Ruster Straße 51. ☎ 62460. Fax: 624609). Modestly priced family concern with excellent home-cooking and car-parking spaces in front of the Gasthof. Located near the railway station.

✰ *Gasthof zum Haydnhaus* (Josef-Haydn-Gasse 24. ☎ 6436 36). Modestly priced and centrally located.

The choice of hotels in Eisenstadt itself is not overwhelming, so travellers might prefer to stay in Rust or Neusiedl (see p 184 and p 188) on the Neusiedler See.

Romantics might like ✰✰✰ *Schloss Bernstein* (see p 195: Familie Berger, Schlossweg 1. ☎ 6382. Fax: 6520. Open May–mid-October), where the elegance of a family home is combined with friendly service and good cooking.

Food buffs might prefer a weekend based on the ✰✰ *Weingut am Spitz* (7083 Purbach, Waldsiedlung 2. ☎ 5519. Fax: 551920. Closed Christmas to Easter). A relatively expensive but worthwhile option here is to participate in the Friday evening gourmet meals accompanied by various excellent wines from the estate.

Restaurants

The choice in Eisenstadt is not very exciting and the best Austrian food is probably served in the above-mentioned hotels, to which might be added the **Haydnbräu** (Pfarrgasse 22).

Cultural events

DONNERSKIRCHEN

Pannonian Concert Days ('*Musikalischer Weinsommer*') are held in the Martinschlössel in **July** and **August**.

EISENSTADT

The *Haydn-Tage* are held in **June** and **September** in Schloss Esterházy and the Bergkirche, with parallel events across the border in Hungary at Esterháza (Fertőd).

BURG LOCKENHAUS

In **July** there is a *Chamber Music Festival* (founded by Gidon Kremer), which is held in the Burg and the parish church. The stress is on informal music-making and the actual programme develops as the festival progresses.

KOBERSDORF

The *Schlossspiele* are held in **July** in the courtyard and there are also performances in the cellar by a troupe unconnected with the *Festspiele*. The programme includes comedy, music, dance, fairytales, etc. (Moving the *Festspiele* to Burg Forchtenstein is currently under discussion).

MÖRBISCH

The *Seefestspiele Mörbisch* (Mörbisch Lakeside Festival) was founded in 1957 and presents operetta each summer on a stage built out over the Neusiedler See. The season lasts from **mid-July to the end of August**. Every performance closes with a firework display. Tickets from Schloss Esterházy, Eisenstadt, ☎ 66210.

ST MARGARETHEN

A **Passion Play** is held every five years in the Roman quarry, the next being scheduled for the year 2001. In addition there are summer productions of operas and musicals.

History of Eisenstadt

The area now encompassed by the city of Eisenstadt was settled from the late Stone Age, its origins lying on a knoll of the Leitha Mountains known as the **Burgstallberg**. Archaeological finds show that this was a centre of Celtic and Hallstatt culture, while a Roman settlement grew up later in the eastern part of the town. This outpost of the empire was later overrun by the Goths, whose cemetery here has been excavated. In the period of the **Great Migrations**, the ethnic hordes coming from the Pannonian Plain washed over Eisenstadt, until it was established as a frontier station of Charlemagne's *Ostmark*. From the late 10C it became a tempting target for Magyar aggression, as the conquerors of the Carpathian Basin (AD 896) stepped up their raids in search of western booty.

The first documentary mention of historic Eisenstadt occurs as *capella sancti Martini de minore Mortin*, or '**Kleinmartinsdorf** (**Little St Martin**) in 1264. In 1371, after the Hungarian noble line of Kaniszai had succeeded the German Gutkeled knights as local lords, the former received permission from Louis the Great of Hungary to build a fortification for the town, the legendary strength of which is supposed to have given birth to the nomenclature '**Eisenstadt**', **the iron city**. However, the Hungarians retained the original reference to St Martin and to this day call the place *Kismarton*. In 1388 Kismarton, which had already received municipal rights from the Kaniszai in 1371, also acquired market rights from the Kaniszai's patron, King (later Emperor) Sigismund (of Luxembourg, 1368–1437). This privilege gave a considerable boost to Kismarton's commerce, opening up the Hungarian market for local traders and encouraging the wine exports to Silesia and Poland. At approximately the same time, the Kaniszai built a powerful moated castle within the city walls, the forerunner of the Esterházy Schloss.

In the following century the Habsburgs acquired Eisenstadt by treaty (1445), together with neighbouring Hornstein, although the now prosperous market remained an apple of discord between Habsburg and Hungarian rulers. During the part-occupation of Austria by Matthias Corvinus of Hungary in the 1480s, it reverted to the latters' control, but by the **Peace of Pressburg** (1491) returned to Habsburg possession, despite its continuing location in Hungarian territory. It was thereafter pledged to various noble families, who generally oppressed the burghers and drained the town's resources. Eisenstadt rose unsuccessfully against Archduke Ferdinand in 1522, was laid waste by fire in 1525 and had its burgher rights removed in a statute of 1526, the year in which the Habsburgs inherited the throne of Hungary after the death of Lajos II at the Battle of Mohács.

Despite the town's supposed invulnerability, the Turkish army overran Eisenstadt on its way to an unsuccessful siege of Vienna in 1529, and thereafter the fortifications were strengthened by Italian military architects. Under **Hans von Weißpriach**, to whom the town was pledged from 1554–71, the burghers were further oppressed, although Weißpriach is also known to have acted as protector of the substantial Jewish community (which had existed here since at least 1296) and was remarkably tolerant of Protestants. The Jewish ghetto was settled against the castle walls, while the Protestants were allowed to have their own church. A man of wide interests, Weißpriach also founded a menagerie in the Schlosspark and a brewery in the town. However, the vociferous complaints of the burghers against the arrogant rule of Weißpriach finally compelled Maximilian II to take action: in 1572 he redeemed the town and confirmed the burghers in their rights, naturally against a substantial payment, as well as issuing an ordinance that the town should never again be sold or pledged.

Despite occasional setbacks, the burghers of Eisenstadt mostly succeeded in holding on to their rights and privileges thereafter: at any rate, when the Esterházys acquired the Burg in 1622, the town remained independent, a status confirmed (again for hefty payments) in **1648** by Ferdinand III, who raised it to a **Freistadt**. In 1671 a new Jewish ghetto, the *Unterberg*, was erected west of the Burg, built on former administration offices of Hans von Weißpriach. This replaced the old Jewish quarter that had been dissolved by imperial fiat.

After some anxious moments in the later Turkish wars and the Hungarian *kuruc* War of Independence (1703–11, see p 174), Eisenstadt boomed in the 18C as the *Residenzstadt* of the glittering Esterházy Princes, two of whom were Palatines of Hungary and all of whom were inestimably rich patrons of culture. Carlo Carlone rebuilt the rugged *Wasserburg* between 1663–72 in Baroque style, while the Esterházys' other great palace in the region was built in the 1670s a short distance away at Esterháza to a design (probably) by Melchior Hefele from Tyrol. Meanwhile, a further rearrangement of border territories in 1655 had returned Eisenstadt to Hungarian administration within the Empire.

Prince Miklós Esterházy (1714–90), nicknamed 'the Magnificent', (his family in the main line were hereditary Princes of the Holy Roman Empire from 1711) summoned Joseph Haydn to Eisenstadt in 1761 and the composer was to serve the family for nearly three decades thereafter. Eisenstadt became a centre of culture and Baroque spectacle, thereby losing its border fortress character completely—indeed even the city fortifications were gradually demolished. A number of families with famous offspring were Eisenstadt burghers or employees of the Esterházy court, among them that of the celebrated dancer, Fanny Elßler (1810–84), of the actress Therese Krones (1801–30), who made her name on the Vienna stage in the bitter-sweet comedies of Ferdinand Raimund, of the distinguished anatomist Joseph Hyrtl (1810–94), who revolutionised the conservation process of human parts and supplied many anatomical museums and colleagues worldwide with his preparations, and of Ignaz Semmelweis (1818–65), the Hungarian discoverer of antisepsis known as the 'saviour of mothers'. The Esterházy court also attracted distinguished visitors over the years, including Ludwig van Beethoven, Admiral Nelson (who thus made the acquaintance of Haydn, the composer celebrating Nelson's great victory at Aboukir Bay by entitling his *Mass in D minor* the *Nelson Mass*) and Franz (Ferenc) Liszt. In the 19C the city steadily expanded, not least due to a strong military presence following the 1848 revolution and the founding of the Imperial Cadet Institute in 1853.

In the difficult period after World War I, the Hungarians at first refused to accept the requirement of the Treaty of St-Germain-en-Laye that Burgenland be yielded to Austria. After intervention by the Western Powers and a plebiscite in Sopron/Ödenburg, the situation was resolved and Eisenstadt became the new province's capital in 1925. In 1926 it was elevated to the honorary status of *Freistadt*. After the Nazi reorganisation and a period of post-war Russian occupation, the city settled into its role as an administrative and commercial centre. In 1960 it became a Diocesan seat and has long been the residence of the Superintendents of the Burgenland Lutheran Community. The present incumbent of this latter post, Gertraud Knoll, is an attractive and media-friendly lady who stood unsuccessfully for the Austrian presidency in 1998.

The old town

The old centre of **Eisenstadt** is reached through remnants of the medieval and Renaissance walls and bastions, which are best preserved to the north and south, and which enclose the three east–west parallel streets of the earliest town's ground-plan. The restored **Pulverturm** (Powder Tower) at the north-east end of town (beyond the Franciscan Church) is a typical part of the Renaissance defences and dates to 1534.

Schloss Esterházy

The central square is officially **Esterházyplatz**, but generally known as **Schlossplatz**, **Schloss Esterházy** lying to the north of it. Its predecessor was the Kaniszai Burg (host to King Sigismund at a Kaniszai marriage in 1392) and is recalled with the Kaniszai coat of arms on the south-east tower, the latter dating to the first half of the 15C. The moated medieval Schloss passed to Miklós Esterházy in 1622, but it was not until 1663 (under Pál Esterházy) that work was begun on remodelling it in Baroque style to plans by Carlo Martino Carlone, executed by Sebastiano Bartoletto and Carlo Antonio Carlone. It has been said that the fruits of their labours display a certain barbaric splendour, perhaps an allusion to the 18 busts of Hungarian warriors fronting the mezzanine level windows, but perhaps also the decision to retain the medieval idea of four massive corner towers contributes to this effect. Notable are Andrea Bertinali's cartouches of mascarons on the volutes of the protruding eaves. Other aspects of Carlone's design (such as onion domes on the towers) fell victim to Pierre-Charles Moreau's further alterations between 1797 and 1805, which added a neo-classical flavour to the building. Moreau was a proponent of so-called 'Revolutionary Classicism', having come to Austria in the wake of the French Revolution and it is to him that we owe the balcony of the façade, which is supported by Tuscan columns, and the Classical portico of the garden façade with its doubled Corinthian columns.

- Those parts of the Schloss that are not leased to the Burgenland administration are accessible for concerts or otherwise from June–Sept, 08.30–18.00, Oct–May, 08.30–17.00, between Easter–Oct daily, from Nov–Easter at weekends only. Guided tours on the hour, 09.00–16.00. The **Burgenländische Landesgalerie**, in the former stables and guardroom of the Schloss, has been installed since 1996 (open Tues–Fri, 10.00–12.00, Sun, PH 13.00–17.00), and is dedicated to contemporary art.

Above the entrance are busts in niches of the first Esterházy owners of the Schloss,

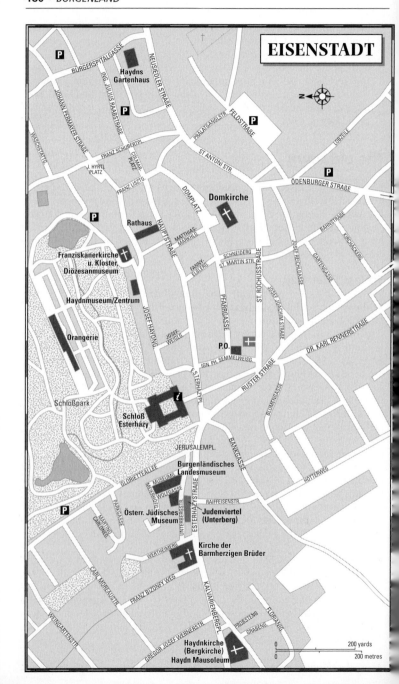

EISENSTADT

Haydns Gartenhaus

BÜRGERSPITALGASSE

NEUSIEDLER STRAße

JOHANN PERMAYER STRAße

ING. JULIUS RAABSTRAße

VASCASSTG

FRANZ SCHUBERTPL

CULMAR PLATZ

J. HYRTL PLATZ

FRANZ LISZTG.

PRÄLAT GANGLSTR.

FELDSTRAße

ST ANTONI STR.

ÖDENBURGER STRAße

LÖBTELE

Domkirche

DOMPLATZ

Rathaus

HAUPTSTRAße

MATTHIAS- MARKHLG.

SCHNEIDERG.

ST. MARTIN STR.

ST. ROCHUSSTRAße

JOSEF REICHL GASSE

BAHNSTRAße

KIRCHÄCKERG.

GARTENGASSE

Franziskanerkirche u. Kloster, Diözesanmuseum

FANNY- ELßLERG.

Haydnmuseum/Zentrum

JOSEF HAYDNG.

JOSEF WEIGLG.

PFARRGASSE

JOSEF JOACHIM STRAße

DR. KARL RENNERSTRAße

Orangerie

P.O.

IGN. PH. SEMMELWEISG.

RUSTER STRAße

ESTERHÁZYPL.

BLUMENGASSE

Schloßpark

Schloß Esterházy

JERUSALEMPL.

BANKGASSE

HÖTTERWEG

GLORIETTEALLEE

MUSEUMG.

MEIERHOFG.

WOLFGASSE

Burgenländisches Landesmuseum

RAIFFEISENSTR.

UNTERBERGSTR.

ESTERHÁZYSTRAße

Österr. Jüdisches Museum

Judenviertel (Unterberg)

MARTINI CARLONEG.

PFARRGASSE

WERTHEIMERG.

Kirche der Barmherzigen Brüder

FRANZ BIZONFY WEG

CARL MOREAUSTR.

KALVARIENBERGPL.

PRÖBSTENG.

FLORIANIG.

WEINGARTENSTR.

GREGOR JOSEF WERNERSTR.

GRABENG.

Haydnkirche (Bergkirche)

Haydn Mausoleum

0 ___ 200 yards
0 ___ 200 metres

Miklós Esterházy, Palatine of Hungary (1582–1645) and his younger son, Pál (1635–1713), the actual commissioner of Carlone's work. Of the interior, the great **Festsaal** in the north wing (also known as the 'Haydnsaal', since he often performed here) is notable, rising through three storeys and showing 16 grisaille medallions of Hungarian generals and kings, these portraits being based on a work published in Nürnberg by Ferenc Nádasdy and entitled *Mausoleum regum ac primorum Ungariae ducum*. The frescoes (richly framed) on the ceiling are by Carpoforo Tencalla of Lake Garda and represent scenes from *The Golden Ass* by Apuleius (including *Amor and Psyche* and *The Hesperides*). They were painted at the end of the 17C and beginning of the 18C as the signature *Tencala pinxit 1701* testifies, but were heavily restored after World War II. In the **Wildschweinsaal** (Wild Boar Room) may be seen a statue (1805) by Antonio Canova of **Leopoldine von Liechtenstein** (née Esterházy), which was originally made for Moreau's memorialising **Leopoldinentempel** built next to an ornamental pond in the garden.

In the **Haydnzimmer** of the west wing stands a huge gilded vase with green malachite cladding made in 1902. Lastly, one proceeds to the richly ornate **Schlosskirche** in the Schlosshof: a separate parish for the Esterházy Schloss was founded in 1655 'for the personal convenience and comfort of the prestigious family' as the Bishop of Győr obsequiously put it, being consecrated in 1660 by the Archbishop of Esztergom himself. Its prestige was further enhanced when Count Pál managed to obtain for it the bones of St Constantine the Martyr, which were placed under a side-altar. It was in this chapel that most of Haydn's Masses were first performed.

The **Schlosspark** was laid out primarily as a utility garden in 1624 (albeit with parterres as well); however its present aspect goes back to alterations made by Moreau, at which time it was transformed in English style, having in addition an orangery, a greenhouse and (from 1803) an early steam water-pump, which is now in Vienna's Technical Museum.

The Esterházy wine production is stored in the Schloss cellars, while in the former **Schlosstaverne** could be seen huge barrel belonging to the vintner Wolf that holds several thousand litres.

Josef-Haydn-Gasse

East of the Schloss the attractive Josef-Haydn-Gasse runs parallel to the old city wall and contains mostly 17C houses. You pass on your left (no. 1) the former administration centre of the Esterházy estates, built in 1792 on the Augustinian cloister dissolved by Joseph II, which in turn stood on the first Jewish ghetto razed on the orders of Leopold I in 1671. This was at a time when Leopold was strongly under the influence of his bigoted Spanish wife, who joined in a conspiracy with the fanatical Cardinal Khlesl to drive the Jews from Vienna's *Unteren Werd* (see *History* p 54; thereafter named the Leopoldstadt). Beethoven stayed in this building when writing his *C Major Mass* to a commission for Miklós II, Prince Esterházy, in September 1807, a visit that ended in a quarrel between aristocratic patron and proud musical genius. Further along the street no. 17 has an attractive Rococo façade with reliefs of the *Four Seasons* (these, however, are unrelated to Haydn's oratorio of the same theme based on James Thomson's *The Seasons*, 1730). Two houses further along at no. 21 is indeed the Haydnhaus, bought by the composer in 1766 and occupied until 1778, when he had to move (not without grumbling) to Esterháza (over the Hungarian border at Fertőd). The **museum** here (open Easter–Oct, daily 09.00–12.00, 13.00–17.00) has materials on Haydn, Franz Liszt and Fanny Elßler, amongst others, the last-named scoring her greatest successes (like Haydn) in London.

To the east of the Haydnhaus you come shortly to the **Franciscan Church and Monastery**, the latter founded by Prince Miklós Esterházy in 1620, the former in 1625 on the site of a Gothic Minorite monastery destroyed by the Turkish invasion of 1529. The high altar (1630) shows *St Michael* flanked by *Sts Mark and Matthew*, and there are notable stucco reliefs for the side-altars (on the left the *Resurrection*, on the right, the *Assumption*), while on the south wall is a copy of the famous *Black Madonna* of Częstochowa (Poland). The Rococo **pulpit** (1752) has carved reliefs of the *Legends of St Francis*, and also notable are the choir-stalls (1630) and the confessional (behind the high altar, with polychrome busts of saints). In the garden wing of the Franciscan monastery is the Esterházy crypt (*Esterházy-Gruft*). A red and white marble tomb for Palatine Pál (d. 1713) and Prince Joseph Esterházy (d. 1721) stands in middle. At the foot of the steps against the east wall of the monastery are two statues showing Prince Paul Esterházy and his wife Ursula, perhaps by the Viennese court artist, Paul Strudel, and made in the early 18C. The **Diocesan Museum** at Haydngasse 31 is open May–Sept, Wed–Sat, 10.00–13.00, 14.00–17.00, Sun and PH 13.00–17.00.

Hauptstraße, Pfarrgasse

A turn to the right from the Josef-Haydn-Gasse down Lisztgasse brings you to the **Hauptstraße**. Immediately on your left at no. 35 is the **Rathaus** (c 1650), with its three bay windows, and showing frescoes of female figures as allegories of the virtues of good city government (*Loyalty*, *Wisdom*, *Strength*, *Hope*, *Charity* and *Moderation*). Further to the east (at Bürgerspitalgasse 2) is the **Haydn-Gartenhäuschen**, a summer house where the composer is supposed to have retreated to compose in tranquillity (it can be visited). However, a turn right (westwards) out of Lisztgasse brings you past the **Plague** or **Trinity Column** (1713), and beyond it to **St Florian's Well** (1628) at the central point of the medieval city (the statue is a 19C addition). Passing several interesting houses you rejoin the Schlossplatz, to the south-east of which (leaving the Landesgalerie on your right) **Pfarrgasse** leads back eastwards to the **Domplatz** and (just to the south) the **cathedral** itself. The latter is dedicated to Eisenstadt's (and Burgenland's) patron, St Martin, and was built on the site of a 12C Romanesque church, the original *capella sancti Martini* founded in 1200. It stands in a cemetery surrounded by a defensive wall and retains other military features on its massive tower. The present building (1629) replaced a 15C late Gothic hall church largely destroyed by fire in 1589, and was itself substantially re-gothicised in 1903–04. This process obliterated most of the Baroque fittings, although the pulpit of 1745 (with a relief of *Jesus and the Scribes*) and the organ loft with Leopold Malleck's organ (1778, built to Haydn's specifications) survive. Although Stefan Dorfmeister's Baroque frescoes have gone, his altarpiece (*The Apotheosis of St Martin*, 1777) has been rehung on the north wall, together with the same artist's *Immaculata* (1777) on the north wall of the choir. In the northern vestibule is a polychrome relief of *Christ on the Mount of Olives* dating to 1495. Of the modern works, note the massive statue of *St Martin and the Beggar* on the right-hand column of the triumphal arch, the stained glass (1960) by Margaret Bilger and a bronze *pietà* by Anton Hanak in the modern crypt.

West of Schlossplatz

The area known as **Unterberg** to the west of the Schloss was the site of the Jewish ghetto. Jews had settled in Eisenstadt since the 13C, their numbers being increased in 1388 by co-religionists fleeing from pogroms in Austria. Their original ghetto had been close to the eastern wall of the Burg and was built under Hans von Weißpriach (see *History*, p 177), but under Pál Esterházy a new ghetto was founded (1671) to the west after the Emperor had ordered the dissolution of the existing one. Enclosed by Museumgasse, Wolfgasse, Unterbergstraße and Wertheimergasse, it remained a self-administrating Jewish quarter until 1938. At Unterbergstraße 6 was the mansion (1719) of the well-to-do Samson Wertheimer, who was both a banker and a rabbi; it now houses the interesting **Austrian Jewish Museum** (open May–Oct, Tues–Sun, 10.00–17.00). The posts with chains on the wall of the house recall that the streets around the synagogue (located inside the Wertheimer house) were closed off on the Sabbath to ensure its rigorous observance. The Wertheimergasse leads north to the Jewish cemetery, which is crowded with inscribed gravestones from the 17C–19C (the earliest dating to 1679), many leaning at crazy angles, and the whole reminiscent of the much described Jewish cemetery in Prague.

On the way to the Jewish Museum you will have passed at Museumgasse 1–5 the **Burgenländische Landesmuseum** (open Tues–Sun, 09.00–12.00, 13.00–17.00) with its departments of Natural History, Archaeology, Cultural History and Folklore. The departments dealing with pre-history and Roman finds (including a fine **Roman mosaic**) are of interest, as also are the rooms devoted to Franz Liszt and Fanny Elßler (see *History*, p 178), the contemporary historical documentation since 1919, and especially the new (since 1989) wine museum. On the western edge of the junction with Wertheimergasse and Esterházystrasse is the **church** (1740) and hospital (since 1713) of the Brothers of Mercy (*Barmherzigen Brüder*, Esterházygasse 26). The high altar (1760) of the former is a free-standing *mensa*, while its altarpiece on the wall of the apse is a representation of *St Anthony* (to whom the church is dedicated) with the *Christ Child* in an ornate Rococo frame, and was painted by a certain Father Wagenstein in 1768. The wrought-iron grille with the Esterházy coat of arms is notable.

From here the road climbs west from the Unterberg to the **Oberberg**, more specifically to the **Calvary Hill**, which one ascends from the **Gnadenkapelle** (Votive Chapel) to the **Chapel of the Cross** (1707) at the summit. The '*Kalvarienberg*' is actually an artificial creation of ashlar blocks erected (1701–07) on the orders of Prince Pál Esterházy I, on which an elaborate **Calvary route** has been laid out in a series of grottos, niches and shrines connected by corridors and steps. The concept, which is based on a similar layout at Maria Lanzendorf but has unique features, was worked out by a Franciscan brother named Felix Nierinck. In total there are 320 vernacular figures of wood and stone, theatrically didactic realisations for the chapels and altars of 24 Stations of the Cross (there are usually only 14 represented).

The **Bergkirche** on the west side of the Kalvarienberg is the stunted realisation of a more ambitious plan to build Hungary's biggest pilgrimage church on this site. In the event only the presbytery was built (1715–22) with Esterházy money, and this came to be called the **Haydnkirche** after the composer was buried here. The composer's original grave is marked under the organ loft with a simple marble tombstone, but a Haydn mausoleum was subsequently built under the north tower of the church in 1932 (the bicentenary of the composer's birth). Haydn actually died (31 May 1809) in his Vienna house and was buried in a suburban cemetery. When his remains were exhumed (1820) to be brought to Eisenstadt, the head was found to be missing—it had been appropriated by Joseph Karl Rosenbaum, who was conducting researches into the skulls of exceptionally gifted people. Haydn was hastily lent somebody else's head for his reburial in the Bergkirche in the same year; his real head found its way eventually to the museum of the Vienna **Gesellschaft der Musikfreunde** (Society of the Friends of Music), where it was displayed from 1895–1954, when the Society was finally persuaded to part with it. On the 5 June of that year Haydn was finally reunited with his skull in his mausoleum. The latter shows allegorical sculptures of the *Four Seasons* and has inscriptions round the cupola recalling Haydn's most important works. The fresco (1772) on the ceiling of the church shows the *Ascension* and is the work of Christian and Wolfgang Köppl. In 1776 an organ on which Haydn had played was built into the church.

Around Eisenstadt: the Leithagebirge

The clement micro-climate of the Neusiedler See to the east of Eisenstadt is due in large part to the barriers of the wooded **Leithagebirge** (Leitha Mountains) which bar the path of the advancing weather from the west. Their seemingly unending tapestry of deciduous woods remain to a large extent in the possession of the Esterházy family. The land between the mountains and the lake is characterised by the vine-clad hills around Rust, producing much of Burgenland's best quality wine, and rolling fertile land stretching along the western shore of the lake and up to the Parndorfer Heide, to the north-east of Neusiedl am See.

A minor road heads north from Eisenstadt towards Stotzing, passing through an area with many attractive ramblers' routes (e.g. up to the **Sonnenberg** or the **Buchkogel**). Beyond Stotzing is the pilgrimage church of **Loretto** (Anton Riebler, 1704), ranged along the side of a picturesque village square and approached through a courtyard with a gateway surmounted by a stone *Madonna*. In the courtyard is a **Marian Column** (1700) decorated with reliefs of scenes from the life of Christ (*Jesus in the Temple*, the *Flight into Egypt*, *Christ and the Pharisees*, the *Crown of Thorns*, the *Deposition from the Cross*, the *Lamentation of Christ*). In the niche over the church entrance is a statue of *St Barbara*, while the niche figures of the tower represent the two *Saint-Kings of Hungary*, István (Stephen) and *Ladislas*, the same figures flanking the altarpiece of the *Immaculata* in the interior with its high altar (1766) of green marble. The rich stucco (c 1660) is by the Carlone workshop, while the sanctuary again alludes to the Marian cult with pictures of the *Visitation* and the *Reception of the Virgin into the Kingdom of Heaven* (both c 1650). There are eight highly ornamented side-chapels dedicated respectively (clockwise from the entrance) to All the Saints, a certain Benitius (an adviser of Rudolf of Habsburg), St Stephen (of Hungary), St John Nepomuk, St Rochus, St Sebastian, St Judas Thaddeus, St Peregrine, and Our Lady of Sorrows. In the inner courtyard, circumscribed by the cloister, is the **Votive Chapel** (1664), an imitation of the Loretan *Casa Santa*, and containing the votive *Black Madonna*.

South-east of Eisenstadt: St Margarethen

A few kilometres south-east of Eisenstadt on the Rust road is **St Margarethen im Burgenland** with its remarkable **open-air museum** (open daily 09.00–18.00, with tours) centred on the 147,000sq m of Roman quarry, one of the most impressive (up to 40m high) and oldest in Europe. Its stone was used for building *Carnuntum* (see p 134) and *Vindobona (*Roman Vienna, see p 51), and it subsequently supplied material for medieval parts of the Vienna Stephansdom and even for the 19C Ringstrassen palaces. The cliffs of the quarry are formed by deposits of chalky sandstone left by the prehistoric sea that covered Pannonia. It has been a rich source of fossils and has a cave in which thousands of bats spend the winter months. The quarry is the location for an international summer school for sculptors and provides the setting for a quinquennial Passion play. A modest museum is devoted to the latter at Siegendorfer Strasse 23 in the village (to visit, apply to the priest's house). The late Gothic parish **church of St John the Baptist** with a modern extension has a notable stone pulpit of the 17C made by the local sculptors' workshop. Next to it is a **charnel house** from the early 14C with a pyramidal roof and Baroque additions. At Hauptstrasse 161 is the medieval Burghof.

THE NEUSIEDLER SEE

The Neusiedler See

The Neusiedler See (Hungarian *Fertő-tó*) is a shallow, salty steppe lake, which is currently 33.5km long, has an average width of 12km, and an average depth of 110cm, in places 170cm. It is so shallow that it can be waded through at the Mörbisch-Illmitz narrows at its southern end, as happens during the annual folk festival. It is girdled by a thick band of reeds known as *das Rohr* (pipe), which is home to many species of birds. The reeds (except at Podersdorf) necessitate long wooden dykes ('*Schluichten*') to reach the open water from the banks. They are also exploited commercially (a harvest of 10,000 tons annually) for roofing, handicrafts, etc. The waters hold 30 species of fish, the most common being carp (130,000 kg caught annually), zander and pike (50,000 kg annually), together with bream, perch and eels, producing total catches of up to 400,000 kg of fish a year.

The entire lake is an ornithological conservation area attracting birdwatchers from all over Europe, its importance being partly due to the fact that it lies on a migration route. Among the 280 different species found here are herons, bustards, spoonbills, sandpipers, lapwings, egrets, rails, bitterns and quail, together with many other kinds of wader, warbler, tit and waterfowl. As a rich biotope, it provides a suitable summer habitat for storks, which can be seen gliding around the rooftops of the surrounding villages, or standing meditatively in the fields wherever a good supply of mice and frogs (their preferred delicacy) is available. The lake is known as *Das Meer der Wiener* (The Sea of the Viennese), since it is easily reached from the capital and offers extensive sporting and recreational potential, and is also ringed by perhaps the most pleasant cycling route in Austria (see also pp 169 and 186).

Typical architecture around the Neusiedler See

The western shore: Mörbisch to Neusiedl am See

From St Margarethen road 52 leads through Rust (see below) and on to **Mörbisch am See** on the Hungarian border, formerly '*Merwisch*' and part of the Sopron/Ödenburg territories from 1385–1848. The atmosphere of its streets lined with Hungarian-style peasant houses with their columned verandahs (*Lauben*) is most delightful in summer when the corncobs are hung out to dry in the sun. A traditional house of this style dating to the turn of the 19C has been turned into a museum and is well worth a visit (**Heimathaus**, Hauptstraße 55, open April–Oct, 09.00–12.00, 13.00–17.00): it shows the living quarters of a peasant family, farm buildings, the kitchen, cellar, winepress, animal stalls and larder. The *Seebühne* for the summer operetta festival (July and August, see **Arts festivals** above) is reached via a dyke across the reeds girdling the lake (there is also a restaurant here). Protection against midges is advisable for those attending the performances. Likewise the **Dammstrasse** leads to the boat station for ferries to Illmitz and Podersdorf.

Mörbisch was for long a cul-de-sac, as there was no crossing from here into Hungary in the days of the Iron Curtain (it is now passable on foot or bicycle). In 1989 the Austrian and Hungarian Foreign Ministers ceremonially cut the barbed wire near here, heralding the fall of the Iron Curtain. However, our route lies back up the west side of the lake to **Freistadt Rust**, distinguished on account of having the biggest stork colony in Austria—some 30 pairs occupy the chimney-top perches between the end of March and the end of August. The name of the town is derived from *Rusterbaum* (Hungarian '*szil*'), a reference to the elm-trees that still grow here, this German name, however, first occurring in 1385. For many centuries, as still today, the place has been famed for its quality wine, ancient wine privileges which allowed exports to Hungary having been confirmed by Matthias Corvinus in the 15C. In 1681 the Protestant 'Free Town of Rust' (a freedom acquired in the mid-century on payment of much wine and 60,000 Gulden) received its city statute from Leopold I.

The **Rathaus** dates to the Renaissance, with Baroque additions in 1637 and 1703, and has an important archive preserving the above-mentioned statute of Leopold I, which lays out the rights and privileges of the city in painstaking detail. A curiosity is the inscription over the entrance to the Rathaus cellar: '*17 is all right by me when I am at least at 26*', a combined reference to the date of the portal (1726) and the possibilities of intoxication available beyond it.

The fortified **church of St Pancras and St Giles** or **Fischerkirche** at Rathausplatz 16 (open daily 10.00–12.00, 14.00–18.00) is an agglutinative Gothic church with remnants of its 12C Romanesque predecessor (the northwest wall). Between 1521 and 1649 it was alternately in the possession of the Catholics and Protestants, reflecting the ebb and flow of religious allegiance in Rust. According to tradition, the Gothic chapel built on to the Romanesque church was founded by Queen Maria of Hungary in gratitude for her rescue by fishermen when she was caught in a storm on the Neusiedler See. Surviving Romanesque frescoes on the lower north wall of the nave show a *Madonna and Child*, while of the frescoes elsewhere dating from the 14C, 15C and 16C, those on the bosses of the vault of the Pankrazi-Chor showing vine-cutters, hoes and fish emblems, and in the nave showing acanthus wreaths, vines, fruit, a man framed by a vine and fishes in the tresses of seaweed, are the emblems of the fishermen's and vintners' guilds of Rust. The whole of the interior is indeed a riot of colourful mural decoration from different periods of the Middle Ages, even the architectural features having painted ornamentation. The Gothic *Three Saints Altar*, also in the Pankrazi-Chor, shows *St Catherine*, *St Florian* and *St Ursula*, while in a side-chapel is a polychrome Gothic *Madonna*. The early Baroque high altar (1642) has an altarpiece of the *Crucifixion* and is flanked by wooden statues of *St Pancras* and *St Giles*. To the south of the church may be seen the remnants of the city walls of Rust.

The **Lutheran Church** to the west has a tower built at the turn of the 19C (Joseph II's Tolerance Patent of 1781 at first forbad the building of towers for Protestant churches). A walk round the town reveals many beautiful old houses, some with Renaissance sgraffiti. The tower of the 17C Catholic **parish church** may be climbed for a good view. The **Seevogel-Museum** (Am Hafen 2, open April–Nov 09.00–12.00, 13.30–18.00) informs about the bird life of the Neusiedler See.

The minor road leads north from Rust through **Oggau**, where at Hauptstraße 40 there are temporary displays of local archaeological finds from Easter to October. After joining the main road 50 coming from Eisenstadt, you reach shortly **Donnerskirchen**, with its Baroque **parish church** surrounded by a medieval protective wall, and a **pillory** of 1666. Further north-west is **Purbach am Neusiedler See**, which preserves much of its anti-Turkish bastions and three city gates. The altarpiece (1788) of the parish church shows the *Trinity* and *St Nicholas as Saviour of Shipmen* by Stefan Dorfmeister. The high altar itself has a free-standing neo-classical tabernacle and the church also possesses a dramatic picture of a shipwreck on the lake. This is a spectacular reminder that the extreme shallowness of the lake (similar to Hungarian Lake Balaton, not far to the east) is by no means guaranteed to make it less harmless. On the contrary, strong winds can whip up the waves to a dangerous fury in a matter of minutes, capsizing the frail shallow-draughted craft suitable for use in such waters. In the Schulgasse at no. 9 is the **Türkenkeller**, an arcaded vintner's house with the stone bust of a Turk on the chimney: according to legend, a Turkish soldier, who did not wish to be parted from the joys of the infidels' delightful wines, hid himself in the chimney of the house when the Turkish army retreated. The returning inhabitants smoked him out of his hiding-place (in fact he got stuck trying to squeeze out of the top of the chimney and had to be rescued), but spared his life, whereupon he turned Christian, married a local girl 'and thereafter populated Purbach with many half-Turks'. The village has numerous buildings from the 16C and 17C, notably the **Weinhauerhaus** '*Fasching*' at Kirchengasse 45, and the '*Nikolauszeche*', a restaurant built into the old city wall.

Breitenbrunn a few kilometres further north-east is dominated by a 32m high Türkenturm erected in 1689 on the foundation of earlier fortifications and now a **museum** (open May–Oct, Tues–Sun 09.00–12.00 and 13.00–17.00).

The five storeys have interesting documentation of the history and natural history of the area. Neighbouring **Winden am See** was an ancient crossroads on the amber trade route and thereby became a Roman settlement of some importance (it featured as '*Ulmus*'—elm-tree—in the *Tabula Peutingeriana*, published (1507) in Augsburg by the humanists Konrad Celtis and Konrad Peutinger, a copy of a 5C Roman road map showing all the Empire's trade routes). In a cave (**Ludl-Loch**) on the western slopes of the Zeilerberg to the north, skeletons of an ice-age bear and hyena were discovered in 1930 and are now displayed in the Breitenbrunn Museum. The **Gritsch-Mühle** above the town is an open-air museum founded by the sculptor Wander Bertoni in 1966—nearby is one of his steel sculptures. The Italian-born (1925) Bertoni was brought to Vienna as forced labour in 1943 and after the war studied under Fritz Wotruba. Among his works are an *Icarus* made for the Vienna International Airport at Schwechat (surely the most unfortunate choice of symbolism from the point of view of passengers about to board their flights) and some reliefs for the Vienna Opera. The parish church at **Jois**, to the north, has provincial Baroque fittings of some charm, notably the figures of *Saint-King Stephen of Hungary* and his son *St Imre*, together with *Sts Sebastian* and *Rochus* on the main altar, and the pulpit with rocaille ornament and representations of *Faith*, *Hope* and *Charity*, above which is an angel blowing a trumpet.

Neusiedl am See and environs

Although the Neusiedl site was inhabited from earliest times and was a market at least since 1209, the modern foundation of it is attributed to German Counts of Győr, and its settlers were described as *hospites*—that is, German immigrants. The New Settlement (*Nuisidel*) of 1282 was part of an attempt to repopulate the territory after the disastrous Tatar invasions of 1240–41, which wiped out hundreds of Pannonian villages. The **Tabor** (fortified tower) dates to the 13C and was later (during the insurgency of the Hungarian *kuruc* armies of the 18C) part of a fortified line running from the Danube (Petronell) to the Neusiedler See, which, however, proved ineffective. The Catholic **parish church** (repeatedly rebuilt from its 1464 Gothic original) has a remarkable **Fishermen's Pulpit** (1780), which is partly in the form of the bows of a ship with mast and sail, and shows St John behind Christ, who is raising his hand in blessing over Peter sinking in the water.

The **Karl Eidler Regional Museum** (Kalvarienbergstraße 40; open May–Oct, Tues–Sat, 14.30–18.30, Sun, PH 10.00–12.00, 14.30–18.30) documents the peasant lifestyle of western Pannonia.

The **Seemuseum** (Seebad Neusiedl; open Easter–Oct, daily 09.00–12.00, 13.00–17.00) concentrates on the region's natural history and includes 280 stuffed birds, together with recordings of bird song. From April to August the *Neusiedler Impulse* features various artistic and gastronomic events.

The large village of **Parndorf** lies north of Neusiedl am See on the edge of the extensive **Parndorfer Heide** or **Platte**, a plateau of arable and heathland with much viticulture on the southern-facing slopes. The 18C fortification line (*Alte Schanze*) to the Danube ran through here, but before its erection Parndorf had been totally destroyed by the Turks in 1529, thereafter (like many such depopulated villages in North Burgenland) being resettled with Croats by the Esterházys. The **parish church**, (originally 1572) was partly rebuilt by Lukas von Hildebrandt in the 18C. The Vienna–Budapest highway now runs close to Parndorf, so Bruck an der Leitha can be reached shortly to the west, or the Hungarian border station Nickelsdorf/Hegyeshalom to the east. However, the main road north from Parndorf heads to **Gattendorf**, close to the site of a battle between Heinrich Jasomirgott of Babenberg and Géza II of Hungary in 1146, at which the Babenberg forces suffered a crushing defeat.

Zurndorf an der Leitha (between Gattendorf and Nickelsdorf) was once a Pechenegg settlement, the warlike tribe that originally drove the Hungarians into the Carpathian Basin in 896 being later used as border troops by the Hungarians themselves. In the church is an altarpiece of the Paul Troger school (the *Departure of the Apostles Peter and Paul on their Mission*).

At **Potzneusiedl**, reached on a minor road to the north-west, the neoclassical **Schloss Potzneusiedl** (1808) houses the **Austrian Icon Museum** (open daily 10.00–17.00), together with a collection of Hungarian Zsolnay porcelain. **Kittsee** to the north of Gattendorf and close to the Slovakian border has a Baroque **Neues Schloss** (1668, enlarged by Antonio Martinelli between 1730–40 to a commission from Pál Esterházy) with a splendid neo-Baroque wrought-iron gate to the park; the gate was originally made for the Austro-Hungarian pavilion at the Paris World Exhibition in 1900. Peter the Great stayed incognito at the Schloss, when visiting the area to spy on the Danube flotilla of the Habsburgs. Notable is the building's noble façade with Atlas figures supporting an elegant balcony, while inside is an **Ethnographical Museum** (open daily, 10.00–16.00, in summer to 17.00) with items of vernacular art from eastern and southern Europe. The **Alte Schloss** of Kittsee was originally moated, and probably built by the Hungarian Árpád kings as a border fortress. In neighbouring **Edelstal** is the celebrated *Römerquelle* factory, which produces the mineral water bottled and sold under the Römerquelle name all over Austria, a product known for its insinuatingly erotic advertisements. Ninth-century Avar graves have been excavated in the Kittsee area.

The eastern shore: Weiden am See to Apetlon

From Neusiedl am See road 51 leads south-east to **Weiden am See**, which has a Bronze Age necropolis from the period of the so-called Wieselburg culture, and from where you can turn down towards the lakeside and Podersdorf (see below). Weiden's parish church (1786) has sculptures of *Sts Augustine* and *Ambrose*, thought to be copies of originals by Lukas von Hildebrandt, and a charming pulpit showing the *Four Evangelists*. This village, together with nearby Gols and Mönchhof to the south-east, are classic areas of Burgenland viticulture. **Gols** was a stronghold of Protestantism, even in the Counter-Reformation, and still has a majority of Lutherans over Catholics of c 4:1, a resultant peculiarity being that very many share the same family name, although in most cases they are not related. There is, of course, a Lutheran Church built in neo-Gothic style in 1818, its altarpiece of the *Adoration of the Three Kings* dating, however, to 1537, but after a wooden relief (1511) of Albrecht Dürer. The Catholic Church retains traces of its Romanesque origin, having a formidable defensive tower, and stands on a formerly fortified hillock.

Mönchhof owes its name to a Cistercian foundation of 1217, when a gift of land was made to the Order by the Hungarian King, András II, and the new cloister was populated with monks from Heiligenkreuz in Lower Austria. When the Habsburgs moved their stud here from neighbouring Halbturn (see below) in 1553, the

Cistercians were given their *congé*, but embarked on a legal claim for restoration of their property which lasted 119 years. Only after the imperial stud was removed to Prague could they return in 1659. On the wall of the **parish church** (1734) the Heiligenkreuz coat of arms may be seen; the altarpieces are by the school of Martino Altomonte (the *Repentance of Mary Magdalene*), while the *Coronation of the Virgin* (1741) on the left-hand side-altar is by Altomonte himself.

Just to the east of Mönchhof is **Schloss Halbturn**, (open April–Oct, daily, 09.00–18.00) now used for (often excellent) extension displays of the Austrian Gallery in the Vienna Belvedere, together with historical exhibitions staged by the Burgenland Department of Culture. After the original settlement had been twice destroyed by Turkish armies, Alois, Count Harrach had Lukas von Hildebrandt build the magnificent Baroque Schloss, the name referring to a 'half tower' ('*halber Turm*') remaining from the previous building. Emperor Karl VI used Halbturn as a hunting-lodge and the substantial park was laid out between 1724 and 1727. Subsequently, alterations to the building were made under Maria Theresia by Franz Anton Hillebrand. The superb ceiling frescoes (1765) in the **Großen Schloßsaal** are the work of the great Franz Anton Maulbertsch and show *Allegories of Light and Time*.

The **Josefskirche** (1714) in Halbturn was enlarged to plans by Josef Emanuel Fischer von Erlach in 1730. There is a *Heuriger* in the courtyard of the Schloss and a wine-shop selling the excellent products of the local vineyards. Behind the Schloss, note the vernacular maize stores known as *Tschakardaken*.

A minor road leads south-east to **Andau**, a nature reserve where it is possible to observe great bustards in their natural habitat. The same minor road leads south-west from Andau to reach the Hungarian border at **Pamhagen**, the latter situated in the marshes of the *Hanság* which were drained on the Hungarian side by 'voluntary' and military labour under the Rákósi regime in the 1950s. The small border crossing here is open only between 06.00 and 22.00.

The main road leads south from Mönchhof to **Frauenkirchen**, with its Baroque **pilgrimage church** (1695) built by Francesco Martinelli and commissioned by Prince Pál Esterházy. The vegetative stucco (1700) of the richly ornate interior is by Pietro Conti, while the frescoes are by Luca Antonio Columba. The Esterházy coat of arms may be seen on the triumphal arch. The 14C votive statue of the *Madonna* is the focus of the grandiose high altar, liberally supplied with gilt, putti and plaster saints, and flanked by over-life-size statues of *St Leopold* (of Babenberg/Austria) and *St Stephen* (of Hungary), expressing the twin allegiances of the Esterházy. The whole with its eight side-altars, together with the oratorium of the Esterházy princes (first side-altar to the north), makes a remarkable Baroque *Gesamtkunstwerk*. Frauenkirchen took in the Jews driven from Mönchhof in 1678, the Jewish community on the **Judenhöhe** between Frauenkirchen and St Andrä numbering 100 in 1696. Of this, only the cemetery remained after the Nazi expulsions in 1939–40.

A minor road leads south from Weiden (see above) to **Podersdorf am See**. Surrounded by vineyards, the town is the largest resort of the Neusiedler See. Its 200-year-old **windmill** with a shingled roof may be visited (Mühlstrasse 26. Open May–Sept daily, 17.00–19.00). The mill was able to process 400kg of corn per hour, due to its sophisticated design of adjustable wings. Two other attractive villages of interest in this low-lying, partly marshy and pond-studded area known as the **Seewinkel** (a National Park where birds such as avocets can be seen in the *Lange Lacke* Nature Reserve around the salty pools or '*Lacken*') are **Illmitz** and

Apetlon. In the former is a Magyar-style *Pusztascheune* (a type of barn typical of the Great Plain), which is built from reeds and has been turned into a *Heuriger* (see p 27). There are also houses with reed roofs at Florianigasse 8 and 8A. In the **parish church** at Apetlon is a fine altarpiece by Lucas Stiberger showing *St Margaret*. Notable is the Baroque house at Raiffeisenplatz 3, with a Baroque gable, a stork's nest on the chimney and a draw well at the front.

South and south-west of Eisenstadt

Road 50 (E69) leads south of Eisenstadt to **Mattersburg**, until 1924 named *Mattersdorf* (in Hungarian *Nagymarton*, Greater St Martin) and a flourishing centre of the wine trade. A feature of the town and its access roads are the *Bildstöcke* (wayside shrines and columns), a notable one being the Gothic **Halterkreuz** (1442) in the Stadtpark. The **Martinskirche** (1344, later barockised) is surrounded by a fortified wall of 2m. The Esterházys were here, as elsewhere, protectors of the Jews, the Jewish community forming one-third of the population by the mid-19C.

A minor road leads to Loipersbach on the Hungarian border, whose church has an altarpiece by Stefan Dorfmeister; it then curls north to **Schattendorf**, whose Baroque **St Michael's Church** has a dramatic depiction on the choir wall of *St Michael Expelling the Rebellious Angels from Heaven* (school of Tintoretto). However, this otherwise insignificant village has entered Austrian history as the place that (ultimately) supplied the spark for the Austrian civil war of February 1934, but more immediately led to the burning of the Palace of Justice in Vienna in July 1927. Following a clash (30 January 1927) in the village between members of the *Frontkämpfer* (right-wing) and *Schutzbund* (left-wing) militias, in which a man and a child were killed, the three *Frontkämpfer* accused of firing the shots were freed by the Viennese court in what looked like a politically-biased decision. Furious opponents of the *Frontkämpfer* rioted in the streets of Vienna, the leaders of the Social Democrats being unable to control their rank and file, and the resultant instability gave the dominant right in Austria a new excuse to tighten their control.

Baumgarten in Burgenland, to the north, has a late Gothic pilgrimage church possessing an impressive example of the Stations of the Cross in paintings and a crucifixion relief with a representation of Jerusalem as background. The adjacent buildings belonged to the former Paulite cloister. At neighbouring **Drassburg**, a relief dating to 4000 BC has been excavated, the so-called *Venus of Drassburg* (now in the Landesmuseum, Eisenstadt). The Drassburg Schloss has an 18C garden laid out by Le Nôtre, the designer of the garden at Versailles, with statues by a pupil of Georg Raphael Donner (Jakob Schletterer). At **Siegendorf im Burgenland** to the north-west is the **Freilichtmuseum Schuschewald** (open all year in daylight hours), consisting of Bronze Age tumulus graves that have yielded important finds, and a **Sugar Museum** (Rathausplatz 2; open May–Sept, Sat, Sun, PH, 10.00–12.00), located next to the sugar processing plant.

Retracing your steps towards Mattersburg, a turn to the west on the S4 (*Schnellstrasse*) brings you to **Bad Sauerbrunn** on the Wiener Neustadt road. The spa became popular after the railway reached it in 1847 and is beneficial for sufferers from kidney and urinary ailments. A very minor road southwards through the **Rosaliengebirge** brings you to **Wiesen**, noted for its jazz festival, although there are other musical high spots between May and October, including programmes of ethnic dance, Reggae and Latin American music, etc. Wiesen is also famous for its strawberries (you can pick your own during the harvest).

South of Wiesen is the historic **Burg Forchtenstein** (Hungarian *Fraknó vára*) on a dolomite spur rising behind the castle to 746m, and built in the 14C by the Mattersdorf Counts (later the 'Forchtensteiner' line) to control the old Wiener Neustadt–Sopron highway. In 1622 it was acquired by the Esterházys and rebuilt from 1652 by Simon Retacco, Domenico Carlone and Bartolomeo Spacio. The castle with its 5–7m thick and 10m high walls is approached across a wooden bridge (formerly drawbridge) over a dry moat. Its 142m well was supposedly bored over a period of 30 years by unfortunate Turkish prisoners of war. The museum shows arms and armour, Turkish artefacts, portraits of Esterházys, pictures of battles, carriages, furniture, etc. (open April–Oct, 09.00–16.00, in winter by prior appointment. ☎ 02626 81212). The **Forchtensteiner Kultursommer** (late July–early Sept) takes place in the surroundings and includes concerts, exhibitions etc.

Road 50 or S31 lead south past **Kobersdorf** with a Renaissance **Wasserschloss** and a **synagogue** (1848) in Romantic style. From Weppersdorf to the south, road 62 leads east to **Lackenbach**, the site of a great battle (1620) between imperial troops led by Miklós Esterházy against his rebellious compatriots under Matthias Tarródy, whose grave stands at the eastern edge of the village. From here a minor road leads south via **Unterfrauenhaid**, which was settled with Croats after the Turkish devastation of 1529, to **Raiding**, the birthplace (22 October 1811) of Franz Liszt. His house (**Liszt Geburtshaus**) is now a memorial to the composer (open Easter–Oct, daily, 09.00–12.00, 13.00–17.00, or in winter by arrangement; ☎ 02619–7220). Also at Raiding is a 14km section of the ancient Roman 'amber route' with an information kiosk.

Returning to road 62, a right turn brings you to **Deutschkreutz** and the Hungarian border crossing at Kopháza, which is very close to the seat of the great Hungarian family of the Széchenyis at Nagycenk. The parents of Károly Goldmark (1830–1915) lived in Deutschkreutz, another distinguished Hungarian-born composer, even if his works such as *The Queen of Sheba* (an opera) are now largely forgotten. His music, however, follows the Viennese tradition, rather than the Hungarian Romantic style of Liszt. A **museum** dedicated to him is at Hauptstrasse 54 (open Easter–Oct, daily 08.00–16.00). The Renaissance Schloss has lovely arcades, re-opened (they were formerly blind) and restored by the present owner, the artist Anton Lehmden of the Viennese 'Magical Realism' school.

West of Weppersdorf (back on road 50) a minor road leads from Markt St Martin to the impressive castle ruins at **Landsee** on a 630m elevation, once the haunt of 16C highwaymen, but acquired by Miklós Esterházy in 1612 and burned down in 1772. The nearby Steinmuseum (permanently open) displays the rocks that constitute the basic geological formations of Burgenland. Road 50 from Markt St Martin leads to **Stoob**, well-known for its pottery, whose Romanesque Bergkirche has 13C frescoes, and where there is a **Lutheran Museum** (☎ 02612 43491, otherwise open Sun and PH at 10.30, after the service), which documents Protestantism in Burgenland and Western Hungary.

Road 50 then leads south to **Oberpullendorf**, where the **Rathaus** (open Mon and Fri, 08.00–12.00, Mon to 16.00) has an exhibition concerning the local prehistorical iron industry. A minor road leads east via Großwarasdorf to the Croatian settlement of **Nikitsch**, with some interesting peasant houses and the frequently remodelled **Schloss Gálosháza**, set in an English park, and a **Ceramic Museum** (open daily 09.00–20.00) situated in a marvellous vernacular Baroque house with huge corner volutes.

To the south-east of Oberpullendorf is the village of **Frankenau**, whose Croat population dates to the 16C and was introduced on the initiative of Miklós Jurisics, the heroic defender of Köszeg against the Turks in 1532, and himself of Croatian origin. There is a monument by Ivan Meštrović to the Croatian poet Mate Meršić (pen-name 'Miloradić') who was born here in 1850. The road signs around here are bilingual and two languages are used for school instruction. A minor road leads west to Mannersdorf, and so to the border crossing and Kőszeg in Hungary. A right turn on road 55 leads to Lockenhaus (see below). Beyond the latter, the winding road 56 leads south to the **Geschriebenstein** peak (884m), the highest in the Günser Gebirge ranged along the Hungarian border and a favoured hiking area.

Rechnitz further south was a stronghold of the Batthyánys, whose coat of arms may be seen over the entrance to the parish church (1679). The latter's 19C altarpiece of *St Catherine* is the background to an elegant columned altar of the High Baroque (1680), flanked by wooden statues of *St Stephen* and *St Ladislas* of Hungary. A regular visitor to the town was Prince Eugene of Savoy, who was a close friend and card-playing partner of the widow Eleonore Batthyány-Strattmann (it was said that he visited her Viennese palace so often that his carriage horses knew their own way there and back). Rechnitz used to be a centre of boot-making, documented in the **Csizmenmachermuseum** (open Mon, 07.30–12.00, 13.00–16.00, Fri 07.30–12.00 otherwise ☎ 033 63 79 202), the Hungarian for a top-boot being '*csizma*'. Here also is the terminus of the South Burgenland Regional railway, now privatised and used for goods traffic. In summer, however, it makes a so-called *Märchen* tour for tourists at weekends, stopping along the way at various tableaux with animated scenes from Grimm's *Fairy Tales* etc.

Schachendorf, through which you pass on the way to Hannersdorf, is another Croatian village, as may be seen from the traditional dress of many of the inhabitants. Croatian culture in South Burgenland is preserved in costume, folklore, music and dance. In 1991 over 19,000 still defined their ethnicity as Croat in Burgenland (7.2 per cent of the province's population), of whom 3000 gave Croatian as their principal language, 16,000 being bilingual; 29 *Volkschulen* teach in Croatian. Their community has tended to be conservative and conservatively catholic.

Ritterburg Lockenhaus

If road 50 is followed south-west from **Oberpullendorf** via Piringsdorf, you reach the **Ritterburg Lockenhaus** (1254, with later alterations) on the Güns river (open Apr–Sept, 07.30–18.00, 08.00–16.00 the rest of the year), one of whose owners was the vicious Ferenc Nádasdy II; his cruelty to his inferiors pales, however, beside that of his wife, the notorious Erzsébet Báthory, a psychopath who is supposed to have tortured and murdered over 600 virgins in a long career of crime. After her grandson, Ferenc Nádasdy III, was executed (1671, in the old Vienna Rathaus) following his involvement in a plot against Leopold I, the castle passed via the Draskovics family to the Esterházys. Now in the possession of the widow of the writer Paul Anton Keller (d. 1976), Lockenhaus hosts the annual **International Chamber Music Festival** in July, jointly founded by the violinist Gidon Kremer and the musically-minded local priest, Josef Herowitsch.

The entire **Burg** is of considerable interest, a complex of buildings built on two levels and with a mighty seven-storeyed keep (1200) at the centre, the oldest part of the castle, which contained the torture chambers. The barockised Romanesque chapel on the north side has remnants of 13C frescoes showing a *knight* and *St Nicholas* and with evident Byzantine influence. The east wing is the **Palas**, and has an impressive **Rittersaal** (Knights Hall), a vaulted space divided by five octagonal columns with a ribbed vault, and said to have been used by the Knights Templar as a Chapter House. However, documentation on the Knights Templar largely disappeared as a consequence of Philip IV of France's barbaric persecution of them, and although the Knights did have possessions in western Hungary, evidence is lacking to show that Lockenhaus was one of these. You enter the castle via the 17C Baroque **Fürstenzimmer** located in the Baroque entrance hall (**Vorburg**) built under Franz Nádasdy by an Italian architect, Pietro Orsolini of Siena. Adjacent is the **Heiduckenstube** (the name refers to the Hungarian border troops, originally cattle drovers known as *Heyducks*, Hungarian *hajdúk*, from *hajtani* meaning to drive).

On the southern side of the **Unteren Burghof** (with its sundial, 1655) an agreeable **Schlosstaverne** operates in summer. A covered flight of steps leads up to the Belfry or Gate Tower (*Torturm*) and thence to the **Mittleren Burghof**, on the south-eastern side of which is the kitchen with a huge stove and chimney. From this level there is access to the famous early Gothic apsidal **Kultraum**, lit by light-well from the **Oberen Burghof** above, and perhaps used for mystical ceremonies by the Knights Templar (dissolved 1312) or by a somewhat similar later order, the Knights of St John (as the two chiselled Johannite crosses suggest). The association with the Knights Templar is based partly on the fact that sanctuaries lit from above in the same way were known to exist in Templar castles of Syria and the Holy Land. However, owing to the uncertainty as to whether the Knights were ever at Lockenhaus, other suggestions have been made, for example, that the space could have been used as a prison, a treasury, a crypt, or even a cistern.

The **Obere Burghof** is reached via steps from the keep (*Bergfried*, *see above*) and from here the aforementioned **Palas** and **Burgkapelle** are accessible. According to legend, the 114m well at the south-east corner connects with a secret passage leading to neighbouring Burg Bernstein (*see below*). The **Burg Museum** includes arms and armour, instruments of torture, works of art and a display of ancient locks and keys, and there is also a hotel located on the premises.

In Lockenhaus village stands the **pilgrimage church** (1669) built by Pietro Orsolini on a Greek-cross groundplan and having an interestingly rich interior showing a high altar with Corinthian columns. The altarpiece (1673, by Georg Kéry) shows the hermits *Paul* and *Anthony*, and over the oblation portal may be seen the church's patrons (*St Nicholas of Tolentino* and his namesake of Bari), together with cornice figures of *St Stephen* and *St Ladislas of Hungary*. The faces of *St Sebastian* and *St Catherine* in the paintings above the sacristy door are those of Ferenc Nádasdy III and his Esterházy wife. In the crypt lie the remains of Nádasdys, with several fine tombs, particularly that of the executed Ferenc Nádasdy III (known as the Hungarian Croesus, owing to the fact that he controlled the lucrative cattle trade between the Great Plain and Venice) and his wife Juliana, with their coats of arms and enchanting puttis at the four corners. The wall frescoes of the *Dance of Death* date to 1772.

Bernstein

A few kilometres to the west (road 50) is the magical **Burg Bernstein** (1249, altered in 1389 and later), built on a site fortified since the 9C, and having a name recalling its propinquity to the ancient amber trade route. From 1546 it was given improved Renaissance fortifications by the imperial architect, Francesco de Pozzo with Antonio de Spacio, and in the following two centuries became a vivid centre of culture under the Batthyánys, after an explosion in the powder magazine had necessitated further extensive rebuilding. Its current owners are related to the now famous Count Almássy, who is the central figure in the novel and film *The English Patient*, the Almássy family having acquired the Burg in 1892.

In the east wing is the **Rittersaal** (now the dining room), with a Renaissance door and rich stucco decoration (1650) by Filiberto Lucchese and Bartolomeo Bianco. The superb cartouche reliefs of the ceiling show scenes from Greek mythology and Ovid's *Metamorphoses*, together with puttis, Amazons, maskarons, etc. as well as cameo portraits of Dante and Ariosto, and hunting scenes in the window niches. The monumental staircase of the south-east wing is attributed to J.B. Fischer von Erlach. Burg Bernstein is now a hotel (☎ 03354 6382, fax 6520, open between May and Oct). Most of the interior is accessible only to hotel guests, but tourist visits to the Rittersaal may be possible with prior notification from Easter–Sept, daily, 09.00–17.00.

Around Bernstein is found the semi-precious serpentine, and a museum, located in 105 metres of tunnels, may be visited (**Felsenmuseum**, Hauptplatz 5, open March–Dec, daily 09.00–12.00, 13.30–18.00). It documents the exploitation of this local speciality, a hydrated magnesium silicate, the exotic name of which is prompted by the fact that it is often found in winding veins. North of the hamlet are Pannonian burial mounds from the 1C and 2C AD.

Road 50 continues past **Mariasdorf** with its beautiful Gothic parish church (1400, albeit with a barockised interior of 1666 and later completely 're-Gothicised'). The portal of the western façade dates to 1409 and shows a relief with Marian symbols (unicorn and lion). The font (Hungarian work of the 1880s) made from colourful glass majolica and with a wrought-iron cover, is notable. A minor road leads south-east to **Stadtschlaining**, with a mighty **Burg** (1271), whose walls are 6–9m thick; since 1993 it has been home to a *Friedensuniversität* devoted to peace studies. The Burg was associated (like Lockenhaus and Bernstein) with the powerful and aggressive Counts of Güssing in the 13C until being acquired by Albrecht I of Habsburg. Of the subsequent owners, an over-mighty Andreas Baumkircher, who organised a rebellion against the Habsburgs of the Styrian nobility in 1471, was summoned to Graz for 'a discussion' with the Emperor and summarily executed. Later the Burg passed into Batthyány hands (1574–1912), whose coat of arms (1648) may be seen on the outer **Burgtor** (while those of Baumkircher,1450, and Stubenberg, 1520, are on the inner one). The **Schwarzer Hof** of the interior has chequered sgraffito decoration on white walls. In a lower Romanesque courtyard on the bottom part of the keep a relief (1450) of Andreas Baumkircher in armour may be seen. From the keep itself there are good views, while opposite it is the Batthyány **Palas** with a barockised Gothic chapel. The living quarters and representation rooms of the Palas contain various displays of peasant furniture, wrought-iron, weapons, hunting trophies etc. and have fine stucco (c 1700) on the ceilings. The Burg is open Easter–Oct, Tues–Sun, 09.00–12.00, 13.00–17.00.

Baumkircher, who owned the fortress from 1446 until his death, also commissioned the **parish church**, which has attractive star vaulting in the nave and a net vault in the choir, together with later Baroque ornament. The **Lutheran church** (1787) has an elegant neo-classical high altar from the beginning of the 18C and galleries overlooking the nave. It was the first *Toleranzkirche* of Austria (that is, the first non-Catholic church to be built following Joseph II's Edict of Tolerance of 1781).

From Stadtschlaining it is possible to reach **Bad Tatzmannsdorf** by very minor roads, or by returning to Mariasdorf and heading south on road 50. The spa here was used by the Romans, if not earlier, and a 'drinking cure' has been offered since 1620, a surgeon named Jakob Rauch building the first bath-house around 1650. The Batthyánys expanded the spa and by the 19C it had been discovered by Adalbert Stifter and the notoriously hypochondriacal Franz Grillparzer. The resort also offers sporting facilities such as a golf course, while the previously mentioned South Burgenland railway also stops here on its weekend trips. A minor road leads north-east to Pinkafeld, the oldest German settlement of Burgenland and documented as early as ad 860, when it was a Carolingian outpost in the possession of the Salzburg Archbishops. In the **Batthyány-Schloss** on the southern periphery the Countess Franziska Batthyány held a religious salon in the early 19C, at which the reforming preacher Clemens Maria Hofbauer (see p 77) was the star turn. The Catholic parish church (c 1773) has a pulpit with sitting figures of the *Four Evangelists* attributed to Philipp Prokopp, and some of the fittings of the **Kalvarienbergkirche** to the south-west are the work of Matthias Steinl. The history of the spa, which has suffered repeated destruction, may be followed in the exhibits of the **Kurmuseum** in the Quellenhof (open Tues 15.30–17.30, Sat, Sun 09.30–12.30).

To the south, road 50 reaches shortly **Oberwart**, with a mixed German, Hungarian, Croat, Romany (and earlier, also Jewish) population. The Romanies were targets of a neo-Nazi bomb attack in 1994 by Franz Fuchs, the self-styled leader, and apparently the sole member, of the 'Bajuvarian Liberation Army', who was finally caught in 1998 and brought to trial in 1999. Apart from injuring various left-of-centre figures in a succession of letter bombs, he killed several Romanies with the Oberwart bomb. The original Romany settlement was established here in 1674 with the permission of the local lord, Count Christoph Batthyány. The name of the town means upper watch-post (**Unterwart**, lower watch-post, is nearby), in Hungarian, *Felső-Őr*, an important defensive section of the endlessly disputed border region (*Őrség*). Another indication of Hungarian influence is the **Calvinist Church**, built in 1769 and a rarity in Austria. In

Oberwart, Calvinism, the religion of the Great Hungarian Plain, had been strong since the Reformation and had the upper hand over Lutherans, whose church was built in 1815. The older **Catholic Church** has remains of Gothic frescoes and a Baroque altarpiece of the *Assumption* by Stefan Dorfmeister. The adjacent new one (by architects Günter Domenig and Eilfried Huth, (1967–69) is one of Austria's most remarkable churches inspired by the reforms of the second Vatican Council. The Magyar peasant's way of life is evoked at the **Unterwarter Heimathaus** *(Alsóőri otthon)* a few kilometres to the south; (to visit, ☎ 03352 34179). To the south of Unterwart at **Rotenturm an der Pinka** is a splendid Romantic-style country house built by Anton Weber for the Hungarian Erdödy family in 1864 on the site of a moated castle. Its striking façade has red brick cladding with Moorish-Romanesque decoration made of white sandstone. Of the interior the stairway, the stucco and the frescoes by Károly Lotz, one of the leading Hungarian painters of Historicism, are notable.

Road 63 leads south to **Großpetersdorf**, from where a minor road heads on south to **Kohfidisch**, site of another **Erdödy-Schloss** whose English park has a number of rare trees and is a conservation area. The minor road south-west leads to St Michael im Burgenland, where a turn north-west on road 57 takes you to **Stegersbach**, where the **Regional and Post Museum** is situated on the first floor of a former Bathyány Schloss (open Easter–Oct, daily 09.00–12.00, 14.00–18.00). It concerns local geology, flora and fauna, history and folklore. The modern church (**Heiliggeistkirche**, 1974) is a remarkable beton construction in the form of a spiral stirway and symbolises the climb up to heaven.

Güssing

Continuing southwards on road 57 from St Michael im Burgenland, you arrive shortly at **Güssing**, whose half-ruined 12C **Burg** (extended in the 16C and 17C, and replacing an earlier wooden fortress) was originally built on the orders of Béla III of Hungary, who evicted the resident Benedictines in 1180 to do so, much to the indignation of the Pope. The Counts of Güssing, starting from a relatively modest base as owners of the castle in the 13C, extended their dominance over a wide area of Burgenland, eventually including some 25 villages and castles. However, they overreached themselves with the unwise decision to back Ottakar II of Bohemia, rather than the Habsburgs, and after the defeat of the former on the Marchfeld in 1278, Güssing was overwhelmed (as were all their allied castles, with the exception of Bernstein) by Duke Albrecht I of Habsburg in 1289. However, in a compromise with the Hungarian King András III in 1291, the Güssing Counts regained their possessions, only to lose them again to Charles Robert (Károly Robert), the Angevin King of Hungary, in 1327.

Güssing later came into the hands of the Batthyány in 1524 as a reward for Ferenc Batthyány's generalship during the Turkish wars, and it was a later Batthyány (Balthasar) who made it a cultural centre where Pieter Breughel the Younger was a guest and painted *The Anabaptist Sermon*, and where also the humanist botanist Carolus Clusius wrote and published his treatise on Pannonian flora, *Stirpium Nomenclator Pannonius* (1583). In the impressive **Hochburg** is a **Burgmuseum** (open 30 April–29 Oct, Tues–Sun, 10.00–17.00) containing ancestral portraits, porcelain and the 16C console organ originally in the chapel. The 15C **Burgkapelle** itself has a graceful net vault and neo-Gothic fittings (including the altar of 1794) made during the fashion for re-gothicising initiated by Ferdinand von Hohenberg in Vienna.

The 18C **Kastell Batthány** on the Hauptplatz of the village is still inhabited by members of this distinguished Hungarian noble line that has seldom been far from the centre of the action in Hungarian history. The Kastell was erected as residence in place of the Burg (which was partly demolished in 1778) in order to avoid Maria Theresia's swingeing 'roof and window tax', introduced to finance military expenditure. Also on the Hauptplatz, the Batthyány-Strattmann crypt is to be found in the Franciscan Monastery (founded 1648) and was possibly built by Filiberto Lucchese. It contains some 100 coffins, of which Balthasar Moll's lead one for Prince Károly Batthány (1697–1772) is notable. In the neo-classical **Schloss Draskovics** (another leading line of Hungarian nobility, especially in the era of the Enlightenment) is a **winged altar** of 1469. In the Schloss estate is a safari park, the park only being open to visitors.

Eighteen kilometres to the east of Güssing and north of road 56 is the **pilgrimage church of Maria Weinberg** (1525) near Gaas, with a delicate net vault and a huge 17C fresco in Renaissance style over the triumphal arch showing a most vivid *Deposition from the Cross*, while the gallery frescoes from the 18C show angels playing musical instruments and saints. The votive icon is a late Gothic carved *Madonna* (1460) on a half-moon, placed in the central niche of the fine neo-classical high altar (1800). The flanking figures are *Joachim*, *Anna* and the *Saint-Kings Stephen* and *Ladislas*. In the choir is another *Madonna* of 1625 placed centrally on a marble column (a rarely surviving arrangement) and elsewhere a Gothic **crucifix**. (If access is difficult, apply at the Pfarramt, Gaas, ☎ 033 23 234). At **Eberau** to the north are the remains of the 13C (Babenberg) and 14C (Habsburg) fortifications and a moated 17C castle, together with a church girdled with 2m high defensive walls, the last named having a notable net vault. In the old Rathaus is a **Heimatmuseum** (open Sat 10.00–12.00, Sun and PH 10.00–12.00 14.00–16.00).

South of Güssing road 57 leads down to the Hungarian border at Heiligenkreuz im Lafnitztal, 6km to the south of which is **Mogersdorf**. On the **Schlösslberg** to the north of the village a béton cross (1964) recalls the great battle at Mogersdorf/Szent Gotthárd (the latter on the Hungarian side of the border), when 25,000 imperial troops under Count Raimund Montecuccoli defeated a Turkish army four times as large under the Grand Vizier Achmed Köprülü on the 1 August 1664. Many fleeing Turks were drowned in the swollen flood waters of the Raab, here at its confluence with the Lafnitz. Unfortunately the 17-year-old Leopold I, under pressure from an aggressive Louis XIV in the west, failed to press the advantage of this victory and signed a generous peace with the Turks at Vasvár shortly afterwards; this act of betrayal (as it was seen) was subsequently to provoke a rebellion of Hungarian nobles who had risked all to hold the southern line of Christendom. Nevertheless, it was almost 20 years before the Turks launched a further major attack after their defeat at Mogersdorf. In the straw-roofed **Kreuzstadel** (1973, open daily 08.00–20.00, also on the **Schlösslberg**) is a documentation of the battle and a memorial chapel. In the so-called 'Turkish Cemetery' on the western periphery of the village a white stone cross (1840) with inscriptions in Latin, German, Hungarian and French marks the location of a mass grave. Not far away is a memorial rotonda (**Anna-Kapelle**, 1670) with an altarpiece (1664) of *St Anne* and a Latin inscription recalling the battle. It was built to honour an Austrian General who fell in the battle, Count Trauttmansdorff, and may have been deliberately sited over the grave of a Turkish pasha. At any rate it is reported that a Turkish delegation came annually to lay a wreath at the chapel up to 1914. The parish church shows a modern fresco (1912) of the battle on the triumphal arch, while over the entrance to the **Gemeindeamt** (Municipal Offices) a Turkish cannon ball may be seen. Rainer Maria Rilke's *Cornet* is set against the background of this historic clash between the forces of Christendom and those of Islam (originally it was to be titled *1664*).

From Mogersdorf it is a few kilometres westwards on a minor road to **Jennersdorf**, a charming country town complete with a Hungarian *Lindencsárda* (Lime-Tree Inn) where gypsy music in the evening helps to whet the appetite for a trip to the east. To the south (road 58) lies the Slovenian border, the route to it passing close to the attractive **Neuhaus am Klausenbach** with a **Heimatmuseum** in the 15C **Schloss Tabor** (open May–Oct, Sun and PH, 14.00–17.00). Equally picturesque is **Neumarkt an der Raab**, to the east of Jennersdorf, with its characteristic peasant houses. It is now the venue for musical workshops in summer.

Steiermark (Styria)

Area: 16,388sq km. Population: 1.2 million

Topography, climate and environment

Territorially the second largest Bundesland, **Steiermark** (**Styria**) borders on Land Salzburg and Upper Austria in the west, on Carinthia and Slovenia in the south, on Burgenland in the east and on Lower Austria and Upper Austria in the north and north-east. Its name is derived from the city of **Steyr** (see p 263), which is now in Upper Austria, but was originally the seat of the Traungauer nobles, one of whom founded the independent Styrian Margrave (see History below). Styria's physical geography made it in part a defensible unit, in so far as it was enclosed by the evocatively named **Totes Gebirge** (Dead Mountains) and the **Dachstein** to the north-west, but the border to the east was always vulnerable to attacks from the east and from the Balkans.

Styria owes its traditional nomenclature of the '*Grüne Mark*' (also 'The Green Heart of Austria') to the fact that it was and is extensively afforested, pine and deciduous woodlands carpeting much of its generally (75 per cent) mountainous or hilly terrain. The most mountainous part, Upper Styria (*Ober-Steiermark*), with its numerous river valleys, was traditionally the *Land der Eisenhämmer*, a region with many iron mines and smithies, also known as the 'Iron Mark' (*Eherne Mark*), whose **Eisenerzer Alpen** provided the iron-ore and siderite mined at least since Roman times. Numerous ranges of highlands traverse the province, including the previously mentioned **Eisenerzer Alpen**, the **Seckauer Alpen**, **Gleinalpe**, **Fischbacher Alpen** and the sparsely populated **Niedere Tauern**, out of which numerous rivers have carved their precipitous courses. The settlements of the last named region cluster along the valleys of the larger rivers (**Mur**, **Mürz**, **Liesing**), while from Voitsberg and Graz eastwards on the periphery of the Pannonian Plain, the land is more densely inhabited with a network of villages. Central and Southern Styria is mostly an area of highland and rolling hills well-watered by rivers (the **Mur**, **Raab**, **Feistritz**, **Kainach**, **Sulm** and others). Southern Styria between the **Drau** (Slovenian *Drava*) and the **Save** (Slovenian *Sava*) was lost to Yugoslavia at the end of World War I, its peripheral remnant being the borderland known as the **Windische Bühel**, the word *windisch* (or *wendisch*) referring to its Slovene character.

The Styrian climate is transitional—in the north and north-west it is subject to Alpine influences, in the south and south-east to Pannonian ones. Fifty-one per cent of the land is forest, more than in any other Austrian province, and constitutes about 26 per cent of Austria's total woodland. Another 25 per cent of the territory is arable and meadowland. Besides the production of maize, wheat, buckwheat, vegetables, fruit and animal feed, in the areas with milder micro-climates there is cultivation of sugar-beet, hops, tobacco and grapes (Steiermark accounts for nearly 5 per cent of total Austrian wine production). A local speciality is the **Kürbis** (pumpkin), which is chiefly harvested for its dark brown oil used in cooking and on salads, and is said to guard against prostate disorders.

Styria's beautiful rolling landscape, its hills carpeted with orchards and vineyards like an Austrian Tuscany, or with alpine meadows and forests, have made it a favourite area for hiking. This and its cultural treasures are the main draw for visitors, although there is some skiing and climbing north and south of the Enns valley (alpine skiing at Schladming, cross-country skiing in the Ramsau region and climbing on the Dachstein and Gesäuse mountains). The province's general unsuitability for mass tourism has made it one of the least spoiled and most seductive parts of Austria, and its rather conservative population is likely to keep it that way.

Economy

Styria is home to important industries, many of which have only recently emerged from the major crises of the 1980s. In that decade the great conglomerate of *VOEST-ALPINE Stahl AG* was compelled to lay off workers and restructure on a massive scale, partly because of over-capacity in the European steel industry. The resultant specialisation and privatisation has yielded better results in the 1990s. Sixty per cent of Styria's products are exported (chiefly steel, paper, electrical goods, motor vehicles, leather goods and timber). In the mid-1990s about 24 per cent of the work force was still employed in industry and 29 per cent in the service sector (inclusive of financial services); agriculture and forestry accounts for a further 10 per cent and only 0.5 per cent work in the now reduced mining industry; tourism employs a further 6 per cent. Despite the small numbers employed, over 50 per cent of all mining in Austria is carried out in Styria, the products including brown coal, iron ore, gypsum, anhydrite, talc, magnesite, sinter and stone. In 1998 Austria's worst mining disaster of modern times occurred in the partially closed talc mines at Lassing, when tunnels collapsed on ten workers of a rescue party sent to extract a trapped miner, who alone survived.

In recent years Styria has rediscovered a valuable economic asset in its superior **spas**, some of which have interesting modern functional architecture. Besides the traditional spas at Bad Aussee and Bad Mitterndorf, there has been vigorous development of 'health holiday tourism' in the *Thermenland* round Loipersdorf, Bad Gleichenberg, Bad Radkersburg and Bad Waltersdorf, together with 'altitude cures' at Aflenz, Laßnitzhöhe, Ramsau and elsewhere.

History

Remnants of Stone Age habitation have been found in Styria, as well as examples of urn burial from the late Bronze Age (1300–700 BC) and traces of the Iron Age Hallstatt Culture (800–450 BC). In the Bronze Age, copper mining was already flourishing and the extraction of salt had begun in Upper Styria, to be followed over the centuries by the multifarious mineral and coal exploitation that was to be fundamental to the region's development. In the 4C Celts settled in the area of Carinthia and Styria, their kingdom of *Noricum* being occupied by the Romans in 15 BC. The Styria of today mostly belonged to the Roman province of *Noricum*, a small part being in Pannonia.

In the last quarter of the 6C the region was overrun by Avars and Slavs, the latter eventually gaining the upper hand in the whole of '*Karantanien*', a large area that included the whole of Carinthia with Styria, East Tyrol, Lungau,

STEIERMARK

OBERÖSTERREICH

SALZKAMMERGUT
TOTES GEBIRGE

Altaussee See
Altaussee
Toplitzsee
Grundlsee
Grundlsee
Bad Aussee

Hallstätter See

Dachstein-
Rieseneishöhle

DACHSTEINGRUPPE

145 Pürgg
Bad Mitterndorf
Trautenfels
Aigen i. Ennstal
Irdning

Gröbming
Öblarn
Stein a.d. Enns

Pichl-
Preunegg
Enns
146
Schladming

Untertal
Riesachfälle

Schwarzensee

NIEDERE TAUERN

GR. BOSRUCK
2009

Bosrucktunnel
Ardning
Liezen

Bosrucktunnel

Strechau
Rottenmann

Admont

Trieben

St. Gallen
Großreifling
Enns

Gam
Hief
Hiefla

ENNSTALER ALPEN
GESÄUSE

146

ERZBE

EISENERZER ALP

E57-A9
Mau
i. S

114

Liesing

SECKAUER ALPEN

Oberzeiring

Seckau
Österreichring
Fohnsdorf
Knittelfe

Oberwölz
Krakaudorf
Schöder
Wölzer Bach

Lind b.S.
Scheifling

S36
Judenburg
Zelt

SALZBURG

St. Ruprecht
ob Murau
Murau

Neumarkt
i. Steiermarkt

KÄRNTEN

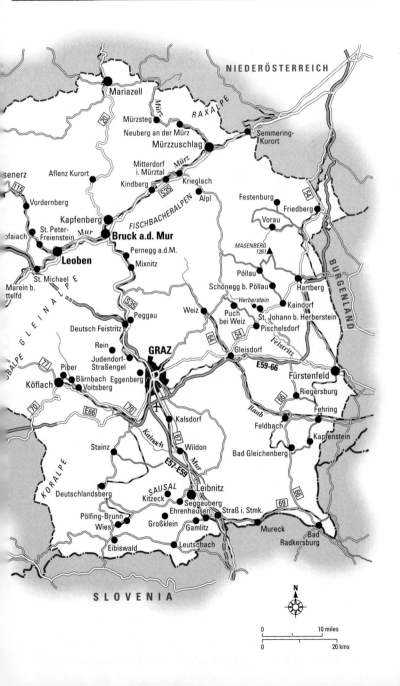

south-east Upper Austria, the southern part of Lower Austria and Carniola ('*Krain*'). In 740 the Bavarian Duke Odilo came to the rescue of the local Slavs against the Avars, using the opportunity to extend his hegemony over the region and reconvert the inhabitants to Christianity. From 803 both Styria and Bavaria were part of the **Carolingian Mark**, albeit under Bavarian control, while the Archbishops of Salzburg exercised the equally important prerogative of religious jurisdiction. In the 10C three Marks subordinate to the Carinthian Duchy were created, of which that on the **middle part of the River Mur** (*marchia Carentana*), ruled by the Eppenstein family, was to become the core of later Styria. In 1035 the Mark passed to Count Arnold of Wels Lambach, whose son inherited it but was murdered in 1050. His successor was Ottakar I of the Bavarian Traungauer line, whose seat was the Burg at Steyr and who called himself *Marchio de Stire*, the term **Marchia Styriae** (Styrian Mark) appearing in documents from about this time. (However the town of Steyr itself vanished from Styrian history in 1254, when it became part of the '*Land ob der Enns*', i.e. Upper Austria.) The Traungauer position was strengthened in 1122 with the extinction of the rival Eppensteins, whose substantial possessions fell to the ruling family, of which **Leopold I** was the first nominally independent Margrave of Styria. Under **Ottakar III** (1129–64), Marburg (Maribor) and Radkersburg were added to his territories in 1147, followed by **Graz** in 1156, which became the Margrave's administrative seat. However, it was not until 1180 that Styria finally became completely free of Bavarian influence, when **Margrave Ottakar IV** was created a Duke, this dukedom devolving in 1192 to the first Austrian dynasty of the Babenbergs as the result of an arrangement with Ottakar IV, who had contracted leprosy and was childless.

Following the interregnum after the extinction of the Babenbergs and the intervention of Ottakar II of Bohemia in Austria, Styria was acquired by Rudolf of Habsburg in 1276, and thereafter was an important factor in the various divisions of their territories that the Habsburgs made amongst themselves (in 1379, in 1411 and in 1564), forming the core territory of '**Innerösterreich**' (Carinthia, Carniola, Görz/Gorizia and Styria) with a court and administration at Graz (1564–1619). The term *Innerösterreich* (in use from 1564 until after 1619) counterpointed the nomenclature of *Österreich ob und unter der Enns* (Upper and Lower Austria with Tyrol) as well as *Vorderösterreich* (the term given to Swiss and German Habsburg possessions that were lost over the years). The division of 1379 between **Duke Albrecht III** of **Habsburg** and his brother **Leopold III** marked a dangerous turn in the history of the dynasty, creating the conditions for the Habsburg equivalent of the 'Wars of the Roses' between the 'Albertine' and 'Leopoldine' lines that was not fully resolved until the uniting of all the remaining Habsburg hereditary lands under Maximilian I in 1490.

Styria was subject to numerous **Hungarian attacks** in the 15C (1418, 1440, 1478 and 1490 were the worst) and was also obliged to defend itself against Turkish incursions (1480, 1532), **Graz** becoming thereby the strategic centre for the defence of the south-eastern border of Christendom. In the Reformation the population of the province, as elsewhere, turned Protestant and for a while Johannes Kepler was teaching at the Lutheran Stiftschule in Graz. By 1565 the Protestant nobles had also built the Landhaus in Graz as a rival power base to the Catholic court. But although **Archduke Karl II** granted nominal religious freedom to the nobles in a document known as the *Brucker Libell* of 1576, his fiercely dogmatic son, Ferdinand II, set the **Styrian Counter-Reformation** in motion. It was spearheaded by the Jesuits and enforced by a peripatetic 'Reformation Commission', accompanied by the military, that swept through the countryside burning the Protestants' texts, closing their churches and expelling their pastors. The triumphal conclusion of the Counter-Reformation in the 17C produced a number of remarkable monuments in the province, of which perhaps its great Mannerist mausoleums are the most impressive: Ferdinand II's in Graz (see p 210), the Eggenbergs' in Ehrenhausen (see p 217) and Archduke Karl II's in the monastery church at Seckau (see p 230).

In the 18C Styria somewhat declined in importance, perhaps because it was no longer a vital element in the struggle against alternative religion or foreign invaders. Indeed its autonomy was severely restricted by **Joseph II**, who placed the province under a governor having joint responsibility for Styria, Carinthia and Carniola. Near the turn of the century it was invaded by the French, who invaded again in 1805 and 1809. Following the revolution of 1848 the ancient Styrian Diet, that had existed at least since 1492, was reformed on the basis of three recognised Stände (the landowners, the burghers and the peasants), and Styria was declared to be 'one indivisible Duchy'. Thereafter the development of the province was strongly influenced by the far-sighted **Archduke Johann** (1782–1859), who had supported the liberation war of Andreas Hofer against the French in Tyrol (see p 363). So unequivocal was his support that, following the betrayal of Hofer by Johann's brother, Emperor Franz I, the Archduke was forbidden to re-enter Tyrol. Instead he became active in Styria promoting its economy and furthering culture and education (see p 209), although his official status was no more than that of landowner and honorary mayor of a small Styrian town. Many of his initiatives in the first half of the century were to bear fruit in the wave of industrialisation and business expansion of the second half, the so-called **Gründerzeit**. With improved transport on the railways, Styria was able to export more of its quality goods, raw materials and steel products, as well as local specialities such as Reininghaus beer that found new world markets via the port of Trieste.

World War I interrupted this progress and by the post-war settlement (Treaty of St Germain, 1919) Austria was obliged to cede **Southern Styria** to the new Kingdom of Serbs, Croats and Slovenes (from 1929 the Kingdom of Yugoslavia); 75,000 German-speaking Styrians (out of a total population of half a million) had to change their nationality. Many of these were inhabitants of the province's second largest city, **Marburg an der Drau**, which was reincarnated as the Slovenian town of Maribor. Another consequence of the change was that the important railway link of Graz–Klagenfurt via Marburg was severed. Twenty years later the southern part of Burgenland was added to Styria, and remained Styrian for the seven years of the Nazi regime. Towards the end of World War II eastern Styria saw heavy fighting between the Wehrmacht and the Red Army, while Styrian industrial centres, together with Graz, were subjected to heavy Allied bombing. Under the Four Powers occupation after the war, Styria was in the British zone.

The province is traditionally conservative, a stronghold of the **People's Party** (*Volkspartei*), the latter's predecessor, the Christian Social Party, having provided the Provincial Governors from 1919–38, and the People's Party having provided them since 1945. Under its feisty lady Governor and her predecessor it has been engaged throughout the 1990s in a bitter war of words with neighbouring Lower Austria (also ruled by the *Volkspartei*) in support of the construction of the new Semmering railway tunnel, which is seen as vital to Styria's economy. The project is equally vociferously opposed (on ecological grounds) by the Governor of Lower Austria, a kingmaker in the party.

GRAZ

• • • • • •

Practical information

Population: 238,000. Telephone dialling code: 0316.

Tourist information

Information is available at the Hauptbahnhof, platform 1, (☎ 91 68 37. Open Mon–Fri 09.00–18.00, Sat to 15.00). Also at Herrengasse 16, (☎ 8075 0 or 83524 11. Open Mon–Fri 09.00–18.00, Sat to 15.00, Sun and PH 10.00–15.00). An *Old Town Walk* leaflet is available at modest charge and has a clear street-plan with sights identified on the reverse. German-speakers may find the *Kulturkarte Steiermark* (published by Karl Portal, Vienna) useful, but it is hard to find. A useful listing of **Styrian spas** is also available at most tourist information points. English language material on Styria may be found at the *Englische Buchhandlung* (Tummelplatz 7). A branch of *Freytag & Berndt* is due to open shortly at Sporgasse 27.

Getting there

There are regular trains every 2 hours from Vienna (fastest journey time 2hrs 40mins). Graz is also well-served by buses running either from the Bahnhof or the bus station at Andreas-Hofer-Platz. The airport is 10km south of the town, with services to Vienna, Munich, Frankfurt & Zürich.

Hotels

✫✫✫✫ *Schlossberg Hotel* (Kaiser Franz Josef-Kai 30. ☎ 80700. Fax: 807070). Elegant hotel furnished with antiques and conveniently located at the foot of the Schlossberg close to the cable railway up to the summit.
✫✫✫✫ *Hotel Erzherzog Johann* (Sackstrasse 3–5. ☎ 81 16 16. Fax: 81 15 15). In a Renaissance building and centrally located. Generously sized rooms.
✫✫✫ *Gollner* (Schlögelgasse 14. ☎ 82 25 21. Fax: 82 25 21-7). Sound-proofed rooms, some overlooking a pleasant courtyard with garden. Friendly service. ✫✫✫ *Hotel-Restaurant Ohnime-di Gallo* (Purbergstrasse 56. ☎ 39 11 43. Fax: 39 11 43 19). Moderately priced for the level of comfort on offer. Situated on the outskirts of the town at Mariatrost.
✫✫✫ *Hotel Pension 'Iris'* (Bergmanngasse 10. ☎ 322081. Fax: 32208 15).

Restaurants

Kaiser Josef Bistro (Schlögelgasse 1). An expensive gourmet establishment with French flavoured cooking and

some *nouvelle cuisine.*
Hofkeller (Hofgasse 8). Mediterranean atmosphere reflected also in the cooking. Middle price range.
Stromberg (Jakominiplatz 12). On the fifth floor of the Steirerhof. A simple menu at midday gives way to gourmet cooking with an Austrian flavour in the evening.
Kepler-Keller (Stempfergasse 6). Located in the house where Johannes Kepler is supposed to have lodged. Typically Austrian dishes and good Styrian wine. Background music in the evening. Moderately priced.
Gamlitzer Weinstube (Mehlplatz 4). Styrian dishes at very moderate prices.

Cultural events

Steirischer Herbst

The Graz **October festival** of the avant-garde was founded in 1968 and has the reputation of being at the cutting edge of Austrian performance art. It includes theatre, exhibitions, film, workshops, etc.; an important element is experimentation with video. Some of the events take place at venues outside Graz.

Styriarte

A **summer festival** of music in Graz founded in 1985. A prime mover is the Graz-born conductor, Nikolaus Harnoncourt, whose interest in early music and music played on the original instruments is reflected in the programme.

History of Graz

Graz (until the 19C '*Grätz*', the name derived from the original Slav nomenclature of '*gradec*', meaning a small fortress) is a city of about 238,000 inhabitants built on both sides of the River Mur, and is the capital of the **Steiermark** (Styria). In the Middle Ages it was often designated **Bairisch-Grätz** (Bavarian Graz) to distinguish it from the Lower Styrian **Windischgraz**, a reminder also that the original town developed out of a Bavarian settlement first documented in 1128. However, there had been a crossing of the River Mur here from earliest times, as well as a settlement on the dolomite protrusion of the Schlossberg.

The importance of Graz grew in the 12C after the Bavarian Traungauer made the Burg their seat of government (see p 204). By 1172 Graz appears in documents as having market rights, by 1189 as *civitas* and nearly a century later as *oppidum*. From 1379, after the division of the Habsburg patrimony, Graz was the residence of the dynasty's 'Leopoldine' line. Friedrich III expanded the Burg from 1438, the latter withstanding Turkish attacks in 1480 and 1532. After a further land division of the Habsburgs, Graz became once more the seat of the rulers of **Inner Austria** (see p 204) under Archduke Karl II (1564–90) and temporarily under his son Ferdinand II, who, however, moved his court to Vienna in 1619 on becoming Emperor. Nevertheless, Graz remained the most important city of the 'Inner Austrian' *Länder* (Styria, Carinthia, Carniola) until the mid-18C.

Expansion of the city had already begun in the Middle Ages, but this had left its suburbs unprotected against Turkish attacks. After 1544 it was decided to modernise the fortifications of both the town and the Schlossberg, the Milanese architect Domenico d'Allio being entrusted with the task. Although Graz became the **Archducal residence** in 1564, the Reformation had by then taken firm root in the city, whose Lutheran **Stiftschule**, under the patronage of the Protestant nobility, attracted even such an illustrious

Archduke Johann (1782–1859)

A major influence in 19C Styria was Archduke Johann of Austria, the liberal-minded younger brother of the reactionary Franz I. Unlike Franz, who sought to portray himself as *pater patriae*, while collaborating with Metternich in the operation of a police state, Johann was genuinely popular and close to his subjects. He favoured the bourgeois notion of putting personal happiness before the exigencies of rank, living in (eventually) conjugal bliss with the postmaster's daughter at Aussee (it was several years before the Emperor allowed the marriage to proceed in 1829). Johann had been given military responsibility in the Napoleonic wars, but had only limited success as a general (he gave up the high command after losing the battle of Hohenlinden, aged 18!). He did, however, lend practical assistance to the Tyrol freedom fighters under Andreas Hofer (see p 363), greatly to the fury of Metternich and Emperor Franz, who were preparing to sell out their Tyrolean subjects for reasons of *Realpolitik*. Johann's subsequent banning from Tyrol was motivated by fear of loyalist demonstrations in his favour.

The Archduke's organisational abilities were demonstrated in the many initiatives he took to modernise Styria. In 1811 he laid the foundations for the **Joanneum** in Graz (see p 214) by turning over his extensive scientific collection to the new body. He was instrumental in setting up a provincial archive (1817) and in providing fire insurance for the peasantry (which led to the abandonment of wooden construction in favour of brick to qualify for the lower premiums). He promoted modern mining technology and modernisation in agriculture (in particular encouraging the planting of potatoes to protect against periodic famine) and was an active patron of the arts. During the revolution of 1848, he opened the brief-lived constitutional assembly which met in the Redoute of the Vienna Hofburg, and was even elected Vice-Regent (of the Empire) by the Liberal Assembly at Frankfurt in the same year, although he resigned after 12 months.

scholar and teacher as Johannes Kepler. Nevertheless in 1573 the Jesuits were able to found a competing school (by 1586 it had university status) and thereafter the Counter-Reformatory grip on Graz steadily tightened. Even before the Turkish menace had finally receded in the second half of the 17C, one of the city's major Baroque monuments (the great **Mausoleum**, see p 211) had been created, the momentum of Baroque building gathering force thereafter.

Graz seems to have been something of a backwater in the 18C and the diminished importance of Styria as a dukedom is underlined by the fact that the inauguration (1728) of Emperor Karl VI as Styrian Duke (followed by the homage of the diet) in Graz was the last ceremony of its kind to take place. When Maria Theresia and Franz Stephan visited the Burg in 1765, she had some of the most precious items of the **Kunstkammer** transported to Vienna and officially bestowed the rest of the treasures on her consort, a connoisseur and avid collector. In a gesture to her loyal Styrian subjects, however, Maria Theresia had eight precious pearls added to the ducal crown and donated the same to the city as 'a special act of grace'. In 1784 the fortifications, long redundant, were finally dismantled, allowing the city to expand.

The early 19C was marked by initiatives of the popular **Archduke Johann**, who founded the **Joanneum** (see p 214) in 1811, an institution that combined curatorship with pedagogic functions. With the connection of Graz to the *Südbahn* in 1844 (after the intervention of Archduke Johann—the route originally planned went through western Hungary), Graz began to reap economic benefits which were further enhanced by the railway link to the lignite mines at Köflach. At the same time the city's congenial climate and somewhat relaxed way of life made it the '**pensionopolis**' of the Dual Monarchy, the preferred place of retirement of many civil servants and military officers on relatively generous government pensions.

The Old Town

Historic Graz is situated on the east side of the River Mur, mostly within an area lying between Kepler-Brücke in the north and Radetzky-Brücke in the south, and formerly enclosed by a defensive bastion (**Glacisstrasse** marks the line of it). It is convenient to begin a tour at the triangular **Hauptplatz**, with its statue of Archduke Johann at the centre and the neo-Renaissance **Rathaus** (1888, generally considered a disturbing element among the 16C and 17C buildings) to the south.

Herrengasse leads south-east out of the square, its south-western side being flanked (no. 16) by the Renaissance **Landhaus** (1565), the seat of the provincial parliament and an expansion (by Domenico d'Allio) of an earlier Gothic building. D'Allio's extension of the **Rittersaal** (Knights' Hall, in the **Rittersaaltrakt** overlooking the Landhausgasse) and the **Landstube** (chamber of the Provincial Parliament) of the interior are beautifully stuccoed by Giovanni Formentini with scenes from Styrian history, but the *pièce de résistance* is the beautiful **courtyard** with three tiers of arcades (the south side dates to 1890, however), that recall Italian precedents. A bronze well-canopy (1590) may be seen to the west. The adjacent **Zeughaus** (Armoury, 1645, the largest in the world) was built by Antonio Solari and reflects Graz's strategic significance in the defensive ring built against the Turkish incursions into southern Austria. It contains some 29,000 weapons, suits of armour, etc., some of them purely ornamental and others for hunting or tournament use (open March–Oct, Tues–Sun, 09.00–17.00, Nov–March by appointment, ☎ 0 316 80 17/4810).

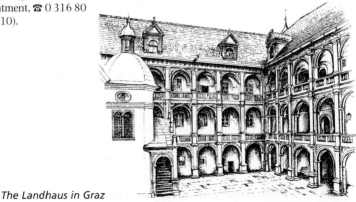

The Landhaus in Graz

Back on Herrengasse, at no. 21 is the **parish church of the Holy Blood** (1519), a Gothic hall church barockised in the 18C and 'regothicised' in the 19C. It boasts an *Assumption* (1594) by Tintoretto in the oval chapel dedicated to John of Nepomuk, and the tomb (in the left-hand aisle) of the sculptor Johann Baptist Erlacher (d. 1649), perhaps made by Johann Baptist Fischer, whose marriage with Erlacher's widow produced (1566, in Graz) the renowned architect Johann Bernhard Fischer von Erlach.

A Baroque **Marian column** marks the end of the Herrengasse, from which a turn left on the Opernring brings you (500m) to the neo-Baroque opera house itself (1899). A few minutes' walk north-east into Zinzendorfgasse brings you at no. 5 to the early Gothic **Leechkirche** (1293), the oldest surviving building of Graz, although its towers are of later date (c 1500). Notable on the portal is the transitional Romanesque-Gothic *Madonna* in the tympanum, while the graceful interior shows strong influence of French Gothic. The stained glass in the choir shows the *Passion*, with the *Evangelists* above (1337). The Marian statue of the Baroque high altar is late 15C.

A left turn brings you via the Burgring into the **Stadtpark**, laid out in 1869. Another left turn along the Erzherzog Johann-Allee brings you back through the old enceinte at the Burgtor to the **Burg** itself (Hofgasse 13, the seat of the Provincial Administration). Built (from 1438) by Emperor Friedrich III as his residence, and extended (1494–1500) under Maximilian I and Archduke Karl II (1570), the Burg mostly retains its early Baroque aspect despite some vandalistic 19C alterations. Its most beautiful Gothic survival is the **double spiral staircase** of 1499 in the north-west wing.

Domkirche Ägydius and the Mausoleum

Shortly to the west in the Hofgasse is the **Cathedral of St Giles** (Domkirche Ägydius), built (1462) on the site of a Romanesque church, perhaps by Hans Niesenberger (the cathedral has normal opening times, but opening times for the Mausoleum are inconvenient: Mon–Sat in summer only, between 14.00 and 15.00). Note on the exterior the motto of Friedrich III (AEIOU, see p 68) and on the south-west side remains of a fresco (1485) depicting the city of Graz afflicted by the divine punishments of that year (hordes of locusts, the plague and Turkish attacks).

The fine **interior** achieves its effects by means of the soaring, narrow and light-flooded choir, to which the eye is drawn from the dark and broad nave of the hall church through a high triumphal arch, the latter thus forming the threshold of light or an emblem of Heaven's Gate. The Baroque fittings introduced by the Jesuits are remarkable and include Georg Kraxner's monumental high altar (1733) with an altarpiece by Franz Ignaz Flurer of the *Miracle of St Giles* (1733) and statuary by Jakob Schoy. The Ignatius Altar in the southern nave has an altarpiece by Pietro de Pomis, the builder of the adjacent Mausoleum (see below), and statuary by Veit Königer. Exceptional are the two lovely Italian **bridal chests** on either side of the triumphal arch, brought to Graz by Duchess Paola Gonzaga of Mantua in 1477 on her marriage to Count Leonhard of Gorizia (the last of his line, which died out with him in 1500). These two beautiful chests (in fact reliquaries) with ivory and horn inlay, perhaps to designs by Mantegna (see also Millstatt, p 353) illustrate Petrarch's *Trionfi*, the triumph of the divine over all worldly things and thus mankind's liberation from the dominion of the senses. This allegory is presented as triumphal processions of antiquity, celebrating the victories of Love, Innocence and Death, which are also (by extension and implication) the triumph of Fame, the Passage of Time and Eternity.

Other interesting features in the cathedral include the devotional picture of Archduke Karl and his family (1591, by J. de Monte) and a number of fine tombs and epitaphs, notably that of Count Cobenzl opposite the pulpit with a lead medallion (1741) of the Count by Georg Raphael Donner.

Adjacent to St Giles is the Mannerist **Mausoleum** (1638) of Ferdinand II (1578–1637), an astonishing cruciform structure designed by Pietro de Pomis, and continued after 1633 by Peter Valnegro, with its lofty copper dome and a cylindrical east belfry. The façade is a sophisticated play of great beauty between the triangular angularity of the tympanum and rounded arches, the crowning one of which is surmounted by statues (1635) of *St Catherine and two angels*. The interior is notable for the stucco decoration of J.B. Fischer von Erlach (1699), where Atlas figures, putti and eagles draw the eye upwards. The ceiling frescoes in the nave by Franz Steinpichler show the liberation of Vienna from the Turks in 1683 and the high altar is also an early work of Fischer von Erlach, with a statue of *St Catherine* by Marx Schokotnigg. In the crypt is a red marble sarcophagus (by Sebastiano Carlone) of Ferdinand's mother, Maria of Bavaria, while Ferdinand himself lies to the right of the altar. In the north aisle is an *Immaculata* altar by Antonio Beduzzi.

At Bürgergasse 2 (opposite the mausoleum) is the former Jesuit College (1597, Vincenz de Verda) with a fine stairway in the south wing, and next to it the Old University (1609) with the imperial coat of arms of Emperor Ferdinand II, together with that of his wife, Maria Anna of Bavaria, on the façade.

Heading north you pass through the Freiheitsplatz with a neo-classical theatre (Peter Nobile, 1825) and climb to the Karmeliterplatz, from which a path ascending west through an archway leads to the **Schlossberg**, and the emblem of Graz, a **clock-tower** (expanded from a Gothic core in 1555–56, the clock itself 1712). The Schlossberg is a dolomite block 473m above sea-level, fortified (1544–88) by Lazarus Schwendi and Domenico d'Allio, although some sort of defences had existed since Celtic times. Its pleasant park was laid out in 1839 by Baron von Welden in Romantic style. The five-storeyed (28m) octagonal **belfry** (perhaps by Antonio Marmoro, 1588) contains the great bell (1587, cast by Martin Hilger) known affectionately as the *Liesl* (or *Lisl*) after the Elizabeth Chapel originally in the fortress; its basement was the town prison and known (not affectionately) as the *Baßgeige* (bass fiddle). Direct access to the old city is provided by the cliff-side steps added in 1918 or the funicular railway (1895). The fortified **Schloss** itself, with its origins in the first fort or *gradec* of the Slavs, was demolished by the French in 1809. There are fine views over the town from the terrace. A right turn from the Karmeliterplatz ascends north-east to the **Paulustor** (1614), the sole remaining gate of the Renaissance fortifications, the outward-facing side of which bears the coats of arms of Archduke Ferdinand and his wife. You reach shortly the **Styrian Folk Museum** in the former Capuchin Convent (Paulustorgasse 11–13A. Open Mon–Fri 10.00–17.00, Sat, Sun, PH 14.00–17.00, due to reopen after re-arrangement in summer 2000).

Descending Sporgasse, you pass (at the corner of Hofgasse) the **Palace of the Teutonic Knights** (1612, Peter Valnegro) with its Renaissance courtyard, opposite which (Sporgasse 21) are picturesque steps up to the **Stiegenkirche** (**St Paul im Walde**) on the site of the oldest church in the city, the present one built

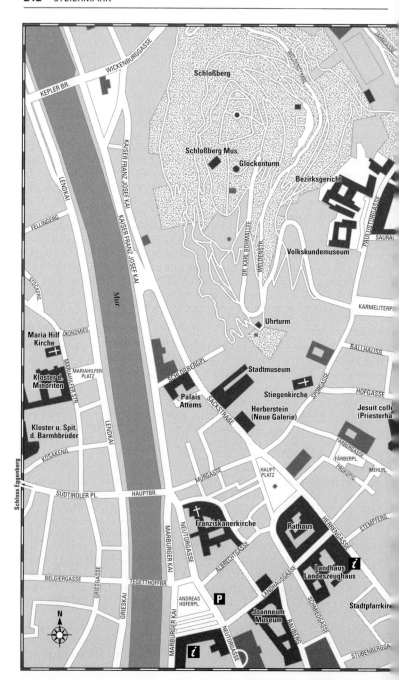

GRAZ

hloßberg

JAHNGASSE

MARIA THERESIA ALLEE

Stadtpark

FRIEDRICH V. GAGERN ALLEE

GLACISSTRASSE

HARRACHGASSE

ezirksgericht

PAULUSTORGASSE

Leechkirche

ZINDENDOREGASSE

SAURAUGASSE

BRANDHOFGASSE

lkskundemuseum

Forumstadtpark

Stadtpark

KARMELITERPLATZ

ELISABETHSTR.

BALLHAUSG.

Burggarten

WILH. FISCHERALLEE

GLACISSTRASSE

Burg

HOFGASSE

Landesregierung

EHZG.

JOHANN ALLEE

LEONHARDSTR

FARBERGASSE

Dom St Ägydius

Kunsthaus

(FÄRBERPL.

Jesuit college
(Priesterhaus)

Mausoleum

BURGGASSE

P

MONTCLAIR ALLEE

Stadtpark

PROKOPIG.

MEHLPL.

BURGRING

ENGE G.

STEMPFERG.

BISCHOFPL.

Akadgymn

EINSPINNERG.

RENGASSE

Bischöflicheresidenz

TUMMELPL.

GLACISSTRASSE

Landhaus
deszeughaus

HANS SACHSGASSE

OPERNRING

FRANZ GRAF ALLEE

Stadtpfarrkirche

P

Opernhaus

SPARBER
BLACHGASSE

GASSE

STUBENBERGGASSE

AM EISERNEN TOR

0   200 yards

0   200 metres

Herz. Jesu Kirche

by the Augustinian hermits in 1627. The *Annunciation* (1686) in a side-chapel is by Adam Weißenkirchner. Sporgasse leads back to the Hauptplatz, from which Sackstrasse leads north-west. At no. 16 is the **Herberstein Palace** with a lush Rococo interior, which houses the **Neue Galerie** that used to feature Austrian art of the 19C and 20C (open Mon–Fri, 10.00–18.00, Sun and PH, 10.00–13.00). Currently (and inexplicably) the permanent collection is in store, but it is hoped that the old pictures will return.

The **Palais Attems** (1716, Andreas Stengg) at no. 17 is perhaps the city's finest Baroque palace with a monumental stairway, mythological frescoes by Matthias von Görz on the ceiling of its **Steinsaal** and rich stucco. The building houses the Styrian Visual and Audio Archive (open Tues 09.00–17.00, Sat 09.00–17.00. Media Service: Mon, Tues, Thur, 08.00–16.00, Wed and Fri 08.00–13.00).

At Sackstraße 18 the **Stadt Museum** (Municipal Museum; open Tues, 10.00–21.00, Wed–Sat 10.00–18.00, Sun and PH 10.00–13.00) is housed in the former Palais Khuenberg and includes an apothecary from the Baroque age. The road leads on past the Mint (1690) to Franz-Josefs-Kai, from where the funicular railway ascends to the Schlossberg.

If the opposite direction from the Hauptplatz is taken, southwards along Schmiedgasse and then to the right along Landhausgasse, the **Palaeontological, Geological, Mineralogical and Natural Historical Collection** of the **Joanneum** is reached to the left at Raubergasse 10 (open all year, Tues–Sun 09.00–16.00).

In the parallel street at Neutorgasse 45 is the main building of the **Landesmuseum Joanneum** (currently open Tues, weekends, PH, 10.00–17.00, but times may be extended), with a notable collection of works from the Romanesque to the Baroque periods. Here is to be found Conrad Laib's **Crucifixion altar** from the cathedral, and numerous other Gothic works, most of them retrieved from Styrian churches. Note the remnants of altars by Michael Pacher, including a depiction of the *Murder of Thomas à Becket*, Marx Reichlich's *Departure of the Apostles* (1490) and works of the Cranach school. The Baroque collection includes works by Rottmayr, Maulbertsch, Kremser Schmidt, Paul Troger, Pietro de Pomis and others. On the first floor is applied art.

West of the Hauptplatz and just south of the Haupt-Brücke is the **Franciscan Church** (14C–16C), its irregular positioning being explained by some that it was originally integrated into the city wall, by others that it was once cut off by an arm of the River Mur. It has suffered from re-Gothicisation and bomb damage in the last war and many of the fittings in the interior are modern.

By crossing the Mur by the Haupt-Brücke and turning right along the bank (*Lendkai*), you reach on the left the Mariahilfer Platz with the **Maria-Hilf-Kirche** and the Minorite cloister. The late Baroque towers (1744) of the church's front elevation are by Josef Hueber and flank the older central structure by Pietro de Pomis, which was inspired by Palladio's San Giorgio Maggiore in Venice. The high altar of the mostly unremarkable interior is also the work of de Pomis and frames a wonder-working icon of Maria-Hilf dated to 1611. Its ornate silver frame (1769) with angelic figures is by Philipp Straub, and the St Michael figure on the external gable is by the same artist. In the Schatzkammerkapelle of the monastery's west wing are frescoes (1711) by Adam von Mölk.

South and slightly to the west at Annenstrasse 2 is the cloister and hospital church of the Brothers of Mercy (*Barmherzige Brüder*). It was built (1735–40) by

Johann Georg Stengg, with an altarpiece of the *Annunciation* (1754) by the Neapolitan Corrado Giaquinto; the side-figures of *Pope Paul V Authorising the Order* (left) and *Carlo Borromeo Offering the Host to a Plague Victim* (right) are by Josef Schokotnigg.

There are at least 12 other churches in and around Graz, of which the barockised **parish church of St Andrä** on the right bank of the Mur, and the neo-Gothic **Herz Jesu Kirche** in the Sparbersbachgasse are the most interesting. The latter is the most ambitious example of Historicism in the area, built (1881–98) by Georg Hauberrisser and boasting a 102m high tower. The vivid frescoes are by Max Godfried and Hans Lukesch.

Two specialist museums may also be of interest: the **Austrian Lock and Key Museum** (Belgiergasse 3. Open Thur 15.00–18.00 or on request; ☎ 0316 71 1625) contains 9000 objects from all over the world; the **Robert Stolz Museum** (Mehlplatz 1, entrance Färberplatz. Open Tues–Thur 14.00–17.00, Sat 10.00–13.00) documents (also with tapes and videos) the life and work of one of Austria's best-loved composers of light music (1880–1975), who was born in Graz.

Schloss Eggenberg

On the western periphery of Graz and reached (3km) via the Annenstrasse and Eggenberger Strasse is the fine Baroque residence (1635) of the Eggenbergs, a family of bourgeois origin that became wealthy from finance and trade (tours of the Schloss take place April–Oct, Tues–Sun at 10.00, 11.00, 12.00, 14.00, 15.00 and 16.00). Hans Ulrich von Eggenberg was made Governor of Inner Austria in 1625 and decided to build himself a palace commensurate with his status. The construction was carried out by Italian masters, including Pietro Valnegro to a design by Laurenz van de Sype.

The ground floor houses the **Museum of Early and Pre-History** (open Feb–Nov, Tues–Sun, 09.00–17.00), which contains the unique **Strettweg chariot of bronze** dating to the 7C BC and found near Judenburg in 1851. It is thought to represent part of a sacrificial procession celebrating the 'Great Mother', i.e. a fertility rite. On the first floor is a **Hunting Museum** and **Coin Collection** (same opening hours).

The design and decoration of the Schloss follows a calendarial theme: its four towers represent the four seasons, its 12 entrances the 12 months, its 365 windows the days of the year. Of the impressively stuccoed and painted interior (mostly the work of Alessandro Serenio), the great **Planetensaal** with Hans Adam Weißenkirchner's superb frescoes (1684–85) is outstanding: on the walls are allegories of animals and the planets, at the centre is Helios (a symbol for Leopold I) floating towards the eagle symbolising the Eggenberg family. In the English park is a **lapidarium**. North of Schloss Eggenberg is the ruined **Burg Gösting**, which belonged to the family from 1622–1707, a 12C castle guarding the road and river approaches to Graz.

The **Pilgrimage Church of Mariatrost** is 5km north-east of Graz. It was built (1714–24) by Andreas Stengg in collaboration with his son, Johann Georg, and its object of veneration is a late Gothic icon of the *Madonna* (1470). There is also statuary of high quality by Josef Schokotnigg and Veit Königer, the latter also being responsible for the decorative pulpit.

South of Graz

Road 67 leads south of Graz, running between the Mur and the A9/E93 motorway. After passing through Kalsdorf and Wildon (from whose castle Tycho Brahe is said to have made astronomical observations) a minor road leads to **Hengsberg**, where a museum of local pre-history has been set up in the undercroft of the church and a museum of peasant life in the tower (open on application; ☎ 03185 2203). The minor road leads on to **Stainz**, whose secularised Augustine abbey was for a while (from 1840) Archduke Johann's residence, and since then has been owned by the Counts of Meran, the title bestowed on his commoner wife. The Archduke instituted here a model agricultural estate, in particular promoting the **Schilcher**, a dry rosé wine that is a celebrated Styrian speciality. It is made from the indigenous **Blaue Wildbacher** grape, a wild species known to the Celts and producing a marvellous range of colour from delicate pink to the purplish glow of red onions.

In 1850 Archduke Johann was elected the first Mayor of Stainz, the only official position he held in the province. The abbey may be visited from April–Nov, 09.00–17.00, a highlight being the refectory with rich stucco and frescoes and the adjacent church (partly by Domenico Sciassia) in which an altarpiece of the *Martyrdom of St Catherine* by Hans Adam Weißenkirchner may be seen. The abundant statuary of the side-altars is by Veit Königer and Andreas Marx, while the ceiling frescoes by Matthias Echter show scenes from the history of the Augustinian order. The folk museum in the Schloss is open April–mid-November, daily 09.00–17.00. **Eichegg bei Stainz** is regarded as the second birthplace of Schilcher, after the grape was replanted here following the phylloxera plague of the 1890s. The area between Stainz and Eibiswald in the south is known as the **Schilcherweinstrasse**, the heartland of Schilcher wine production.

Road 76 leads from Stainz to **Deutschlandsberg**, whose medieval Burg has been restored and now houses a hotel in one wing, the restaurant of which is in the former **Knights Hall**, and a Museum of Early and Pre-History (open April–15 Nov, daily 09.30–12.00, 13.00–17.00). **Schloss Hollenegg** (1577) is just to the south, while a loop eastwards on road 74 brings you to **Pölfing-Brunn**, where there is documentation of mining located in a former coal-mine (viewing by arrangement; ☎ 034 65 30 00 0). A minor road leads south-west to **Wies**, where the old smithy has been turned into a museum (☎ 034 65 22 01 0 or enquire at the town hall), and then to Eibiswald, where a small museum is dedicated to the local '*Groß-Deutsch*' poet and doctor, Hans Kloepfer, also showing ethnographic items (☎ 034 66 43 117).

Retracing the route as far as Pölfing, road 74 runs east from Gasselsdorf, a turning south beyond Maierhof bringing you to **Großklein**, where the **Hallstattmuseum** (open Tues, Wed, Fri–Sun, 10.00–12.00 and 14.00–16.30) contains the largest preserved grave from the period of Hallstatt culture (750–450 BC, early Iron Age). Returning to the main road you continue east through the very attractive **Sausal Weinstrasse** area, a detour to the north bringing you to **Kitzeck im Sausal**, where the **Styrian Wine Museum** (open April–Nov, Sat, Sun, PH 10.00–12.00, 14.00–17.00) is to be found at Steinriegel 16. At 621m, Kitzeck is one of the highest wine-growing regions in Austria, also one of the oldest, looking back on a 1000 year tradition. A feature of the museum is the *Klapotetz*, a clattering wind-driven wheel placed in the vineyards between the 25 June and 11

November to keep marauding birds away. In the Sausal region, not only wine but chestnuts, pumpkins (producing the famous black oil) and fruit are grown.

To the east of Kitzeck is **Seggauberg**, where **Schloss Seggau** has a display of Roman reliefs and inscriptions in the courtyard. The neighbouring **Tempelmuseum Frauenberg** has a lapidarium (open April–Oct, Mon and Sat 10.00–16.00, Sun, PH, 10.00–18.00) containing part of the temple of Isis at Noreia (AD 100). At nearby **Kaindorf an der Sulm** is a school of horticulture and viticulture, while at **Leibnitz Schloss Retzhof** (open Mon–Fri, 08.00–12.00, 13.00–17.00) was formerly the property of the Seckau bishopric and is now partly a college. The town is the centre of the local wine trade and originally grew up close to the Roman settlement of *Flavia Solva*, now **Wagna**, reached by a minor road to the south-west. The **Museum Flavia Solva** (open Easter–Oct,Tues–Sun, 10.00–17.00) has exhibits from the Roman excavations here.

You continue to **Straß**, the Schloss of which houses the **Truppenmuseum** of the Erzherzog-Johann Barracks (open on application, ☎ 03453 2611/5088) with a display of 140 years of Austrian military history.

To the west (road 69), overlooking the town of **Ehrenhausen**, is the superb Mannerist **Mausoleum** (1680) of the Eggenbergs. It was built by Johann Walter to plans by Pietro de Pomis for Ruprecht and Wolf von Eggenberg, who died respectively in 1611 and 1615. Ruprecht (b. 1545) was a soldier, celebrated for his victorious battles against the Turks. The most illustrious of the line was Johann Ulrich von Eggenberg (1598–1634), a Catholic convert and trusted adviser of Ferdinand II. He urged severity after the defeat of the Bohemian Protestants at the Battle of the White Mountain, and became one of the richest men of his age with possessions in four Habsburg hereditary lands, as well as estates in Bohemia confiscated from the exiled Protestant nobility. The 5m-high portals with the Eggenberg coat of arms, the majestic stone watchmen (portrayed as armed giants) and the stucco representing the heavenly choir (by Alessandro and Giuseppe Serenio), combine to create a formidable impression of power and glory. The interior was designed by J.B. Fischer von Erlach and the altarpiece of *Mary Interceding for Victory over the Turks* (1691) is by Hans Adam Weißenkirchner. The Burg, for long in possession of the Eggenbergs, preserves a 12C keep. The **parish church** dedicated to Our Lady of Sorrows was built (1755) by Johann Fuchs, the Rococo high altar with theatrical statuary and the altarpiece being by Philipp Straub; there is also a 15C *pietà*, while the statues (1760) for the side-altars are the work of Veit Königer. At Ehrenhausen begins the south Styrian Weinstrasse, an attractive region of vine-covered hills which it is worth taking at a leisurely pace. At **Gamlitz** the Schloss contains a **Wine Museum** and a small gallery (open May–11 Nov, Tues–Sun, 10.00–12.00, 14.00–17.00).

From Straß road 69 runs east parallel to the Slovenian border (here formed by the River Mur) to the south-east corner of the province and the frontier town of **Bad Radkersburg**. On the way it passes **Ratschendorf** with a Roman burial ground, which may be visited (key from the house adjacent). At Bad Radkersburg itself there is a **municipal museum** in the former Armoury (1588) with limited opening hours (Nov–March, Tues and Fri 14.00–17.00). The town was the first in Austria to receive the Europa Gold Medal for conservation and its old centre is girdled with the remnants of Italian fortifications from the 16C. The parish church of St John the Baptist (1402) has a fine sandstone portal from the 16C and a late Gothic crucifix (1510).

Around Bärnbach

Hundertwasser church, Bärnbach

Road 70 loops south and west of Graz to Voitsberg, with its open-cast lignite mines, just before which a turn to the north brings you to **Stallhofen**, where the deaf sculptor and poet Gustinus Ambrosi (1893–1975) retired (for visits to the Ambrosi Haus, ☎ 031 42 220 38). A follower of Rodin, he sculpted many of the most important figures in the arts and politics of his day, including Rilke, Stefan Zweig, Strindberg, Karl Renner and Julius Raab. In the north of the village is a former smithy with an end-wall shaped like a human visage and known locally as the *Eisenfresser* (Iron Eater). At **Bärnbach**, just to the north of Voitsberg is the splendid **Kirche Bärnbach**, built after the war, but completely remodelled by Friedensreich Hundertwasser in 1987–88. The playful effect of its dual-toned wall decoration, the variegated tiled roof and the gold onion dome make this a particularly pleasing example of post-modern exuberance. Nearby, the Renaissance **Schloss Alt-Kainach** with finely restored coffered ceilings and an impressive knights hall may be visited between May and Oct, Tues–Sun 10.00–12.00, 14.00–17.00. At the **Stölzle Glass Centre**, Hochregisterstraße 1, Bärnbach (open Mon–Fri, 09.00–17.00, Sat, 09.00–13.00) is an interesting exhibition on glass production with the opportunity to try your hand at glass-blowing (Sun and PH May–Oct, 09.00–13.00).

The Lipizzaner Stud

A minor road leads north and west to the famous Lipizzaner stud at **Schloss Piber**, which is an experience not to be missed. Open from the Monday before Easter to Nov, daily 09.00–10.15 and 14.00–15.00 (waiting time can be passed pleasurably in the Schloss Taverna). The Piber stud was originally for military use (from 1798), but in 1920 horses were brought here from Laxenburg and Kladruby, where they had passed the war. The excellent lecture tour shows some characterful horses that obviously enjoy posing for the cameras with one foreleg crooked while the groom gives a flattering account of their talents. Information is given on the breeding techniques, how the horses are hardened and trained, and the criteria for selection to appear at the famous Spanish Riding School in Vienna. The Lipizzaner had such an aura that General Patton organised a bold (and totally unauthorised) dash into Czech territory at the end of the last war to save a large number from falling into Russian hands (they were being used as work horses).

East and south-east of Graz

Lipizzaner horses

At **St Johann/Herberstein**, north-east of Graz (turn off Road 54 beyond Pischelsdorf) is the great Baroque Burg of the Herbersteins, a rebuilding of earlier Renaissance and Gothic edifices dating back to 1230, but in the family's possession since 1320. More than most Schloss owners, the Herbersteins have bestirred themselves to 'market' their home, offering an exhibition of Life in the Schloss (i.e. at the turn of the 19C) and conscientiously restoring the **historic garden of Schloss Herberstein** (laid out in the 17C and lovingly reconstructed by the garden historian and architect, Maria Auböck, in 1997, whose source was an etching by Georg Mattäus Vischer of 1681). Other interesting features of the Schloss include an arcaded courtyard, the ancestral portrait gallery, the porcelain collection and the chapel. Burg Herberstein is open from April–Oct, daily, 10.00–16.00, ☎ 0 3176 88250) The **Wildlife Park** with animals from five continents is open April–Oct, daily 08.00–18.00, Nov–March, 10.00–16.00.

On a minor road to the west, **Puch bei Weiz** is reached with an open air **Museum of the Urn Burial Period** (open May–Oct, Mon–Sat, 09.00–17.00, Sun 10.00–18.00) nearby on the Kulmberg. A curiosity is the **Haus des Apfels**, all you ever wanted to know about apples in history, religion, art and custom from Neolithic times (open 16 April–Oct, Tues–Sun, 10.00–17.00).

You continue north-west to join road 72 and turn south on the latter to **Weiz**, whose Taborkirche (dedicated to Thomas à Becket in 1188) retains Romanesque features and is girdled by a defensive wall incorporating dwellings. The high altar has a depiction of *St Thomas* and there is an 18C view of Weiz (Josef Adam Mölk, 1771). The frescoes of the 13C, 14C and 15C were restored and partly extended in 1933. On a hill on the eastern edge of the town (**Weizberg**) is the **Pilgrimage church of the Sorrowing Virgin Mary**, a late Baroque edifice (1758) on the site of earlier churches. The interior is richly frescoed by Josef Adam Mölk (1771, the *Celebration of the Virgin*, the *Passion* and illusionist architecture representing the temple in Jerusalem). The high altar (1771) is by Veit Königer, with a 15C *pietà*, while the richly decorative **pulpit** (1775) is by Jakob Peyer. At **Dürntal bei Weiz** to the north-west of the town are spectacular stalactite caves (**Grasslhöhle**: open April–Oct, Sat, Sun, PH 09.00–17.00). Road 64 goes on to join the Graz–Bruck an der Mur road.

If road 54 is followed north-east from Pischelsdorf, a turn south-west at Kaindorf brings you to **Schloss Obermayerhofen** (now a hotel open between March and December). The **Festsaal** has frescoes of animals and plants (1780) by Franz Moser. Road 54 continues to **Hartberg** with the 17C **Schloss Hartberg** and **Schloss Klaffenau** (1560), the latter with an exhibition and shop of peasant handwork (open Fri–Sun, 10.00–18.00). The parish church is notable for its Romanesque charnel house to the south, later probably used as a baptismal chapel, as the theme of its frescoes suggests. At Herrengasse 5 is a Renaissance house containing the local museum (open Wed 15.00–17.00, Sat 09.00–11.00) with exhibits from the Roman period.

The **church of St Anne** on the southern slopes of the Masenberg massif between Hartberg and Pöllau is a small Gothic gem of 1499 with a remarkable *St Anne with Mary and Jesus* (1520) on the otherwise Baroque main altar. In the nave is a winged altar with similar iconography dating to 1522.

South-west of Hartberg at **Löffelbach** a 1C Roman villa has been excavated and may be visited. North-west of this a minor road leads to Pöllau, where the pilgrimage church **Maria Pöllauberg** has decorative Gothic tracery in sandstone in the choir and on the sacramental niches. Above the high Gothic façade with its cylindrical tower a rather awkward Baroque superstructure was built in the 1670s. The votive *Madonna* (1480) on the intricately carved high altar by Marx Schokotnigg is flanked by figures sculpted by Schokotnigg and his son Josef, while the frescoes (1691) of the *Life of Mary* over the organ loft are by Antonio Maderni. Notable are the Gothic sitting niches of the choir and the consoles with sophisticated stone carving, including the symbols of the Four Evangelists. In Pöllau itself the church of the former Augustinian abbey has powerful illusionist ceiling frescoes (1718) by Matthias von Görz, whose general theme is the *Glorification of the Lamb of God*, the *Exaltation of the Cross* and the *Expulsion of the Rebellious Angels from Heaven*. The altarpiece of the *Martyrdom of St Vitus* is by J.A. Mölk, while the fabulously ornate Rococo pulpit (perhaps by Jakob Peyer) shows allegories of *Faith, Hope and Charity*. The southern altarpiece showing St Augustine writing (1788) is also by Mölk.

Stift Vorau

North of Hartberg (turn west from Rohnbach off Road 54) is the **Augustinian Abbey at Vorau**, beautifully situated in a valley with the Masenberg to the south and the Wildwiesen to the west. Founded in 1163 by Margrave Ottakar III of Steyr, the monastery is celebrated for the *Imperial Chronicle* (30,000 narrative verses written here in the late 12C, some of the earliest medieval poetry in Austria). Other rare treasures include poetry by Ava (see p 159) and a history of the times of Friedrich Barbarossa, as well as 84 codexes and 392 incunabula. The monastery declined during the Reformation, revived in the Baroque period and survived Joseph II's dissolutions because of its educational and cultural activity, which continues to this day.

The present **monastery** and **parish church** (1662) is mostly the work of Domenico Sciassia and has a dazzling Baroque interior. The frescoes (1705) by Johann Kasper Waginger (in the entrance hall and side-chapels) and the Viennese masters Karl Ritsch and Josef Grafenstein (in the nave and choir), also Karl Unterhuber (the western gallery, behind the organ) have three themes: the *Promise of the Kingdom of God as Foreseen by the Sibylls* (at the entrance) and the *Prophets and Patriarchs* (in the side-chapel arches), the *Coming of God's Kingdom through Christ* (on the entrance ceiling and chapel walls); a further representation of the *Fulfilment of God's Kingdom through Christ* (five large frescoes in the vault of the nave); and the *Glorification of his Saints, the founder, Margrave Ottakar III, St Augustine, St Thomas, Mary at the Assumption and the Heavenly Throng* (from the entrance moving inwards). The high altar (1704) is by Matthias Steinl with an altarpiece of the *Assumption* by Antonio Bellucci, beneath which is a plastic group of the apostles around the coffin. In front of the choir are four statues of the *Fathers of the Church*. Steinl was also responsible for the pulpit, showing God the Father on the canopy in a gloriole on a globe surrounded by angels: on the rear wall Cyriak Hackhofer's portrayal of Christ flanked by figures representing the Old and New Testaments. On the pulpit steps are scenes taken from the teaching of Christ that dovetail with the iconography of the frescoes. The finest frescoes (1716), however, are to be found in the sacristy and are by the Italian-influenced Johann Cyriak Hackhofer. They show on the ceiling the *Last Judgement*, a horrifying vision of hell on the west wall, elsewhere the *Passion*.

In the north wing of the so-called *Prälatur* is the **library** decorated with frescoes (Ignaz Gottlieb Kröll) and stucco symbolising *Philosophy, Theology* and *Law*. In the manuscript room is a fresco of the *Three Divine Virtues* (Georg Mayr, 1713) and an *Immaculata* by Hans Adam Weissenkirchner.

A minor road leads to the north and to **Burg Festenburg** near Bruck an der Lafnitz, since 1616 a possession of the Vorau monastery, with its fine **church of St Catherine** (1617). Hackhofer has again supplied the frescoes (1710) which ecstatically represent the *Triumph of Piety*, the culmination of a cycle beginning in the six chapels of the Burg and charting the path to joy through the Cross and suffering, as symbolised in the Rosary and the martyrdom of St Catherine. Festenburg is associated with the vernacular poet, Dr Ottakar Kernstock (1848–1928), who wrote new words for Haydn's *Kaiserlied*, as for the national anthem of Austria between the wars.

Returning south-east to road 54 by minor roads, you turn left for **Friedberg**, where there is a permanent exhibition of the furniture made by the famous **Thonet firm** founded in 1825 (open Sat, Sun, 10.00–12.00, 14.00–16.00) who had a factory here. The town was founded by Leopold of Babenberg, probably using part of the ransom moneys he got for the release of Richard Coeur de Lion. From Friedberg the road continues into Lower Austria.

An alternative southern route from Graz is to take road 65 to Gleisdorf, then road 68 to the south-east, reaching shortly Feldbach. In **Schloss Kornberg** annual exhibitions of Styrian handicrafts are held around Easter and Christmas (open daily, 10.00–18.00). The **Feldbacher Museum im Tabor** is located in the 15C fortifications and has a permanent exhibition of different aspects of Styrian life (open May–Oct, Mon–Fri, 09.00–11.00, 14.00–17.00, Sat, Sun, PH, 09.00–12.00).

Striking north on road 66, you reach the mighty castle of **Riegersburg**, built (1100) on a basalt outcrop and never successfully besieged (the Turks dubbed it 'the strongest fortress in Christendom'). It was much extended by Elisabeth Katharina, Baroness von Galler in the 17C and since 1822 has been in the possession of the Liechtensteins. Highlights of the tour include the *Fürstenzimmer* (with the bed of the spendthrift 'Gallerin'), the Roman room with scenes (1589) from mythology and Roman history, and the Knights Hall *(Rittersaal)* with a fine coffered ceiling. In the Burg the **Witch Museum** has an interesting exhibition on this theme, and in summer there are **falconry displays**. The Burg is open April–Oct, daily 09.00–17.00.

South of Feldbach on road 66 is the delightful **Bad Gleichenberg**, a spa known to the Romans, and a leading player in the increasingly sophisticated 'spa tourism' of Styria. The park around the spa has a nostalgic Biedermeier ambience and is planted with exotic species, and there is also an **Alpengarten** worth visiting. From here the road leads on south to Bad Radkersburg, and so over the Slovene border; alternatively you head back to the north in the direction of Feldbach.

North of Graz: the Mur Valley

Stift Rein

The main *Autobahn* A9 north of Graz runs shortly past **Judendorf-Straßengel** to the west, whose Gothic pilgrimage church (1355) has a fine octagonal belfry surmounted by an openwork steeple. In the choir is 14C and 15C stained glass showing biblical scenes, while above the south doorway is a carved tympanum showing the *Deposition from the Cross*. Further north is the oldest of the surviving Cistercian monasteries in Austria at **Rein** near Gratwein, founded in 1129 and rebuilt at the end of the 17C after being sacked by the Turks in 1480. The main Barockisation took place in the 18C (1737–47) under Johann Georg Stengg. The church has an elegant and rhythmic façade showing the allegorical figures of *Faith, Hope and Charity*, behind which rises the clock-tower and onion dome. The virtuoso *trompe l'oeil* frescoes (1766) of the interior are by J.A. Mölk (the *Fallen State of Rome and St Benedict*, the *Virgin*, *St Bernard of Clairvaux's Vision of the Cross*, the *Cardinal Virtues*, *Mary in the Temple*, *St Joseph with Jesus* and (beneath) *Joseph sold by his Brothers*). The high altar is also the work of Stengg, with a superb altarpiece (1779) of the *Holy Night* by Kremser Schmidt.

In the Gothic **Kreuzkapelle** to the north is the tomb of Archduke 'Iron' Ernst (1377–1424), and in a neighbouring chapel that (in red marble) of Margrave Ottakar III, both men being decisive figures in Styrian history. Ernst was the last Habsburg to be invested as Carinthian Duke on the Zollfeld and spent much of his life struggling with his brothers for a larger share of the hereditary lands. The monastery church can be visited without formality, or for the frequent concerts.

Just to the north of Rein is the **Austrian open-air Museum** at **Stübing** (open April–Oct, Tues–Sun, 09.00–17.00) with 85 examples of farm buildings and implements etc. from all over the country.

At **Deutschfeistritz** to the north is a factory that made scythes (until 1984), the hammer being driven by six huge waterwheels (*Sensenhammer Deutschfeistritz*: open April–Oct, Mon–Fri, 14.00–17.00, Sat, Sun, PH 10.00–17.00).

At **Peggau** the road branches and the right-hand fork (S35) continues to **Lurgrotte** (stalactite caves: open April–Oct, daily 09.00–16.00), where the temperature is a constant 10°C and the humidity 95 per cent. An underground river flows from a karst spring for 2km inside the cave.

Burg Rabenstein to the north-west was built above the Mur valley to guard the trade route. It is not normally visitable, except for concerts, when the Barockised interior of the **Knights Hall** with stucco by Alessandro Serenio may be seen. **Pernegg an der Mur** is a few kilometres further up the valley and has a 15C Gothic hall church barockised in 1775. Nearby are two natural wonders, a gorge with a river at the bottom (*Bärenschützklamm*), for which the walk (c 2hrs) starts at Mixnitz, and the Dragon's Cave (*Drachenhöhle*).

Bruck an der Mur (Roman *Poedicum*) is reached shortly, an industrial town lying at the confluence of the Mürz and the Mur rivers. The Hauptplatz has a Marian column (1700) with statues of six saints; at the north-east corner of the square is the notable **Kornmesserhaus** (1505) with a balustrade of astonishingly intricate stonework above ogee arches, the vaulted loggia behind being influenced by Venetian models. The house belonged to a prosperous smith (*Hammerherr*). On the square is a well with an ornate wrought-iron canopy (1626), while the **Apothecary's House** in the Anzengrubergasse has an attractive closed arcade of 1530. On the northern outskirts is the early Gothic parish church of 1272 with a 15C *Crucifixion* in a side-chapel. The **sacristy doors** (1500) with a rhombus design in wrought-iron and especially the key-mounting and door ring are notable. At the western periphery of the town is the **St Rupert Church** with a well-restored fresco of the *Last Judgement* (1420), while to the east is the former **Minorite Church** (13C) below the **Schlossberg**, with remains of 14C frescoes. Ottakar II Premysl of Bohemia built a castle on the Schlossberg in 1265, but only a clock-tower survived a fire of 1792.

Leoben and Göss

West of Bruck an der Mur, Road H6 or S6 leads to **Leoben** in the Mur valley, the research and development centre for the Styrian iron and steel industry. The town's economic ascent may be traced to privileges and tolls connected with the iron trade that were bestowed on it in 1314. In 1797 the Treaty of Leoben was signed here between the Austrians and the French, bringing a temporary halt to the Napoleonic war (in fact a truce into which the Austrians were forced, and which preceded the Treaty of Campo Formio). The **parish church** in Leoben was originally that of the Jesuit College, hence its dedication to St Francis Xaver. It was built (1665) by Peter Franz Carlone, its façade recalling the Jesuit church of Vienna. The heavily ornate gilded and black Baroque furnishings of the interior achieve an impressive unity, enhanced by Ägydius Meixner's over-life-size statues of the *Apostles*, *Peter and Paul* and the *Salzburg bishops*, *Rupert and Virgil*. The graceful pulpit with its baldachin held aloft by angels is probably also the work of Meixner. The altarpiece shows the *Apotheosis of St Francis Xaver* by Johann Heinrich Schönfeld. The former Jesuit college is adjacent to the north.

In the former **Burg** is the **Municipal Museum** with a newly constituted display concerning technological development in Styria ('*Made in Styria*': open daily 10.00–12.00, 14.00–17.00). The **Hauptplatz** has a number of historic buildings, including the Alte Rathaus (1485, with a Renaissance corner tower and a frieze recalling the visit of Karl VI in 1728), the **Hacklhaus** (no. 9, with stucco of 1680 showing allegories of the *Four Seasons and Christian Virtues*, in the stairway Max Fendler's frescoes (1851) of *Mining and Hunting Scenes*) and the **Gasthof zum Schwarzen Adler** (no. 11, with a Renaissance portal and Gothic courtyard). South of the Jesuit College is the 17C century **Mautturm** (customs tower), now known as the **Schwammerlturm** (mushroom tower) and rebuilt by Carlone in 1615. Across the river is the church of **Maria am Waasen**, which preserves 54 panels of Gothic stained glass in the choir, showing *Apostles, Saints, the Founder of the church* and a remarkable *Passion* cycle.

In the western suburb of **Göss** is the lovely church of the former **Benedictine nunnery**, founded in 1020 and initially settled by nuns from the Nonnberg in Salzburg. It was dissolved by Joseph II and the convent became the residence of the bishops of Leoben, an office that only existed briefly.

The **Stiftskirche** (now the parish church) is exceptional: the looped vaulting of the three-aisled late-Gothic nave rests on massive octangular block columns, of which the two at the east end (16m) are turned like the thread of a corkscrew (an intriguingly different technique to the later Salomonic or 'barley sugar' columns of the Baroque). Another beautiful feature of the church is the late-Gothic south portal (1520), having an ogee arch at its centre with a rectangular frame of four ribs beautifully counterpointed above the door by looped tracery and foliage in a semi-circular bow. Over the ornate choirstalls hangs the Romanesque **Gösser crucifix**, probably Italian work dated to c 1180. The southern side-altar has an altarpiece by Kremser Schmidt of the *Holy Family* (1791), while above the altar of the cross to the north is a *Crucifixion* by the same artist. Other notable features of the church include the polygonal **font** (1612) and the early Romanesque crypt.

Adjacent to the church is the two-storeyed **St Michael's Chapel**, the lower part Romanesque, the upper part (where the only Bishop of Leoben used to celebrate mass) known as the **Bishop's Chapel**, a fine example of early Gothic. The **Zackenstil** frescoes (1271) show, besides saints and biblical scenes, a vivid *Song of Solomon* on the south wall, this erotic poem being (as the guidebook hastens to explain) an allegory for Christians of the 'bonding of the human soul with Christ'. The tour includes the small museum, which documents the history of the nunnery, besides having various pictures and treasures of some interest, most amusingly a *Klappsarg*, or re-usable coffin from the Josephin era (it has a false bottom from which the corpse was ejected). This sensible and economic device was furiously rejected by the populace, who were much attached to their coffins, and indeed all the other pomp and ceremony of a Baroque funeral.

Göss is also famous for its brewery, which has operated in a dependency of the nunnery at least since 1459, taking over the entire cellar of the secularised convent in 1860. There are guided tours of the Stiftskirche and the showrooms of the former convent but these require a minimum number of people. For these and access to the Stiftskirche (if closed) apply at the Pfarramt Leoben-Göss (☎ 0 38 42 43 236 or 22 148). The interesting Göss **Brewery Museum** in the former malthouse is open 26 April–26 Oct, Mon–Fri 09.00–18.00.

West of Leoben and Bruck an der Mur

Vordernberg, Eisenerz and the Erzberg

Road 115 leads north from Leoben, shortly passing through **St Peter Freienstein**, its 16C **Schloss Friedhofen** having a small museum relating to salt-mining (open on application: ☎ 0 38 42 227 62). The road leads on to **Trofaiach**, where **Schloss Stibichhofen** may be visited (Sat 10.00–12.00, 15.00–17.00, Sun 10.30–12.00), once the home of a celebrated plague doctor, Anton Adam Lebaldt von und zu Lebenwaldt (1624–1696), who was ennobled for his services in 1659, and who was also a poet. There is a small museum of local history.

The town of **Vordernberg** was a mining settlement, as was **Eisenerz**, whose fortified Gothic parish church retains some unusual Gothic features, including the relief over the portal showing Adam and Eve as ur-miners (!). However, the interior was remodelled in neo-Gothic style to plans by Friedrich Schmidt between 1890 and 1899. The massive **Schichtturm** (1580) in the town is a clock-tower, so-called because its bell summoned the miners to their shifts. There are Gothic and Renaissance houses in the old town on the Bergmannplatz (however, the fountain here, with a figure of a miner dates to 1874) and in the surrounding streets.

In the Krumpentalerstrasse at no. 12, with a Renaissance portal is the **Kammerhof**, former seat of the mining overseer, now a **Municipal Museum** (open May–Oct, daily, 09.00–17.00, Nov–April, Tues–Fri 09.00–12.00). A dramatic insight into the miners' world may be gained by visiting the **Schaubergwerk am Steirischen Erzberg**, a labyrinth of tunnels with all the tools of the trade on display. It is open May–Oct, daily 10.00–15.00.

The **Erzberg** itself is to the south-east of Eisenerz, a gigantic wound in the hillside rising in a series of terraces to a height of 1465m, its 1870 peak of 1532m having gradually been eroded by surface mining. The mountain is mostly siderite, yielding 32 per cent iron, and has been quarried from time immemorial. Formerly the iron was transported by river from Hieflau to Steyr, but it is now sent direct to the blast furnaces in Linz or Donawitz. Between May and October there are 'adventure' excursions with a converted iron-ore carrier ('*der Hauly*'), whereby visitors are ferried between the different terraces of the mine. (Information from *Voest Alpine*, Erzberg 1. ☎ 0 38 48 32 00).

North and west of Hieflau: Großreifling, Admont, Ardning

Beyond Eisenerz, road 115 forks at **Hieflau**, road 25 leading north-east to **Gams bei Hieflau**, where there is a gypsum cave named after its discoverer, Franz Kraus (Kraushöhle, open April–Oct, 09.00–17.00). The road continues over the border into Lower Austria. Road 115 leads due north to **Großreifling** (**Landl**), where the interesting Austrian Forestry Museum is located in a Baroque grain store (1771). It gives a wealth of information about tree-felling, timber transport and the many ways in which wood can be used (open May–Oct, Tues–Sun, 10.00–12.00, 13.00–17.00). The hairpin road leads on to the border with Upper Austria, leaving to the west St Gallen, reached by a minor road. The ruins of **Gallenstein** here afford fine views of the **Gesäuseberge** (to the south) and the **Voralpen**.

Stift Admont

Bearing west from Hieflau along road 146 brings you to Styria's oldest male monastic institution (founded in 1074 by Archbishop Gebhard of Salzburg), the **Benedictine abbey of Admont** (the monastery and museums may be visited April–Oct, daily, 10.00–13.00 and 14.00–17.00, PH 10.00–12.00, Nov–March only in groups, ☎ 0 36 13 23 12/601). The barockised buildings were largely destroyed by fire in 1865, as was also Johann Gotthard Hayberger's Baroque church of 1734. Parts of the Romanesque portal (e.g. the stone lions) remain, together with the base of the tower, but the rest is neo-Gothic. Gothic and Baroque fittings were, however, rescued from the fire, including a celebrated Baroque crib (1755) by Joseph Thaddäus Stammel of Graz (1695–1765) and a representation of the *Dead Christ* by the same artist. On the Marian altar is Martino Altomonte's *Immaculata* (1726) surrounded by 15 medallions (by Stammel) representing the mysteries of the Rosary. In the sacristy is a monumental *Crucifixion* (over 2m high) dating to 1518.

The superb **Baroque library** (1774) by Hayberger and Josef Hueber survived the 1865 fire, and is the last and one of the most beautiful of its kind to be built in Austria. The ceiling fresco of the elegant red, gold and white interior with finely carved bookshelves is by Bartolomeo Altomonte and shows *Religion and the Church as Protectors of Art and Knowledge*, with architectural decoration by Johann Georg Dallinger. Inserted into the general scheme are superb lime-wood sculptures (later bronzed) by Stammel, an eschatological and didactic ensemble based on the number four; it features *Death and Judgement, Heaven and Hell*, the *Four Cardinal Virtues*, *Moses, Elias, Peter and Paul*, the *Four Evangelists*, the *Judgement of Solomon* and *Jesus in the Temple*.

Examples of the 900 incunabulae in the library's possession are periodically on display, as well as treasures such as **Luther's Bible** (1539), and a Greek and Latin New Testament edited by Erasmus. Admont also has an **Art Historical Museum** and a **Natural History Museum**, the latter containing a unique insect collection made by a Benedictine monk named Gabriel Strobl.

Six kilometres west of Admont on road 146 is **Ardning**, near which the A9 *Autobahn* is reached northwards through the Bosrucktunnel into Upper Austria. Perched on the Kulmberg which rises abruptly out of the Ennstal is the **Frauenberg church** (1687) at Ardning, built by Carlantonio Carlone and containing further striking works by Joseph Stammel (*Saints and Angels*) and rich Baroque fittings. Stammel also created the *Altar of the Cross*, where the wooden Marian statue of 1410 is an object of veneration. The frescoes (1695) in the nave are by Antonio Maderni, in the choir (1794) by Johann Lederwasch.

Road 146 crosses the motorway and heads west through **Liezen**, from where road 113 leads south and east, eventually back to **St Michael in Obersteiermark** on the Leoben/Judenburg road (see below). On this stretch (parallel to which runs the A9 *Autobahn*) you pass the Renaissance **Burg Strechau** near Rottenmann with a beautiful arcaded courtyard and a unique Protestant wall-painting (1579) in the Lutheran chapel, while in the later Catholic one is an altar and crucifix (1637) by J.H. Stammel (open May–Sept, weekends and PH, 14.00–16.00).

Further south at **Mautern** is a small zoo (Natur-und-Tierpark, open May–Oct daily, 09.00–17.00, weekends, PH, 09.00–18.00). The **parish church**

of St Nicholas has a fine tabernacle relief by Johann Stammel on a side-altar (the 'Altar of the Cross', whose miraculous cross has been transferred to the high altar), which shows *Moses and the Burning Bush*. The altarpiece of *Christ on the Mount of Olives* (1798) is by Johann Lederwasch. Stammel also supplied the statuary (1740) in the choir of the convent **church of St Barbara** (1676), which was probably built by Domenico Sciassia.

Around Pürgg

Bearing west of Selzthal (Liezen), road 113 becomes road 308, then road 146. On a hill close to **Pürgg** (just beyond Stainach) is the Romanesque **Chapel of St John** (1160), with exceptional **frescoes** (the oldest preserved in Austria) painted between 1160–70: on the north wall, the *Feeding of the Five Thousand*; elsewhere the *Driving out of the Devil from the Possessed, Joseph's Dream;* on the south wall, the *Annunciation* and the *Nativity*. Also a celebrated depiction symbolising the struggle against the evil one, and known as the '*Cat and Mouse War*'. On the triumphal arch are to be seen the spiritual and secular founders of the church, above them *Cain and Abel*. In the chancel is the *Lamb of God surrounded by the symbols of the Evangelists*. In the lunettes are personifications of the *Four Empires of the World*. The Romanesque **crucifix** on the altar dates to the 13C. The **parish church of St George** in Pürgg retains Romanesque features, including its defensive wall and its belfry, in the porch of which are early 14C frescoes (the *Legend of St Catherine* and the *Passion*).

To the south-east of Pürgg at **Aigen im Ennstal** is a castle now used as a youth hostel and nearby the allegedly warm **Putterer See**; however, the real feature of interest at Aigen is the **modern church of St Florian**, completed in 1992 to plans by Volker Giencke of the contemporary Graz School. Approached across a bridge, this striking building has a greened, 'environmental' roof and an irregular ground-plan enclosed by colourful glass walls, while the interior has a slightly inclined floor. Altogether it is an exhilarating example of how a modern materials-focused design can yet evoke an atmosphere of reverence and contemplation.

If you recross the river via Irdning, you come to **Schloss Trautenfels**, a celebrated Baroque castle of 1664, actually a reconstituted medieval fortress (*Neuhaus*) that guarded the valley here and which is overlooked by the massive Grimming opposite. It was in this castle that Ottakar IV was named Duke of Styria by Friedrich Barbarossa. The interior contains stucco by Alessandro Serenio and frescoes (1670) by Carpoforo Tencala (the *Four Seasons*, the *Four Cardinal Virtues* and mythological scenes). In the free-standing chapel are further examples of the Serenio workshop's stucco and more frescoes by Tencala. The Schloss has been lovingly restored and now houses a **Landscape Museum** with a good display on the life of the Enns region. The Schloss and museum are open from Palm Sunday–31 Oct, daily 09.00–17.00.

Around Bad Aussee

Road 145 bears north-west from Pürgg for Upper Austria (the **Salzkammergut-Bundesstrasse**) and reaches shortly **Bad Mittendorf**, a spa known to the Romans and a popular ski resort. In the parish church the altarpiece (the *Beheading of St Barbara*) is by Kremser Schmidt and there is a dodecagonal Gothic font of red marble.

The main road continues to **Bad Aussee**, another spa set in beautiful landscape, but owing its importance originally to its salt-mines. The local citizens were hereditary lessees of the mines from the time they received the privilege from Duke Albrecht in 1290 until compelled to relinquish it by Friedrich III, the Habsburgs thereafter exploiting the salt production for their own profit. This was a remunerative enterprise—in 1510 there were no less than 15 saltworks. The town contains a number of buildings (*Hallingerhäuser*) from the time of salt extraction (the **Kammerhof, Herzheimerhaus, Hoferhaus,** etc.). In the **parish church** of St Paul are two notable sacramental niches (1523) and in the Marian Chapel a fine stone *Madonna* of 1420. In the apse of the **Spitalkirche** (1395) is a winged altar (1449) donated by Friedrich III, a gesture perhaps following his expropriation of the salt monopolists, the shrine of the altar showing the *Holy Trinity*, on the wings scenes from the childhood of Jesus. The **Kammerhof** (1500) on the Chlumeckyplatz was the former office of the saltworks and now houses a museum with information on the history of salt-mining etc. (open April–June, Oct, Tues 15.30–18.00, Fri 09.30–12.00, Sun 10.00–12.00; 15 June–30 Sept, daily 10.00–12.00, 16.00–18.00). The 1200sq m of **Alpengarten** with 2500 species of Alpine plants and shrubs, is also worth a visit. Anna Plochl, daughter of the local postmaster, was born in Bad Aussee in 1804. Archduke Johann met her when she was 15 and was able to marry her ten years later. Her house may be seen on the Meranplatz, so-called because Anna Plochl was created Countess of Meran in 1844.

From Bad Aussee there are pleasant excursions in the Ausseer Land and the Styrian Salzkammergut, including the **Altausseer See** overlooked by the Loser (1.838m) and (to the east) the Trisselwand (1735m). The **Grundlsee** is the biggest lake in Styria at 4.3sq km and receives its water from the **Toplitzsee** and **Kammersee**. It was at Toplitzsee that Archduke Johann and Anna Plochl met on an excursion and the area became popular with artists and intellectuals in the 19C, who justly referred to it as a *Seelenlandschaft* (a landscape to soothe the soul).

In the disused salt-mines (first exploited in 1147) at **Altaussee**, thousands of works of art pillaged from European collections by the Nazis were stored during World War II, the full extent of the plundering being first documented by Lynne Nicholas in her brilliant book *The Rape of Europa*. There is a small **Literature and Local History Museum** (open May–Sept, daily, 10.00–16.00) in the **Kurhaus**. Altaussee has a famous local son in the actor and director, Klaus Maria Brandauer, who was born here in 1944, and who impressed international audiences with his performances in *Colonel Redl* and *Mephisto* (both directed by the Hungarian, István Szabó). Of his hometown Brandauer once remarked that 'Altaussee has 1800 inhabitants, only two months of summer and 500 cows. That's it.' However, his affection for it obviously remains undimmed, as he still has a house here.

At the Toplitzsee a huge number of forged pound notes were discovered at the end of the war, part of Hitler's plan to undermine the British currency.

Beyond the **Kammersee** tarn rise the peaks of the **Toten Gebirge**, the highest being the **Grosser Priel** (2525m). The main road leads on from Bad Aussee over the **Pötschenhöhe** into Upper Austria for Bad Ischl.

West of Pürgg to Schladming

If road 146 is followed due west from Pürgg, passing by Schloss Trautenfels (see p 227), **Öblarn** is skirted shortly to the south, home to the poetess Paula Grogger (1892–1984), who wrote a play based on the romance of Archduke Johann and Anna Plochl, a performance of which is given in the Kirchplatz every five years and involving the whole village (giving thus a new dimension to the term 'passion play'). Further west on the same minor road is **Stein an der Enns**, the entrance to the **Sölktäler Naturpark**, an attractive nature reserve with hiking routes around the lakes (**Schwarzensee** and **Hohensee**). The scenic Erzherzog Johann Strasse leads over the **Sölkpass** (1788m) into the **Murtal**.

Just to the north of the main road 146 is the town of **Gröbming**, whose parish church has an exceptional late Gothic **winged altar** (c 1520, from the workshop of Lienhart Astl), with (in the shrine) gilded relief figures of the *Twelve Apostles* and *Christ enthroned* above, on the inner wings four gilded reliefs of the *Passion*, and another four passion scenes on the exterior wings, evidently influenced by Albrecht Altdorfer and the Danube School. The 16C Schloss Moosheim, with its Renaissance sgraffitoes, is now a luxury hotel.

The road leads on to **Schladming**, whose local **Stadtmuseum** (open Tues–Fri, 10.00–12.00, 17.00–20.00, Sun and PH 11.00–14.00) at Talbachgasse 110, formerly the house (1618) of the market supervisor, documents the history of the mines. On display is a letter written in 1408 setting out the rules governing their exploitation, that served as a model for mine regulation elsewhere in Austria. There is also material on the Reformation and Counter-Reformation in the region. The tourist information office will give details about visiting the local silver and lead mines, which operated between 1520 and 1875.

The Protestant miners of Schladming actually defeated an army sent against them in 1525 by the Styrian governor, Sigmund von Dietrichstein, the town subsequently being burned to the ground by the troops of Count Salm as revenge (a monument on the Hauptplatz recalls the victory of 1525). Although Protestantism was forbidden in 1600, after Joseph II's Tolerance Patent of 1781, the majority of the local population announced their allegiance to Lutheranism. The **Lutheran Church** (1862) in the upper Martin-Luther-Strasse is the largest in Styria, a lofty hall church containing remnants of a Renaissance altar (1570).

The famous Loden cloth is manufactured in the town: Archduke Johann's adoption of the grey '*Steirische Rock*' (a stylish jacket), with its antler buttons and green-bordered styling, made it *de rigueur* for the prosperous bourgeoisie, and indeed it is still worn, though much less than it used to be.

The town is also a ski resort (the Alpine World Championships were held here in 1982) and there is a summer music festival (*Schladminger Musiksommer*). A few kilometres to the west road 146 (E651) passes into Land Salzburg via the Mandlingpass of the Enns Valley. Some kilometres to the south of the town are the **Riesachfalle**, reached on a minor road running parallel to the Unterthalbach, whose waters partly spill out of the Riesachsee.

South-west of Leoben:
Seckau, Knittelfeld, Judenburg

Road S36 runs westwards, crossing the north–south *Autobahn* at St Michael in Obersteiermark and following closely the north bank of the River Mur. At **St Marein bei Knittelfeld**, on a hill to the north of the road, the founder of the Seckau abbey (see below) erected a fine hall church during the reign of Friedrich III, as the dual inscription (1445) to Friedrich and Duke Albrecht indicates. In the left-hand side-altar is a late Gothic winged altar (1524), together with painted wooden statuary of *Sts Mary Magdalene and Martha* of about the same period.

Stift Seckau

A minor road just to the west leads up to the **Benedictine Abbey of Seckau**, founded originally in St Marein in 1140 for the Augustinians by Adalram von Waldeck, and transferred here two years later, evidently on the grounds of this location's greater security. It became a bishopric in 1218, was dissolved in 1782 and refounded in 1883. The highlight is the unforgettable Romanesque **Abbey Church of the Assumption** (1164), to which a groined vault (remaining in the lateral naves) was added in 1259 following a fire, the same being remodelled in the main nave as somewhat severe star vaulting at the end of the 15C. This and the massive Romanesque columns topped by block capitals set the ascetic tone of the interior, the whole having been built to a single measure of 7.9m (the width of the central nave) or multiples thereof. The enlargement of the building at the crossing in the 19C has not disturbed its impressive dignity, further enhanced by the superb Crucifixion figures suspended in the choir (the *Crucified Christ*, 1220, flanked by *Mary* and *St John*, 1150). The façade of the church was rebuilt in neo-Romanesque style between 1891 and 1893. Its other Romanesque or early Gothic features include the stone lions of the portal, a *Madonna and Child* (c 1260) in the western entrance and the frescoes taken from the exterior to the south wall of the crossing (*Life of John the Baptist*, 1270).

The **Mausoleum** (or **Prince's Chapel**) built for Karl II (ruler of Inner-österreich from 1564–90) is notable as a uniquely exuberant embodiment of the transition from Renaissance to Baroque. It was begun in 1587 by Alessandro de Verda of Lugano and completed by Sebastiano Carlone in the early 17C, the paintings being the work of Theodoro Ghisi. Its iconography follows the themes of *Resurrection* and *Enlightenment*, expressed through 50 statues and 150 relief figures, together with more than 60 heads, as well as pictures, coats of arms and wrought-iron decoration.

In the chapel of the south tower there is a carved remnant of a winged altar (*Madonna and Child*, 1488), while on an octagonal column in the northern side-aisle are six reliefs of the *Passion, Death, Resurrection* and *Glorification of Christ*. On the northern side-altar is a remarkable 14C pietà (the 'Seckauer Marienklage') by Hans von Judenburg. In the **Engelkapelle** (Angels' Chapel) of the northern nave is Herbert Boeckl's challenging fresco of the *Revelation of St John the Divine* (1960), a successful mingling of the bleakly linear asceticism of Boeckl's schematic modern style with the similarly ascetic Gothic and Romanesque surroundings. Boeckl also designed the cross, the lighting and the doors of the chapel. In the adjacent **Sacramental Chapel** is a Venetian alabaster relief (c 1200) of *Mary Enthroned* (*Nikopoia*, the Bringer of Victory), showing Byzantine influence and now in a modern gold frame (1953).

The **Bishops' Chapel** is closed by a wrought-iron grille (1720) with a remarkable altar showing the *Coronation of the Virgin* (1489), a rare South Tyrolean carved scene of Mary being received by the Three-in-One God of the Trinity.

The early Baroque façade (1625) of the monastery is by Pietro Carlone and the interior boasts a stuccoed **Imperial Hall** and **Hall of Homage**, as well as a chapel with decorated capitals on its Romanesque columns. The inner courtyard (1628) has three levels of arcades with Tuscan columns, while the Renaissance cloister (1588) has two arcaded storeys. The abbey buildings, formerly surrounded by ramparts with octagonal corner towers, were rebuilt in the late 16C by Bernhard de Silvo and Thomas Solari.

Returning to the main road S36, you soon reach Knittelfeld (to the south), and just beyond it (to the north) **Zeltweg**, where **Schloss Farrach** has a noble Baroque façade (1680) and is open daily in the periods when exhibitions are being held here. Nearby is the Austrian Grand Prix circuit (*Österreichring*) which reopened in 1997 after a long closure. At Fohnsdorf to the west is the **Montanmuseum** (open May–Oct, daily 09.00–17.00) documenting the history of what used to be the deepest lignite mine in the world (1130m), before it closed in 1978.

Judenburg, situated on a terrace of glacial debris above the Mur, is reached shortly to the west, its Burg formerly the seat of the Liechtensteins. The family's famous poetical scion, Ulrich von Liechtenstein (1200–76), lived nearby (15km west of Judenburg) in the romantically situated Frauenburg (Unzmarkt). The name of Judenburg is said to be derived from a colony of Jewish merchants that was resident here until wiped out by a pogrom in 1496. At any rate the town is of ancient origin, having an Illyrian population in the Hallstatt period, to which time is dated the famous **Strettweg cult waggon** found near here and now in the Grazer Landesmuseum at Schloss Eggenberg (see p 215). In its boom period of the 14C and 15C, the market town minted the first gold Gulden in Austria and was a flourishing art centre: at the end of the 14C the Master of Großlobming, one of the most important sculptors of the Gothic soft style, was active in the neighbourhood, as was the painter and sculptor Hans von Judenburg in the years 1411–24. In the 18C Judenburg was a centre of Baroque art (*Judenburger Werkstätte*).

The **parish church of St Nicholas** with a choir of 1513 was rebuilt by Domenico Sciassia in 1673. Its **All Saints Chapel** off the right-hand nave has a late Gothic wooden *Madonna and Child* (1480), while the **St Andrew Chapel** shows ten over-life-size and gilded statues of the *Apostles* (c 1750) by Balthasar Prandstätter (or Brandstätter) of the Judenburger Werkstätte, who also made the St Nicholas group on the high altar. North of the choir is the Gothic '*Beautiful Madonna*' of c 1420, made from sandstone, perhaps by Hans of Judenburg. The 75m free-standing tower (on the main square) was built between 1448 and 1520 and can be climbed (253 steps!). In the **Stadtpfarrhof** is a late Gothic *pietà* of c 1510, while the former Jesuit cloister to the east has a noble stairway of 1660. North-eastwards, across the river, is the **church of St Mary Magdalene** (1330), with a fine fresco of St Christopher (c 1500) on the southern wall and Gothic stained glass (1380–1420) in the choir, the latter featuring scenes from the *Life of Mary*, the *Lives of the Apostles* and the *Old Testament*. On the northern wall of the choir are frescoes from the 14C (*Crucifixion, Dormition of the Virgin, Apostles*). Of the Baroque fittings, Balthasar Prandstätter's *Immaculata* (1730) on the right-hand side-altar is of notable quality.

The former **Schloss Neu-Liechtenstein** to the east received its Baroque decoration in the 17C; above it are the ruins of an earlier castle (c 1140), the ancestral home of Ulrich von Liechtenstein, whose somewhat uncompromising approach to personal privacy was emphasised by the fact that the castle was only accessible by ladder.

West of Judenburg

A short detour on road 114 leading north from road 96 to the west of Judenburg leads to **Oberzeiring**, where a former silver-mine has partly been converted into a sanatorium for sufferers from respiratory diseases. The display mine may be visited (open by appointment, ☎ 0 3571 28 11 or 23 87, and guided tours May–Oct, 09.45, 11.00, 14.00, 15.00, 16.00). Continuing west on road 96 you reach the town of **Scheifling**, an important road junction from earliest times and the site of a Roman post station '*ad Pontem*'. The parish church contains a strikingly expressive *pietà* (c 1430, *Scheiflinger Marienklage*) and reliefs on the Altar of the Fourteen Holy Helpers (c 1490).

The little town of **Oberwölz** just to the north (via road 75) is encircled by defensive walls built after 1317, and preserves its medieval aspect with five city gates and two towers. The parish church has frescoes on the vault (1777) and an altarpiece showing the *Legend of St Martin* by J.A. Mölk. On the southern wall is a *St Christopher* of 1500. Of the two other Gothic churches, that of St Sigismund is interesting for the Baroque calvary pictures by Johann Lederwasch in the organ loft.

Road 83 from Scheifling leads southwards to **Neumarkt in Steiermark** where **Schloss Lind** (11C, enlarged 17C) houses a local museum (open Mon–Fri 09.00–12.00, 15.00–17.00). The castle was used as an extension of the Mauthausen concentration camp during the war. Twelfth-century **Burg Forchtenstein** at the north-west corner of the Neumarkt fortification now houses a mining museum (open daily, 08.00–17.00). However, the greatest attraction in the area is for birdwatchers who visit the neighbouring **Naturpark Grebenzen** around the Furtnerteich, where more than 200 species of bird have been recorded.

Stift Lambrecht

A minor road leads west to the isolated Benedictine **Abbey of St Lambrecht**, founded in the 11C by Count Marquard of Carinthia and his son, Heinrich III. Its three-aisled Gothic hall church was built in the 14C replacing a Romanesque structure, and the choir was again altered in 1639, while Domenico Sciassia rebuilt the west façade and added the marble portals between 1640–45. The Romanesque portals of the entrance were uncovered in 1975, as also were their Gothic frescoes, including a *St Christopher*. Michael Hönel's *Mother of God*, depicted on top of a globe, was painted in 1642. Of the interior, the soaring main altar (1632) of false marble by Valentin Khautt is striking, as is the richly ornamented Benedictine altar (1638) by Christoph Paumgartner. A highlight is Balthasar Prandstätter's **pulpit** (1732), with its dynamic ensembles of figures. The Renaissance tomb of Abbott Johann Trattner (d. 1591) and that for Abbott Johann Schachner (with its Renaissance frame) catch the eye. Sciassia also barockised the abbey buildings, which were subsequently extended in the 18C (unfortunately of these only the beautiful **Prälatensaal** with stucco (1739) by Johann Kajetan Androy, is accessible). On the other hand the **Art Collection**, the **Heimatmuseum** and the **Peter Blasius Hanf Bird Collection**, together with the **library**, are visitable, but with limited opening times and only with a guided tour (weekdays: 10.45, 14.30, Sun & PH 14.30). Of the art collection, the highlights are mostly Gothic, including works by the Master of Großlobming and late Gothic works from the Villach workshop, although there are also many Baroque items. Peter Blasius Hanf (1808–92) was a self-taught ornithologist who documented the birdlife of the Grebenzen area with incredible diligence; the fruits of his labours are the 2000 stuffed birds to be seen here.

To the west of the abbey is the **Peterskirche** with a late Gothic winged altar (c 1515) from the Villach workshop and panels by the Master of St Lambrecht, a striking *Crucifixion* picture (1435) in the left-hand side-altar and a Marian statue of 1430 on the right-hand side-altar.

The main road 83 leads on south to the ruins at Dürnstein, an 11C castle built by the Eppensteins and owned by all the local rulers at one time or another (the Counts of Steyr, the Babenbergs, finally the Habsburgs). The road continues into Carinthia reaching shortly Friesach (see p 339).

Continuing west from Scheifling on road 96 you come to **Murau**, whose Schloss Obermurau (open June–Sept, guided tours ☎ 03532 2302) has belonged to the Schwarzenbergs since 1624, when the 30-year-old Count Georg married the wealthy 82-year-old, one-generation noble, and fiercely Protestant Anna Neumann or Neumanin von Wasserleonburg (1535–1623). Anna had already been married several times, including to Christoph II of Liechtenstein, whose massive tax arrears and those of his brothers she paid off by buying the Murau castle from them in 1574. Anna's father, a Villach burgher, had made a fortune in the Gailtaler mines and acquired a noble title by buying the Wasserleonburg estate. She married altogether six times, accumulating massive fortunes and assets along the way, and at her death the Schwarzenbergs scooped the lot, Count Georg being the only husband to outlive her. Her success in burying husbands aroused accusations of witchcraft, but it was the accusers themselves who ended up on the executioner's block; meanwhile her Protestant inclinations kept the Counter-Reformation in check in Murau for a generation. However (according to the *Österreichisches Lexikon*), the Catholic church took revenge, if rather a petty one, by forbidding her burial in the parish church. The story goes that a compromise was reached, whereby the wall was broken through and a niche created, most of Anna Neumann's remains lying inside, but her head remaining outside, the building.

Sadly, this enjoyably bizarre tale is almost certainly invented: at any rate there is a great marble tomb (1624, by Martin Pocabello) for the lady in the town's Capuchin Church, which is said to have been transferred there from the Spitalskirche in 1873. The **parish church of St Matthew** itself (1296) has a

14C fresco cycle and (in the southern crossing) a painted winged altar of 1500. In the north of the crossing is the Liechtenstein crypt. The Baroque remodelling of the high altar has incorporated a Gothic crucifixion group of 1500.

The **church of St Leonard** also has interesting features, notably a 17C ivory crucifixion group and late Gothic (1520) statues on the high altar (*Sts George, Florian* and *Eustace*), which are products of the Villach workshop. The **church of St Eustace** is the oldest in the town and has a beautiful beamed ceiling (1500) painted with late Gothic motifs. The old town of Murau is delightful, having many historic houses dating from the 15C to the 17C. The brewery is 500 years old and another interesting relic is the narrow-gauge railway (*Murtalbahn,* 1891) that runs through the town on a route from Unzmarkt to Tamsweg.

A detour north brings you on road 96 and then minor roads to **Schöder**, where the great Styrian horse fair takes place on the last Saturday in August amid general merry-making. At **Krakaudorf** the parish church of St Oswald has a fine coffered ceiling with a rosette pattern. Yearly on St Oswald's feast day a giant (6m) Sampson figure is paraded through the town, a custom dating to 1635.

Road 97 runs on to St Ruprecht ob Murau with the **Styrian Wood Museum** (open April–Oct, daily 09.00–16.00). From here the main road leads into Land Salzburg.

East of Bruck an der Mur: along the Mürz Valley

Kapfenberg, just north-east of Bruck an der Mur, is an industrial town that grew prosperous from its involvement in iron and steel manufacture. Its parish church has a delightful Rococo interior, graceful side-altars containing statues by Veit Königer (also responsible for the Holy Sepulchre, 1780), and a main altar-piece showing *St Oswald* (1738) by Johann Veit Hauck. Above the town is a ruined Kapfenberg castle and below it the **Oberkapfenberg** (1378), which has been turned into an excellent hotel and restaurant.

Road 20 northwards from Kapfenberg leads to the health resort of **Aflenz**, renowned for its benevolent climate (also a ski resort). Notable in the parish church is the ornate pulpit (1710) with figures of the *Four Evangelists* in a state of exaltation and elaborate stylised floral decoration. The reliefs of the apostles on the interior walls date to 1520 and there is also a Romanesque crucifix of 1175.

Mariazell

Continuing on road 20 you reach the celebrated pilgrimage town of Mariazell on the border with Lower Austria, founded in 1157 by Benedictine monks from St Lambrecht. It has a particular importance for Hungarians, after Louis the Great, the Angevin king of Hungary, gave money for the **Gnadenkapelle** (to house the wonder-working icon) following military successes in the 1350s (perhaps specifically the conquest of a large part of Dalmatia, including Zara (Zadar), in 1357–58). In 1599, with the Counter-Reformation in full swing, 23,000 persons pilgrimaged to Mariazell.

The great **Parish and Pilgrimage Church of the Nativity** is Romanesque in origin, converted to a Gothic triple-naved church between 1380 and 1396, and altered in Baroque style by Domenico Sciassia after 1644. At this time the body of the church was widened to include chapels with galleries above. A transept replaced the Gothic choir with a new sanctuary under a cupola, while the two Baroque towers were added to the façade either side of the Gothic one. The interior is especially distinguished by J.B. Fischer von Erlach's superb high altar (1704) with its over-life-size silver crucifixion group (1714) following a design by Lorenzo Mattielli and executed by Johann Kauschbauer. Below it is a silver globe (1702, Augsburg work) with a diameter of 2m, flanked by the figures of *St Mary and St John*. The copper snake writhing on it is also enamelled. The concave ensemble is framed by four columns using variegated marble, above which rises a gilded heaven of angels with the *Holy Ghost* represented by a dove at the centre, from where the heavenly rays shoot out. The costly tabernacle is by Johann Drentwett (1727) and the stained-glass window (1905) beyond the altar shows Jerusalem. Under the cupola on a 5m column is a late Gothic *Madonna and Child* dating to c 1520.

Archangel Raphael, Mariazell

The main focus of the church, however, is in the east of the central nave, the extraordinary **Gnadenaltar** (Altar of Mercy), in the tabernacle of which hovers the 48cm high limewood icon *Mater Magna Austriae* (c 1266): the Virgin embraces the infant Jesus cradled in her right arm, the latter (but hidden by the dress) holding an apple in the right hand while stretching towards a pear with the left (symbols respectively of Sin and the Peace of God). The dresses for the statue and the gold crowns are 19C additions. The setting for the icon is the most striking part of the ensemble, the altar design being by Fischer von Erlach the Younger (Josef Emanuel), its execution by an Augsburg goldsmith, Johann Drentwett. Its background is a Gothic arch converted into a chapel c 1653, when the Baroque cornice was added. In the broken pediment, note the sandstone busts of Louis the Great of Hungary (*Nagy Lajos*) and his wife Elisabeth. A beautiful **silver grille** (1756) with an acanthus arch in the centre closes the chapel at the front and was donated by Franz Stephan I and Maria Theresia. On either side under the Gothic baldachin are the statues of *St Benedict and St Lambert*, but the virtuoso statuary is that resting on the entablature, three characteristically vivid figures (1734) by Lorenzo Mattielli (the *Prophet Joachim*, father of Mary, flanked by *St Anne and St Joseph*).

The **interior** of the church is richly **stuccoed** and **marbled**, the finest stucco being the work of Matthias Camin in the central nave (1649–69), in the two sacristies by Alexander Serenio, and under the cupola by Giovanni Bertoletti. The cupola itself shows rather heavy stucco (1703) by Domenico Bosco and Francesco Casagrande, while its frescoes (1680, by Georg Hansen and Giovanni Battista Colombo) show three patron saints of the Empire (*Leopold of Babenberg*, *John of Nepomuk*, *Stephen of Hungary*), together with the *Four Evangelists*.

The **pulpit** (1691) is magnificently monumental Baroque (albeit recalling the

Renaissance in many individual elements), the work of Andreas Grabmayr. Over its entrance is the striking figure of *St Paul*, the model for all preachers, while the reliefs on the variegated marble sides show the *Four Evangelists* with their symbols. The side-chapels also show high quality works, and include the **Emmerich Chapel** to the north with an altarpiece by J.A. Mölk (the chapel was endowed, in 1670, by the Hungarian Count Draskowitch, its dedicatee being the revered and early deceased son of King Stephen of Hungary). A neighbouring chapel, also endowed by a Hungarian (Count Nadasdy), is dedicated to St Stephen himself and has an altarpiece (1665, Tobias Pock) of *St Stephen before the Mother of God* (in King Stephen's time Hungary was converted to Christianity and placed under the special protection of the Virgin by the King). The same artist painted the *Beheading of St Catherine* in the adjacent chapel endowed by Prince Esterházy. The chapels on the south side are endowments of the Styrian Diet, the Convent of St Lambrecht etc., and contain mostly Baroque works by minor masters. Note their ornate wrought-iron grilles with acanthus patterns and grotesque masks, mostly the work (c 1673) of Blasius Lackner. The organ loft (1740) and the organ (partly 1689) are notably elaborate. The relief on the underside of the loft commemorates the founding of the pilgrimage church: the monkish founder is shown riding through the Styrian countryside with the Marian icon in his hand.

The two **Treasuries** are over the sacristy and the Pilgrim's Chapel and display the valuable votive offerings accumulated here over the centuries, including Louis the Great's offering (1380) of a **Marian icon** (note the enamel background of fleur-de-lys, symbolising the Angevin dynasty). This icon is thought to have been painted by Andrea Vanni c 1360 in Siena, its ornate frame showing coats of arms of the Anjoux of Hungary, Poland, etc., having probably been made by a Neapolitan goldsmith. Another unusual treasure is a carved cedarwood cross (1531) from Mount Athos.

The brave and stubborn Cardinal Mindszenty was buried in the Ladislaus Chapel in 1975, but had written in his will that his remains should be transferred to his native Hungary as soon as the east was liberated from Communist tyranny; accordingly, in 1991, he was reburied in Esztergom, seat of the Primates of Hungary and site of the baptism of King Stephen, first Christian king of Hungary.

Continuing east from Kapfenberg on the S6, you reach shortly **Kindberg**, where **Schloss Oberkindberg** may be visited (open May–Oct, Fri, Sat, Sun, 14.00–18.00). The interior has Rococo decoration and wall-painting, while the chapel has a *St Jerome* (c 1690) by Hans Adam Weißenkirchner. The Schloss houses the **Austrian Montanmuseum**, an imitation mine documenting local iron-ore extraction. At **Mitterdorf im Mürztal** to the north-east are the ruins of **Lichtenegg** with a small local museum (open weekends and PH from 15.00–17.00), while at **Krieglach** the parish church has a fresco (1420) of the *Last Judgement* in the choir and a Renaissance marble tomb made for the Lord of Lichtenegg, Georg Stadler (d. 1557). The Styrian vernacular poet, Peter Rosegger (1843–1918) was born in the countryside nearby and his house at Roseggerstraße 44 may be visited (open April–Oct, Tues–Sun, 09.00–17.00, Nov–March 10.00–16.00). In the later part of his career he was increasingly associated with the *Heimatkunstbewegung*, which idealised the life of the peasantry and of the village milieu, in marked contradistinction to the supposedly decadent literature of the metropolis (especially of the narcissistic *Jung Wien*, whose leading protagonist was Hermann Bahr). At Alpl, to the south of Krieglach, is Rosegger's birthplace, now a museum (open April–Oct, Tues–Sun, 09.00–17.00, Nov–March to 16.00).

Mürzzuschlag, a few kilometres to the east lies at the confluence of the Mürz and Fröschnitz and in previous centuries was a centre of the Mürztal iron-working industry. The **Brahmshaus** (Wiener Straße 4, open May–Oct daily, 10.00–12.00, 14.00–18.00, Nov–April, daily 14.00–17.00) recalls the composer (who wrote his 4th symphony in Mürzzuschlag) with a small exhibition, while at Wiener Straße 79 is the **Wintersport Museum** (open Wed–Sun, 09.00–12.00 and 14.00–17.00). The **Kunsthaus** (Wiener Straße 56) has continually changing exhibitions of modern art (open Wed–Sat, 10.00–18.00, Sun 10.00–16.00).

Road 23 leads north from Mürzzuschlag towards the Lower Austrian border, reaching shortly **Neuberg an der Mürz**, where a Cistercian cloister was founded by Duke Otto 'the Merry' (son of Albrecht I of Habsburg) in 1327. Their former hall church (completed in 1496), with exceptionally graceful ribbed vaulting, was painstakingly restored between 1950 and 1986. Notable features are the huge Gothic windows of the north and east walls that flood the church with light, and the rosary window in the western façade. Note also the restored floral decoration (1470) of the vaulting.

The gilded main altar (20m high) dates to 1612, the combined work of Hans Mader from Überlingen on Lake Constance, Hans Huldi from Ulm and Thomas Steinmüller from Olmütz (Olomouc). It shows (in the shrine) the *Assumption* flanked by *Sts Bernard and Benedict*, with a crucifix above. On the lateral volutes are statues of *St Ruprecht* and *St Ulrich*. The rear was painted by Giovanni Terzano of Como. A large fresco (1505) on the west wall shows the *Holy Family*, the *Crucifixion* and the *Holy Helpers*. On an altar of the south wall is the so-called *Neuberger Madonna* (1350), a stone statue that fell from the western façade in the 17C, miraculously remaining unbroken. Also on the south side is the Baroque Marienaltar, but displaying a sitting *Madonna* dated 1450. On the third set of columns from the church entrance are panels from late Gothic winged altars, to the north *Christ on the Cross* with the *Passion* and the *Discovery of the True Cross* on the rear (1505), to the south, the *Deposition from the Cross*, with the *Passion* and the *Life of St Bernard* (1518). The **pulpit** (1670) resting on an angel is particularly striking.

The monastery buildings, preserving almost exactly their medieval aspect, are extremely atmospheric and include a lovely late Gothic cloister with fine carvings of animals (a lion, a pelican, a unicorn, a partridge, etc.) serving as Christian symbols (2C AD), based on the celebrated *Physiologus*, illustrating correct behaviour in the secular and monastic worlds.

The hexagonal well-house in the south wing dates to the 15C. The tympanum of the refectory, opposite the well-house, shows a relief of the *Crucifixion* of c 1470. The Chapter House (1344), on the east side of the monastery, has columns with richly decorated capitals, while in the crypt below it rest the remains of the founder.

Road 23 continues past Mürzsteg, a hunting-lodge of Franz Joseph which is now the summer residence of the Austrian President, and descends (road 21) to Mariazell (see p 234) after skirting the Lower Austrian border. The **Mürzsteger Punktation** concluded here in the autumn of 1903 between Franz Joseph and Czar Nicholas II was a document addressed to Turkey, demanding better treatment of its Macedonian subjects who were then in revolt. From Mürzzuschlag road 306 leads over the Semmering Pass (see p 132) into Lower Austria.

Oberösterreich (Upper Austria with the Salzkammergut)

Area: 11,979sq km. Population: 1.34 million

Topography, climate and environment

The Land of Upper Austria stretches from the **Böhmerwald** (Bohemian Forest, a granite massif whose south-eastern periphery encompasses the Upper Austrian **Mühlviertel**) to the jagged Alpine ridge of

the **Dachstein**, which forms a triple border between the provinces of **Oberösterreich**, **Salzburg** and **Steiermark**. To the east of it is **Niederösterreich** (Lower Austria) and to the west is Bavaria, a second international border being with the Czech Republic in the north.

Upper Austria is divided into four geographical areas ('*Viertel*'), of which the northernmost is the above-mentioned Mühlviertel, a rolling landscape north of the Danube so-called after the **Große Mühl** and **Kleine Mühl** rivers that traverse it; the (western) **Obere Mühlviertel** is quite densely populated, while its (eastern) **Untere Mühlviertel** is a land of isolated farms and romantic castles, the two sub-regions being divided by the **Grosse Rodl** river that runs into the Danube at Ottensheim.

The second region is the **Hausruckviertel**, a 30km long forested ridge in the Alpine foothills dividing the **Innviertel** from the rest of the province. The Innviertel itself (officially **Innkreis**, its principal town being **Ried im Innkreis**) is named after the River Inn that forms the border with Bavaria and is a fertile part of the Alpine approaches to the west. It contains reserves of oil, natural gas, and lignite, although its brown coal mines were closed in 1994.

The **Traunviertel** (*Traunkreis*) is centred on the river of the same name. It has some of the most fertile land in Austria (the **Welser Heide**) and includes important industrial centres (**Steyr**, **Enns**, **Linz**, **Lambach**, **Wels**, etc.). A further region, the **Pyhrn-Eisenwurzen** may be encountered in the tourist brochures and is really the eastern part of the **Traunviertel** irrigated by the waters of the **Krems**, **Steyr** and **Enns** rivers. The name refers to its role in the ancient iron industry (see also p 225 on the Styrian Erzberg). The most scenic part of Upper Austria, however, is undoubtedly the **Salzkammergut**, which comprises the western part of the Traunviertel.

The landscape of Upper Austria is extremely varied, including the limestone Alpine barrier of its southern periphery, the picturesque mountain lakes of the **Salzkammergut** (including the **Mondsee**, **Attersee**, **Wolfgangsee**, **Hallstätter See** and **Traunsee**, all of them formed by the retreat of prehistoric glaciers), and the drainage basins or valleys of rivers emptying into the Danube. Its climate is largely determined by prevailing west winds bringing substantial precipitation (more than 2000m annually in the Salzkammergut), and the warm south-westerly *Föhn* blowing through the Alpine valleys. The climate of the Bohemian Massif (Mühlviertel) is considerably harsher than that of the Alpine foothills. The area's extended summers (*Altweibersommer*—'old wives' summer' in German) are the best time to visit, and perhaps it is no accident that the most celebrated work of the Upper Austrian writer, Adalbert Stifter (1805–68), is entitled *Der Nachsommer* ('Indian Summer', 1857). On the other hand winter sports and skating on the smaller lakes are also attractions, although everything in Upper Austria is on a more modest scale than that of the commercialised winter tourism of the money-spinning resorts in Tyrol or Vorarlberg.

The mountain areas are characterised by typical alpine flora, including dwarf-pines, gentians, alpine roses and Edelweiß. In the valleys and lower mountain slopes are extensive deciduous woodlands, typically of beech, oak and maple. On the conservation area of the **Ibmer Moos** (see p 280) in the south-western Innviertel, highly specialised flora may be encountered, especially rare species of reeds and orchids. Game is plentiful (deer, pheasant and partridge) as are waders in the boggy areas and lakesides (quail, lapwings, herons and many others). It seems amazing that Franz Joseph did not single-handedly wipe out the chamois (*Gemse*) population in the mountains above **Bad Ischl**, since he was proud to have slaughtered some 2000 of these luckless beasts, which nevertheless survive in considerable numbers. The goat-like chamois live high in the mountains (800–2500m) and supply the famous *Gamsbart*, the bushy decoration for hats popular in Bavaria and Austria, which is composed of hairs from the back parts of the chamois.

Economy

Much of Upper Austria is extremely fertile and agricultural produce plays a significant part in the economy, especially fruit which is turned into fruit juice or schnapps. There is also considerable beef production and horse-breeding. However, the drift from the land that began in the 19C has intensified in the 20C and the young generation finds work in the industrial towns along the Danube valley and in the Traunviertel. Building on the considerable Nazi investment in Hitler's home province, and in particular in Linz, post-war Austria has developed a significant steel-based industry employing new technology *(Linz-Donawitz-Verfahren)*. The successor to the Hermann Göring Works (founded 1938) was the state-owned *Vereinigte Österreichische Eisen-und Stahlwerke*, known as VÖEST AG, later (1973) merged with *Alpine-Montan AG* to create *VOEST-Alpine*, which, however, fell victim to the worldwide crisis in steel production of the 1970s and 1980s. After successful restructuring, the business was privatised in 1994, its part-flotation on the stock exchange being the biggest in the history of the Second Republic. Successful smaller industries include the aluminium works at Ranshofen, cement in Vöcklabruck, motor parts in Steyr, wood and paper production and quarrying in the Mühlviertel. Mining and textiles, previously important, have recently declined in the province, but 'quality tourism' has been expanded with some success, although recent years have been difficult.

History

That the territory of **Oberösterreich** has been inhabited since the early Stone Age is testified by major archaeological finds, the most recent of which (1983) were the stone implements discovered in a cave of the **Toten Gebirges**. The *Mondseekultur* existing around the lake of that name has yielded archaeological discoveries for the period between 3000 and 2000 BC, while the salt-based *Hallstattkultur*, centred on the shores of the **Hallstätter See** from about 800 BC, represents a transition from the late Bronze to the Iron Age, and from the urn burial of ashes to inhumation. *Hallstattkultur* appears to have been a society of artisans and peasants which was dominated by a military caste, the latter building fortresses on strategic hilltop sites and burying its dead in the tumuli raised exclusively for the aristocratic rulers. Celtic influence is evident from around 450 BC, from which time there is transition to the so-called *La-Tène-Kultur* of the early Iron Age, so-called since 1874 after significant finds at Lac de Neuchâtel in Switzerland. In these early civilisations the influence through trading links of Mediterranean cultures (primarily Greek, Etruscan and Roman) is evident, but so also are links with the Pontic steppe in the east.

The exact parameters of 'Upper Austria'—and indeed its independent status—have undergone radical changes in the 2000 years since it formed the northern part (*Ufernoricum*) of the Romano-Celtic province of *Noricum*. By the 8C the population of Romanised ur-Celts had been diluted by immigrant Bavarians and Slavs in the eastern and south-eastern parts. In 788 and 800 the Bavarian Agilolfinger dukes acquired much of Upper Austria as vassals of Charlemagne. The pious Agilolfinger founded a monastery at Mondsee in 748 and then (in 777) at Mattsee, Kremsmünster (see p 261) and St Florian (see p 257). The future *Land of Oberösterreich* was for long the subject of dispute after the East Carolingian dynasty died out in 911, and was also a prey to frequent Magyar attacks. Its early modern history begins with the Babenberg Margraves, who were awarded 'Ostarrichi' (then consisting only of the *Land unter der Enns*, i.e. Lower Austria) in 976 by Otto II, a time at which the Upper Austrian region was still ruled by various Bavarian nobles. However, the influence of the latter gradually weakened and in 1192 the Babenbergs were able to acquire the Duchy of Styria (**Steiermark**), formerly under the Traungauer counts, from which base they gradually expanded their lands to include much of today's **Traunviertel**, **Hausruckviertel** and **Mühlviertel**. During the interlude when Ottakar II of Bohemia ruled in most of Austria, the land between the **Hausruck** and the **Ybbs** river is referred to for the first time as the *Land ob der Enns*, the core of what became *Oberösterreich*; it was confirmed in the titles of Albrecht I of Habsburg, who was made governor of the region by Rudolf of Habsburg in 1281, a few years after his great victory over Ottakar.

The Habsburg Albertine line ruled Upper Austria until this part of the dynasty died out with Ladislaus Posthumus in 1457; thereafter Emperor Friedrich III awarded the *Land ob der Enns* to his brother, Albrecht VI, who established his residence in Linz from 1458–63, during which period his patrimony was elevated to the status of the Habsburg hereditary *Land* of '*Österreich ob der Enns*'. On Albrecht's death it reverted to the main line and under Maximilian I was enlarged at the expense of Bavaria in the **Mühlviertel**, with territories around the Mondsee and Wolfgangsee.

During the Reformation, Linz, Enns and Freistadt became bastions of Protestantism, so that by the second half of the 16C two-thirds of the local population were Lutheran. However, the **peasant revolt in 1549** provoked a closing of ranks between the Catholic church and the nobility against a

OBERÖSTERREICH

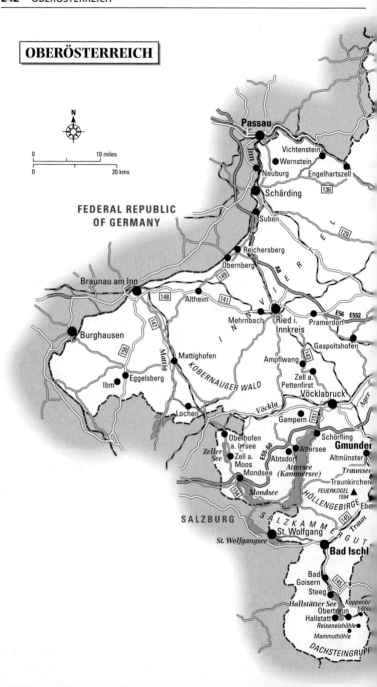

N

0 ____ 10 miles
0 ____ 20 kms

Passau
Vichtenstein
Wernstein
Neuburg
Engelhartszell
Schärding
136
Suben
129
FEDERAL REPUBLIC
OF GERMANY
Reichersberg
Obernberg
Braunau am Inn
148
Altheim
141
Mehrnbach
Ried i. Innkreis
Pramerdorf
E56 E552
Gaspoltshofen
143
Ampflwang
Mattighofen
Burghausen
156
Zell a. Pettenfirst
Vöcklabruck
Eggelsberg
Ibm
Lochen
Gampern
151
Schörfling
Oberhofen a. Irsee
Gmunden
Zeller See
Zell a. Moos
Attersee
Abtsdorf
Altmünster
Mondsee
Attersee (Kammersee)
Traunsee
Mondsee
FEUERKOGEL 1594
Traunkirchen
154
SALZBURG
HÖLLENGEBIRGE
Ebe
St. Wolfgang
145
St. Wolfgangsee
Bad Ischl
Bad Goisern
145
Steeg
Koppenbr höhle
Hallstätter See
Obertraun
Hallstatt
Reiseneishöhle
Mammuthöhle
DACHSTEINGRUPPE

INN
AB
INNVIERTEL
Mattig
KOBERNAUßER WALD
Vöckla
Ager
E55-60
SALZKAMMERGUT
Traun

CZECH REPUBLIC

BÖHMER WALD

chbühel 877 ▲ Aigen i. Mühlkr
Schägl
Haslach a.d.M.
Reichenthal
Waldburg Freistadt
Kefermarkt
M Pürnstein Königswiesen
Neufelden St. Peter a. Wimberg
Kl. Mühl
Gr. Rodl
Gmühl
Feldaist
Gramastetten
Wartberg obd. Aist
130 Walding Ottensheim
Eferding Donau
Waldhausen i. Strud.
PÖSTLINGBERG 539 LINZ
E55 A7
Ebelsberg Mauthausen 3 Perg
Klam Grein
Enns Arbing
STRUDENGAU
Ansfelden Baumgartenberg
Kremsdorf A1 E60
Wels Markt St. Florian
Weißkirchen a.d.T.
A1 E60
Traun
ESS E56 E60
A1
nbach Sattledt Steyr
adl- Fischlham Kremsmünster
aura 122 NIEDERÖSTERREICH
Krems Bad Hall
122 Schlierbach
Inzersdorf
RAUNSTEIN 891 Micheldorf 115 Enns
Grünau i. Almtal Frauenstein
138 SENGSENGEBIRGE
Windischgarsten

STEIERMARK

common and (as they believed) Protestant-inspired enemy. The Counter-Reformation was then pushed forward under successive emperors during the Thirty Years War. After the **Peace of Westphalia** in 1648, most of the Lutherans of the **Salzkammergut** were resettled in **Siebenbürgen** (Transylvania), where there was religious tolerance under Hungarian princes. Some remained, however, and *Salzkammergut* still has the largest number of Protestant parishes of any Austrian region. This is one peculiarity of an area that enjoyed several unusual privileges because of the importance of the salt trade to the imperial exchequer: the miners and refiners were excused military service and also enjoyed tax concessions, together with a special legal status.

In the **War of the Spanish Succession** (1700–14), and at the beginning of Maria Theresia's reign, Bavaria attempted to regain portions of Upper Austrian territory, but failed in both instances. In the **Seven Years War** (1756–63) the position was reversed, with Austria claiming Bavarian territory, some of which indeed she later gained, the border between the two states finally being settled in 1779. In the **Napoleonic War** Upper Austria was again occupied by Bavarian troops and liberated from the same by the **Congress of Vienna** in 1815. Thereafter **Oberösterreich** was united with **Land Salzburg**, until the latter gained independent status as a result of the 1848 revolution; at this time a small part of the Salzkammergut was joined with Salzburg, the majority of it remaining with Oberösterreich.

The status of the administratively autonomous 'Archduchy of Austria beyond the Enns', as Upper Austria was officially called, was confirmed by Franz Joseph in his **February Patent** of 1861 and lasted until the end of the Austro-Hungarian Monarchy in 1918. During the 'Founders' Period' (*Gründerzeit*, 1860–90) of industrialisation and Liberal politics, the province enjoyed a railway boom, the first (horse-drawn railway) in Austria between Linz and Ceské Budějovice/Budweis (Bohemia) having been instituted in 1832. The Emperor's choice of **Bad Ischl** as the imperial summer resort also did wonders for the local economy, attracting to the town the officials of the Dual Monarchy with their families, together with elements of the *beau monde* anxious to exploit the social cachet that a Bad Ischl address now attracted.

Upper Austria suffered badly in the economic crisis during and after World War I, which was doubtless the main cause for the population's enthusiasm for union with Germany: there were even treasonable negotiations between local politicians and their counterparts in Bavaria at the end of the war. In the light of this emotional climate, it is perhaps not so surprising that **Adolf Hitler** (1889–1945), who was born in the Upper Austrian town of Braunau am Inn, should have been so contemptuous of his native land, once declaring that the entire history of Austria had been one long catalogue of treason. During World War II Oberösterreich was designated the *Gau Oberdonau* and Hitler planned to make Linz one of his five '*Führerstädte*'; heavy industries were founded and the Führer's architect, Albert Speer, drew up grandiose plans for transforming Linz into a utopian city displaying the evil genius of Nazi power in Ceausescu-type triumphalist architecture.

Since the end of World War II Upper Austria has developed its industry with the help of extensive hydro-electric damming on the Danube and (controversially at Lambach) on the Traun. Early success was overshadowed, however, not only by the 1970s crisis of the steel industry, but by the most spectacular post-war criminal trial in Austria. This involved the VOEST associated firm of *Noricum*, which illegally sold weapons to countries at war (chiefly Iran), transactions that were strictly forbidden under Austria's neutrality law. More agreeably, tourism has boomed in the beautiful **Salzkammergut**, so much so that a special provision had to be made when Austria negotiated her entry into the EU allowing a legal prohibition on foreigners buying up properties in the region. It was aimed principally at Germans, in order to prevent outsiders scooping the benefits of the tourist trade and cutting out the locals.

Upper Austria is politically conservative: the right-of-centre **People's Party** (ÖVP) has supplied the Provincial Governor continuously since 1945, while the Upper Austrian, Rudolf Kirchschläger, who was officially the Socialist candidate but with strong bipartisan support, occupied the Austrian presidency from 1974–86. Nevertheless the province has demonstrated a willingness to adapt and modernise; while it is therefore certainly no backwater, it retains a strong sense of its core identity.

Cultural traditions

Upper Austria boasts a long tradition of Christian art and architecture, the earliest examples being the lovely Romanesque **Tassilo Chalice** kept in the monastery at Kremsmünster (see p 261) and the (much reduced) **Martinskirche** in Linz, the latter dating to the Agilolfinger era (8C). The Romanesque style (remnants survive in the monastery churches of **Wilhering**, **Lambach**, **Kremsmünster** and elsewhere) gave way to the Gothic style in the late 13C, of which many examples remain in the form of parish churches and castles (*Burgen*).

The province is particularly rich in **late Gothic winged altars**, the most celebrated being that (1481) by Michael Pacher (c 1435–98) in the church of St Wolfgang (see p 321), while another important workshop was led by Lienhard(t) Astl or Astel of Gmunden (active 1505–23). Many such altars, with their powerfully realistic representations of biblical figures and saints, some of which double as contemporary portraits of the commissioner of the work or founder of an institution, already display the expressive naturalism of the Renaissance, together with the rudiments of perspective. The very large number of such works dating from the late 15C and early 16C century are an indication of the economic boom in Upper Austria around this time, when the exploitation of salt and mineral mines was at its height. The consequent expansion of burgher affluence and administrative autonomy during the Renaissance led to the building of city-towers, fortifications, *Rathäuser* (town halls) and dwelling houses for prosperous merchants and traders, typically in the important commercial centres like **Steyr**, **Wels**, **Linz** and **Enns**. The rise of the burghers was also a factor in the spread of Lutheranism, which provided an ideological basis for resistance against the Habsburg central power and its ally, the Catholic church, although in artistic terms the onset of the Reformation was generally a destructive phenomenon.

The Counter-Reformation set out to win back the hearts and minds of the populace through the sensual dynamics of display and spectacle. It was at this time (from the mid-17C) that almost all the churches were barockised with little expense spared, while the great cloisters such as **St Florian** and **Wilhering** were extended or remodelled. Beside the many Italian masters involved in this process, two names of local sculptors recur: firstly, the **Schwanthaler dynasty**, active between the 17C and 19C (21 artists working through seven generations), the last Schwanthaler being a neo-classicist working in Munich who made the Austria Fountain for the Freyung in Vienna (see p 79); secondly, **Meinrad Guggenbichler**, a sculptor who settled in Mondsee in 1679 and whose vividly plastic Baroque altars decorate many a church of Upper Austria. Another important sculptor dynasty was that of the **Zürn family** in the 17C, the two gifted brothers Martin and Michael Zürn likewise receiving many commissions to ornament Baroque churches. The commissions for Baroque architecture in Upper Austria involved a number of Italian masters, most notably the Carlone dynasty (who were actually Swiss Italians from Lake Como), of whom no less than 12 were active, running through several generations. Some were architects, others Baumeister or (like Giovanni Battista Carlone) specialists in decorative and stucco work. The most important native architect was **Johann Michael Prunner** (1669–1739), a native of Linz who was trained in Italy but was influenced by Lukas von Hildebrandt and Jakob Prandtauer. He developed his own manner out of these influences and built many churches, chapels and *Schlösser* in Upper Austria, his most idiosyncratic masterpiece being the **church of the Holy Trinity** at Stadl-Paura (see p 282). South German influence is evident in the sophisticated Rococo architecture and decoration to be found in many churches of Upper Austria. One of the most notable representatives of this trend was Johann Georg Üblher (1700–63, also spelled Ueblher, Ueblherr, Übelherr and Übelhör) a leading stuccoer and sculptor from Wessobrunn whose exceptional work may be seen at Wilhering and Engelszell (see pp 257 and 277).

After the Middle Ages, there were few really notable painters who were natives of Upper Austria, although there were a number of workmanlike Baroque and Rococo masters. A modern artist of note was the book illustrator and author **Alfred Kubin** (1877–1959), whose somewhat morbid but powerful drawings and etchings reflect both a modern pessimistic sensitivity and the artist's own troubled psyche, a projection of uncompromising intimacy that was a feature of Austrian Expressionism. Folk art in the region is most commonly identified with the whirling green-on-white patterns of **Gmunden ceramics**, which became a middle-class fashion in Austria, despite their somewhat overpowering vernacularism which makes them hard to integrate with other objects in an interior. Another Gmunden pattern showing flowers on a white background is more subtle and less likely to unbalance its decorative environment.

The most famous scholar associated with the region is **Johannes Kepler** (1571–1630), who moved from Prague (where he had been Court Astronomer) to Linz in 1612 on the death of his patron, Rudolf II. In Linz he completed his *Harmonice Mundi Libri V* and his *Epitome Astronomicae Copernicae*, before moving to Regensburg shortly before his death. The university at Linz was named after him. The best-known Upper Austrian writer is a giant of 19C Austrian literature, namely **Adalbert Stifter** (1805–68), who was also a gifted water-colourist. A quintessentially Biedermeier figure,

Stifter unfolded his 'gentle law' of a well-ordered evolution of mankind equally in harmony with nature and reason in his celebrated novel *Der Nachsommer* (Indian Summer, 1857), which reflects also the rural idyll of his Upper Austrian homeland. Like several gifted Austrian writers in the 18C and 19C, Stifter was employed in the imperial bureaucracy: as a reforming official in the field of education, he irritated his conservative superiors with his humanitarian zeal, while in his capacity as inspector of monuments he was one of the first conservationists in the modern sense, rescuing and restoring a number of important and neglected works of art in provincial churches (see pp 283 and 285). Unfortunately he was also a creature of his age and was swept up in the craze for the 're-Gothicisation' of churches which had been barockised in the Counter-Reformation. Often this was a well-intentioned attempt to recreate the original structure and atmosphere of a building in the spirit of Historicism, but equally as often it produced unhappy results.

The critic and essayist **Hermann Bahr** (1863–1934), founder of the *Jung Wien* movement at the turn of the 19C, was an *Oberösterreicher* born in Linz, although his career as a literary propagandist and arbiter of taste was pursued exclusively in Vienna. This did not prevent his enemy Karl Kraus from disparaging his provincial origins by referring to him satirically as 'the gentleman from Linz', an especially cruel put-down in view of Bahr's notably multi-cultural promotion of European modernism, not to mention Kraus's own origins in a provincial Bohemian town .... The philosopher **Ludwig Wittgenstein** and the poet **Rainer Maria Rilke** were also partly educated in Linz. A contemporary writer who has been mentioned elsewhere (see p 62) is the novelist and playwright Thomas Bernhard (1931–89), who lived in Upper Austria for much of his life at his Ohlsdorf house near Gmunden. His love-hate relationship with his homeland was sealed with his testamentary stipulation that none of his works should be given new productions in Austria for 70 years after his death—a move presumably designed to obviate the Austrian tendency to 'cash in' after their deaths on the works of creative artists who were ignored or even vilified during their lifetimes.

The musical traditions of Upper Austria live in the shadow of its greatest composer, **Anton Bruckner** (see below), but two modernists are worthy of mention: Helmut Eder (b. 1916), whose opera *Mozart in New York* was played to acclaim at the 1991 Salzburg Festival, and the prolific Johann Nepomuk David (1895–1977), whose output includes a number of impressive choral works in the tradition of Bruckner, as well as symphonies, chamber music and sacred pieces. An Upper Austrian by choice was the immensely successful Hungarian operetta composer, **Franz Lehár** (1870–1948). He visited Bad Ischl in 1906 (see p 272), where the operetta provided the undemanding form of music that was ideal for the holidaying bureaucrats, and decided to settle there, moving to a house on the banks of the Traun in 1910. Nor should it be forgotten that the great tenor Richard Tauber (1892–1948) was born in Linz.

Last but not least, mention should be made of two folk dances known as **Ländler** and (the more formal) **Landler**. The name is derived from the core area of Upper Austria, signifying the *Hausruck-* and *Traunviertel*, which (in contradistinction to the *Innviertel*) were never under Bavarian rule. At least from 1500, dances in 3/4 time, often accompanied by yodelling, clapping and stamping, were performed by the peasantry of the '*Landl*' (the term at that

Anton Bruckner (1824–96)

Anton Bruckner earned the appellation 'God's musician' not only because of his well-attested piety, but also because of the spark of divine genius that runs through his idiosyncratic oeuvre of symphonies and sacred music. His father was a provincial schoolmaster, and when he died in 1837 leaving the family penniless, Bruckner was accepted as a chorister at the abbey of St Florian. His patron was the prior, Michael Arneth, who seems to have taken to the gauche but gifted boy, and accepted him even though Bruckner's voice was already breaking. Bruckner subsequently followed his father into teaching, but at the same time was encouraged in his musical studies by his godfather and by teachers who had spotted his talents. In 1848 he was appointed organist at St Florian and began composing sacred music, in 1856 becoming the organist of Linz Cathedral. In the following decade he began work on his first symphony after hearing Wagner's *Tannhäuser*, the latter making a tremendous impact on him and (as he thought) showing him the musical path he should pursue. In 1868 (after constant rejections of applications for other posts) he was finally appointed a teacher at the Vienna Conservatoire.

After a nervous breakdown in 1866–67 (possibly brought on by one of his many disappointments in love), Bruckner embarked on writing and endlessly revising his nine great symphonies through the 1870s and 1880s. His work frequently met with incomprehension or contemptuous rejection (especially by the critic Eduard Hanslick, who had originally been a Bruckner supporter), and only gradually, in the last years of his life, did he enjoy more general acceptance by the musical establishment and the concert-going public. Although he was not the naïve soul often portrayed, Bruckner certainly suffered greatly on account of his simplicity, uprightness and chronic under-confidence, all his life collecting examination certificates and testimonials as lesser men collect postage stamps. He paid the price of being a man devoid of malice, whereas there was, and is, an inexhaustible reservoir of malice among the denizens of the cultural hothouse of Vienna. He also suffered from a condition known as numeromania, counting the number of prayers he said each day and numbering all the bars in his scores, even counting the leaves on the trees and the stars in the sky. Moreover, he shared the traditional Austrian obsession with death, being particularly partial to exhumations. When he received the Order of Franz Joseph in 1886, the Emperor asked him kindly if there was anything he might be able to do for him. 'Yes, Majesty,' came the doleful reply; 'You could stop Hanslick.' (According to another, version of the same story, he asked the Emperor if he 'could please stop the wind blowing in Vienna'.) In the event, the Emperor gave him the gate-keeper's lodge at Schloss Belvedere rent-free for the last year of his life.

time being contemptuous and implying a society of country bumpkins). This form of music and dance spread into neighbouring *Länder*, and from the 18C into polite society. It is generally considered to be the origin of one of the most successful musical forms of all time, namely the *Wiener Walzer*. The first waltz to be played in the capital is recorded in 1786, part of a theatrical performance entitled *Una cosa rara* by Martin y Soler. The intimacy involved in the dance, and the energy expended in performing it, attracted hysterical criticism both on the grounds of its supposed immorality and the danger it posed to health (there were many predictions that waltzing would lead to early death). Despite (or perhaps because of) these dire warnings, the Viennese took to the waltz and the dance became a symbol of their preference for merry-making instead of attending to the important but disagreeable realities of everyday life. When the news of the catastrophic defeat of the Austrians by the Prussians at Königgrätz came through to Vienna in 1866, the Viennese thronging the dance halls are said to have hardly paused in their waltzing. Indeed it was following this defeat that Johann Strauss wrote his celebrated *Blue Danube Waltz*.

LINZ
• • • • •

Practical information

Population: 203,000. Telephone dialling code: 0732 Linz.

Tourist information
Hauptplatz 1 (☎ 7070-1777, fax 0732 77 2873). Open: Mon–Fri, 07.00–19.00, weekends 08.00–11.30, 12.30–19.00. Nov–April, 08.00–18.00. A useful *Stadtplan* may be obtained here. Hauptbahnhof (in Sparda Bank). Open: Mon–Fri 08.00–19.00, Sat 08.00–12.00, 15.00–17.00, Sun 08.00–12.00.
The *Landesverband für Tourismus in Oberösterreich*/provincial tourist office for Upper Austria is at **Schillerstrasse** 50, A-4010 Linz. ☎ 0732-771 264. It is advisable to buy a day ticket covering all of the city public transport network (but not the *Pöstlingbergbahn*) at a *Tabak/Trafik*. The ticket must be validated at a bus or tram stop before boarding for the first trip.

Getting there
By train Linz is on the main Vienna—Salzburg line and served by regular express trains. The Bahnhof is 2km south of the city centre and the bus terminal is on the Bahnhofplatz. Trains to and from the Mühlviertel arrive at Linz-Urfahr on the north bank.

By boat Although river journeys have become progressively slower as more hydro-electric dams have been built and are only suitable for leisure travel, there is a boat service between Linz—Passau and Linz—Vienna between April (Passau) or May and September. The DDSG station (☎ 77 1090) is at Untere Donaulände 10 on the South Bank, east of the Nibelungen Brücke.

By air Linz Airport is at Hörsching 10km south-west of the city, with flights to Germany and Switzerland, but mostly used by businessmen. For flight information ☎ 07721 727 00224. At Schulertstrasse 1 *AVA* and **Swissair** share an office.

Hotels
☆☆☆ *Wolfinger* (Hauptplatz 19, ☎ 7732 91. Fax 77 32 91 55). Although it has the drawback that only a few rooms actually look on the Hauptplatz, this is the most central place

to stay with modern comfort in a nostalgic Biedermeier atmosphere.

✩✩✩ *Hotel Drei Mohren* (Promenade 17. ☎ 7726 26. Fax: 7726 266. Smart modern city hotel, centrally located.

✩✩ *Goldener Anker* (Hofgasse 5. ☎ 77 10 88. Fax: 77 10 88). Good value and just off the Hauptplatz. Garage nearby.

Restaurants

✩✩✩ *Der Neue Vogelkäfig* (Holzstrasse 8). First-class regional cooking.

✩✩✩ *Kremsmünster Stuben* (Altstadt 10). Gourmets' choice for game dishes and local specialities such as *Innviertler Knödeln*.

✩✩ *Linzer Stuben* (Klammstrasse 7). The weekday lunches with a fixed menu are a bargain.

✩✩ *Klosterhof* (corner of Bischofstrasse and Landstrasse). Attractive dining

rooms in a 17C building. Modestly priced Austrian fare.

There are no cafés of particular distinction in Linz. However most of the cafés and *konditoreien* around the centre are comfortable enough, and almost all serve the local speciality of *Linzer Torte*, a layered sponge cake.

Cultural events

Internationales Brucknerfest Linz. An annual celebration of Anton Bruckner's music held in **September**, most performances are in the modern **Brucknerhaus**, a combined auditorium and congress hall on the riverside. **Ars Electronica** A festival of electronic and computer music with multi-media animation (founded 1980s) is held at the same time as the Brucknerfest.

History of Linz

The historic site of Linz was situated on the south side of the Danube, which at this point breaks through the Linz Gate (*Linzer Pforte*) at the rim of a granite plateau and flows into the fertile Linz Basin (*Linzer Becken*). The capital of **Oberösterreich** (Upper Austria) and the third largest town in the country, Linz does not seem a very bustling place, at least around its huge rectangular **Hauptplatz**. The business end of modern Linz, with its vast iron- and steelworks, is located in the southern suburbs; and the extensive Danubian port is situated to the east, beyond a loop of the river, which flows serenely between the two central residential districts. A compact view of Linz, ancient and modern, may be obtained from the delightful **Pöstlingberg** to the north, which is reached by a railway from the **Bergbahnhof Urfahr** (*see below*).

The Linz region has been settled since the Stone Age, but it was the Celts who first built a fort on what are now the upper reaches of the *Altstadt*, to which the Romans gave the name *Lentia*. Despite the Danubian flotilla stationed here, *Lentia* was of considerably less significance than neighbouring *Ovilava* (Wels) or *Lauriacum* (Lorch bei Enns). At the close of the Dark Ages, the town known as 'Linze' from the 8C fell under Bavarian and Carolingian control, although direct authority was exercised by the bishops of Passau. It became more important after 1200, by which time Enns, Wels, Steyr and Linz were all under the control of Leopold VI of Babenberg. His successors extended the fortifications from 1236 while the graceful **Hauptplatz** was laid out in 1260, during the hegemony of Premysl Ottakar II of Bohemia. Linz meanwhile began to prosper from the trade in wood, salt and the iron from Styria. Under the Habsburgs the town significantly increased its privileges, obtaining the licence for a mint in 1458, and building the first bridge over the Danube in 1497. The Danubian toll, levied from some time in the 13C, was one of the most profitable in the whole Austrian territory. In 1489 Friedrich III even moved his residence to Linz, and died here in 1493, thus placing Linz at the nerve-centre of the Habsburg hereditary lands.

Notwithstanding its imperial tradition, Linz became Protestant for a while in the late 16C and early 17C, at a time when Johannes Kepler was teaching at the *Landschaftsschule* for the local nobility. This did not prevent it from becoming the capital of the *Herzogtum ob der Enns* (The Archduchy beyond the Enns) in the 16C, a position it was never to relinquish. Its industrial ascent may be traced to 1672 and the founding of a wool factory on the *Untere Donaulände*, which had become one of the biggest in Europe by the 18C. This, the most successful of all the dynasty's mercantilist projects, was built by Johann Michael Prunner, the province's leading architect of the day, and at one time employed some 1000 workers in the city, many thousands more as 'home-workers' doing piece-work. In 1722 it was taken over by the ill-fated Ostend Trading Company, the Habsburg firm designed to break into the East Indian trade. The British regarded this concern as competition in their own backyard and successfully demanded its dissolution in return for recognition of the Pragmatic Sanction of Karl VI.

After occupation in the Napoleonic War, the 19C saw the development of rail and river connections to Linz that greatly benefited the economy of the city, as also did the incorporation of the suburbs of Urfahr and Ebelsberg. Growth continued in the 20C and Hitler had plans to transform and expand the city he remembered with some affection from his spell at the *Realschule* after 1900, although little remains of his utopian vision other than the buildings between the north end of the Hauptplatz and the Nibelungenbrücke. Today Linz remains an important industrial city and port, the seat of the Upper Austrian *Landtag* and the provincial administration, a university town (since 1962) and a bishopric (since 1783), also the proud home of a top football club (*Linzer Athletik Sportklub* or *LASK*).

Sights of Linz

It is simplest to begin a tour of the city with the beautiful **Hauptplatz** (laid out in 1260), a huge (219 x 60m) rectangular space just to the south of the southern bridgehead of the **Nibelungenbrücke**. At its centre is a **Trinity Column** (1723, perhaps by Antonio Beduzzi), which, besides its allusion to the Christian doctrine of the Trinity, also embodies the triple symbols of Emperor, Land and City, represented by three coats of arms. Deliverance from past perils is reflected in the protective saints chosen to ornament it: *St Florian* against fire, *Sts Sebastian* and *Carlo Borromeo* against the plague and the *Maria Immaculata* as protagonist of the faith against the infidel Turks and heretical Protestants.

The attractive and gracious house façades from the Renaissance, Baroque and Rococo periods that line the square were those of prosperous merchants, their ground-plots originally being distributed in equal proportions on the same principle as those of the merchants along the canals of Amsterdam; later they were often combined in twos or threes under a single rich owner. The originally Renaissance **Rathaus** on the east side of the square was built by Master

Christoph in 1513 after the great fire of 1509, but combined with the neighbouring building in 1658–59, when it was given its present Baroque façade.

If you follow Hofgasse west from the square, you find yourself climbing to the **Schloss**, whose origins lie in the 8C, but which was rebuilt by Friedrich III in the late 1470s (note his motto AEIOU on the Friedrichstor), and again rebuilt for Rudolph II by the Dutchman Anton Muys around 1600. The interior has served as a hospital, prison and barracks and now houses a branch of the **Upper Austrian Landesmuseum** (Schloß Museum) (open Tues–Fri, 09.00–17.00, Sat, Sun, PH, 10.00–16.00), one of the richest of its kind. The contents include archaeological finds, a weapons collection, sculpture, musical instruments, ceramics etc. and a picture gallery with works by Ferdinand Waldmüller, Gustav Klimt and Egon Schiele, amongst others. There are also portraits of Johannes Kepler and Anton Bruckner.

A walk through the rear battlements of the castle and along the **Römerstrasse** brings you on the right to the ancient **Martinskirche**, which was formerly three times as large as its present size and is perhaps the oldest surviving church in Austria, originating in the era of the pre-Carolingian Agilolfingian overlords (before 788). Note the Roman gravestones integrated into the walls. The fresco (c 1440) on the church's north wall imitates in the medium of painting the celebrated *Volto Santo* of Matteo Civitali's tempietto in the cathedral at Lucca (Italy), a crucifix said to have been carved by angels. On the triumphal arch of the choir is a Gothic 'radiant Madonna'.

Returning south-east via the Römerstrasse through the old town, you pass the neo-classical **Landestheater** (1803), remodelled by Clemens Holzmeister in 1957–58. A detour down the Theatergasse brings you to the Renaissance **Mozarthaus**, where the *Linz Symphony* was composed in 1783 (there is a 1957 bust of the composer in the entrance hall by W. Ritter). From here you return to the **Promenade**, some way along which on the left is the **Landhaus**, the seat of the Provincial Parliament and Governor, and a fine Renaissance edifice built (1564) on the site of the Minorite monastery, whose church is adjacent.

In the beautiful three-storeyed, arcaded courtyard is Peter Guets' **Fountain of the Planets** (1582), the central column of which features representations of the *Moon, Mercury, Venus, the Sun, Mars and Saturn*, these surmounted by *Jupiter*. Between 1612 and 1626 Johannes Kepler taught mathematics and astronomy at the Protestant **Landschaftsschule** situated here. The north portal is especially fine Renaissance work (perhaps by the Venetian, Caspar Toretto) with a graceful *Rundbogen* window over the red marbled doorway; note the two putti in between the architrave and the window, bearing aloft the coats of arms of Lower Austria, Upper Austria and (in the middle) Imperial Austria.

The **Minorite Church** was rebuilt in 1751 by Johann Krinner as a single-naved Rococo church with ornate white, yellow and pink stucco by Kaspar Modler. Above the main altar is Bartolomeo Altomonte's *Annunciation* and there are four works by Kremser Schmidt (*Joseph of Copertino, St John of Nepomuk*, the *Vision of St Francis on Mount Alverna* and a *Crucifixion*). The subject matter of these celebrates the mystical gifts of the Franciscans, hence the rare representation of the ecstatic Joseph of Copertino (or Cupertino, 1603–63). The saint was a sickly and slow-witted Calabrian youth known as 'the gaper', who found employment as a stable boy with the Franciscans at La Grottella.

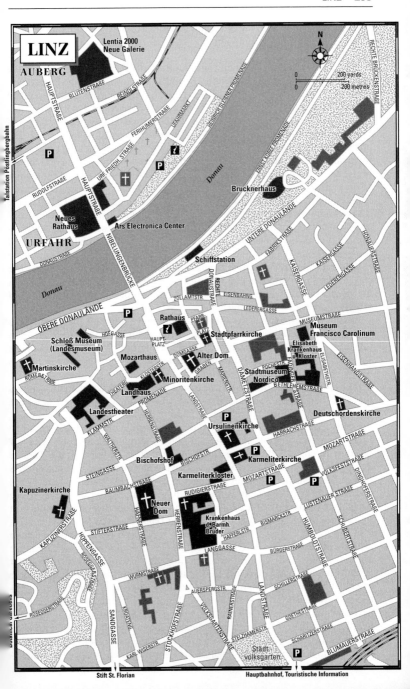

LINZ

AUBERG

Lentia 2000
Neue Galerie

Talstation Pöstlingbergbahn

HAUPTSTRASSE

BLUTENSTRASSE

REINDLSTRASSE

HEINRICH-GLEISSNER-PROMENADE

RECHTE BRUCKENSTRASSE

N

0   200 yards
0   200 metres

FERIHUMERSTRASSE

URFAHRMARKT

URF.-FRIEDH. STRASSE

P

i

Donau

ERNST-KOREF-PROMENADE

Bucknerhaus

RUDOLFSTRASSE

HAUPTSTRASSE

P

Neues
Rathaus

URFAHR

Ars Electronica Center

NIBELUNGENBRÜCKE

UNTERE DONAULÄNDE

FABRIKSTRASSE

KAISERGASSE

LEDERERGASSE

HONAUERSTRASSE

Schiffstation

DONAUSTRASSE

RECHTE DONAULÄNDE

EISENBAHNG

DONAUSTRASSE

Donau

OBERE DONAULÄNDE

P

ZOLLAMTSTR.

EISENBAHNG.

LEDERERGASSE

MUSEUMSTRASSE

HOFGASSE

Rathaus
i

PFARR
PLATZ

Museum
Francisco Carolinum

Schloß Museum
(Landesmuseum)

HAUPT-
PLATZ

Stadtpfarrkirche

POCHESTR.

Elisabeth
Krankenhaus
u. Kloster

EISENHANDSTRASSE

Martinskirche

ROMERSTRASSE

Mozarthaus

DOMGASSE

Alter Dom

GRABEN

MARIENSTR.

Stadtmuseum
Nordico

BETHLEHEMSTRASSE

ELISABETHSTR.

KLOSTERSTR.

Minoritenkirche

DAMETZSTRASSE

Landhaus

THEATERGASSE

PROMENADE

HERRENSTRASSE

LANDSTRASSE

Deutschordenskirche

Landestheater

KLAMMSTR.

Ursulinenkirche

HARRACHSTRASSE

MOZARTSTRASSE

WALTHERSTR.

STEINGASSE

P

Bischofshof

BISCHOFSTR.

Karmeliterkirche

P

VOLKSFESTSTRASSE

DINGHOFERSTRASSE

Kapuzinerkirche

BAUMBACHSTRASSE

Karmeliterkloster

MOZARTSTRASSE

P

LUSTENAUER STRASSE

HUMBOLDTSTRASSE

SCHUBERTSTRASSE

KAPUZINERSTRASSE

HAFNERSTRASSE

RUDIGIERSTRASSE

Neuer
Dom

HERRENSTRASSE

Krankenhaus
d. Barmh.
Brüder

BISMARCKSTR.

BÜRGERSTRASSE

STIFTERSTRASSE

HAFFERLSTR.

HOPFENGASSE

ROSEGGERSTRASSE

LANGGASSE

WURMSTRASSE

AUERSPERGSTR.

LANDSTRASSE

SCHILLERSTRASSE

SANDGASSE

STOCKHOFSTRASSE

VOLKSGARTENSTRASSE

RATHENSTRASSE

STELZHAMERSTR.

GOETHESTRASSE

SCHARITZERSTRASSE

ROSEGGERSTRASSE

KARL-WISER-STR.

KUDLICHG.

Städt.
volksgarten

P

BLUMAUERSTRASSE

Volksgarten

↓
Stift St. Florian

↓
Hauptbahnhof, Touristische Information

Later he was admitted to the order and performed many apparently miraculous acts, his speciality being levitation.

If you turn off the Promenade and head south on the Herrenstrasse, you pass the **Bischofshof** (no. 19) built between 1721 and 1726 to plans by Jakob Prandtauer, originally for the Abbots of Kremsmünster, and having a fine wrought-iron **grille** on the stairway by Master Valentin Hofmann. Shortly beyond it is the huge neo-Gothic **Cathedral**, the largest church in all Austria and designed in the manner of French cathedral-Gothic by Vinzenz Statz. It took 62 years to build (1862–1924) and can accommodate 20,000 people, but hardly compares with the same architect's work on Cologne cathedral. The reactionary tendency in the Austrian church of the day regarded the cathedral as a mighty visual offensive against the secular Liberalism of contemporary politics. The steeple is 134m high, but was not permitted to exceed the height of the south tower of St Stephen's in Vienna (137m). These statistics may serve to impress the visitor, for it is hard otherwise to enthuse about such unremittingly sterile architectural precision, the end-result of which is a soulless desert of all-encompassing gloom that would surely strike a chill in the heart of the most self-sacrificial church-mouse. Still, the vastness of the space must have made the première of Bruckner's *E-minor Mass* here in 1869 sound impressive. The stained-glass window depicting Linz history is much admired, as is Sebastian Osterrieder's nativity scene in the crypt. The vast statues of *St Peter* and *St Paul* (1663) also have a monumental dignity.

West of the cathedral is the **Capuchin Church** (1661) on the street of the same name, where Count Montecuccoli, the victor over the Turks at Szent Gotthard in Western Hungary in 1664, lies buried. Just to the south on Herrenstrasse is the **church of the Brothers of Mercy** (*Barmherzige Brüder*) built by J.M. Prunner with an elegant concave façade.

Herrenstrasse joins Rudigierstrasse east of the cathedral, which in turn crosses the axial Landstrasse, on the far side of which you will see the **Carmelite church of St Joseph**, completed in 1726 and with a façade (1722) by J.M. Prunner. The interior can be viewed through a grille and contains stucco by Diego Francesco Carlone and Paolo d'Allio. The main altarpiece (1724) by Martino Altomonte shows the *Holy Family*, while another of the Carlone dynasty (Carlo) painted the altarpiece showing *St Anne*. Next to this church is that of the **Ursulines** (Johann Haslinger and Johann Matthias Krinner, 1757) dedicated to St Michael, and now a cultural centre. The altarpiece of the *Archangel Michael* is by Bartolomeo Altomonte, as is another on the south-west side of the church showing *St Ursula with St Leopold*.

If you follow Harrachstrasse to the east, you reach on the left the former **church of the Teutonic Knights** (1739, *Deutschordenskirche*), a diminutive and strikingly elegant elliptical structure hugging the seminary wall. It was built to plans by the great Lukas von Hildebrandt, although the realisation of these was chiefly the work of Johann Michael Prunner. The coat of arms on the attractive concave façade is that of the founder, Prince Harrach, and the allegorical figures above of *Vigilance*, *Generosity*, *Chastity* and *Obedience* (by Johann Georg Kracher) allude to the virtues theoretically espoused by the Teutonic Knights, although their record in East Prussia and Lithuania leaves room for scepticism. The clock-tower continues the angle of the tympanum and is capped by a mushroom-shaped dome with a cross.

A little to the north at Dametzstraße 23 is the **Stadtmuseum Nordico** (open Mon–Fri, 09.00–18.00, Sat, Sun, 14.00–17.00), which is often given over to temporary exhibitions, but which also contains an archaeological collection and materials relating to the history of Linz. Its name recalls the fact that Scandinavian students were originally sent here to be raised in the Catholic faith by the Jesuits, hence the coats of arms on the portal of the canonised nordic kings, Knut, Eric and Olaf. Nearby is the **church of the Elisabethan Sisters** dedicated to St Francis Seraphicus, a transitional Baroque to neo-classical building. The architectural painting in the cupola is by Bartolomeo Altomonte and Matthias Dollicher. Also worth visiting is the **Francisco Carolinum**, the **Landesmuseum**, at Museumstrasse 14 (open Tues–Fri, 09.00–18.00, Sat, Sun, 10.00–17.00) which displays the natural history of the region. The frieze on the façade by Bruno Schmitz shows scenes from Austrian history, together with allegorical representations of the main occupations pursued by Upper Austrians (mining, agriculture, Danubian shipping, etc.). Not far to the west is the **Old Cathedral** (Jesuit church of St Ignatius) encompassed by the Graben and Domgasse. It was built by Pietro Francesco Carlone for the Jesuits between 1669 and 1678, fell into decay with the dissolution of the order in 1773, but was made the cathedral church when the Linz bishopric was set up in 1783. On the completion of the new Linz cathedral in 1924 the Jesuits were reinstated. The *Assumption* over the high altar is by Antonio Bellucci, but more remarkable is the effect of the gold-bordered drapery covering much of the east wall and held by 18 angels. Also striking is the altarpiece showing *St Aloysius* by Bartolomeo Altomonte. The beautiful 17C choirstalls are by a Benedictine monk named Michael Obermüller and the Baroque organ (frequently played by Bruckner between 1856 and 1868 in his capacity as cathedral organist) was constructed by a famous craftsman in the branch, Franz Xaver Krismann. The organ was modified for Bruckner.

The **parish church** standing slightly to the north has Romanesque and Gothic origins (visible, for example in the structure of the tower) but was rebuilt in Baroque style in 1648 and boasts (on an exterior wall of the choir) a marble statue (1727) of *St John of Nepomuk* by Georg Raphael Donner, which is set in a frame designed by Lukas von Hildebrandt. The modest interior of the church has an altarpiece of the *Assumption* by Karl von Reslfeld and an oval baptismal chapel dedicated to John of

The Old Cathedral, Linz

Nepomuk which, however, was originally endowed and designed by the Linz architect, Johann Michael Prunner, as his own burial chapel. The grave of Friedrich III in the choir also contains the Emperor's embalmed entrails and heart, an early example of the Habsburg necrolatry that was to reach its apotheosis in Counter-Reformatory Vienna. As you make your way back to the Hauptplatz via the Rathausgasse, you pass at no. 5 the house where Johannes Kepler lived as a guest of the Altenstrasser family, and where he wrote his *Tabulae Rudolphinae* (on the movements of the planets, extending the minutely detailed work of his mentor in Prague, Tycho Brahe).

Immediately to the north of the Hauptplatz the **Nibelungenbrücke** crosses the Danube. Downstream, on the south bank, is the **Brucknerhaus**, a congress house and concert hall much praised for its acoustics and built (1974) by the Finnish architect, Heikki Siren. The opening concert or *Klangwolke* (literally: 'cloud of sounds') of the annual **Brucknerfest** in September takes place on the embankment.

A few minutes' walk or a tram ride brings you across the river to the suburb of **Urfahr**. Immediately on the north bank at Hauptstrasse 2 you will see the impressive **Ars Electronica Center** (open Wed–Sun, 10.00–18.00) which is opposite the new city hall, identifiable by its rather bleak concrete balconies. Known as *Museum der Zukunft* (Museum of the Future) its main attraction is the CAVE (standing for Cave Automatic Virtual Environment and a reference to Plato's ideas about reality and perception). For CAVE, you need to book a time at the entrance desk, but other features, such as the virtual reality room (for which a special 3-D viewfinder is needed) in the rooftop cybercafé can be sampled on spec. Further north a right turn into Blütenstrasse will take you shortly to the **Neue Galerie der Stadt Linz** (open Mon, Tues, Wed, Fri 10.00–18.00, Thur 10.00–22.00, Sat 10.00–13.00) at no. 15 in the **Lentia** shopping precinct. It is also known as the **Wolfgang Gurlitt Museum** after the Berlin art dealer on whose collection it was based when founded in 1952, and contains mainly Austrian works from the turn of the 19th century to the present. Besides works by Schindler, Romako, Moll, Klimt, Schiele and Kokoschka, there are contemporary paintings by Arnulf Rainer, Hermann Nitsch and others.

Pöstlingberg Bergbahn

If you return to the tram-stop where you alighted for the Neue Galerie and take tram 3 to the northern end-stop, you will find yourself at the terminus for the **Pöstlingberg Bergbahn**, opened in 1898 and designed by Josef Urbanski, who is said to have been cheated out of his royalties by the Viennese construction firm that built the railway (*plus ça change*). It appears in the *Guinness Book of Records* as the steepest adhesion railway in the world, although it was originally planned as a cogwheel system.

The 2.9km **Bergbahn** climbs 255m to a fortified area designed (1837) by the Italian father of the French novelist, Emile Zola. Steps lead up to the **Pilgrimage Church of the Seven Sorrows of Mary** (1771), built by Johann Matthias Krinner on the site of a wonder-working icon by Ignaz Jobst placed on the Pöstlingberg in 1716 after effecting a miraculous cure on Prince Gundomer von Starhemberg. The church is now in the possession of the Oblates of St Francis de Sales and was made a *basilica minore* in 1964 by Pope Paul VI. The turn of the century fresco of the interior (*Coronation of the Virgin*) is by Andreas Groll. Close to the church is a **Grottenbahn** (open 09.00–18.00 in summer, 10.00–17.00 Sept–Nov), a poor man's Disneyland ride with dwarves, dragons, etc.

Around Linz

Eight kilometres west of Linz on the south bank of the Danube is the Cistercian **Abbey Church of Wilhering** (1733, Johann Haslinger, perhaps in collaboration with Andreas Altomonte) with a superb Rococo interior. The abbey itself was founded in 1146 and to this day continues the agricultural activity typical of the order in the Middle Ages, with market gardening and forestry being practised on an economic basis, and money also flowing in from the boarding school (*Gymnasium*) run by the monks. The massive clock-tower dominating the church façade, impressive though it is, is not in keeping with the traditionally ascetic Cistercian building norms.

The astonishing **interior** boasts the largest ceiling fresco of any church in Austria, a depiction of *Mary as Queen of Heaven* as eulogised in the Loretan Litany, perhaps the greatest work by Bartolomeo Altomonte. The white, pink, green and gold stucco in the nave, with its sophisticated rocaille motifs, is by Franz Joseph Holzinger, while that in the crossing and the choir is the work of Johann Michael Feichtmayr and Johann Üblher. The Marian theme recurs in the fresco of the cupola over the crossing, where the *Virgin* is represented as the *Fount of Wisdom, Justice and Mercy*, accompanied by depictions of *Adam and Eve* and *The Fall*. Our Lady is further celebrated by the chorus of angels painted in the choir and in Altomonte's altarpiece, which shows the *Assumption*. The white sculptures above it represent the *Trinity*, while Üblher's masterly sculptures for the side-altars depict the various saints to whom they are dedicated. The same sculptor did the pulpit figures and those of the organ loft. The ensemble is a remarkable example of Rococo *Gesamtkunstwerk*, where didacticism and aesthetic effect are mutually reinforcing, the general atmosphere of mystical spirituality being enhanced by light streaming into the church (as if from heaven itself) via the elevated windows.

The **cloister** is reached to the left of the entrance, and leads to the Romanesque **Chapter House**. In the monastery's **picture gallery** (open 15 May–15 Oct, daily 10.00–17.00) can be seen sculptures and paintings by the Linz artist Fritz Fröhlich (b. 1910), who has lived in Wilhering since the 1960s. His often openly satirical works owe something to George Grosz, but it was his lyrical side that originally impressed the monks, typically in the frescoes he painted at Engelszell (see p 277).

Stift St Florian

The minor road no. 296 leads a few kilometres south of the Linz suburb of Ebelsberg to **Markt St Florian** and the celebrated **Stift St Florian**, which rivals Melk and Klosterneuburg in magnificence and architectural sophistication. There has been a cloister here since the Carolingian era, followed by a refoundation in the 11C, when it changed (1071) from Benedictine to Augustinian control. The monastery grew rich from the astute economic exploitation of its extensive lands in Lower and Upper Austria, while its secular influence resided in the

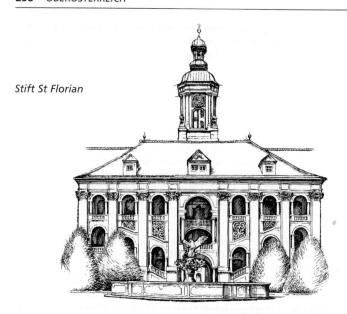

Stift St Florian

administration of no less than 33 parishes. After the decisive defeat of the Turks at the siege of Vienna in 1683, Abbot David Fuhrmann decided to celebrate by rebuilding the entire monastery and engaged Carlo Antonio Carlone for the task, over which Carlone presided from 1686 until his death in 1708. His successor (engaged by Fuhrmann's successor in office, Johann Baptist Födermayer) was the great Jakob Prandtauer, who built the south wing and the marble hall. After Prandtauer's death (1726), the library wing was completed (1751) by Gotthard Hayberger.

From the 18C St Florian was a noted centre of learning and culture. It is, however, most famously associated with **Anton Bruckner**, who joined its choir in 1837, but had to be employed as a violinist, because his voice was already breaking. The Prior, Michael Arneth, needed his considerable reserves of indulgence in dealing with his protégé, who does not seem to have been such an unconventionally pious young man as legend suggests. At any rate he was once rebuked by Arneth for his drinking sessions, the Prior (according to Bruckner's own account) telling him he would have both Bruckner and the organ thrown out if the visits to the tavern didn't stop. Bruckner hastily wrote a cantata 'for the Herr Prior's name-day', which seems to have mollified him. After a decade of study and apprentice teaching beginning in Linz in 1838, and (most implausibly) a brief spell in the National Guard during the 1848 revolution, Bruckner returned to St Florian to occupy the official post of organist. Even after his subsequent move to Vienna, where he was subjected to so much humiliation, he returned for holidays to the friendly and welcoming environment of Sankt Florian, and it was here that many of his sacred works were first performed. On his death in 1896, his body was brought here and his coffin lies in the crypt beneath the monastery's organ.

St Florian has regained its old lustre since restoration was completed in 1996.

Proceeding towards the main entrance, the visitor is struck by the imposing elegance of the monastery's 214m long western façade, with its rows of 34 windows. The magnificent doorway (by Prandtauer) is flanked by four monumental Atlas figures with sculptured allegories of the *Cardinal Virtues* by Leonhard Sattler above, these surmounted by a small balcony with ornamental stone vases and finally a tower known as the **Bläserturm**, presumably because musicians would have played here on ceremonial occasions. Beyond the gateway is a large courtyard studded with box-trees, having at the centre an ornate fountain ('**eagle fountain**', 1757, by Johann Jakob Sattler), the backdrop being the eastern (library) wing of the monastery. From the gateway the **grand staircase** is reached, one of the loveliest in Austria, a seven-axial double stairway standing proud of the building, with two storeys of open balustraded arches divided by pilasters, below which are openwork panels. Its two sets of stairs slope gracefully inwards to the focal arch at the centre. The original concept was Carlone's, but the peculiar genius of the stairway's elegant ornamentation with its Palladian allusions is the result of Prandtauer's alterations completed in 1714. It should be viewed from the fountain before ascending.

The monastery may be visited with a guided tour lasting c 1.5 hours from 16 April–end Oct, daily at 10.00, 11.00, 14.00, 15.00 and 16.00. The tour includes the **State Apartments** in which a carved Turkish bed once belonging to Prince Eugene of Savoy may be seen, together with the bed in which Bruckner died, the latter having been brought here from the Belvedere gate-lodge in Vienna. The adjacent **Altdorfer Gallery** contains the superb *St Sebastian Winged Altar* (c 1518), eight panels by Albrecht Altdorfer of the Danube School depicting scenes from the *Passion*; on the reverse of the outer wings is represented the *Legend of St Sebastian*. The altar was commissioned for St Florian by Abbot Peter Maurer, who is depicted on the predella, together with *Sts Margaret and Barbara* (the missing paintings of the *Burial and Resurrection of Christ* were removed to the Kunsthistorisches Museum in Vienna). There are other examples of the Danube School in the gallery, notably two paintings by Wolf Huber (c 1485–1553).

In the centre of the south wing is the **Marble Hall** (*Marmor-* or *Kaisersaal*, 1724), with ceiling frescoes by Martino and Bartolomeo Altomonte (father and son) of the *Victory of Austria over the Turks* and the *Glorification of Peace*, as well as portraits of Prince Eugene of Savoy and Karl VI at either end. The Rococo library (1750) with 120,000 volumes, designed by Gotthard Hayberger, has an attractively ornate gallery and a ceiling fresco by Daniel Gran and Bartolomeo Altomonte (the *Marriage of Virtue and Learning Inspired by Religion*), Religion being depicted as a cleansing force driving out ignorance and vice.

The monastery **church of the Assumption** (1715) at the north end of the west wing is one of the masterworks of Carlo Antonio Carlone. Between its twin Baroque towers is an entrance with adjacent niche statues representing *St Florian* and *St Augustine*, while in the gable above may be seen the *Virgin Enthroned with John the Baptist and John the Evangelist*.

The imposing white **interior** has monumental half-columns on tall plinths joined by arches supporting galleries, above which is an ornate cornice. The wrought-iron grille (1699) that closes off the main church from the porch is by Hans Meßner. The lavish stucco of the walls is by Bartolomeo Carlone, brother of Carlo Antonio. The frescoes (1695) are by Johann Anton Gumpp and Melchior Steidl (in the porch, *Christ on the Mount of Olives* and prophetic scenes from the *Old Testament*, over the organ loft, *St Cecilia*, in the main nave the *Martyrdom and Transfiguration of St Florian*, in the choir the *Glorification of the Virgin Mary of the Loretan Litany* and the *Assumption*). The altarpiece (1687) by Giuseppe Ghizi also shows an *Assumption*. The marble altar itself (1690) is the work of Giovanni Battista Colombo and other features of note include the delicately carved choirstalls and a pulpit of black marble.

The **Bruckner organ** (1774, by Franz Xaver Krismann) is world famous for its size and the mellifluous quality of its sound: it has 7343 pipes and 103 possible tones. Anton Bruckner was employed as organist between 1848 and 1855 and lies at rest in the Romanesque crypt below, together with Valeria 'a matronly woman from Traun', who is supposed to have buried the body of St Florian here. St Florian is, of course, the patron saint of firemen and at Stiftstrasse 2 in the village you can visit the **Austrian Fire Brigade Museum** (open May–Oct, Tues–Sun, 09.00–12.00, 14.00–18.00).

Two kilometres to the south near Enzing is **Schloss Hohenbrunn**, built by Jakob Prandtauer and formerly the hunting-lodge of the St Florian abbots, now housing the **Austrian Hunting and Fishing Museum** (open Tues–Sun, 10.00–12.00, 13.00–17.00).

Two kilometres east of the monastery is the **open-air Museum of Upper Austria** *(Freilichtmuseum Samesleiten-Sumerauerhof)*, which is open between April–Oct, daily, 10.00–12.00, 13.00–17.00 and offers a display of peasant life, folk art and furniture etc. At **Ansfelden**, a few kilometres to the west of the abbey is the **Anton-Bruckner-Geburtshaus** (open April–Oct, Wed 14.00–17.00, Sun 10.00–12.00 and 14.00–17.00), with a display documenting the composer's life and work and a preserved school classroom of the period. Adjacent is a **Pfarrhof** built by Carlo Antonio Carlone.

THE TRAUNVIERTEL

The historic town of **Wels** (from Celtic *vilesos*) is reached on road 1 heading south-westwards from Linz, the name of the town referring to a meander of the River Traun which seems, however, to have been straightened somewhat with the passage of time. As a river crossing on a trade route, it flourished in Roman times as *Ovilava*, being raised to a *municipium* by Hadrian, later (under Caracalla) to a *colonia*, and becoming capital of the province of *Ufernoricum* (*Noricum ripense*) in AD 300 under Diocletian. It prospered in the Middle Ages as *Castrum Uueles* (first mentioned as such in a document of 776) and was favoured by Maximilian I, who died here on 12 January 1519. It has a particularly attractive main square with 64 Baroque house façades, most of them fronting an original Gothic building; there is also one surviving tower (the **Ledererturm**, 1376, in the west) of the old city fortifications.

The fine Rococo **Rathaus** (1748) at no. 1 on the Stadtplatz is the work of J.M. Prunner, while the fountain in front of it is a reconstruction of the 1593 original. A narrow street to the west leads to the early Gothic former Minorite Church, which was chosen to house the Upper Austrian Exhibition in the year 2000, the Minorites' former cloister being destined to become the Wels archaeological museum. The **Sigmarkapelle**, also known as the **Barbarakapelle**, is one part of the monastery that has not been deconsecrated and is entered from **Am Zwinger** on the south-east side. Its chief features of interest are the frescoes of 1480–90 and the reticulated vaulting.

Further to the west is a **water-tower** of 1577. The **parish church of St John** at the east end of the Stadtplatz retains Romanesque elements, notably the stepped portal of the western porch under the tower, the tower itself (1730) again being the work of J.M. Prunner. The porch also contains marble epitaphs of the Lords of Polheim. The church's most important feature is the Gothic stained glass in the choir: to the north, *Prophets*, Personifications of *Virtue and Vice*, the *Nativity* and the *Adoration of the Kings*; in the middle, the *Lives of John the Baptist and John the Evangelist*, the *Last Supper* and the *Four Evangelists*; to the south, the *Tree of Life* and the *Passion*. It has been pointed out that the cycle is designed to be read from north to south, in other words moving from darkness into light.

South of the church at Stadtplatz 24 is the **house of Salome Alt** (1568–1633), from 1600 Salome von Altenau, the mistress of the Prince-Bishop of Salzburg, Wolf-Dietrich von Raitenau (see p 295). She retreated here when Wolf-Dietrich was imprisoned by his rivals in the Salzburg fortress, and lived with a cousin married to a Protestant. The house has elegant late-Gothic corner bays and a red and cream patterned façade of illusionist architecture, showing also three painted coats of arms.

The former **Imperial Burg**, where Maximilian died, is further south and probably dates to the 8C, but was modernised in 1222 and now houses several museums as well as hosting drama performances and concerts in summer. The **Agricultural Museum**, the **Town Museum**, as well as **Bakery and Confectionery Museum** are open Tues–Fri, 10.00–17.00, weekends and PH 10.00–12.00. The Town Museum (*Stadtmuseum*) is notable for the Roman *Wels Venus* (1C or 2C AD), while the **Museum of Exiles** (*Gedenkraum der Heimatvertriebenen*: ☎ (0 72 42) 235-0) documents the history of German minorities in Central Europe (Danubian Swabians, Transylvanian Saxons, Sudeten and Carpathian Germans).

Near the hamlet of **Pucking** reached by crossing the Traun to the south of Wels and turning east on a minor road through Weißkirchen and on towards the A1/A25 *Autobahn* junction, is the 15C **church of St Leonard**. Notable are the finely painted lunettes in the vaulting of the choir, showing the *Archangel Michael* and *Sts Barbara and Catherine*, *Christ on the Mount of Olives*, the *Crucifixion*, *Christ with the Angelic Host*, below these an unknown bishop and a figure possibly representing the church's founder, further the *Twelve Apostles*. In the nave are medallions, against a background of stars, and showing the *Church Fathers* and the *Evangelists*.

Stift Kremsmünster

The **Benedictine Abbey of Kremsmünster** is reached south of Wels via roads 138 and 122. It was founded in 777 by Duke Tassilo III of Bavaria, who, however, was deposed in 788 for his treasonable manoeuvrings against Charlemagne. The monastery was destroyed by the Hungarians in the 10C, but was rebuilt and enjoyed two flourishing periods in the 13C and 17C, its mostly Baroque aspect being the result of intense building activity between the mid-17C and mid-18C. It was always a centre of learning, housing a **Ritterakademie** (an academy for the sons of the nobility) founded by Maria Theresia (but dissolved by Joseph II), which was a forerunner of Linz University, and a **Gymnasium** attended by Adalbert Stifter (see p 246).

The outer **Stiftshof** is entered through Jakob Prandtauer's so-called **Eichentor** (oak gate, 1723). To the east of it are the unique **fish-ponds** (Fischkalter, 1691), a series of five stone water-basins surrounded by antler-embellished arcades with Romano-Tuscan columns, three of the ponds having been designed by Carlo Antonio Carlone, and two added by Prandtauer in 1717. The ponds are fed by fountains incorporating sculptured mythological or biblical figures that are thematically associated with fish.

Proceeding south, you pass through the **Brückenturm**, built over the medieval moat, and cross the **Prälaten-Hof** to reach at the south-east corner the mid-13C church built in a transitional Romanesque and Gothic style, but remodelled in Baroque after 1680 by Antonio Carlone. The lofty and richly stuccoed (G.B. Carlone and G.B. Barberini) interior has 12 altars distributed in the choir and aisles, each with an altarpiece under a red damask baldachin held by angels, this being tilted at an angle towards the viewer. The altarpiece (1712) of the high altar represents the *Transfiguration* and is by Johann Andreas Wolf. More impressive than the rather average paintings are the kneeling angels made from marble which decorate the altars of the choir, together with standing ones on the side-altars; two of these (on the high altar) are by Johann Anton Pfaffinger, and six of them are by Johann Baptist Spaz (1713, on the western side-altars). Pfaffinger also made the monumental figures of *Sts Benedict and Scholastica* in front of the pillars of the crossing. However, the finest angel sculptures are the 16 others (1686) by Michael Zürn the Younger, a pupil of Bernini, whose benign influence is readily apparent.

On the right, near the entrance to the church, is the **Gunther Grave**, a relief stone sepulchre (c 1300) moved here from the crypt in 1948. 'Gunther' (perhaps a corruption of 'Theoto') was the son of the monastery's founder, Duke Tassilo, and died in a hunting accident near where Kremsmünster was subsequently built. The sepulchre's various decorative features (a sword, a hunting horn, a hound and a wild boar) recall this legend. In the lateral naves are frescoes by the Grabenberger brothers showing a cycle of Old Testament and New Testament scenes. The **Frauenkapelle** (reached from the east bay of the southern side-aisle) was built at right-angles to the church by Carlo Antonio Carlone in 1676–77. The frescoes here showing the *Life of the Virgin* are by Johann Benedict Dallinger, the stucco is by Johann Peter Spaz and Giovanni Battista Mazza, and there is an early 17C *pietà* on the right-hand side-altar.

From the southern end of the **Hof** there is access to the **Kaisersaal** (with Habsburg portraits), which has a ceiling fresco (1696) of the *Triumph of Light* by Melchior Steidl and stucco (1719) by Diego Francesco Carlone. The former imperial bedchamber is now the **Treasury**, containing the celebrated **Tassilo Chalice** (c 781) made of gilded copper with niello plaques on a silver background, a unique example of Carolingian workmanship. The plaque shows *Christ and the Symbols of the Evangelists*, and (on the foot) various saints. In addition to the chalice there is a disc-cross of c 1180, the *Codex Millenarius* (c 800) and other precious sacral objects, including two fine gold candlesticks from the turn of the 10C/11C. There is also an arms and armour collection.

The monastery's **picture gallery** includes works by Wolf Huber, Jan Breughel the Elder (*The Four Elements*), Jan Gossaert, Kremser Schmidt and others. The carved elephant stool (1553) is all that remains of the unfortunate beast brought to Vienna with the young Emperor's Spanish bride by Maximilian II in 1552—unhappily the climate did not agree with it and it expired a year later in the imperial menagerie at Kaiserebersdorf. Its first appearance near the Kärntnertor caused panic among the Wiener *Pöbel* (rabble), but it was later put on display outside the Stubentor and became something of a celebrity. The **library** has fine Italian stucco and possesses 400 MSS and 797 incunabula.

On the eastern periphery of the monastery buildings is the 70m **Observatory**, or 'Mathematical Tower' (1758, P. Anselm Desing), an eight-storey edifice accommodating collections in the fields of geology, palaeontology, mineralogy, physics, zoology, anthropology and astronomy, this last department including a 'Tychonic' sextant (named after Tycho Brahe) perhaps used by Johannes Kepler. There is a fine view from the roof terrace above the chapel: the latter was placed on the top storey to symbolise the fact that all the eight sciences culminated in an appropriately humble contemplation of God's glorious creation (the inscription over the entrance reads: *Ad Gloriam Altissimi*). Kremsmünster may be visited with a guided tour from Easter–end Oct, daily at 10.00, 11.00, 14.00 and 16.00; Nov–Easter at 11.00 and 14.00.

STEYR

● ● ● ● ● ●

Road 122 leads east from Kremsmünster to the ancient town of Steyr, the road passing through the spa of **Bad Hall**, known for its iodine waters taken by Bruckner, Grillparzer, Stifter, Mahler and other celebrities, and having several Jugendstil buildings from its boom time at the turn of the 19C/20C. The '*Stirapurch*' (fortified castle) of Steyr was built c 980 by the Traungau line, later to become the dukes of Styria; however, Steyr itself was incorporated into Upper Austria in 1254, together with the rest of the Traungau.

History

Lying at the confluence of the Enns and Steyr rivers, the town profited from the transport of pig-iron from Eisenerz to the Danube along the Enns (see p 266). Its staple right stipulated that wood and pig-iron produced north of the Erzberg had to be landed in the city, stored for at least three days and offered for sale; this enabled the burghers to acquire raw materials relatively cheaply, so that Steyr became a centre for the manufacture and export of weapons, especially to Germany and Venice.

Acquired by the Babenberg dukes in 1192, Steyr passed to the Habsburgs in 1282 and was given its urban statute in 1287. Subsequently the close trading contacts with Germany ensured that Lutheranism rapidly took root in the city. According to a contemporary account, there were only 16 Catholics left in Steyr in 1618, the year of the Defenestration of Prague, after which the tide turned against the Protestants. During the Counter-Reformation many of the artisans left the city, the entire company of cutlers, for instance, moving to Solingen in the Rheinland. Other factors in the city's decline were the repeated peasant revolts in the 16C and early 17C, as well as Turkish incursions, periodic flooding of the rivers and devastating fires.

After the Napoleonic occupation, Steyr revived in the 19C, largely through the invention (by Joseph Werndl, 1831–89) of a gun with an improved loading technique, the arms factory founded by Werndl in 1830 laying the basis of Steyr's modern prosperity. Perhaps because of its industrial development, Steyr was one of the first cities on the continent to acquire electric lighting in 1884. Today's industrial area is to the north-east of the main town, where the *Steyr-Daimler-Puch* works are situated, the successor (after two mergers) of Joseph Werndl's concern. From 1894 the firm also produced bicycles, and from 1918, motor cars. Göring switched the emphasis back to weapons production during World War II, which occasioned heavy bombing of Steyr; however, in the post-war period it was again motor production that predominated, the Steyr-Daimler-Puch four-wheel drive system becoming a world leader in auto-technology.

The old town is situated on a narrow strip of land between the Steyr and Enns rivers and retains three gates of its medieval fortifications. The attractive main square (**Stadtplatz**) has Gothic, Renaissance, Baroque and Rococo houses, of which the **Rathaus** (1778) was built by J.G. Hayberger, who was also the mayor at the time, and who created with this an exceptionally fine example of Rococo city architecture. Opposite it at no. 32 is the **Bummerlhaus** (1497), the usual emblem for the city, which retains its beautiful Gothic features: a soaring gabled roof, blind windows and Gothic tracery. Maximilian I stayed here on occasion while attempting to raise loans from the wealthy burghers to pay his mercenaries, evidently with some success, since a grateful Emperor granted Steyr the right to free election of its mayor in 1499. In the house at no. 6, Franz Schubert repeatedly stayed between 1825 and 1827 with his friend Sylvester Paumgartner, who presided over the *Steyrischen Musikverein* (Music Association), and who commissioned the immortal *Trout Quintet*. Schubert wrote appreciatively to a Viennese colleague about the beauties of the neighbourhood, including the female ones ('in the house where I live there are eight girls, nearly all of them pretty'). Notable also is the Baroque façade at no. 9 and the Gothic and Baroque **Star House** at no. 12, so-called from the star above the portal borne by two griffins. In the medallions above the second-storey windows are allegorical depictions of the human senses: *Smell*, *Taste*, *Hearing*, *Sight* and *Touch*.

In the southern part of the square is the former **Dominican Church** (1647), with a Rococo interior. The northern end of the square leads into the Enge Gasse and to the small **Zwischenbrücken Platz** (i.e. lying between the Enns bridge to the east of it and the Steyr bridge to the north). A plaque shows the high water mark here of the 1572 floods. Crossing the Steyr bridge, you come to the **Michaelerkirche** (1677) with a vivid fresco in the gable of the *Archangel Michael* (restored 1977), mirroring the theme of the altarpiece (1769) of the interior by Franz Xaver Gürtler. Nearby to the left is the former **Bürgerspitalkirche** (1305), remodelled in the 16C and now divided into dwellings. In the Kirchengasse leading north-west from the Michaelerplatz is the **Apothecary of the Holy Spirit** at no. 16, with a remarkable arcaded courtyard from the late 16C.

Continuing into the Gleinker Gasse, you reach the 16C customs gate (*Schnallentor*) with sgraffiti. The Taborweg to the right runs alongside the old cemetery, the name referring to the camp in 1467 of the Protestant Bohemian (Hussite) army which was involved in Friedrich III's struggle to obtain the city from a certain Jörg von Stein, to whom it had been pledged.

Returning towards the river, the **Museum Industrielle Arbeitswelt** (Museum of the World of Work) in a former factory in the Wehrgraben documents (since 1987) the life and work of the Steyr working-class over the last 100 years, specifically with reference to Catholic social doctrine (open Tues–Sun, PH 09.00–17.00).

Recrossing the River Steyr from here by the footbridge, you arrive below **Schloss Lamberg**, to which steps ascend. It retains the mighty keep of the original *Stirapurch*, itself built on the site of a Roman camp. It belonged to local, then to all-Austrian rulers, until acquired by Count Lamberg in 1666, was thereafter destroyed by fire in 1727 and rebuilt primarily by Johann Michael Prunner. In the courtyard is a fountain in the form of a deer-hound spewing water, the hound being a feature of the Lamberg coat of arms. It is surrounded by dwarf figures (J.B. Wuntscher, 1720) inspired by the *Augsburger Book of Dwarves* (1716), which satirised the human character, differently represented dwarves showing the diversely ludicrous aspects of the latter.

Passing through the extensive **Schlosspark**, the **Werndl Monument** (see Josef Werndl, above) is reached at its south-eastern end on the Enrica-Handel-Mazzetti-Promenade. If the promenade is followed south-west, a left turn brings you into the Bruckner-Platz, and (on the east side) to the **parish church of St Giles and St Koloman**, which was rebuilt by Friedrich Schmidt in neo-Gothic style in the 1880s, an idea originally favoured by the writer and conservationist, Adalbert Stifter, much earlier in the century (see p 247). The original Gothic church was built by the great Hans Puchspaum, one of the architects of St Stephen's Cathedral in Vienna. The plans for the Steyr church are preserved in the Vienna Academy of Fine Arts, but this edifice was destroyed by fire in 1522 and rebuilt in Baroque style in 1636.

In the interior Puchspaum's Gothic **sacramental niches** have survived on the north side of the apse, unusually conceived as miniature spires and recalling similar work in Nürnberg's St Lorenz church. The stone baldachin in the choir is also the work of Puchspaum. In the front windows of the south aisle is to be found 14C stained-glass, brought from Schloss Laxenburg near Vienna in exchange for windows sent from here for the Emperor Franz's folly of the Franzensburg, and showing *Sts Leopold and Agnes* (his consort) together with figures resurrected to eternal life at the Last Judgement. The **Marian window** in the east dates to 1523, while the **font** is Renaissance work (1569) with reliefs on the pewter cover. The tomb (1513) of one of the church's builders, Wolfgang Tenk is also notable. The north portal of the church is original Gothic, containing niche statuary (c 1410) attributed to the Master of Großlobming; in the tympanum, however, the scenes from the *Life of the Virgin* are mostly from the early 16C.

Adjacent is the Gothic **Margaretenkapelle** (originally a burial chapel) by Hans Puchspaum and dated to c 1430. Karl von Reslfeld painted the altarpiece (1727) of the *Fourteen Holy Helpers*. Nearby is the Gothic *Priest's House* where Bruckner stayed (and composed) several times between 1886 and 1894.

At Grünmarkt 26 to the south-west of the Stadtplatz is the **Municipal Museum** (open Nov–March, Wed–Sun, 10.00–15.00, April–Oct, Tues–Sun, 10.00–15.00), which contains objects of vernacular culture and in particular items relating to the iron industry. At the south end of the Grünmarkt (i.e. the vegetable market) is the impressive **Neutor** (1573), a survival of the fortifications. From mid-June to the end of September the **Steyrtal narrow gauge railway** (1889) runs from the city up to Grünberg on Sundays at 09.30, 14.00 and 18.30; from Grünberg to Steyr at 07.30, 11.30 and 17.00 (☎ 0732 2352433).

Around Steyr

On the western outskirts of Steyr is **Christkindl**, with a Rococo pilgrimage church (1725) begun by Giovanni Battista Carlone and completed by Jakob Prandtauer. The cupola fresco of the *Assumption* (1710) in the interior is by Karl von Reslfeld, who also painted the *Nativity* for the left-hand side-altar. The focus of the church is the tiny (12cm) wax icon of the *Christ child* (*Christkind*), from which the church and hamlet take their name, and which has been set in a Rococo frame with rocaille ornamentation. Throughout Advent a remarkable **mechanical crib** made by Karl Klauda, and having 300 figures driven by a chain mechanism and accompanied by organ music, is operating in the *Pfarrhof* (parsonage) here. Since 1950 a special post office has been set up each year in the church at Christmas to answer letters addressed by Austrian children to the 'Christkind' and to send greetings to philatelists worldwide.

Garsten to the south on road 115 was originally a Benedictine monastery built (1693) by Pietro Francesco and Carlo Antonio Carlone (father and son), but since 1850 used as a prison. Its **Church of the Assumption** is also the work of the Carlone family, Giovanni Battista having been responsible for the rich white and pink stucco, the latter being so pervasive (as one commentator puts it) that it suggests a veritable *horror vacui* on the part of the builders. The stucco contrasts spectacularly with the turned columns and gold and black colour scheme of the altars and pulpit. The frescoes in the nave and summer sacristy are by the brothers Grabenberger and Antonio Galliardi, and show the *Life of the Virgin*. Under the organ loft the *Life of King David* is represented and elsewhere there are depictions of Old Testament figures traditionally regarded as the forerunners of the Virgin Mary, together with the *Apostles* etc. In the presbytery the frescoes (1627) dealing with the *Triumph of the Eucharist* are inspired by Rubens tapestries. Altar paintings of considerable quality are by Peter Strudel, Innozenz Turriani, Joachim von Sandrart, Karl von Reslfeld, Andreas Wolff and Johann Heiss, while Reslfeld's frescoes celebrating the 1683 victory over the Turks above the music gallery are especially notable.

ENNS

The River Enns forms the border between Upper and Lower Austria (and in the distant past that between the Bavarian Eastern March and the area settled by Slavs) as it runs from Steyr to Enns, which claims to be the oldest town in Austria.

History of Enns

Enns was raised to a *municipium* by Caracalla in 212, and received its charter exactly 1000 years later in 1212 from the Babenberg duke. (However, St Pölten believes its charter of 1159 decides the matter in its favour.) Enns stands on the west bank of the river, close to the site of Roman *Lauriacum* to the north-west, so-called from the Celtic tribal name of *Laurios* which has been preserved in the district of the city called *Lorch*. In late Roman times, *Lauriacum* became the base for the Danubian naval flotilla for the Province of

Noricum. Charlemagne encamped near Enns during his successful campaign against the Avars in 791. The town also has ancient Christian associations, since Florian, a converted Roman official, was martyred here by drowning with a millstone round his neck in AD 304. In the following century it was also associated with the missionary and diplomatic activity of St Severin (see p 120).

St Florian

St Florian is one of the most often represented *Schutzheilige* (guardian saints) of Austria, usually being depicted as a Roman soldier pouring water on a burning house, occasionally, however, with a millstone round his neck and watched by an eagle. His story is not without pathos: at the time of Diocletian he had exchanged his military calling for a post in the administration, in which capacity he learned that 40 soldiers had been incarcerated in *Lauriacum* for their Christian beliefs. He entered a powerful plea on their behalf with the authorities, confessing at the same time his own allegiance to Christianity. After torture failed to move him from this persuasion, he was to have been thrown into the river from the bridge at Enns, but none of his fellow Romans among the soldiers of the garrison would undertake to do the deed. Finally, a man wishing to ingratiate himself with the Roman Governor pushed him into the water. His body was washed up by neighbouring cliffs and an eagle is said to have settled by the corpse to protect it from desecration. Subsequently a matron from Traun named Valeria collected the body and buried it at a place where a chapel was later built, eventually to become the site of the great monastery of Sankt Florian (see p 257).

The medieval (1193–94) fortifications of the city are rather well preserved with no less than six towers or remnants of them surviving. On the **Hauptplatz** is the 60m high **Stadtturm** (1568), perhaps built by a certain Hans von Mainz and combining the functions of observation tower, clock-tower and firewatch, a typical expression of the self-confidence and presumption of self-governance vested in the Protestant burghers. However, a tactful sop to the authorities may be seen below the picturesque clock-face on the south side, namely the Habsburg coat of arms showing the double-headed eagle. The view from the top of the tower is worth the strenuous climb of 157 irregular steps.

At no. 19 on the Hauptplatz is the **Alte Rathaus** (c 1489), formerly the Mint, which now houses the **Stadtmuseum Lauriacum** (open Nov–March, Sun and PH, 10.00–12.00, 14.00–16.00, April–Oct, Tues–Sun, 10.00–12.00, 14.00–16.00). Its most important exhibits are from the Roman period, especially a rare fresco of *Amor and Psyche* taken from the ceiling of a Roman villa, and 25 bronze statuettes of Roman legionaries. In the Rococo former Council Chamber may be seen a copy of the Enns city charter, dated 12 April 1212.

From the north end of the Hauptplatz the so-called **Frauenturm** is reached, part of the afore-mentioned fortifications and owing its name to a church (now demolished) built on to it (*Kirche Unsere Liebe Frau am Anger*). On the north wall of the tower may be seen Maltese crosses, the symbol of the Knights of St John, who had a hospice adjacent and a chapel inside the Frauenturm. The 14C Gothic frescoes of the interior, which may be visited with group tours of the city, show the *Passion* and a rather unusual *Christ Crucified on the Tree of Life*.

South of the Hauptplatz is the **parish church of Our Lady of the Snow** (1300, a reference to the foundation legend of Santa Maria Maggiore in Rome) which formerly belonged to the Minorites. On its south side is a late Gothic cloister, restored to its pristine state in the 1970s, the galleries that had been added above it being removed at this time. The monastery church was originally a Gothic hall church, but converted to two aisles in the early 15C, when the rib vaulting of the nave was added. The modern (1975) stained glass of the choir (*St Francis's Song of the Sun*) is by Markus Prachensky. The **Wallseerkapelle** attached to the northern wall was endowed around 1343 by the brothers Reinprecht and Friedrich von Wallsee, whose family supplied the Burgraves of Enns up to 1345 and were the scions of an ancient Swabian line that came to Austria with Rudolf of Habsburg in the 13C. The chapel's design is unusual, having a double nave opening into a triple-aisled choir, where the altar stands centrally between four columns, thus creating an ambulatory. The sandstone *Madonna* in the choir dates to 1300.

In the western district of the town (*Lorch*) is the **Church of St Lawrence**, built on three preceding sanctuaries, the earliest having been a Celtic-Roman temple of c AD 180, which was superceded by a Roman *cella* at the time of Caracalla, then by a Carolingian church. The excavations in the choir revealing these earlier buildings are the subject of a display in the undercroft and presbytery. A limewood *Madonna* (1330) and a *pietà* of 1430, together with parts of a **winged altar** (1530) graphically showing the *Massacre of the Innocents* are the main objects of interest in the interior. The adjacent **charnel house** dates to 1507 and has a Baroque *Ecce homo*, in which Pontius Pilate is represented wearing the robe of the Turkish Grand Vizier!

THE PYHRN-EISENWURZEN
• •

Continuing south (12km) from Kremsmünster (see p 261) on road 138, you pass **Schlierbach** in the **Pyhrn-Eisenwurzen** region, most of which is in Lower Austria (see p 117). Its name alludes to the iron ore reserves of the area (*Eisenwurzen*), while *Pyhr* is the Celtic word for a mountain.

The **Cistercian former Nunnery** (1355) at Schlierbach is sited, uncharacteristically, on a hill (the order's rule normally required foundations to be in valleys or hollows as a symbol of humility, because Eberhard of Wallsee offered them a castle here. After dissolution in 1556, the convent was refounded as a monastery (1620), with monks from Stift Rein in Styria. The monastery's Baroque church (1683) was built by Pietro Francesco Carlone and his son Carlo Antonio. Its interior is considered by many to be over-cluttered with Baroque stucco in brown, red, black and gold, effectively set off, however, by the dazzling white of the vault. It is the work (1683–85) of Giovanni Battista and Bartolomeo Carlone. The entire decoration of the church is an unparalleled example of the Marian cult, showing the Virgin's symbolic forerunners in the Old Testament her relatives and her companions through life, the eulogistic instances of the Loreto Litany, Mary's role as Queen of the Patriarchs, the Prophets and the Martyrs, etc., and all of this culminating dramatically in the high altar showing the *Assumption* and *Glorification of the Virgin*. The monastery buildings and cloister may be visited on application to the porter (visits are possible May–Nov). In the cloister is a striking Gothic wooden *Madonna*, and there is a Rococo library (1712) with *trompe l'oeil* frescoes, probably designed by Johann Michael Prunner. The **Bernhardisaal** was reserved for imperial use, and has a ceiling fresco eulogising Karl VI as *Apollo, God of the Arts*.

At **Inzersdorf im Kremstal** to the south-west of Schlierbach is the modern **Marienkirche** (1975), containing a gilded *Madonna and Child* dating to 1430. Rejoining road 138, you continue south to **Micheldorf**, nestling below the 'Calvary Mountain' of St George, excavations in whose church have revealed pre-Christian and early Christian sanctuaries. The late Gothic pilgrimage church at **Frauenstein**, 4km to the south, has a *Madonna sheltering Supplicants with her Cloak* (c 1515) on the high altar, attributed to Gregor Erhart of Ulm, and one of the finest examples of this much-loved image. Among the supplicants are to be seen Kaiser Maximilian I and his minister, Florian Waldorf (on the left), while the female figures on the right are headed by Maximilian's wife, Bianca Sforza.

Road 138 leads south to **Windischgarsten**, the name recalling that it was originally colonised by Slavs; beyond it is **Spital am Pyhrn**, named after a hospice founded by Bishop Otto II of Bamberg in 1199. Its **Church of the Assumption** was splendidly rebuilt in Baroque style in the 1730s, probably by Johann Michael Prunner, and has striking illusionistic frescoes by Bartolomeo Altomonte, some of his finest work, showing the *Apostles round the empty Coffin of the Virgin* and *Mary carried to Heaven by Angels*. The tempietto of the high altar (1769) is by Veit Königer of Graz, while the richly ornamented pulpit is counterpointed by a glorification of St John of Nepomuk opposite. To the south of the village is the 15C **church of St Leonard** (a note on the door indicates where the key is kept), which has upper and lower parts separated by spiral steps. In the lower church is a fresco of 1476 showing the *Heavenly Jerusalem*, while the upper church has fine reticulated vaulting.

The **Felsbildermuseum** in the town (open May–Oct, Tues–Sun, 10.00–12.00, 14.00–17.00, Dec–April, Wed & Sun 15.00–18.30, Sat 10.00–12.00 and 15.00–18.30) has extensive documentation of the pre-history of the region.

THE SALZKAMMERGUT
• • • • • • • • • • • • • • • • • • • •

Beyond Wels (see p 260) the road enters the region of the **Attergau**, which spreads to the north of the attractive **Attersee**. Road 1 leads west to **Vöcklabruck**, one of the larger towns of the area, and the gateway to the **Salzkammergut**. It was founded at a crossing-point on the Rivers Vöckla and Ager and grew prosperous under the patronage of Duke Albrecht the Wise and his son Rudolf the Founder in the 14C. After being pledged to Bavaria, it returned to the Habsburgs in 1816 and developed rapidly in the 19C. The 16C gate-houses at either end of the Stadtplatz are decorated with frescoes, the **Untere Stadtturm** featuring Maximilian I flanked by the coats of arms of Austria and Burgundy (he married Mary of Burgundy in 1477). The **church of St Giles**, north of the bridge over the Vöckla, is a fine work by Carlo Antonio Carlone with ceiling frescoes of the *Life of the Virgin* and the *Passion*. In the southern

Schöndorf part of the town is the remarkable cemetery **church of the Assumption**, with its unusual western towers placed one behind the other, the result of an incomplete rebuilding in 1450. In the interior the organ loft, with its donkey-arched balustrade in a wave-like horizontal rhythm, is also a rarity. The four Baroque statues (1772, to the west) of *Sts Anthony, Wolfgang, Blaise* and *Erasmus* are by Johann Georg Schwanthaler. The neo-Gothic altar enshrines a *Madonna* of 1440.

At **Gampern**, reached by minor roads to the south-west of Vöcklabruck, the **parish church** has a **winged altar** (c 1500), a major work by Lienhart Astl of Gmunden. In the shrine, the crowned *Mother of God* is shown with a Turkish head at her feet; next to her are the patrons of the church, *Sts Remigius and Pantaleon*. The wings show the *Annunciation, Visitation, Nativity* and *Presentation in the Temple*. Above is *Remigius* again with *Pantaleon* and *Sebastian*, at the top the *Resurrected Mary* and *John the Evangelist*. These are relief panels for feast-days; the work-day panels are painted and show scenes from the *Passion*. With the *Last Judgement* on the rear, the iconography encompasses all the cardinal points of the Christian faith.

The Attersee

At **Schörfling** on the northern tip of the **Attersee** is a Gothic hall church attributed to Stefan Wultinger, but more interesting for most visitors is the lovely **Schloss Kammer** on a promontory jutting into the lake, and reached by an *allée* of lime-trees; one of Gustav Klimt's most appealing works is his picture of this *allée* with the Schloss beyond, painted during one of his regular summer holidays (1908–12) at Villa Oleander in Kammer. 171m deep, the Attersee is the largest of the necklace of Salzkammergut lakes (**Mondsee, Wolfgangsee, Attersee** and **Traunsee**), which constitute the area known as the **Äusseres Salzkammergut**. The lake is fed by the Seeache in the south-west, in fact an overspillage from the Mondsee, and flows out at Kammer via the Ager river. It is rich in fish, especially the indigenous *Reinanke*. At **Abtsdorf** just to the south of Attersee, the **Laurentius Church** has some fine statuary by Meinrad Guggenbichler. Above the village was situated the 9C Carolingian palace of Atarnhova (885), later a powerful medieval castle.

The *Autobahn* A1, heading west, skirts the northern end of the Attersee, the eastern shore of the lake having little of artistic interest, although **Steinbach** will attract Mahlerians. The composer stayed here in the summers of 1893–96, erecting a hut (*Schnitzelputzhäusl*) in the garden of his lodgings, where he composed parts of the 2nd, 3rd (*Steinbacher*) and 4th Symphonies (to visit the hut, enquire at the adjacent Gasthof, where the composer was a guest). However, the *Autobahn* goes on to **Mondsee**, a picturesque resort on the lake of the same name, which is dominated by the **Schafberg**.

The area has been settled from earliest times, the remains of lacustrian dwellings on piles having been of sufficient significance to merit the term *Mondseekultur* (neolithic, c 3000–2000 BC) among archaeologists. A **Museum (Österreichisches Pfahlbaumuseum)** documents the local archaeological finds and is well worth visiting on Marschall-Wrede-Platz (open May–mid-Oct, Tues–Sun, 10.00–18.00, mid- to end Oct weekends and PH only, 10.00–17.00). A monastery existed at Mondsee from the mid-8C (founded by the Bavarian Duke

Odilo II), of which the barockised church survives. This handsome building with its lightly concave façade (1730) is characterised by a raised choir and features five altars carved after 1679 by Meinrad Guggenbichler. In particular the **Corpus Christi altar** (1684, in the north aisle) is regarded as his masterpiece, with its columns wreathed with gilded vine-leaves framing a picture of the *Last Supper* by C.P. List, each column resting on a group of four putti draped in bunches of grapes. The church retains Gothic elements such as the net vault and a remarkable late Gothic **portal** (1487) to the sacristy on the north side of the choir, surmounted by seven Gothic statues (*Sts Wolfgang, Benedict, Peter, Paul, Mary* and *John the Evangelist*, with *Christ the Redeemer*). Its iron door of 1482 is also of rare quality. Mondsee's other sight is the **open-air museum** at Hilfbergstraße 7, which has examples of peasant architecture, and is open April: weekends & PH, 10.00–18.00; May–mid-Oct: Tues–Sun, 10.00–18.00; rest of Oct, weekends & PH, 10.00–17.00.

North of the Mondsee stretches the **Zellersee** (or **Irrsee**), on whose northern shore the hamlet of **Oberhofen** has a church with three Guggenbichler altars (a key may be obtained at the priest's house). Road 154 leads south from Mondsee, however, to St Gilgen in Land Salzburg and the Wolfgangsee. (The picturesque village of St Wolfgang with its parish church and Michael Pacher's celebrated altar are described on p 321).

INNERES SALZKAMMERGUT

The **Innere Salzkammergut** describes the area around the **Obere Trauntal** (Upper Traun Valley) and the **Hallstättersee**, a roughly oval slab of land stretching out from Upper Austria between Land Salzburg and Styria, and boxed in by the **Toten Gebirge** in the east, the **Dachstein** in the south, and the **Höllengebirge** in the north. The western periphery is constituted by the **Gosau Valley** backing up to the spectacular **Gosaukamm** and the **Tennengebirge** beyond.

Bad Ischl

From St Gilgen, road 158 runs along the south-western shore of the Wolfgangsee past Strobl to the spa of Bad Ischl (Celtic '*Iscla*'), lying between the **Ischl** and **Traun** rivers, and famous for its salt production. The 'white gold' was first extracted here in the mid-13C and exploitation was encouraged under Maximilian I, although the business subsequently declined in the years of strife between the strongly Protestant Ischler and the ruling house, whereby for a while the former were punished with the withdrawal of market privileges. In the 19C, after the first salt-water bath was opened in 1823, Bad Ischl became fashionable for its cures, a particular boost to its fortunes being the cure apparently effected by the waters for the Archduchess Sophie's childlessness: the remarkable result was the birth of Franz Joseph (1830), followed by Maximilian (1832) and Karl Ludwig (1833), who were thus somewhat irreverently dubbed the 'salt princes'. On 19 August 1853, Franz Joseph was betrothed in Bad Ischl to his cousin, Elizabeth of Bavaria, in his parents' house at Esplanade 10 (now the Municipal Museum). Franz Joseph and Elisabeth received the former villa of a certain Dr Eltz as a wedding gift in 1854, and thereafter Bad Ischl became the focus of the *beau monde* of the Austro-Hungarian monarchy, a favoured resort of literati, actors, and especially composers (Bruckner, Mahler, Brahms, Strauss, while Franz Lehár even owned a villa here from 1910 until his death). There is much architecture from the 19C, Ischl's heyday, including the **Stadttheater** (1827), a drinking hall for taking the cures (1831), a casino (1840, now a store) and the **imperial villa** (*Kaiservilla*, enlarged 1857).

The **Kaiservilla** stands at the foot of the Jainzenberg and is Biedermeier in origin, the additions of 1857 being a slightly more pompous form of neo-classical. Its left wing is still inhabited by a Habsburg (the great grandson of Franz Joseph), but the rest can be visited with a tour (open Easter, and at weekends in April, and May–mid-Oct, daily 09.00–12.00, 13.00–16.45). It was in this villa that Franz Joseph signed the ultimatum to Serbia and also dictated the declaration of war on 28 July 1914. If this does not sufficiently lower your spirits, the 50,000 hunting trophies on the walls assuredly will (the luckless 2000th chamois to receive the imperial bullet has even been stuffed and put on display). The villa is perhaps the dreariest sight in all Austria, the gloomy sanctuary of a mediocre personality and singularly lacking in taste, gaiety or comfort. The extensive garden (**Kaiserpark**) with its ornamental fountain by Viktor Tilgner is a breath of fresh air in more senses than one. The **Photography Museum of Upper Austria** is located in the **Marmor Schlößl** (once a summer house) of the Kaiserpark and is open April–Oct, daily 09.30–17.00.

The **Municipal Museum** (Esplanade 10, open Tues, Thur–Sun, 10.00–17.00, Wed 14.00–19.00; Feb–Easter, Fri–Sun, 10.00–17.00) has vernacular objects and documents the history of the Salzkammergut with particular reference to the salt-mining. At Sulzbach 132 there is a **Motor Museum** (open April–Oct, daily 09.00–18.00) of more than passing interest. The **Lehár Villa** (open at Easter and May–Sept, daily 09.00–12.00, 14.00–17.00; see p 247) is at Lehárkai 8 and may be visited with a guided tour. Of interest also is the **Haenel-Pancera-Familienmuseum** at Concordiastrasse 3 (open May–Sept, daily 09.00–17.00) featuring seven rooms decorated in various styles and with pictures by Rembrandt, Caravaggio and others, together with autographs, furniture etc.

The **Salzbergwerk** (salt-mine) at **Perneck** to the south-east may be visited (open daily mid-May to end of June 09.00–16.00, July–mid-Sept 10.00–17.00). For many visitors one of the most appealing attractions of Bad Ischl is the **Hofkonditorei Zauner** in Pfarrgasse, which was patronised by Edward VII on his visit to Franz Joseph in 1907. It was on this occasion that the English monarch persuaded his Austrian counterpart to a short ride in a motor car, an experience Franz Joseph took care never to repeat.

The **Salzkammergut Bundesstrasse** leads south along the River Traun to **Bad Goisern**, with its iodine spa, lying between the **Ramsaugebirge** and the **Predigstuhl**. The market-town is famous for its hand-made shoes with side-lacing known as '*Goiserer*' (Franz Joseph himself had a pair), examples of which may be seen in the **Heimatmuseum** (open June–Sept, daily 09.30–11.30). The contents of the latter include also models of peasant houses. In the **Marian chapel** of the Catholic parish church are late Gothic statues from the Lienhard Astl school, as well as panels from the workshop of Rueland Frueauf the Elder of Salzburg. The nearby **open-air museum** at Anzenau 1 (open May–Sept) is chiefly concerned with vernacular wooden building, but also has a traditional bakery operating on Saturdays.

Hallstatt

South of Bad Goisern a minor road leads south from road 166 along the Hallstätter lakeside, and reaches, towards the far end of the lake, the ancient town of Hallstatt. This is a favourite excursion for Austrians because of the scenic drive along the western shore, as well as attractions such as the salt-mine, which has been in operation for 2800 years, the cable-car trips up the Dachstein (the highest point reached is Krippenstein, 2074m) and the ice-caves at Obertraun. Because of overcrowding, the town is closed to vehicles and you will be directed to car parks outside the periphery. When the summer season is in full swing, it may be better to arrive by ferry from the north-east bank of the lake (Obersee), the north-west bank (Steeg), the south-east bank (Obertraun), or from the railway station opposite the town: access by boat was indeed the only possibility until the west bank road was built in 1890.

The early Iron Age habitation (**Hallstattkultur**, 800–500 BC) has left many remnants and is documented in the **Museum of Pre-History** at Seestrasse 56 (open 22 March–30 April, daily 10.00–16.00, May–Sept 10.00–18.00, Nov–March, 14.00–16.00). A footpath leads from the market square to the Iron Age excavation area (*Gräberfeld*) and to the above-mentioned **salt-mine** (open daily, May–26 Sept, 09.30–16.30, 27 Sept–1 Nov, 09.30–15.00), or you can take the charming **Salzbergbahn** (funicular) from the **Lahn** district of the town. Its terminus is close to the **Rudolfsturm** (with a superb view of Hallstatt), part of a ruined castle built in 1284 to protect the mines from the predations of the Salzburg Prince-Bishops, the town's great rivals in the salt trade. From 1607 the salt was conveyed in solution along channels (*Soleleitungen*) to Ebensee, 15km north of Ischl, where it was refined and taken by barge to Gmunden.

A climb up the cliff-steps overlooking the town brings you to the Catholic **parish church of the Assumption**, with a fine Romanesque tower (the Baroque upper part is a 1750 addition). The church was rebuilt at the beginning of the 16C, having as elsewhere (e.g. Hall in Tyrol) separate naves for the burghers and the miners. In the southern choir is the late Gothic **Marienaltar** (c 1520), a masterwork of Lienhart Astl commissioned by the miners and having an iconography based on the *Seven Joys of Mary*. The painted wings show (during Lent) *Jesus as a Twelve-Year-Old Boy in the Temple*, the *Marriage Feast at Cana*, *Jesus's Leave-Taking of his Mother*, and *Christ Resurrected*. On minor feast-days and during Advent, the outer wings are open and various scenes are visible: *Mary in the Temple*, the *Meeting of Joachim and Anne*, the *Parents of Mary*, the *Golden Gates*, the *Visitation*, *Mary's Betrothal to Joseph*; and beneath these *Joseph's Dream*, *the Circumcision*, the *Adoration of the Three Kings*, and the *Flight into Egypt*. Normally the altar is kept open, showing the shrine with relief figures of *Mary as the Queen of Heaven* flanked by *Sts Catherine and Barbara* (the former being the patron of the wheelwrights, the latter of the miners); on the wings to right and left of the shrine may be seen the *Birth of Mary*, the *Annunciation*, the *Presentation in the Temple* and the *Dormition*. In the confessional chapel to the north is a small winged altar of 1450 with a *Crucifixion* on the middle panel. To the north side of the church is the remarkable **ossuary** (c 1600), which is the lower part of St Michael's Chapel, and has rows of skulls (some 1200 in all) arranged above stacks of bones, the dates of death being painted on them, together with floral and plant decoration, crosses, etc., also the names of the deceased. It is still in use.

Along the southern shore of the Hallstätter See the road leads to **Obertraun**, near to which (2km) the **Dachsteinseilbahn** (cable car) takes you to the extraordinary **Dachstein-Riseneishöhle** (Ice Caves, guided tours May–15 Oct, daily 08.30–17.00). Adjacent is the largest of this cave-system, the so-called **Mammuthöhle**, a limestone labyrinth of 40km with beautiful stalactite features (guided tours from May–15 Oct, daily 08.30–15.00). Next to the cable-car station on **Schönbergalm** (1338m) is the **Cave Museum** (open May–Sept, daily 08.45–16.30). Twenty minutes' walk from the *Gasthaus Koppenrast* in the valley is the **Koppenbrüllerhöhle** with an underground stream flowing through it (guided tours May–Sept, daily, 09.00–17.00). The main caves were first explored in 1910 by a Wagner admirer, Hermann Bock, who named the ice-chambers after Wagnerian characters or places (*Tristandom, Parsifaldom*, etc.). The ice in the caves is up to 25m thick and produces some magnificent spectacles; obviously warm clothing is required for visiting. From Obertraun the road climbs sharply, with fine views of the lake, before crossing the border into Styria and heading for Bad Aussee.

Around the Traunsee

North of Bad Ischl road 145 heads along the Traun valley to **Ebensee** at the southern tip of the **Traunsee**, above which a cable car ascends to the **Feuerkogel** (1592m), a peak in the **Höllengebirge**. Modern salt refineries at Ebensee have replaced the earlier (1607) evaporating houses; after processing, the salt was conveyed across the lake, originally on barges, but from 1839 by a steamship operated by two Englishmen.

The Traunsee is the second largest lake of the Salzkammergut after the Attersee and the deepest in Austria at 191m; to the Romans it was the *lacus felix*, and is certainly less gloomy than the Hallstätter See, although the water is cold and the **Traunstein** (1691m) to the east is a brooding presence.

The road runs along the western shore to **Traunkirchen**, where the parish church is worth visiting for its remarkable **Fisherman's Pulpit** (1753), representing the miraculous draught of fishes (*St Luke, Ch.5, Vv. 1-11*). The pulpit (carved by an unknown local master) is in the form of a fishing boat and shows the brothers James and John hauling up a net bursting with fish: behind them is Jesus in the act of blessing Peter, who kneels before him. On the overhead canopy is the figure of St Francis Xaver, suggesting a Jesuit commission, the idea of christ as 'fisher of souls' being appropriate to the order's mission, and of course also appropriate in a village where so many earned a living from harvesting the waters of the lake. A local custom also unites religion with the traditional life of the lakeside dwellers: each year at Corpus Christi, Christ's sermon on the Sea of Galilee is symbolically re-enacted on the Traunsee, the priest celebrating mass from a boat.

At **Altmünster**, further north, the Gothic parish church of St Benedict (1480, the only relic of an earlier Benedictine abbey) has an altarpiece (1636) by

Joachim Sandrart showing the *Death of St Benedict*. The altar's fine statues of *Sts George and Florian with angels*, together with that of the *Archangel Michael* under the organ loft, are the work of Michael Zürn the Younger and were additions made at the end of the 17C. The church also possesses a Romanesque font behind the pulpit showing a lamb (*Agnus Dei*), a fish, a goat, a dove and an eagle as Christian symbols. In the **All Saints Chapel**, to the right of the entrance, is an epitaph for Count Adam Herberstorff, who put down an uprising of the local peasants in 1626 with great ferocity, while another feature of interest is a sandstone altar of 1518, showing influence of the Lombardy Renaissance. At nearby Traunblick Wagner was a guest of Otto and Mathilde Wesendonk (to whom his celebrated song-cycle was dedicated) and composed part of *Tristan and Isolde* here.

The road continues north to **Gmunden**, passing at 2km **Seeschloss Orth**, situated on an island reached by a wooden footbridge. The Schloss dates to the 14C, although a fortified tower stood here as early as the 12C, and was later being remodelled in Renaissance style, when the arcades of its triangular courtyard were made. In the barockised chapel are remnants of frescoes (c 1634) and a **statue** of the *Madonna* dating to 1450. The rooms are now partly taken up with the Municipal Museum for periodic exhibitions, and there is also a restaurant and café. At the landward end of the footbridge is the **Landschloss Orth** (1626), built by Count Adam Herberstorff and now belonging to the Austrian Forestry Commission. It was bought in 1876 (two years before he bought the **Seeschloss**) by Archduke Johann Nepomuk Salvator of the Tuscan line of the Habsburgs, who was a nephew of Franz Joseph. He renounced his title in 1889 to marry a commoner, taking the name of 'Orth', and thereafter was banned from living in Austria-Hungary. In 1890 he sailed in a cement freighter for La Plata from Hamburg, and from La Plata set off round Cape Horn in another ship he commanded himself. The vessel disappeared without trace, but is thought to have sunk in the night of 20–21 July 1890, with no survivors. Schloss Orth is the setting for a long-running and very popular TV soap opera.

Gmunden

The town of Gmunden was strategically placed on the salt transport route from Hallstatt, prompting the Habsburgs to erect a customs and tax post on the bridge at the north end of the lake, which flowed into the now expanded River Traun. It became the centre of the economically important Salzkammergut, whose commercial secrets were considered so valuable that a special pass was still required of travellers in the 19C. A subsidiary export of the town from at least the 18C was the Gmundner faience, with its decorative motifs taken from religious tradition or from peasant and artisan life. A tour of the ceramics factory at Keramikstrasse 24 takes place in July and August (Tues and Thur, 09.30).

The **Rathaus** on **Rathausplatz** is Renaissance in origin, later barockised and with an 18C **Glockenspiel** in the top arcade; the bells of the latter are made of Gmunden ceramic, and play different tunes at different hours (a poster on the wall lists these). Under an arcade in the Kammerhofgasse is the entrance to the interesting **Stadtmuseum** (open May–Oct, Tues–Sat, 10.00–12.00, 14.00–17.00, Sun & PH 10.00–12.00). It contains sections showing Gmunden faience, sculpture of the 16C to 18C, documentation of the salt trade and memorial rooms to two prominent summertime visitors to Gmunden: Johannes Brahms and the playwright Friedrich Hebbel (1818–63). The latter wrote dramas ahead of their time in their treatment of feminist issues. A splendid new *Museum für historische Sanitärobjekte* (Trauhgasse 4) displays decorative toilets (open May–Oct, Tues–Sat, 10.00–12.00 and 14.00–17.00, Sun & PH 10.00–12.00).

The **parish church of the Virgin Mary and the Epiphany** in the upper part of the town contains a particularly impressive *Adoration of the Magi* (1678) by Thomas Schwanthaler on the high altar, while the flanking figures of *Elisabeth* and *Zacharias* are works (1685) by Michael Zürn the Younger, whose workshop was in Gmunden from 1681. A long-standing custom in Gmunden is for the 'Three Magi' to arrive by boat at the town on the eve of 'Three Kings' Day' (i.e. Epiphany, 6 January) and to process with musical accompaniment into the Epiphany Church.

Gmunden is a pleasant place to stay and flâneurs will find a wealth of historic architecture to admire around the town, such as picturesque galleries, corner bays, and towers, not a few of these dating back to the Renaissance or Gothic periods. Across the River Traun to the north-east of Gmunden is **Schloss Cumberland** (1886), home to the last Duke (son of George V) who died here in 1923. The Traunsee itself is plied by the oldest Austrian lake steamer, the *Gisela*, named after Franz Joseph's daughter and in operation since 1872. A fine view may be had from the *Grünberg* (1004m) rising from the east bank of the lake, and reached by cable-car from the suburb of **Weyer**.

If you follow road 120 east from Gmunden and bear south at Mühldorf, you come (after a 23km climb) to the delightful **Grünau im Almtal**, whose **parish church** contains an unusual high altar brought here from Kremsmünster, of which the church was a dependency. It was made in 1618, primarily by the Bavarian Hans Degler, but incorporates late Gothic remnants. The figures in the lower part (*James the Elder, Melchisedek, John the Baptist*) are attributed to Degler, while the superstructure and its carved figures date to 1531 and are by Johannes Peysser (note the representation of *God the Father*, with one foot resting on the globe). In the left-hand side-altar are sculptures of the *Nativity* and *Christ Pantocrator* by Michael Zürn the Younger. Enquire at the priest's house to see the late 15C *pietà* and a sculpture of *St Wolfgang* from the circle of Lienhard Astl.

Grünau began to profit from summer tourism when the railway reached it in 1911, at which time several comfortable hotels were built. One of the most attractive of these is the *Romantik Hotel Almtalhof* (☎ 07616-82040), situated on the rushing River Alm amongst birch, chestnuts and sycamores and with a garden where the lilac blooms. Its well appointed rooms have pine furniture made by the proprietor (Karl Leithner) himself, and there is gourmet Austrian cuisine.

THE INNVIERTEL

Road 129 leads west of Linz to **Eferding**, whose late Gothic **church of St Hippolytus** (completed 1505) contains tombs of the local lords (Schaunbergs, and later Starhembergs). The south portal (1471) impresses with its Gothic tracery and statues (1497) of the *Virgin Mary* at the centre, flanked by *St Giles* (right) and *St Hippolytus* (left). **Schloss Starhemberg** to the north-east dates to the 16C with 18C alterations and contains a display concerning the family history of the owners (open Sun and PH, 09.00–12.00). The **Spitalskirche** near the south-east corner of the **Stadtplatz** has frescoes of 1430 in the **Magdalene**

Chapel and an elegant high altar (1623) and pulpit. Among the tombs is that of the founder of the church in 1325, Rudolf von Schifer.

Stift Engelhartszell

Road 130 leads along the Danube beyond the **Schlögener Schlinge**, a dramatic near 180 degree meander of the river, eventually reaching **Engelhartszell**. Austria's only Trappist Monastery, originally a Cistercian foundation of 1295 called **Engelszell**, i.e. *Cella Angelica*, situated here since 1975. It was intended to provide a retreat for the hard-working monks of Wilhering and also to minister to travellers on the Danube. Its church dates to the mid-18C, after a fire destroyed its predecessor in 1699.

The semi-abstract frescoes in the nave are modern works by Fritz Fröhlich and show the *Virgin Mary accompanied by the Nine Choirs of Angels*. Otherwise the ornamentation is Rococo, with fine stucco and (in the choir) Bartolomeo Altomonte's fresco of the *Angelic Throng*, together with (in the chancel) the *Coronation of the Virgin*.

The striking stucco figures of the high altar and pulpit are the work of Johann Georg Üblher, while the three archangels and one guardian angel in the chancel niches are by Franz Anton Zauner, a major neo-classical sculptor who worked mostly in Vienna. Altomonte was responsible for the main altarpiece of the *Assumption*, while Üblher's figures are now thought to represent *Archbishop Konrad II of Salzburg, Pope Eugene III, Bishop Reginbert of Passau* and *Bishop Otto of Freising*, all benefactors of the Cistercians. Üblher's remarkable pulpit shows angels symbolising the Old and New Testaments, and (on the canopy) a dramatic representation of *St Bernard of Clairvaux Triumphing in his Disputation with Peter Abelard*. The saints on the side-altars are also the work of Üblher. To the right of the entrance of the church are late Gothic epitaphs of Jörg Pernpeck (1516) and the Albrechtsheimers, husband and wife (1508). In the monastery may be seen Gothic remnants of the earlier building (e.g. the **chapter house**), and (in the **library**) more frescoes by Bartolomeo Altomonte, with fine stucco by Johann Kaspar Modler. For a guided tour of the monastery apply at the porter's lodge.

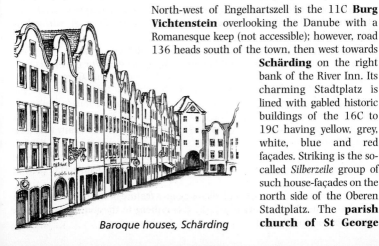

North-west of Engelhartszell is the 11C **Burg Vichtenstein** overlooking the Danube with a Romanesque keep (not accessible); however, road 136 heads south of the town, then west towards **Schärding** on the right bank of the River Inn. Its charming Stadtplatz is lined with gabled historic buildings of the 16C to 19C having yellow, grey, white, blue and red façades. Striking is the so-called *Silberzeile* group of such house-façades on the north side of the Oberen Stadtplatz. The **parish church of St George**

Baroque houses, Schärding

close to the Marktplatz was rebuilt after severe damage in the Napoleonic war, and has an altarpiece above the left-hand side-altar of *Christ Appearing in a Vision before St Theresia* by Johann Michael Rottmayr. Of the castle at Schärding there remain only the Zwinger, the moat and the outer gate, in which there is now a **Heimatmuseum** (open Wed, Thur, 15.00–17.00, Fri, Sat, 10.00–12.00).

The main road leads north, parallel to the Inn and past **Burg Wernstein**, a forward post for **Neuburg** castle on the heights above the river, which is already on Bavarian territory. Just before Wernstein is the village of **Zwickledt**, where the artist Alfred Kubin lived from 1906 until his death in 1959. It was here that he conjured his frightening dystopian visions, and wrote a bizarre, ghoulishly illustrated work reminiscent of Edgar Allen Poe entitled *Die andere Seite* (*The Other Side*, 1909). The **Kubin-Haus** at Zwickledt 7 is open April–Oct, Tues, Wed, Thur, 10.00–12.00 and 14.00–16.00, Fri 17.00–19.00, Sat, Sun, PH 14.00–17.00.

Across the Bavarian border a few kilometres to the north is the historic city of Passau, whose powerful bishopric (founded 731) divided jurisdiction over much of medieval Austria with its rival Salzburg, the two of them often competing for influence as, for instance, in Vienna. Churches dedicated to St Stephen in Austria are normally those formerly under the influence of Passau, while those (far fewer) associated with St Rupert were Salzburg oriented. With a Vicar General sitting in Vienna, Passau maintained its administrative dominance in Upper and Lower Austria right up to the time of Joseph II, who, however, placed its Austrian territories under local control between 1783 and 1785. At Passau the Inn flows into the Danube at a massive confluence, whereby the waters of the latter are more than doubled in volume.

South of Schärding road 142 passes through **Suben**, where the former Augustinian monastery is now a prison. However, its Rococo **church** (Simon Frey, 1770) is worth visiting to see the stucco of Johann Baptist Modler, together with the altars and their statuary of the church fathers, evangelists and archangels by Josef Deutschmann. The ceiling frescoes by Johann Jakob Zeiller show the *Conversion of St Augustine*, the *Augustinian Rule* and apocalyptic scenes. **Reichersberg** further south has another ancient Augustinian **abbey** (founded 1084 and still operating) with an attractive marble fountain in the outer courtyard topped by a gilded copper statue (1697) of *St Michael* by Thomas Schwanthaler.

The church (1779), built by Christian Weiß from Ried im Innkreis, has ceiling frescoes by Christian Wink of Munich (to the west, *St Augustine giving his Rule to the Monks*, at the centre, the *Archangel Michael on Monte Gargano*, in the chancel *Angels and Saints Praising God*). Notable for their quality are the choirstalls and the pulpit. Near the left-hand side-altar is a red marble tombstone (1470) showing the monastery's founder, Werner von Reichersberg, together with his family. The dependencies, including a richly decorated **library** with frescoes (1771) illustrating the monastery's history by Johann Nepomuk Schöpf, and the refectory (1695) by C.A. and G.B. Carlone, may be visited. Tours of the monastery and its small museum take place from Easter–All Saints' Day, daily at 15.00.

The stucco of Johann Baptist Modler is again a feature of the house façades on the picturesque **Marktplatz** of nearby **Obernberg** to the south-west, once a flourishing port of the Inn.

Braunau am Inn

Road 142 leads on, however, to Altheim, where an eastward turn brings you on road 309 to Braunau am Inn, rather undeservedly linked in most people's minds with the name of Adolf Hitler, who was born here in 1889 in the suburban Salzburger Vorstadt 15 outside the medieval **Torturm**. In front of the house is a granite slab from Mauthausen (see p 287) bearing the inscription: 'For peace, freedom and democracy/Never again fascism/In memory of the millions who died.'

History of Braunau am Inn

The name of the town comes from the *'braunen Au'*, which described the once adjacent river meadowland whose vegetation was presumably more brown than green. Quite unconnected with 'Braunau', brown became the trademark colour of Hitler's Nazis, the expression 'brown' being to this day a reference in Austria to Nazi or neo-Nazi sympathies. Braunau was a Bavarian possession until 1779 and grew prosperous from the Inn water traffic, besides being at the conjunction of roads (partly Roman in origin) leading to Linz, Passau and Salzburg, and so profiting from itinerant cloth traders and salt merchants. Although Napoleon had most of the town's fortifications demolished, the remnants that survive contribute in part to a romantic river frontage. The town lost much of its prosperity after becoming Austrian, although Hitler himself was to revive its fortunes by locating an aluminium works at nearby Ranshofen in 1939. As is well-known, Hitler was born the son of a minor customs official, Alois Schicklgruber, who changed his name to Hitler in 1893, and moved to Passau three years after the birth of his son, then to Leonding near Linz. Hitler went to school in Linz, moving to Vienna at the age of 18; there he fell under the influence of the racist doctrines of Lanz von Liebenfels and imbibed the (also racist) political philosophies of Mayor Karl Lueger and the vicious Georg von Schönerer. This motley crew of one gifted, if unscrupulous, politician (Lueger), and two mentally unstable cranks has therefore got a lot to answer for, even if Hitler added his own inimitable flavour.

The long central **Stadtplatz** running north to south has attractive period façades, notably that of the **Gnändingerhof** (1530) at no. 32, to the west of which are picturesque alleys and lanes. Dominating the square is the Gothic tower (96m) of the **parish church of St Stephen**, begun in 1492. The clock on the tower dates to 1646 and a Baroque onion dome was added in 1752. The interior has fine net vaulting and intriguing columns with the heads of saints and angels serving as capitals. Most of the Baroque high altar fell victim to re-Gothicisation in the 19C, but Michael Zürn's over-life-size figures (1642) remain (the *Virgin and Child enthroned in Clouds*, with *Sts Stephen* and *Lawrence*, further saints in the choir). A feature of the church is the red marble tombstone of the Passau Bishop Mauerkircher (d. 1485) by Hans Valkenauer of Salzburg. The stone pulpit (1490) has reliefs of the *Church Fathers*, and statues of *Christ and the Evangelists* beneath the canopy, with the *Prophets* below. The many chapels around the walls were endowed by the various guilds of the city—smiths, bakers, weavers, brewers, merchants, etc. The exterior walls are studded with tombstones, of which the most celebrated is that (1567) on the north wall of the *'man* *with the long beard*' (it reaches to his feet), actually Hans Staininger, a city governor. According to legend, his beard proved to be his downfall when a fire broke out in Braunau: not having enough time to wind it around his neck as usual, he tripped over it in his flight and broke his neck.

The former **Bürgerspitalkirche of the Holy Spirit** to the east dates to the 15C and is notable for the hall-like area around the western entrance, now closed, but formerly opening onto the hospital, so that the sick could participate in the mass (the space on the left reserved for women, on the right, for men).

Ranshofen, once the site of a Carolingian palace, is 4km upstream to the south-west of Braunau. Here are Hitler's aluminium factories, as well as a former Augustinian convent with a church of 1751 having fine Baroque pews. The **charnel house** to the west of it is a notable late Gothic construction.

THE HAUSRUCKVIERTEL

The **Hausruck** is a 30km long and densely forested ridge dividing the Inn from the valley of the Vöckla and Ager rivers and having reserves of oil and natural gas. Its extensive deposits of brown coal are no longer worked. Road 147 runs south-east parallel to the River Mattig, reaching at 7km **St Georgen an der Mattig**. The small church is distinguished by superb examples of Michael and Martin Zürn's statuary (1645–49) on three altars, showing the *Martyrdom of St Sebastian* (on the right-hand side-altar), *St George and the Dragon* (on the high altar) and *St Martin and the Beggar* (left-hand side-altar). To the south is **Mattighofen** with an early classical church (1779) by Franz Anton Kirchgrabner of Munich with frescoes of the *Assumption* (1780) by Nepomuk della Croce and Thomas Schwanthaler's high altar statues (1676) of *Sts Peter* and *Paul*.

South-west of Mattighofen (on road 156) is **Eggelsberg** with a 15C church having unusual star vaulting spreading out from a central hexagonal column. **Ibmer Moos** bordering on Land Salzburg to the south is a swampy conservation area that will be of interest to bird-lovers: large numbers of lapwings, herons and various species of waders, some rare, are to be found here.

Fifteen kilometres to the south of Mattighofen is **Lochen**, whose **parish church** contains masterwork (1709) of Meinrad Guggenbichler, in particular the high altar showing in the shrine a *Sacra Conversazione* with *Mary as Queen of Heaven*, together with *St Barbara* and *St Catherine* flanked by *St George* and *St Florian*; above these *St Bartholomew* with the plague protectors, *Sts Sebastian* and *Rochus*. Guggenbichler was also responsible for the pulpit (1713), as well as a **crucifix** and statues of *Our Lady of Sorrows*, the *Good Shepherd* and the *Man of Sorrows*. These are considered to be the major works of the artist's monumentalising classical style of Baroque. A few kilometres south-west and close to the Salzburg border, the church of **Gebertsham** (from which there are fine views of the Alps and Mattsee) has a winged altar of 1520 showing the *Passion*, a work attributed to Gordian Gugg of Salzburg.

North of Mattighofen minor roads lead east through the **Kobernausser Wald** (map required) to **Ried im Innkreis**, or alternatively the main road (148 then 141) leads there direct from Braunau. The original settlement was founded in the 12C by one Dietmar, the son of a miller, a monument (1665) to whom stands on the **Marktplatz**. This Dietmar seems to have made both his name and a fortune by participating in the Third Crusade and distinguishing himself at the siege of Jerusalem in 1189, receiving a generous plot of land as his reward.

The town has several old streets and squares (unfortunately many of them choked with traffic) and was the home of the Schwanthaler dynasty of sculptors who had their workshop here between 1632 and 1838. A **Schwanthaler Museum** in the **Volkskundehaus** may be visited at Kirchplatz 13 (open Tues–Fri, 09.00–12.00, 14.00–17.00, Sat 14.00–17.00). (This is not the family house, however, which was at Schwanthalergasse 11). The museum also contains 19C and 20C works by Innviertel artists. The **parish church** contains Schwanthaler works, of which the most impressive is Thomas Schwanthaler's life-size group of *Christ on the Mount of Olives* in the north-west confessional chapel, a work filled with emotion, movement and drama. In the Chapel of the Guild of Cobblers is an altar dedicated to St Martin by the brothers Martin and Michael Zürn, while Johann Peter Schwanthaler's fine *pietà* is in the Chapel of the Guild of Weavers.

South-east of Ried is **Gaspoltshofen** (reached by a minor road from Haag), where the parish church has a remarkable **Fisherman's Pulpit** (1770) similar to that at Traunkirchen (see p 274). At the foot of this one is a vast fish's mouth, represented in the act of spewing out an understandably relieved-looking Jonah. South of Ried on road 143 beyond Ampflwang is **Zell am Pettenfirst** (actually in the Attergau), where the late Gothic **parish church of the Visitation** has attractive net and star vaulting, together with works by Thomas Schwanthaler. Of note is the lovely main altar (1667) showing the *Virgin* with *Sts Afra* (to the left, holding a torch) and *Mary Magdalene* in the shrine, these figures having been taken taken from an original Gothic winged altar on the instructions of the commissioner, and put by Schwanthaler into a new Baroque setting. The flanking figures of *St John* and *St Matthew* are by Schwanthaler, as is the *Nativity* scene above, flanked by the other two Evangelists, *Luke* and *Mark*.

Stift Lambach

South-east of Gaspoltshofen at the confluence of the Ager and Traun rivers is Lambach, the site of a Benedictine Abbey founded in 1056 by the powerful noble line of Wels-Lambach. The abbey was rebuilt in the 17C and its entrance has an impressive **marble portal** (1693) by Jakob Auer. The treasury possesses a celebrated Romanesque **Adalbero chalice**, named after Bishop Adalbero of Würzburg, the son of Arnold II of Wels-Lambach. Adalbero took the Pope's side in the mid-11C investiture dispute and thus fell foul of Henry IV, who had him forcibly removed from his Würzburg bishopric. Despite the support of Bishops Gebhard of Salzburg and Altmann of Passau (who were also dismissed), and of course of the Pope himself, Adalbero failed to make a comeback and died in retirement in Lambach, subsequently being canonised.

The **library** in the north wing (part of the so-called *Neuen Konvent*) has a ceiling **fresco** by Melchior Steidl, and the **refectory** has stucco by D.F. Carlone, together with appropriate frescoes by Wolfgang Andreas Heindl. However, the most unusual aspect of the monastery is the **theatre** with Rococo scenery; the first performance held in it was for Marie Antoinette, who stopped at Lambach on her ill-fated bridal journey to France in 1770.

In the monastery **church of the Assumption** (1656, perhaps by Filiberto

Lucchese, but retaining its Romanesque tower) is Joachim von Sandrart's monumental altarpiece of the *Assumption* (1655), together with a Rosary picture by the same artist. In 1868 **Romanesque frescoes** were uncovered in the area that had been the west choir of the predecessor church, but were only restored in the second half of the 20C. The complex cycle from the 11C is of extremely high quality and shows *Scenes from the Nativity, Childhood and Ministry of Christ, Joseph's Dream*, the *Rise and Fall of Herod Agrippa*, etc. and is clearly influenced by the North Italian masters with affinities to Byzantine art. It is assumed that these unique works were commissioned by Adalbero himself, since the scenes follow no known iconographical scheme; moreover, the unflattering depiction of Herod Agrippa may plausibly be interpreted as an allusion to Bishop Adalbero's great secular opponent, Henry IV. Unfortunately, visiting times for the monastery are limited: Easter–All Saints' Day, once daily, at 14.00. ☎ 072 45/2 17 10.

Stadl-Paura

On a hill overlooking the south bank of the Traun, south of Lambach, is the unusual **triangular pilgrimage church** (1725) at **Stadl-Paura**, its form being part of a symbolic plan based on the Holy Trinity, to which the church is dedicated. Thus its towers, doors, altars (dedicated respectively to God the Father, God the Son, and God the Holy Ghost), as well as its apses, organs and confessionals are three in number. The church was designed by Johann Michael Prunner, while the stucco of the interior is by the Holzinger brothers, the frescoes by Carlo Carlone (in the cupola, the *Holy Trinity*) and Francesco Messena (who supplied the *trompe l'oeil* decoration), the sculptures by the Spaz brothers with Leopold Mähl and Josef Matthias Götz. The church is a masterpiece of the Rococo and represents not only the summit of Prunner's achievements, but also the apotheosis of Counter-Reformatory triumphalism (see, for instance, the representation of *Faith* on the Altar of God the Father triumphing over a humiliated male figure holding a portrait bust of Martin Luther in his left hand).

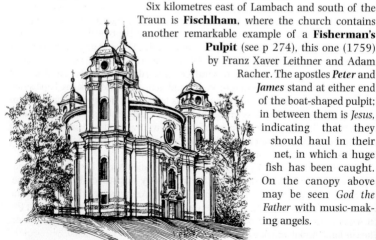

Six kilometres east of Lambach and south of the Traun is **Fischlham**, where the church contains another remarkable example of a **Fisherman's Pulpit** (see p 274), this one (1759) by Franz Xaver Leithner and Adam Racher. The apostles *Peter* and *James* stand at either end of the boat-shaped pulpit; in between them is *Jesus*, indicating that they should haul in their net, in which a huge fish has been caught. On the canopy above may be seen *God the Father* with music-making angels.

Stadl-Paura church

THE MÜHLVIERTEL

Oberes Mühlviertel (Upper Mühlviertel)

Leaving Linz to the north-west by road 127 through Urfahr on the north bank of the Danube, you pass medieval **Schloss Ottensheim** overlooking one of the Danube's hydro-electric dams (there is also a ferry across the Danube here). A minor road leads north-east off road 127 from Walding north of Ottensheim to **Gramastetten**, with its 15C **St Lawrence church**, which has fine star-vaulting and Gothic tracery.

At **Pesenbach** (reached from Ottensheim on road 131 to the west) the parish church has a late Gothic **winged altar** (1495), restored and returned to its original position in 1854 on the orders of Adalbert Stifter in his capacity as curator of monuments. The shrine shows *St Leonard* flanked by *St Bartholomew* (left) and *St Michael* (right), while the relief panels show scenes from the *Life of St Leonard*, as do the painted panels on the rear.

Continuing north-west on road 127, you reach Neufelden, to the north of which (2km) is **Burg Pürnstein**, a 10C castle belonging to the Bishops of Passau until 1803, but permanently pledged to various noble families. There is a small weapons collection (open May–Oct, Wed–Mon. Guided tours at 10.00, 11.00, 14.00, 15.00, 16.00 and 16.30).

Road 127 continues north to **Schlägl**, which is just before Aigen on the Große Mühl river. The Premonstratensian monastery on the riverbank dates to 1218 and was founded (originally as a Cistercian cloister) by Calhoch von Falkenstein. The monastery **church of the Assumption** dates from the 13C and 15C, and was barockised between 1626 and 1630. Steps lead up the portal of 1654 showing a *Madonna with Angels* together with the Falkenstein coat of arms, the rising effect being maintained with steps up to the Gothic porch and again rising (steeply) to the choir, the cumulative drama being heightened by the light flooding in through the windows of the same in contrast to the darkness of the nave. A fine wrought-iron gate closes off the choir from the rest of the interior, isolating thus the area below which the Romanesque crypt is situated. The roof of the crypt is supported by a central column having a gemmiform capital, and the Romanesque part connects with a Gothic part having groined vaulting. In the monastery is a **picture gallery** with works of the Danube School as well as paintings by Italian and Dutch masters; also a medieval *Madonna with Corn Mantle*, an allusion to the Immaculate Conception. There is in addition an attractive **library** with Biedermeier furnishings and Rococo frescoes, as well as a collection of 17C sculptures by Johann Worath, who was also responsible for most of the statuary in the monastery church. Tours of the monastery are possible from 15 May–26 Oct, Tues–Sun, 10.00–12.00 and 13.00–17.00.

In the parish church at **Aigen** is a charming late Gothic *Madonna* in the choir, a work of the international soft style, dated to c 1400. **Haslach** to the south-east stands at the confluence of the **Steinerne Mühl** and the **Große Mühl**, and has a parish church with fine late Gothic net vaulting. At Kirchplatz 3 is a **Weaving Museum** (open April–Oct Tues–Sun, 09.00–12.00), and at Windgasse 17 a **Trade and Merchants' Museum** (*Handels- und Kaufmannsmuseum*, open May–Oct, Tues–Sun 09.00–13.00).

Freistadt and environs

Road 125 leads north-east of Linz to the medieval city of **Freistadt**, still surrounded by its moat, in which orchards and gardens have now been planted. The name '*Freistadt*' recalls that this was a city of free burghers ('*Stadt der Freien*'), who received their privileges from the Babenbergs and grew rich from storing and trading the salt and iron being transported to Bohemia.

The enceinte (completed in two phases, c 1300 and c 1400) is almost entirely preserved, of note being the **Linzertor**, showing the Freistadt emblem. Many of the burgher houses lining the extended **Hauptplatz** are also Gothic, while the **Marian column** at its centre is Baroque. At the southern end is the Gothic **church of St Catherine** with a conspicuous Baroque clock-tower by J.M. Prunner; its interior boasts particularly beautiful **ribbed vaulting** and a fine choir built (1483) by Mathes Klayndl. In the choir (which was subsequently barockised by Antonio Carlone) may be seen an altar of 1520 showing the *Fourteen Holy Helpers*, with relief panels of the *Life of King Wenceslas* (on the left), and (on the right) *St George and the Dragon*. The main altarpiece (1640) is by Adriaen Bloemaert.

At the north-east of the town is the nine-storeyed **keep** of the Freistadt Schloss, a late 14C building with an arcaded courtyard inside, which now houses the **Mühlviertler Heimatmuseum**. The museum (Schlosshof 2) contains an important collection of *verre églomisé* (glass decorated by unfired painting or gilding, sometimes engraved), but has odd opening times: 2 May–31 Oct, Tues–Sat 10.00 and 14.00, Sun and PH at 10.00; Nov–May, Tues–Fri at 10.00, Tues and Fri also at 14.00, closed at weekends and PH). The **Liebfrauenkirche** (1345) near the **Böhmertor** of the city wall has 14C stained glass in the northern window of the choir, showing *Mary with the Infant Jesus*. A peculiarity are the Gothic **Totenlaterne** (lamps for the dead), perhaps also by Klayndl and dated to 1484; they used to stand in the cemetery, but are now displayed in the choir.

Reichenthal, 10km north-west of Freistadt, has a 19C church with an unusual **pulpit**: it is shown as resting on a tree, around which is twined a snake with seven human faces, each of which represents (and most vividly) one of the *Seven Deadly Sins*. A few kilometres to the west of Freistadt is **Waldburg**, with no less than three late Gothic **winged altars** in its parish **church of St Mary Magdalene**. The two side-altars (1520) dedicated to St Lawrence and St Wolfgang, are of rather average quality; but the **main altar**, with its shrine showing the *Virgin*, *Mary Magdalene* and *St Catherine*, together with relief scenes of the *Passion* and painted panels of the *Life of Mary Magdalene* is a masterpiece of 1517, attributed to Gregor Erhart.

Six kilometres north-east of Freistadt (road 38) is **Oberrauchenödt**, above which on a knoll of primary rock is the **church of St Michael** (from a bench south of the church there are superb views over the Mühlviertel). According to the geologists, the knoll rises above a watershed, between the Feldaist and Maltsch rivers, and thus between the water flows to the North Sea and to the Black Sea. The church is usually open at weekends, when the fine **winged altar** may be admired. It shows in the shrine *St Nicholas* and *St Stephen*, flanking an almost girl-like *St Michael*, whose effeminate features are framed with ringlets. The inside relief panels show the *Life of St Nicholas* and the *Stoning of St Stephen*, while the closed wings (painted) show the *Passion*. The quality of the carving is, however, noticeably more refined than that of the painting.

Unteres Mühlviertel (Lower Mühlviertel)

Kefermarkt

At Kefermarkt, south-east of Freistadt, the parish **church of St Wolfgang** possesses a huge (13.5 m) late Gothic **winged altar** made of limewood, an astonishing work described by Adalbert Stifter in his novel *Der Nachsommer* (Indian Summer), and restored on the writer's initiative in the mid-19C. Up to that time, the altar had been gradually crumbling from woodworm, following years of neglect. In the shrine may be seen *St Wolfgang*, the *Bishop of Regensburg*, flanked by *St Peter* (to the left) holding the symbolic key to Heaven, and *St Christopher* to the right, staff in hand and with the infant Christ perched on his shoulder. The reliefs on the wings show (from left, above) the *Annunciation*, the *Nativity*, the *Adoration of the Magi* and the *Dormition of the Virgin*. The shrine is surmounted by carving of great delicacy and complexity, with statues of the *Madonna and Child*, together with female saints (*St Catherine* and *St Barbara*, below *St Agnes* between busts of the prophets, with *St Helena* at the pinnacle). The creator (or probably creators) of this beautiful and refined artefact, which pulses with human character and emotion in the realistically depicted faces of individuals, is not precisely known, although there are many suggestions ranging from Veit Stoß to Michael Pacher. What is known is that the formidable features of St Wolfgang are a likeness of Albert Schöndorfer (d. 1493), the Bishop of Passau who consecrated the Kefermarkt church. With such an ambitious work, it was usual for the master to carve the central figures (in the shrine) and leave the side-panels to assistants, as seems to have been the case here.

On the north-east edge of Kefermarkt is **Schloss Weinberg** (1305, but much altered in the Renaissance and now an educational institution). Road 124 from Wartberg to the south leads east to **Königswiesen**, where the parish church has superb **groined and star vaulting** of immense complexity: it grows out of the three main octagonal columns to create 480 geometrically diverse fields that coalesce centrally in star forms.

South-east of Königswiesen you come (via road 119) to **Waldhausen im Strudengau**, which is close to the Lower Austrian border. The church of the former Augustinian monastery that was known as *Silvia Domus* (much of the latter having been demolished so that its stones could be used for Emperor Franz's Laxenburg folly of the Franzensburg, see p 116) is the work (1650) of Carlo Canevale. The interior is richly frescoed by Cristoforo Colombo and stuccoed by Giovanni Battista Colombo, the frescoes showing *St John on Patmos*, the *Assumption*, the *Conversion of St Paul* and the *Stoning of St Stephen*. On the high altar are over-life-size figures of *St Augustine* and *St Ambrose* by Johann Seitz, while the altarpiece of the *Last Judgement* is by Joachim von Sandrart. The parish **church of St John** is an oddity, built in the 17C, but retaining the Gothic style for the interior, with a Renaissance portal on the south side—an architectural time-warp.

STRUDENGAU

The stretch of the Danube between **Grein** (reached on road 119 to the west of Waldhausen, see below) and the Lower Austrian border is called the **Strudengau** on account of its formerly dangerous currents and maelstrom ('*Strudel*') in the proximity of a reef that cost many Danube shipmen their lives over the years. A folksong records these unhappy events in the *Greiner Strudel 'wo der Tod seine Herberge hält*' ('where Death has his domain'). In 926 the illustrious Bishop of Freising was also drowned here. The dangers decreased with detonations of the reef in the late 18C, while the building of the Ybbs-Persenbeug hydro-electric dam in 1958 resulted in an effective regulation of the most treacherous currents. The Strudengau still looks spectacular, however, and is overlooked east of Grein (and opposite the Danubian island of Wörth) by the medieval **Burg Werfenstein**, of which chiefly the keep remains.

Grein

Grein itself, a town that prospered from levying a Danube toll, is dominated by **Schloss Greinburg**, a castle of 1493 enlarged in the 17C. Since 1823 it has been in the possession of the Sachsen-Coburg-Gotha family, but the southern wing may be visited and has stunning views of the Danube from its windows. Its three-storeyed arcaded courtyard is one of the loveliest in Austria, a unique feature being (at the south-east corner) the Renaissance room with massive **rhombic vaulting** (*Zeltengewölbe*), which has a touch of Surrealism about it. No less interesting is the **Museum of the Danubian Shipmen** on the first floor (open May and Oct Tues–Sun, 10.00–12.00, 13.00–17.00. June–Sept, Tues–Sun, 10.00–18.00).

Down in the town is the delightful Rococo **Stadttheater** (1790), located on the first floor of the **Rathaus**, and having lockable wooden seats for the burgher patrons. Guided tours are available from April–Oct, daily at 10.30 and 14.30. A feature of the theatre's interior (which was formerly a salt store) is the convenient loo, separated from the auditorium only by a curtain, so that its user could continue to watch the play while performing his or her ablutions.

Just west of Grein is **Klam**, whose **Burg Clam** (the family name spelled with a 'C') is a well-preserved castle from the 12C. Highlights of the **Burgmuseum** include the chapel with 14C frescoes, an apothecary, weapons and porcelain collections and documentation of the Clam line that is still in possession of the Burg (open May–Oct, daily 10.00–16.00). August Strindberg stayed in the **Grillenberger House** of the village in 1895–96, writing here his *Inferno* and *Damascus*.

Two kilometres to the west on road 3 is **Baumgartenberg** in the fertile **Machland** (the Lords of the Machland being the original builders of Burg Clam), an area which is encompassed by a loop in the Danube. Otto von Machland founded a Cistercian abbey here in 1141 (suppressed under Joseph I in 1784), of which the former church has an exceptionally beautiful Baroque interior from the late 17C, probably by Carlo Antonio Carlone. The decorative harmony between the icing sugar stucco with floral and vegetative motifs and the medallion **frescoes** of the nave and choir, together with the quadrilateral wall frescoes in the nave, strikes an unusually pleasing aesthetic balance. The frescoes show the history of the Cistercian Order, while those in the vault

(Giacomo Antonio Mazza, 1696) show prophets and scenes from the *Life of St Bernard*. The frescoes in the choir depict the *Secrets of the Rosary*. Also of note are the finely carved choirstalls and the **pulpit** (1670) in the form of the *Tree of Jesse*; from the recumbant figure of St Bernard grows the fruit-laden tree of the Cistercian community.

Arbing to the north-west has a parish church with fine reticulated vaulting, while at **Perg** the church of St James boasts an early 16C statue of the *Madonna*; and at **Altenburg** (north-east of Perg on the Münzbach road) the crypt of the church has well-preserved frescoes from the early 16C. These were commissioned by a local lord, Prager of Pragthal (who is buried here), and feature a *Crucifixion* and *Christ Pantocrator*, as well as coats of arms. To the north-west of Perg is **Schloss Schwertberg** on the banks of the River Aist, transformed in Renaissance style by Antonio Canevale at the beginning of the 17C.

Mauthausen

Road 3 continues west of Perg to Mauthausen, situated at the confluence of the Enns and the Danube. Three kilometres north-east of the town is the notorious **Mauthausen concentration camp** of the Nazis, the principal one in Austria and built promptly after the *Anschluß* in 1938 by prisoners from the already functioning camp at Dachau. It is maintained as a memorial with a museum located in the camp's sick quarters, the latter containing grim photographs and documents (there is a leaflet in English). Underneath the sick quarters were the gas chambers, the use of Zyklon B being an Austrian contribution to the war effort. It was first tested at Schloss Hartheim, near Linz, which had been turned into a euthanasia centre. The experimental centre here was run by a Linz doctor named Rudolf Lonauer, who presided over the deaths of 12,000 sick and mentally ill patients brought from all over Austria.

A track leads from the Mauthausen camp to the **Wiener Graben**, where more than 2000 prisoners were put to work in a granite quarry, hundreds dying on the so-called *Todesstiege* ('*Stairway of Death*', actually the steps that lead down from the quarry) or being pushed to their deaths over the sheer cliff that overlooks it. Among the survivors of this hell on earth was Simon Wiesenthal, who subsequently worked (1945–47) for the US War Crimes Office, and founded in 1947 the Jewish Documentation Centre in Linz, which moved to Vienna in 1961. Information collected by the Centre has led to the apprehension of some Nazi war criminals, although most escaped, in some cases with the assistance of the Vatican. In Mauthausen and its 49 ancillary camps, it is estimated that around 100,000 people were murdered or worked to death. The Mahn- und Gedenkstätte KZ Mauthausen is open daily Feb–March, 08.00–16.00, April–Sept, 08.00–18.00, Oct–15 Dec, 08.00–16.00. It is closed from 16 Dec–31 Jan.

The ancient market town of Mauthausen itself has been settled since the Stone Age and derives its name from the **Mautstätte** (toll station) erected here in the Babenberg era. It has a number of attractive burgher houses around the **Marktplatz**. On the south side of the parish church is an octagonal Romanesque **charnel house** with 13C frescoes (the *Virgin Mary* and *St John*, also the *Lamb of God* and medallions of birds, ancient symbols of the departed human souls). On the Leopold-Heindl-Kai is **Schloss Pragstein** (1491), originally built on a cliffspur forming an island in the river and known as the *Wellenbrecher* (wavebreaker), its function being to guard the river crossing. It houses a **Heimatmuseum** (open mid-May–mid-Sept, Mon, Wed, Fri, 17.00–19.00).

Salzburg City and Province

Area: 7154sq km. Population: 482,000

Topography, climate and environment

Salzburg is the principal town of Land Salzburg, which borders on Upper Austria in the north and north-east, on Styria and Carinthia in the east and south-east, on East Tyrol and South Tyrol in the south, on North Tyrol and Germany in the west and north-west. It is a landscape of rugged karst mountains, through which run the Saalach, Enns and Mur rivers, while the Salzach itself runs east from its source in the **Oberpinzgau** near the Tyrol border, and then follows the edge of the **Hohe Tauern National Park**. After flowing through the centre of the provincial capital, the river forms for a while the border between Germany and Austria before joining the Inn at Überackern. The scenically spectacular **Großglockner** panoramic road to the south straddles Austria's highest pass between Salzburg and Carinthia, close to the border with East Tyrol. West of this is the next highest peak of the province, the **Großvenediger** (3666m) in the Hohe Tauern. Land Salzburg includes wholly (**Zellersee**, **Fuschlsee**, **Wallersee**, **Mattsee**) or partially (**Wolfgangsee**) several scenically enchanting lakes and a narrow strip of the **Salzkammergut**. The province is administratively divided into six districts: **Salzburg and environs**, **Flachgau**, **Tennengau**, **Pongau**, **Pinzgau** and **Lungau**.

The northern edge of the Alps is subject to prevailing west winds and high precipitation, producing the famous Salzburg drizzle (*Schnürlregen*) all the year round. However, in the Lungau and the high Mur region, the climate is continental, often with very low temperatures, earning it the nickname of the Austrian Siberia. In the mountains there are golden eagle, white-headed vultures and ravens, as well as chamois and ibex. The flora is generally typical of the Alpine area, flourishing in river valleys, alpine pastures and coniferous forests.

Economy

The moist climate and abundant pasture favours dairy farming and market gardening is a feature of the Salzburg environs. In the alpine meadows cattle and sheep are raised, while the horses bred in the Pinzgau include the Noriker, which take their name from the Roman province of *Noricum* and are said to be descended from the horses of the legionaries, and the heavy work-horses of the Pinzgau breed. (The 19C Viennese, wishing to damn what they regarded as the excessively stout Pegasuses adorning the roof of Van der Nüll's new opera house, referred to them slightingly as '*Pinzgauer*', an insult that finally compelled their removal and substitution by slim-line quadrupeds of indeterminate race.)

The original sources of Salzburg's wealth (the mining of silver, gold and iron ore) declined from the second half of the 17C, not least because of competition from the more cheaply obtained supply of precious metal from the New World. The 20C has seen the final demise of the trade in 'white gold', the salt from which the area takes its name, again because the expense involved in extraction made the product uncompetitive on the world market. However, a dynamic light industry of machinery and electrical goods has ensured Salzburg's increasing prosperity since the 1960s. This is supplemented by a profitable trade in locally produced food products and beer, as well as a strong service sector with tourism supplying a major share of the local revenue and every third job. Salzburg's ever-expanding arts festivals generate huge income, but the year-round possibilities for skiing and hiking in the mountains and summer lakeside holidays, together with the cure centres of Badgastein and Bad Hofgastein, ensure that almost all parts of the province share in the prosperity.

Cultural traditions

Music

The rich musical tradition of Salzburg goes back to the patronage of the immensely wealthy Prince-Archbishops from at least the 15C. While the names of composers like Finck and Hofhaymer, Muffat and Biber, are largely forgotten, that of **Johann Michael Haydn** (1737–1806, brother of the more famous **Joseph**) is not. He was the Director of the Court Music at Salzburg from 1763 and known as a great teacher. It is uncertain whether he or **Leopold Mozart** composed the *Toy Symphony*, but in any case Leopold, father of **Wolfgang Amadeus Mozart**, left his mark on Salzburg in other ways, working as court composer and publishing his famous violin manual (1756), as well as composing church music and symphonies. His son was born in Salzburg, also in 1756, and first appeared in public as an infant prodigy in 1761. The young Mozart found employment at the court of Archbishop Colloredo, but was dismissed in 1778 for his airy disregard of protocol and general insolence. In the 19C the dissolution of the temporal powers of the archbishops in 1803 caused Salzburg's cultural life to sink into insignificance (a fact commented on by Schubert on his visit to the city in 1825), but Franz von Hilleprandt's founding of the **Dom-Musikverein** (Cathedral Music Association) in 1841 heralded a new dawn. In the same year this cultivated lawyer founded a museum at Mozart's birthplace and in 1856 the first Mozart festival worthy of the name was held, followed by the foundation of the **Internationale Mozartstiftung** in 1870. Salzburg thus became once more a centre of musical performance and pedagogy, while the musical reputation of the *Stiftung* itself was to grow exponentially under the direction of the great Bernhard Paumgartner (1917–38, 1945–59).

In the 20C the city has become world famous through its realisation of the dream of the Mozartstiftung's founders to hold regular festivals of Mozart's music. In 1920 the first festival also saw the première of Hugo von Hofmannsthal's reworking of the 15C English mystery play, *Everyman* (in German, *Jedermann*) held on the cathedral square; thereafter the **Festspiele**, under the guidance of Max Reinhardt, Alfred Roller, Richard Strauss and Franz Schalk, rapidly gained an international reputation. Hofmannsthal's expressed wish was that the festival should be 'a spiritual possession of the world', an idealistic attempt to focus on the healing and binding power of great art after the horrors of World War I. From the beginning the *Festspiele* included theatrical, operatic and concert performances with world-class

LAND SALZBURG

N

0 ——————— 10 miles
0 ——————— 20 kms

Michaelbeuern

Oberndo

**FEDERAL REPUBLIC
OF GERMANY**

Berchtesgaden

St. Martin
b. Lofer

Maria
Kirchental

National Park
Berchtesgaden

SAALACHTAL

372

311

Saalfelden

TIROL

311

KITZBÜHELER ALPEN

Zell a. See

Paß Thurn

168   Salzach

Bruck a.d.
Großglocknerstraß

Paß Gerlos

Mittersill

Kaprun

Krimmler Fälle

161

Stausee
Wasserfallboden

H O H E   T A U E R N

Felbertauerntunnel

Edelweiß straße
Großglockner-
Hochalpenstraße

OSTTIROL

Heiligenblut

I T A L Y

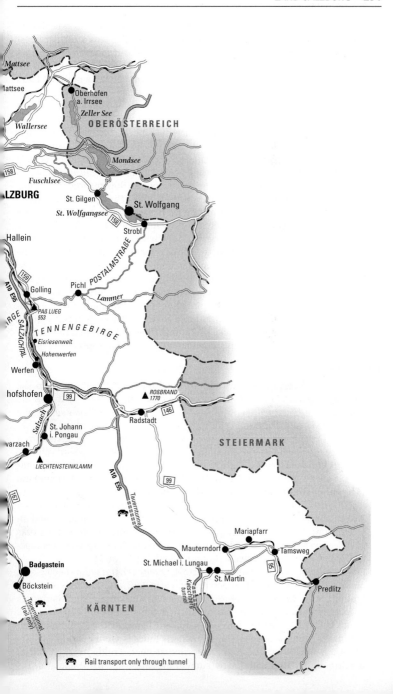

Rail transport only through tunnel

performers and producers, many of whom, however, went into exile during the Nazi period. After the war, **Wilhelm Furtwängler** was a regular guest conductor, but the festival became a fixed item on the agenda of Europe's cultural and social élite under the subsequent (1956–60 and from 1965 to his death) musical direction of **Herbert von Karajan**, himself a native of Land Salzburg (he was born in Anif).

A new auditorium designed by Clemens Holzmeister was opened in 1960 and a new Easter festival (originally concentrating on the music of Richard Wagner) was initiated by Karajan in 1967, to be followed by the Whitsun Festival founded in 1973. Seventy per cent of the notoriously costly **Salzburger Festspiele** are covered by sponsorship and ticket sales, deficits being made good by the state and Land Salzburg. However, indirect earnings from tourism stimulated by the festival are put at 900 million ATS. Since Karajan's death in 1989 a conscious attempt (under the artistic directorship of the Belgian, Gérard Mortier since 1992) has been made to modernise the image of the festival with premières of contemporary opera and drama, but these have not always found favour with the hard core of rich, conservative patrons. In 2000 a new (German) artistic director, Peter Ruzicka, takes up the reins promising no 'breach with tradition or modernity,' which would seem to leave him free to do almost anything. Experimental and avant-garde work has also been encouraged outside the range of the festival events and music education was expanded through the foundation of the Orff Institute by the composer Carl Orff (1895–1982). There has also been collaboration between the **Camerata Academica** (founded by Paumgartner in 1952) and the masterclass of the distinguished Hungarian conductor, **Sándor Vegh** (1992–97).

Literature

Literary traditions in Salzburg also have deep roots, reaching back to the *Salzburger Annalen* (1150) which record events of the 8C–10C, as well as the late medieval *History of the Conversion of the Bavarians and Karantanians* (the first-named being of German stock, the second being Alpine Slavs). In addition 100 poems designed for musical settings written by one Hermann, a Salzburg monk who was active in the second half of the 14C, afford valuable insights into the literary culture of the late Middle Ages. A scholar and writer of European significance was the doctor and alchemist **Paracelsus** (**Theophrastus Bombastus von Hohenheim**, 1493–1541), whose medical diagnoses and researches did (as he claimed) partly establish medicine on a scientific basis, but whose successes were marred by charlatanism and an intemperate disposition that caused him to make a public bonfire of the works of Avicenna and Galen. Even his adopted name was chosen to assert his superiority to Celsus, a celebrated writer and physician of the 1C.

As a religious centre, Salzburg nurtured many scholars and theologians, among them Bishop Pürstinger in the early 16C and Luther's superior, Staupitz, who was briefly Abbot of St Peter's. In the Baroque Age, Salzburg's University Theatre enjoyed a European-wide fame, while the educationalist Franz Michael Vierthaler, was an important figure of the Enlightenment. Salzburg's greatest literary son of modern times is **Georg Trakl** (1887–1914). A late Romantic and Expressionist poet, Trakl's work is full of moving, partly mystical, partly surreal evocations of his homeland. His patrons were Ludwig von Ficker, editor of the celebrated literary journal of Innsbruck, *Der Brenner*, and the philosopher Ludwig Wittgenstein. A melancholic, Trakl had a nervous breakdown while serving in World War I and died in Cracow after overdosing on cocaine. The **Georg-Trakl-Forschungs-und Gedenkstätte** (Georg Trakl Research Centre and Memorial Rooms, tours Mon–Fri at 11.00 and 14.00) is at Waagplatz 1A (☎ 84 52 89).

Lastly, no one has depicted provincial life with more unremitting bleakness than **Thomas Bernhard** (1931–89) in his first novel *Frost* (1963). He moved to Salzburg after the war and completed his music studies at the Mozarteum in 1957. Although he is later associated more with Vienna, where several of his plays enjoyed success, Bernhard was deeply rooted in the Salzburg ethos, no doubt because his formative years had been spent there. It was here also that his incurable lung condition was first diagnosed in 1949.

Art and architecture

As far as the fine and visual arts and architecture are concerned, the relative wealth and influence of the Salzburg archbishopric ensured that patronage for architecture and art was always available. There were significant Romanesque buildings in the city, including the cathedral itself, but most of the Romanesque architecture still visible has been incorporated into later Gothic structures. The defensive city walls built in 1280 stood (with additions) until their demolition in the 19C after the Napoleonic Wars. In Salzburg two of the greatest Gothic masters of the region were active: Conrad Laib (b. c 1410, d. after 1460) and Michael Pacher (c 1435–98). The latter's wing altar for the **parish church of St Wolfgang** on the Wolfgangsee (see p 321) is considered the high point of the late Gothic style in Austria.

Under the autocratic rule of Wolf Dietrich von Raitenau (1587–1612), Salzburg experienced a flowering of the visual arts and city architecture: the foundations were laid for the transformation of a medieval town into a magnificent early Baroque and Italianate city—the 'German Rome' as it came to be called. Instead of the piecemeal addition or alterations of the Middle Ages, Wolf Dietrich's Italian architect, Vincenzo Scamozzi, embarked on ambitious planning inspired by the Renaissance idea of the 'ideal city', as conceived by aestheticians who rediscovered Vitruvius, and based on the work of Andrea Palladio, whose follower and pupil Scamozzi was. In the spirit of his mentor, Scamozzi drew up ambitious plans for a new cathedral, although these were subsequently to be scaled down by his successor as architect and city planner to the Archbishop, Santino Solari. At the same time as the cathedral was being planned, new street-lines were created and squares laid out, all of which necessitated the demolition of over 100 houses. It was primarily Italian trained (Hans Waldburger) or Italian born (Santino Solari) artists and architects who assisted in this great project, the basis of the rather impersonal beauty (emphasised by the use of forbidding grey limestone) that characterises the city's rationally planned spaces and buildings.

Italians were still active in the High Baroque period (Giovanni Antonio Dario, Gaspare Zucalli), but were followed by the Italian-trained Johann Bernhard Fischer von Erlach (1656–1723), who built the monumental **Kollegienkirche**. His great contemporary and rival, Lukas von Hildebrandt (1668–1745), rebuilt the **Residenz** of the Archbishops in collaboration with the sculptor Georg Raphael Donner (1693–1741), the same team also transforming **Schloss Mirabell** and **Schloss Klessheim**. In the mid-18C, distinguished Baroque artists such as Johann Michael Rottmayr and Martin Johann ('Kremser') Schmidt carried out contracts for secular and sacred decoration in the city, the extreme prolificacy of the latter being explained by the fact that his workshop frequently carried out most of the detailed work on his projects.

The 19C saw regulation of the Salzach and other significant practical measures such as the removal of the old bastions and the institution of public parks. Thereafter the only significant aesthetic addition to the city's patrimony is the work of Clemens Holzmeister (1886–1983), who first altered part of Wolf Dietrich's extensive stables to create the small Festspielhaus in the 1920s, and after World War II completed the building's modern transformation with the construction of the Grossen Festspielhaus. A law of 1967 (the first of its kind in Austria) strictly regulated building or alterations in the old city; for modern architecture one must go, for example, to the suburb of Parsch, whose remarkable parish church (1956) was built by the **Arbeitsgruppe 4** team of architects with the involvement also of the sculptor Fritz Wotruba and the painter Oskar Kokoschka. Modern painting first became established in Salzburg with the formation of the **Wassermann Group**, which gave new life to a rather tepid 19C tradition of local painting, notwithstanding that Austria's most significant painter of Historicism, Hans Makart, was born (but never worked) in Salzburg. The leading painter of *Der Wassermann* was Anton Faistauer (1887–1930), who frescoed the foyer of the Festspielhaus. In 1953, Oskar Kokoschka and the prominent gallery owner, Friedrich Welz, founded the **Schule des Sehens**, a summer academy offering instruction in all artistic genres, and now including stage design, photography, video and film.

History of Salzburg and Land Salzburg

The Salzburg region has been settled since the Stone Age, its early major Celtic civilisation of the Iron Age typically basing itself on the commanding heights above the Salzach, for example on the Kapuzinerberg and the Festungsberg. The Celts were already mining and trading in salt (the original basis of Salzburg's wealth): the ancient word 'ha -' (as in Hallein, Hall etc.), signified saltworks and is thought by some scholars to be of Celtic origin, although others ascribe it to West Germanic and point to an association with the word *Halle*. Following their usual practice, the Romans cleared the Celts from their hilltops (around AD 15) and founded a new town (*Iuvavum*) on the shores of the Salzach river, the latter being granted municipal rights under Claudius (AD 45). An indigenous romanised population appears to have held out through the Dark Ages on the fortified Nonnberg, but Salzburg really enters history when Bishop Ruprecht of Worms acquired the settlement from the Bavarian Duke and founded the monastery of St Peter at the end of the 7C.

The name 'Salzburg' becomes current in the 8C and the town was raised to a bishopric in 739 under the Wessex-born Benedictine, (St) Boniface (c 673–754), who was known as the Apostle of Germany (he also founded the bishopric of Passau). Fifty-nine years later in 798 the city was raised to an archbishopric. Under the Irish Bishop Virgil (746–84), who was the Abbot of St Peter's, Salzburg developed rapidly as an ecclesiastical and artistic centre. By the mid-9C, the Salzburg Archbishops were also chaplains to the Holy Roman Emperor, a privilege they lost, however, when Archbishop Herold unwisely involved himself in a rebellion against Emperor Otto I, and was blinded and exiled for his pains. In 996 Otto III awarded Salzburg market and toll rights, as well as the right to mint coins. In the 11C and 12C, Salzburg consistently backed the papacy in the investiture dispute between the latter and the Emperor, a policy that made it vulnerable to imperial retribution, culminating in the city being burned to the ground by Friedrich Barbarossa in 1167. Ten years later Salzburg's reconciliation with the secular power was sealed with the Peace of Venice and thereafter the city was rapidly rebuilt. From around 1278 the area on the right bank of the Salzach was fortified with a city wall, later to be extended and strengthened (1465–80) in order to contain the not infrequent peasant revolts. The Salzburg Archbishopric reached its greatest territorial extent by the end of the 14C under Pilgrim II, when for a brief period it included much of Tyrol, Bavaria, Carinthia and Krain (modern Slovenia).

The salt industry revived from 1190, when the monks of St Peter started mining on the Dürrnberg overlooking Hallein. The revenues from mining were to provide the basis of Salzburg's subsequent political and cultural rise. A visible sign of the renewed prosperity and cultural revival was the building of an impressive Romanesque cathedral under Cardinal Konrad III, completed under Archbishop Adalbert III in 1198. However, in the following two centuries, Salzburg went through periodic crises under weak archbishops, a low point being reached under Friedrich V, whose concubine assumed control of secular affairs, dispensing offices and emoluments to her admirers. The strong-minded Archbishop Leonhard von Keutschach began to reverse the decline in 1511, forcing the Bürgermeister and city councillors to forego the extensive civic rights granted to them by Emperor Friedrich III (in the *Grossen Ratsbrief* of 1481) by the simple expedient of locking them up until they agreed. He also had a short way with the Jews, instituting a brutal pogrom against them in 1498.

In 1587 perhaps the most significant figure in Salzburg's history was elected Prince-Archbishop: **Wolf Dietrich von Raitenau**. A Renaissance *uomo universale* and a man of unbounded ambition, he single-mindedly developed the salt industry at Hallein, in the hope of liquidating the Bavarian competition. His attempt to establish a virtual monopoly in salt eventually led to a Bavarian invasion, which revealed him to be virtually friendless after years of erratic and arbitrary diplomacy that had offended many of his potential supporters. He was forced to abdicate as ruler and imprisoned in the fortress of Hohensalzburg, where he died in 1617. He was replaced by his cousin, **Marcus Sitticus of Hohenems**, who beautified and expanded the city. Under him and his successor, **Paris Lodron** (1619–53), Santino Solari rebuilt the cathedral, the Residenz was constructed, as also the Italianate villa or **Lustschloss** at Hellbrunn with its magnificent gardens and ingenious waterworks.

Shrewd diplomacy kept Salzburg out of the Thirty Years War, during which period the University was founded (1622), and six years later the great

Salzburg domes and towers with Hohensalzburg above

Baroque cathedral consecrated. Under **Archbishop Thun** (1687–1709), the Italian Baroque style of sacred and secular architecture gave way to the work of the native Austrians, Johann Bernhard Fischer von Erlach and Lukas von Hildebrandt. The latter rebuilt the Schloss Mirabell for Thun's successor, **Franz Anton Harrach**, scion of one of the most powerful noble families in Austria, on whose estates near the Hungarian border Joseph and Michael Haydn were born. **Archbishop Anton Freiherr von Firmian** felt strong enough to break with the limited toleration of his predecessors and expelled 20,000 Lutherans from Salzburg Land in 1731, an event commemorated in Goethe's *Hermann und Dorothea*. The large number was an indication of how well Protestantism had managed to survive in mountainous regions, as compared with other parts of the Crown Lands, and the expulsion proved to be short-sighted, leaving an acute shortage of skilled craftsmen. Those expelled emigrated mostly to East Prussia and Holland, some going on to found a colony in Georgia.

In 1756 **Wolfgang Amadeus Mozart** was born in Salzburg and in his youth enjoyed, with others of his family, the patronage of Sigismund III, Count Schrattenbach. On the death of the latter, Mozart became dependent on the less easy-going **Hieronymus Colloredo** (1772–1803), who was disliked by his subjects for his economy measures. Notwithstanding his unpopularity, Colloredo was an able ruler, a true son of the Enlightenment who put the finances of his archbishopric in order and encouraged learning and the arts. He was, however, to be the last Prince-Archbishop to rule the city: during the Napoleonic War he had to flee Salzburg and in 1803 the city was secularised and handed over to a branch of the Habsburgs. Subsequently (1805) Emperor Franz I of Austria took the additional title of 'Duke of Salzburg'. This was not quite the end of the changes to Salzburg's status—the city was under French governance between 1809–10, then ruled by the King of Bavaria. Finally in 1816, following a decision of the Congress of Vienna, Salzburg with Land Salzburg (but shorn of Berchtesgaden and the Rupertigau) officially became Austrian territory and was thereafter administered from the Upper Austrian capital of Linz.

In 1818 a fire destroyed much of New Salzburg on the right bank of the Salzach, including substantial parts of Schloss Mirabell. It was in this same year, one of economic depression accentuated by local commercial difficulties resulting from the post-Napoleonic settlement, that **Franz Xaver Gruber**'s *Stille Nacht! Heilige Nacht!* was first played on Christmas Eve in the parish church at Oberndorf on the Salzach. In 1850 Land Salzburg became one of the Crown Lands of the Empire, having regained its archbishopric in 1823 (but without the secular powers previously pertaining thereto). The year 1860 saw the city connected to the international railway grid when the Empress Elisabeth Westbahn, running between Vienna and Munich, was opened.

The 1860s was also a 'founders' period' in Salzburg, if not on the same scale as the industrial development driven by the Liberal politics of Vienna. Nevertheless the city's infrastructure was modernised, the old bastions were demolished and luxury hotels were built. The Mozart Monument had been erected as early as 1842, but in 1877 came the first festival of Mozart's music, the forerunner of the ambitious **Salzburger Festspiele** that began to take shape with the formation of the Association of the Salzburger Festspielhaus in 1917 by Richard Strauss, Max Reinhardt and Hugo von Hofmannsthal. In 1920, Salzburg (city and province) became one of the nine (future) Bundesländer of the Austrian Republic, as it remains today, and the same year saw the first Festspiele in the city.

During World War II, Salzburg was degraded to a '*Reichsgau*' by the Nazi regime and seriously damaged by waves of Allied bombing before its liberation by the Americans on the 4 May 1945. Until the end of the occupation of Austria in 1955, it was the headquarters of the American occupation zone. The return to normality brought with it the first **Mozartfestspiele** in1956 and the re-opening of the University (1962). A strict conservation law (*Lex Salzburgensis*) to protect the ancient fabric of the city and stop reckless development was passed in 1961. Since then Salzburg has prospered from burgeoning tourism and, moreover, acquired the status of one of the cultural capitals of Europe.

SALZBURG

Practical information

Population: 144,000. Telephone dialling code: 0662.

Tourist information

The tourist information office is at Mozartplatz 5 (☎ 889 87 330. Fax 889 87-32). Open from Easter–Oct 09.00–17.00 (to 20.00 between May–Oct). Nov–Easter it is open 09.00–18.00, Mon–Sat. A city map costing a few Schillings may be obtained here. A separate counter sells tickets for events (plus commission). Useful is the **Salzburg card** (24, 48 or 72 hrs) giving concessions on museums etc. as well as unlimited use of public transport. The tourist office for Land Salzburg is in the same building. There are **smaller information offices** at entry points to the city:

Hauptbahnhof (main station), Platform 2A: Open daily 09.00–20.00 (May–Oct 08.30–21.00).

Flughafen (Airport), Arrivals Hall:
Open daily 09.00–18.00 (June–Oct to
19.00).

Getting there
The **Hauptbahnhof** and **bus
station** is on the right bank at Südtiroler
Platz 1. Salzburg is on the main trans-
continental routes. Train information
☎ 1717 (07.00–20.00). Fast trains to
Vienna (3hrs 20mins) leave hourly and
every 2hrs for Innsbruck (passing
through Germany). There is at least one
train per hour to Munich. Bus informa-
tion ☎ 87 2150 (railway buses),
☎ 167, 517 22–238 (post buses).
   Autobahn exits: Salzburg Mitte,
Münchner Bundesstrasse 1: Open
Easter–Oct, daily 09.00–20.00
(Nov–April 11.00–17.00. Salzburg Süd,
Park and Ride, Alpenstrasse: Opening
hours as for Salzburg Mitte. Salzburg
Nord, Autobahnstation Kasern: Open
June–Sept Mon–Sat 09.00–19.00 (July,
Aug 09.00–20.00).

Public transport
It is advisable to buy either the
Salzburg card (see Tourist information)
or a 24-hour or weekly pass (*Netzkarte*)
from a *Tabak* shop; the pass is valid for
all city buses and trolley buses, also
buses to Hellbrunn. At night a special
'city taxi' operates between 23.30 and
01.30 (details from the terminals at
Hanuschplatz and Theatergasse). If a
pass is not bought, tickets must be purchased from the bus driver. Ticket offices
at Griesgasse 21, Südtiroler Platz and at
Alpenstrasse 91.

Taxis
☎ 874400, 1715, 1716, 8111. Taxi
ranks are on the Residenzplatz, by
Tomaselli's café, by the Mönchsberg lift,
at the Hauptbahnhof, on Makartplatz
and elsewhere.

Accommodation
The tourist information bureau
supplies a listing of hotels and pensions
and the main office will help with bookings for a modest commission. All telephone numbers given below should be
prefaced with the local dialling code for
Salzburg, if calling from outside the city
(☎ 0662). Salzburg is expensive, with
premiums added for festival periods, for
which hotel rooms must be booked well in
advance. Those travelling on a tight bud-
get might consider staying in private
rooms, of which the tourist office has a
list (but you must make the booking yourself). Some proprietors will collect from
the station. There are eight **youth hostels**, including the *International Youth
Hotel* at Paracelsus Strasse 9
(☎ 879646), the attractive
Naturfreundehaus at Mönchsberg 19c
(☎ 841729) accessible via the
Mönchsberg lift, or the church-run
Institut St Sebastian (Linzer Gasse 41,
☎ 871386), which is more peaceful than
the others.

Hotels
☆☆☆☆☆ *Goldener Hirsch* (Getreidegasse
37. ☎ 8084-0. Fax: 843349). Top end
of the market and situated in the same
street as Mozart's House. Valet parking
service (extra charge). Rooms are spread
across three Baroque houses.
☆☆☆☆☆ *Hotel Österreichischer Hof*
(Schwarzstrasse 5-7. ☎ 88977. Fax.
88977-551). The hotel has fine views of
the Salzach and the city and is the
favoured watering-hole of the *beau monde*.
☆☆☆☆☆ *Schloss Mönchstein* (Mönchsberg
Park 26. ☎ 848555. Fax. 848559).
Elegant Schlosshotel in a pleasant setting, but further out of the city centre.
☆☆☆☆ *Altstadthotel Wolf Dietrich* (Wolf-
Dietrich Strasse 7. ☎ 871275. Fax
882320). Facilities include an indoor
pool, sauna, restaurant and garage (for
which extra payment is required).

☆☆☆☆ *Hotel Weisse Taube* (Kaigasse 9.
☎ 842404. Fax. 841783). Right in the
centre of town. Garage parking space
available.

☆☆☆ *Goldene Krone* (Linzer Gasse 48.
☎ 872300 or 878352). Pleasant mid-
priced hotel on the right bank, but
within walking distance of the old town.

☆☆☆ *Hotel Restaurant Hofwirt*
(Schallmooser Hauptstrasse 1.
☎ 872172–0. Fax. 881484–99). Free
parking is a bonus. There is a good
restaurant with a set lunch (good value)
and moderate price à la carte in the
evenings.

☆☆☆ *Blaue Gans* (Getreidegasse 41-43.
☎ 841317. Fax: 841317–9). Good
value considering its central location,
but not every room has its own shower.

☆☆☆ *Weisses Kreuz* (Bierjodlgasse 6.
☎ 845641. Fax: 845 6419). Tiny hotel
for which you pay a small premium for
being right behind the Cathedral
Square. Garage available.

☆☆☆ *Junger Fuchs* (Linzer Gasse 54.
☎ 875496). Relatively cheap and
cheerful.

Outside Salzburg
Pension Nocksteinblick (Heuberg 11.
☎ 64 50 40). On the hilly eastern outskirts of the city. Handy for quick access
to Fuschlsee and Wolfgangsee (see p
321).

Restaurants
Gourmet restaurants
Paris Lodron Schlossrestaurant in
Schloss Mönchstein (Mönchsberg Park
26).
Auerhahn (Bahnhofstrasse 15).
Purzelbaum (Zugallistrasse 7).
Riedenburg (Neutorstrasse 31).

Local cooking
Sternbräu 'La Stella' Trattoria (in the
courtyard between Getreidegasse 34
and Griesgasse 23).
St Peters Stiftskeller (in the courtyard of

St Peter's Abbey).
Zum Mohren (Judengasse 9).
K & K Stieglbräu Restaurant
(Rainerstrasse 14, on the right bank).

Cheaper places to eat
The *Blaue Gans* and *Weisses Kreuz*
hotels (see above) both serve modestly
priced food, the latter offering Balkan
specialities, the former Mexican.
Weingut Buschenschenke at
Neutorstrasse 34 is a wine tavern with
food.
St Paul's Stuben (Herrengasse 16)
serves pasta and pizza.
Restaurant Wegscheidstuben
(Lasserstrasse 1, right bank) offers
Austrian cooking.
Self-service of good quality is offered
by the *Nordsee* fish restaurant at
Getreidegasse 27.

Coffee houses
Tomaselli (Alter Markt). Unrivalled in
Salzburg and an institution.
Kaffeehäferl (Universitätsplatz 6).
Mozart (Getreidegasse 22).
Glockenspiel (Mozartplatz 2).
Café Winkler (Mönchsberg 32, access
by lift from the town, see p 301).

Main post office
Makartplatz 6. Also at Hauptbahnhof.

Police
Alpenstrasse 90. ☎ 63 83-0.

Cultural events
Since the inception of the Salzburger
Festspiele, the city has had an increasing number of annual arts festivals with
the emphasis naturally falling on music.
In addition, almost every year is marked
with a historical exhibition and accompanying events recalling some aspect of
Salzburg's rich past. **Information and
tickets for the Salzburger Festspiele**
may be obtained from the *Kartenbüro der
Salzburger Festspiele*, Postfach 140.

A-5020 Salzburg, Austria. ☎ (43 662) 84 45 01. Fax (43 662) 84 66 82.

Mozartwoche/Mozart Week
Staged over Christmas and New Year by the Stiftung Mozarteum, this short festival involves major symphony orchestras (such as the Wiener Philharmoniker) and chamber music groups playing Mozart favourites and less familiar works.

Osterfestspiele/Easter Festival
A week of symphony concerts, chamber music and opera over Easter.

Pfingstfestspiele/Whitsun Festival
Opera and concerts at the end of May and the beginning of June.

Salzburger Festspiele/Salzburg Festival
From late July to the end of August, the festival includes several opera productions, drama, solo and orchestral concerts, and of course, the hardy perennial *Jedermann* (*Everyman*) performed on the Domplatz.

Salzburger Jazz Herbst/Autumn Jazz Festival
In early November Salzburg plays host to international jazz stars.

Salzburger Festungskonzerte
Concerts in the Salzburg Fortress. All the year round chamber concerts are held in the *Fürstenzimmer* and *Wappensaal* of Festung Hohensalzburg.

Salzburger Schlosskonzerte/Salzburg Palace Concerts. All the year round chamber concerts are held in Schloss Mirabell.

Salzburger Mozartserenaden
Mozart Serenades . Chamber music from Easter to the end of the year in the Gotischen Saal and the Mozarteum.

Konzertsaison im Mozarteum
Concert Season in the Mozarteum. **Lieder**, chamber music, orchestral concerts in the Mozarteum in the spring and autumn.

Konzertring der Kulturvereinigung
Concerts of the Cultural Society. Up to May and from the beginning of September a series of major concerts are held in the Grossen Festspielhaus.

Landestheater Salzburg
Salzburg Provincial Theatre. Until the middle of June and from the middle of September a programme of opera, operetta and drama is on offer.

Salzburger Kunst und Antiquitätenmesse
Salzburg Antiques Fair. The fair is held in early April in the representation rooms of the Residenz.

Sightseeing tours

Leaflets at the tourist information bureau give details of the many possible tours of Salzburg and the nearby sights. For many of these (**Hellbrunn**, the **salt mines**, the **Großglockner**) a bus tour is only advisable if you are without a car. However, the tour to Hitler's **Eagle's Nest** (over the Bavarian border above Berchtesgaden on the Obersalzberg) is more convenient than driving, since the last part of the journey may in any case only be made with the official bus. Moreover, there are various **Sound of Music Tours**, which are somewhat kitschy attempts to milk the scenic potential of places featured in the film of the same name. Contact: Salzburg Panorama Tours ☎ 0662 874029; or ALBUS/Salzkraft ☎ 0662 881616.

Altstadt ~ the Old City

Writing in his journal of 1936, Karl Heinrich Waggerl vividly records an experience that many a Salzburg visitor may have shared:

> *It is night and a heavy rain sluices out of the sky. A little earlier, the surrounding landscape had been gently irradiated by the gleam of starlight—until the cloud brought the darkness into the valley. I saw how it overtook and swallowed up the moon as she tried to escape, likewise the anxious stars, and was indeed about to eclipse the entire firmament. Satiated at last, it laid itself down on the mountain as the last faint glimmers of light were snuffed out. I myself went out into the streets clothed in black. This Salzburg darkness is completely without form or shape, but all the same you can sense its unearthly measure as it moves; and I, a mere speck of life, seem to be floating in an abysmal void. And in this void I feel the beating of my heart.*

Such black and rainy nights of Salzburg are complemented by its frequently damp grey days, the greyness being emphasised by the rough and forbidding limestone used for so many of its historic buildings. The old city is crammed between the craggy heights of the Mönchsberg and the grey-green waters of the Salzach, as they rush importunately through the town and on to their appointment with the Inn. When you contemplate Marcus Sitticus's unfinished layout for an ideal city from the heights of the **Festung**, the grey-green panorama of the roofs and squares stretched out below you exudes a melancholy beauty that scarcely lifts the heart. And yet it is possible to be gradually seduced by the city's wealthy stoicism and epicurean masochism, to admire the restraint of Tomaselli's waiters when a party of 14 Japanese visitors occupy three tables and order two coffees, and even to aestheticise the constant, gentle rain as it silently settles on buildings and statues, when not also on the soul.

The city authorities have sensibly banned cars from the centre, so that motorists will be directed to one of several car parks which give direct access to the main sights. The Altstadt Garage (1500 places) inside the **Mönchsberg** (follow signs to *P-Zentrum*) is conveniently situated, with several exits, one of which is next to the **Sigmundstor** (or **Neutor**) at the north-eastern end of the tunnel under the mountain built between 1764 and 1768. The Baroque ornamentation of the Sigmundstor (including a medallion of the tunnel's commissioner, Archbishop Sigmund III) is by the brothers Johann and Wolfgang Hagenauer. Nearby is the **Hofmarstallschwemme**, once a pool for washing horses, as the backdrop of (heavily restored) frescoes by F.A. Ebner recalls. The *Horse Breaker* sculpture (1695) in the centre is by Bernhard Mandl, probably to an original design by J.B. Fischer von Erlach.

Before plunging into the main sights, it is worth making a detour westwards on the Bürgerspitalgasse to the **Hospital Church of St Blasius** (1330), which boasts a rare sacramental reliquary (1481) on the north side of the main altar. The church was used by the burghers and by the prebendaries of the **Bürgerspital** (1556–70), a fine arcaded structure just to the south, which now houses the **Spielzeugmuseum** (Toy Museum, open Tues–Sun 10.00–18.00. Closed in November.).

Continuing north-west you pass the lift which ascends the rockface to the *Café Winkler* and the **Casino**, with fine views of city from the summit. An interesting panoramic representation of Salzburg (made by Johann Michael Sattler in 1825)

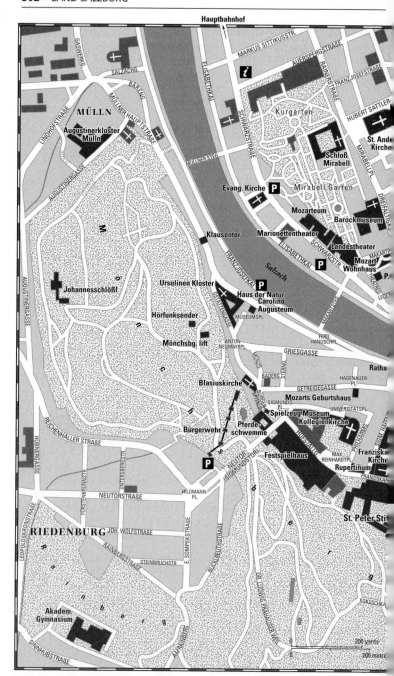

Hauptbahnhof

MÜLLN

Augustinerkloster Mülln

Kurgarten

St. And. Kirche

Schloß Mirabell

Evang. Kirche

Mirabell Garten

Mozarteum

Barockmuseum

Klausentor

Marionettentheater

Landestheater

Mozart Wohnhaus

Johannesschlößl

Ursulinen Kloster

Haus der Natur Carolino Augusteum

Hörfunksender

Mönchsbg. lift

Griesgasse

Ratha

Blasiuskirche

Mozarts Geburtshaus

Spielzeug Museum

Kollegienkirche

Bürgerwehr

Pferde-schwemme

Festspielhaus

Franziska Kirche

Rupertinum

St. Peter Sti

RIEDENBURG

Akadem. Gymnasium

200 yards

200 metres

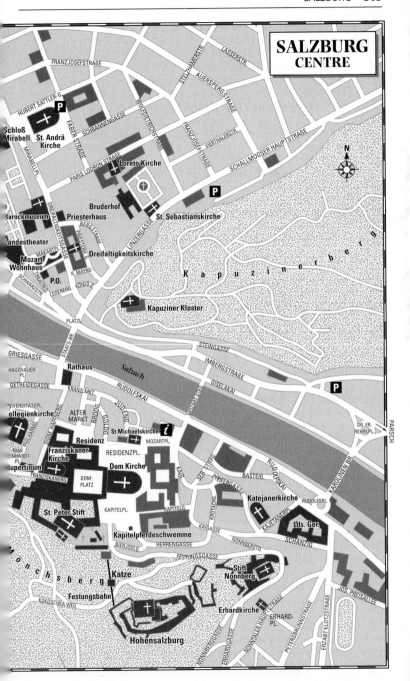

SALZBURG
CENTRE

FRANZJOSEFSTRAßE
LASSERSTR.
STEINAMETSTR.
AUERSPERGSTRAßE
WOLFDIETRICHSTRAße
FRANZ-JOSEF-STRAße
VIERTHALERSTRAße
SCHALLMOOSER HAUPTSTRAße
N
HUBERT SATTLER-G.
P
FABER STRAße
SCHRANNENGASSE
Schloß
Mirabell
St. Andrä
Kirche
MIRABELLPL.
PARIS LODRON STRAße
Loreto Kirche
P
Barockmuseum
Landestheater
BERGSTRAße
PRIESTERB.
DREIFALTIGKEITSGASSE
Bruderhof
Priesterhaus
LINZERGASSE
St. Sebastianskirche
MAKARTPL.
Mozart
Wohnhaus
R. MAYRG.
Dreifaltigkeitskirche
THEATERG.
P.O.
LEDERERG.
KÖNIG. G.
SCHWARZSTR.
K a p u z i n e r b e r g
Kapuziner Kloster
PLATZL
STAATS BR.
STEINGASSE
GRIESGASSE
IMBERGSTRAße
Rathaus
Salzach
HAGENAUER
PL.
GETREIDEGASSE
KRANZLMKT.
RUDOLFSKAI
GISELAKAI
P
*NIVERSITÄTSPL.
ALTER
MARKT
JUDENG.
BRODG.
GOLDG.
MOZARTSTEG
PARSCH
ollegienkirche
SIGM. HAFFNERG.
St Michaelskirche
i
DR. FR.
REHRLPL.
*MAX
EINHARDT-
PL.
Residenz
Franziskaner
Kirche
MOZARTPL.
RESIDENZPL.
RUDOLFSKAI
upertinum
FRANZISKANERG.
Dom Kirche
KAIG.
SEB. STIEFG.
PFEIFERGASSE
BASTEIG.
St. Peter Stift
DOM-
PLATZ
KAPITELPL.
KAPITELG.
KROTACHG.
KAIGASSE
Katejanerkirche
RUDOLFSPL.
KAJETANERG.
Lds. Ger.
SCHANZlG.
Kapitelpferdeschwemme
BIERJODLG.
HERRENGASSE
NONNBERGSTG.
M ö n c h s b e r g
FESTUNGSGASSE
Katze
Stift
Nonnberg
Festungsbahn
KOKOSCHKA WEG
Erhardkirche
ERHARD-
PL.
NONNTALER HAUPTSTRAße
PETERSBRUNNSTRAße
ERZABT KLOTZSTRAße
JOS. PREISALLEE
Hohensalzburg
NONNBERGGASSE
ERHARDGASSE

may be seen in the café entrance hall. Beyond the lift at street level is the former **Ursuline Convent** which houses the spectacular **Haus der Natur** (Natural History Museum, open daily 09.00–17.00). Close by is the former Ursuline Church, which became the **Markuskirche** when rebuilt in 1669 to plans by J.B. Fischer von Erlach after destruction by a rockfall. Its rich interior stucco is attributed to the Carlone workshop, while the ceiling frescoes (1756, featuring the *Apotheosis of St Ursula* and the *Fathers of the Church*) are by Christoph Anton Mayr.

Across the street at Museumsplatz 1–6 is the **Salzburger Museum Carolino Augusteum** (open Tues–Sun 10.00–18.00, Thur to 20.00), the city's important historical museum. It was founded in 1834 and named after the widow of Emperor Franz, Carolina Augusta of Bavaria (d. 1873). The basement contains Roman mosaics, while the first floor has artefacts from the Iron Age and Hallstatt period of Celtic civilisation, together with Gothic sculpture and painting. The second floor displays Baroque painting, landscapes of Salzburg in the Biedermeier period, musical instruments, furniture and reconstructed interiors. Highlights include a fine **Rosary picture** of the late 16C, a portrait (1589) of the formidable Wolf Dietrich von Raitenau aged 30 by Kaspar Memberger, *Jesus Teaching in the Temple* (1697) by J.M. Rottmayr, and two powerful works by Paul Troger, both dating to 1749 (*Daniel Defending Susanna* and the *Judgement of Solomon*). From the 19C collection, William James Grant's intensely romantic *Mozart Composing His Requiem* (1854) stands out, as does the genially ironic *Sunday Walk* (1841) by the Munich painter, Carl Spitzweg: the fact that Spitzweg was said to be Hitler's favourite painter should not be allowed to obscure his talent for gently satiric observation and his skill in evoking the ambience of Biedermeier *Gemütlichkeit*. The 20C section has pictures by leading members of **Der Wassermann**, Felix Albrecht Harta (1884–1967) and Anton Faistauer (1887–1930).

Mozart sights in Salzburg

Retracing your steps to the south-west, you reach the entrance to the Getreidegasse with its picturesque shop signs, the oldest house of which (no. 21) dates to 1258. At no. 9 is the **Mozart House**, where the composer was born on 27 January 1756. The museum displays memorabilia of Mozart's childhood, instruments (open July and Aug, daily 09.00–19.00, Jan–June and Sept–Dec, 09.00–18.00).

Apart from **Mozart's birthplace**, there are several other places associated with the composer in Salzburg. It is well worth acquiring the booklet *Mozart in Salzburg* on sale at the house, which gives a detailed description of what each of these has to offer, as well as a chronology of Mozart's career and brief biography. The **Mozart Wohnhaus** (Mozart family residence) is at Makartplatz 8 (open July and August, 09.00–19.00, Jan–June, Sept–Dec 09.00–18.00) and was rented by Leopold Mozart from a dancing mistress, Anna Maria Raab, between 1773 and 1787. It had to be substantially rebuilt after wartime bombing and was reopened in 1996. There are five rooms, one of them Leopold's library with some of his books on display, another dedicated to Mozart's sister, Nannerl, and a room with a large wall map showing Mozart's journeys round Europe. Perhaps its most interesting section is the **audio-visual museum**, whose mission is to collect every single Mozart interpretation that has been mechanically preserved. Visitors currently have access to some 11,000 audio- and 1000 videotapes.

Wolfgang Amadeus Mozart (1756–91)

Mozart was baptised Johannes Chrysost Wolfgang Theophilus and nicknamed 'Amadè' or 'Amadeus' from 1777, a joking reference to Theophilus, 'Gottlieb' in German. His music, regarded by some to be the finest ever written, and the details of his hectically creative life first became the subject of a romantic cult in the 19C. He was only moderately successful in terms of hard cash in his own lifetime, being dismissed from Archbishop Colloredo's employ (literally booted out by the Chamberlain) and receiving only a lukewarm reception at the Vienna court. His operas were well received in Prague, however, and *Die Zauberflöte* (*The Magic Flute*) quickly became a favourite with the Viennese. Nor should the spectacular success of *Mitridate, Rè di Ponto* in Milan (1770) be overlooked and the bestowal of the Order of the Golden Spur on the 13-year-old prodigy in Rome in 1769. If Mozart is not the neglected or maligned genius of romantic fancy, neither did the world fall at his feet: he took risks with his career and some of these failed to pay off.

As the protagonist and perfector of the *Wiener Classik*, who expanded the musical horizons of his friend and mentor, Joseph Haydn, Mozart stands at the turning-point between Baroque and Classicism, between the ages of Counter-Reformatory zeal and rational Enlightenment. His richest period of creative production in Vienna between 1781 and 1791 coincides almost exactly with the reign of the Enlightened absolutist, Emperor Joseph II, himself a figure who bridges the world of the *ancien régime* with that of the modern state. If Sir Thomas Beecham curiously chose to see *Così fan tutte* as the swan-song 'in praise of a civilisation that has passed away', *Le Nozze di Figaro* (*Marriage of Figaro*) mocks the anachronistic privileges of feudalism with civically self-confident irreverence. The ability of Mozart to stand simultaneously in two worlds is underlined by Aaron Copland, when he writes: 'Mozart in his music was probably the most reasonable of the world's great composers. It is the happy balance between flight and control, between sensibility and self-discipline, simplicity and sophistication of style that is his particular province...'

The **Internationale Stiftung Mozarteum** was founded in 1841 and its collection of manuscripts by Mozart and other members of his family are housed in the basement. The collection is based on the bequest of Mozart's son, Franz Xaver, which included all the composer's manuscripts and personal library, but has been considerably enlarged through acquisitions. The **Mozarteum** itself (Schwarzstrasse 26, open Mon–Fri, 09.00–12.00 and 14.00–17.00) was built between 1910 and 1914 in Munich *Jugendstil* and houses a music school, research library and two concert halls. In the foyer of the larger one is Edmund Hellmer's *Mozart-Apollo* sculpture; in the garden is the **Little House of the Magic Flute**, a summer house transported here from the garden of the Theater auf der Wieden in Vienna. Allegedly the impresario and lyricist for *The Magic Flute*, Emanuel Schikaneder, locked Mozart into this house until he completed the score of the opera, which was then premiered at the adjacent theatre. Access is only possible during concert intermissions in the summer months.

Finally, the **Mozart Monument** by the Munich sculptor, Ludwig von Schwanthaler, was set up on Mozartplatz on 4 September 1842, in the presence of the composer's two sons. The local historian Karl Heinz Ritschel remarks that this 'awful' statue neither 'looks like Mozart nor evokes his genius' but seems more like 'the brazen representation of a boring bureaucrat'.

At the east end of the Getreidegasse is the Baroque **Rathaus** (1618) with attractive rocaille decoration on the façade. In the niche over the portal is an allegory of *Justice* by Hans Waldburger. The whole street has attractive five- or six-storeyed Baroque houses and intimate passageways leading through or into courtyards.

A right turn beyond the Sigmund-Haffner-Gasse (named after the rich burgher for whom Mozart wrote a well-known serenade to accompany a family wedding) brings you into the **Alter Markt**, at the south end of which is the **Florianibrunnen** (Floriani Fountain) with a figure (1734) of *St Florian* sculpted by Josef Anton Pfaffinger and a Renaissance basin (1587) with elegant acanthus volutes. Close by is the famous *Tomaselli café* founded by a Milanese in 1730 and frequented by the Mozart family. The historic core of Salzburg stands to the south, but before visiting it, turn left (skirting the **Residenz** and Residenzplatz) to reach the **Church of St Michael**, founded before 800 but completely rebuilt between 1767 and 1776. There are Roman reliefs (one showing *Dionysius and Ariadne*) attached to the north wall and the interior has extensive Rococo decoration by minor masters.

Further east along Pfeiffergasse the former **Kajetanerkirche** (Cajetan Church) is reached, built by Johann Kaspar Zugalli (actually 'Giovanni Gaspare Zuccalli', one of the many Italians active in Salzburg, although in this case an Italian-Swiss). The church is named after St Cajetan (1480–1547), founder of the Theatine Order, whose cloister adjoins it, and who were called to Salzburg to train priests. The order devoted itself to the remedy of abuses in the church and its members were allowed neither property, nor to beg for alms. However, their pedagogic activity brought them into conflict with the Benedictines, who jealously guarded their teaching monopoly at the University, and who managed to hinder progress on the church between 1687 and 1696. Of interest is the cupola fresco (1728) by Paul Troger of *St Cajetan being received into Heaven*, and the same artist's altarpiece featuring the church's patron (the *Martyrdom of St Maximilian*, 1777). Above the left-hand side altar is is J.M. Rottmayr's *St Martin* (1708), above the right-hand one, Troger's *St Cajetan comforting the Victims of the Plague* (1735). Note also the white marble sculptures of Matthias Wilhelm Weissenkircher (*Praying Angels*, the *Immaculata*).

Residenzbrunnen and Residenzgalerie

Retracing your steps eastwards along the Kaigasse, you pass the **Archbishop's Palace** (since 1864) on your left and enter the **Kapitelplatz**, which has another horse-washing pool (*Kapitelschwemme*) decorated with a *Neptune* sculpture (1732, Joseph Anton Pfaffinger, after a design by Georg Raphael Donner). Skirting the east end of the cathedral, you cross the **Residenzplatz** with its magnificent **Residenzbrunnen** (Residenz Fountain) of 1661 ascribed to Tommaso di Garona. The imposing sculptural ensemble shows four sea-horses galloping out of grottoes, these below Atlas figures bearing the fountain's basin entwined with dolphins, the whole crowned with a Triton. In the context of the 'ideal city', such fountains represented *abundantia*, the ruler's generous exercises of his virtues (and also, of course, hard cash) on behalf of his suitably grateful subjects.

The **Residenz** of the Archbishops itself is entered from the west side of the square under a portal bearing the arms of Franz Anton Harrach. At the end of the central courtyard is the **Hercules fountain** (1615), to the left of which steps climb to the starting-point for a tour of the interior. The original building dates to the Middle Ages, but was extended and altered by Wolf Dietrich in Renaissance style and by his successor, Marcus Sitticus, who built the wing along the Alter Markt; further extensions were commissioned by Paris Lodron, Guidobald Thun and finally Hieronymus Colloredo, who added the Toskanatrakt. The **representation rooms** on the second floor can be visited with a 40-minute tour (April–Sept, daily 10.00–17.00), provided they are not being used for official functions. Highlights include ceiling frescoes by J.M. Rottmayr (*Vulcan's Smithy*, *Atalante's Boar-Hunt*, *Neptune stilling the Winds for Aeneas*), and rooms created by Lukas von Hildebrandt and Antonio Beduzzi with fine stucco by Alberto Camesina and painting by Martino Altomonte (the **Throne Room**, **White Room** and the **Emperor's Chamber**).

On the floor above is the **Residenzgalerie** with paintings from the 16C–19C, including Rembrandt's portrait of his *Mother at Prayer*, some appealing Dutch landscapes by van Goyen, Ruysdael, Cuyp and others, Rubens' *Allegory of Karl V as Ruler of the World*, Carlo Dolci's *St Catherine Reading*, two Guercinos, Maulbertsch's *Last Supper*, some charming Biedermeier works, and Johann Fischbach's attractive *View of Salzburg*. The superb **frescoed wall maps** in the Toskanatrakt, whose restoration was completed in 1995, may be seen on application to the University, whose Law Faculty uses the room as a library.

Across the square is the **Residenz-Neugebäude**, from whose tower a Dutch **glockenspiel** (1702) plays a changing programme of various (including Mozartian) themes at 07.00, 11.00 and 18.00. By walking through the arches southwards from the Residenzplatz, you reach the **Domplatz**, on which Max Reinhardt's production of *Jedermann* is played each year during the festival against a backdrop of the cathedral façade. In the middle of the Domplatz is the **Marian Column** (1771, by Wolfgang and Johann Baptist Hagenauer), aligned with the cathedral façade in such a way that, when viewed from the back of the square, the two angels on the the second storey of the façade appear to be placing a crown on the head of the Madonna of the column.

Dom Sankt Ruprecht

The Dom (Cathedral) is the oldest bishopric church in Austria, founded under Bishop Virgil in 774 on the remains of the Roman town, rebuilt in 1181 after a fire, and planned anew by Wolf Dietrich's architect, Vincenzo Scamozzi. His ambitious design envisaging a building 139m long and 100m wide, was modified by the actual builder of the cathedral between 1614 and 1628, Santino Solari. The elegant façade with its twin towers is richly decorated with statuary by Tommaso di Garona (the *Four Evangelists* on the balustrade, above them *Christ*, *Moses* and *Elias* in the gable). Note also the emblems of Marcus Sitticus (an ibex) and of the Archbishopric (a lion).

In front of the triple-arched entrance are statues of the local patrons, *Sts Rupert and Virgil* on the outside (Bartholomäus van Opstal, 1660), and on the inside *Peter* and *Paul* by Bernhard Mandl (1698). The hugely monumental **interior** with a wide processional nave is richly decorated with greyish white

Cathedral of Saint Rupert

stucco reminiscent of Lombardy Baroque. The nave opens out into the light-filled crossing, the graceful proportions of which testify to the architect's almost hubristically bold realisation of Luca Pacioli's 'golden section' (*sectio aurea*), whereby the smaller proportional feature is to the greater as the greater is to the whole. Note the four organs at the four corners of the crossing, which create a magnificent acoustic harmony when played in conjunction with the main organ at the rear.

The fresco cycle of the Dom (by Arsenio Mascagni, a Servite monk from Florence) has a complicated iconography and was heavily restored between 1878 and 1880, and again after 1945. (Rebuilding after wartime bombing lasted until 1959.) The nave frescoes feature the *Passion of Christ*, with the *Miracles of Jesus* in the cartouches. The *Life of Christ* continues in the presbytery, while the main altarpiece represents the climax of the entire cycle with the *Resurrection*. The *Transfigured Christ* appears on the vault and the *Glory of God in Heaven* on the vertex. The south transept shows the *Life of Mary*, the north transept, that of *St Francis*. The 16 divisions of the cupola recall references to the Old Testament in Christ's teaching, and the Holy Spirit hovers above. The *Four Evangelists* are depicted on the drum spandrel. The north altar paintings again feature the *Life of Christ*, while those in the south depict saints and apostles.

The *Gesamtkunstwerk* of architecture and decoration is designed to produce an artistic and spiritual unity focused on the single most important article of Christian faith, namely the Resurrection. Of the 17 century paintings of the side-altars, Joachim Sandrart's *St Anne* and the Bohemian Karel Škréta's *Christ on the Cross* (north aisle), and Škréta's *Descent of the Holy Ghost* (south aisle) repay study. The other paintings of saints in the south aisle (Rochus, Sebastian, Carlo Borromeo—all associated with protection from the plague—and Martin, Gregor, Jerome and Nicholas) are by Johann Heinrich Schönfeld. Around the crossing are fine polychrome **marble tombs** of the Archbishops by Konrad Asper and Josef Anton Pfaffinger. The **crypt** displays a mosaic of the ground plans of earlier churches on the cathedral site and a Romanesque crucifix. The **font** has survived from the pre-Baroque cathedral, its lion-base being 12C, the basin itself, with reliefs of bishops and abbots, dating to 1321.

The **Cathedral Museum** (entrance in the southern vestibule; open mid-May–26 Oct, Mon–Sat 10.00–17.00, Sun, PH 13.00–18.00) contains an intriguing *Kunst- und Wunderkammer* (1662).

Leaving the Domplatz towards the west, a right turn brings you almost immediately to the **Franziskanerkirche** (Franciscan Church), whose high and narrow Romanesque nave (c 1223) opens out of mystical gloom into a 15C Gothic choir by Hans von Burghauser. Striking is the single column rising at the centre of the choir, against which is set the pink and gold Baroque high altar (1708) by J.B. Fischer von Erlach, the focus of a circumductory ambulatory with its wreath of 17C chapels. The middle one of these has a fine marble altar of 1561. The Baroque decoration of the main altar frames the late Gothic (1498) *Madonna* by Michael Pacher, part of a much bigger work now lost. The *Christ Child* set in the middle of it dates to 1825, however. The marble pulpit is Romanesque, having at the foot of its steps a rather cheerful-looking lion, considering that a knight lying beneath him is stabbing him vigorously with his sword. The hand raised in blessing on the west portal of the church signifies that it once disposed of the right of asylum for those fleeing the law.

An alley leads south from the Franziskanergasse into the courtyard of the Benedictine **abbey of St Peter**, founded in 696 by St Ruprecht and seat of the bishops until 798, then the archbishops until 1110. On the middle one of three internal courtyards stands a hexagonal fountain with a statue of *St Peter* (1673); on its east side is the entrance to the oldest wine cellar of Salzburg, *St Peters Stiftskeller*, a good place to stop for lunch.

Romanesque tympanum, Abbey of St Peter

The entrance to **St Peter's Church** (tours for a minimum of five persons take place on the hour 10.00–17.00, May–Sept) is adjacent, the latter now presenting a chiefly Rococo aspect after alterations in 1770, but in origin a Romanesque basilica built in 1147. The interior is closed off by a wrought-iron screen (1768, Philipp Hinterseer) showing the arms of Abbot Beda Seeauer (1753–85), in whose abbotship the church was barockised.

All but two of the Baroque altarpieces inside are by Kremser Schmidt or his school, while the wall paintings include *Christ carrying the Cross* (1591, Kaspar Memberger) in the right-hand nave and Ignazio Solari's *Erection of the Cross on Calvary Hill* (1632) to the left. J.B. Weiss painted the frescoes of the *Life of St Peter* on the flattened vault of the centre aisle, with its attractive eau-de-Nil stucco (Benedikt Zöpf) on a white background. The organ (1620, rebuilt 1763) is topped by statues of *Sts Peter, Vitus and Rupert* (1625, Hans Waldburger). The putative tomb of *St Rupert* is in the south aisle, but his remains, if briefly deposited here, were soon transferred to the cathedral.

Adjacent to the church is the **cemetery** partly encompassed by Christoph

Gottsreiter's arcades (1626), a place of unearthly calm once celebrated by Georg Trakl in verse. Santino Solari (d. 1656) is buried here, together with Michael Haydn and Mozart's sister, Nannerl.

At the entrance to the municipal crypt is a powerful representation of the *Dance of Death* reminiscent of Hieronymus Bosch. Nearby are the so-called catacombs (daily tours on the hour May–Sept, 10.00–17.00, Oct–April at 10.30, 11.30, 13.30, 14.30 and 15.30) dating to the 3C and 4C and later used as hermitages by the monks of St Peter. The tour includes the **Gertraude Chapel** of 1178, above whose entrance is a 15C fresco of the *Murder of Thomas à Becket*, an event that took place eight years before the dedication of this chapel. From the east end of the cemetery you reach the terminus of the cable railway up to the *Festung* (see p 311), after passing on your left the Stift bakery; but we return to the Max-Reinhardt-Platz west of the Franciscan Church.

In Wiener-Philharmoniker-Gasse (leading north out of the square) at no. 9 is the **Landessammlungen Rupertinum** (open Tues, Thur, Fri, Sat, Sun 10.00–17.00, Wed 10.00–21.00, in summer also on Mon) containing 20C painting, graphics, sculpture and photographs. On the south side of Max-Reinhardt-Platz is the Kleines Festspielhaus, extending into the Grosses Festspielhaus, and occupying the former site of the Archbishop's stables. The **Kleines Festspielhaus** was built to Clemens Holzmeister's design in 1926 as a conversion of the impressive Felsenreitschule and Winterreitschule (the latter having a 600sq m ceiling fresco (1690) by J.M. Rottmayr and Christoph Lederwasch, the so-called *Türkenstechen*). The Kleine Festspielhaus has a foyer decorated with frescoes by Anton Faistauer. These featured the architect and builder themselves, the dinner scene from *Jedermann*, allegories of the power of music and beauty, and a representation of the path of life from birth to death, then St Cecilia (as patron of music) etc. The Nazis considered these to be '*entartete Kunst*' (degenerate art) and had them removed, but they returned in 1956. In the central foyer is Alfred Hrdlicka's *Orpheus* sculpture and a tapestry decoration of the sun and the moon by Oskar Kokoschka. The latter also did the tapestry design of *Amor and Psyche* for the Upper Circle corridor of the **Grosses Festspielhaus**, which Holzmeister completed in 1960. Tours of the Festspielhaus take place at 14.00 in Oct, Nov, Dec, April, May, and at 09.30, 14.00, 15.30 from June–Sept.

The last major sight of the old town is the **Kollegienkirche** (University Church, 1707) by J.B. Fischer von Erlach, with its imposing convex façade and two ornate clock-towers, which stands on Universitätsplatz north-west of the Festspielhaus. Its dedication to the Immaculate Virgin reflected a dogma rigorously upheld by the University's Faculty of Theology, even though it was not as yet an official dogma of the church (it became such only in 1854 under Pius IX).

The **interior** of the church is austere, the icy clarity generated by the generous space and the height of the cupola being emphasised by the paucity of colourful decoration and the severity of the white stucco. The high altar is closed off by two monumental pillars, supposedly an allusion to those of Solomon's temple. Above it rise exuberant stucco clouds, a feature that breaks out of the rigidity of the church's formal decoration and celebrates the Immaculata with apocalyptic brio. The two windows at the centre supply the effect of dazzling light penetrating the clouds. The rest of the church's decoration is generally unremarkable, with the exception of J.M. Rottmayr's paintings for the two side-altars featuring the lives of the patron saints of the University, *St Carlo Borromeo* and *St Benedict*.

Festung Hohensalzburg

The Salzburg fortress (119m above the city on the south-east peak of the Mönchsberg) is reached with a formerly water-driven cable railway starting from the east end of St Peter's cemetery (Festungsgasse 4, open May–Sept 09.00–21.00, Oct–April 09.00–17.00). The fortress itself (the largest surviving intact in Central Europe) is open daily from 09.00–17.00 and may be visited with a guided tour (45mins). It was built in c 1077 on the site of a Roman *castrum* and was considerably enlarged and altered by several archbishops, notably Leonhard von Keutschach (1495–1519), a monument to whom (Hans Valkenauer, 1515) stands by the Church of St George towards the Festung's east end. Generally, the fortress was used as a retreat for the rulers when the going got rough, and then as a barracks until the first tourists were admitted in 1870.

In 1953 Oskar Kokoschka's School of Seeing (see p 294) was installed here. In recent years the walls have reacquired their white patina, a return to their original medieval aspect, or so the historians claim. The tour includes the **Stallgebäude** with portraits of the archbishops who built and extended the fortress, the **Alte Schloss** with the decorative **Fürstenzimmer**, the **Goldene Stube** with an impressively ornate tiled stove of 1501, and the **Goldene Saal** with its marble columns, coats of arms and inscriptions. There is a modest Burgmuseum and another exhibition devoted to the Salzburger House Regiment of the Archduke Rainer, which was quartered here between 1871 and 1918.

Stift Nonnberg

If you descend eastwards from the fortress by foot, a ten-minute walk (bearing right) will bring you to **Stift Nonnberg** founded by St Rupert in AD 700, at which time he appointed his niece (Erentrudis or Arintraud) as its first Abbess. Now run by the Benedictines, it is the oldest nunnery of the German-speaking region. (It is perhaps better known to millions as the convent featured in *The Sound of Music* where Maria is a somewhat flighty novice, and where, in a scene beyond parody, the generously proportioned Mother Superior bursts into song with '*Climb Every Mountain*'.)

St Erentrudis is buried in the crypt of this strangely inspiring Gothic church, the atmosphere of which becomes even more romantic if you catch the dulcet tones of the nuns singing Evensong in the screened gallery at the west end. Romanesque elements from the earlier church may still be seen, chiefly the tympanum and banked columns of the south portal, and the Byzantine-influenced frescoes (1140) under the nuns' choir, which show six not definitively identified saints, but possibly *Benedict*, *Rupert*, *Stephen*, *Agnes*, *Florian* and *Vincent of Saragossa*.

The **Johanneskapelle** in another part of the convent has a fine Gothic wing altar from 1498 attributed to the circle of Veit Stoßof Nürnberg and may be visited on application to the porter's lodge. Steps descend north from the Nonnberg to the Kaigasse, but if you follow the Nonnberggasse south-west and descend via steps to the Nonntaler Hauptstrasse, you will see on your left the **church of St Erhard** built by Giovanni Zuccalli. The high altar (1689) has an altarpiece by J.M. Rottmayr of the *Healing of the Blind Man*.

The right bank of the Salzach

By crossing the River Salzach at the centrally located Staatsbrücke, you find yourself at the busy Platzl junction, from which a main street (Linzergasse) heads north-east. Through an archway at no. 14 the road climbs to the

Kapuziner (*Capuchin*) **cloister** and **church** (1602) and the **Kapuzinerberg**, from which there are pleasant views. At Linzergasse 41 is the **Sebastiankirche**, the façade of which shows two angels acting as caryatids to support the door columns and above them a bust of St Sebastian pierced by an arrow, twin allusions to his martyrdom and his function as a saint protecting against the 'arrow of the plague'. A fire of 1818 destroyed much of the church's interior, but a wrought-iron gate (Philipp Hinterseer, 1752) has survived, while a *Madonna* (1600) by Hans Waldburger has replaced the altarpiece by Paul Troger. More interesting is the **cemetery**, in particular the impressive late Renaissance tiled and domed **Mausoleum** or **Gabrielskapelle** (1603, Elia Castello) of Archbishop Wolf Dietrich, and the arcades (1600) built by Andrea Bertoleto of Como, which so strongly recall the tradition of the *campo santo* of his homeland.

Wolf Dietrich von Raitenau (1559–1617)

One of the most vivid figures in Salzburg's history, Wolf Dietrich of Raitenau (in Vorarlberg), became archbishop when only 28 years' old after an education in Italy that convinced him of the need to replan his city according to the ideal tenets of the Renaissance and likewise to elevate it politically and economically. His ideal city was never realised, although he did initiate a new cathedral and rebuild the archbishop's residence, as well as clearing about one-third of the existing houses in the old town in preparation for his great project. He also changed the face of Salzburg with measures such as draining the Schallmoos area and laying out new streets, primarily on hygienic grounds to reduce the rapid spread of plague. Under his regime, plague victims were immediately isolated or interned outside the city. The archbishop's ruthless realism was also evident in his healthy disdain for relics, the bones of the city's most revered figures, including St Rupert, being for some time piled up unceremoniously in a corner of his palace during building works. Similarly, when he needed to clear the old cathedral cemetery, he simply had the contents of the graves tipped into the Salzach, much to the outrage of the Salzburgers. Another source of scandal was his unblessed 'marriage' to the bourgeois Salome Alt, whom he persuaded Emperor Rudolf II to ennoble as Salome von Altenau, and who bore him some ten children, and for whom he built Schloss Altenau (later the Mirabell Palace). His orthodoxy in ruthlessly persecuting Protestants could not rescue him from pious (envious?) condemnation of this irregular, but lastingly happy, liaison.

As a politician, Wolf Dietrich attempted to shore up the influence of Salzburg by having an intimidated Cathedral Chapter pass a statute forbidding the election of any member of the House of Bavaria, or of Habsburg, to the post of archbishop. When he overreached himself in trying to suppress Bavarian competition in the salt trade, his archbishopric was invaded and he was deposed, then kept prisoner on the Hohensalzburg by his successor and cousin, Marcus Sitticus of Hohenems. His confinement was merciless— Marcus Sitticus even had his windows sealed after failed escape attempts—and he finally died of an epileptic fit at the age of 58. His corpse was carried to his mausoleum, in accordance with his instructions, at night and accompanied only by two Franciscan monks, with no tolling bells nor princely obsequies.

The other distinguished figure in the cemetery of St Sebastian is **Theophrastus Paracelsus** (1493–1541), whose tomb abuts the chuch vestibule. Scientist, philosopher, doctor or quack, according to taste, Paracelsus correctly described kidney and bladder stones and the pathology of infected wounds, as well as discovering many natural remedies that have come to be looked on more favourably with the advance of alternative medicine. Also buried here are various members of the Mozart and Weber families.

Returning to the Platzl, a little to the north of it you encounter the **Dreifaltigkeitskirche** (Holy Trinity Church, 1702) on Makartplatz, J.B. Fischer von Erlach's first ecclesiastical commission in Salzburg having an elegant concave façade evidently influenced by Borromini's Sant'Agnese in the Piazza Navona in Rome. The fresco of the *Coronation of the Virgin Mary* (1700) in the cupola is by J.M. Rottmayr. On the south side of the Makartplatz is **Mozart's House** (see p 304), also known as the *Tanzmeisterhaus* on account of the owner's profession.

Schloss Mirabell and the Barockmuseum

Leaving the Landestheater on your left, you proceed from the north-west of the square to the delightful **park** of Schloss Mirabell, laid out by Fischer von Erlach and subsequently altered in the 1730s by Franz Anton Danreiter, the reconstruction of whose late Baroque garden has been the aim of post-war restorers after some unhappy 19C interventions. The focal point of the central part of the gardens is Ottavio Mosto's **fountain** (1690), symbolising the elements of Earth, Air, Fire and Water, here allegorically represented as *Proserpine and Helen, Aeneas and Anchises, Hercules and Antaeus*. The geometrical arrangement of the garden follows the embroidery style of Le Nôtre (*broderie parterre*) employed at Versailles, but the asymmetry of the cultivated areas is an idiosyncracy that was determined by the plot available. In the raised western part of the garden (*Rosenhügel*) is a circle of stone dwarves set up under Anton, Count Harrach (archbishop from 1709–27) who himself kept a dwarf at his court. The scheme of Bernhard Mandl's originally 24 creations was to be 'a world in miniature' representing all sorts and conditions of men from rope-dancers and craftsmen to merchants and Turkish lords. Around it were planted dwarf trees, the whole an ironic caricature of the 'real world'. In the upper gardens is to be found the so-called '**hedge theatre**' (1718), whose bushes replicated contemporary stage settings, and on another level is the **Pegasus fountain** (1661, Kaspar Gras), originally part of the *Pferdeschwemme* on Kapitelplatz and brought here in 1913.

Schloss Mirabell, originally Salome von Altenau's residence (built in 1606), acquired its present name in 1612, Marcus Sitticus wishing to obliterate the memory of his cousin's *mèsalliance*. It was rebuilt (1721–27) by Lukas von Hildebrandt and reconstructed by Peter von Nobile after a fire in 1818. Hildebrandt's fine **staircase**, with sculptures of putti pointing the way upwards (by Georg Raphael Donner) survived the fire and may be seen when entering the west wing. The statue of *Paris* (1726) halfway up is also by Donner. The **Marble Hall** in the centre of the west wing is impressive, with its marble-clad walls and gilded stucco, and is now a popular venue for concerts, while the neo-classical **chapel** in the east wing is also worth a visit, the altarpiece (1830) of *St Nepomuk* being by Michael Hess. The rest of the palace is given over to the offices of the Mayor and municipal government.

To the west of Schloss Mirabell's bastion runs Schwarzstrasse, leading to the Mozarteum (see p 304) at no. 26 and the adjacent (no. 24) **Marionettentheater**, a world famous puppet theatre playing operas (inevitably much Mozart, but other works as well) and founded in 1913 by Anton Aicher.

To the east of the Schloss is the Orangery and entrance to the **Barockmuseum** (open Tues–Sat 09.00–12.00, 14.00–17.00, Sun 09.00–12.00) based originally on a collection of sketches and models acquired by one Karl Rossacher on his travels. The exhibits interestingly chart the progress of many Baroque projects from commission to their final form via *Pensiero* (first idea) and *Bozzetto* (provisional scale model). Many of the leading Baroque masters are represented in this way either with 'work in progress' or autonomous creations, among them the sculptors Georg Raphael Donner and Balthasar Permoser, and the painters Cosmas Damian Asam, Franz Anton Maulbertsch, Kremser Schmidt, Paul Troger and J.M. Rottmayr. Note also Bassano's fine portrait of Vincenzo Scamozzi, Wolf Dietrich's principal architect.

Salzburg province

Parish church of the Precious Blood in Salzburg-Parsch

East of the Kapuzinerberg is the district of Parsch, whose parish church in the Weichselbaumsiedlung is a significant example of modern ecclesiastical architecture in Austria. It was built (1955/56) by the architects known as the **Arbeitsgruppe 4** (Wilhelm Holzbauer, Friedrich Kurrent and Johann Spalt), who embarked on a complete remodelling of an old farmhouse, of which structural parts remain. The roof is partly glass, being surmounted, however, by a further splayed pitched roof, the free angle of which serves as a belfry. The decidedly ascetic mode of the architecture represents a symbolic return to the origins of Christianity, more precisely to the simplicity of early Christian shrines. Over the main portal is Fritz Wotruba's béton *Crucifixion*, while the church doors on the south side bear the freely sketched images of *The Fall* and the *Baptism of Christ* from original designs by Oskar Kokoschka.

Schloss Hellbrunn

Reached via the Nonntal to the south, on the left bank of the Salzach (or by bus 55 from the *Hauptbahnhof*), **Schloss Hellbrunn** (1615) was designed by Santino Solari for Archbishop Marcus Sitticus and is famous for its sophisticated waterworks (**Wasserspiele**) in the garden, which can be explored with a guided tour. Highlights include the *al fresco* dinner table with concealed water-jets to drench the archbishop's guests after their resistance had been lowered and their attention blunted with copious food and drink; a marvellous mechanical theatre showing an opera-like scene with 138 figures whose movements are water-driven; and an organ likewise water-powered. All over the garden are grottoes and mythological sculptures of Mannerist exuberance, the majority created by Hans Waldburger. There is also a formal Baroque garden (*Ziergarten*) laid out in the mid-18C and an English garden (c 1790) which Archbishop Colloredo instituted to replace an existing vegetable patch. Edmund Hellmer's statue of Empress Elizabeth (1900), originally in front of Salzburg Hauptbahnhof, was placed here in 1925.

The villa (Schloss Waldems) on the nearby Hellbrunner Berg was built inside a month by Solari in 1615 in order to win a bet that Marcus Sitticus had made with a rival estate-owner that this could be done. It now houses an Ethnology Museum (open Easter–Oct, 10.00–18.00). The **Lustschloss** of Hellbrunn itself is an Italianate villa, a place to cultivate the *vita solitaria* held up as an ideal by Petrarch and enjoyed by potentates such as the Medicis in their Tuscan retreats. The **Festsaal** was frescoed by Arsenio Mascagni, whose illusionistic architectural features again recall the 'ideal city' envisaged both by Wolf Dietrich and Marcus Sitticus, whose emblem of an ibex (together with that of the Archbishopric, a lion) may be seen above the doors. Mascagni also decorated the octagonal **Music Room** and painted the huge sturgeon in the **Fischzimmer**. (In one of the pools of the garden, you can see black, hammer-headed *sterlet* cruising the gravel bottom.)

A combined ticket for the (obligatory) guided tours of the Schloss and Wasserspiele may be purchased at the entrance, where there is also a pleasant and modestly priced restaurant. The garden and villa are open in April and Oct, 09.00–16.30; May, June, Sept, 09.00–17.00; July, Aug, 09.00–22.00. The **Fest in Hellbrunn** (opera, drama, dance, readings) takes place in the first two weeks of August.

Closer to the city and south-east of Festung Hohensalzburg is **Schloss Leopoldskron**, built between 1736 and 1744 by a Scots Benedictine named Bernard Stuart for Archbishop Firmian, originally in Rococo style, but with neo-classical alterations in the 19C. The theatre director, Max Reinhardt, owned it between 1918 and his forced emigration in 1938 and it is now the centre for the Salzburg Seminars in American Studies'. Access is limited although some of the rooms are rented out commercially. A number of other Baroque Schlösser in the neighbourhood between Leopoldskron and Hellbrunn may be seen only from the outside (**Freisaal**, **Fronburg**, **Emsburg** and **Emslieb**), as they are either institutions or private property.

SOUTH OF SALZBURG – TENNENGAU

Continuing south from Hellbrunn on the *Autobahn* (A10) you soon reach the **Tennengau**, consisting mostly of the Salzach valley and the adjacent mountains.

Hallein

The first town of significance is Hallein, the name derived from the salt-mines (see p 288) on which its wealth was based even before the 13C, when its name first appears on documents. The salt was extracted from the Dürrnberg overlooking Hallein from the south west and now close to the German border. It is thought to have been worked as early as the *La-Tène* period, between 600 and 400 BC. Celtic remains have been found in abundance, including a finely tooled bronze jug, now in the Museum Carolino Augusteum in Salzburg. An **open-air museum** here shows an excavated grave and a farmstead. Perhaps of greater interest are the **saltworks** (open daily 27 April–30 Sept, 09.00–17.00, Oct–March 11.00–15.00), that only ceased operation in 1989.

Down in Hallein itself, the important **Celtic Museum** (Pflegerplatz 5, open daily April–30 Sept, 09.00–17.00) is worth a visit. It is located in the former salt office and has a room on the second floor with 75 oil paintings (1757) showing how the salt was extracted and processed, before being shipped down the Salzach. There is also a memorial room to Franz Xaver Gruber, composer of *Silent Night* (the original MS may be seen). Gruber's grave lies in front of the family house opposite the **parish church of St Anthony the Hermit**; in the house there is a small **museum** dedicated to him, which, however, only opens its door in Advent (November 11–17) and closes again after Christmas. The present **church** with a hideous modern tower—its predecessor burned down during the war—has an unusual neo-classical design with two quadrangles divided at the centre by triumphal arches, the whole interior being painted an icing-sugar white. It preserves a late Gothic font and a Baroque organ on which Gruber (organist from 1835 to his death in 1863) first played some of his compositions.

Following the Salzach upstream from Hallein, you soon reach **Golling**, an ancient staging-post for travelling merchants on their way to the **Lueg Pass** (554m) between the Tennengebirge and Hagengebirge, and thus wealthy enough to have a row of attractive burgher houses. In the Torren district of the town is a scenic waterfall, dropping its icy torrent over 80m into the Salzach. The road to the east and south towards the Lammertal and the Salzburger Dolomitenstraße is extremely picturesque, while a turn left near the beginning takes you over the hairpin toll road (Postalmstraße) to Strobl and the Wolfgangsee (see below). Continuing south, however, you reach the astonishing **Eisriesenwelt**, the world's largest **ice caves**, consisting of a 47km labyrinth with an ice surface of some 30,000 sq m. The approach is 6km from the main road, then on foot, by cable-car and again on foot, c 45mins required. The tour (70mins) take place from 1 May to 8 Oct daily, 09.30–15.30, to 16.30 in July and August. Warm clothing and sensible shoes are mandatory.

The caves are close to the town of **Werfen** and the **Burg Hohenwerfen**, built by Archbishop Gebhard in 1077, who took the part of the Pope in the investiture struggle, and needed a stronghold to defend the Lueg Pass against Henry IV's troops. Wolf Dietrich (see p 312) was briefly imprisoned here before being put in the Salzburg Festung—a bitter poem bemoaning the arbitrariness of fate inscribed on one of the walls is thought to be by him. Access to the Burg is possible from the car-park below. Between May and October there are spectacular falconry shows held in the castle precincts.

The Pongau

The *Autobahn* forks left before Bischofshofen along the Fritztal towards the Roßbrand and through the Pongau region. Its main settlement is **Radstadt**, well-preserved fortified town of the 13C. From here road 146 follows the River Enns into Styria. Alternatively the A10 runs south, partly through the **Tauern** and **Katschberg** tunnels into Carinthia. Just before the border at St Michael is the exit to **Mauterndorf** and **Tamsweg**. The former has a 13C castle left to Hermann Göring by his Jewish godfather, Hermann von Epstein. Together with some 72,000 German soldiers, Göring was captured here at the end of the war.

A little further south is **Schloss Moosham** (tours May–Sept, daily at 10.00, 11.00, 13.00, 14.00 and 15.30. Oct–April 11.00, 13.00 and 14.30), an ancient district court where, according to the records, supposed witches were regularly tortured and condemned from about 1580, when this particular bout of righteous Christian slaughtering started, right up to the middle of the 18C. The Schloss contains a museum, a serendipity of furniture and objects of folk art collected from many lands by Count Wilczek (1837–1922). (The latter was a multi-talented man, amongst other things a Polar explorer after whom one of the islands of Franz-Josefs-Land was named.) Tamsweg, a little to the west, is the capital of the Lungau region with a 15C pilgrimage **church of St Leonhard** on a rock terrace overlooking the town. The church is notable for the survival of its 15C painted glass.

Bischofshofen itself is the largest town of the Pongau and boasts a Romanesque tower (*Kastenhof*) next to the parish church. In the *Pfarrhof* is an 8C Irish cross (*Rupertuskreuz*) and the church also houses the **Gothic tomb** of Bishop Sylvester Pflieger (1453, Hans Baldauf) decorated with a life-sized relief of the occupant. **St Johann in Pongau** further south gives access to the resorts of the **Grossarl** region. Where the river of the same name flows into the Salzach close to **Schwarzach im Pongau** is the **Liechtensteinklamm**, a spectacular gorge and waterfall. In Schwarzach's town hall is the locally celebrated **Salzleckertisch**, at which, in 1729, 19,000 Protestants from Land Salzburg swore they would either compel tolerance of their religion by the Salzburg archbishopric or emigrate. In 1731 Archbishop Firmian graciously relaxed the three-year notice period required for emigration, so that by the spring of the following year 3184 Protestants had left the area.

Bad Gastein

West of Schwarzach the road to Bad Gastein leads south down the Gasteinertal, bypassing **Bad Hofgastein** near where the Salzburg archbishops had gold-mines in the 15C and 16C. The road then climbs to Bad Gastein (formerly 'Wildbad Gastein') dramatically situated in a gash of the wind-grieved Tauern Mountains. A Roman road through the Alps followed the Gasteiner Tal: notwithstanding a romantic legend concerning Ritter von Goldegg's pursuit of a wounded deer that was healed of its wounds when it stumbled on the warm springs, it is probable that the Romans already exploited the mineral waters here, as also the surrounding gold-mines. The *Minnesänger* Neidhart von Reuental celebrated the spa in the Middle Ages and Paracelsus analysed the composition of its springs in 1500 and recommended their healing powers. From the end of the 18C, the town became rapidly fashionable due to the patronage of distinguished visitors such as the popular Archduke Johann, and soon the place was awash with kings and princelings staying in well-appointed hotels. From the completion of the Tauernbahn in 1905, however, Bad Gastein began a slow but steady trajectory downmarket, losing first its rulers and aristocrats, then its glamorous literati and well-heeled professional classes, finally becoming a haunt of people paid for by their health insurance—and now, with the recent cuts in benefits, having rather fewer even of them. Centrepiece of the town is the beautiful **waterfall** of the Gasteiner Ache, best viewed from Steinbrücke in the main street. The small 15C **church of St Nicholas** has fine star vaulting and Gothic frescoes of 1480 by the Master of Schöder showing the *Calvary* and *Christ rescuing Adam and Eve from Hell*.

Around Bad Gastein and at neighbouring Böckstein ski resorts have been developed, to offset decline in income from the spa. Cars can be transported through the Tauern railway-tunnel from Böckstein over the border into Carinthia.

Großglockner

Großglockner Hochalpenstraße and Zell am See

Road 311 continues west past the mouth of the Gasteiner Tal to the rather sombre **Zeller See**, which lies in a cleft between the Dientener Berge and the Kitzbühler Alpen. Just before you reach the south end of the lake you pass through Bruck, from which the road runs through the Fuscher Tal towards the **Großglockner Hochalpenstraße** (open end of April– early Nov, snow conditions permitting, 05.00–22.00. Toll). On the way it passes the **Alpenwildpark** at Ferleiten where bears, wolves, lynx and species of deer may be observed in their natural environment (open daily from 08.00–dusk). Falconry displays are held at 15.00, between June and September also at 11.00. There are several outlook points, information booths and descriptive placards as the Hochalpenstraße becomes increasingly spectacular up to the **Hochtor** (2503m), the highest point and the border between Salzburg and Carinthia. The 48km road with 27 hairpins over Austria's highest mountain passes was built under engineer Franz Wallack in the depression of the 1930s as a job creation scheme employing 3200 men and was completed in 1935. It follows a medieval (and prehistoric) trade route over the Tauern range linking Venice with Germany: fruit, wine, oriental silks and spices travelled north on this route, while salt, wood, furs and precious metals travelled south. One of the best views of the **Großglockner**, Austria's highest peak (3798m/12,460ft) is from the Carinthian side at the **Franz-Josefs-Höhe** reached by a turning to the west (*Gletscherstraße*: Glacier Road). From here the **Gletscherbahn** descends to the crevassed Pasterze glacier. The village of Hof below is commonly called **Heiligenblut** from the phial of 'holy blood' brought from Constantinople in 914 and preserved in the parish **church of St Vincent** (completed 1490). The latter boasts a superb **polychrome altar** (1520) by Wolfgang Asslinger and Marx Reichlich, which is heavily influenced by the art of Michael Pacher. The altar is 10.6m high, and thus the largest surviving example of such a work. It shows the *Coronation of the Virgin* below *Christ* and martyr figures, and has an additional 12 painted panels. There is also a sacramental holder dating to 1494 in the choir and a **Veronica Altar** (1491), perhaps by Lukas Tausmann in the north aisle. With its beautiful Gothic angularity and slender spire, at 1300m Heiligenblut perfectly harmonises with its backdrop of mountain peaks.

The Pinzgau

Zell am See on the west side of the lake is the capital of the Pinzgau, a summer and winter resort with a railway terminus and a *Lokalbahn* that makes the 55km trip westwards to the spectacular **Krimmler Fälle** (see p 395). Just to the south of the town is **Kaprun** with a highly scenic hydro-electric dam at nearby

Wasserfallboden, which can be viewed from the Kitzsteinhorn ascended by the *Gletscherbahn* (also used by skiers).

North of Zell am See is **Saalfelden**, which picturesquely describes itself as being '*am Steinernen Meer*' ('on the stone sea', the name of the mountains north-east of it). The road continues up the small peninsula of Land Salzburg sandwiched between Tyrol and the German territory of the *Deutsches Eck*, the Bavarian enclave that cuts off Salzburg from part of its hinterland and Tyrol. Most of this land was once under Salzburg hegemony, then briefly under that of Austria, but lost by the Habsburgs at the Treaty of Schönbrunn (14 November 1809) imposed by Napoleon, and subsequently never recovered. West of the town of St Martin bei Lofer is the pilgrimage church of **Maria Kirchental** (1701), built by J.B. Fischer von Erlach to a commission from Count von Thun-Hohenstein, and reminiscent of the Salzburg Kollegienkirche in miniature.

West of Zell am See road 168 traverses the Oberpinzgau up to the Tyrol border. The main town is **Mittersill**, from which a road leads south into **Osttirol** (East Tyrol) via the Felbertauern Tunnel. The town has associations with the last war—British officers gave shelter to Vaslav Nijinsky in the Schloss (1540), who was fleeing Eastern Europe. Less happily, the composer Anton von Webern (1883–1945), who was staying with his son-in-law at Marktplatz 10, was shot dead by an American soldier in circumstances that remain unclear, but possibly because he was confused with a wanted black marketeer.

NORTH OF SALZBURG ~ FLACHGAU

The northern part of Land Salzburg comprises the attractive **Flachgau**; with its meadows, woods and lakes it has been described by the poet Carl Zuckmayer as a 'little paradise'. There are several places worth visiting.

Pilgrimage church of Maria Plain

Due north of Salzburg, close to road 156, is the pilgrimage Church of Maria Plain (1674) built by Giovanni Antonio Dario. Among the altarpieces of the various side-altars of the interior founded by abbots and bishops is a *Crucifixion* (1724) by François von Roethiers (left-hand side-altar) and there are sculptures of quality by Thomas Schwanthaler; Frans de Neve painted the *Betrothal of Mary* and the *Flight into Egypt* on the right-hand side-altar. There are eight paintings (1765) on the walls by Kremser Schmidt (*Leonhard comforting Prisoners*, together with Benedictine saints including *Maurus*, *Benedict* with his sister *Scholastica*; further *St Benedict's Miracle of the Wine*, *Sts Wolfgang and Placidus*, and lastly *Mary* and *St John*). On the pulpit is a relief of the fire in Regen (Bavaria) which a Marian icon (1480) miraculously survived (thus providing the impulse for founding the church) and which is now on the high altar. On either side of the altar are the figures of *Sts Vitalis* and *Maximilian*, while above it is a depiction of the *Holy Trinity* (Frans de Neve).

Some 20km further north is **Oberndorf**, a village that used to be subject to flooding from the Salzach, thus necessitating the demolition of its vulnerably situated **St Nicholas parish church** in 1909. It was here that *Silent Night* was first performed in 1818, with a text by the local chaplain, Joseph Mohr, and music by the teacher from neighbouring Arnsdorf, Franz Xaver Gruber (see p 316).

Stille Nacht! Heilige Nacht!

At the end of the Napoleonic War the salt trade that had supported the ship-men of **Oberndorf** was ruined, a further blow being the cession of the sister village (**Laufen**) across the river to a hostile Bavaria at the peace treaty. In this time of poverty and desperation, **Joseph Mohr** was appointed curate to the unamiable local priest, Georg Nöstler. Mohr was the illegitimate child of a soldier in Salzburg service and a seamstress from Hallein, and he supplied the words for this most famous of Christmas carols.

Franz Gruber wrote some 285 folk-influenced works for the church, none of the other 284 being as remotely successful as the tune for *Stille Nacht! Heilige Nacht!* The Christmas song rapidly gained in popularity after 1825, probably via an organ-builder from the Zillertal, who worked with Gruber repairing the rickety Oberndorf organ. He may have passed the song to the *Tiroler Sängergesellschaften* of his homeland (see p 394), which in turn popularised it as a folksong on their world tours. It has since been translated into 170 languages and according to researchers is the best known song ever written. It was famously sung by troops on opposing sides in the trenches of the Western Front during a Christmas lull in the fighting.

A **Gruber-Mohr Memorial Chapel** was erected in 1930 on the site of the old St Nicholas Church and contains the skull of Joseph Mohr. The stained-glass windows (1935) depict Mohr and the church (north side) and Gruber at Arnsdorf (south side). Nearby at the **Bruckmannhaus** is the **Stille-Nacht-und Heimatmuseum**, displaying a collection of stamps with the song as motif and a substantial collection of recordings (chapel and museum are open daily, 09.00–12.00, 13.00–17.00, to 18.00 till 24 Dec). At neighbouring **Arnsdorf**, a museum is dedicated to Franz Gruber in the old schoolhouse (visits by arrangement: ☎ 06274 7453 or 6937).

At the northern tip of Land Salzburg is the Benedictine abbey of **Michaelbeuern**, whose history goes back to the Carolingian period, and which at one time included even the Michaelerkirche in Vienna amongst its substantial possessions. The cloister buildings (tours from Easter Mon–31 Oct, Fri, Sat, Sun 14.00, or ☎ 062 74/8116) include a refectory dating to the 11C, while the **Abbot's chamber** contains frescoes (1771) by Franz Nikolaus Streicher (*Abraham and the Three Angels*, allegories and landscapes), as well as fine stucco from 1720. The library is attractive, as is the former tavern (*Mezger-Stöckl*), again frescoed (1770) by Streicher (*Sts Benedict, Michael* and *Scholastica*). The **Stiftskirche** was built in 1072, but the Gothic and Romanesque parts can only be glimpsed in the now Baroque ensemble. The high altar (1691) is impressive, with florid Baroque sculpture by Meinrad Guggenbichler (*Sts Rupert* and *Ulrich, Benedict* and *Scholastica*) and early paintings by J.M. Rottmayr (*Resurrection, St Michael*), the artist having been a chorister in the abbey.

East of Salzburg

Only 12 per cent of the beautiful area of lakes and mountains known as the Salzkammergut actually lies in Land Salzburg (16 per cent is in Styria, 72 per cent in Upper Austria), but it forms a homogeneous economic, cultural and historical area and is described as a single unit elsewhere (see p 269), with the exception of the **Wolfgangsee** which straddles Salzburg and Upper Austria (see below).

A few kilometres to the east of the city lies the beautiful **Fuschlsee** on the edge of the Salzkammergut. It has one of the most delightful hotels in Austria at the north-west end, namely *Schloss Fuschl* (built in 1450), once the hunting-lodge of the Salzburg archbishops (guided tours once a week, ☎ 06229 22530). During the war bunkers for the Nazi leaders were built into the hillside close to the hotel. In the nearby **Jagdhof Fuschl** (above road 158) is a hunting museum that also contains a collection of pipes (open daily 09.00–18.00).

The road continues to **St Gilgen am Abersee**, at the western (Salzburg) end of the enchanting lake more generally known by the name of its eastern (Upper Austrian) part, the **Wolfgangsee**. St Gilgen has been favoured for many years by the German ex-Chancellor, Helmut Kohl, for his summer holiday. Mozart's mother was born here and his sister returned to live in St Gilgen after her marriage in 1784. (The *Mozart-Gedenkstätte* in the courthouse is open June–Sept, Tues–Sun 10.00–12.00, 14.00–18.00.)

St Wolfgang

Seven kilometres further east is the turning for the car ferry that crosses the lake to picturesque St Wolfgang (the ferry is recommended, since the town is crammed in high season and you can leave your car in the parking area provided). The time capsule of St Wolfgang with its 16C and 17C houses has unfortunately become a tourist trap since being made famous by Ralph Benatzky and Robert Stolz's operetta *The White Horse Inn*, (1930), supposedly set in one of its lakeside hostelries (but the original inn of the story was actually at Lauffen bei Bad Ischl).

The town's principal artistic attraction is the unique late Gothic **winged altar** (1481) in the **church of St Wolfgang**, considered to be the masterpiece of Michael Pacher, and containing four wings with 16 scenes. Originally the inner wings (showing the *Life of Christ*, the *Miracles* and the *Raising of Lazarus*) would have been closed on Sundays; on weekdays the whole was closed, showing four panels (by Friedrich Pacher) of the *Life of St Wolfgang*. Today the altar is generally kept open and its central iconography, which exalts the Virgin Mary as interceder for mankind and points to the auxiliary roles in this task played by St Benedict and St Wolfgang, may be enjoyed at leisure after insertion of the necessary coins for the automatic lighting on the right.

The four outer panels show scenes from the *Life of Mary* (the *Birth of Christ*, the *Circumcision*, the *Presentation in the Temple* and the *Death of the Virgin*), and are notable for Pacher's Italian-learned mastery of perspective. The predella shows the *Adoration of the Three Kings* flanked by the *Visitation* and the *Flight into Egypt*, while on its reverse (if the altar is closed) are vivid portrayals of the *Fathers of the Church*. The central focus of the shrine is a magnificent figural group of which the focal point is the *Crowned Mother of God receiving the Blessing of Christ*.

This immensely spiritual yet lyrical tableau, framed by ecstatic choirs of angels, represents a high point in the redemptive mariolatry of the western church. Flanking it are the statues of the church patron, *St Wolfgang* (on the left) and *St Benedict* (on the right). Both are depicted with remarkable naturalism, the austere features of St Benedict being especially powerful and forbidding. The latter holds in his hand the vial in which his fellow monks were said to have placed poison, in a fruitless attempt to liberate themselves from the harshness of Benedict's rule. The symbolic dissipation of the poison is represented as snakes spiralling out of the cup.

Only a little less impressive than Pacher's masterpiece is the church's centrally located **Baroque altar** (1676), a work by Thomas Schwanthaler which is surrounded by a fine wrought-iron screen. On the left-hand sacramental altar, the *Holy Family* is depicted, on the right, *St Wolfgang*. The side-figures are *St Benedict* and *Scholastica*, and above them is the *Coronation of Mary*. Schwanthaler has taken care to harmonise his work with the spirit of Pacher and the Gothic ambience of the church, which can be immensely inspiring when late afternoon sun shines through the open west door, creating a numinous rippling effect across the pulpit due to reflection from the lake's surface. The three northern side-altars and the pulpit were decorated by the sculptor Meinrad Guggenbichler, while in the tiny **Wolfgangskapelle** is another altar (1713) by Guggenbichler. A terrace runs along the western wall of the church, affording magical views of the Wolfgangsee.

From St Wolfgang a cogwheel railway conveys sightseers to the top of the **Schafberg**. Road 158 leads east past the town of Strobl at the end of the lake and over the border into Oberösterreich, reaching shortly the town of Bad Ischl (see p 271).

Kärnten (Carinthia)

Area: 9533sq km. Population: 548,000.

Topography, climate and environment

The southernmost Land of Austria, **Kärnten/Carinthia**, borders on Styria in the east and north-east, on Salzburg in the north-west, on East Tyrol in the west, on Italy in the south-west and on Slovenia in the south-east. Upper Carinthia (*Ober-Kärnten*) is mostly mountainous, while Lower Carinthia (*Unter-Kärnten*—the southern and eastern part of the region), is veined with river valleys and long narrow lakes. Of the four largest lakes, the holiday paradise of the **Wörther See** is the best known (the other large ones are the **Ossiacher See**, the **Millstätter See** and the **Weißensee**). The most important river is the **Drau**, which rises in South Tyrol and flows through East Tyrol and Carinthia before becoming the *Drava* in Slovenia and Croatia, eventually joining the Danube below the town of Osijek. Two hundred and sixty-one kilometres of its 749km length are in Austria, and the main Carinthian traffic routes follow its west-east course through Spittal an der Drau to Villach, after which the river loops south of Klagenfurt, passing through several artificial lakes. The province is virtually enclosed by mountains: the southern boundaries are formed by the **Karnische Alpen** and the **Karawanken**; in the east is the **Koralpe**, while in the north are the **Nockberge**. The last-named is part of a national park, covering an area consisting of gneiss, mica schist and limestone formations that are rich in alpine fauna and flora, and containing many high altitude lakes left behind by the Ice Age. The north-west of Carinthia is part of the **Hohe Tauern** range (also a national park) with the great **Großglockner** (see p 318) guarding the pass into Land Salzburg. The capital of Carinthia is **Klagenfurt** (c 90,000 inhabitants) and the only other town of significant size is **Villach**.

Carinthia's mountain barriers protect it from the worst northern weather, so that it enjoys a happy combination of year-round sunshine and plenty of snowfall in winter, turning to fairly substantial rainfall in the warmer months. Several of the Carinthian lakes are rather deep (the **Millstätter See** is 141m at its deepest point) and were mostly formed in the last Ice Age. The water is relatively warm by Austrian standards, the four larger lakes reaching maximum temperatures of between 23° and 26°C in the hottest months.

Examples of the indigenous flora of Carinthia may be seen in the Botanical Gardens in the old quarry of the **Klagenfurter Kreuzbergl** (see p 333). A rarity is the blue *wulfenia carinthiaca*, named after its 19C discoverer, Baron Franz Xaver von Wulfen, which is to be found growing naturally in a small area under the **Gartnerkofel** on the Italian border. The Himalayas are one of the very few places elsewhere that it is found. The enormous variety of Carinthian flora (which includes Continental, Illyrian and some Mediterranean species) reflects its varied micro-climatic and environmental conditions, the greater part of it being nevertheless autochthonous Alpine and Central European. A local feature are the unusually large clusters of the Swiss stone pine (*Zirbelkiefer*). Carinthia is also rich

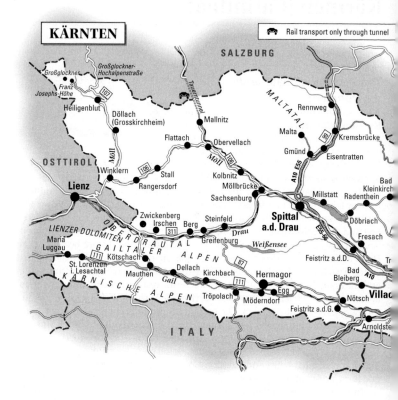

in animal species, some of them the descendants of creatures driven from the north by the last Ice Age, and others (such as the various species of lizards) reflecting the fact that Carinthia is simultaneously the southern border of Central Europe and the northern border of Southern Europe. The two species of (harmless) scorpions and one type of bird spider are also at the northernmost extent of their usual warm habitat. In the mountains are eagles, rock partridges, capercaillie and blackcock, while animals that were nearly wiped out by 19C 'sportsmen' (moufflon, ibex, lynx) have been rescued from extinction. Wandering bears and wolves from the Balkans are occasionally sighted (of the former, the animal researcher Bernhard Gutleb estimates a figure of 12 resident or occasionally resident around the 'triangle of three provinces': Carinthia, Slovenia and Friaul/Friuli).

Economy

As elsewhere in Austria, agriculture's contribution to the economy is in retreat in Carinthia, although the possibility of developing a 'second leg' in tourism (farm holidays and associated leisure pursuits) saves some of the local farms

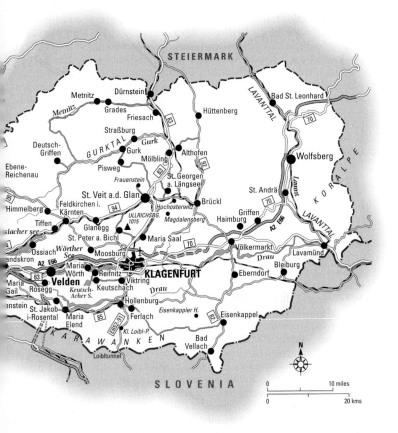

from going under. The decline of agriculture's share in the economy (only 7 per cent of the population is engaged in it) is balanced by an explosion of activity in the services sector, now employing some 58 per cent of the people. Otherwise timber production (albeit stagnating), cattle-breeding and horse-breeding are the significant land-based industries, while paper and wood manufactures, iron goods, electronics and textiles, prefabricated building materials and (a local speciality) the production of sporting guns are the important wealth producers after the increasingly important summer tourism. Carinthia does not really compete for skiers with the highly developed resorts of Tyrol and Vorarlberg, and indeed in winter the number of visitors falls by up to 80 per cent. In addition to the above activities, there are successful specialist industries filling market niches, such as those producing marine couplings, or making an ingredient for anti-rust coatings, or wristwatch straps etc. Industry is concentrated around Villach and Klagenfurt, where the machines, tools and electrical components are produced.

History

Eastern Carinthia has been inhabited from the Stone Age, as remains found in stalactite caves of the **Griffener Berg** testify. A skeleton from the 'String Ceramic' period (2500 BC) was discovered in the **Metnitztal** in 1937, one of the earliest such discoveries in the Alpine region. By the Bronze Age Carinthia had thriving agricultural and mining settlements, perhaps originally populated by Etruscans and Italians who are thought to have migrated northwards from the Po Valley and the Veneto, but later almost certainly inhabited by Illyrians of the so-called Hallstatt culture. The Illyrians were in turn subject to Celtic immigration from about 250 BC. Around 200 BC the Celtic settlement on the **Magdalensberg** was founded and a powerful Celtic kingdom grew up, which the Romans called *Regnum Noricum*, and which grew rich from iron exports. In the late 2C BC, *Noricum* was attacked by the Germanic Kimbern, a fierce tribe driven from their North German-Danish homeland by the rise in sea-level that flooded their territories. They delivered a stunning defeat to the Romans in 113 BC at *Noreia*, whose location in *Noricum* has not been discovered. However, the Kimbern then turned west to attack the Helvetic Celts and thereafter the relatively peaceful assimilation of *Noricum* to Roman control continued, the process being complete by about 15 BC. Sixty years later the town of *Virunum* (with a Roman governor) was founded on the **Zollfeld** (see p 334) below the Magdalensberg, the Celtic inhabitants of which were also settled on the plain. In the Roman period it was discovered that gold was so easily recoverable in the Tauern range, that the gold price fell dramatically throughout Italy.

It was to *Virunum* that the Christian missionaries came in the early 4C, the governor's seat, together with *Teurnia* (St Peter im Holz) becoming bishoprics under the Aquileian Patriarchate. However, Christianity was eclipsed during the invasions of the Dark Ages that followed the first attack of the Goths in AD 408. The last Romans withdrew in AD 488, and in the following three centuries the region became a buffer zone between competing powers until the coming of the Slavs in the early 7C. In AD 740 the now Slav inhabitants of Carinthia under their ruler Boruth called on the Bavarians for help against the Avar armies, and the Bavarians (the first German-speaking settlers) used the occasion to occupy the area and reconvert the people to Christianity. The early Romanesque parts of the existing church of **St Peter im Holz** date to around this time as also did the predecessor (767) of **Maria Saal**, the oldest documented church of Carinthia. After the overthrow of the Bavarian Duke Tassilo III in 788, Carinthia was absorbed into Charlemagne's empire under Bavarian control. At the local level there was a struggle for power in Carinthia between the Salzburg Archbishop Arno and the Aquileian Patriarch Ursus. Charlemagne resolved this dispute by an order given in Aachen on 14 June 811, which divided the province between the two, making the River Drau (Drava) the border of their respective competences.

Roman relief, Maria Saal

Although by the late 9C Arnulf of Bavaria was actually referred to as *Bagoariorum et Karantorum Dux* (Duke of Bavaria and Carinthia), in 976 Carinthia became virtually independent, and in the following century Adalbero von Eppenstein founded the first Carinthian dynasty. In 1016 the most important town of his dominion, **Friesach**, acquired market and customs rights, followed by **Villach** in 1060. By the 12C today's borders of Carinthia had been established, a number of monasteries had been founded (**Ossiach, Gurk, Millstatt, St Paul im Lavanttal**, all founded between 1028 and 1096) and Romanesque art was flourishing. In the 13C Carinthia (together with Styria and Carniola) came under the control of the Dukes of Görz-Tirol, finally becoming part of the Habsburg patrimony in 1335. In 1414 Duke Ernst of the Habsburg Styrian line became the ruler of the 'Inner Austrian' territories, which included Carinthia, Carniola, the Windische (Slav) Mark and Austrian Istria.

Perhaps because of its complicated and turbulent history, its subjection to competing cultural, political and religious influences, and its eventual emergence as a distinctive Germano-Slavic region with Italian features, Carinthia exudes an air of quintessential ur-Austria, lying (as Grillparzer so quaintly put it) 'between the Italian child and German man'. Earthquakes, plague and repeated Turkish attacks in the 1470s made Carinthia an insecure place in the 14C, 15C and 16C, as the surviving fortified churches testify. There were also peasant uprisings and terrible fires—Klagenfurt was burned to the ground except for a single house in 1514. Then came Lutheranism that found many adherents among the peasantry, as also among the miners, for in the 16C silver and gold was still being extracted in large quantities in the Tauern and Lavanttal region (1560–80 was the peak period of production). The Counter-Reformation (from 1600) led to an exit of many miners and artisans and of the Protestant nobility, a defining moment being the issuing of an edict by Ferdinand II in 1628 compelling people to choose between Catholicism and Protestantism. Although this caused economic decline, the proselytising enthusiasm of the Jesuits produced a cultural upswing with the founding of numerous schools and a theatre in Klagenfurt. An ugly aspect of the religious struggle, however, were the witch trials that reached hysterical proportions between 1640 and 1680.

Under Emperor Karl VI Carinthia enjoyed an economic boom as the importance of the towns on the trade routes to Italy (especially Klagenfurt and Villach) continued to grow. Carinthia benefited from the reforms of Karl's daughter and successor, Maria Theresia (1740–80) and of her son Joseph II (1780–90), who, however, dissolved many monasteries that he regarded as unproductive, only those that could demonstrate their usefulness for education and social or medical provision escaping the axe. The province's history in the 19C was similar to that of the other *Länder*—occupation by French armies on two occasions, a revolution in 1848 that finally freed the peasants from feudal impositions and established a *Landtag* (Provincial Parliament), and finally an economic boom (the so-called *Gründerzeit*) in the second half of the century, when Carinthian timber was much in demand. The railway lines between Leoben and Villach, Villach and Franzensfeste, and Villach and Tarvisio were all opened between 1868 and 1873.

At the end of **World War I** the new Kingdom of Serbs, Croats and

Slovenes, later to be called Yugoslavia, tried to press Slovenian claims to large portions of Carinthia with Slovene inhabitants, and its troops occupied an area up to and including Villach and Klagenfurt. However, the Carinthians successfully organised themselves into a *Heimwehr* (Home Guard) and forced a Yugoslav withdrawal, being at least tacitly supported by the majority of the Slovene population. On the 14 January 1919, a truce was called and the American Miles Commission began its work to determine the wishes of the Carinthians. Realising that their appeals to nationalism were falling on deaf ears, the Yugoslav army twice broke the truce in an attempt to create a *fait accompli*, reoccupying Klagenfurt in June, but were forced to withdraw by the Allies shortly afterwards. The subsequent plebiscite was planned to be held separately in the southern part of Carinthia with a large Slovene population (Zone A), and the northern part (Zone B) with its German-Austrian majority. However, the vote in Zone A (10 October 1920) was so decisive in favour of remaining Austrian (59 per cent to 41 per cent) that the Zone B poll was abandoned.

Notwithstanding the Carinthian loyalties of the majority of Slovenes, the **ethnic minority issue** has been a running sore of post-war provincial politics, typically with disputes over dual-language schools and dual signposting generating passions and some racist attitudes. The strongly 'German national' faction in local politics is noisy and sporadically dominant. For a brief period after 1989 the Provincial Governorship was held by the head of the right-wing Freedom Party, Jörg Haider, supported (unwisely, as it turned out) by the conservative People's Party; however, he was obliged to resign after claiming in Parliament that the 'Nazis at least had an effective employment policy'. He returned as Governor in 1998. Social Democracy, which also absorbed *Großdeutsch* elements, supplied the Governor for no less than 40 years, a length of tenure that inevitably led to corruption.

KLAGENFURT

Practical information

Population: 90,000. Telephone dialling code: 0463.

 Tourist information
Fremdenverkehrsamt des Magistrates, Rathaus, Neuer Platz. ☎ (0463) 53 72 23. Fax 53 72 95. Open Mon–Fri 08.00–20.00, Sat, Sun 10.00–17.00. Oct–April, Mon–Fri 09.00–18.00.

Touristenzentrum Europapark, Völkermarkter Strasse 225.

☎ (0463) 236 51. Open May–Sept, 10.00–20.00.

If you are staying for some time in Carinthia it is worth obtaining the **Kärnten Card** (photo required) which, for a sum of around 400 ATS, entitles you to discounts on some services, as well as the free use of many lake ferries and cable-cars and gratis entrance to a number of museums. It is usually valid from mid-May–mid-October. Schubert & Frankel's *Kultur Ausflug Kärnten* is a useful summary of sights with details of location etc, albeit only in German.

Getting there

By train There are train connections from Klagenfurt to Graz and to Villach (including destinations in Slovenia and Italy).

By bus Buses depart from the main station, 1km south of Neuer Platz.

By air There are five flights daily to Vienna with *Tyrolean Airways*, two a day to Zürich (*Crossair*) and Frankfurt (*Tyrolean Airways*).

Steamers run on the Wörthersee from May to mid-October

Hotels

☆☆☆☆ *Arcotel Musil* (10 Oktober Strasse 14. ☎ 511 660. Fax: 511 66 04). Stylishly furnished with antiques: an elegant and comfortable hotel.

☆☆☆☆ *Hotel Palais Porcia* (Neuer Platz 13. ☎ 511590. Fax: 51159 030). Luxury hotel in the city centre.

☆☆☆ *Hotel Garni Blumenstöckl* (10 Oktober Strasse 11. ☎ 577 93. Fax: 57 79 35). Attractive Renaissance building overlooking a courtyard.

☆☆ *Hotel Liebetegger* (Völkermarkter Strasse 8. ☎ 56 935. Fax: 56835–6). One of the few cheaper hotels in the city centre.

☆☆ *Frühstückspension Stadt Eger* (Karfreitstrasse 20. ☎ 54320. Fax 54709). Cheap, cheerful and quite central.

Restaurants

Restaurant à la Carte (Khevenhüllerstrasse 2). Small, gourmet establishment.

Gasthaus Wienerroither (Neuer Platz 10). Good, traditional food.

Gasthaus Pirker (corner Adlergasse and Lidmanskygasse). Austrian cuisine.

History of Klagenfurt

The original settlement of Klagenfurt ('*Furt an der Glan*') lay on the north bank of the River Glan, in the northern part (*Spitalberg*) of the present town, and was founded by Hermann von Spanheim in the 12C. However, the area was subject to constant flooding, prompting his son, Duke Bernhard, to move its centre to the south bank between 1246 and 1252. This move was also designed to consolidate the secular power of the Duke, who was to some extent in competition with the chief landlords in the town, the Bishops of Salzburg and Bamberg. Municipal rights were first awarded to medieval Klagenfurt by Albrecht II of Habsburg in 1338.

After a fire destroyed the entire town in 1514, the perennially cash-strapped Maximilian I turned the site over to the Carinthian Estates in 1518, on the grounds that he had no money to finance rebuilding. His simultaneous withdrawal of all burgher privileges at first added to the bitterness of the former inhabitants, but Klagenfurt (which was designated the Provincial Capital after reconstruction) soon began to boom under noble administration, and indeed 800 burghers cooperated in the rebuilding. By 1527 a canal (the **Lendkanal**) had been built in order to link the city to the **Wörthersee** (it also channelled water to a defensive moat), while between 1534 and 1594 the Italian military architect, Domenico de Lalio (or dell'Allio) of Lugano gave Klagenfurt an entirely new aspect. His fortifications survived until they were demolished by the French in 1809.

The Carinthian nobility went over to Protestantism in the Reformation and subsequently built the greatest Protestant church of Austria in Klagenfurt, together with the impressive Landhaus (1574–94), the seat of the Provincial Diet.

They also erected a mighty castle (in fulfilment of their promise to the Emperor to defend the Empire's southern rim), to which was attached an agricultural college for nobles. However, despite some concessions such as the Graz Religious Pact of 1572, which for a while guaranteed the nobles free exercise of their religion, the Counter-Reformation slowly gathered momentum from 1580 and eventually resulted in the expulsion of the Protestant nobles and burghers in two waves under Ferdinand II (1600 for the burghers and peasants and 1628 for the nobility). These persecutions increased the economic malaise, since they happened to coincide with the decline of the local reserves of precious metals. At the same time, the upsurge of intellectual activity in the Counter-Reformation saw the publication by Hieronymus Megiser of the first history of Carinthia (*Annales Carinthiae* by M.G. Christalnick) in Klagenfurt (1612), together with the appropriation and reform of the schools by the Jesuits and the founding of a theatre.

Religious intolerance depressed the local economy for a century or more until the gradual rise of the importance of the port of Trieste also increased the prosperity of Klagenfurt. The latter's advantage as a trading centre on the route from Inner Austria to the Mediterranean was greatly enhanced by the improvements to the Loibl Pass in the 18C under Karl VI. In the 19C several industries developed (notably textiles) and the coming of the railway led to a boom in commerce and tourism. As the century progressed, the Slovene minority in Carinthia increasingly began to oppose domination by the German-Austrian majority and to rediscover a Slovene cultural and linguistic identity. Nevertheless, the attempt of the new Yugoslav state to 'reclaim' Klagenfurt (and other areas, see p 328) at the end of World War I came to nothing. After World War II Klagenfurt was the centre of the British Zone of the Allied occupation of Austria until 1955. It was mostly from Klagenfurt that the British despatched both Cossacks and Chetniks to certain deaths in their homelands in 1945.

Sights of Klagenfurt

It is simplest to begin a tour of the city at the **Tourist Information Büro** on the **Neuen Platz**. Also on this square is the Klagenfurt emblem, the **Lindwurmbrunnen** (Dragon Fountain, 1590), sculpted by Ulrich Vogelsang with a later mace-swinging Hercules figure (1636) added by Michael Hönel. This huge sculpture made from chlorite was ceremonially carried to its plinth in 1593 by a procession of 300 youths dressed in white. According to the legend, a dragon lived in the dangerous marshes beyond the city gates, devouring man and beast alike, until he was eventually captured by some townsmen using a clever ruse. The story is probably a metaphor for the reclamation of the marshes by the city. The cranial bone of an animal thought to be the dragon was discovered in the Middle Ages, but in 1840 the zoologist Franz Unger demonstrated that it came from a rhinoceros living at the time of the last Ice Age.

At the end of the square is the **Neue Rathaus**, a Renaissance building (formerly Palais Rosenberg) preserving original features such as the ceremonial stairway of the interior. The Kramergasse leads north into the **Alten Platz**, with the **Alten Rathaus** of 1600 and a Trinity Column of 1680. The fresco on the

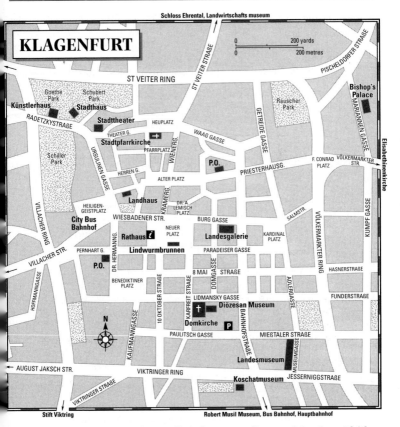

Schloss Ehrental, Landwirtschafts museum

KLAGENFURT

Rathaus (by Josef Ferdinand Fromiller) shows an allegory of *Justice* with the coats of arms of Klagenfurt and Carinthia.

Just to the west of the Alten Platz is the great Renaissance **Landhaus** (built between 1574 and 1581 by Hans Freymann and Giovanni Antonio de Verda), with its arcaded courtyard to the east and its onion domed towers with lanterns. Its famous **Große Wappensaal** is a unique feature of the **interior**: the walls are decorated with 665 coats of arms (1741, by Fromiller) of Carinthian noble families. The ceiling fresco, also by Fromiller, shows the *Diet Paying Homage to Karl VI* (in 1728), the *Investiture of the Carinthian Dukes* (see p 335), and *Maximilian I donating the City to the Landstände*. In the **Kleinen Wappensaal** are another 298 coats of arms by Fromiller and a ceiling fresco of *Truth as the Daughter of Time*, while in the **Assembly Hall** Suitbert Lobisser's painting commemorates the defence of Carinthia against Yugoslav troops in 1918–20. There also used to be an allegorical depiction (1930) of Carinthian history by the Expressionist Anton Kolig (1886–1950, see p 332), which was removed by the Nazis. The artist's grandson, Cornelius Kolig, an avant-garde artist who has scandalised conservatives in the past with an exhibition involving tampons, urine-soaked underwear and excrement, has recently been given the commission to replicate and partially replace these frescoes. He was chosen unanimously by a panel of experts, despite near-hysterical opposition from the right-wing Freedom Party, who have dubbed him the 'faecal artist'. After further attacks on him in the press he suspended his work in early 1999.

To the north of the Landhaus is the **parish church of St Giles** (1697, replacing a medieval church on the site damaged in the earthquake of 1690). St Giles is one of the Fourteen Holy Helpers and the patron of cripples and nursing mothers, but perhaps was chosen for the church in his capacity as protector of blacksmiths. The frescoes in the choir by Fromiller show the *Trinity* and celebrate the survival of Carinthia, despite the plague, famine, Turkish attacks and Protestantism, a somewhat disingenuous linking of historic phenomena. In the nave Joseph Mölckh has painted a scene of *St Giles' Head presented to the People by Angels*. The Franco-American writer, Julien Green (1900–98) was buried in St Giles at his own request in a chapel off the right-hand nave. This was partly in recognition of the fact that in the 1980s the local arts festival rediscovered his work, which had fallen into neglect. Apart from the autobiographical *Memories of Happy Days* (1942), most of Green's work was written in French.

North of the Pfarrplatz is the **Heuplatz** (former hay market) with its neo-classical **St Florian Monument** (1777), raised after the city centre was successfully saved from a serious fire in the suburbs. Just to the north-west of the square is the attractive *Jugendstil* **theatre** (1908) erected for Franz Joseph's 60-Year Jubilee, and recently renovated. Retracing your steps south via the Neuer Platz, follow Burggasse from its north-east corner to no. 8 for the entrance to the **Landesgalerie** (open Mon–Fri, 09.00–18.00, Sat, Sun & PH 10.00–12.00). It displays the work of Carinthian artists, including the best-known among them, **Herbert Boeckl** (1894–1966), an autodidact whose work shows the influence of Lovis Corinth and Oskar Kokoschka. He was associated with the **Nötscher School** of colourists (see p 350), to which Anton Kolig also belonged. The gallery is situated in the **Burg** built by Giovanni de Verda as a Protestant college for the nobility, but after the Counter-Reformation the seat of the burgraves. Its chapel has a fresco by Fromiller of the **Apotheosis of St Domitian**, the first Christian Duke of Carinthia and the province's unofficial patron saint, together with a view of Millstatt (see p 353) where Domitian's relics are to be found. There are also representations of a number of somewhat obscure local saints, such as Modestus (buried in Maria Saal, see p 334; Brictius, Hemma von Gurk, see p 338; Hildegard von Stein and others).

A walk down the Domgasse south from the Burg brings you to the **Cathedral Church of St Peter and St Paul**, built as the Trinity Church by the Lutherans between 1581 and 1591 and acquired by the Jesuits in 1604. The Jesuits' barockised church was substantially damaged by fire in 1723, although some of Gabriel Wittini's beautiful stucco survived the blaze. The present late Baroque interior has stunning ornate stucco (1725) by Kilian and Marx Josef Pittner. The frescoes of the *Assumption* and (in the choir) *Christ and the Divine Light of Mount Tabor* have been much altered through repeated restoration, while the four modern frescoes that are also in the choir are by Suitbert Lobisser (the *Lives of St Peter and St Paul*, 1928). The two altarpieces (1752) of the impressively monumental high altar are by Daniel Gran (*St Peter and St Paul before their Martyrdom* and above it the *Trinity*). The many side-altars show 11 different shades of marble, possibly the work of the Venetian, Francesco Robbia. The first one on the right has an altarpiece by Paul Troger showing *St Ignatius*. Note also the tabernacle designed as a gilded tempietto, and Fromiller's *Apotheosis of St John Nepomuk* placed contrapuntally to the pulpit. The **Diözesanmuseum** on Domplatz is open May–Oct, Mon–Sat 10.00–12.00, June–Sept also 15.00–17.00.

From the cathedral it is a short walk via the Mießtaler Strasse to the **Landesmuseum** (Museumgasse 2, open Tues–Sat, 09.00–16.00, Sun and PH 10.00–13.00). It documents every aspect of Carinthia, with departments devoted to history, art and folk art, as well as mineralogy and zoology. Of special interest are the Roman remains and the archaeological finds of the Bronze and Iron Ages. The fossilised rhinoceros head, originally thought to be that of the *Lindwurm*, is on show here.

A walk north past the Baroque **Bürger Spitalkirche** (1664) brings you into the Kardinalplatz, from where you head north-east for the **Gurker Bishop's Palace** (Mariannengasse 2, 1776) by Nikolaus Pacassi and the **Elisabethinenkirche** on neighbouring Völkermarkter Strasse, both associated with the crippled Archduchess Maria Anna (1738–89, commonly called 'Marianne') the oldest surviving daughter of Maria Theresia: the palace was originally built for her and her tomb (by Balthasar Moll with a *Crucifixion* group as ornamentation) is in the crypt of the Elisabethans' Church. In the former apothecary of the Elisabethan cloister are mementoes of the Archduchess, a philanthropist who had connections (through Ignaz von Born) with a masonic lodge (*Zur wohltätigen Marianna*) founded in Klagenfurt in 1783, and was also a patron of art, being herself a gifted etcher. In 1783 she brought her brother, Emperor Joseph II, to see the nuns: Joseph commented on their cheerfulness, which he contrasted favourably with the gloomy religiosity of other convents and took the opportunity to justify his dissolution of superfluous monasteries, remarking: 'Many will curse me for that, but many will thank me for it.'

Other sights

Bordering on the Lendkanal and close to the Wörthersee in the west is the celebrated **Minimundus** (Villacher Strasse 241), with 160 miniature (1:25) models of buildings from all over the world (open April–Oct, 09.00–17.00, May, June, Sept 09.00–18.00, July, August to 19.00). In summer a jazz band plays here on Saturdays. Nearby is a **Zoo** and **Reptile House**, and a **Planetarium** (Villacher Strasse 239, Lectures in May and June at 14.00, 15.00 & 16.00; Sun & PH 11.00 and 17.00).

On the north-west outskirts of the city is an **Observatory** (*Sternwarte Kreuzbergl*; open April–Aug from 21.00, Sept from 20.00, Oct, Nov from 19.00) and just beyond it are the **Botanical Gardens** (Prof.-Dr.-Kahler-Platz 1) which are adjacent to the **Mining Museum** in the former air-raid shelter inside Kreuzbergl (Bergbaumuseum; open April–Oct, daily 09.00–18.00). Somewhat further north at **Schloss Ehrental**, Ehrentaler Strasse 119 is the **Agricultural Museum** (*Landwirtschaftsmuseum Klagenfurt*; open June–Aug, daily except Sat 10.00–18.00, May, Sept, Oct, 10.00–16.00), which includes informative sections on healing plants, herbs and ecosystems.

Two other museums are worth a visit: the **Robert Musil Literature**

Museum (Bahnhofstraße 50, open Mon–Fri, 10.00–17.00, Sat 10.00–14.00) which documents Musil's life and work, as well as having sections devoted to the local poet Christine Lavant (1915–73), and the writer Ingeborg Bachmann. You can walk from the Robert Musil museum down to the **Koschatmuseum** at Viktringerring 17, which celebrates the local composer and poet Thomas Koschat (1845–1914), who wrote Carinthian folk music (open 15 May–15 Oct, Mon–Fri, 10.00–12.00).

Around Klagenfurt

The main road 91 south of Klagenfurt passes the former Cistercian **monastery of Viktring**, notable for its 56 surviving panes of Gothic stained glass in the choir of the monastery church. The windows are unrestored and show the *Life of the Virgin Mary* (left), the *Life of Christ* (centre), together with the *Apostles* and Carinthian coats of arms (right). The church itself was consecrated in 1202 but the façade was much altered in 1843, and not for the better. The mostly austere interior has an early Baroque altar (1622) of some grandeur. From **Ferlach**, somewhat to the south-east, once reputed for its gunsmiths, it is not far to the spectacular **Tscheppaschlucht gorge** (the walk through it takes 1.5hrs). To the south is the steep **Loibl Pass** over the **Karawanken** to Slovenia.

North-west of Klagenfurt on road 95 is **Moosburg** where the 16C **Schloss Neue Moosburg** has a remarkable columned **Knights' Hall**, but is seldom accessible. The small **Carolingian Museum** (open June–Sept, Mon–Sat, 10.00–12.00 and 15.30–18.00) narrates the history of Moosburg, and in particular of King Arnulf of Carinthia (850–899). The town was a swampy Carolingian palatinate (*Mosapurch*) under King Karlmann, the father of Arnulf, who was probably born here. The ruins of his palace with the the so-called '*Arnulfsturm*' may be seen nearby (**Burgruine Etzelburg**).

A few kilometres due north of Klagenfurt is the **Pilgimage Church of Maria Saal** overlooking the **Zollfeld**, the historic heart of Carinthia. The church has its origins in pre-Carolingian times and was ringed with a defensive wall in the second half of the 15C (a cannonball dating to a Hungarian attack in 1480 may be seen embedded in the south wall of the church). There are also a number of Roman reliefs incorporated into the masonry, including the so-called 'Roman post-chaise', in which the cloak of the driver identifies him as one of the region's Celtic inhabitants. Note the *Keutschacher Epitaph* in red marble (early 16C), a work by Hans Valkenauer showing the *Coronation of the Virgin*.

The church's most distinguished feature is the **Arndorfer Altar** (1520), showing *St Elisabeth, Mary Magdalene, St Anne with Jesus and St John, St Genevieve and St Ottilia* in the lower shrine; above it the *Coronation of the Virgin*. On the right-hand panel are the *Fourteen Holy Helpers*, on the left-hand one, *St Ursula* and companions with an *Annunciation* above. In the southern apse the **Georgsaltar** (1526) features a splendidly theatrical St George killing a suitably dismayed dragon. Interesting also is the large fresco (1928) by Herbert Boeckl on the south wall, showing *Christ Walking on the Water*. St Peter has been given the features of Lenin, to suggest the inability of Bolshevism and atheism to save itself. The fine **organ** (1737) by Johann Martin Jäger is set in a graceful Baroque organ loft. The 41 painted fields (1491) of the fan vaulting are also unusual and represent the genealogical tree of Jesus. Beside the church is the '*octogon*', formerly a baptismal and burial chapel, in front of it an intricately carved late Gothic column (1497), the function of which was to shelter a night-light to ward off evil spirits so that the dead should rest in peace.

The minor road leads north past an **open-air museum** of Carinthian farm buildings to the historic **Herzogstuhl** (3km), a massive double throne constructed out of Roman slabs, the east-facing seat for the Duke of Carinthia, the west-facing one for the Palatine Count. After acclamation on the Fürstenstein in Karnburg (see below), the Carinthian Dukes took their oaths here and invested their subjects with grants of land, all of which have been documented for the period between 1161 and 1651. This historic seat is seen as the 'navel of Carinthia', in the middle of the **Zollfeld** (plain) of the Glan basin, where the three ceremonies of the ducal inauguration took place, ending with a mass in Maria Saal, but it was also the focus of the earlier Celtic and Roman *Noricum*. The Roman capital *Virunum*, was slightly to the north, many of its buildings and monuments lying just below the soil, although individual artefacts have been recovered and placed in the Landesmuseum in Klagenfurt.

The Magdalensberg and Ulrichsberg

To the north-east the road winds steeply (8km) to the romantic Magdalensberg (1058m) with plenty of good views on the way, all surpassed, however, by the ones from the restaurant and the church at the summit. Just below the peak are the excavations of a Celtic-Roman settlement existing at the turn of the Pre-Christian and Christian Ages, which can be visited. Its most celebrated find, a bronze of a youth (perhaps Mars or Mercury) is displayed in replica. A Romanesque church was built at the top of the hill on the site of shrines dedicated to Mars and Latobius, but replaced by the present one in 1500 and dedicated to St Helena, a finely carved statue of whom adorns the high altar. The predella and wings show the legend of the *Discovery of the True Cross*, while above are the *Madonna*, a *Man of Sorrows* and *Mary Magdalene*. The last-named became the church's patron only after 1583, until when the hill was called the Helenenberg.

The Magdalensberg faces (across the Zollfeld and the River Glan) the equally historic **Ulrichsberg** (1015m), known in the Middle Ages as *Mons Carantanus*, and in 1485 still being referred to as *Kernberg* (i.e. **Kärntner Berg**). This appears to have been a place of worship to Isis-Noreia in pagan times and later an early Christian shrine, and has, like the Magdalensberg, a quasi-mystical significance in the local culture. The two mountains are destinations in the annual pilgrimage (*Vierberge-Wallfahrt* or *Vierberge-Lauf*), which also includes the Veitsberg and Lorenziberg and takes place on the second Friday after Easter. The custom was once thought to be of pagan origin, but is now considered Christian, despite the collecting of pagan-seeming evergreens along the way. In recent years the annual Ulrichsberg meeting of Austrian war veterans has attracted adverse comment because of the tendency of even mainstream politicians to honour surviving members of SS units, as if they were indistinguishable from ordinary soldiers 'just doing their duty' (in ex-President Waldheim's exculpatory phrase), an attitude welcomed and exploited by the right-wing Freedom Party.

The mountain summit can only be approached on foot (c 45mins) via Karnberg-Pörtschach from Kollerwirt. There is a ruined late Gothic church

(1483, destroyed by lightning in 1897) which, since its restoration in 1959, has served as a memorial to the dead of Carinthia in two World Wars and in the struggle against Yugoslavia in 1919–20. In front of the church is a huge white cross, visible for many miles around. The resultant 'Caspar David Friedrich meets Richard Wagner' effect would doubtless seem more appetising if the Nazis had not so contaminated the heroic element in German romanticism.

Hochosterwitz

A minor road leads from road 83 north and east of the Magdalensberg to the dramatically situated **castle** at **Hochosterwitz** on a 150m outcrop of jurassic limestone, still known in the early Middle Ages by its Celtic-derived name of *Astarvizza*, a corruption of *arx taurisca* or 'fortress of the (Celtic tribe of) Taurisker'. Its medieval owners were descendants of the powerful Sponheimer, who claimed descent from Emperor Arnulf and were cupbearers to the Carinthian dukes. Subsequently, one of their number was deputed to gather an army to resist the imminent Turkish invasion of 1473. In 1478 the last cupbearer gave the castle to the Emperor, but it later came into the hands of the bishops of Gurk, then of the Khevenhüller family, who had the buildings greatly extended (1571–86) and strengthened them with bastions designed by Domenico dell'Allio. The road up to it winds round an almost sheer rockface, passing through 14 gates on the way, many with inscriptions, frescoes of banner-waving lansquenets, etc.

The **Castle Museum** (open Easter–Oct, daily, 08.30–18.00) contains weapons and suits of armour and a gilded bronze altar (1580) with a relief of the *Resurrection* and the marble figure of Georg Khevenhüller (1534–87) kneeling in front of it. The charming small chapel has frescoes of the *Apostles* (1570) on the ceiling and New Testament scenes in the lunettes, together with an altarpiece of 1673 surmounted by a roundel of the *Baptism of Christ*. From the Bergfried there are fine views across the Zollfeld. The castle (still in the possession of the Khevenhüllers) is open from Easter to the end of October and may also be entered on the west side by means of a lift up the cliff. A turning to the right after the 13th gate on the approach road leads to the **church of St Nicholas and St John Nepomuk**, where Protestant services were held in the 16C. Several Khevenhüllers turned Protestant and went into exile in 1628.

Hochosterwitz

St Veit an der Glan and the Gurktal

Located a few kilometres west of Hochosterwitz, the town of St Veit an der Glan was for nearly 400 years (until 1518) the seat of the Carinthian dukes, one of whom (Duke Bernhard, 1202–56) was married to a daughter of the formidable King Ottakar II Přemysl of Bohemia, the splendour of whose court he tried to emulate. Lustre was lent for a while to his residence at St Veit in 1220 by the presence of the *Minnesänger* Walther von der Vogelweide, which explains the monumental fountain (1676) on the Hauptplatz dedicated to the poet (the bronze statue is a contemporary work by L. Szadai, 1960). Other features of this exceptionally picturesque square are the Plague Column (1716) at its centre and the **Schüsselbrunnen**, a fountain whose basin is taken from a Roman one found in *Virunum*, to which a late Gothic bronze figure has been added, possibly a representation of a town councillor.

The **Rathaus** (1648) on the Oberen Platz has an impressive late Baroque façade and a graceful arcaded courtyard, while both of the town's substantial squares are lined with decorative patrician houses dating to St Veit's 15C boom period, when the Dukes ordered that all the iron mined in the nearby Hüttenberg had to be transported via the town (the so-called *Straßenzwang*). For the burghers this amounted almost to a licence to print money, which in fact St Veit also did, or rather minted, between 1220 and 1725. The Romanesque and Gothic parish church has a charnel house incorporating a carved stone from the Carolingian era. Its Baroque altars and the pulpit are mostly the work of Johann Pacher, whose workshop was here.

Road 94 bears west from St Veit to the Ossiacher See (see p 352), passing Glanegg to the south on the way to **Tiffen**, where the fortified parish church has 15C and 16C frescoes by Thomas Artula and Urban Görtschacher of Villach. Frescoes by Friedrich von Villach may be seen in the church at **St Gandolf**, south of Glanegg and also (a dogleg to the east) at **St Peter am Bichl**.

North-west of St Veit is the impressive castle of **Frauenstein** (the present remnants dating to 1519 on a 12C base) and nearby the ruins of the two Schlösser at Hochkraig and Niederkraig, the principal fortresses of the Carinthian dukes in the 12C. A minor road leads on to the Gurktal past **Pisweg**, where there are Romanesque frescoes from around 1280 in the well-preserved charnel house next to the parish church. If the main road (83) is followed north of St Veit, **Althofen** is reached after several kilometres, situated on a hill just east of Mölbling. Its Gothic church is dedicated to St Thomas of Canterbury, the saint being represented in the neo-Gothic high altar surrounded by angels, while on the north wall is a painting of his reception into heaven. In the cemetery and embedded in the walls of the church are some interesting Roman tombstones, some apparently dedicated to freed slaves from the local population, others recalling the Dionysian cult. The town was an important staging-post on the trade route between the Adriatic and the Danube.

Road 93 now bears west up the valley of the River Gurk, after passing the Baroque Schloss (1780) at **Pöckstein** built by J.B. Hagenauer; for a brief while (1780–87) it was the seat of the Gurk bishops, and is now the administration for the bishopric's forestry.

The historic town of Straßburg is shortly reached to the west, having on its outskirts the hilltop village of **Lieding**, the church of which has a carved tympanum over the main door showing an angel, a lion and a dragon; in the interior a fine Gothic chancel. A certain Hemma from this village is the legendary 11C founder of the Monastery of Gurk a few kilometres further west. It was founded in memory of her husband, the Count of Zeltschach, who died returning from a crusade, but also in expiation for the crimes of her two horrible sons who oppressed the local miners and made off with their wives. In 1072 the Gurk bishopric was founded and the building of the Romanesque cloister began in 1140. St Hemma's tomb (1174) with a Baroque marble relief showing her death (Antonio Corradini, 1714, note also the wrought-iron screen by Michael Gaissl and Corradini's mourning figures) is in the crypt of the extremely impressive cathedral. The crypt is made intensely dramatic by its thicket of 100 columns on which the choir rests, and it also contains the '**Hemma Stone**' on which the founder supposedly sat in 1043 watching the construction of her convent.

Monastery and Cathedral of Gurk

● Guided tours take place from Ash Wednesday–All Saints' Day, weekdays 09.30, 11.00, 14.30, 16.15; also at 13.30 May–Oct. On Sun and PH at 10.30, 11.00, 14.30, 16.15 (13.30 May–Oct).

Gurk Cathedral – crypt

The marvellous Romanesque cathedral of Gurk has been aptly described as a *Gesamtkunstwerk* harmonising the finest aesthetic products of different styles and ages. To the triple-aisled basilica was added the reticulated vaulting in 1591. The superb seven-arched western **Trichterportal** of c 1200 has palmette and rosette decoration, together with frescoes in the entrance hall (c 1340) illustrating 32 scenes from the New Testament which are said to show Giotto's influence.

A rare Romanesque survival is the **Bishop's Chapel**, a double-bayed cross-vaulted gallery above the western barrel-vaulted porch, which is reached by a spiral staircase next to the font. Its frescoes (1263) were painted according to the original scheme (1220) of Master Heinrich, whose work was destroyed in a fire, being evidently by a later hand (1263) and in the new *Zackenstil* (with angular serrations in the carved folds of the drapery). In the eastern cupola is the *Earthly Paradise*, in the western one the *New Jerusalem*. On the eastern wall is a somewhat obscure theological programme, with *Mary and Jesus on the Lion Throne of Solomon* and allegories of the *Virtues and the Prophets*. On the west wall the the *Transfiguration of Christ on Mount Tabor*, to the south, the *Three Kings*, to the north *Christ's Entry into Jerusalem*. (This complex iconography is explained in detail in the booklet obtainable at the rear of the church.) In the western roundel window is a *Deposition from the Cross* dating to 1270.

Of the many treasures in the body of the church, the Romanesque *Sampson* tympanum (c 1200) is notable on the north wall, showing Sampson (emblematic of Christ) tearing apart the jaws of the lion (emblematic of Satan). Beyond it on the north and south walls of the choir are six reliefs of the *Hemma tableau* (1515) by L. Pampstel, which show the legend of Hemma's founding of the convent and the subsequent miracles at her tomb. The Baroque high altar is by Matthias Hönel of Pirna and is of stunningly vivid complexity. The 16m high gilded retable is adorned with 72 figures and 82 angels' heads. It focuses on a carved *Rosary Madonna* at the centre, accompanied by *Angels holding scrolls of the Loretan Litany,* beneath her the *Apostles,* above her the *Trinity.* Ranged below are the *Four Evangelists* (of which the head of Luke may be a self-portrait of Hönel), the *Fathers of the Church, St Hemma* and her husband *Count Wilhelm, Emperor Heinrich II and Kunigunde,* etc. The altar table has rare *cosmati work* of coloured stones, mother of pearl, glass, and goldleaf, outside Italy only to be found in Westminster Abbey.

The *pietà* of the Altar of the Cross (in front of the choir, in the centre) is the last masterwork of Georg Raphael Donner with a tabernacle by his follower, Balthasar Moll.

The **pulpit** (Giovanni and Antonio Bibiena, 1741) shows the victory of the church over false doctrine (above) and six lead reliefs by Donner of biblical scenes. In the north crossing is a huge fresco (c 1250) of *St Christopher,* one of the earliest of its kind. The image, painted on a vast scale, became a popular motif of the external walls of parish churches, on account of the belief that anyone seeing St Christopher would not die on that day without the comforts of the faith (St Christopher was seen as carrying Christ to the dying). In the south crossing are frescoes (c 1380) of the *Conversion of St Paul* and the *Twenty-Four Elders of the Apocalypse,* on the north wall a representation (c 1200) of Sampson slaying the lion.

The greatest treasure of the monastery (since 1932 in the hands of the Salvatorians) is its **Lenten Cloth** (9 x 9m) or *Biblia pauperum,* one of only nine that have survived. On the left half are 50 scenes from the Old Testament and on the right 49 from the New Testament. The cloth was painted on linen in 1458 by Konrad of Friesach and is hung on the high altar of the cathedral during Lent. Also of note is the modern (1955) reliquary of St Hemma made by Anni Perner-Sturmayer. The **charnel house** opposite the main porch was made octagonal in 1450 and contains a representation of *Christ on the Mount of Olives* (1722) by Anton Artl, together with remnants of early frescoes.

Further west along the Gurktal a road leads north to **Deutsch Griffen** with an impressive fortified church whose walls are over 3m high and 80cm thick; the covered stairway to the church is later (1755).

Friesach

If the main road 83 (E7) is followed north instead of turning off to Gurk, Carinthia's most ancient town (1215) of Friesach is soon reached, only a few kilometres short of the border with Styria. The strategic town guarded the valley and retains much of its medieval walls and part of the moat (9.5m deep, 15.5m wide) to the east and north-east. Its name is probably derived from Slav '*bresah*' ('near the birches'). It was in the possession of the Salzburg Archbishops from 860–1803, despite many attempts to dislodge them. In 1192 Richard Coeur de Lion was hiding in the town before going on to Vienna, where he was arrested by agents of Duke Leopold of Babenberg. In the 12C and the 13C the Friesach silver penny was an important currency and Friesach weights and measures were used all over Carinthia. In the 13C also the 'summit conference' (1224) so vividly described by the *Minnesänger* Ulrich von Liechtenstein (in his *Friesach Tourney* (Tournament) and *Venus Voyage*) took place, and involved several days of jousting and junketing. The upshot was a territorial agreement between the quarrelling Carinthian Dukes and Margraves of Istria. It is a stiff climb from the Hauptplatz to the **Petersberg** overlooking the town from the west with a 13C church built over a Carolingian edifice (pre-927). An even stiffer climb awaits visitors to the massive 13C **Bergfried** (28m high) on the south-eastern edge of the adjacent castle area, which now houses the **Municipal Museum** (open May–Oct, Tues–Sun, 10.00–12.00 and 13.00–17.00), but was originally the residence of the Salzburg bishops. Highlights of the museum include a Romanesque *Maria lactans* (c 1200) sculpted in stone, a late Gothic shrine and two wings of a 15C altar painted by the artist of the Gurk Lenten Cloth, Konrad von Friesach, together with rare Romanesque frescoes. The north-west of the Petersberg is occupied by the remains of **Burg Lavant**, so-called because it was formerly the residence of the Lavant bishops.

Returning to the Hauptplatz, note its beautiful **Renaissance fountain** (1563), with reliefs of *Poseidon, Acteon and Artemis*, the *Rape of Europa, Amphitrite as a sea monster, Perseus and Andromeda, Hercules and the Centaur, Leda and the Swan, Castor and Pollux* and *Persephone in the Underworld*. To the north the **parish church of St Barthlmä** (Bartholomew) was officiously restored in the 19C, but retains fine 14C stained glass in the choir (The *Wise and Foolish Virgins*, the *Life of Jesus*). Outside the moat to the north is the **Dominican Church of St Nicholas**, the first to be built on German soil by the Dominicans after their foundation in 1217. The church is transitional between Romanesque and Gothic and contains an early Gothic painted sandstone *Madonna* and a 14C *Crucifixion*, probably by a Salzburg master. The early 16C wing altar shows Sts Florian and George with Christ and scenes (some of them apocryphal) from the life of John the Evangelist (his refusal to worship Artemis, his drinking from the poisoned chalice, his writing of the Revelations on Patmos, finally his descent into the prepared grave following his final sermon).

To the south of the town is the **church of St Blaise** (to visit apply at the hospital) that belongs to the Teutonic Order (with both 'sisters' and 'brothers' living here uniquely under one roof), the knights originally having set up the hospice in 1275 (there is still a hospital adjacent). The Romanesque and Gothic church was barockised in the 18C and given a new tower. The ruined 12C frescoes in the choir show the *Feeding of the Five Thousand*, the *Wise and Foolish Virgins* and fragments of an *Annunciation* and a *Nativity*. The impressive late Gothic winged altar shows *Mary as Queen of Heaven* with *Sts Catherine and Margaret*; above is the *Coronation of Mary* with *Sts Anthony and Lawrence*; the *Nativity* and *Adoration of the Magi*; in the tabernacle, the *Annunciation*, with New Testament and Old Testament scenes on the wings, also a charming *hortus conclusus* representation of Mary with the unicorn, symbol of purity. On the north wall of the choir is a late Gothic winged altar from Frankfurt showing in the shrine *Christ Pantocrator* above the *Saved and the Damned* with various saints depicted on the wings, the predella and the neo-Gothic superstructure.

Friesach has a dance festival in summer and there are concerts accompanying the Friesach Academy week in September. Details of these and local sights from the Tourist Information at Hauptplatz 1 (☎ 04268-4300. Fax: 4280).

Beyond Friesach a minor road leads west up the Metnitztal to **Grades** where both the parish church with its Romanesque frescoes and stained glass, and the fortified **St Wolfgang Church**, are of interest. The church at **Metnitz** has fine Gothic vaulting and a *Dance of Death* cycle of frescoes on the north wall, moved here from the charnel house.

East of Klagenfurt

Brückl and Hüttenberg

If you take road 70 due east of Klagenfurt and turn shortly north-east on road 92, you soon reach **Brückl** on the old Roman road running between *Virunum* and the iron ore mines of Hüttenberg. The late Gothic **parish church** dominates the village and has an especially elegant late Baroque columned altar (1758) by Johann Packer with a carved group of the *Baptism of Christ*. Following the road some 25km towards the Styrian border you reach **Hüttenberg** itself, a centre of iron production for 2000 years, the famous *ferrum noricum* having been produced from pre-Roman times until the closure of the mines in 1978. The inhabitants have done their best to keep its memory alive with the institution of a research centre (Geozentrum), an impressive **Exhibition Mine**, **Mining Museum** and **Mineral Display**, all of which are open May–Oct, daily 10.00–17.00 (last guided tour of the mine at 16.00). A new attraction is the **Heinrich-Harrer-Museum** (open

Heinrich Harrer (1912–)

In his youth Harrer was the Austrian student skiing champion and the first to scale the North Wall of the Eiger (with three companions) in 1938. His book *The White Spider* describes this remarkable achievement. In 1939 he was a member of the German Nanga-Parbat Expedition, but the outbreak of World War II found him in India, where he was interned by the British at Dehra Dun. However, he escaped in 1944 and made his way with one companion across the Himalayas to Lhasa, where he was later an adviser to the Dalai Lama between 1946 and 1951. He returned to Europe when the Chinese gained control of Tibet and thereafter embarked on a series of expeditions to remote areas of the world. His autobiographical classic *Seven Years in Tibet* was recently made into a film starring Brad Pitt, but the publicity surrounding its release led to the German magazine *Stern* exposing Harrer as having Nazi sympathies in the late 1930s.

Harrer's fascination with Tibet may have been partly inspired by the theory then current that it was the original home of the 'Aryan race'; however, the country still exerts a (happily non-racial) spell in Austria, the singer Hubert von Goisern being one of the stoutest supporters of the Dalai Lama and a doughty campaigner against Chinese attempts to destroy Tibetan culture.

May–Oct, 10.00–17.00) showing the ethnographical collection of the celebrated traveller (see above). The museum is in the former school attended by Harrer and was opened in the presence of the Dalai Lama. Artefacts and cult objects from Africa, South America, Tibet, the Andaman Islands, Borneo and New Guinea may be seen here; it is also worth venturing on the **Tibetan pilgrims' path** located on the rock face opposite the building (the climb is not demanding for humans, although a cow fell off the rockface a few years ago). Harrer himself lives on the nearby Knappenberg, his house recognisable by the Tibetan decoration of the garage. After his death it will become a centre for Tibetan studies.

Völkermarkt, Unteres und Oberes Lavanttal

Some 30km east of Klagenfurt is the town of **Völkermarkt**, the scene of bitter fighting between Yugoslav troops and the local *Heimwehr* after World War I, and occupied by the former from November 1918 to May 1919. Close by the town is a large reservoir formed from the damming of the Drau river. The **parish church of St Mary Magdalene** has a 15C painted *pietà*, star vaulting and 15C frescoes, while the earlier church of **St Rupert** to the north has an 11C tower, but has otherwise been spoiled by heavy-handed restoration in the 19C. The **Alte Rathaus** on the Hauptplatz has attractive arcades dating to 1499, while the **Neue Rathaus** is neo-classical. Several of the other houses of the square have pleasing Biedermeier façades.

North-east of Völkermarkt is **Haimburg**, where the parish church has a well-preserved Lenten Cloth dating to 1504 and Gothic frescoes in the choir of angels with musical instruments. To the south of the hamlet are the ruins of the Burg. At **Griffen** nearby are caves (open July–Aug, daily 09.00–17.00, May and June, Sept and Oct 09.00–12.00, 13.00–17.00; guided tours last 30mins.) discovered during World War II when the authorities were searching for suitable air-raid shelters. The bones of a number of extinct species of animal were subsequently found here, including prehistoric bears, hyenas, lions, mammoths, deer and woolly rhinoceros. The caves also appear to have been used as refuge by Stone Age hunter gatherers.

Monastery of St Paul in Lavanttal

Road 70 leads on to the right-hand turning south-east for the Lower Lavanttal (**Unteres Lavanttal**), and shortly the richly endowed **Monastery of St Paul** founded by Benedictines from the Black Forest in 1091, and refounded in 1809 after dissolution under Joseph II. The church retains Romanesque features, but the dependencies were rebuilt in the 17C. In the shallow crypt beneath the choir of the monastery church are the graves of 13 Habsburgs brought here from St Blasien when the monks returned in 1809. The majestic effect of the basilical church (1170–1220), which opens into three apses at the eastern end, is enhanced by the lovely Gothic vaulting of the choir (1367) and of the nave (1468) together with the elegant Baroque fittings. The ornate Romanesque capitals have palmetta, rosette and foliage decoration, while Romanesque features in the apses include carved dragons, snakes and other representations of evil spirits. The *Fathers of the Church* and *Saints* shown on the 23 keystones and in the vaulting are by Michael and Friedrich Pacher from the Pustertal (East Tyrol), whose work is found in a number of Carinthian churches.

The tympanum relief of the west door is Romanesque and shows *Christ giving his Blessing*, with a kneeling *St Paul* beside a figure who is perhaps the first Abbot. In the tympanum of the south door, of which the portals are a reconstruction (1618) of the Romanesque original, is a relief of the *Adoration of the Three Kings*. The high point of the **interior** is the celebrated foundation fresco (1493) in the crossing by Thomas of Villach, which shows *Count Engelbert of Sponheimer and his spouse, Hadwiga, protected by St Benedict and St Catherine;* the accompanying angels hold the coats of arms of the monastery and of Carinthia. On the east wall *St Peter and St Paul* are depicted, together with the *Vernicle* and (in the peripheral decoration) a self-portrait of the artist. The main altar is a late Gothic triptych of 1460, at the centre a *Throne of Grace* flanked (left) by *Sts Erhard* and *Barbara*, and (right) by *John the Baptist* and *St Catherine*. Of the many tombstones, that of the Sponheimer is exceptional, showing Engelbert and Hadwiga holding a model of the church they founded, from the tower of which a bird takes wing—a delightful symbol of the departing soul. Also notable is the Renaissance tomb (1520) of Ulrich Pfinzing, perhaps by an Augsburg master.

In the monastery itself, rebuilt after 1618, fine coffered ceilings of the 17C may be seen in some of the rooms, as well as beautiful 18C stucco. In the refectory are modern (1932) frescoes by Suitbert Lobisser (the *Arrival of the Monks from Hirsau in 1091*, *The Turkish Army Camp in front of St Paul in 1476* and *The Four Orders of Benedictine Monks*). The monastery's art collection and library may be visited and contain early MSS, an ecclesiastical treasury and Baroque sketches and paintings. There are guided tours daily at 10.30 and 15.00 from May–Oct and the church is open 09.00–17.00.

Turn back north to rejoin road 70 and continue north to **St Andrä im Lavanttal**, the seat of the Prince-Bishops of Lavant from 1228–1859, when the bishopric was transferred to Marburg (Maribor, now in Slovenia). The Gothic parish church is unremarkable, except for its arcaded passageway that connected the bishop's residence with the church, but the **Pilgrimage Church of Maria Loreto** (1687) has an impressive high altar. Its statuary (Markus Claus, 1691) shows the crucified Christ flanked by St John and Mary Magdalene, and the altar is encompassed by a striking architectural fresco of 1793 by an unknown master: God the Father, enveloped in a mantle of mercy, looks down on the Crucifixion in a gesture of blessing, while Jeremiah and Isaiah (in the columned side-niches) foretell the sacrifice of Christ for mankind. The tomb of Bishop Stadion (1704), the founder of the church, shows his portrait and graceful late Baroque decoration.

Five kilometres north of St Andrä is **Wolfsberg**, founded by the Bishop of Bamberg in the 11C, and overlooked by an originally Renaissance Schloss that was altered (1853) in 'Windsor style' by its 19C owner, who married an English lady. The Romanesque and Gothic **parish church of St Mark** has Renaissance and Baroque features in the interior. Romanesque survivals include the west portal and a pillar in the south-east part of the church with a remarkable marble relief of the *Lion of St Mark* and the *Evangelist's head* behind it, evidently influenced by the style of Roman funerary sculpture. The altarpiece of the high altar is Kremser Schmidt's depiction of St Mark. The figures on the consoles in the choir are Emperor Heinrich II with his consort St Kunigunde; they crop up again in the second chapel on the north side where a picture of *Kunigunde's Trial by Fire* (J.B. van Rüll, 1667) may be seen. This recalls the regrettable episode when the Emperor wrongly suspected Kunigunde of adultery, whereupon she proved her innocence by walking barefoot on red-hot ploughshares. The **Anna Chapel** behind the church was the guild chapel of the bakers and has a fine late Gothic altar with a *Madonna and Child*, the wings showing reliefs of saints on the inside, scenes from the *Life of Mary* on the outside; on the predella *Christ with the Apostles*. The town centre (Hoher Platz) has attractive 16C houses and a Marian column of 1718.

Bad St Leonhard to the north (road 70, then road 78) is so-called from its radioactive sulphur springs, but grew into a rich town from the mining of precious metals in the Middle Ages. The 14C fortified parish church dedicated to St Leonard is surrounded by an iron chain, a reference to the saint's role as the liberator of prisoners—the current chain is modern (1912), however, since Joseph II had the original removed. The interior preserves 139 ancient panes of stained glass, the earliest being early 14C. They depict the legend of the church's foundation, as well as saints, prophets and the lives of Mary and Christ. The high altar dates to 1646, while in the choir is a Gothic winged altar (1513) with a graceful carving of *St Anne, the Virgin and Jesus* in the shrine. The church possesses a Lenten Cloth (1570) showing New Testament and Old Testament scenes. Nearby is a charnel house dating to c 1400.

South of Völkermarkt

To the south-east of Völkermarkt is the frontier town of **Bleiburg**, so-called from the lead mining that was carried on in the local Petzen mountains. In the centre there are attractive historic houses and the Renaissance Schloss is an imposing presence (but not accessible). The **Werner-Berg-Gallery** (open 15 May–15 Nov, Tues 14.00–17.00, Wed–Sun 10.00–12.00 and 14.00–17.00) celebrates the work of a German artist who settled here aged 27 and documented peasant life in a style that mixes the naïve with Expressionistic elements, recalling the Hungarian painter Tivadar Csontváry Kosztka.

On the main road due south of Völkermarkt is **Eberndorf** with its former Augustinian Abbey, of which the church is now the parish church. It has an impressive free-standing tower like a campanile. On the main altar is a Gothic *Madonna* (c 1470), in the Franz Xaver Chapel a *St Anne with Mary and Jesus* dating to 1530 and a vivid *Annunciation* relief of 1510. The highlight is perhaps the **Ungnad Chapel** with its late Gothic relief on the tomb of the Knight Christoph Ungnad, who died in 1490 and was the Lord of nearby Sonnegg. The raised choir is unusually 12 steps above the nave with a crypt (1380) beneath it, and the early Gothic vaulting is also notable. A turn eastwards onto road 81 to the south brings you to **Globasnitz-Hemmaberg** and the remains of Roman *Iuenna*, the hoard of coins dating to the 3C that was found here now being in the Landesmuseum in Klagenfurt. *Iuenna* was destroyed by the Avars at the end of the 6C, at which time the inhabitants retreated to the Hemmaberg. In the **Archaeological Museum** (open May–Oct, Mon–Sat 10.00–12.00, 14.00–17.00) exceptional early Christian mosaics may be seen. The open air museum of the Hemmaberg is accessible all year round.

Road 82 leads on towards Slovenia, passing through **Eisenkappel** ('*Kappel*' until 1890) on the way, a town that lay on an important medieval trade route for salt, iron and lead, and that became even more significant after the Habsburgs obtained Trieste in 1383. Remains of defensive roadblocks (*Türkenschanze*) may be seen on the nearby Trobelfelsen. The parish church has a **Plague Chapel** of 1680 with powerful representations of the plague protectors, Sts Sebastian, Florian and Rosalie. The **Pilgrimage Church of Maria Dorn** to the north has external and internal frescoes (c 1490) and a carved *Madonna* of c 1410. Eisenkappel lies at a point where the valley of the River Vellach narrows sharply and was consequently often exposed to flooding in the spring thaws: the custom whereby children float lighted models of churches on the river on 1 February goes back to an early attempt to appease the raging waters with token sacrifices. The Vellach flows south to Slovenia and the extremely scenic southernmost road of Austria follows its course to Bad Vellach and the Seebergsattel of the Steiner (Slav: *Kamniske*) Alpe, which straddles the border. Another attractive route runs along the minor road to the west from Eisenkappel to Ferlach via Zell (Sele), passing through one of the heartlands of the Slovene minority in Carinthia.

Between Klagenfurt and Villach

The north and south banks of the Wörther See

The main road 83 and *Autobahn* A2 (E7) run along the north bank of the **Wörther See**, one of Austria's favourite summer resorts. At picturesque **Pörtschach** an EU summit was held in 1998 when Austria held the EU presidency for the first time. The town was a popular 19C resort for the well-to-do and consequently has many fine Historicist and turn of the century villas. Johannes Brahms visited in 1878–79, composing his 2nd Symphony and Violin Concerto here. He stayed at **Schloss Leonstein** (still a hotel), once a Renaissance castle, that retains an arcaded courtyard in which there is a fountain with a lion ornament. At the far end of the lake is another popular resort called **Velden**, **Schloss Velden** (a hotel) having been built (1603) by Barthlmä Khevenhüller for his retirement.

There is rather more to see along the southern shore of the lake. Passing through **Maiernigg**, where Gustav Mahler bought a summer villa in 1902 and composed his 5th, 6th, 7th and 8th Symphonies, you reach after 11km the village and monastery of **Maria Wörth**, originally situated on an island until the lake level dropped suddenly in 1770, and now picturesquely nestling on a peninsula. In the 9C, Bishop Arnold of Freising obtained the island and one of his successors enhanced its attractions by bringing the remains of the Roman martyrs Primus and Felician here (the lake for a while bore their names). A monastery was founded by a Babenberg bishop and is now an offshoot of the Benedictine monastery of St Paul im Lavanttal. The former monastery church (1151) is reached by a covered stairway and has a Romanesque south portal and crypt. Its chief treasure is the large **Altar of the Cross**, where the pompous Baroque fittings frame a Gothic crucifix and *Madonna* (1469) showing affinities with the Byzantine icon of Santa Maria Maggiore in Rome. The Baroque high altar dates to 1685 and is flanked by statues of the church's patrons, *Sts Primus and Felician*.

A late 13C charnel house stands near the church and lower down the slope is the **Rosenkranzkirche**, the parish church from 1155, which has Romanesque frescoes in the choir: on the east wall, the *Apostles* (originally grouped beside the now obliterated figure of Our Lord), and on the north wall a further row of *Apostles* painted 200 years later. The Gothic window showing *Mary and the Child Jesus on a Half-Moon* is notable. A road south of Maria Wörth leads to **Keutschach** and the **Keutschacher See**, a popular bathing area with its adjacent string of small lakes. The masonry of the Romanesque **St George's Chapel** incorporates an interesting Carolingian (or perhaps 8C) stone showing a primitively carved symbol of the *Resurrection*. South-west of Maria Wörth, and reached via the Keutschacher See, is the 850m **Pyramidenkogel**, with an outlook tower offering superb views of the surrounding countryside.

The minor road leads along the southern shore of the Wörther See to Velden (see above), south of which is **Rosegg**, lying in a bend of the River Drau and an important river crossing from earliest times. This had always made it vulnerable in wartime and its buildings suffered again in the Napoleonic War and in 1919. It is now overshadowed by a vast hydro-electric installation. Much of the Gothic parish church was destroyed in 1813 but some Baroque fittings remain, while the 12C fortress of **Altrosegg** is completely ruined but picturesquely sited on a commanding point over the river crossing. **Schloss Rosegg** (1772) belongs to the Liechtensteins and has a **Waxworks Museum** (open May–11 Oct, 10.00–18.00, not Mon, but daily in July and Aug). The **Wildpark Rosegg** (open daily April–Nov, 09.00–17.00, July and Aug 09.00–18.00) is decidedly user-friendly with a 'petting zoo' for children.

South of the River Drau between Klagenfurt and Villach

If you continue on road 91 (E94) from Viktring (see p 334), you cross the river near the strategically situated 16C **Schloss Hollenburg**, from which there are fine views of the Karawanken Mountains and the Rosental (only the courtyard of the Schloss is accessible). **Ferlach**, south of the river, has a **Gunsmiths Museum** (open May–Oct by appointment. ☎ 042 27 49 20) of some interest, Ferlach having been an ancient centre of gunmaking, later of weapons research when a Technical School was founded here under the Dual Monarchy. The E652 (road 91) leads on over the Loibl Pass to Slovenia, but a turn westwards along road 85 brings you to **Maria Elend** with its Gothic hall church, which is associated with St Hemma of Gurk (see p 338). The fresco in the choir, perhaps by Fromiller, shows the saint's vision of the church she was to found, with *Our Lady enthroned* above it. The late Gothic **winged altar** (1525) in the south nave shows the *Madonna with Sts Rochus and Sebastian*, then the *Fourteen Holy Helpers* on the wings, the *Passion*, the *Four Evangelists* and (on the predella) the peculiarly horrible *Martyrdom of St Achatius* and his companions by impaling, finally (on the reverse) the *Vernicle*.

Pilgrimage Church of Maria Gail

After passing by St Jakob and the extension of the A11 motorway from Villach heading for the Karawanken tunnel and into Slovenia, you fork right on to road 84 for **Maria Gail**, with its pilgrimage church, the place taking its name from the nearby tributary of the Drau. According to local tradition, the church of Maria Gail was 'founded by pagans', a reference to the supposed foundation at the time of the Longobards. The parish was originally placed under the patriarchate of Aquileia, like all those south of the Drau, after Charlemagne was obliged to adjudicate in the territorial dispute between the Patriarch of Aquileia and the Bishop of Salzburg.

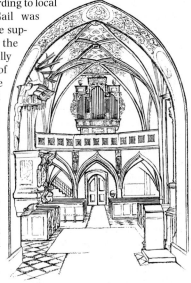

The Pilgrimage Church of Maria Gail

The church is defensively built with its Romanesque tower situated between the nave and the choir to provide refuge in times of trouble, which was frequent enough in the border region. The net vaulting is late Gothic (1450) with painted ornamentation while the organ loft rests on a turned column springing from Gothic stone lions. On the **exterior** a painted Gothic frieze may be seen, together with Romanesque and Gothic ornamentation, including a *Last Judgement*. The church's finest artefact is the delicately carved Gothic winged altar (c 1525) showing the *Coronation of Mary by the Trinity* (in the shrine) and (on the inside wings) reliefs of the *Nativity*, the *Pentecost*, and the *Dormition of the Virgin*. On the painted exterior is a complicated presentation of the Marian cult with quotations and prophecies, including the *hortus conclusus* with a hunted unicorn seeking refuge with Mary, a *Visitation*, the *Infant Christ in the Temple* and the *Resurrection*. Of the Baroque fittings, the high altar with its monumental columns (c 1700) and vivid statuary of saints and angels is particularly fine, as is the charmingly intimate detail of the **Annakapelle**, showing St Anne teaching the Virgin Mary to read.

Landskron

The motorway runs north, then north-west from Maria Gail to pass the spectacular ruined castle of Landskron, built on a commanding spur (676m) of the hills to the east of Villach. The same Khevenhüller family who had possession of Hochosterwitz (see p 336) acquired this castle in 1542 and the Carinthian governor, Christoph Khevenhüller, invested vast sums in the extension of the ancient building; like his relation, Georg, he made the place a refuge for Lutherans in the 16C, indeed, he went further and set up a printer's that produced 16,000 Protestant Bibles. However, the Khevenhüllers paid a high price for adhering to their faith when the castle was confiscated in 1628 and given to the Catholic (and ultra-loyalist) Dietrichsteins. In the restaurant (from which there are magnificent views) Roman fragments and a rare Celtic portrait may be seen. The 'Crown of the Province' has acquired an almost mystical significance for Carinthia, and references to it recur in Austrian verse and prose, for example in the novels of Heimito von Doderer. A special attraction is the **eagle display** in summer (May, June, Sept at 11.00 and 15.00 daily; July, Aug, at 11.00, 15.00 and 18.00), when birds of prey are shown working the thermal currents of Landskron, with accompanying commentaries on their habits and habitat.

VILLACH

The unappealing city of Villach has become important as a transport hub and the tourist's springboard for Italy. There are three express train routes (to Salzburg, Lienz and Klagenfurt), plus direct connections to Venice, Ljubljana and Zagreb. Cross border *Autobahnen* pass close to the city. The local buses leave from the railway station.

To the south-west of the town is a spa that attracted the Romans to the area, which they called *Santicum*. By the 9C it had become *Pons Villah*, on account of its importance as a Drau crossing, and was given by Heinrich II to the diocese of Bamberg in 1007, the latter holding it until 1759, when the Habsburgs felt obliged to buy it. It suffered its full share of catastrophes, including wars, plagues, floods and fires, but with the extra refinement of earthquakes. The one it suffered on 25 January 1348 (simultaneous with a major landslip at Dobratsch in the Villacher Alpe to the south of the town) nearly destroyed it altogether; there was another earthquake in 1690 and the town was also dangerously close to the great Friulian earthquake of 1976. Villach experienced an economic and cultural boom in the 15C and 16C, when it was the centre of an artistic workshop whose masters painted major works all over Carinthia. In the 16C it was also home (1502–34) to the apothecary Wilhelm von Hohenheim, father of Paracelsus (see p 313), who himself spent much time in the city. Between 1809 and 1813 Villach belonged to the short-lived Kingdom of Illyria set up by Napoleon. More recently, it suffered from heavy bombing in World War II because of its strategic railway junction and rolling stock repair sheds.

The focus of the town is the vast, spacious square running from the parish church down to the main bridge over the Drau, from which narrow streets lead, often with overarching beams between the houses on either side. There are some attractive façades of Renaissance, Baroque and 19C houses: the 16C Paracelsushof at no. 18 is one example, with reliefs on a wall of the courtyard showing Paracelsus and his father.

The **parish church of St James**, with its formerly free-standing, and nearly 100m tall campanile, has a 14C choir and a 15C nave, the neo-Gothic connection between campanile and church having been made only in the 19C. Rebuilding of an earlier church began after the devastating earthquake and fire of 1348, while the complex star and net vaulting was probably added after a major fire in 1524. The Baroque and Rococo high altar (1784) is strikingly baldachined and frames a late Gothic *Crucifixion* of 1502. The much restored fresco of *St Christopher* in the choir is from the 15C as is also the relief on the adjacent arch of the *Three Kings*.

The highly unusual **pulpit** (1555, Georg von Kynsberg) dates to the time of the Protestant possession of the church (1526–94) and was made in celebration of the Peace of Augsburg, the compromise between Ferdinand I and the Electors of Germany stipulating that subjects should adopt the religion of their lords (*cuius regio, eius religio*). From the breast of the carved figure of Jesse lying on the ground a tree rises with half-figures of the descendants of King David (the son of Jesse) appearing on the branches. The reliefs on the pulpit's panels show symbolic instances of the life and death of Christ. The numerous **tombs** in the church are of high quality, by masters such as Heinrich von Valkenauer (the tomb of Balthasar von Weißpriach, 1484, on the southern side), Anton Colin (on the south wall, the tomb of Georg Khevenhüller, 1587) and Ulrich Vogelsang (another monument to the Khevenhüller family dating to 1580). The tower can be climbed (generally open Mon–Sat 10.00–16.00, longer in summer) and affords a superb view over the city.

The **Pilgrimage Church of the Holy Cross** (Hans Ederer, 1738) in Perau on the right bank of the Drau has an elegant concave façade between two pilastered towers and a complex ground plan in which internal cupolas blend into the form of a cross. The frescoes (1960) in the vault are by Franz Fröhlich and harmonise well with the Baroque interior, while in the Chapel of the Cross to the north (1771) are further Rococo frescoes of the foundation legend of the church and scenes from the life of Mary.

The **Villach City Museum** (Widmanngasse 38, open May–Oct, Mon–Sat 10.00–16.30) documents the history, art and culture of Villach and environs. It includes stone monuments and archaeological finds from prehistoric, Roman and medieval Villach, objects relating to crafts and trades and a picture collection including a number of works by local masters painted in the period of the medieval painter workshops.

In the **Schillerpark** is a huge **relief** (1889) of Carinthia (182sq m, scale 1:10,000; open May–Oct, Mon–Sat 10.00–16.30). It is worth making the excursion to **Warmbad Villach**, 4km to the south, to see the remains of a Roman road with deep grooves in it caused by the wheels of carts carrying the locally produced iron.

Around Villach: to the south-west

Road 83 leads south-west of Villach to Arnoldstein with its bizarre **Schrotturm** (1843), an industrial monument that was once used for casting lead balls, and on to **Thörl-Maglern** close to the Italian border, whose mostly 15C and 16C **church of St Andrew** is well worth visiting for the remarkable late Gothic frescoes on the north wall of the choir, the east side of the triumphal arch and the vaulting. The attribution of these to the greatest Carinthian medieval master, **Thomas of Villach**, was made by Professor Walter Frodl and since then other works by the same artist have come to light. The greatest protagonist of the Gothic soft style of his age, Thomas was active in the second half of the 15C and lauded by contemporaries such as Paolo Santino, an official of the Aquileian bishopric, as a 'second Apelles'.

The frescoes on the north wall show, with astonishing realism and pathos-filled empathy, the journey of Christ through this vale of tears to his destiny on the cross, then the miracle of the Resurrection and the Pentecost. The central and dominating representation of the 'living cross' is a powerful symbolic depiction (probably worked out for the painter by Abbot Christoph Manfordin of neighbouring Arnoldstein) that illuminates the spiritual meaning of the

Crucifixion: namely the triumph over death, the conquest of hell and the supplanting of Judaism ('*Synagogue*') by the Christian church ('*Ecclesia*'). These antitheses are brilliantly worked out in the images of the Christ frescoes, as also in the figure of the **Mother of God** to the left, who plucks golden apples from the Tree of Life and transforms them into the Host, which she passes to the Christian masses through the mediation of the Pope; and to the right, the contrasting figure of *Eve*, whose plucked fruit is transformed only into skulls. Adjacent, to the east, is the **Eucharist** and its foreshadowing in the Old Testament; in the centre is the '*Ährenchristus*', Our Lord's wounds highlighted by vine leaves and ears of corn (*Ähren)* that symbolise the wine and the bread of the Eucharist. On the east wall of the triumphal arch is the **Last Judgement**. In the vaulting the Fathers of the Church are represented with corresponding symbols of the Evangelists and of the elements (thus *Air* is for Sts Augustine and John, *Fire* for Sts Gregory and Mark, *Earth* for Sts Jerome and Matthew, *Water* for Sts Ambrosius and Luke). In the fields of the vaulting in the nave are sparse later frescoes (1510–20) showing various saints, and over the triumphal arch is a remarkable carved **Rosary** from the 17C showing the *Madonna and Child* at the centre with a sunburst in the background and seven ecstatic angels.

West of Arnoldstein: along the Gail Valley

Road 111 leads west from Arnoldstein and follows the valley of the River Gail. At **Feistritz an der Gail** is the fortified **St Martin's Church** with an impressive west tower and 15C frescoes by Friedrich von Villach, but in poor condition. At the town of **Nötsch** just beyond it is a museum devoted to the **Nötscher Kreis** (in Haus Wiegele, open March–Oct, Thur–Sun 14.00–18.00 or by appointment, ☎ 04256 3664). The four artists of this circle (Sebastian Isepp, Anton Kolig, Franz Wiegele and Anton Mahringer) were subject to the various influences of the age (notably Symbolism, Expressionism and Neue Sachlichkeit), but remained rooted in their Carinthian milieu—the chief factor that unites their work. Mahringer and Kolig worked together on the project for the Klagenfurt Landhaus in 1929 (see p 331).

From Nötsch a minor road leads north and curves back east to Villach, passing through **Bad Bleiberg**, where the old lead and zinc mines have been turned into a multi-media 'experience', which is aimed principally at children, including adult ones (**Terra Mystica**: open Palm-Sunday–June 10.00–15.00, July–mid-Sept 09.30–16.00, 16 Sept–Oct 10.00–15.00). **St Stefan an der Gail**, a few kilometres further west on road 111, has a parish church with late Gothic frescoes in the choir (half-figures of apostles and saints) and an archaic (Celtic?) stone head incorporated into its west wall. On the main altar is a vivid late Gothic relief of the *Stoning of St Stephen*, and above it the *Martyrdom of St Lawrence*.

At **Hermagor**, further west, the late Gothic church (1485) is dedicated to the early Christian martyrs St Hermagor and St Fortunatus and has a *Madonna and Child* in the south chapel dating to 1510. At the foot of the supporting wall of the church is a monument recalling the Austrian liberation from the Napoleonic occupation in 1813.

From Hermagor road 87 leads north-west to the **Weißensee** and on to the junction with road 100 at Greifenburg (see below). Just south of Hermagor

St Michael's Church at **Egg** preserves two fine stained-glass windows (1490) in the burial chapel of Gandolf von Khuenberg and his wife Dorothea. Continuing on road 111, however, you reach shortly **Kirchbach**, where the cemetery of **St Martin's Church** has a remarkable Gothic entrance to the south, with frescoes by a master from the Pustertal. They show St Martin on his white horse cutting his cloak for the beggar; above the scene hover a host of angels, holding the future bishop's mitre. The flanking figures are Sts Achatius, Ursula, John the Baptist and Rochus. The theme of the vivid Baroque interior of the church is also the life of St Martin. At **Dellach**, further west, the **Church of St Daniel** has a Baroque high altar showing *Daniel in the Lions' Den*, a favourite motif of the Roman catacombs, but rare thereafter (it is a modern work, despite its Baroque mood, dating to 1902).

The church at **Kötschach**, some kilometres further west, has perhaps the loveliest vaulting (1527) of Carinthia, a unique design of delicate swirling tendrils that recalls a wild vine and which was made by Bartlmä Firtaler from Innichen. Firtaler's plant decoration suggests abstract symbols of Christ, vines of course, but also lilies and forget-me-nots. Rococo decoration and frescoes (1750) of the life of Mary have replaced Firtaler's vaulting in the choir, an incredible piece of vandalism by the local ecclesiastical authorities in the 18C, but sadly not uncommon. However, the frescoes (1499) by Nikolaus Kentner on the north wall showing the *Dormition, Assumption and Coronation of Mary* have survived. Similar themes are treated in the **parish church of St Mark** at **Mauthen**, just to the south, in the frescoes of the south wall by two unknown masters and dating to 1514.

To the north (on road 110 leading up to **Oberdrauburg**) another example of Firtaler's marvellous vaulting may be seen in the church at **Laas**, the only one of his three masterpieces that has been preserved in its entirety. The nave vaulting, as at Kötschach, is a swirling mass of abstract vegetation whose delicate stems end in flowers or acorns. On the keystones of the ribs are coats of arms of Austrian noble families, while in the fields between them are delicately painted buds and blooms. These appear also in the fields of the equally graceful but more formally geometrical star vaulting (1516) of the choir. The creator of this unique masterpiece is portrayed near to the sacristy door with the inscription '*Maister partholome firtaler hat gemacht die Kirchen 1535*'.

St Lorenzen im Lesachtal, further west on road 111, has Gothic frescoes in the parish church, including on the north wall a *Last Judgement* similar to that at the monastery in Millstatt (see p 353). Passing through **Maria Luggau**, where Firtaler's work in the **pilgrimage church of Our Lady of the Snow** has been mostly obliterated (except in the tower vault) by the Servites in 1736, you soon reach the border with East Tyrol, joining eventually road 100 for Lienz. Perhaps it is unjust to hurry by Maria Luggau without seeing the ornate Baroque interior of the church with its delicate tracery of stucco and Johann Georg Grasmair's *The Sorrows of Mary* (1728, left-hand side-altar), together with Cosroe Dusi's *St Luke* (1833, right-hand side-altar, a good copy of an earlier Baroque picture). The name *Luggau* is possibly derived from '*Lukas Au*' (St Luke's meadow) and St Luke is revered here as the local protecting saint.

North-east of Villach: Ossiacher See, Nockgebiet

Stift Ossiach

North-east of Villach is the caterpillar-shaped **Ossiacher See**, along the northern bank of which runs road 94, while a winding minor road follows the southern shore to charming **Ossiach** (from Slavic '*osoje*' , i.e. 'living in shade'), which faces the 1909m high Gerlitzen mountain across the lake. The fortified Benedictine abbey here was the order's oldest in Carinthia (founded 1028) until its dissolution in 1783.

The former **monastery church** delights with its pastel-shaded stucco by masters of the Wessobrunn school and especially the exhilarating frescoes of Josef Ferdinand Fromiller: in the main nave, the *Assumption* and the *Empty Tomb* with the *Apostles*, to the west *St Margaret* and to the east *St Catherine*. Above the crossing *God the Father* in a *trompe l'oeil* cupola, above the altar the *Eye of God with Angels*. On the side-walls are Benedictine saints enraptured by a *Vision of the Madonna*; in the choir and the crossing the *Life of Mary* and the *Childhood of Jesus* are depicted. The *St Sebastian* in the north aisle has a visage represented on his sleeve, supposedly the artist's self-portrait. Over the windows is depicted the *Legend of Boleslaus*, a Polish king who murdered the Archbishop of Cracow in 1079 on the altar of the latter's cathedral. He repented of the deed (according to the story) and made a pilgrimage to Rome for absolution, remaining in Ossiach on the return journey and performing the most menial tasks for the monastery until his death in c 1082. Over the organ loft is another curiosity, namely the depiction of Abbot Werner (1307–14) receiving three crystal balls from an angel prompted by Our Lady. With these crystal '*Kugeln*' he 'cured' patients by 'burning' them, using the crystal glass as a reflector, on the application of which they are said to have fallen into a healing sleep. Unlikely as it may seem, this treatment apparently attracted many patients to Ossiach.

In the north chapel is a late Gothic winged altar (c 1505) showing the *Madonna and Child between Sts Catherine and Margaret*, with the *Twelve Apostles* on the inner wings; on the external ones, paintings of the *Annunciation*, *Nativity*, *Mary's Return Home*, and the *Resurrection*. A plaque in the church recalls the concert pianist Wilhelm Backhaus, to whom the organ is dedicated (he gave one of his final performances here on 26 June 1969 and died a few days later). In the sacristy are two glass paintings donated (1905) by the German writer of Westerns, Karl May, whose works were immensely popular in the German-speaking world. The donation was in gratitude for a pleasant stay in Ossiach, where he wrote one of his tales.

The former monastery is now a hotel and has frescoes by Fromiller in the **Benedictussaal** (illusionistic architecture and the *Apotheosis of St Benedict*) and in the **Fürstensaal** (Habsburg benefactors, the *Inauguration of the Carinthian Dukes on the Zollfeld*, the *Transfer of Klagenfurt to the Diet by Maximilian in 1518*, together with historically interesting depictions of the Ossiach Monastery and the Klagenfurt fortress). The ceiling fresco shows the last occasion that the Carinthians paid ceremonial homage to their Duke, in this case the Habsburg Emperor Karl VI, which took place in Klagenfurt in 1728, thus breaking with the Zollfeld tradition. A curiosity is the sundial on the exterior north wing—it counts the time both in the 'Greek' ('*Kriechisch*') and 'Italian' ('*Welsch*') hours, underlining the difference between the Eastern Orthodoxy and the Western Church.

The **Carinthian Summer Festival** takes place in Ossiach from the end of

June to the end of August each year and features drama, concerts, lectures and exhibitions in the ceremonial rooms of the monastery and in the church (also at Villach venues).

The roads flanking the Ossiacher See lead either to Feldkirchen, the treasures of whose church have unfortunately been stolen, and St Veit an der Glan (see p 337), or north to the Styrian border (road 95) via Himmelberg (passing the Renaissance Schloss Piberstein) and the town of **Ebene Reichenau**. Here, there is a fossil museum '**Zirbenhof**' (open May–Oct, Mon–Sat, 09.00–17.00, mid-Dec–Easter, Mon–Sat, 09.30–12.30 and 14.00–17.30). The town makes a good base for excursions into the **Nationalpark Nockberge**. From the north-west end of the lake, road 98 leads northwards to **Treffen**, where the parish church is dedicated to the local St Maximilian, a 3C itinerant preacher who was a native of *Noricum*. Its exterior has (partly ruined) frescoes of *St Christopher* and *Christ on the Mount of Olives* from the workshop of Thomas of Villach. The frescoes of the interior (the *Assumption and Coronation of the Virgin*, and the *Four Evangelists* in the nave) were uncovered in 1965 and date to 1700.

At Radenthein turn east for **Bad Kleinkirchheim** nestling in the **Nockgebiet** mountains, one of the oldest spas in Austria and popular for its unique combination of ski runs and warm waters. The parish church has a monumental modern painting (1928) by Jonas Ranter of the *Victory of Otto the Great over the Hungarians on the Lechfeld in 955*. The **Pilgrimage Church of St Catherine in the Spa** was built over a healing spring in the 15C, the water originally being collected in the undercroft area.

North-west of Villach

Millstatt

A turn to the west at Radenthein brings you past Döbriach at the north-east shore of the atmospheric, if sometimes gloomy, **Millstätter See** and after 8km you reach the town of **Millstatt** itself, its centre located on the shore, above which is an upper town with many attractive villas. Millstatt makes a comfortable base for motorists from which to travel round the main sights of Carinthia and is well supplied with moderately priced hotels.

In the 11C the Benedictines founded a cloister at '*Milistat*' and began building their **church**, the place acquiring in the following 200 years a reputation as a centre of learning that produced several important manuscripts. In the 15C the Order of St George (founded in 1469 to combat the Turks) took over the monastery, but the buildings fell into decay after the order was dissolved in 1598. Subsequently, the monastery was given to the Jesuits but closed after their dissolution under Maria Theresia in 1773.

The **portal** is particularly fine, with a tympanum of *Christ Pantocrator*, serene and almighty amidst the sun, moon and stars, and depicted in the act of blessing the Abbot who founded the church. Unusually, the master mason has identified himself with an inscription (*Rudger me fecit*), this Rudger having left his mark elsewhere with a depiction (on the north tower) of a bird sheltering youths, a symbol of the protection of the church. On the east wall are frescoes of the *Passion* (1473) signed by Friedrich of Villach, and an earlier

Madonna and Child. The Jesuits incorporated some of the red marble tomb-stones of the members of the Order of St George into the side-walls, including that of the first Grand Master. On the south wall is the huge fresco of the *Last Judgement* (6 x 4m), an early Renaissance work by Urban Görtschacher, transferred here from the exterior west wall of the north tower. It shows *Christ Pantocrator with St Mary and St John* pleading the cause for humanity, adjacent the *Twelve Apostles* on a bank of cloud, appearing here as assessors at the Day of Judgement. Below is the *Awakening of the Dead on the Day of Judgement* and their division into the *Saved and the Damned*, the artist taking care to flatter contemporaries such as Pope Leo X and Emperor Maximilian by including their portraits among the Saved. The commissioner of the work (Augustus Reinwald of Gmünd), is featured together with his family.

The **cloister** shows other superb and justly celebrated examples of decorated Romanesque capitals, some of the columns also resting on sculptures of wild beasts. The **Monks' Portal** leading to the church is guarded by sculptures of *St Paul and St Michael killing the dragon*; on the bases of the door columns, two bearded men are shown being tormented by women (one of them is having his beard pulled), supposedly an emblem of the victory of Christianity over the heathen world, although males ignorant of this symbolism might be inclined to a different interpretation.

The former Grand Master's Lodge is now the charming *Hotel Lindenhof* ('Lime-Tree Court', the lime is very ancient) while the **Stiftsmuseum** has interesting documentation of the Benedictines, the Knights of St George and the Millstatt Jesuits, as well as the magnificent **Gonzaga Wedding Chest** (the counterpart is in Graz Cathedral, see p 210). The museum incorporates the 16C dungeon and is open June–Sept, daily 09.00–12.00 and 14.00–18.00, April, May, Oct by appointment ☎ 04766 3039.

A further attraction of Millstatt are the many 19C and turn of the century villas in the Upper Town, where well-to-do Austrians from the military, intellectual, commercial and artistic milieux of the monarchy spent their summer holidays as, for example, did the Nobel Prizewinning physicist, Erwin Schrödinger at Villa Waldheim-Mansbart. Anyone deciding to make Millstatt their base could do worse than stay at the very moderate *Villa Waldheim* in the Upper Town with spacious rooms recalling a more leisured age, it even has a Bösendorfer for spontaneous *Hausmusik* (Villa Waldheim: A-9872 Millstatt am See, Mirnockstrasse 110. ☎ 04766 2061. More expensive is the excellent *Familienhotel Post* where the cooking is unrivalled and the menu includes fresh fish from the lake (Mirnockstrasse 38. ☎ 04766 21 08). Road 98 runs from Millstatt north-west along the shore of the lake to Spittal an der Drau (see below).

Unteres Drautal: from Villach to Spittal an der Drau

The south-western Unteres Drautal shore of the Millstätter See may be approached direct from Villach on road 100 or *Autobahn* A10 (E14), which runs north to Spittal along the Drau Valley. A few kilometres north of Villach you pass **Feistritz an der Drau**, on the western periphery of which is a **chapel** (*Unsere Liebe Frau am Bichl*). The frescoes (1440) of the interior are by the workshop of

Friedrich of Villach, and show scenes from the *Life of Christ*, including a touchingly realistic circumcision.

To the east of the road and a little further north is **Fresach**, where there is a Lutheran Museum (**Evangelisches Diözesanmuseum**: open Thur 09.00–12.00 and 14.00–18.00, Sun 10.00–12.00) in the former Lutheran chapel. It documents Protestantism in the so-called *Toleranzgemeinden* of Upper Carinthia, founded after Joseph II issued his Edict of Tolerance on 13 October 1781. The lifting of restrictions on the free exercise of religion revealed that there were still 14,000 Protestants in Carinthia, despite the efforts of the Counter-Reformatory Emperors to enforce conformity or expulsion. The majority of these hitherto closet Protestants were to be found in the Gegendtal, the central Drautal, in the Liesertal and around the Weißensee.

Spittal an der Drau (the name is derived from a 12C hospice/hospital) is most notable for the handsome Renaissance **Schloss Porcia**, begun by the Spanish treasurer of the Archduke Ferdinand I, Gabriel of Salamanca, in 1533, although he did not live to see its completion in 1597. His coat of arms with Baroque ornamentation (1703) may be seen above the main entrance, flanked by those of his two wives. The name Porcia comes from a later owner, Hannibal Alfons Porcia (1698–1738). The Schloss has a courtyard (modelled on the early Renaissance *palazzi* of Florence) with arcades running along three storeys and a graceful open stairway to the first floor, where it is closed by an ornate Renaissance grille. The upper floors house a **regional museum** (open mid-May–Oct, daily, 09.00–18.00, Nov–May, Mon–Thur, 13.00–18.00) and there are drama performances in the courtyard in summer. At nearby **Seeboden** is the intriguing **Kärntner Fischereimuseum** (open June–Sept, daily, 10.30–18.00) in a vernacular building with various artefacts relating to fishing.

North-east of Spittal

Road 99 and the *Autobahn* A10 continue north-east of Spittal towards **Gmünd**, overlooked by its castle ruins. In the parish church with its fine net vaulting the brother of Salzburg's most famous Prince-Bishop, Wolf-Dietrich von Raitenau, is laid to rest in the circular burial chapel (1642) attached to the choir. The adjacent charnel house of St Michael has frescoes of 1370 showing North Italian influence. In Gmünd the first Porsche motor car was built by the legendary Ferdinand Porsche and enthusiasts will warm to the **Porsche Museum** at Riesertratte 4, where examples of most of the Porsche models are on display (open daily, mid-May to mid-Oct, 09.00–18.00, Oct–May, 10.00–16.00).

Just beyond Gmünd the road forks left at the Maltatal (poetically described by a 15C Swiss traveller as 'the valley of the tumbling waters'—an allusion to its 30 waterfalls), where the **church of St Leonard and St Catherine** at **Dornbach** has frescoes (1461) in the vaulting of the choir of the saint serenaded by angels, on the north wall the *Burial of St Catherine*, on the east wall, the *Annunciation*, on the south wall, *St Catherine before Emperor Maximinus*. By the hand of the same Salzburg master is the remnant of a winged altar (1463) showing the *Betrothal of St Catherine*.

The church at **Malta** itself has 14C frescoes, an iconographical rarity on the south wall of the choir being *St Mary in Labour*, to which many pregnant women go on a pilgrimage (Carinthia has one of the highest rates of extra-marital pregnancy in Austria, a tradition that has happily co-existed with peasant piety).

Beyond the village a picturesque road (toll) leads 15km up to the **Kölnbreinspeicher**, the highest reservoir in Carinthia. The A10 continues north-east to **Eisentratten**, where iron ore was mined, also gold, lead and arsenic. The Türk-Haus (1592) in the village, with a sun-dial on its wall, was named after a local mine-owner, Jakob Türgg. The Historicist sculptor Hans Gasser (1817–68) was born in Eisentratten and was responsible for some of the statuary for the Vienna Burgtheater and for the Fountain of the Danube Nymphs in the Vienna Stadtpark.

The road continues up the **Liesertal** to Krems, where a scenic hairpin road (*Nockalmstrasse*, toll) heads for Ebene Reichenau, passing through the health spa of **Karlbad** (1650m), whose waters are said to be effective against gout. A10/road 99, however, continues past **Kremsbrücke**, one of 13 bridges on this stretch of road and at 2.6km the longest. The **parish church of Maria Trost** was refounded (1640) on the site of an earlier church, by Emperor Ferdinand III, to combat Protestantism in the area, which had evidently survived *sub rosa* despite the Edict of the Emperor's father (Ferdinand II) in 1628 expelling Lutherans. The imperial eagle may be seen over the pulpit, emblematic of imperial protection for the true faith and a not very subtle reminder to the preacher, should he be tempted to stray from the orthodox line. At **Rennweg** there is a former arsenic mine with an accompanying exhibition which can be visited on application to *Gasthof Schoberblick* (☎ 04734 8380). The road continues north through the Katschbergtunnel (toll) into Land Salzburg.

From Spittal along the Mölltal to Heiligenblut

Four kilometres beyond Spittal a turning left from road 100 leads to **St Peter im Holz** on the historic Lurnfeld, partly occupying the site of Roman *Teurnia*, which in turn absorbed an earlier Celtic settlement on the Holzerberg plateau. Teurnia became the capital of *Inner Noricum* towards the end of the Roman hegemony, inheriting the role from *Virunum* (see p 326) which was less secure. On the site of an 8C bishop's church, founded during the reconversion of the Karantanians from the paganism into which they had lapsed following the Roman withdrawal, the parish church was built in the 14C. It has late 14C and early 15C frescoes (including two of *St Christopher*, one brought inside from the external wall, and scenes from the *Life of Mary*, the *Passion* and the *Legend of St Dorothy*). The **Teurnia Museum** (partly excavations, and open May–mid-Oct, Tues, Sun, 09.00–12.00 and 13.00–17.00) is of interest, particularly the early Christian relics and a remarkable **mosaic** with Christian symbols and images, an early example of a *biblia pauperum*. It bears the inscription of a certain (Bishop? or Governor?) Ursus and his wife, Ursina, who evidently commissioned the work.

At **Möllbrücke** is a fortified Gothic church (1473) with a superb late Gothic winged altar (1510) showing the patron of the church, *St Leonard*, in the shrine holding his bishop's staff and his emblem of a chain (as patron of prisoners), flanked by *St Rochus* and *St Sebastian*. The wing reliefs show two bishops, one of them *St Rupert*, the other *St Erasmus*. The closed wings of the altar show *Emperor Heinrich II and his wife Kunigunde* between *St Wolfgang* and *St Martin*. On the predella wings, *St Helena* and *St Elisabeth* (of Hungary) representing the piety of rulers, and *St Mary Magdalene* and *St Afra* representing the repentance of sins. The road (106) follows the Mölltal to the north-west, reaching shortly

Kolbnitz, above which, on the **Danielsberg**, an originally Romanesque church (rebuilt 1516 and re-dedicated to St George) stands on the site of a Roman temple of Hercules. Further on you pass (to the right) the impressive **Schloss Oberfalkenstein** (12C–15C) perched on a southern spur of the Pfaffenberg, with its huge keep surmounted by a wooden superstructure. In **Stallhofen** the late Gothic **pilgrimage church of Maria Tax** has an elegant stone organ loft, star vaulting and extensive frescoes by Josef Ferdinand Fromiller.

At **Obervellach**, another former mining community, the fortified parish church contains, in the north chapel, a **triptych** (1520, the present combination and setting of the panels, however, dating to 1692) by **Jan van Scorel**, painted by the master when he stopped here on the way to Italy. The middle panel shows the *Holy Family*, to the left is *St Christopher*, to the right *St Apollonia*, who were the patron saints of the commissioners, Count Christoph Frangipani and his wife, Apollonia. The doors of the church retain their original furniture, including a decorative door-knocker on the southern one.

From Obervellach road 105 heads north to the Tauerntunnel (8.5km), which gives access to Land Salzburg and Badgastein (see p 317): cars are put on the train just beyond the ski resort of Mallnitz and unload at Böckstein on the far side.

Forking left onto road 106 at Obervellach, you continue up the Möll Valley, passing through Flattach, to the south of which is a natural wonder, the 800m long **Raggaschlucht** (gorge), carved out of the mountainside over the centuries by the Raggabach stream. Further along the road is the oldest settlement in Mölltal (documented since 977), the village of **Stall**, whose church has early frescoes. **Rangersdorf** is reached shortly, with its late Gothic parish church containing a winged altar of 1425, the latter showing the *Freeing of Peter from Prison* and the *Departure of the Apostles on their Missions* and their subsequent *Martyrdoms*.

At **Winklern**, where there was a customs post in the Middle Ages, the road forks, road 107A heading north to Döllach im Mölltal (the parish having now reverted to its ancient name of **Großkirchheim**), once the seat of the local mines inspector, whose house may be seen at no. 47 in the high street. The **Schloss Großkirchheim** houses a museum documenting the gold mines of the Hohen Tauern region (☎ 04825 226 or 429). Shortly beyond is the village of **Heiligenblut** at the foot of the Großglockner, with its graceful Gothic pilgrimage church of St Vincent (see p 318). Leaving the Franz Josephs-Höhe to the west, you begin the climb from here over the Großglockner Hochalpenstraße, perhaps the most scenic drive in all Austria.

ALONG THE OBERDRAUTAL

From Spittal (see p 355) you head north-west, bearing west on to road 100 at the Lurnfeld confluence of the Möll and the Drau and passing **Sachsenburg**, with remains of ancient town walls on its north and west side, together with late Gothic houses on the **Marktplatz**.

At 15km from Sachsenburg is the village of **Gerlamoos** nestling in the hillside on the edge of pinewoods (it is just to the north of the main road before Steinfeld). The **church of St George** above the village is a little gem of preserved Romanesque architecture (with alterations in the 16C and 17C). The key for it must be obtained from no. 13 in the main street, opposite the well, and the church itself is 5 minutes' walk above the highest street of the village.

The Gothic **cycle of frescoes** (1470–80) by Thomas of Villach is the exceptional feature of the church, still magnificent despite retouching in the 19C. It shows the *Life of St George*, the *Virgin sheltering Supplicants with her Cloak*, and the *Life of Christ* (30 scenes from the *Annunciation* to the *Resurrection*). On the external eastern wall are late 14C frescoes, including *St Christopher* and *St George fighting the Dragon*, together with a *Crucifixion*.

A Baroque sculptural group (early 1700s) in the interior also repays study: it shows St Wilgefortis (*Kümmernis*, in England called '*Uncumber*'), a Princess of Portugal whose vow of virginity obliged her to reject the suit of the King of Sicily; God caused a beard to grow on her face, whereat the Sicilian king lost interest and her enraged father had her crucified.

Further along the Drautal, the late Romanesque **parish church of Maria Geburt** at **Berg** is of interest, with lovely Gothic vaulting, of which the fields between the ribs are painted with flower motifs. Romanesque also are the frescoes on the tympanum of the west portal (the *Crucifixion* with the figures of the *Virgin Mary and St John*), and in the choir (the *Lamb of God* with symbols of the *Evangelists* and the *Life of Christ*). The nave has late Gothic frescoes of apostles, coats of arms, etc. On the otherwise Baroque high altar is a stone *Madonna* from the early 15C, an example of the Gothic soft style. Especially delightful is the wooden Baroque chandelier, in which figures of the *Twelve Apostles* and *Christ* serve to hold the candles (now electrified), a visual metaphor for the Light of the World as embodied in the life and teaching of Our Saviour and his Disciples. The centre of the chandelier's superstructure is rounded off with an *Annunciation*. The charnel house beside the church also has frescoes (1428) of a *Last Judgement* and *Apostles*, but the restoration seems unrefined.

Further west at **Stein im Drautal** a castle belonging to the Counts of Rosenberg overlooks the valley. The 12C keep lours above the cliff-face. In the castle to the rear is a remarkable Romanesque **double-level chapel**, the upper chapel containing frescoes by Simon von Taisten of the *Church Fathers*, and the *Evangelists*, further the coats of arms of Carinthia, of the *Counts of Görz-Tirol* and of the *Gonzagas*. The last-named coat of arms is a reminder that the castle once belonged to Leonhard of Görz-Tirol who married Paola Gonzaga (see pp 210 and 354).

Opposite Stein, north of the Drau, on a minor road is **Irschen**, the name supposedly a corruption of the Latin for bear (*ursus*), and being associated not with wild animals in the area, but rather with a Patriarch of Aquileia named Ursus, the founder of its 12C church of St Dennis. The latter has a pleasant situation overlooking the valley; in the interior are frescoes (c 1330) on the north wall of the choir (the *Coronation of the Virgin, with saints and the Evangelists*). The *Last Judgement* in the apse is a work from the 16C. The Gothic winged altar, perhaps by a Tyrolean master from the Pustertal, shows *St Dennis* in the shrine with *St John the Evangelist* and *St Leonard*. The reliefs of the inside wings show *St Andrew* and *St Oswald* (the latter being the patron of brides, hence the raven on a globe with a ring in its beak).

The road continues to **Oberdrauburg**, a favoured base for hiking excursions in the Gailtaler Alpen, the Lienzer Dolomiten and the Kreuzeckgruppe. A minor road leads north of Oberdrauburg to **Zwickenberg**, where the parish church has frescoes from the 15C. They include two vivid representations of St Christopher on the external south wall painted at different times (13C and 16C), the later one full of vivid details such as the pagan spirits in the water seeking to make the giant lose his footing, the hermit who lights the way of the saint with his lamp, etc. There is also an early 15C cycle of frescoes showing the *Life of St Leonard*. In the interior the *Four Evangelists* (1438) may be seen in the vault of the choir, shown hard at work writing the gospels. The early 16C winged altar focuses again on *St Leonard*; on the interior wings are reliefs of the '*Four Saintly Maidens*', on the exterior *St Sebastian* and *St Christopher*, painted perhaps by Simon von Taisten. Road 100 continues north-west to Lienz in East Tyrol.

Tirol (North Tyrol & East Tyrol)

Area: 12,648sq km. Population: 632,000

Topography, climate and environment

Seven-eighths of Tirol (*Tyrol*) is mountainous, making it only the fifth largest *Bundesland* in terms of population, although the third largest in terms of territory. The two most easily negotiable Alpine passes linking Central Europe with the Mediterranean, the

Brenner (1370m) and the **Reschen** (1504m), are situated in the province (popularly known as 'the Land in the Mountains'), and have endowed Tyrol with great strategic significance. Since the Treaty of St-Germain-en-Laye (1919), the **Austrian province of Tyrol** has consisted of *Nordtirol* (North Tyrol) and *Osttirol* (East Tyrol). The land lying in between them and to the south (*Südtirol*, Italian *Trentino-Alto Adige*) has a German-speaking majority overall in *Provinz Bozen* i.e. *Alto Adige* (68 per cent in 1991, Italian 27.6 per cent, Ladin 4.4 per cent) and Italian speaking majorities in the urban areas. The region was ceded to Italy as a result of a secret agreement (Treaty of London, 3 May 1915) between the Entente and Italy designed to bring the latter into World War I on the side of the Allies.

North Tyrol is watered by the beautiful **River Inn** (so-named from the Celtic word '*Ine*' meaning 'that which flows'). It rises near the Malojapass of the Swiss Engadine south of St Moritz and flows into Tyrol via the Finstermünzpaß, finally entering the Danube at Passau and increasing the waters of its sister river by 50 per cent at this point. The Inn Valley is divided into the **Oberinntal** (Upper Inn Valley, as far as Innsbruck) and the **Unterinntal** (Lower Inn Valley), stretching almost to Kufstein on the Bavarian border. For **Osttirol** (East Tyrol) see p 399.

From **Innsbruck** westwards the climate is surprisingly mild, being influenced by the warm south wind *(Föhn)* blowing off the Alps, which, however, causes migraines, lassitude and circulation problems in the susceptible. At **Zirl** it is even mild enough for wine production. **Lienz**, the principal town of East Tyrol, claims the highest average yearly hours of sunshine in Austria. In general, the summers are short and the winters long, so the area is a paradise for winter sports (although recent warming has resulted in the steady melting of glaciers and less reliable snowfall). Nature lovers will encounter up to 100 species of flower, including the famous *Edelweiß* and delicately beautiful gentians. A third of the area is forested with the usual quick-growing varieties of tree (spruce, larch), while the hardy Swiss stone pine (which produced a rhapsodic outburst from Goethe when he first encountered it) may be found at surprisingly high altitudes. Marmot and ibex can sometimes be seen, also eagles soaring above the valleys. In the forests are chamois, red deer and martens, black game and capercaillie.

Economy

Tyrol was traditionally an area of smallholdings, but in the 20C light industry and tourism have become important. The pattern of agriculture and forestry is determined by local conditions, 35 per cent of the workable land is forestry and another

35 per cent pasturage. The most important industries are metalworking, machine production, glass and chemicals, while the formerly significant textiles and mining sectors are in decline. Tourism (especially summer tourism) has been hit in recent years by the increasing availability of cheap holidays abroad for Austrians and the relatively high prices that deter some potential non-Austrian visitors. On the other hand Tyrol offers exceptional all-year-round possibilities for leisure pursuits, including hiking in the East Tyrol sector of the **Hohe Tauern National Park**, the **Kaisergebirge** and the **Karwendel**, mountaineering and summer skiing on glaciers, as well as the ever-popular winter sports for which **Kitzbühel** is the most fashionable resort. An environmental problem is caused by the heavy volume of north-south transit traffic, alleviation of which involved tortuous negotiations when Austria applied to join the EU; the problem is intensified by the Swiss ban on lorries over 28 tons. Night-time bans on lorry traffic and transfer to the railway for part of the journey have proved to be only a partial solution; what is really needed is major infrastructural investment in rail transport from Southern Germany through to Italy.

History

Tyrol was inhabited even before the last Ice Age, but significant civilisation came with the Bronze Age Celts, who had flourishing settlements in the Inn Valley. The Romans (for 500 years from about 15 BC) pacified the wild Rhaetian tribes and secured the Alpine passes, in particular the Via Claudia Augusta (which includes the **Reschenpass**), a route that led north to *Augusta Vindelicorum* (Augsburg). Strabo describes in his *Geographia* how Augustus cleared the roads of robbers, but also stresses the physical dangers of journeys through territory subject to fearful natural disasters. After Roman withdrawal (476), the area was invaded by Langobards, Slavs and others during the great migrations (6C–9C AD), but Rhaetoroman/Ladino peoples preserved their culture in isolated valleys of the high Alps and Dolomites. Christianisation was undertaken both from the south and north (via Bavarian 6C invasions) with the first bishopric being founded as early as the 5C. In the 9C Tyrol came under the influence of Charlemagne and his successors, who in turn devolved it to the control of the Trento and Brixen bishops. Tyrol's aristocracy were appointed secular governors by the bishops, but gradually assumed total control of the area, which was consolidated into a single holding by Albrecht III in 1248 through marriage (his coat of arms became that of Tyrol). Later Tyrol was inherited by the Tirol-Görz line under Meinhard II, passing to the related Dukes of Carinthia in 1253. When this line expired with the widowed Margarete 'Maultasch', on her son's premature death (1363), the Habsburgs acquired it through the decisive and skilful negotiation of Rudolf IV.

Rudolf IV guaranteed the traditional freedoms of the fiercely independent Tyroleans, who profited further from the initially turbulent reign of Friedrich IV (1402–39), founder of the short-lived 'old Tyrolean line' of the Habsburgs. Friedrich's backing of the 'anti-Pope' John XXIII, deposed by the Council of Constance for his scandalous living, proved a disastrous miscalculation and for a while he was a fugitive stripped of his lands. (These had included the original Habsburg property in the Aargau which was lost at this time to the Swiss Confederation.) Friedrich, however, made an astonishing comeback with the help of the peasants and burghers, eventually compelling the allegiance of the dissident nobility. While this ensured greater power for those of non-noble

TIROL

FEDERAL REPUBLIC
OF GERMANY

Füssen
Tannheim
Reutte
Vilsalpsee
Bichlbach
Fernpaß
Ehrwald
Bschlabs
Hahntennjoch
Nassereith
Telfs
Bach
Lech
L E C H T A L
Imst
Inn
Stams
Lech
VORARLBERG
Zürs
Arlbergpaß
St. Anton
A. Arlberg
Arlbergtunnel
Landeck
Roppen
Oetz
Jerzens
Umhausen
Stuibenfälle
Ö T Z T A L
Fiß
Serfaus
Tösens
P I T Z T A L
Längenfeld
Mutterbergalm
S A M N A U N G R U P P E
Inn
Pfunds-Stuben
St. Leonhard
i. Pitztal
Mittelberg
Sölden
Zwieselstein
Finstermünzpaß
Stausee-
Gepatsch
K A U N E R T A L
HINTERER
BRUNNENKOGEL
Nauders
V E N T E R T A L
GURGLTAL
Vent
Obergurgl
SILVRETTAGRUPPE
SWITZERLAND

ZUGSPITZE
2962
Mittenwald
Seefeld
i. Tirol
SEEFELD
2074
REITHE
2374
INNSBR
A12 E60
171
Götzens
Axamer Lizum
Tel
Fulpm
STUBAITAL
Ne
i. St

origin than elsewhere, an upturn in trade and profits from the silver-mines also brought new prosperity; indeed, the apparently mocking nickname '*Friedl mit der leeren Tasche*' ('Freddy with the empty pocket', originally a contemptuous description of Friedrich coined by his enemies), became an affectionate indication of the Duke's popularity amongst the population at large.

Under Sigmund '*der Münzreiche*' ('the Rich', 1477–90) and Emperor Maximilian I (1490–1519), Tyrol grew prosperous from copper- and silver-mines, enjoying a cultural and economic boom. It was Maximilian who allowed the peasants to bear arms, on condition that they assumed responsibility for defending Tyrol— in this way the celebrated *Schützen* (marksmen militia) came into being in 1511. Maximilian also confirmed the importance of the Tyrolean inheritance by moving his residence to Innsbruck.

In 1525, a peasant uprising led by Michael Gaismair aimed to turn Tyrol into

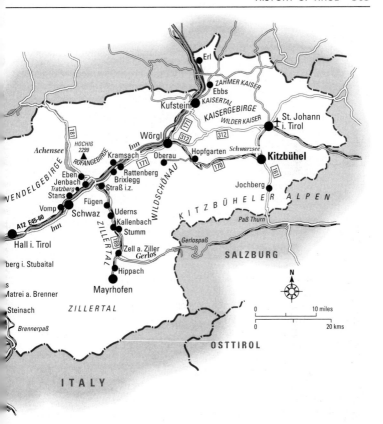

a radical democracy underpinned by Protestantism; but Gaismair was assassinated in 1532 before his plans could be realised. The Tyrol line of the Habsburgs became extinct in 1665 when Claudia Felicitas, daughter of the last Archduke (Ferdinand Karl), became the second wife of her second cousin, Emperor Leopold I, and the province thus fell under the direct control of Vienna. The heroic *Schützen* repelled Bavarian invaders (1703) in the **War of the Spanish Succession**, but could not resist Bavarian overlordship imposed by Napoleon a century later. However, in 1809 Andreas Hofer led his countrymen successfully against the occupiers, winning a famous victory at Bergisel (see p 378). Unfortunately Emperor Franz I, who had issued a proclamation in May promising that he would sign no peace treaty separating Tyrol from Austria, did just that in September by the **Treaty of Schönbrunn**. Only after the **Treaty of Paris** (1814), following the defeat of Napoleon, did the territory return to Habsburg rule.

Margarete Maultasch (1318–69)

Reliable information about the character of Margarete Maultasch, the unfortunate inheritor of Tyrol (daughter of Duke Heinrich of Carinthia and Tyrol) is hard to come by, since opposed and biased contemporaries endowed her with a range of irreconcilable qualities from chastity to promiscuity, ugliness to beauty, and always with equal vehemence and in equal measure. Even the origin of her nickname is unclear: it has been suggested it could be a reference to one of her estates (Schloß Maultasch at Terlan) or a slighting allusion to her (reportedly) disfigured mouth. In Südtirol a '*Maultasch*' is a person who can never stick to the point and thus brings about a general confusion, the expression conceivably having its origin in Margarete's erratic behaviour after her 19-year-old son, Meinhard III, died of pneumonia in 1363.

Margarete's first marriage to Johann Heinrich of the Luxembourg dynasty was so unhappy that she eventually refused her husband entry to the Tyrol residence, causing him to retire aggrieved to Bohemia. Without divorcing, she then married (1342) the son of Ludwig of Bavaria, also called Ludwig. For this irregularity, she was excommunicated by Pope Clement IV, who was a supporter of the Luxembourgs. Margarete soon discovered that the Wittelsbachs were an even worse fate for her and her people than the Luxembourgs, and this despite the fact that '*Der große Freiheitsbrief*' (Great Letter of Freedom, 1342) had confirmed all Tyrol's noble and burgher privileges as a condition of the Wittelsbach marriage. Before his death in 1361, Ludwig had dispossessed many nobles and instituted the first Jewish pogrom in Tyrol's history.

As soon as Rudolf IV heard that Margarete's son and heir was dying, he rushed to Tyrol, and confronted the bereaved and desperate mother, who was recklessly dispensing her heritage to all and sundry. By adroit and firm diplomacy, Rudolf managed to secure the region for himself and his two younger brothers (Albrecht III and Leopold III), thus preventing its further slide into chaos. As was his wont, Rudolf could not resist forging a document to reinforce his claim, but in any case Margarete seems to have welcomed him with open arms. On the 2 September 1363 she resigned all claims to Tyrol and followed Rudolf to Vienna. Here she lived unhappily in the quarter of the city subsequently named after her (*Margareten*, 4th District), becoming increasingly homesick for her beloved homeland, to which she was prevented from returning by the Habsburgs. She died aged 51 in 1369, an embittered exile, referred to as a whore by the pious and uncharitable Viennese, and later the heroine of several romantic historical novels including one by Lion Feuchtwanger.

World War I saw some of the bloodiest fighting on the monarchy's southern front, specifically around the Südtirol territory later ceded to Italy (see above) by the Treaty of St-Germain. During **World War II** Mussolini and Hitler forced many German-speaking inhabitants to leave Südtirol for resettlement elsewhere in the Reich. The rest of Tyrol, which had mutated from being a Crown Land to a Bundesland in 1918, was the centre of the area known as '*Gau Tirol und Vorarlberg*' (excluding Osttirol) under the Nazis. After the war

Karl Gruber, the Landeshauptmann (Provincial Governor) of re-established Land Tirol was also Austrian Foreign Minister (1945–53) and in this capacity took a leading role in negotiations concerning Südtirol with the Italian Prime Minister, De Gasperi.

After 1955, Tirol's integration into Europe was emphasised by the building of the Brenner *Autobahn* and the **Europabrücke** (p 388), which opened up tourism and increased trade, while Innsbruck gained prestige from hosting the Winter Olympics in 1964 and 1976. In 1995, Austria entered the EU and plans were drawn up to create a 'European Region' out of Tyrol and South Tyrol, something which should assist in normalising relations between the two areas. Meanwhile the issue of minority cultural and political rights for the German-speaking population in South Tyrol was defused with the signing of the so-called **Südtirol-Paket** in 1969, an agreement guaranteeing the status of both German and Ladin speaking inhabitants. The agreement officially came into force in 1972, but with a period allowed for examination of its workings; in 1992 Austria finally signed an official declaration that the dispute was resolved. The 'packet' has been hailed as a potential model for the resolution of historically-based conflicts involving minorities.

INNSBRUCK

• • • • • • • • • •

Practical information

Population: 118,000. Telephone dialling code: 0512

 ### *Tourist information*
Burggraben 3. ☎ 5356 36. Fax 5356 43. Open Mon–Sat 08.00–19.00, Sun, PH 09.00–18.00. The office sells tickets for public transport and ski passes, as well as a fixed price museum card which entitles the bearer to admission to local museums over a three-day period without further charge. Another useful concession is a general discounted transport and museums admission card. The **Club Innsbruck Card** is obtainable from your hotel and with purchases from certain shops; it allows discounts of various kinds, including one for the underground car-parks.

Other information offices are at the East and West Autobahn city approaches and on the Brenner Pass (open March–Nov, 12.00–19.00 or 21.00). Hotel reservations at the Hauptbahnhof (☎ 5837 66), open daily 09.00–21.00 or 08.00–22.00 in high season.

Getting there
By air 4km west of the town at Fürstenweg 180. ☎ 22 5 25. *Tyrolean Airways* is the local carrier with domestic and some international flights (Amsterdam, Frankfurt, Paris and Zürich). ☎ 22 22 77. Direct flights from London Stansted with *Air UK* every Wed and Thur.

By train ☎ 1717. Express trains leave daily from the Hauptbahnhof for Bregenz, Salzburg, Vienna and through to international destinations (Munich, Brussels, Zürich, Milan, Rome, Zagreb).

Taxis ☎ 53 11 or 45 500, 1718.

City transport

There are 24-hour and seven-day passes for the city transport network of trains and buses, obtainable at *Tabaks*.

Hotels

✯✯✯✯ *Goldener Adler* (A-6020 Innsbruck, Herzog-Friedrich-Str. 6. ☎ 512 58 63 34). Modernised hotel going back 600 years—everyone who was anyone stayed here. Situated right next to the Goldenen Dachl.

✯✯✯✯ *Hotel Maria Theresia* (A-6020 Innsbruck, Maria-Theresien-Str. 31. ☎ 512 5933).

✯✯✯ *Weisses Kreuz* (A-6020, Innsbruck, Herzog-Friedrich-Str. 31. ☎ 512 59 4 7990). 500-year-old inn where Mozart stayed aged 13. Comfortable, spacious rooms if you book the doubles.

Pensions

✯✯ *Riese Haymon* (Haymongasse 4. ☎ 58 98 37).

✯✯ *Pension Paula* (Weiherburggasse 15. ☎ 29 22 62).

Hotel/Restaurant

Weisses Rössl (Kiebachgasse 8). Homely restaurant and small ✯✯✯ hotel (14 rooms) of considerable charm. Renowned for its local dishes.

Restaurants

Altstadtstüberl (Riesengasse 13). First-class Tyrolean cooking.

Gasthaus Goldenes Dachl (Hofgasse 1). Tyrolean specialities.

Stiegl Bräustube (Wilhelm-Greil-Straße 25). Beer cellar, moderate prices.

Self-service

Andrä Hörtnagel (Maria-Theresien-Str. 5).

Café

Café Central (Gilmstraße 5).

Cultural events

The **Innsbrucher Festwochen der Alten Musik** (Festival of Early Music) is at Schloss Ambras (see p 378) in August. Booking is possible at the Tourist Information office. Inquire also at the tourist office for details of folk music ('Tyrolean Evenings'). Between May and September a brass ensemble plays on the balcony of the Goldenen Dachl on Sundays at 11.30.

History of Innsbruck

Innsbruck (the first city of the Earldom of Tyrol from 1420 with central administrative functions, officially capital of the province of Tyrol since the mid-19C) owes its name to a bridge apparently built over the River Inn in the late 12C by the Bavarian Counts of Andechs, the name '*Innsprucke*' (sometimes *Inspruk/Inspruke/Insbruke*) occuring first in 1187. In the 15C the name *Pontina* was also current. However, it was in 1180 that an agreement between Berchtold V of Andechs-Meranien and the Premonstratensians of Wilten Abbey established a market on the right-hand bank of the river (the market had previously been on the other side), thus laying the foundation for what became the **Altstadt** or historic inner city. The town grew rich from a transport monopoly of salt and fish going south and west along the Oberinntal and the return traffic of wine and spices. Money was also made from Innsbruck's entrepot function (levies, storage charges and customs duties). The Habsburg rulers, who acquired Tyrol in 1363 (see above) and moved their residence here from Meran in South Tyrol in 1420, built the 15C Hofburg, the celebrated 'Goldenes Dachl' (Golden Roof), and other monuments. At the end of the 15C, the city reached the zenith of its prestige when Maximilian I set up his court here (1493). Another important patron was Archduke Ferdinand II (1529–95) who reconstructed Schloß Ambras and (like many Habsburgs before and since) incurred huge debts to finance his extravagant lifestyle, his mania for building and collecting, as well as his expensive campaign to acquire the Polish throne.

Innsbruck University was founded by Leopold I in 1669. In the 18C the city also expanded as a commercial centre. It passed into Bavarian hands during the Napoleonic Wars, but resistance was led by Andreas Hofer (p 374), whose victories over the occupiers were chiefly at Bergisel on the south-eastern outskirts of the city. With the 19C expansion of railway lines (east-west completed in 1884, north-south in 1867) Innsbruck grew in importance. At the turn of the century it became culturally significant with the founding by Ludwig von Ficker of what became Austria's most important literary journal, *Der Brenner*, of which Karl Kraus wrote that it was the 'only honest review in the country'. The city was reduced almost to starvation by the Entente blockade in World War I. At the end of World War II, the German 9th Army surrendered at Innsbruck (5 May 1945). In 1965 the city was awarded the honorary title of 'City of Europe' in recognition of the achievements of post-war reconstruction.

Sights of Innsbruck

The obvious place to begin your tour is the museum now known as the **Maximilianeum** (north end of Friedrichstraße) with its celebrated **Goldenes Dachl** (Golden Roof) rising above a Gothic loggia, itself surmounting a frescoed façade and oriel window. 'Golden' refers to the 2738 fire-gilt copper tiles of the crocketed roof, which was constructed between 1494 and 1496 as part of the **Neuer Hof** or **Fürstenberg**, a palace originally commissioned by Duke Friedrich of Tyrol, but radically modified in the 19C. The lower frieze consists of the coats of arms of Maximilian's various territories; above it are frescoes (by Jörg Kölderer, 1500) of two figures holding banners with the coats of arms of the Holy Roman Empire and Tyrol. The balustrade reliefs (copies of the originals, now in the **Ferdinandeum;** see p 375) show Maximilian in the middle with his two wives, Maria of Burgundy (on his left) and Bianca Maria Sforza; then Maximilian again, with his chancellor and court jester. The outer reliefs are of Moorish dancers: acrobatic and grotesque dancing was a feature of contemporary entertainment and the dance depicted here is of Andalusian origin. Jörg Kölderer's frescoes on the interior of the loggia show scenes from contemporary aristocratic life. Maximilian commissioned the gallery from Nikolaus Türing the Elder at the time of his marriage (1493) to Bianca Sforza so that he and the court could watch festivities on the city square.

In the **Maximilianeum** (entrance beneath the Goldenes Dachl, open daily 10.00–18.00; combined ticket includes **Zeughaus** and **Ferdinandeum**) there is an excellent video show concerning the life and times of Maximilian, together with a small museum on the same theme.

The Herzog-Friedrich-Straße running to the south from the Maximilianeum is lined with Gothic arcades (*Lauben*) and historic houses. The **Helblinghaus** (no. 10) on the corner is notable for its splendid Rococo façade (1732) by Anton Gigl. West of the Dachl at no. 6 is the **Goldener Adler** inn, where innumerable travellers of distinction have stayed, including Joseph II, Goethe, Paganini and Ludwig I of Bavaria. On the other side of the street at no. 21 is the former **Rathaus** with a 15C tower (open 10.00–17.00, to 18.00 in summer, and the view from the tower is worth the climb). The rest was built in 1358 but renovated by Georg Türing in 1543 with a façade barockised (supposedly) by Johann Martin Gumpp the Elder in 1691. However, we head north up the Domgasse to the Domplatz and the **Domkirche St Jakob** (Cathedral of St James).

Maximilian I (1459–1519)

Maximilian I was elected 'Roman King' in 1486, inheriting the Habsburg lands and becoming Emperor in 1493. Known as 'The Last Knight' for his (by then) anachronistic love of jousting and tournament, Maximilian was the last Emperor to take part in a battle personally. For the propagation of Habsburg dynastic ambitions, his reign was decisive: not only did he marry two of the richest dowry-bringers of Europe (Maria of Burgundy, whom he loved, and Bianca Maria Sforza of Milan, whom he did not), but through the marriage of his son Philip the Fair to Johanna ('the Mad') of Castile and Aragon, Spain, later Portugal, as well as the American New World, fell into Habsburg hands. Through the famous double marriage (1515) of Maximilian's grandson and granddaughter to the Jagellonian heirs of Wladislaw II, Bohemia and Hungary were to follow. Maximilian was indeed fulfilling the maxim (adapted from Ovid) of Friedrich III's court poet, Aeneas Silvius Piccolomini, later Pope Pius II: *Bella gerant alii, tu felix Austria nube!* (Let others make war; you, fortunate Austria, marry!). In 1511 he even contemplated adding to his secular titles that of the office of Pope, in one sense a logical extension of the traditional alliance between throne and altar cultivated by the Habsburgs, but the plan was dangerously unrealistic.

Maximilian had to fight the French for his Burgundian inheritance even before he and Maria were married, and he continued to wage wars on various fronts (25 campaigns in 40 years) for the rest of his life. Despite his huge dowries and revenues, these military struggles exhausted his coffers and sometimes put him at the mercy of his enemies. He was imprisoned for 14 weeks by the burghers of Ghent in 1488, and just before his death, he was turned away from his beloved Innsbruck because the unpaid innkeepers and merchants refused to supply his followers.

The emperor was a patron of learning and culture, and a relentless self-publicist. This last characteristic extended beyond the grave with his great (uncompleted) project for a magnificent pantheon of the dynasty (albeit involving some creative genealogy) to be set up in the **Hofkirche** (see below). In addition Maximilian wrote up his own exploits in the epic *Theuerdank*, *Weißkunig*, and *Freydal*, works adorned with beautiful illustrations like medieval books of hours. 'He who has no memorial in his own lifetime,' he wrote, 'will surely not have one after he is dead; such a man will be forgotten with the last knell.'

INNSBRUCK

Alpenzoo

Hungerburgbahn
Riesenrundgemälde (Panoramic Bergisel Battle Painting)

Hofgarten

HÖTTING

Inn

Dom St Jakob

Dom Platz.

Landestheater

Stadtsäle

Stadtarchiv

Hofburg

UNIVERSITÄTS-

Alte Universität

Goldenes Dáchl

Hofgasse

Stadtturm

Jesuitenkirche

Helblinghaus

Hofkirche

Volkskunst-museum

Airport

Tourist Information

BURG GRABEN

Ferdinandeum

MUSEUMSTRASSE

MARKT-GRABEN

Spitalskirche

INNRAIN

Adolf-Pichler-Platz

Annasäule

Rathaus

Hauptbahnhof

Bozner Platz.

MERANER STRASSE

Altes Landhaus

Alpenvereins-museum

P.O.

Triumphpforte

MAXIMILIANSTRASSE

SALURNER STRASSE

Bus Station

ANDREAS HOFER

SCHÖPFSTRASSE

LEOPOLDSTRASSE

WILTEN

0   200 yds

0   200 metres

OLYMPIA STRASSE

Glockenmuseum Grassmayr

EGGER-LIENZ STRASSE

Westbahnhof

Kaiserschützen-museum

Stiftskirche Wilten

Pfarr- und Wallfahrtskirche

Kaiserjägermuseum
Olympia-Sprungstadion
Bergisel

Domkirche St Jakob

The **Cathedral** dates back to a Romanesque parish church established with the new market in 1180 ('*ecclesia in foro*'), which was under the control of Wilten Abbey (see p 366). It suffered damage or destruction due to fire and earthquakes and was largely rebuilt in 1438, its enlargement being financed by the humanist Bishop of Brixen, Nikolaus von Cues. The earliest visual record of the church is a watercolour by Albrecht Dürer, made in 1494 on his journey to Venice. In 1551 it was converted from a triple-aisled into a hall church and subsequently (1643) gained its independence from Wilten. The present Baroque church (1722) is mostly the work of Johann Jakob Herkomer (who won the commission in competition with Georg Anton Gumpp), and was finished by his nephew, Johann Georg Fischer.

The elegant concave façade of the church is surmounted by twin towers with lanterns. Modern sculptures of Tyrolean saints are featured in the wall niches, with a statue of the *Virgin* in the central gable, below one of *St James* on horseback. The illusionist ceiling frescoes (1723) of the *Life of St James* in the interior were by the renowned Munich artist, Cosmas Damian Asam, but have been virtually recopied after extensive bomb damage sustained in 1944. In the fresco of the main dome, St James appears before the Spanish army as it prepares to fight the Moors, in the transept he points to a Marian altar, in the nave he intercedes with God on behalf of suffering humanity and above the organ he champions the cause of Innsbruck, Tyrol, Austria and the Catholic church. Notable also is the stucco by Cosmas Damian's brother, Egid Quirin Asam, and the variegated marble floor attributed to Cristoforo and Teodoro Benedetti from the Trentino. The high altar displays the church's greatest treasure, Lukas Cranach's *Madonna of Mercy* (c 1530), donated by Archduke Ferdinand Karl in 1650. The miracle-working icon is one of the most popular objects of veneration in Christendom, having 60 chapels and churches dedicated to it in Tyrol alone. The icon is coordinated with Joseph Schöpf's altarpiece (1789) showing *Sts James and Alexis* in ecstatic veneration of it, but on feast days it is provided with a frame of silver angels and gilded rays. The patron saints of the Brixen (South Tyrol) diocese (*Ingenuin and Albuin*) flank the high altar, a reminder of Innsbruck's former subordination to the Brixen bishops.

Other notable features of this striking interior are Nikolaus Moll's pulpit (1725) and the organ decoration by the same master. The **Tomb of Archduke Maximilian III** (1618), a Grand Master of the Teutonic Order of Knights, is in the north transept, a Mannerist work featuring a kneeling Maximilian with St George and mourning figures bearing torches at the four corners. Maximilian was the first Habsburg to become Grand Master, an illustrious and powerful office at that time: nine more were to follow him, the last (Eugen) outliving the collapse of the Empire by retaining the office until 1923. A feature of the tomb is its beautifully wrought Salomonic columns with a decoration of vines, birds and animals.

The Hofburg

South-east of St Jakob's is the Hofburg (Rennweg 1, open daily 09.00–17.00), the **interior** of which is still being painstakingly restored. Note at the entrance the Emperor Maximilian's family tree, somewhat fancifully tracing the Habsburgs back to the Merovingian dynasty. The present extent of the palace dates to the late 15C (when Dürer painted it) but it was extensively remodelled

(1754) under Maria Theresia by Johann Martin Gumpp, and then by her court architect, Nikolaus Pacassi, the interior and a new wing being completed only in 1776. The tour passes through the chapel (the room in which Franz I Stephan, Maria Theresia's husband, suddenly died of a stroke in 1765 during the marriage celebrations for their son Leopold and the Spanish Infanta). The grisaille in the altar niche depicting God and the mourning angels (A. Leitensdorfer, 1766) is striking. On the altar is a noble *pietà* flanked by obsequial figures by Anton Sartori (1766). The portrait of Maria Theresia in the ante-chamber depicts her initiating the Foundation for Elderly Gentlewomen, who were deputed to say prayers for the soul of Franz Stephan twice daily in the chapel.

After passing through the **Guard Hall**, you enter the magnificent **Riesensaal** (Giants Hall, 31x13m), actually a celebration of the dynasty's achievement in driving out the Turks from the Habsburg lands, although Maria Theresia in her homely way called it the 'family hall'. The portraits (partly by the school of Martin van Meytens) include all of her vast family, but the splendid ceiling frescoes (1776) are by the great and prolific Franz Anton Maulbertsch, with the assistance of his pupil, J.J. Winterhalder. They celebrate the victories of the house of Habsburg-Lorraine (recalling the Great Gallery in Schloß Schönbrunn) and the liberation of Hungary and Vienna from the Osman menace, with allegorical allusions to the renewal of dynastic might. The beautiful limewood chandeliers are by J. Stark.

More family portraits are to be seen in the **Lorraine Room**, while the **Chapter Room** has a table set for an imperial banquet in the time of Franz Joseph. There are several more apartments, of which the most interesting is the **White (or Mirror) Room** with its fine portrait of Maria Theresia and her family, and the **Audience Room**. The last named has a remarkable **tableau** (1769) by Balthasar Moll bearing relief medallions of Emperor Franz I Stephan with his wife and their children. The **Hofgarten** to the north was laid out in English style in 1858 and has a monument to the handsome Archduke Eugen (see above) by Clemens Holzmeister and a fountain with the figure of the *Frog King* by Albin Lanner (1948). On the Rennweg opposite the Hofburg, note the **Leopoldsbrunnen**, an equestrian statue and fountain featuring *Archduke Leopold V* (1619–32) and figures from classical mythology (including *Neptune, Diana, Amphitrite*), all copies of Kaspar Gras's originals in the Tiroler Landesmuseum.

Hofkirche

South of the Hofburg is the Hofkirche (*Franziskanerkirche*) containing the **Funerary Monument of Maximilian I**, begun by Gilg Sesselschreiber (1502) and completed by Stefan Godl of Nuremberg, finally (1584) Gregor Löffler. The black marble cenotaph (1580, designed by Florian Abel of Cologne, the Court Painter in Prague) is surrounded by a wrought-iron grille (1573, Georg Schmiedhammer) and flanked by figures symbolising *Justice, Prudence, Temperance and Fortitude* (by Alexander Colin). The Emperor is featured in his coronation robes kneeling in prayer. The alabaster reliefs (also by Alexander Colin) show scenes from the Emperor's life. The tomb is empty as Maximilian was actually buried in Wiener Neustadt (see p 130).

Placed between the columns on either side of the tomb are the extraordinary **Schwarze Mander** (Black Statues), 28 over-life-size representations of the Emperor's relations and ancestors by different hands and sculpted over 80 years (originally 40 were planned). The scheme also includes chivalric heroes whom Maximilian regarded as his spiritual forebears (Clovis, founder of the Kingdom of the Franks, Theodoric the Goth and King Arthur of England). Originally it was planned to place them in a mausoleum at Falkenstein above the Wolfgangsee, chosen as the focal point of an interlocking network of monasteries, hospitals and castles in Habsburg possession. The memorial was also to include 34 busts of Roman emperors and 100 of the saints venerated by the house of Habsburg, the whole designed to underline the dynasty's claims to divinely sanctioned secular power.

In the table below, the initial in **bold** preceding the name of the statue is an abbreviation of the artist's name:

> **G**: Stefan Godl
> **S**: Gilg Sesselschreiber
> **V**: Peter Vischer
> **PL**: Peter Löffler
> **GL**: Gregor Löfffler

Starting from the entrance and moving up the left-hand row towards the choir the statues are as follows:

1• **G** Emperor Albrecht II (1397–1439). His wife was Elisabeth of Hungary.

2• **G** Emperor Friedrich III (1415–93), father of Maximilian I.

3• **G** Saint Leopold III, (1073(?)–1136), Babenberg Margrave of Austria from 1095, canonised 1485. Founder of many monasteries including Klosterneuburg. Patron saint of Austria.

4• **G** Albrecht IV of Habsburg (d. 1240), father of the first Austrian Habsburg, Rudolf I.

5• **G** Duke Leopold III (1349–86) (killed at the Battle of Sempach fighting the Swiss Confederation).

6• **G** Duke Friedrich IV 'of the empty pockets' see p 362 (1382–1439).

7• **G** King Albrecht I (1248–1308, assassinated). Married to Elisabeth of Görz-Tirol.

8• **G** Godefroy de Bouillon, 'King of Jerusalem' (i.e. the Crusader State), otherwise Godefroy VI of Lower Lorraine (1061–1100).

9• **G** Elisabeth of Hungary (1396–1443), wife of Emperor Albrecht II.

10• **S** Maria of Burgundy (1457–82), first wife of Emperor Maximilian I and daughter of Charles the Bold.

11• **S** Elisabeth of Görz-Tirol (1263–1313), wife of King Albrecht I.

12• **S** Kunigunde of Bavaria (1465–1520), sister of Emperor Maximilian I.

(*Left-hand side of entrance to choir*):

13• **G** Ferdinand of Aragon (1452–1516), husband of Isabella of Castile and father of:

14• **G** Juana 'the Mad' of Spain (1479–1555), wife of the Habsburg Philip the Handsome.

(*Right-hand side of entrance to choir, then moving back down the church*):

15• **G** Philip the Good of Burgundy (1396–1467), father of:

16• **G** Charles the Bold of Burgundy (1433–1477), father of Maria of Burgundy, first wife of Emperor Maximilian I.

17• **S** Zimburgis of Masovia (d. 1429), wife of the Habsburg Duke Ernst, the Iron Duke.

18• **G** Archduchess Margarete (1480–1530), daughter of Emperor Maximilian I.

19• **G** Bianca Maria Sforza (1472–1511), second wife of Emperor Maximilian I.

20• **G** Archduke Sigmund 'the Rich' of Tyrol (1427–96), son of Duke Friedrich IV.

21• **V** King Arthur of England (d. c 542).

22• **S and PL** Ferdinand of Portugal (1345–83), grandfather of Maximilian's mother, Eleonore of Portugal (1436(?)–67). (The visor is closed, since his appearance was unknown to the artist).

23• **S** Duke Ernst, 'the Iron Duke' (1377–1424), husband of Zimburgis of Masovia, grandfather of Emperor Maximilian I.

24• **V** Theodoric the Great, Ostrogothic King of Italy (454–526).

25• **G** Duke Albrecht II, the Wise (1298–1358), son of King Albrecht I and grandfather of Ernst, 'the Iron Duke'.

26• **S** Rudolf I of Habsburg (1218–91), founder of the dynasty in Austria.

27• **S** Philip the Handsome of Castile (1478–1506), son of Emperor Maximilian I by Maria of Burgundy, father of Charles V and Ferdinand I, husband of Juana 'the Mad'.

28• **GL** Clovis I, Merovingian King of the Franks (465–511).

Although the statues vary in quality, two are outstanding, namely the figures of *King Arthur* and *Theodoric the Great*, which were based on drawings by Albrecht Dürer and cast by Peter Vischer the Elder. Of the women, the highly expressive statues of *Zimburgis of Masovia* and *Elisabeth of Görz-Tirol* (probably from a model by Gregor Erhart) and that of *Kunigunde of Bavaria* (designed by Hans Leinberger) are worth closer attention. The court painter Jörg Kölderer is thought to have supplied the designs for the *Juana the Mad*, *Charles the Bold*, *Sigmund the Rich*, *Friedrich III* and *Friedrich 'of the empty Pockets'*.

The Hofkirche itself was built on the orders of Maximilian's grandson, Ferdinand I, to plans by Andrea Crivelli and perhaps constructed by Nikolaus Türing the Younger, whose grandfather created the Goldene Dachl. The late Baroque high altar, flanked by Balthasar Moll's statues of *St Francis* and *St Theresa*, is by Nikolaus Pacassi, and there is a historic organ of 1558 (still functioning) by Jörg Ebert. A flight of stairs leads to the **Silberne Kapelle** (Silver Chapel), where Archduke Ferdinand II (d. 1595), the builder of Schloß Ambras (see p 378), lies in a marble tomb by Alexander Colin, while another tomb by Colin contains his commoner wife, Philippine Welser (d. 1580).

On the way out of the church you pass the **tomb of Andreas Hofer**, an uncomfortable figure for the Habsburgs, whose successes against the occupying Bavarians in 1809 were brought to nought by the Treaty of Schönbrunn (see p 363) signed (under duress) by Franz I. On either side of Hofer lie two comrades in arms, Josef Speckbacher and the Capuchin friar, Joachim Haspinger.

Andreas Hofer (1767–1810)

Of striking appearance with his huge stature and long black beard, Hofer was a publican and vintner from South Tyrol who became the leader of the independence struggle against the French-inspired Bavarian occupation of Tyrol in the Napoleonic Wars. A deeply religious Catholic and Habsburg loyalist, Hofer led the Tyrolean marksmen against the occupiers, three times defeating them at Bergisel (see p 378), on the last occasion after the Emperor he revered had already made his accommodation with the enemy following the defeat of imperial forces at Wagram.

Hofer's victory inspired a rather poor sonnet by Wordsworth, in which he compared him to William Tell. Like many heroes who catch the spirit of the hour, he was in many respects an ambivalent figure, the defender of superstitious religious fundamentalism against a more sophisticated regime influenced by the Enlightenment, which only fell out of favour with the local population when a faltering economy began to cause hardship. The innkeepers (including Hofer's lieutenant, Peter Mayr) were losing business, while the church was furious at reforms which curbed its influence.

Hofer's greatest **Bergisel victory** (13 August 1809) was achieved at a time when the French and Austrians had already agreed a truce. The Kaiser nevertheless sent him a golden chain as a token of his gratitude in October, but ten days later signed a treaty returning Tyrol to Bavaria. The abandoned Hofer fought on with increasing lack of success, and lost the fourth Battle of Bergisel in November. He was subsequently captured in his mid-winter mountain hideaway, having been betrayed by a former comrade, and was executed in February 1810 in Mantua on the express orders of Napoleon.

The **Tiroler Volkskunstmuseum** (Museum of Tyrolean Folk Art, Universitätsstraße 3, open Mon–Sat 09.00–17.00, Sun, PH 09.00–12.00. July and Aug, daily, 09.00–17.30) is reached from the same entrance as the Hofkirche's and is well worth a visit. It is on three floors of the former Franciscan cloister overlooking a Renaissance courtyard. Its 30,000 items include Christmas cribs, beautifully finished models of typical Tyrolean houses, historic interiors rescued from buildings that were to be demolished, all manner of household objects and carved furniture, and ceramic stoves.

Further east in the Universitätsstraße is the **Alte Universität**, the east wing of which is the work of Johann Martin Gumpp the Elder. Next to it is the somewhat forbidding **Jesuit Church** (1646), the University Church built by members of the order. The building has a chequered history, Matthias Kager of Munich's first effort having fallen down in 1626. The design of his successor (the Südtiroler Father Paul Fontaner) is inspired by the cathedral in Salzburg, whose Italian architect (Santino Solari) had been called in to give advice after the church's collapse. The attractive façade is the work of the court architect in Innsbruck, Christoph Gumpp, except the towers (designed by Friedrich Schachner), which were only completed in 1901. The ambitious and fiercely counter-reformatory Archduke Leopold V (d. 1632), who was for some time Bishop of Passau but later married (in 1626, with a papal dispensation) Claudia of Medici (see p 382) (d. 1648), shares a mausoleum with his wife in the crypt and bought the land for the Jesuits to build on.

About 1km further east is Maximilian I's former arsenal (**Zeughaus**, 1500) which houses the **Tiroler Landeskundliches Museum** (Zeughausgasse; open daily May–Sept 10.00–17.00, late opening Thur to 21.00; Oct–April Tues–Sat 10.00–12.00 and 14.00–17.00, Sun, PH 10.00–13.00) and is part of the **Ferdinandeum** (see below). It was originally not only a depot but also an armaments factory supplying weapons for Maximilian's mercenaries. The **geological and butterfly collections** here are substantial, and other displays of interest cover mining, cartography, musical instruments, public transport and the history of the defence of Tyrol.

Tiroler Landesmuseum Ferdinandeum

Parallel to and south of the Universitätsstraße is the Tiroler Landesmuseum Ferdinandeum (**Provincial Museum of Tyrol**) at Museumstraße 15 (open May–Sept 10.00–17.00, late opening Thurs to 21.00; Oct–Apr Tues–Sat 10.00–12.00 and 14.00–17.00, Sun, PH 09.00–13.00). The museum is named after Emperor Ferdinand (*der Gütige*) the Benevolent, who was its patron. Ferdinand was epileptic and a simpleton, but it was in his reign that the Academy of Sciences was founded (1847) in Vienna (admittedly largely due to the efforts of Metternich). In Tyrol his record was mixed—in 1837 he ordered the expulsion of the Zillertaler Lutherans (see p 394), despite their appeal for a reprieve based on Joseph II's Edict of Tolerance (1781), which guaranteed freedom of worship. On the other hand, he was received with genuine warmth (after his less than popular father) on the 12 August 1838, when the Tyrol and Vorarlberg Diets foregathered in the Riesensaal of the Innsbruck Hofburg to pay him homage. It was to Innsbruck that Ferdinand and the court fled in May 1848 after the first phase of the Revolution of that year, staying until August in the comparative safety of the conservative-minded province.

The Ferdinandeum was founded in 1823 and is the second oldest such institution after the Styrian Joanneum in Graz. It begins (**first floor**) with archaeological displays from the Hallstatt period and La Tène culture, but perhaps the most notable part consists of medieval and Renaissance painting and sculpture, including work by the great Michael Pacher, sculpture made for the Goldenes Dachl by Nikolaus Türin the Elder, the **Annenberger Altarpiece** (1517) with one of the earliest views of Innsbruck, and Bernhard Strigel's striking portraits of Maximilian I and Bianca Maria Sforza. Note also the rare cloths for Lenten altars with scenes of the passion dating to 1460. On the **second floor** are Dutch and Flemish works by Lukas Cranach, Gerhard ter Borch, Rembrandt and others; also a fine altarpiece by Pierre Raymond. There are several interesting portraits, including that of Claudio Monteverdi by Bernardo Strozzi (1630), of the Innsbruck-born cardinal and opponent of Josephinism, Christoph Migazzi by Pietro Longhi (1760) and Paul Troger's fine self-portrait (1730). Josef Anton Koch's *Macbeth and the Three Witches* is fun, while a curiosity is Simon Troger's group of ivory figures depicting *St Michael casting out Lucifer*. One of the museum's greatest treasures is the *Schwazer Bergbuch*, a unique illuminated manuscript of 1556 with details of the duties and rights of the miners of silver and copper at Schwaz (see p 391).

Maria-Theresien-Straße

From the west end of Museumstraße, the Burggraben and **Maria-Theresien-Straße** are rejoined. On the west side of the latter is the **Spitalskirche**, a single-vaulted church built by Johann Martin Gumpp (1701), which has extremely fine stucco by Constantin Reiser, Michael Hann and Benedict Fries. The vivid modern **frescoes** (1962) by Hans Andre show the *Sermon on the Mount*, the *Descent of the Holy Ghost on the Day of the Pentecost* and *Saints effecting Cures for the Plague*.

Further south opposite the **Rathaus** is the **Annasäule** (St Anne's Column), so-called because it commemorates the deliverance of Tyrol from Bavarian invaders on St Anne's Day, 1703, during the War of the Spanish Succession. The column, built in 1706 by Cristoforo Benedetti of Trento, carries a statue of the *Virgin* on a throne carved as a crescent moon, a copy of Benedetti's original in the Benedictine church at Fiecht. The street is rich in Baroque architecture by the Gumpp dynasty (no. 39 and opposite, and no. 45), in particular the **Alte Landhaus** (1728), the seat of the provincial administration and the most important work by Georg Anton Gumpp. Ascending the impressive staircase of this fine building, you pass statues (1728) by Nikolaus Moll on the second floor representing *Diana* and *Apollo*, together with busts of *Jupiter* and *Juno*. The splendid **Landtagssaal** (Parliamentary Chamber) has allegorical frescoes of Tyrolean landscape as the god-given riches granted to Meinhard II (Cosmas Damian Asam, 1734). Gumpp also designed the **chapel** (1729) with an altarpiece of *St George* (c 1732) by Johann Georg Grasmayr.

On the other side of the street and further south is the **Servite Church** (1626), whose frescoes were destroyed in wartime bombing and have been replaced by the work of Hans Andre, the latter also having painted the *Holy Trinity* on the exterior. The mid-17C carved pews and Martin Pollack's altarpiece (*The Marriage of Mary*, 1628) make the interior worth a visit, as also does the Pellegrini Chapel's reliquary altar decorated with ivory. It supposedly contains the head of St Christina and the bones of St Vitalis (Felicity), both saints of doubtful authenticity. Beyond the Servite Church is the Roman-style **Triumphpforte** (Triumphal Arch, 1765) erected, like several others in her realms, for the triumphal entry of Maria Theresia and Franz Stephan, on this occasion to celebrate the marriage of their son Leopold II. On the north side, Balthasar Moll added mourning emblems (1774) for the Emperor, who died during the festivities (see Hofburg Chapel above), while on the south side the reliefs commemorate the marriage.

Smaller museums and other attractions

The **Alpenvereinmuseum** at Wilhelm-Greil-Straße 15 (open Mon–Fri 10.00–17.00, Wed to 19.00, May–Oct also Sat 10.00–13.00) documents the history of mountaineering in the Alps with reliefs, cartography and paintings. Notable among the latter is *Bergraum I* by the distinguished Tyrolean artist, Albin Egger-Lienz. The **Olympia Museum**, is soon to be installed in a new home at the Bergisel Stadium next to the ski-jump.

On the northern periphery of the old city at Rennweg 39, near the terminus for the *Hungerburgbahn* (funicular), is the great **panoramic picture** (*Riesenrundgemälde*, 1896) of the most significant battle at Bergisel (13 August 1809, see **Andreas Hofer** above) by Michael Diemer and Franz Burger (open daily 09.00–17.00). It required 5000kg of canvas and 4726kg of paint to complete and is one of only a handful of historical panoramas on this scale that survive from the 19C, when there was a vogue for such things.

If you take the *Hungerburgbahn* you can reach the **Alpine Zoo** (open 09.00–18.00 in summer, 09.00–17.00 in winter) which is home to 140 animal species found in Alpine regions. Above the zoo is the Hungerburg villa quarter, whose **Theresienkirche** has a remarkable modern fresco of the *Crucifixion* (1947) by the best-known contemporary artist of Tyrol, Max Weiler (b. 1910). The work is highly controversial, featuring characters in contemporary dress and a Tyrolean marksman piercing the side of Christ with his spear. Only slightly less controversial is the fresco that Weiler did for the Innsbruck *Hauptbahnhof*, but both are worth the detour to see.

Close to the centre is the **Innsbrucker Stadtarchiv** and **Historisches Museum der Stadt Innsbruck** (Badgasse 2, open Mon–Thurs 08.00–12.00, 14.00–18.00, Fri 08.00–13.00) which displays its contents in a revolving programme of temporary exhibitions on specific aspects of the city. The postcards and photographs of Innsbruck have charm, while the early prints and etchings of the city are of aesthetic as well as historical value.

Wilten, Bergisel, Schloss Ambras

Wilten Abbey

On the southern periphery of the city is Wilten Abbey, the highlight of which is the **Abbey Church of St Lawrence**, according to legend remorsefully founded by the local giant, Haymon, after he had slain his rival, Thyrsus. (He also had a dragon to contend with during construction, which destroyed the fruits of his day's labour every night until Haymon lay in wait for it and cut its tongue out). Impressive statues of the two giants by Nikolaus Moll flank the main entrance. Ill-advised searches for Haymon's bones caused the old Romanesque church to collapse in the 17C, after which it was rebuilt in the 1650s by Christoph Gumpp the Younger, who also remodelled the adjoining Premonstratensian Abbey. The later façade (1716) is by Georg Anton Gumpp. The entrance is barred by a notable wrought-iron grille (Adam Neyer, 1707) with motifs of ivy and gilded roses, but the interior can be viewed beyond it (or with a tour, see below). The ceiling frescoes by Kaspar Waldmann (1707) that survived World War II feature the *Coronation of the Virgin* and the *Virgin handing St Norbert* (founder of the Premonstratensians) *a monastic Robe*. The post-war frescoes are by Hans Andre (1962). The impressive high altar (1655) is the work of Paul Huber, who was the court cabinet maker, and Egid Schur painted the altarpiece (1671) of the *Virgin as Queen of the Rosary with St Lawrence, St Stephen and the company of Angels*.

Wilten Abbey arose in the early 12C near a former Roman customs post, but suffered several fires and catastrophes; it began to flourish only in the 17C, with the completion of the Baroque buildings under the energetic Abbot Stremer (1693–1719). The highly decorated interior is worth seeing; it includes the **Norbertisaal** (St Norbert's Room) with frescoes of the *Life of St Norbert* by Kaspar Waldmann, the **Altmuttersaal**, so-called from the 19C landscapes and exotic animals by Franz Altmutter, and more work by Kaspar Waldmann in the **Jagdzimmer** (Hunting Room) and Refectory. The abbey, together with its church and the interesting museum, may be visited in tour groups only (☎ 0512 58 30 48).

The **Pfarr-und Wallfahrtskirche Unser Lieben Frau unter den vier Säulen** (Wilten Parish and Pilgrimage Church of Our Lady under the Four Columns), built by Franz de Paula Penz in 1756, is situated nearby and is regarded as the finest Rococo church in Tyrol. Particularly striking is the stucco of the dazzling **interior** by Franz Xaver Feichtmayr and the ceiling frescoes by

Matthäus Günther of Augsburg (*Mary interceding for Mankind*, *Esther interceding with the Persian King for the Jews* (an Old Testament theme symbolic of protection for the common man) and *Judith as the Jewish Patriot vanquishing the Assyrian General*, interpreted in the Counter-Reformation as the victory over sin. Above the high altar is the magnificent baldachin (Franz Karl Fischer, 1775), which gives the church its name, and encompasses the much venerated 14C sandstone *Madonna* with its added neo-Baroque aureole. (From mid-June to the end of Oct the church is open from 08.30 to 17.00; otherwise the interior can only be viewed from the entrance.)

Just to the north of the abbey is the **Tiroler Kaiserschützenmuseum** (Klostergasse 1, open May–Sept, Mon–Sat 10.00–16.00, Sun, PH 10.00–13.00, Oct–April by appointment. ☎ 58 74 39), which documents the defence of Tyrol by the special alpine force (often including voluntary fighters who were under- or over-age) awarded the honorary title of *Kaiserschützen* by Emperor Karl I in 1917 for the heroic defence of the province against the Italians in World War I. North of this museum is a bell foundry (**Glockengießerei Grassmayr**, Leopoldstraße 53, open Mon–Fri 09.00–18.00, Sat 09.00–12.00) dating to the 16C. The trade secrets of bell casting were passed through 14 generations of Grassmayrs after Bartlme Grassmayr learnt his trade in the Aachen foundry of Joan von Treer. From the museum you can see (through a window) men at work casting bells, and in the *Klangraum* you can test the results.

Bergisel

Bergisel (746m) to the south of the abbey is the site of the Olympic ski-jump (1964: jumps up to 104m), beneath which the Brenner *Autobahn* and railway pass through tunnels. It is about 15 minutes' walk from Wilten. At its summit is the Olympia Ice Stadium, but Bergisel's historic significance is that Andreas Hofer (see p 374) defeated French and Bavarian forces here three times in May and August of 1809, and was himself defeated in November. On the north side of the hill below the ski-jump is the **Andreas Hofer Monument** (1893) and a memorial chapel (1909). Behind this is the **Tomb of the Tiroler Kaiserjäger** and a **museum** dedicated to them (open March, Tues–Sun, 10.00–15.00, April–Oct 09.00–17.00, Nov–Feb closed). The museum possesses objects belonging to Hofer and has a section dealing with World War I, the latter with important pictures by Albin Egger-Lienz, Felicien von Myrbach and Franz von Defregger.

Schloss Ambras

Two kilometres south of Wilten is Schloß Ambras (Schloßstraße 20, open April–Sept, Tues–Sun, 10.00–17.00), one of Austria's finest Renaissance castles. It contains a fabulous **Kunsthistorisches Museum** based on the (originally military) collection of its Habsburg owner, Archduke Ferdinand II (1529–95). Although the name of the gloomy medieval castle of the Andechs Counts was derived from '*ad umbras*' ('lying in the shade'), Ferdinand transformed it (1564–67) into a glittering residence for a Renaissance *grand Seigneur*, more especially for his commoner wife, Philippine Welser, a patrician from Augsburg. So much did he love his unacceptably low-born spouse (the marriage was kept secret until two years before her death), that he built for her the unheard-of luxury of a personal bathroom (in the Hochschloss), complete with copper bath.

After Philippine's death in 1580, Ferdinand married Anna Katharina Gonzaga of Mantua and the Schloss became a humanist centre of learning, the ducal collection being systematically arranged for public exhibition.

To the left of the entrance the **Unterschloss** displays suits of armour (partly from the collection of Archduke Sigmund and Emperor Maximilian) from different countries and different periods, the whole conceived as a glorification of military might, but also reflecting lustre on the Habsburgs themselves. The armour for a giant on the Archduke's payroll, Giovanni Bona, is a curiosity: Bona (2.4m tall) was kept as a live exhibit in the museum and contemporaries report the bizarre spectacle of him walking through the Innsbruck streets hand-in-hand with the court dwarf. Another wing of the Schloß houses the magnificent **Kunst-und Wunderkammer**, founded on the universalist principle of the Renaissance and including *Artificialia* (the products of artifice), *Naturalia* (phenomena of nature), *Mirabilia* (curiosities and wonders) and *Scientifica* (scientific items). These are in fact the original concepts from which modern museums sprang and they formed the basis for the ambitious museum projects of the 19C. The collection is fascinatingly diverse, a *theatrum mundi* that greatly impressed such cultivated visitors as Goethe and Queen Christina of Sweden. Many of the items (coral, ivory, whales' teeth, rhinoceros horn, etc.) are of great natural beauty, while others (the depiction of the hirsute man and his children, of dwarves, giants and cripples) have a somewhat grotesque fascination.

On the way to the **Hochschloss** you pass the magnificent 43m long **Spanish Banqueting Hall** (c 1572) by Giovanni Lucchese, with 27 over-life-size portraits of Tyrolean rulers probably painted by Giovanni Fontana. There is a fine (partly gilded) coffered ceiling with a stucco frieze, and the elegant doors inlaid with various woods are by the same master, Conrad Gottlieb of Hall. The courtyard walls of the Hochschloss are decorated with mythological scenes and Christian allegories, together with *trompe l'oeil* architectural decorations by Heinrich Teufel (1568). The **Portrait Gallery**, spanning the period 1400–1800, contains more than 250 pictures and is perhaps the finest genealogical showcase in Europe. For those interested in the mind-boggling ramifications of the House of Austria's dynastic expansion, a catalogue is available in German, which also supplies useful family trees. However, the artistic interest of the portraits is even greater, since a number of the pictures are by major artists (some attributions doubtful), and constitute rare (on occasion, unique) representations of the rulers concerned.

In the medieval **Bergfried** (keep) is a collection of Gothic sculpture, the highlight being the **St George Altar** by Sebastian Scheel and Sebald Bocksdorfer, which was commissioned by Maximilian I and dates to around 1510. Apart from the astonishing vividness of St George, clad in elegant contemporary armour as he gives the dragon the *coup de grâce* while the Princess and her pet sheep look on from a safe distance, the dynastic symbolism of the piece is worth remarking: the two saints in the wings are supposed to be concealed portraits of Habsburgs, while the coats of arms above (*left to right*: Austria, Hungary, Portugal, the Holy Roman Empire, England, Bohemia and Naples) suggest not only the political aspirations of Maximilian, but also allude to his actual and imagined forebears in a manner reminiscent of the **Schwarze Mander** (see p 372) in the Hofkirche in Innsbruck.

Last but not least the **Schloßpark**, now mostly a 19C landscaped garden on the English model, but structurally redolent of its Renaissance origins, makes a delightful setting for a stroll after lunch at the excellent Schloss restaurant.

The so-called **Wildpark** to the east of the Hochschloss boasts a picturesque waterfall. South of the Spanish Hall is a formal garden, laid out in 1974 but having regard to existing 19C features. To the west is the 19C **landscaped garden** with winding paths and a wooden observation pavilion on the site of an earlier chapel. These divisions hark back to the Renaissance concept of Italian garden design which generally offered a formal decorative part with flowers, a *boschetto* (wooded area) for intimacy and a *selvatico* (wild area) for the triumph of nature. Descriptions of Ferdinand's original Renaissance garden speak of an ambitious botanical and architectural structure, as well as technical wonders (for example, a huge circular maplewood table for summer banquets, which was made to revolve by means of water pressure and had hidden refresher sprays).

From Schloß Ambras it is a short detour south via Lans to the health and ski resort of **Igls** (900m) where there is another place of interest to garden enthusiasts, the **Innsbruck University Botanical Gardens for Alpine Plants**. Also at Igls is one of the earliest golf courses in Austria (opened 1930). A cable-car ascends over the bob-sleigh run to a station 295m below the summit of the **Patscherkofel** (2247m), the last stretch being on foot or by chair-lift.

Götzens is not far west of Igls, but separated from the latter by the valley of the River Sill, and so has to be reached from Wilten via Mutters. The village has an attractive setting on the Axamer Lizum plateau and derives its name from a corruption of Latin *casa*, there having been a Roman settlement here. The extremely elegant Baroque **parish church** (Franz Singer, 1775) has a delightful gilded and grey-white Rococo interior with ceiling frescoes by Matthias Günther (1775), a pupil of Cosmas Damian Asam. They illustrate the *Lives of St Peter and St Paul*, the patrons of the church, with further scenes on the same theme in the spandrels. On the chancel arch is the inscription (in Latin): 'Peter pastures the sheep, Paul teaches you how to love.' Most striking is the cupola fresco of the choir, where St Peter, enthroned on a cloud, commends the Götzens church to the protection of the Trinity and the Virgin. The altarpiece (*Christ Resurrected, Peter and Paul interceding for Mankind* and an *Allegory of the Church Triumphant*) has been ascribed to Franz Anton Maulbertsch, or his pupil, Andreas Nesselthaler. The wooden sculptures (and perhaps the whole design of the high altar) are by Johann Schnegg: amazingly sophisticated and convincing imitations of marble, they are considered his masterworks. On the altar are the patrons of the Brixen diocese, *Sts Ingenuin and Albuin*, with two Roman martyrs, *John and Paul*; elsewhere are extraordinarily graceful angels, the *Archangel Raphael with Tobias*, and other saints on the side-altars (notably *St Notburga* carrying an enormous scythe see p 393).

West of Innsbruck

The *Autobahn* (A12) runs straight to the Arlberg and on to Bludenz in Vorarlberg, but there are several worthwhile detours on the way, so it is advisable to take the parallel road 171 as far as **Landeck**. Just before **Zirl** is the **Martinsbühel**, where Emperor Maximilian was once trapped in a steep ravine when out hunting. Only after the monstrance from the Zirl church was brought to the spot was it possible for a peasant to rescue the Emperor, in memory of which the latter had a shrine built on the **Martinswand**. The **Maximiliansgrotte**, north of Zirl, can be reached on foot from the Zirler Weinhof, and the whole episode was written up in Maximilian's epic account of his life, *Theuerdank* (see p 368), besides being a favourite theme for painters even as late as the 19C (including a well-known picture by Moritz von Schwind).

Seefeld in Tirol

Shortly after Zirl the route forks right on to road 177, a branch of the ancient Via Claudia Augusta connecting Tyrol with Augsburg, and ascends to **Seefeld in Tyrol**. In this otherwise less than exciting but mysteriously fashionable summer and ski (*Langlauf*) resort (it has implausibly been compared with St Moritz), the **parish church of St Oswald** should not be overlooked, being a rare surviving example of work by the medieval Guild of Masons in Innsbruck. It became a pilgrimage church after a miracle in 1384: a local freebooting knight, Oswald Milser of Schloßberg, haughtily demanded to be given the consecrated wafer first at communion. No sooner was the wafer in his mouth than he began to sink through the floor, as did the altar table when he clutched it for support. All returned to normal when the wafer (now blood-coloured) was removed from his mouth. Parseval of Weineck made a monstrance for the miraculous host (see below), an object of veneration ever since.

The present church, begun in 1432, has an interesting interior with fine reticulated vaulting. The choir (perhaps a remnant of an earlier sanctuary) is considerably lower than the nave, with simpler vaulting and early painted scenes on the north wall (*Mary Magdalene*, *St Oswald*, the *Mount of Olives* and *Christ crowned with Thorns*). The ancient Gothic altar table (now surmounted by a neo-Gothic altar incorporating some original Gothic sculptures including the *Madonna*, *St Oswald* and *St Leonhard*) still shows a mark, supposedly the imprint of Oswald Milser's hand; those of a credulous disposition will be pleased to note the hollow left in the floor when he began sinking. The pulpit on the north side of the chancel arch dates to 1524 and on the south wall of the choir is a panel painting (by Jörg Kölderer, 1502) of the miracle of the host related above. On the south wall of the sanctuary is the Miraculous Host itself. Notable also is the Gothic font with a renaissance canopy.

From the north aisle a marble stairway leads to the **Blutkapelle** (1576), built by Alberto Lucchese for Ferdinand II. There is fine 18C stucco on the ceiling and an elegant wrought-iron screen (1724). On the tympanum of the impressive late Gothic portal on the south side of the church are reliefs of the *Miracle of the Host* and the *Execution of St Oswald* (it is apparently accidental that the church's patron shares a name with the protagonist of the miracle). The Scottish coat of arms above it refers to Eleonore (1433–80), daughter of James I of Scotland and wife of Archduke Sigmund 'the Rich' (1427–96, so-called because he reformed the currency). Eleonore is supposed to have translated the famous French epic *Pontus and Sidonia* into German for Sigmund's court, her skills being the legacy of a childhood spent at the Valois court of Charles VII.

Climbers can enjoy fine views from Seefeld's neighbouring peaks, notably the **Seefelder Spitze** and **Reither Spitze**, and there is also an Olympic Sports and Congress Centre (the Nordic skiing competitions were held here). The main road leads on to the German border at Scharnitz with (to the east) an extensive area of mountainous nature reserve (the limestone **Karwendel**) of which the ancient maple groves are a feature. There used to be a fort on the Scharnitzpass, built (1632) for defence against the Swedes in the Thirty Years War by the Medici widow of Archduke Leopold V, and known after her as the *Porta Claudia*. In 1805 its defenders against Napoleonic forces were commanded by an Englishman in Austrian service, one Colonel Swinburne, a forebear of the poet.

Stift Stams

Baroque putto, Stift Stams

About 10km further west along the Inn Valley from Zirl, on the south side of the river, is the **Cistercian Abbey of Stams** (tours: July–Aug, daily 09.00–11.00, 13.00–17.00 every half hour; April–Oct on the hour; Nov–March on the hour 09.00–11.00, 14.00–16.00. Museum open mid-June–Sept, 10.00–11.30, 13.30– 17.00) built in 1284 by Count Meinhard II of Tyrol at the prompting of his wife, Elisabeth of Bavaria, and also intended to provide a mausoleum for Tyrolean rulers. Elisabeth specifically wanted to commemorate her son who had been executed in Naples by Charles of Anjou. The medieval abbey was sacked in a peasants' revolt (1552), and much of it was destroyed by fire in 1593. The present church (1699) was remodelled by Georg Anton and Johann Martin Gumpp. It was used as a depot during the last war, when the abbey was a transit camp for emigrants from South Tyrol (see p 364). Its subsequent superb restoration was recognised by the Europa Nostra prize and the Pope gave it *Basilica minor* status in 1984. There are summer concerts of Baroque music in the **Bernhardisaal** (see below) of the monastery, and an idiosyncratic feature of the extensive educational activity of the monks is the **Skigymnasium**, where future medal-winners are subjected to intellectual and spiritual discipline as well as physical training.

The superb **Stiftskirche** presents a dazzling array of white stucco, gilded ornament, delicately carved stalls (some with pewter inlay) and Johann Georg Wolker's colourful frescoes (1734) in the vault, showing the *Life of the Virgin*. Notable are the wrought-iron screens by Bernhard Bachnitzer and Michael Neurauter separating the porch from the church. To the south is the ornate **Heiligblut-Kapelle** with a beautiful rose screen. The ornate stucco, among the most beautiful in the South German region, is by Franz Xaver Feichtmayr and Josef Vischer, while the gilded pulpit (1740) and four chapel altars are by Andreas Kölle. The **Fürstengruft** (Princes' Crypt), at the entrance to which is Andreas Thamasch's *Crucifixion* group and other figures, contains the tombs of Sigmund '*der Münzreiche*' ('the Rich') and his wife Eleanor Stuart (see above) as well as those of Bianca Maria Sforza (second wife of Maximilian I). Unique is the **high altar** with the fabulous limewood **Lebensbaum** (*Tree of Life*, 1613) by Bartholomäus Steinle and Wolfgang Kirchmayr, once movingly celebrated by the poet Georg Trakl (1887–1914) in a famous lyric entitled *A Winter Evening*:

Many a wanderer on paths unlit
Approaches here the gate:
Golden shines the tree of grace,
From earth's cool sap arisen.

At the bottom of the tree are the figures of *Adam and Eve*, the source of natural life, while its supernatural essence streams from *Jesus Christ* at the top. From the trunk springs an ornate mesh of gilded branches and figures, a total of 84 saints carved in wood, who represent the fruits of the union between natural and supernatural forms of life. The noblest fruit is the *Virgin Mary*, placed at the centre. The work's symbolic allusions play on the religious significance of trees in Christian tradition: the Old Testament Tree of Life springing from *Jesse*, father of King David, but also the Tree of Knowledge in the Paradise Garden, which is superseded in New Testament terms by the resurgent tree of life as represented by the redemptive cross.

Notable features of the **Stift** itself (accessible only with the guided tours) are the **staircase** of the Prelates' Wing with wrought-iron railings and a ceiling fresco of angelic musicians by Franz Michael Huber (1729) and the lavishly ornamented **Bernhardisaal** (St Bernard Room or Hall of Princes, 1770) by Georg Anton Gumpp, with a cycle of frescoes and paintings of the *Life of St Bernard* by Huber and Anton Zoller. The ceiling opens to a gilded gallery with frescoes on the roof above.

Ötztal

A little further on road 171 is a turning south into the picturesque **Ötztal** (road 186), where the Ötztaler Ache flows into the River Inn. At **Oetz** there is an attractive parish church, a vivid feature of which is St Michael's Chapel below the choir. The altar (1683) by Ignaz Waibl shows scenes of *St Michael expelling the Rebellious Angels*. The walls of the Gothic *Gasthof Stern* in the village have colourful Renaissance and Baroque frescoes (1573, 1615—they include a delightful *St Christopher* with a tiny *Christ* perched on his shoulder like a bird, and an exuberant *Adam and Eve*); other houses round about are similarly decorative. **Umhausen**, further south and climbing, has remains of Gothic frescoes in the church; shortly beyond it the spectacular **Stuibenfall** may be reached to the east by a footpath. The 150m waterfall is fed from higher glaciers, its energy now being harnessed for hydro-electric generation. **Längenfeld** (1180m) is a health resort with sulphur baths and an open-air museum. **Sölden** is a popular resort with access to high runs making summer skiing possible. A cable-car ascends to the Geislacherkogel (3058m) with panoramic views of the Ötztal Alps. From **Zwieselstein** a minor road forks south-west along the **Venter Tal** towards **Vent**, from which the **Niederjoch** on the frontier with Italy is reached. Near the **Tisenjoch** (3287m) the famous man from the ice, 'Ötzi', was discovered in the early 1990s, and became a Stone Age celebrity overnight.

The main road from Zwieselstein climbs steeply into the **Gurgltal** at the head of which is the ski resort of **Obergurgl**. Professor Piccard landed on the Gurgler glacier on 27 May 1931 after his first balloon ascent of 16,000m. A road over the **Timmelsjoch Pass** (closed early Oct–mid-June) brings you to the Italian border. In the South Tyrol/Alto Adige valley beyond, Andreas Hofer (see p 374) was born near St Leonhard im Passeier (San-Leonardo in Passiria) in 1767.

'Ötzi', the 'Man from the Ice'

The most sensational anthropological find of recent years was made by German hikers on 19 September 1991 on the **Niederjochferner** of the **Hauslabjoch**. Discovering the mummified body of a man that had recently emerged from the glacier, they alerted the local warden, who in turn alerted police on either side of the Austro-Italian border. Both the discoverers and the authorities believed that they had stumbled on the remains of an unfortunate climber who had met with an accident in the not so distant past. Closer inspection revealed that the corpse was that of a man, about 30 years old according to later radio carbon tests made in the University of Innsbruck, who had died on the mountain at least 2000 years before Christ. The glacier had conserved not only the bones, but all the main organs and much of the flesh, together with patches of animal-skin clothing, wooden, stone and bone tools, a quiver full of arrows, a bow and a wooden-hefted copper axe; this extensive equipment, together with his decorative necklace and body tattoos, suggests he was a personage of some importance.

The **photographic exhibition** in **Vent** concerning the discovery of Ötzi is well worth a visit and stresses the co-operation between Italy and Austria in the exploitation of the find (Ötzi was actually found some 90m over the Italian border). 'Alpine Adam', '*Homo tyroliensis*' or 'Frozen Fritz' as he is variously known, has already provoked excited reactions, some of them bizarre: several women have applied to be impregnated with his Stone Age sperm (unfortunately the relevant parts of Ötzi are no longer intact). In 1998 Ötzi was taken to Bolzano Südtirol/Alto Adige and put on display in a special museum.

Pitztal

Parallel to the **Ötztal** in the Ötztaler Alps is the Pitztal, reached by a turn up a minor road at **Arzl** just before Imst on road 171. The main town is **Wenns**, which has a house (**Platzhaus**) on the main square richly decorated on the exterior with Renaissance frescoes of biblical and mythological scenes. Further along the valley is **Jerzens**, and beyond it **St Leonhard**, whose parish church has some fine carving and an altarpiece by Philipp Jacob Greil. The drive is worth it for the last dramatic stretch running between the mountains with emerging views of the **Mittagskogel**. From Mittelberg it is two hours' trek to the **Mittelbergferner** (the glacier), which is also accessible by an underground railway built in 1984 and known as the '*Pitz Express*'. Earlier this century the glacier reached as far as the valley itself, but has since receded. From the Mittelbergferner the highest cable-car in Austria takes you to the **Hinteren Brunnenkogel** (3440m).

North of Imst to Reutte, Füssen and the Lechtal

From Imst (see below) road 314 heads north towards the German border over the **Fernpaß** (1209m). At **Nassereith** the **Fasnacht-Museum** (Fasching or Carnival Museum, open on application; ☎ 05265-52120) in the town hall documents a pagan custom still enacted, whereby the peasants indulge in a pre-spring carnival frolic recalling a stamping dance (*Schellerlaufen*) over the frozen fields in late winter, designed to awaken the buried seeds to life; a similar custom is preserved in Imst, Telfs and other places around Innsbruck. On the **Fern Paß** beyond is the ruin of the Sigmundsberg hunting-lodge (1460) and the Schloss Fernstein almost opposite it (originally a roadblock and toll-house, now a hotel). A fork right leads to Ehrwald, from where access is gained to the dramatic peak of the **Zugspitze** (2968m), Germany's highest mountain peak, the last stretch by cable-car. Back on road 314 **Bichlbach's** 15C **church of St Lawrence** was largely destroyed in the Reformation by Maurice of Saxony's troops, who caused untold damage in Tyrol, but its later Baroque frescoes by the Zeiller family (in the nave, the *Condemnation and Assumption of St Lawrence*, in the choir, the *Feeding of the Five Thousand*) have considerable charm. The market town of **Reutte** in the Lech Valley has some historic houses, especially the so-called **Zeillerhäuschen** at Untergsteig 1 with its illusionist Baroque decoration by Franz Anton Zeiller. Wernher von Braun, developer of the Nazis' V2 rockets, was captured in Reutte by the Americans in 1945, the latter subsequently arranging comfortable facilities for him and his team to continue their work in the United States.

From Reutte to **Füssen** and the German border is a short stretch, or alternatively road 198 runs back south-west along the **Lechtal** towards Vorarlberg and eventually Lech (p 424) itself. The picturesque **Tannheimer Tal** (road 199) from Weißenbach leads to Emperor Maximilian's fishing grounds at **Haldensee** and **Vilsalpsee** in a nature conservation area. A number of scenically attractive routes lead up mountain valleys from the main Weißenbach-Warth road. In particular the **Bschlaber Tal** gives access to the pass over the **Hahntennjoch** (1895m) and so back to Imst.

The oldest settlement in the Lech Valley is **Elbigenalp** with colourfully painted houses (the painting looks Baroque, but is 19C). The town was always a centre for artists and craftsmen and is the birthplace of the landscape painter Josef Anton Koch (1768–1839). His great-niece, Anna Knittel, became famous for mountaineering exploits, in particular for robbing inaccessible eagles' nests; her life-story was turned into a sentimental novel by Wilhelmine von Hillern (*Die Geier-Wally*, 1875) and even into an opera in 1892 (unfortunately called *La Wally*, by Alfredo Catalani, but Callas has sung it) as well as providing material for three subsequent films. In the **parish church of St Nicholas** is a Gothic fresco of the *Last Judgement* (1450), together with a fresco in the nave by Johann Jakob Zeiller representing *Christ Victorious*, while the nearby chapel for the ossuary has a notable 19C fresco cycle of the *Dance of Death* by a local man, Anton Falger.

Imst and Landeck

Imst once enjoyed a reputation as a centre for bird breeders, their line in canaries being much sought after in Europe. This idiosyncracy was the inspiration for Carl Zeller's operetta *Der Vogelhändler* (1891, the tenor comic hero is a canary fancier from Tyrol). The parish church has fine star and ribbed vaulting and a Gothic crucifix of 1520 by Hans Kels.

Landeck to the west developed on the ancient junction between north–south and east–west routes, its strategic importance being underlined by Meinhard II's decision to extend an existing fortress that had existed since the early 13C. **Burg Landeck** is built on a crag above the town and houses a **Museum of Local History** (open daily, June–Sept 10.00–17.00, Oct daily 14.00–17.00) which has a well-presented display concerning peasant life in Tyrol (from which it may be seen that, besides the other rigours of peasant existence, sleeping often had to be undertaken in a sitting position and bread was hung from the rafters to outwit the mice!). There is also interesting documentation of the life and career of Jakob Prandtauer (see p 122), the great architect of the monastery of Melk on the Danube, who was born at Stanz nearby. His portrait shows his qualities clearly; as the staunchly patriotic guidebook puts it: 'From the energetic mouth, dark eyes and sharply etched nose, one recognizes a man of Tyrolean origin'. Also part of the museum is a picture gallery and an account of the pioneer of Alpine skiing at St Anton, Benno Rybizkai (1904–92). Landeck's **parish church of the Assumption** below the castle was founded on a spot where (according to legend) the children of two peasants who had been abducted by a bear and a wolf were discovered in what was then forest. The story is depicted in four large panels on the south side of the Gothic church, which is otherwise unremarkable. Finely carved *Totenschilde* (funerary plaques) hang over the altar, that on the right by Sebald Bocksdorfer having been used for the obsequies in 1497 of a local lord, Oswald von Schrofenstein.

The Oberinntal: south and west of Landeck

The valley (road 315) follows the Upper Inn (river) towards its source in the Swiss Engadine as the river gathers volume from glaciers in the **Samnaungruppe** and **Kaunergrat**. The bridge at **Prutz**, was a strategic point, defended in 1703 and 1809 by Tyrolean freedom fighters, who are commemorated with a bronze eagle monument.

At Prutz, the secondary road for the Kaunertal leads off through mountainous terrain, eventually reaching the **Gepatsch-Stausee** (reservoir), fed by the second longest glacier (19km) in the Alps. A panoramic road (**Kaunertaler Gletscherstraße**) leads along the shore (toll) up to the skiing area of the **Weißseeferner**, which boasts the highest bus-stop in Austria at 2570m.

The main road from Prutz leads up the **Oberinntal** past **Ladis**, **Fiss**, and **Serfaus**, which compete with Lienz for claiming the highest number of hours of sunshine in Austria (hence their name '*Sonnenterrasse*'). Before reaching Prutz, however, it is worth stopping at the parish church of **Fließ**; in the cemetery there are attractive wrought-iron crosses, while a remarkable gilded Rococo grave-ornament on the south wall of the church is a memorial to the priests of the parish. On the exterior of the tower is a huge fresco of *St Christopher* (1500, but much restored after a fire in 1933). The astronomical clock above dates to 1696, whereas the clock with coats of arms, including the Imperial and Tyrolean eagles, was made in 1547. In the interior is a late Gothic font (1523) with a Rococo cover showing a puttee (perhaps the Christ Child) stepping on a serpent in front of a globe with a representation of Original Sin. The high altar (1698) is flanked by turquoise Salomonic columns and has an altarpiece of the *Assumption* (Matthias Gasser), while to the left and right are Andreas Kölle and Jakob Auer's Baroque statuary (*Tobias and the Angel*, *St Magnus and the Dragon*). In the crypt, dedicated to a much loved 18C priest of Fließ and two others who were killed in World War II, is an impressive modern bronze and glass monument in the form of a fountain with a bird drinking at the pool (Engelbert Gitterle). The pilgrimage church (**Pfarrkirche Unsere Liebe Frau im Walde**, 1400) at **Serfaus** claims to be the oldest Marian Pilgrimage Church in Tyrol; it has a very early Romanesque statue of the *Madonna* on the altar (light switch by the door), on the back of which is the date 804, supposedly the year when pilgrimages began. The hollowed-out niche in the back may indicate that it was used as a reliquary.

South of the *Sonnenterrasse* is **Tösens**, where there is a church with 15C frescoes, while at **Pfunds**, there is a Rhaetoroman settlement whose name is derived from Latin *fundus*, or 'usable land'; according to the pamphlet issued by the parish, it has had a dramatic history, punctuated by warfare, fire, plague and waves of emigration, all determined by its position as a strategic border town on the Roman-built north–south route (*Via Claudia Augusta*) from Germany to Italy. An interesting footnote is that a peasant named Josef Schwargl killed the last bear of the Upper Inn Valley near here in 1897. There are Gothic houses in the main town, while in the quarter known as **Stuben** on the valley slopes, is the **church of the Assumption** (1470), its entrance flanked by ancient poplars. Some 15C frescoes of high quality (the *Agony in the Garden*, *Deposition from the Cross*, *Calvary*) may be seen in the interior, as also a Baroque altar of 1680 that ingeniously integrates some surviving late Gothic elements and depicts the *Annunciation* and *Nativity*, the *Three Magi*, the *Circumcision* and the *Madonna with Saints*.

From Pfunds it is not far over the **Finstermünzpass** to **Nauders**, very close to the Swiss and Italian borders. A few kilometres to the south is the **Reschenpass**, which brought not only commerce and soldiers (it had a customs post even in Roman times), but also glimmerings of the new faith in the 5C, when the first chapel was built here. The oldest part of the **parish church of St Valentine** is early 16C, however, and the font (1519) and St Michael's altar in the presbytery (1515) also date to this period. In the 19C the church doubled in size with neo-Romanesque elements being added, while the well-known Viennese academic and Nazarene painter, Carl von Blaas, contributed the portrait of *St Valentine* for the high altar. Modern artefacts were added when intensive renovation took place in 1980–82. The most remarkable aspect of the church is the late Baroque **Heilige Grab** (tomb of Christ) by local masters which is only displayed at Easter and combines a picturesque provincialism with extreme theatricality.

South of Nauders the small museum in the privately owned **Schloß Naudersberg** (guided tours Tues–Fri, 16.00, Sun 11.00) is worth a visit and contains a gallery of local artists including Carl von Blaas (1815–94), who was born in Nauders; it also documents the history of skiing in the area and (more interestingly) the castle's role as a regional courthouse. Nauders lay in the so-called **Oberen Gericht**, an area of governance that included the entire Upper Inn Valley and had its centre at Schloß Laudeck lower down the valley at **Ladis**. The **St Leonhard Chapel**, also on the southern outskirts of Nauders, contains 12C frescoes (the oldest in North Tyrol) of *Christ Pantocrator and the Apostles*.

South of Innsbruck to the Brenner Pass

The European transport artery to the south (E6/A13) runs from Innsbruck through the **Wipptal** across the Adriatic/Black Sea watershed to the **Brenner Pass** and the **Alto Adige** (**Südtirol**). The increase in heavy traffic on this route has become a controversial issue which the (as yet unrealised) plan of a railway tunnel between the Inn Valley and Bolzano is designed to alleviate.

The sightseer should avoid the *Autobahn* (toll) and take the old road 182, passing beneath the **Europabrücke** (820m long, 180m high), a stunning feat of engineering (also a favourite with suicides until higher side-barriers were erected to discourage them), which spans the Sill Valley from Patsch to Schönberg and was built between 1959–63. Just beyond it road 183 forks south-west along the **Stubaital** towards Mutterbergalm with a number of churches built by the local priest-architect, Franz de Paula Penz (1707–72), whose masterpiece is the Abbey Church at Wilten (see p 377). Penz formed his own team of builders and himself planned and financed a total of 14 churches needed to cater for a growing population at that time. The church in **Schönberg** (1749) is his work and has a fresco of the *Transfiguration of the Virgin* in the cupola by Giuseppe Cru of Verona. As at Nauders, a Baroque **Heiliges Grab** (*Tomb of Christ*) of theatrical vividness is displayed here at Easter. The walk from Schönberg up to the **Gleinser Höfe** is worth it for the view over the Stubaital and the Serles peak. At **Mieders** Penz barockised the 15C church and planned the parish church at **Telfes**, where he died, and of which parish he was the priest. The **church of St Vitus** (with elegant Rococo stucco by Anton Gigl) in **Fulpmes** is by him, as is the **parish church of St George** at **Neustift**, his last work. The narrowing valley ascends to **Mutterbergalm** (1728m) surrounded by peaks and glaciers.

The main road leads on to **Matrei am Brenner**, the oldest (Celtic) settlement in the **Wipptal**. The *Gasthof zur Uhr* in the town centre is a Gothic inn, once the customs and exchange house, with a vaulted ceiling in the expansive ground-floor hall and a monumental stairway at the rear. The coat of arms on its east wall is that of the Heurling family, who combined two local houses into one in 1471. The **parish church of the Assumption** is notable for its **frescoes** by the Viennese Josef Adam von Mölk (1755) showing *Karl VI victorious against the Turks*, thanks to the protection of the *Rosary Madonna* and of *St Dominic*. The cupola fresco shows *Solomon conducting his mother, Bathsheba, to the Throne*, an allegory of *Christ and the Virgin Mary*. Mölk was also something of an architect and was responsible for alterations to the church in the second half of the 18C. The **Chapel of St John** in the cemetery is a little Gothic gem of 1509 ascribed to the workshop of the Türing family of 'Goldenes Dachl' fame. The intricate rib vaulting has beautiful ornamentation at the cruces and in the spandrels (heads of saints, angel faces, fruit, a bear's head, etc.).

The **parish church of St Erasmus** at **Steinach** was built in the 19C after Franz de Paula Penz's Baroque church was destroyed by fire, but the fine **altar** by Johann Perger survived. Its snow-white figures represent the *Fourteen Holy Helpers*, of whom Erasmus was one (four statues were lost in the fire), while the picture of the church's patron and two other altarpieces are by Martin Knoller, a native of the village. From Steinach it is only a few kilometres to Italy.

East of Innsbruck

Hall in Tyrol

Ten kilometres east of Innsbruck on road 171 is the important town of Hall in Tirol, once walled, which housed the ducal mint and was for a long time the region's main saltwork and depository (the '*Halle*' was the salina, documented since 1263). In Roman times the salt was transported over the Brenner and traded in Italy for wine and other goods. Later, a barrage was erected on the Inn at Hall to catch the logs floated down from the forests in the Upper Inn Valley, which were then processed locally. In 1303, Duke Otto II of Carinthia and Tyrol granted Hall a city charter which raised it to the same privileges as Innsbruck, and in 1477 Sigmund the Rich (of Habsburg) established the mint; the Haller Thaler became thereby the first large silver coin in Europe. Although the town was a significant river port in the 18C (Franz Stephan I's corpse was returned to Vienna from here in 1765, passing down the Inn and the Danube), it declined in the 19C as Innsbruck became the main transport hub.

From the car park by the bastion at the south-west corner of the old city, **Hasegg Castle** and the **Münzerturm** (Tower of the Mint) are quickly reached. The castle (1489) dates to the time of Archduke Sigmund, while Archduke Ferdinand II moved the mint into it the following century. The impressive dodecagonal tower to the south houses the **Old Mint** and is now part of the **Municipal Museum** (Untere Stadtplatz, open July and Aug, 10.00–15.00). The latter's collection includes sacred art by local masters, the history of the town, and documentation of salt-mining. Note in particular the astonishingly plastic and vivid **Waldauf Altar** by Marx Reichlich (see Waldauf-Kapelle below). The **Prince's Hall**, with its Gothic-timbered ceiling and the chapel built by Nikolaus Türing the Elder (1519) are also well worth visiting.

Duke Sigmund founds a currency

In the mid-15C the rich silver veins near Schwaz were discovered, prompting Archduke Sigmund (thereafter known as '*der Münzreiche*'—'the Rich') to found the mint in 1477, which thus overtook the function of the historic, but less defensible one of the Tyrolean Counts at Meran in South Tyrol. The silver *Pfundner* with Sigmund's likeness was the first portrait coin in the German-speaking world. A subsequent and larger coin, the *Guldiner*, was widely used in Europe and soon imitated, particularly in Bohemia's Joachimsthal, where a large number of *Guldiner* were produced and known as *Joachims-Taler*, later simply *Taler*. The famous *Taler* lives on in the English corruption of the word, *dollar*. Sigmund's intelligent currency reform of 1482–86 was highly successful (the money being a precursor of the Euro in its universal exchangeability), and the monetary system he created was to last until the early 19C.

At the heart of the old town, reached up the Langer Graben from the Stadtplatz, is the **parish church of St Nicholas**, consecrated in 1281. The spacious interior is notable for the lack of alignment between the nave and the choir due to the later church being built (1437) on to an earlier chapel. The **frescoes** by Josef

Adam von Mölk (1752) depict scenes from the *Life of St Nicholas*, patron saint of miners and sailors. There are high quality Baroque statues of apostles and church fathers, while the Gothic *Palm Sunday group* (1420) in the choir is a rarity. Note also the fine *Ecce homo* panel (1500) by Marx Reichlich. The Renaissance stoop of 1506 is complemented by a decorated font (1570, the painting on the sides is later). The altarpiece (1657) of the *Madonna with Saints* is by a pupil of Rubens, Erasmus Quellinus. In the **Waldauf Chapel** to the north-east, separated from the nave by an ornate **Gothic grille** is a late Gothic statue of the *Madonna* attributed to Michael Pacher's circle; along the wall are glass cases containing the donor's (Ritter Florian Waldauf von Waldenstein, d. 1510) bizarre collection of relics gathered from all over Christendom, the result of an oath sworn by Florian in 1489 when he and the future Emperor Maximilian I nearly perished on a sea journey. Florian Waldauf was a powerful man who played a crucial role in persuading Sigmund to give up (1490) Tyrol in favour of Maximilian, the deal involving a promise to support Sigmund's estimated 40 illegitimate children. A formidable military man and astute diplomat, he had helped to negotiate Maximilian's release from imprisonment (1488) in Bruges. In Hall he founded a humanist circle of learning (*die Stubengesellschaft*, 1508) with the scholar Dr Johannes Fuxmagen, and in the **Municipal Museum** (see above) may be seen the remarkable wing altar commissioned by him (1505) from Marx Reichlich and featuring portraits of both him and his wife Barbara.

The **Magdalena Chapel** to the south-east of the parish church has a late Gothic carved altarpiece and a superb fresco of the *Last Judgement* (1466) on the south wall. To the north is the Gothic **Rathaus**, once residence of the Counts of Tyrol, while to the west, along the Mustergasse, is the former **Jesuit Church of All Saints** (Father Stefan Huber S.J., 1610), adjoining its monastery with a fine Baroque courtyard. On the way you pass the **Bergbaumuseum** (Mining Museum, Oberer Stadtplatz 1, open April–Oct, Mon–Sat, guided tours on the hour 09.00–11.00, 14.00–17.00). To the south-west is the **Damenstiftskirche** (former church of the Noblewomen's Convent) attributed to Giovanni Lucchese and with fine stucco by Munich masters. Further south, opposite the Castle of Hasegg, is the Rococo **Spitalskirche** (1727). From 1607 the distinguished doctor to the convent was Hippolyt Guarinoni (Guarinonius, 1571–1654), who published his medical textbook *Vom Greuel der Verwüstung des menschlichen Geschlechtes* (*On the Horror of the Ravages of Mankind*) in 1610, a work which, despite its dramatic title, is full of sensible advice on personal hygiene written in rhyming couplets. Unfortunately, Guarinoni was also responsible for writing up the anti-semitic *Legend of Anderl von Rinn* (1621), an inflammatory tale of a Christian boy murdered by Jewish merchants. The story stimulated a cult based on a pilgrimage church built at nearby Judenstein, where the 'murder' had occurred; only in the 1980s did the Bishop of Innsbruck see fit to forbid it.

The *Autobahn* continues east to **Volders**, where the picturesquely idiosyncratic **church of St Charles Borromeo** (1654) stands close against a lay-by. It was built for the Servite Order with money given by Hippolyt Guarinoni (see above), who also planned its architecture. Three subsidiary domes cluster round the main one, symbolising the Holy Trinity merging into doctrinal unity (the motif is repeated in the tower). The interior was altered in Rococo style in 1766 with stucco by Georg Gigl, the main cupola's fresco of the the *Apotheosis of Charles Borromeo* being painted by Martin Knoller.

Schwaz

Further east is Schwaz, a town with a mining tradition reaching into pre-history, but booming from 15C and 16C exploitation of silver and copper (at **Falkenstein** and the **Alte Zeche**). This immensely profitable business was destined to fall largely under the control of the Fuggers of Augsburg (see below). In 1500 there were some 12,000 miners active in Schwaz and its population of 20,000 made it second only to Vienna in size. By 1516 the yearly production of silver had reached 14,000 kg. Tyrolean miners were considered the best experts in Europe and were called to Italy, Sardinia, Brunswick and even England. The richly illustrated *Schwazer Bergbuch* (1566), now in the Ferdinandeum at Innsbruck, was a descriptive and prescriptive document regulating the work of the Schwaz miners, but the latter were not afraid to strike for better wages. They also organised a basic form of social security, much needed when one considers that their life-expectancy was just 35 years. More about local and mining history can be learned in the **Museum der Stadt Schwaz auf Schloß Freundsberg** on a hill east of the town (open April–Oct Fri–Wed, 10.00–16.00), which also has a picture and sculpture gallery showing the work of masters from the region.

In the town below (at the beginning of Franz-Josef-Straße) may be seen the impressively arcaded **Rathaus** (1509), with a façade painted in 1760 by Christof Anton Mayr, while the **Fuggerhaus** (1525) has a modern monument (left-hand corner) to Ulrich Fugger, the first representative of the family to come to Schwaz. The house is just above the **Franciscan Cloister and Church** (1508), the latter's main treasure being a crucifix of 1520 by Loy Hering of Eichstätt.

The jewel of Schwaz, however, is the **parish church of the Assumption**, the original enlarged by Erasmus Grasser in the late 15C to become the largest church in Tyrol, whose great roof required 15,000 copper tiles. The **interior** is revealed as a Gothic hall church with four aisles, its reticulated vaulting supported by three rows of 18 massive columns of black Dolomite. On one of these a bronze epitaph (Stefan Godl, 1531) honours Ulrich Fugger. One half of the church was reserved for the wealthy burghers, the other for the miners, a wooden partition (removed in the 19C) having separated them. Much decoration has been lost, but the surviving **baptismal font** (1470) of red marble is noteworthy for the reliefs of the *Baptism of Christ* and *John the Evangelist*. Also of interest is the *Madonna and Child* (1430, the child is a Baroque replacement) in the north side-altar. In the south choir is another *Madonna*, together with statues of *Sts Anne, Elisabeth and Ursula* dating to c 1500. Note also the Gothic tombstones of Christian Tänzl (1491) and Anna Hofer (1493) by Wolfgang Leb of Wasserburg.

The two-storeyed **Burial Chapel of St Michael** (1507) in the cemetery should not be overlooked: on the lower level are carved scenes of the *Crucifixion* and *Christ on the Mount of Olives* (1510), and on the upper, a late Gothic wing-altar (1506) by Christof Scheller, showing scenes from the *Life of St Vitus*. (Note the carved snakes and lizards on the handrail to the steps, symbolic of the putrefaction of the flesh.) The inscription over the left portal of the chapel reads (in an English paraphrase): '*Here lie we, levelled by Death's law/Knight and nobleman, rich* *and poor–1506'*. Visits to the chapel are by appointment (☎ 05242-63240, or with the city tour starting from *Tourismusverband*, Franz-Josef-Straße 26, every Tues at 10.00).

The Fugger Banking House

In the mid-14C, the Fuggers were Augsburg weavers of fustian, but from 1440 they became involved in commerce and finance; eventually they came to dominate the copper, silver and gold production of Central Europe. Maximilian I was almost completely dependent on Jakob Fugger 'the Wealthy' (1459–1525), mortgaging for cash (of which there was never enough to finance his extravagance) countships, trading privileges, customs duties and mines (silver production for eight, copper production for four years). In the end the Emperor was paying 35 per cent interest on Fugger loans. It was again Jakob Fugger who 'financed' the election (1519) of Karl V to the office of Holy Roman Emperor, bribes to the Electors reputedly costing a cool 1 million Gulden. The irony is that Schwaz and the Fuggers helped to realise Karl's New World expansion, thus opening up such a quantity of gold and silver reserves in the Americas that Schwaz, with its more costly extraction, was eventually priced out of the market. In the mid-17C, the Fuggers withdrew from the loss-making enterprise in Schwaz, although extraction continued in increasingly adverse economic conditions until the mines were closed in 1827.

A visit to the **Schausilberbergwerk** (the medieval silver-mine) is recommended (Alte Landstraße 3A, open in summer daily, 08.30–17.00, in winter 09.30–16.00. Tours last 2hrs).

Two kilometres north of Schwaz, above Vomp, is the erstwhile Benedictine **Abbey of Fiecht** (Jakob Singer of Götzens, 1750). The stucco and symbols of the apostles in the church are by J.G. Üblher and Franz Xaver Feichtmayr (who was also responsible for the high altar), while the frescoes (in the nave) of *Jesus in the Temple*, the *Adoration of the Shepherds*, the *Betrothal of the Virgin*, (in the transept) of the *Three Magi*, the *Four Continents*, (in the choir) of the *Death of St Joseph* and the *Holy Family*, are all by Matthäus Günther (completed 1755).

A few kilometres west is the late Gothic and partly Renaissance **Schloß Tratzberg** above **Stans** (access from the

Schloß Tratzberg

car park, 10mins on foot. Guided tours April–Oct, daily except Mon at 10.00, 11.00, 12.00, 14.00, 15.00, 16.00. Tours last about 1hr). The rich mining family of Tänzl began rebuilding the Schloß in 1500 after its predecessor, a border fortress against the Bavarians, was destroyed by fire. Christoph Reichartinger, *Baumeister* of the Schwazer parish church, was commissioned to produce a luxurious residence (not a fortress) surpassing all other Tyrolean castles. The tour is an experience, not least because the show rooms retain their Gothic decoration and in some cases unique Gothic furnishings (tables, cupboards, commodes and even a bed). The **Armoury** and **Fugger Rooms** are of interest (the Fuggers having owned the Schloß for a while), but the high point is the **Habsburgersaal**. In this room, with its mighty coffered ceiling resting on red marble columns, 46m of wall is covered with the family tree of the dynasty, comprising 148 of Maximilian's forebears. Since Maximilian's granddaughter, Maria of Hungary is featured as a three-year-old, the painting could not be earlier than 1508, and is thought to be by a Schwazer painter, appropriately named Hans Maler.

East of Tratzberg is the town of **Jenbach**, beyond which, at **Wiesing**, narrow-gauge or cogwheel railways leave for the **Zillertal** and the **Achensee** (930m), the latter being the largest lake in Tyrol and lying between the **Karwendelgebirge** and the **Rofan**. The Achensee cogwheel railway (1889) claims to have the oldest steam engines operating in Europe. The **Achental** beyond the lake continues towards the German border, but before the Achensee is reached, you come to the village of **Eben**, where the **Notburga-Kirche** preserves the supposed remains of St Notburga (c 1265–c 1313).

St Notburga: from domestic drudge to popular saint

St Notburga (d. 1313) is the patron of hired hands in Tyrol and Bavaria, having once been dismissed from nearby Schloß Rottenburg for giving surplus food to the poor, instead of to the pigs as ordered. When the peasants she subsequently worked for in Eben refused her permission to take Sunday off for her devotions, she tossed her sickle dramatically into the air, where (wonder of wonders!) it remained suspended as a sign of divine solidarity. Later she appears to have been recalled to the castle, and it was there that she died. Evidently, the descendants of the castle's owners wished to make reparation for Notburga's mistreatment, since one of them (the Countess of Tannberg) went to considerable lengths to 'discover' Notburga's bones in 1718. Since the Barockisation of the parish church in 1738, the silk-clad skeleton has a place of honour on the colourfully decorated high altar: she has been placed upright, holding her sickle in her bone hand, with her skull veiled. Frescoes in the church by Christoph Anton Mayr relate the legends associated with her. The focus of affection for all exploited drudges, Notburga found little favour with the church in the heyday of her cult, but was finally canonised in 1862.

ZILLERTAL

From **Strass** to the south, road 169 leads 30km down the beautiful but now rather touristy Zillertal with its foaming mountain streams falling precipitously from rugged peaks.

History of the Zillertal

Since the 6C the Zillertal has been inhabited by tough, industrious and independent-minded people of *bajuwarischen* (ur-Bavarian) stock. Lying on the border of the Brixen (now Innsbruck) and Salzburg bishoprics, as also (until 1504) on that of the governance of Bavarian Dukes and Tyrolean rulers (who shared the proceeds of the local mines up to the 16C), the Zillertal was always an area of conflicting interests and confessions. Its hard-working people also gained a reputation for their specialist production of healing oils and ointments made from local recipes, as well as scythes, blankets, gloves and other products. The Zillertaler were also renowned for their music making: an early performance (1822) of Franz Xaver Gruber and Josef Mohr's *Silent Night* (see p 320) was given by the noted Rainer family choir before Franz Joseph and the Russian Tsar at Schloß Fügen in the days when this enduringly beautiful carol was still regarded as a 'folksong'. The Rainer Family and other Zillertaler singing groups toured Europe and America in the 19C, popularising the musical idiom of their homeland.

The divided competence of Salzburg and Tyrol in the Zillertal until 1803 was the main reason that Protestantism survived *sub rosa* in the valley. However, after a number of villagers had publicly left the Catholic church in 1826, the authorities reacted in 1837 by expelling all the *Inklinanten* (430 families who preferred Lutheranism to Catholicism), who opted to go to Prussian Silesia. Although the order came from the Emperor Ferdinand (and had been prepared under his narrow-minded predecessor, Franz I), the main pressure for expulsion came from the local aristocracy in league with the church. These persecuted families were to prove doubly unlucky—their descendants were expelled in their turn from Silesia after 1945, this time by the Poles. Lutheran parishes remained forbidden in Tyrol until 1873.

On a hill above **Fügen** is a 15C Gothic church of St Pankraz with intricate net and star vaulting and frescoes of New Testament scenes on the walls. The parish church is less interesting, although the Baroque wooden sculptures along the walls of the nave by Franz Xaver Nißl make a visit worthwhile. The parish church at **Uderns** has a painting (under the organ loft) of the *Nativity* attributed to Franz Anton Maulbertsch and carved figures of *Mary Magdalene* and *St Anne with the Virgin*, again by Franz Xaver Nißl.

From **Kaltenbach** the panoramic **Zillertaler Höhenstraße** (toll; closed in winter) begins its semi-circular course, returning to the main road either at Aschau or (if the steep and windy main section is taken) at **Hippach**. The latter is a favoured winter sports and climbers' resort, one of several in the valley. **Zell am Ziller** (the name derived from the cells of its 8C monks) grew prosperous from goldmining in the 17C. Its **parish church of St Vitus** has a Gothic tower, the rest of the building (1782) being Rococo and designed by Wolfgang Hagenauer of Salzburg, but built by his Tyrolean rival, Andrä Hueber. In the massive dome is a fresco of the *Trinity* (1779) by Franz Anton Zeiller.

To the south lies picturesque **Mayrhofen**, beyond which is the frontier range of the glacier-rich Zillertaler Alpen. The town is a favourite resort for skiing and hiking. In the summer, cable cars take walkers up to the Penken and Ahorn peaks. To the east runs road 165, passing into Land Salzburg via the **Gerlospaß**, beyond which a switchback toll road leads (beyond the province border) to the **Krimmler Wasserfälle**, the highest waterfalls in Austria with a dramatic triple-tiered drop of 380m.

From **Brixlegg**, north-east of Schwaz on road 171, a minor road leads up to **Alpbach**, host to the European Forum in the last week of August, which is attended by luminaries from all over Europe (the new conference centre opened in 1999). A central figure of these open-ended discussions ('conducted', said Ernst Bloch, 'in a spirit of Utopian tolerance and freedom') was Sir Karl Popper, but figures as diverse as Indira Gandhi and Friedrich Dürrenmatt have also featured. The forum grew out of the 'High School Weeks' founded jointly at the end of the war by a philosophy professor at Innsbruck (whose brother owned a hotel in Alpbach) and the publisher, Otto Molden.

Further east on road 171, atmospheric **Rattenberg** (Bavarian territory until 1504) grew rich like neighbouring Brixlegg from copper-mining and likewise declined with the latter. The **parish church of St Virgil** (1437) resembles Schwaz in that burghers and miners worshipped in separate naves. The delicate stucco is by Anton Gigl, the frescoes in the choir (the *Light of Mount Tabor* and the *Assumption*) are by Simon Faistenberger, while those in the north nave (the *Last Supper*), under the organ (an *Allegory of Faith* featuring the Bavarian born *Emperor (St) Henry II and his wife* (*St Cunegund*), and in the south nave (*Scenes from the Life of the Virgin*) are by Matthäus Günther (1737). The fine wooden sculptures of saints on the altar in the south choir include the church's patron, Fergal ('*Virgil*'), an 8C Salzburg Abbot of Irish extraction, and are the work of Johann Meinrad Guggenbichler from Mondsee. There are other elegant Rococo altars and a pulpit with colourful stucco lustro.

The **Servite Church of St Augustine** close to the River Inn was altered to Baroque in 1707–09 by a member of the Carlone dynasty of architects and has frescoes (1711) by Johann Waldmann (the *Four Evangelists*, the *Apotheosis of St Augustine* and scenes from the latter's life). The ruins of the old castle (built in the 11C and much extended by Maximilian I) lour above the town. It has indeed unhappy associations, since the distinguished jurist and Chancellor of Tyrol, Wilhelm Bienner (or Biener), was tried on framed charges by nobles, who feared the limitations he sought to put on their power, and executed here in 1651 before an Archducal pardon could reach him. Across the river in the *Gemeinde* of **Kramsach** is the **Museum Tiroler Bauernhöfe** (Farmhouse Museum, open Easter–31 Oct, daily 09.00–18.00).

At **Wörgl** on the edge of the attractive **Wildschönau** (the valley of the Wildschönauer Ache river) the road divides three ways, road 170 leading to **Kitzbühel** via **Hopfgarten**, road 312 to **St Johann in Tirol**, the *Autobahn* and road 171 to **Kufstein**. Perhaps the most delightful village of the Wildschönau is that of Oberau, which boasts a substantial Baroque parish church (Hans

Holzmeister, 1752) frescoed by Josef Adam von Mölk with scenes from the *Life of St Margaret*, to whom the church is dedicated. The octagonal **Antonius Chapel** (1674) has an idiosyncratic fresco in the cupola, featuring the *Life of St Anthony* painted around 1700, but in an archaising style.

Road 170 leads up the Brixental to the ancient market town of **Hopfgarten**. The **church of St Leonard and St James** (1764, Kassian Singer and Andrä Hueber) has a striking façade, its effects being due to the unusual arrangement of decorative windows above the main entrance and handsome twin towers.

Kitzbühel

Not far from Brixen is famous Kitzbühel (once '*Chizzo*'—the town's coat of arms showing a young chamois or goat ('*Kitz*'), is a mistaken etymon). In this winter sports paradise for the glitterati (the 3.5km *Hahnenkamm* ski-run down the 'Streif' racing route is world famous), the winter prices ascend into the stratosphere, but are a little more moderate in summer, when there is also an important tennis tournament. Riches are nothing new to Kitzbühel, which has been a staging-post on the Italy-Bavaria trade route at least since Roman times, and was also a centre of silver- and copper-mining. Initially it lay under German influence, being in the possession of the Bamberg bishopric from its first mention in documents (1160), until Maximilian I annexed it for Tyrol in 1505.

The colourful burgher houses of the **Hinterstadt** recall the prosperous mining and trading eras, as does the generous number of places of worship (six in all). Of the latter, the **parish church of St Andrew** is notable for the **high altar** (1663) by the sculptor member (Benedikt Faistenberger) of an important local dynasty of artists and the superb *Kupferschmiedepitaph* (1520) by Hans Frosch with sandstone and red marble passion scenes. The altarpiece of the *Virgin Mary* and the *Fathers of the Church* is by a German painter, Johann Spillenberger. The **Rosa-Kapelle** adjoining the choir should not be overlooked, with its fresco of the morbidly penitential *St Rose of Lima* by Simon Benedikt Faistenberger (grandson of Benedikt) and its Gothic *Madonna* (1450). (The rather odd choice of patron for the chapel may have something to do with the fact that Rose's punishing way of life was initially determined by her parents' financial losses in a mining venture, and with her demonstrative fellow-feeling for the poor and under-privileged.)

The **Liebfrauenkirche** nearby, at the north end of Vorderstadt on the Kirchbichl is a two-storeyed Gothic burial chapel with Baroque (1735) frescoes in the upper part, featuring the *Coronation of the Virgin*, the *Virgin Mary as Protector of Mankind*, *St Mary with St Andrew* and (over the organ loft) *King David*, all by Simon Benedikt Faistenberger and considered his best work. The representation of *Our Lady of Succour* over the altar is a copy of the same by Lukas Cranach in the Innsbrucker Stadtpfarrkirche.

The diminutive neo-classical **Bürgerspitalkirche** (1837) also nearby, has a Gothic crucifixion group of note (*Christ, Simon of Cyrene and a Myrmidon*), while the main interest of the **Katharinen-Kirche** is the 16C winged altar showing *St Anne, St Christopher, St Florian* and (on the wings) *Sts Denis and Sebastian*. The oval Chapel of Johann Nepomuk at the foot of the Kirchbichl again has frescoes by Simon Benedikt Faistenberger (1727) and is lavishly stuccoed. Kitzbühel's modern Lutheran Church (1962) is the work of Clemens Holzmeister, who also built a chapel (1959) on the Hahnenkamm. The **Heimatmuseum** (Hinterstadt 32, open Mon–Sat, 10.00–12.30, longer in summer) in the former grain store documents the history of mining in the Kitzbühel region and also has a section about skiing. Perhaps the most vivid recorder of mountain activities in painting is the Kitzbühel artist, Alfons Walde (1891–1951), also an architect who designed the termini of the *Hahnenkammbahn*, and whose naturalist evocations of the region may be seen in the **Alfons-Walde-Galerie** (part of the museum).

Close to Kitzbühel at **Hinterobenau** to the north is the **Tiroler Bauernhausmuseum** (open daily 13.00–18.00), located in a 500-year-old farmhouse equipped and furnished as it would have been 100 years ago. **Kapsburg** south of the town is a 17C mansion, whose land borders on that comparative rarity in Austria, a golf course, while the 16C **Schloß Lebenberg** to the north-west belonged (like Kapsburg) to the Lamberg Counts, who had grown rich from copper-mining (it is now a hotel). Two kilometres north-west is the **Schwarzsee**, a popular bathing resort fed by warm springs that keep the temperature to a pleasant 27°C, and just beyond it the 15C **Schloß Münichau**, another attractive hotel. At **Oberaurach** (8km south-west) is the **Wildpark Tirol** (open daily 09.00–17.00, feeding time 14.00, closed Nov–Dec) where some 200 animals may be viewed in natural surroundings.

At Kitzbühel the road forks, road 161 leading to Jochberg, thence to Paß Thurn and into Land Salzburg. The same road heading north leads via Oberndorf to **St Johann in Tirol**, the latter lying in the broad valley where several mountain streams converge. The **parish church of the Assumption** contains frescoes of *Mary* and the *Holy Trinity* by Simon Benedikt Faistenberger in the choir and has a fine high altar by Anton Gigl. Nearby is the **Antoniuskapelle** with a cupola fresco of the *Transfiguration of St Anthony* against a background of the grim **Wilder Kaiser** massif of limestone and dolomite.

Kufstein

The E17 (road 312) leads back from St Johann towards **Wörgl**, a right turn on to road 173 at Hauning bringing you along the **Weißache** towards Kufstein (first mentioned as *Caofstein* in a document of 788, and so-called because of the shape of the crag on which the Burg is situated). The town lies on the Bavarian border, being the historic and strategically vital gateway to Tyrol. In the 14C there was a drawbridge over the inn here—now there is an *Autobahn*, whose partial collapse in the middle of the tourist season a few years back caused tailbacks on half the *Autobahns* of Germany. Maximilian I acquired Kufstein in 1504, though not without a fight: he had to bring his huge new cannons (affectionately known as '*Purlepaus*' and '*Weckauf*', i.e. 'Wake up') along the river from Innsbruck, and bombard the **Burg** into submission, when its constable (Hans von Pienzenau) changed his allegiance to the advancing German troops. Pienzenau was executed for his pains. Maximilian's claim to the town was based on his successful mediation in the Bavarian inheritance dispute, for which Kufstein (together with Rattenberg and Kitzbühel) were to be his reward. It had already briefly been in Habsburg possession between 1363 and 1369 under Margarete Maultasch, before reverting to Bavaria. However, the Wittelsbachs were to intervene once more in its chequered history when their troops burned it to the ground (1703) during the War of the Spanish Succession.

The oft-disputed **Festung** (Fortress) of Kufstein (reached by lift from

Römerhofgasse) was greatly enlarged by Maximilian, who added the **Kaiserturm** with cannon positions on four floors, the tower later serving as a prison. The **Obere Schloßkaserne** was built at various times between the 16C and 18C, while the medieval part (including the Bürgerturm) lies to the north. Located in the fortress is the **Heimatmuseum** (open April–26 Oct daily 09.00–18.00. Guided tours 10.30, 13.00 and 15.00), one of the best of its kind and containing pre-historical archaeological remains from the nearby **Tischoferhöhle** (Tischofer Cave), as well as ethnological, folkloristic, fine art, geological and zoological displays relating to the region. In the **Bürgerturm** is a celebrated **Heldenorgel** (Heroes' Organ, 1931), the biggest in the world with 4307 pipes and 46 stops, which is played daily at noon (May–Sept also at 18.00) in memory of those who died in the two World Wars, and can be heard over a distance of 6km.

The **parish church of St Vitus** in the town below is the latest on a site where the earliest sanctuary was built in Carolingian times. Notable on the south wall are the late Gothic tombstones, especially Wolfgang Leb's extraordinary **tomb of Hans Paumgartner** (d. 1493): beneath the latter's portrait, the sculptor has gleefully represented his corpse half-devoured by worms, a *memento mori* designed to concentrate the minds of epicures. There are likewise Gothic gravestones against the walls of the nearby **Dreifaltigkeitskapelle** (Chapel of the Holy Trinity, 1500), together with a fine guilloche screen in the lower chapel. The Rococo altar (1765) in the upper chapel has elegant gilded carvings.

Kufstein is surrounded by a landscape of great beauty with fine views from the **Stadtberg** to the south-east, the **Duxer Köpfl** to the north-east and **Pendling** to the south-west. The **Kaisergebirge** (or simply '*Kaiser*') to the east is a scenically superb nature reserve with precipitous crags and dramatic gorges. The northern **Zahmer Kaiser** (or 'Tame Emperor') is separated by the **Kaisertal** from the **Wilder Kaiser** ('Wild Emperor'), whose highest point is the **Ellmauer Halt** (2344m). At **Thiersee**, 5km to the west of Kufstein, a Passion play is held every six years (since 1799).

North-east of Kufstein is the town of **Ebbs**, with a parish church built by Abraham Millauer (1750), and frescoed by Josef Adam von Mölk with scenes from the *Life of the Virgin*. The town is also noted for its stud of Haflingers (named after the South Tyrolean town of Hafling), sturdy little chestnuts (135–145cm) with white manes and tails whose uniform colouring and configuration goes back to a half-bred stallion ancestor, born in 1874. At **Erl** further to the north, Passion plays have been held every four years since 1613; they are now performed in an attractive modern theatre (1959) designed by Robert Schuler (there are also concerts and opera).

Osttirol (East Tyrol)

LIENZ
• • • • • •

Practical information

Tourist information
Europaplatz 1. ☎ 04852 65265. Fax 65265-2.

Hotels
☆☆☆☆ *Hotel Sonne* (A-9900, **Lienz**, Südtiroler Platz 8. ☎ 04852 63311. Fax. 04852 63314). A Best Western hotel; quiet, own garage, good restaurant.
☆☆☆ *Hotel Goldried* (Goldriedstraße 15, A-9971 **Matrei in Osttirol**.
☎ 04875 6113–0). A well-appointed hotel with 'Austrian-Swedish' ambience in its *Hirschenstube* restaurant and pleasant al fresco eating on the terrace in summer.

Restaurants
Adlerstüberl, Andrä-Kranz-Gasse 7. Traditional restaurant with local specialities.
Gasthof Neuwirt, Schweizergasse 22. The speciality is fish and there are also vegetarian dishes. Outdoor seating in summer.

The principal town of mountainous **Osttirol** (East Tyrol) is **Lienz**. Geographically the area encompasses the **Oberen Drautal** (Upper Drau Valley), the **Iseltal** (Isel Valley) with its offshoots of the Defereggen, Virgen, Tauern and Kalser valleys, and finally the headwaters of the River Gail. To the north it is bordered by the **Hohe Tauern** mountains, including the Großglockner and Großvenediger, to the east by the **Schober** range, to the west by the **Rieserferner** mountains, and to the south by the **Karnische Alpen** (Carnic Alps) and the **Lienzer Dolomiten**.

History of Osttirol

Since South Tyrol (Südtirol; in Italian, Trentino-Alto-Adige) became part of Italy in 1919, East Tyrol's direct link to Innsbruck was severed and its economic orientation is now towards Carinthia, of which indeed it was originally a part as the 'Windisch-Matrei', a name alluding to its early Slav inhabitants. It was for long attached to the territories of the Görz (Gorician) counts before passing (by an inheritance treaty dating to 1394) to the Habsburgs in 1500, at which point it was united with Tyrol. The Nazis incorporated the region with Carinthia and after the war it was in the British occupation zone for ten years. A railway corridor (**Eisenbahn-Korridor**) was agreed with the Italians, so that people passing from one part of Austria to another through Italian territory (South Tyrol) could do so without border formalities. (Similar arrangements exist elsewhere in Austria, for example, with Bavaria and (surprisingly) even with Hungary, a train having run from north to south Burgenland via Sopron throughout the Cold War).

The building of the **Großglocknerstraße** in the 1930s reduced East Tyrol's isolation, while in the 1960s, the **Felbertauern Tunnel** made a new link between East Tyrol and the Salzburger Pinzgau.

OSTTIROL

The area is less developed for tourism than most other parts of Austria and retains a natural charm that attracts in the main hikers and alpinists, for whom there is an extensive network of *Hütten* (alpine huts) offering rest and refreshments. There are, of course, plenty of skiing facilities as well. The **Hohe Tauern** is a national park with well signposted information routes (*Lehrwege*) and numerous observation points, as well as wildlife parks, waterfalls, local museums, etc. (Information: Nationalparkrat, Rauterplatz 1, A-9971, Matrei in Tyrol. ☎ 04875 5161-0. Fax: 04875 5161-20). Among the wildlife that can be encountered are ibex, chamois, marmots and golden eagles; in summer also white-headed vultures. Of smaller creatures, the snowmouse and snowfinch and alpine salamanders are specialities, besides various plant and flower rarities that thrive in high altitudes and around the glaciers.

East Tyrol can be approached from Kufstein (see p 397) over the Kitzbüheler Alpen via Kitzbühel itself, Mittersill and the Felbertauern Tunnel. However, the approach may be more convenient from Carinthia, along the Drau Valley from Spittal.

The main town of **Lienz** (population 12,000) has an agreeable southern ambience, no doubt due to the high annual number of hours of sunshine, as well as the lively cafés spreading on to the pavements in summer and the colourful façades of the houses. Its name first occurs in the 11C as *locus luenzina* (from Celtic *loncina*, perhaps a reference to the broad bow of the River Drau at this point). The Gorician counts settled their residence here (1280) in **Schloss Bruck** and enlarged the town, which was growing prosperous from its situation at the intersection of the Felbertauern and Pustertal trading routes. In 1500 it became Habsburg property and was thereafter pledged to various lords until in 1785 it was re-acquired by the Habsburgs during the centralising drive of Joseph II.

On the **Hauptplatz** is the **Liebburg** (now the **Rathaus**), built in 1604 and twice burned down until placed sensibly in the protection of St Florian, which proved efficacious. Over the Renaissance portal is the coat of arms of the Wolkenstein counts, the first builders of the Liebburg and at that time the local rulers.

To the north-west (along the Muchargasse) is the former **Franciscan** (and earlier Carmelite) **monastery**, whose 15C church has frescoes of 1440 on the south and west walls. Sebastian Gerum is the creator of the three scenes (1468) over the second side-altar on the right, while in the choir, the *Passion* and *Coronation of the Virgin* (the latter showing the Trinity as three persons under the coronation mantle) are later works of c 1500. The wooden *pietà* on the furthest side-altar on the left is also notable.

Heading west along the Schweizergasse, you come at the end (left) to the oldest house of Lienz (the **Rieplerhaus**) and nearby the **Rieplerschmiede**, a former forge that has been made into a museum showing the original workplace, together with a medieval bath etc. The museum is open from Palm Sunday–Oct, 10.00–17.00, in summer to 18.00). The so-called **Klösterle** (the Convent and Church of the Dominican sisters) is close to the bridge on the other side of the road junction from the Rieplerschmiede, and dates to Romanesque times (1220) with Gothic alterations and additions. Inside the church is Hans André's fresco of the *Virgin Mediatrix*, together with a massive wooden sculpture by Hans Troyer (the *Visitation* and *St Hyacinth*, the founder of the order). The nuns' choir to the west has a fine wrought-iron grille by Hermann Pedit.

A right turn from Schweizergasse to the north brings you across the Isel river and shortly to the **parish church of St Andrew** (1457). In the stellar vaulted vestibule are some fine tombs of red marble by Christoph Geiger made for the last Count of Görz (Leonhard I) (1507) and Michael of Wolkenstein (d. 1525) and his wife (1510). The **interior** has a number of interesting features, including J.A. Mölk's ceiling fresco in the presbytery (1761) of *St Andrew interceding for the City of Lienz in time of Trouble* and elsewhere the *Four Evangelists* by the same artist. The altarpiece (1761) is by Anton Zoller and shows *St Andrew taking up the Cross*, while the altar statues (1765) of *St Peter*, *St Paul*, and the Salzburg Bishops *Rupert* and *Virgil*, are by Franz Engele. On the right-hand **Altar of the Cross** is a striking relief of *Abraham sacrificing Isaac* (1776) by Johann Paterer, who also created the standing figures (1775, the *Virgin Mary*, *St John*, *Mary Magdalene*). In the crypt is a crucifixion group dated to 1510 and a fine *pietà* (after 1400). Note also the late Gothic *Christ Pantocrator* on the triumphal arch.

The arcades and war memorial chapel (1924–25) of St Andrew's cemetery

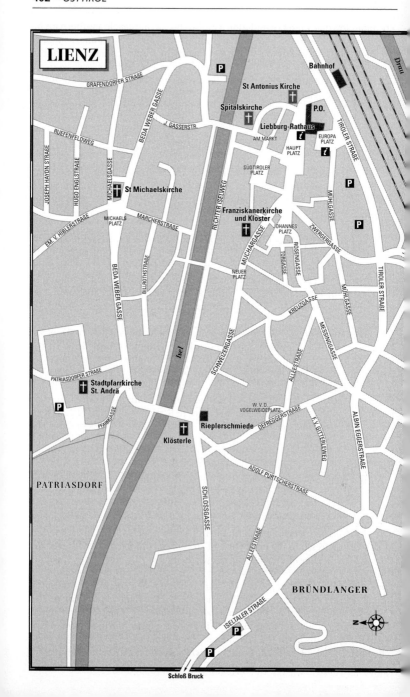

LIENZ

Drau

GRAFENDORFER STRAßE

P

Bahnhof

St Antonius Kirche ✝

BEDA WEBER GASSE

J. GASSERSTR.

Spitalskirche ✝

P.O.

Liebburg-Rathaus

RUEFENFELDWEG

AM MARKT

ℹ

EUROPA PLATZ

TIROLER STRAßE

JOSEPH HAYDN STRAßE

HUGO ENGLSTRAßE

MICHAELSGASSE

HAUPT PLATZ

ℹ

St Michaelskirche ✝

SÜDTIROLER PLATZ

RECHTER ISELWEG

MÜHLGASSE

P

E.M. V. HIBLERSTRAßE

MICHAELS PLATZ

MARCHERSTRAßE

Franziskanerkirche und Kloster ✝

JOHANNES PLATZ

ZWERGERGASSE

P

BEDA WEBER GASSE

BILLROTHSTRAßE

MUCHARGASSE

NEUER PLATZ

TÖRGASSE

ROSENGASSE

TIROLER STRAßE

KREUZGASSE

MÜHLGASSE

Isel

SCHWEIZERGASSE

ALLESTRAßE

MESSINGGASSE

PATRIASDORFER STRAßE

P

Stadtpfarrkirche St. Andrä ✝

W.V.D. VOGELWEIDEPLATZ

DEFREGGERSTRAßE

F.V. GITTERLEWEG

ALBIN EGGERSTRAßE

PFARRGASSE

✝ Klösterle

Rieplerschmiede

ADOLF PURTSCHERSTRAßE

PATRIASDORF

SCHLOSSGASSE

ALLESTRAßE

BRÜNDLANGER

N

P

ISELTALER STRAßE

P

Schloß Bruck

were designed by Clemens Holzmeister, the chapel having important paintings (see below) by Albin Egger-Lienz (1868–1926), whose grave is here. His astonishing and idiosyncratic **cycle of pictures** begins with the *Sower and the Devil* (creative and destructive forces); then comes *The Nameless* (a horrifying evocation of soldiers surging en masse to death), followed by *Sacrificial Death* and finally *The Resurrected*. The last-named, a vision of hope, shows an unconventional version of the risen Christ, derided *inter alia* as 'an Indian chieftain of which only the ring was missing from the nose' (casual racism comes naturally to over-pious art critics). The Vatican Holy Office forbad religious services in the chapel and the local clergy at first obstructed the artist's wish to be buried here. Egger-Lienz's work was also too *outré* for the Viennese artistic establishment, which refused to admit him as a teacher at the Academy in 1899, although Vienna did make amends with a retrospective exhibition in 1925.

A worthwile detour to the east along Beda-Weber-Gasse to Michaelsplatz brings you to the interesting **church of St Michael** *('am Rindermarkt')*, a small late Gothic edifice having Andrä and Bartmä Viertaler's marvellous vaulting, the latter luxuriously, even self-indulgently decorative and having given up any pretence of functionality. The flower-shaped bosses and branch-like ribs of the choir vault are especially striking examples of the Viertalers' work. On the Baroque high altar (1683) is a monumental statue of *St Michael* and elsewhere a large number of early 16C tombs of local lords (Graben, Sumereck, etc.). The coat of arms (1531) of Andre von Graben, together with frescoes and inscriptions, may be seen on the rear wall of the gallery.

Returning across the Isel by the same bridge, the Schlossgasse is taken to reach the Schlossberg and **Schloss Bruck** (1280: the keep, main gate and living quarters; 16C, the outer bailey, towers, moat, etc.). In the chapel with a ribbed vault are some remnants of Romanesque frescoes (1270) by the south window and later painting on both the vault and walls, together with a throne of grace (*Gnadenstuhl*, 1452) in the soft Gothic style by Nikolaus Kentner. The notable murals on the north, east and south walls (c 1499) are by Simon von Taisten (the court painter of Leonhard I), and show the *Virgin protecting Supplicants under her Cloak* and a lovely *Annunciation*. Notwithstanding his astonishing talent, Simon was treated badly by his patron, who was always short of money to pay him. After Leonhard's death, the artist addressed a letter to the new lord, the Habsburg Maximilian I (who was also perennially short of money), requesting that his outstanding honorarium be paid, but received no reply.

In the **Upper Castle** the little Görzer altar (*Görzer Altärchen*) is also by Simon. The Schloss is now a museum displaying finds from the archaeological excavations of the Celtic and Roman periods, together with Tyrolean artefacts of various kinds. It also has a selection of pictures by two of Tyrol's greatest artists, Albin Egger-Lienz (see above) and Franz von Defregger (1835–1921), the latter a student of Piloty in Munich. Notable here is Egger-Lienz's *Dance of Death*, together with a much-reproduced motif of the *Two Alpine Mowers*, a highly stylised treatment of a theme reminiscent of Jean-François Millet. Later works by Egger-Lienz were strongly influenced by Expressionism. A notable picture by Defregger is his rendering of *The Cross* (1901), showing Pustertaler peasants bearing a crucifix into battle against the French in 1809. The Schloss is open April–Oct, Tues–Sun, 10.00–17.00, to 18.00 in summer.

West of Lienz: along the Drau Valley

Road 100 follows the Upper Drau valley (part of the *Pustertal*) to the Italian (South Tyrol) border at Vierschach/Versciaco, close to a watershed for the Mediterranean and Black Sea directed rivers (the Rienz and the Drau). To the north are the **Defereggen Mountains** and to the south the **Lienzer Dolomiten** and the **Karnischen Alpen**.

At Leisach, where only a portal (1660) of the fortress survives, a major battle of the Tyrolean War of Liberation took place in 1809, depicted by Defregger (see above). From Thal-Assling a few kilometres further west, the Pustertaler Höhenstrasse winds up over the sunny terraces of the lower Defereggen mountain slopes.

At **Oberassling** is a 15C Gothic **church** dedicated to St Korbinian, a local saint of French origin, the net vault having representations of him on the bosses. There is a fresco cycle (1579) by André Peuerweg with 30 scenes from the *Passion* and a winged altar (1430) by the Master of St Sigmund. Friedrich Pacher (brother of the more famous Michael) made the Korbinian altar (1480) and the Magdalene altar (1498). The **pilgrimage church of St Justina** to the west also has an altar by Pacher, a statue of the dedicatee saint (1430) and a fresco of *St Christopher* (1513) on the outside wall. (The obscure Justina was much revered in Padua and even honoured with a medieval forgery claiming that she had been baptised by a disciple of St Peter and martyred under Nero.)

Further west is **Anras**, which was the summer seat of the Bishops of Brixen up to 1803, the Baroque residence now being a cultural centre. The **parish church of St Diakon and St Stephen** (13C, rebuilt after a fire in the 15C) has a cemetery chapel where the winged altar (1513) and frescoes from the old church are displayed (access on Sun and PH). The new **church of St Stephen** was built (1757) adjacent to it by Franz de Paula Penz and has frescoes (1754) by Martin Knoller, a pupil of Troger (*St Stephen*, the *Eucharist*, etc.) and an altarpiece (1755) of the *Stoning of St Stephen* by Anton Zoller.

North of Straßen is the Schloss at **Heinfels**, where the parish church has a *Befreeing of St Peter* (1500) by Simon von Taisten. Just before the border is **Sillian**, with fine views over the Pustertal from the Baroque **parish church** (1760), in whose cemetery some of the Görz counts are buried. The frescoes in the vault are by Josef Adam von Mölk (1760) and there is a statue of the *Madonna* dating to 1450 on the altar. In Strassen itself, **St James's Church** has some remarkable Gothic frescoes in the choir showing the *Life and Passion of Christ* and the *Workings of Mercy as answer to God's Love*. Below on the outskirts of the village is the Baroque **Holy Trinity Church** (1641), with a cupola painted (1768) by Franz Anton Zoller showing the *Mission of St Francis Xaver*, and the *Life of the Virgin*. Just to the north of Straßen, the village of **Tessenberg** is worth visiting for the frescoes (c 1500) by Ruprecht Pötsch of Brixen in the **parish church**. They concern the *Life of John the Baptist* (to whom the church is dedicated) and illustrate in didactic manner the fulfilment of Old Testament prophecies.

The Gailtal (Lesachtal)

A turning south-east off road 100 at Strassen leads along the Karnische Dolomitenstrasse, which runs between the mountains of the same name and the Lienzer Dolomiten towards the Carinthian border at Maria Luggau. It passes over the Gail/Gailbach watershed via the **Kartitscher Sattel** (1525m) to

Obertilliach, a village settled by Silesian migrants in the 17C. In the **Nikolauskapelle** here are frescoes of 1490 by Simon von Taisten. This area is perhaps the most remote and unspoiled in Tyrol.

North-west from Lienz: along the Isel Valley

Road 108 leads north-west from Lienz through **Oberlienz**, with its attractive peasant houses and a mill that can be visited. At **Ainet** nearby the last (vain) battle of the Tyrolean War of Liberation took place on the 8 December 1809, but Andreas Hofer was already a hunted man (see p 374). Beyond the ruins of the **Kienburg** on your left, you come to a junction at **Huben**, the western road leading along the Defereggen Tal, and on to Italy; the north-eastern one along the Kalser Tal. The picturesque western route leads soon to **St Veit in Defereggen**, whose **parish church** has frescoes (1420) showing the *Annunciation*, *Nativity* and *Epiphany*; and others (1440) of the *Twelve Apostles* and various saints. There is also a statue (1741) of *St Vitus*, the church's patron, by Johann Paterer. At nearby **St Jakob** the parish church has frescoes painted by associates of Simon von Taisten.

A right-hand turn takes you to Kals am Großglockner (1325m), beyond which is Austria's highest peak, the **Großglockner** (3798m, see p 318); there are also fine views from here of other peaks in the Hohe Tauern, Schober and Granatspitz ranges. Kals is an orientation- and starting-point for hikers and alpinists in summer and for *Langlaufen* fanatics in winter. There is a small 14C **church of St George** with remnants of Romanesque frescoes. Local environmentalists scored a victory in the 1990s by preventing the building of a hydro-electric dam and reservoir in the area.

Matrei in Osttirol

Retracing your steps to Huben, road 108 leads on to Matrei in Osttirol with its 12C **Schloss Weissenstein**, modified in Romantic style in the 19C and standing on a commanding height. The Baroque **parish church of St Alban** (Wolfgang Hagenauer, 1780) retains the Gothic tower of the predecessor church and has a richly decorative and cunningly unified interior making adroit use of light sources. The ceiling frescoes (1783) are by Franz Anton Zeiller (in the choir, the *Honouring of God's Name*; in the nave, the *Feeding of the Five Thousand* with cartouches showing the *Life of St Alban*; in the cupola, the *Apotheosis of St Alban*; and in the spandrels, the *Four Fathers of the Church*); most of the statuary on the side-altars, together with the processional statues, are by the local Johann Paterer, while the figures of *St Peter* and *St Paul* on the high altar are by Petrus Schmid. The somewhat isolated **church of St Nicholas** of Matrei has 14C frescoes of the *Crucifixion* depicted on the outer walls, as well as assorted saints and a *St Christopher* dating to 1530. In the tower are two choirs, one above the other, each with groined vaults and linked by a stone stairway. Romanesque frescoes in the choir (late 13C, perhaps by a Padua master) include the story of *Adam and Eve*, *Jacob and the Ladder*, the *New Jerusalem*, *Apostles and saints*. The fine statues of *St Nicholas* (upper choir), *St Alban* (gallery) and the *Madonna and Child* (lower choir) date respectively to 1420, 1440 and 1430. Unfortunately the danger of theft means that the key to the church is kept at the church warden's house.

To the west of the town is the **Zedlacher Paradies** at the entrance to the

Virgental with a larch forest conservation area, some of the trees being 600 years old. The Virgental follows the Isel up to its headwaters near the border with South Tyrol. In **Virgen** the **parish church of St Virgil** has some remaining Romanesque elements, in particular the baptismal font. On the walls are 18C wooden statues by Johann Paterer, and there is a tomb of Valentin Fercher (d. 1616), and a Lenten Cloth of 1598 signed by Stephan Flaschberger. Above the village are the **Rabenstein** ruins, where the Görz counts sat in judgement in the 12C. Reached by a path from Rabenstein and high above the valley is the extraordinary **All Saints' Chapel** hewn out of the rock, perhaps on the site of a pagan shrine. It has a flat wooden ceiling and three 14C wooden sculptures inside. The view from here makes the climb well worthwhile. At nearby **Mitteldorf** is a 17C silver-mine, which can be visited.

At **Obermauer** further west is the charming pilgrimage **church of Our Lady** (1456) with a striking marble relief on the southern exterior showing the *Adoration of the Three Kings*, and another (to the left of the side-door) showing *St Peter*; elsewhere on the north wall is a *Madonna and Child*. Parts of a substantial 14C cycle of frescoes also remain on the exterior (the *Annunciation*, the *Last Supper*, *Christ on the Mount of Olives* and, to the north, a *Madonna with Angels* and a *St Christopher* signed (1468) by Meister Sebastian Gerum of Lienz). The sundial with coats of arms of the Görz, Wolkenstein and Fercher families, dates to 1601. On the large bosses of the net vault of the interior are portraits of various saints. There is also a remarkable **fresco cycle** (1488) by Simon von Taisten, a beautiful child-like *biblia pauperum* showing (on the two nave arches) vivid scenes of the *Passion*, in the choir, the *Life of the Virgin*, with *Our Lady protecting Supplicants under her Cloak* (north-east corner) and *God the Father shooting an Arrow at the sinful World*. Above the right-hand side-altar may be seen Simon's vivid *St Sebastian* (1484), on the edge of which is a representation (1484) of Rueland Stral, a former Lord of Rabenstein, together with his wife (they were the joint founders of the church). The figures of *St James* and *St Peter* (1430) flank the late Gothic shrine of the main altar, which has Baroque additions dating to 1680, while the busts of saints on Baroque pedestals date to 1525. The pulpit made of calcareous tufa is notable, as elsewhere are the Gothic wooden sculptures of *Sts Florian, George, Barbara and Elizabeth* (probably originally intended for the high altar), and a *Crucifixion* of 1490.

At the end of the Virgental the spectacular **Umbalfälle** are reached, two stretches of fiercely cascading and maelstromic waterfalls dropping into a gorge, the total fall between the **Ochsner Hütte** at the top and the **Islitzeralm** at the bottom being 420m. The area is under conservation—it is a good place to watch water-wagtails, wrens, dippers and other avian lovers of fast-flowing streams in their natural environment.

East and south-east of Lienz

As you cross the Drau river to leave Lienz heading eastwards, you pass by the **Cossack Cemetery**. Cossack soldiers who had fought with the Germans in World War II were rounded up here by the British in 1942, in order to be sent back to execution or imprisonment in labour camps in the Soviet Union. A number chose death or suicide in the River Drau in preference to such a fate, while others were shot by the British while trying to escape.

Just to the south-east of Lienz a minor road leads to Tristach and the **Tristacher See** in the Lienzer Dolomites, the largest lake of East Tyrol and a popular summer resort. From here the **Dolomitenstrasse** (toll) winds up to a peak with fine views. However, the main road 107A runs 4km across a small plain to the east, reaching shortly the excavations at **Aguntum** on the left bank of the Debant river. *Aguntum* was originally an Illyrian settlement of the Hallstatt era (1100–500 BC), but was inhabited just prior to the Roman era by the Celtic Laianci tribe under the suzerainty of *Noricum* (see p 326). After Roman annexation c 15 BC, Emperor Claudius raised it to a *municipium* (AD 50) and it became exceedingly prosperous (evidence survives of heated villas, thermal baths and the like); following Roman withdrawal it was overrun by West Goths and finally destroyed by Slav invaders in the Dark Ages (c AD 610).

Lavant (opposite, on the south side of the Drau) was a hill of refuge for the people of *Aguntum* and has the ruins of an early Christian church (5C), a baptistery and a bishop's seat (collectively known as the '*Lavanter Kirchbichl*'), together with the relics of a prosperous Romano-Celtic settlement. The parish and pilgrimage **church of St Ulrich** (1770) was built by Thomas Hatzer on the Kirchbühel over an earlier Gothic edifice and has attractive Rococo ornamentation and frescoes. Above St Ulrich, the late Gothic **church of St Peter and St Paul** (1485) is well preserved and has three winged altars (c 1530, but brought here in 1873), of which that of the *Coronation of the Virgin* is notable. The wood-panelled ceiling dates to 1516, while beneath the chancel lies an early Christian chapel with a priest's bench. The altarpiece is attributed to Simon von Taisten. However, the winding road leads on to **Dölsach** and the ruins of 13C **Burg Walchenstein**, while nearby (on the way to the Iselsberg) are also those of **Burg Edenfest**, the origins of which are obscure. The neo-Romanesque **parish church of St Martin** has (on the left-hand side-altar) a picture (1882) of the *Holy Family* by Franz Defregger. The little Gothic **church of St Margaret** (1439) received its ornamental vault in 1662 and has much faded frescoes (1490, *Madonna with Saints* [?]) near the entrance. The road (now no. 107) leads on to the Mölltal in Carinthia and then to Heiligenblut and the Großglockner (see p 318).

From the junction at *Aguntum*, road 100 leads south-east, likewise to the Carinthian border and along the Drau valley on the north bank. At **Nikolsdorf** (on the parallel minor road) the **parish church of St Bartholomew** retains elements of its 15C origins, including a delicate net vault in the choir. The later groined vault of the rosetted nave (1612) is purely decorative and the rest of the internal ornament dates to the 19C. Nearby **Schloss Lengberg** was built in the 12C and for 600 years was in the possession of the Salzburg archbishops, who appointed the constables to administer it. After 1480, when the fortress was modernised and made less bleakly military by Virgil von Graben, the place experienced something of a cultural boom. In the 1920s it was owned by an Amsterdam banker and was a favourite holiday home of Queen Wilhelmina and Princess Juliana of the Netherlands, but since 1955 has been owned by Land Tirol.

Vorarlberg (Vorarlberg)

Area: 2601sq km. Population: 332,000

Topography, climate and environment

Since the beginning of the 18C, the area lying between the Upper Rhine and the Upper Inn valleys has been known as **Vorarlberg** owing to its location 'before' the **Arlberg**, and thus geographically isolated from the rest of Austria. After Vienna, it is the second smallest *Bundesland* of Austria and also has the second smallest population. It borders on Germany (Bavaria) in the north, Liechtenstein in the south-west and Switzerland in the west and south. There are few towns of any size in the province and even the capital **Bregenz** has only 27,000 inhabitants, being surpassed only by **Dornbirn** (c 41,000). The densest population is in the **Rhine Valley**. The greatest waterway of Western Europe rises in Switzerland, flows along the Swiss border with Liechtenstein and Vorarlberg, and then into the **Bodensee** (Lake Constance). Another significant river valley is that of the **Ill**, which courses from the **Silvretta Mountains** through the **Montafon** and **Walgau** regions to meet the Rhine near **Feldkirch**. Smaller tributaries of the Ill and the Rhine run off the **Rätikon** and **Verwall** ranges to the south, while the **Bregenzerwald** is watered by the **Bregenzerach**, which rises at the **Jaunberg** and flows into Lake Constance at Bregenz itself.

The population of the *Ländle*, or 'little province' as the locals call it, is centred around the main rivers and in numerous picturesque valleys reaching deep into the mountains. Winter resorts provide substantial employment, but some of these (for example **Zürs**) are virtually ghost towns in the summer. The Atlantic climatic influence, with prevailing west winds, influences the micro-climate of Vorarlberg, which has substantial precipitation and plenty of winter snow. The **Bregenzerwald** lying between Lake Constance and Hochtannberg is partly mountainous (the **Hinterwald**) and partly (the **Vorderwald**) grazing. It is characterised by a lively folk culture and an unusual type of wooden peasant house with wooden tile-hangings constituting the outer walls.

Lake Constance (in German 'Der Bodensee', named after the Carolingian Palatinate of *Bodama*) was the Roman *Lacus Brigantinus*. It is 369m above sea-level, has a maximum depth of 252m, a maximum width of 13.7km and a length of 67km, only a small part of which is in Austria. Remains of Celtic fishing settlements have been discovered along the banks and 35 species of fish may still be found in the lake. The indigenous *Blaufelchen* (powan) is similar to the White Fish of Loch Lomond. In the Rhine delta some 312 bird species are regularly present. The lake has two peculiarities, its hitherto unexplained thunder sound or '*Seeschießen*' and the *Rheinbrech*, a drop in the lake-floor causing high waves on the Austrian shore when there are strong west winds. Since 1972 an international **Bodenseekonferenz** involving all riparian Cantons or States has co-operated on economic and ecological issues regarding the lake.

Economy

Despite the obvious disadvantages of its topography (only 20 per cent of the land surface is in valleys) Vorarlberg is the second most industrialised Austrian province, possessing 35 per cent of the country's textiles capacity with its centre at Dornbirn. The industry grew up from the early 19C onwards, impelled by increasingly sophisticated exploitation of water power and strong local demand for traditional costume. Beginning with the long-established linen-making, production expanded into cotton in the course of the century, with spinning, weaving and embroidery all playing their part. While some 37 per cent of Vorarlberg's workforce is employed in the textile industry, ski-related service industries and food processing, together with paper manufacture and quarrying, are also important. Despite picturesque appearances to the contrary, the economic significance of agriculture in the province is relatively modest. However, the Montafoner cattle produce more milk per head than any other breed, and 60 per cent of Vorarlberg milk production goes into making excellent cheese, including a local speciality called *Bergkäse*. Skiing is the most important aspect of tourism, but considerable strides have been made in developing summer tourism as well, the Vorarlberger having organised themselves to cater for walkers, climbers and families with children. The **Bregenzer Festspiele** in mid-summer attracts increasing patronage and offers the added attraction of performances on a floating stage against a backdrop of lake and mountains.

History

The Vorarlberger have much in common with the Swiss and indeed the majority of them wanted to become part of Switzerland after World War I (the victorious powers forbade it). The province's strategic position west of the European watershed of the **Arlberg** and as gateway to the important Swiss alpine passes for Italy encouraged habitation at least from the early Stone Age. Celtic immigration dates from 400 BC and Roman occupation followed in 15 BC, when the area became part of the province of *Raetia*. The population was Romanised and *Brigantium* **(Bregenz)** grew into a *municipium*. From the 5C, the influence of the German Alemannic tribe slowly increased, eventually replacing the Romanised population. The Vorarlberg dialect (similar to dialects spoken in neighbouring Switzerland, Liechtenstein, Germany and the Lechtal area of Tyrol) is Alemannic, while the speech of all other parts of Austria belongs to the Bavarian dialect group.

The area around the **Bodensee** was christianised by the Irish missionaries Columban and Gallus in the early 7C. Around 1310 the Walser (Valais) people (who have left their imprint on many place names) entered the region, soon occupying about a quarter of the territory. The Alemannic power was subdued by Charlemagne and subsequently (1043) the Counts of Bregenz emerged as rulers, founding the Benedictine Abbey of Mehrerau (see p 414) in 1097. From the 13C, the progressive Counts of Tübingen-Montfort (whose coat of arms became that of Vorarlberg) ruled energetically, founding settlements and improving communications. The Habsburgs purchased the strategic Burg Gutenberg in 1309 and from then on extended their influence through further acquisitions, a process that continued up to 1814. There was, however, a period when Vorarlberg fell under Swiss hegemony during the first Appenzell War with the Swiss Confederation in the early 15C.

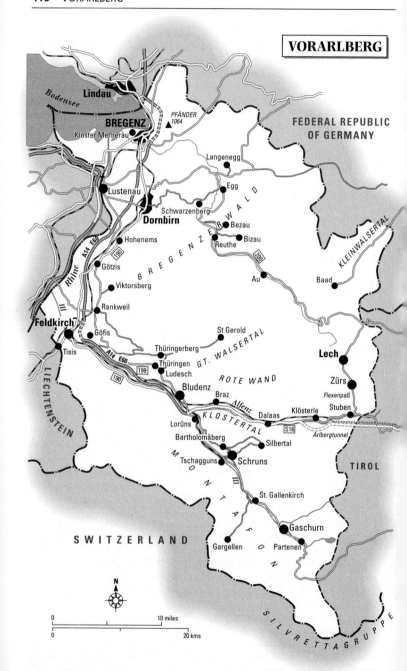

VORARLBERG

Bodensee

Lindau

BREGENZ

PFÄNDER
1064 ▲

Kloster Mehrerau

FEDERAL REPUBLIC
OF GERMANY

Langenegg

Egg

Lustenau

Schwarzenberg

Dornbirn

B R E G E N Z E R W A L D

Bezau

Bizau

Reuthe

Hohenems

Au

Baad

Götzis

K L E I N W A L S E R T A L

Rhine

Viktorsberg

Rankweil

R
h
i
n
e

Ill

St Gerold

Feldkirch

Göfis

G T.   W A L S E R T A L

Lech

Tisis

Thüringerberg

Thüringen

R O T E   W A N D

Zürs

Ludesch

Flexenpaß

Bludenz

Braz

Alfenz

Dalaas

Klösterle

Stuben

L I E C H T E N S T E I N

Lorüns

K L O S T E R T A L

S16

Arlbergtunnel

Bartholomäberg

Silbertal

Tschagguns

Schruns

M
O
N
T
A
F
O
N

TIROL

St. Gallenkirch

Ill

S W I T Z E R L A N D

Gaschurn

Gargellen

Partenen

N

0   10 miles

0   20 kms

S I L V R E T T A G R U P P E

Vorarlberg was administered by Habsburg governors (*Vögte*) and for most of its history was under the regional jurisdiction of Innsbruck. Bregenz was successfully defended in the War of the Spanish Succession (1701–14), and the Vorarlberger joined the Tyroleans in fighting the Bavarians and French in the unsuccessful independence struggle of 1809, returning to Austrian rule in 1814 after the Napoleonic Wars. The region's special status is reflected in Vorarlberg's retained right to call itself a '*Staat*' and certain other peculiarities in the electoral arrangements.

Saints Kolumban (Columban) and Gallus (Gall)

Saints Columban and Gall were the first missionaries in the region of Bregenz and Lake Constance. **Columban** (c 543–615) was of noble Irish origin and dedicated himself to the religious life at an early age. In c 590 he set out on a mission to Gaul, where his group founded three centres of monasticism (Annegray, Luxeuil and Fontaine). However, he quarrelled with the Frankish bishops over the calculation of Easter (which differed in Celtic practice from that of Rome) and made a powerful enemy of Theoderic II of Burgundy, whom he denounced for immorality on account of his numerous illegitimate children. After his expulsion on the king's orders, he eventually reached Bregenz after many hardships and began to convert the Alemannic people on the shores of Lake Constance. Unfortunately, Burgundy conquered this area in 612 and Columban had to flee to Lombardy, where he founded a monastery at Bobbio.

Columban's faithful follower, **St Gall** (c 550–645), accompanied him on his wanderings but broke with him before his departure for Italy, and remained in Switzerland. Some writers explain the split as being due to the irascible Columban's impossible demands on his acolyte, a plausible view since the Columban rule involved alarming rigours, including corporal punishment for any backsliding in spiritual or communal duties. Gallus appears to have become ill and may have been accused of malingering by Columban, who never suffered from ill health himself and therefore did not see why others should (appropriately enough, Columban's emblem is a bear). The penance imposed on the junior missionary was that he should not celebrate Mass again in Columban's lifetime. After Columban's death, his followers evidently had a bad conscience about their mentor's treatment of Gall, and sent him the great man's pastoral staff as a token of reconciliation. Gall is the patron saint of birds, either because of the association of Italian *gallo* (rooster) with his name, or perhaps (but illogically) because the demon he expelled from King Sigebert's fiancée made its departure from her mouth in the form of a blackbird. The monastery of St Gall grew up on the site of his hermitage near the River Steinach on the Swiss shore of Lake Constance and was an important centre of learning in the Middle Ages.

BREGENZ

Practical information

Population: 27,000. Telephone dialling code: 05574.

Tourist information
Vorarlberg Römerstraße 7/1 A-6901 Bregenz. ☎ (05574) 425250. **Bregenz** *Tourismus:* ☎ 05574 433 91-0. Fax: 05574/43 3 91-10. Anton-Schneider-Straße 4A. (Also sells fishing permits for the lake.)

Taxis ☎ 1718.

Getting there
By train From the train station at the west end of the lakeside park (and adjacent to the bus station) there are services to Innsbruck and Vorarlberg destinations, as also to Münich and Switzerland.

By boat Boat services run on the lake from May to October, serving Constance via Lindau (about 3.5hrs), plus ÖBB excursions (weather and numbers permitting). Contact *Bodensee Schiffahrt*, Seestraße 4, ☎ 055 74 42868, Fax: 05574 6755 520.

The sights of Bregenz are easily visited on foot, but a day pass for buses is available at the bus station.

Hotels

✩✩✩ *Hotel Germania*, Am Steinenbach 9. ☎ 055 74/427 66-0. Fax: 42766-4. Garage, sauna, and even a bicycle workshop.

✩✩✩ *Hotel Weisses Kreuz*, Römerstraße 5. ☎ 055 74/49 88-0.

✩✩ *Hotel Garni Bodensee*, Kornmarktstraße 22. ☎ 055 74/42 300-0. Fax: 45168.

✩ *Hotel Krone*, Leutbühel 3. ☎ 055 74/42 117. Fax: 45943. Central location, pleasantly old-fashioned, large rooms (doubles only).

Restaurants

Gösser Bräu, Anton-Schneider-Straße 1.

Schwärzler, Landstraße 9.

Deuring Schlößle, Ehre-Guta-Platz 4. (Luxury ✩✩✩✩ hotel with gourmet restaurant). ☎ 055 74 478 00. Built between 1660 and 1689, this historic Schloß rests on Gothic foundations, and is an atmospheric place to stay.

Cultural events
Bregenz's **Summer Festival** takes place in July and August. The *Seebühne* (floating stage) and Festival Hall are located a little to the west of the harbour, and no expense is spared in lavish productions making ingenious use of the setting. Besides a major opera production, there are symphony and chamber concerts featuring top-class artistes, together with theatrical productions.

For information on the **Bregenzer Festspiele** ☎ 05574 407-5. Postal booking c 9 months in advance from *Kartenbüro, Bregenzer Festspiele*, Postfach 311, Bregenz, A-6901 Vorarlberg, Austria. Brochures and ticket sales: *Bregenzer Festspiele GmbH*, Platz der Wiener Symphoniker 1, 6900 Bregenz. ☎ 05574 407-6. Fax: 407-400.

The capital (population 27,000) of Vorarlberg (Roman *Brigantium*, *Castrum Brigancia* in a document of 802, refounded by Hugo of Tübingen around 1170) was acquired by the Habsburgs in two transactions in 1451 and 1523 and has been the seat of the Landtag since 1861. Lying at the eastern end of the **Bodensee**, it is backed by hills rising steeply from the shore to the **Pfänder** (1063m, cable-car from the south-eastern end of the Schillerstraße, open 09.00–18.00, to 19.00 in summer), from where there are fine views of the lake, the Rhine Valley, and the city, as well as some 240 Alpine peaks in the Allgäu, the Bregenzerwald, the Rätikon and in Switzerland. Nearby is an Alpine wildlife centre, an **Adlerwarte** (hawking centre: performances May–Oct, 11.00 and 14.30) and a restaurant at the **Berghaus** (open 10.00–18.30). Bregenz itself is most pleasant in the upper old quarter, where most of the sights are. From the

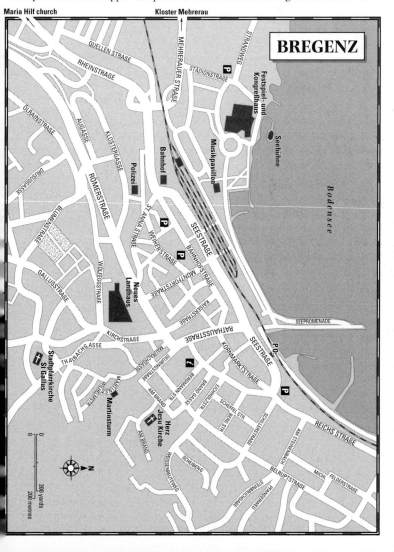

pier there are boat excursions to other towns and to the islands on the lake.

Most of the sights of the city are clustered in the **Obere Stadt** (Upper Town), but the impressive ultra-modern **Kunsthaus** (Peter Zumthor, 1997) for exhibiting contemporary art and architecture is worth a visit on Seestraße before you leave the shore area.

A climb from the harbour via the Rathausstraße, Kirchenstraße and Thalbachgasse brings you to the **Sankt Gallus Kirche** just to the west of the Upper Town, a Gothic church barockised by Michael Kuen (1673), with a mighty tower, Bregenz's spiritual conterpart to the secular Martinsturm (see below). The wide interior contains notable stucco and ceiling frescoes of the *Ascension*, the *Assumption* and the *Holy Ghost* (Ignaz Wegschneider, 1738). Among the shepherdesses featured in the altarpiece of the *Adoration of the Magi* is one with the features of Maria Theresia, who donated 1500 Gulden for the altar. The statues on the altar are of *St Ulrich* (?), *St Peter, St Paul* and *St Gall* (see p 411). An unusual feature is a clock over the chancel arch. On the way to the church you will pass close to the Vorarlberg **Landhaus** (1982, situated between Wolfeggstraße and Römerstraße), a work by Wilhelm Holzbauer who was a pupil of Clemens Holzmeister. (The latter was responsible for the interior (1980) of the **parish church of Maria Hilf** in the Vorkloster District of the town.)

In the **Martinsturm** to the north-east, the Bregenzer Counts collected the provender due from the peasants in a room below a first floor 14C chapel (frescoes). Benedetto Prato extended it in 1599–1601 to make a viewing platform for fire-watchers, while the huge onion dome and lantern were added a century later. The building is said to be the first on the lake shore to be built in the Baroque style. It houses a modest display of military uniforms, but is worth the entrance fee for the view.

Further to the north-east is the **Herz-Jesu-Kirche** (Joseph Cades, 1908), a vast neo-Gothic edifice lent distinction chiefly by its size. Interesting are the 24 modern stained-glass **windows** (Martin Häusle, 1958) describing the *Promise and fulfilment of Christ's Message*. Returning to the lower town, you encounter on the Kornmarkt Straße the attractive rotunda of **St Nepomuk's Chapel**, probably built by Johann Michael Beer in 1757. It is worth a look inside for the ceiling frescoes of the *Apotheosis of St John Nepomuk*; however, it is only open on Saturday afternoons. Also on the Kornmarkt at no. 1 is the **Vorarlberger Landesmuseum** (open daily except Mon 09.00–12.00, 14.00–17.00) with an extensive ethnological, cultural and historical collection relating to the region. It is strong on the pre- and early history of *Brigantium*, cult objects, and (for the modern period) vernacular furnishings. There is some Gothic painting and sculpture, notably the work of the local master, Wolf Huber (1485–1553). One room is devoted to Rudolf Wacker and Angelika Kauffmann (see p 417) with a fine portrait of the Prince of Denmark (1768) by the latter.

On the western outskirts of Bregenz is **Kloster Mehrerau**, an 11C foundation in the possession of the Cistercians since 1854, after the Benedictines were chased out by the Bavarians in 1806. Little remains of the abbey's former glories, but some treasures have been collected in the neo-Romanesque church (a 1582 wing-altar by Durs von Aegeri, a late 15C *Calvary* in the eastern side-chapel by Aelbert Bouts and an *Annunciation* dating to 1480). The modern marble tabernacle is by Hans Arp (1963), while the extraordinary external wall sculpture in béton (1962) is by a contemporary Vorarlberg sculptor, Herbert Albrecht. It shows the **Mother of the Messiah** and **St Michael's Victory over the Dragons** based on the twelfth chapter of the Book of Revelations. On the bottom row contemporary mankind, in its ethical confusion, supports the dragon as it strains upwards towards the mother of God.

Around the Bregenzerwald

Lying between the Bodensee and the Hochtannberg, the Bregenzerwald is drained by the Bregenzerach and sub-divided into the **Vorderwald** and the **Hinterwald**. The area became part of the Habsburg patrimony (together with the Countdom of Feldkirch) at the end of the 14C, but the peasants enjoyed considerable freedom up to the Bavarian occupation (1805–14). At Bezegg on the pass between Bezau and Andelsbuch a monument recalls the site of the *Wälderparlament*, which had four storeys and was only accessible by ladder, the ladder then being removed until all outstanding decisions had been taken by the local representatives.

BEZAU
• • • • • • •

Practical information

Hotels

✩✩✩✩ *Hotel Post*, A-6870 Brugg 35.
☎ 055 14/2207, Fax: 220722.
✩✩ *Pension Rößle*, A-6870 Bezau.
☎ 055 14/2335.

Restaurants

Gasthof Sonne. Moderately priced local cuisine. Also 20 rooms.
Pizzeria Fröwis. Italian specialities with flair, just below Hotel Post.

Bezau is a good base for exploring not only the Bregenzerwald, but most of Vorarlberg, being strategically placed with quick access to Bregenz and thence to the *Autobahn* for sights in the south and south-east of the province, as also to most of the picturesque alpine passes. It has a substantial number of hotels and pensions and good restaurants.

Bezau is within easy reach of ski slopes in winter (*Langlauf* is a major feature) and convenient for hiking in summer. A narrow gauge railway (*Wälderbahn)* built in 1902 to link the town to Bregenz (36km) now functions as an excursion railway (*Museumsbahn*) only between Bezau and neighbouring Bersbuch (6.1km, the evening excursions with live music are recommended). Cable-cars run to the Sonderdach (1208m) and Baumgarten (1624m) peaks. The **Heimatmuseum** (☎ 22 95, open by arrangement or four half-days in the week) has exhibits concerning local lifestyle and ecclesiastical art from the Bregenzerwald.

Almost on the outskirts of Bezau is the hamlet of **Reuthe,** whose **parish church** contains 15C frescoes on the chancel arch and in the choir. They represent (in two rows, beginning from the north-west of the choir) the 12 apostles and 15 scenes from the *Life of the Virgin*. In addition the arch features *St Anne with the Virgin and Child*, *Thomas Aquinas*, the *Virgin of Mercy*, *The Vernicle*, *St Martin* and the *Martyrdom of St Sebastian*. The statues of the *Madonna* to the left of the entrance and on the north wall are by Johann Peter Kauffmann, nephew of Angelika (see below) and a native of Reuthe.

Schwarzenberg

Not far to the north-west of Bezau is Schwarzenberg, where the ladies of the village may be seen in their folk costume streaming out of church after Sunday mass. An annual festival (Sept 14–15) the so-called *Alpabtrieb*, features animals colourfully draped, as well as herdsmen and dairy-maids in traditional costume, with a procession and dancing. A number of houses show the the typical Bregenzerwald architecture, and there is a reconstructed (1948) **Tanzlaube** (wooden pavilion used for dancing and socialising) near the church. The **Museum Schwarzenberg** (open May–Sept, Tues, Thur, Sat, Sun 14.00–16.00, Oct, Thur and Sat, 14.00–16.00) has further displays of folk costume and local culture. It also has exhibits relating to the artist Angelika Kauffmann (1741–1807). Her father's house is near the main square (Angelika was born in her mother's home town of Chur (Coire) over the border in Switzerland, but spent her youth here). Johann Joseph Kauffmann was also an artist and in 1757 received the commission to renew the interior of the **parish church of the Holy Trinity**, which had been damaged by fire. The 16-year-old Angelika assisted him by painting the apostles on the walls of the nave above the calvary scenes by her father. In 1802 she donated the altarpiece (the *Coronation of the Virgin*). On the left wall is a bust of her by C. Heweston.

Apart from the work of the Kauffmanns in the church, it is notable for a highly decorative Rococo canopy over the pulpit consisting of protective angels floating gracefully above the symbols of the four evangelists. The statues flanking the altarpiece represent two of the church fathers, *Augustine* and *Ambrose*, and are by a Bezau sculptor.

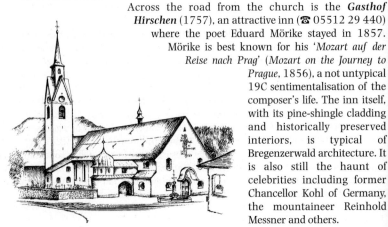

Across the road from the church is the *Gasthof Hirschen* (1757), an attractive inn (☎ 05512 29 440) where the poet Eduard Mörike stayed in 1857. Mörike is best known for his '*Mozart auf der Reise nach Prag*' (*Mozart on the Journey to Prague*, 1856), a not untypical 19C sentimentalisation of the composer's life. The inn itself, with its pine-shingle cladding and historically preserved interiors, is typical of Bregenzerwald architecture. It is also still the haunt of celebrities including former Chancellor Kohl of Germany, the mountaineer Reinhold Messner and others.

Parish church of the Holy Trinity

Angelika Kauffmann

One of the very few famous and successful female artists in history, Angelika Kauffmann studied in Italy, becoming a member of the Accademia S. Luca in Rome by 1765. It was in Rome (where she met Johann Joachim Winckelmann, whose portrait she painted) that she had her first successes. She was even more successful in London (1766–81), where she was a founding member of the Royal Academy (1768). Influenced by Reynolds (it was rumoured they had an affair), she became a fashionable portraitist, while her contacts with Goethe, Herder and Winckelmann in Italy inspired here to work with classical subjects. She married the Venetian artist Antonio Zucchi, but remained childless. Buried in the Roman Chiesa Sant'Andrea delle Fratte, she was posthumously honoured with a bust in the Pantheon. Angelika was essentially a decorative painter whose works were used to ornament porcelain and enamels, as well as being widely disseminated in prints by Francesco Bartolozzi; but she was also an accomplished musician (as her allegory in the church at Schwarzenberg [1760] of herself hesitating between music and painting suggests), and the keeper of a brilliant salon in Rome frequented by Tischbein, Canova and many other artists and intellectuals.

A winding road leads towards Bödele and Dornbirn from Schwarzenberg. To the north-west, however, a picturesque route runs through the Hinterwald to the German border. Nearby, almost at the centre of the Bregenzerwald, is the village of **Egg**, whose brewery produces some of the best beer in Austria, continuing a tradition of brewing in the Bodensee area that dates back to the 9C. Between Egg and Krumbach is **Langenegg** with its fine Baroque parish church. Notable are Johann Michael Koneberg's frescoes (1776), particularly the *Expulsion of the Money Changers from the Temple* under the organ loft, which anachronistically features a woman in local costume. *St Dominic* is represented in the altarpiece with his faithful dog next to him, a burning candle for the faith in its mouth. In the choir is a favourite scene of the local Baroque masters, *Esther pleading for her People before the Persian King, Ahasuerus* (Xerxes I, 486–465 BC), a reflection of Vorarlberg's aspirations to autonomy.

South-east of Bezau is the attractive village of **Bizau** with typical vernacular architecture. At **Au**, further south, road 193 leads south-west for the marvellously scenic **Furkapaß**, which ultimately leads through the mountains to Rankweil (see p 419). The views as you pass the Mittagsspitze at the top (2095m) encompass the major peaks of Vorarlberg. However, there is another good reason for taking this road, namely the **church of St Nikolaus** at **Damüls**, originally built in the 14C on the site of a hunting-lodge. It was twice burned down and the present church dates from 1484–85, the builder signing himself 'Rolle Maiger'. The panels of the coffered ceiling were painted by Johann Purtscher (1693) and show the *Assumption*, the *Coronation of the Virgin*, and *Mary as Queen of the Rosary*, together with saints and the evangelists. The earlier (1500) wall frescoes by an unknown master are of high quality and show scenes from the Bible, with the *Last Judgement* on the arch of the choir. The frescoes only came to light in 1950 under a Baroque covering of cow-hair plaster. The statue of *St Theodul* in the right-hand side-altar is dated to 1480, while the powerful *Plague Crucifix* on the left-hand altar is early Baroque (1635), attributed to Erasmus Kern.

From Dornbirn to Bludenz

Dornbirn, lying at the western periphery of the Bregenzerwald, is the main manufacturing and textile town of the province. The neo-classical **parish church** near the market and at the junction of Riedgasse and Pfarrgasse is notable for the colourful modern mosaic (1924) in the gable of the porch showing *Christ's Entry into Jerusalem*. The town's other attraction is the **Rote Haus** (1639, now a restaurant), a fine example of the vernacular architecture of the Upper Rhine Valley. Good homecooking may be enjoyed in the six *Stuben* of the inn, rooms retaining their historic fittings and made welcoming in winter by the warmth from their decorative ceramic stoves. The **Natural History Museum** (Marktstraße 33, open July–Sept daily 09.00–12.00, 14.00–17.00, otherwise Tues–Sun) was founded by one of the local textile magnates named Fussenegger and gives a good overview not only of Vorarlberg's fauna, flora and geology, but most interestingly of the exploitation of natural features to produce energy for light industry (see p 421 on the Douglas family). A road from the south-eastern suburb of Dornbirn leads up the Ebniter Tal, the route required for the **Rappenlochschlucht**, a dramatic gorge through which the Dornbirner Ach flows in a scenically superb setting.

Hohenems to the south and west boasts a 16C palace of the same name lying below the ruins of the old Alt-Ems castle high up on the Schlossberg, which once marked the boundary between Alemannic and Rhaetian territory. The Renaissance palace (**Schloß Hohenems**) was commissioned by Cardinal Markus Sittich, Papal Legate and Prince-Bishop of Constance, and later extended by his nephew, Count Kaspar of Hohenems (1573–1640). It was Kaspar who had ambitions of creating in 1620 an independent state between Switzerland and Austria; this came to nothing, however, and the line eventually died out in 1759, the possessions passing to the Counts Waldburg-Zeil via the Harrachs. The original design (1567) of the palace was by the papal architect, Martino Longo. A feature is the 'blind wall', a *trompe l'oeil* architectural effect on the cliff side of the Renaissance inner courtyard. The courtyard and the Knights Hall were formerly the venues for *Schubertiad*s in June (they are now in Feldkirch) and are still used for concerts of the Bregenzer Festspiele (July–Aug); a further cultural distinction of the palace is the fact that manuscripts of the *Nibelungenlied* were discovered in the library during the 18C.

The nearby parish church of St Carlo Borromeo, whose present aspect dates to 1757, owes its name to the fact that Markus Sittich's brother, Jakob Hannibal I, the real founder of the Sittich line's fortunes and the first Imperial Count, was married to a step-sister of St Carlo Borromeo. He and his wife, Hortensia, are featured on the winged altar inside as founders of the predecessor (1581) of the present church. The Renaissance altar, by various hands, although the figures are attributed to Hans Dieffolt, is of high quality and depicts the *Coronation of the Virgin*, the *Three Magi*, the *Nativity*, the *Annunciation* and the *Crucifixion*. Note also the red marble sarcophagus of Count Kaspar, which is probably Italian workmanship. The other seat of the Sittich line, the impressive **Burg Glopper**

(1407), is further back on the mountain ridge behind the Alt-Ems ruins, but can only be viewed from the outside. In the town a **Jewish Museum** (Schweizer Str. 5, open Wed, 10.00–12.00, Thur–Sun, PH 10.00–17.00) recalls the Jewish community settled here by Count Kaspar and also gives an account of the history of the Vorarlberg Jews. Hohenems was also the birthplace of the epic poet Rudolf von Ems (c 1200–54) who embarked on, but did not finish, a chronicle of world history.

Worth the detour is the **parish church of St Ulrich** at **Götzis**, a single-naved Gothic church (1514) with star-vaulting in the choir. The frescoes (c 1600) are dramatic, notably the *Last Judgement* on the chancel arch, together with the *Last Supper* and a delightful *Manna from Heaven* in the choir. Above the left side-altar is an over-life-size statue of the *Madonna and Child* (c 1700). A climb up a hairpin road north-eastwards from nearby Sulz to the south brings you to **Viktorsberg**, with breathtaking views from the little **church of St Victor** on the peak. The Bertle dynasty of local painters is responsible for the (by then) anachronistically Baroque frescoes painted for the church in the 19C. The puzzling depiction of *St Eusebius* carrying his own head, refers to the Irish hermit who lived in the first hermitage on the site and was beheaded by irate peasants when he remonstrated with them for working on Sundays. Also depicted is a bishop proffering the skull of St Victor, whose remains (as also those of St Eusebius) are supposedly in the two Baroque reliquaries under the side-altars.

Not far from Sulz, continuing south, is the pilgrimage **church of the Visitation** (*Kirchenburg 'Unsere Liebe Frau Mariä Heimsuchung'*) at **Rankweil**, situated on a precipitous crag, the site of a wonder-working cross supposedly washed ashore in the stream near Sulz. The latter is a superb combination of Romanesque and Baroque work and dominates the east end of the church, being made even more striking by the bronze wreath of angels that encircle it. It weighs 30kg, is believed to have been made by Byzantine masters in Pisa and features reliefs on the front of *Christ's Entry into Jerusalem*, the *Women at the Tomb* and the *Resurrection*; on the back, *Christ Enthroned*, *Mary at Prayer*, *John the Baptist and John the Evangelist*. The silver mantling was made in 1728 by the Augsburg master, J.C. Lutz. The wooden wreath of angels (Ulrich Henn, 1983) is an extremely happy modern addition. Another Romanesque crucifix may be seen on the wall near the **Gnadenkapelle**, the latter containing Hans Rueland's statue of the *Madonna and Child* (1460), the main object of pilgrimage and veneration in the church. An interesting aspect of the building is the defensive corridor that surrounds it, affording fine views over the town, the Rhine Valley, and south towards the **Schesaplana** (2965m) in the **Rätikon Massif**.

Feldkirch

Located where the River Ill joins the Rhine, Feldkirch has been a trade centre from earliest times. It was for a while in the possession of the Counts of Montfort and was sold to the Habsburg Duke Leopold III (1390), on condition that the traditional rights and privileges of the Bürgerturm were respected. It suffered in the Appenzell Wars, then in the Thirty Years War, when the Swedes pillaged it. The Jesuit college founded in 1658 (from 1856–1938 and again from 1946–79, the celebrated *Stelle Matutina Gymnasium*), was part of a lively academic and cultural environment, but even earlier the town produced artists of distinction, notably Wolf Huber of the Danube School.

Feldkirch is dominated from the south-east by the 12C **Schattenburg**, originally built (1200) by Hugo of Montfort, later enlarged and the seat of the Habsburg governors. In the courtyard there is an attractive open-air restaurant in summer; in the chambers of the Schloss is a **Heimat Museum** (open daily except Mon 09.00–12.00, 13.00–17.00) containing old locks and keys, arms, coins, medals and folkloristic items. The chapel has a fresco of 1500 showing *Adam and Eve and the Tree of Knowledge*. In the room devoted to local artists is an altarpiece by the father of Angelika Kauffmann, possibly intended originally for Rankweil.

Bordering the **Neustadt** below is the Gothic **Rathaus** (reconstructed in Baroque times) and just to the north-east, the **Cathedral of St Nicholas** (1478) built by Hans Sturn from neighbouring Göfis. Impressive are the tall and slender sandstone columns that divide the interior and the net vaulting. To the right of the crossing is Wolf Huber's *pietà* (1521), in which the brilliantly coloured robes of the sorrowing group ministering to Christ contrast starkly with the bilious tones of the Vorarlberg landscape at sunset. The same artist executed the predella picture of the *Vernicle* borne by two angels, after a motif by Dürer. Also notable is the **pulpit**, with its delicate ironwork finishing (1500), originally part of a tabernacle.

A short walk to the north-west of the cathedral is the late 15C **Katzenturm**, part of the old fortifications of the town, and due south of it the Baroque **Palais Liechtenstein**, now used for cultural events and exhibitions. Further west (reached via Kreuzgasse) is the **Churertor** (1491), the 'Swiss Gate' close to the **Frauenkirche St Sebastian**, barockised in 1678, but built in 1473 and also attributed to Hans Sturn. Beyond it to the west stands a water-tower at the head of a bridge over the River Ill. The Monfortgasse and Kreuzgasse lead back to the long Marktgasse with its medieval arcades, at the southern end of which is the **Johanneskirche** (1218, later much altered). It was founded by Count Hugo de Montfort as part of a Johannite cloister, the Knights of St John here as elsewhere being responsible for hospitality and assistance offered to travellers at local passes and bridges (in this case the route to the Arlberg). On the south-western outskirts of Feldkirch is the border with the **Principality of Liechtenstein** (160sq km, population 30,000) founded in 1719.

On the eastern outskirts of Feldkirch, **Göfis** is worth visiting for its exciting modern church (1975), which has been built on to a small Gothic choir. The play of angles of the sloping pinewood ceiling, its rhythm broken sporadically by architectonic square blocks, and the ingenious solution of filtering light from side windows partly shielded by geometrical greenery-draped concrete panels, is remarkably effective. From the back of the church, the eye is drawn to the focal point of the choir, although the general atmosphere strikes one as rather secular, as if the space would function equally well as a modern lecture hall. The architect was a local man, Rudolf Greußing. A feature of the likewise modern design of the cemetery are the sculptures of Albert Wider, in particular a striking *pietà* and crucifix.

Continuing south-east on the minor road from Feldkirch (road 193) you reach the small town of **Thüringen**, birthplace of the writer Norman Douglas (1868–1952) and boasting a '*Douglas-Stüberl*' on the main road. If you climb up through the town following signposts to Thüringerberg, and turn off left halfway up, you will come to the Douglas house called *Falkenhorst*, part of which has been acquired by the *Gemeinde* and will soon contain some sort of memorial to the family. John Sholto Douglas's climbing gear, which he was using when he fell to his death in the Klostertal, is hanging in the hall.

John Douglas, John Sholto Douglas and Norman Douglas

In 1837, John Douglas, the 14th Laird of Tilquhillie, founded a textile mill in Vorarlberg which survived (from 1904 under different ownership) until 1966. The energetic Douglas saw a way of harnessing the water power of the **Montjola** torrent at the entrance to the **Große Walsertal**. By 1839 the Imperial Inspector for the region was reporting the considerable expansion of the mill with the help of turbines and a labour force of 150 men. The official also visited Falkenhorst, expressing astonishment that a factory owner should also be a scholar 'quoting Homer and Anacreon extensively in the original', and plain incomprehension that an aristocrat like Douglas should engage in commerce. The previous year, however, the two practically-minded brothers of Franz I, the Archdukes Rainer and Johann, had visited Thüringen and declared the factory to be the most impressive of its kind in the Empire. By 1856, it had made enough profit to pay back most of the enormous mortgages raised on the family's highland seat, repayment having been Douglas's main motivation in starting the business. But Thüringen and Vorarlberg had also profited enormously: even in the 1970s 64 per cent of Thüringen's much expanded population were engaged directly or indirectly in the textile business founded by the Scottish laird.

The founder's son, John Sholto Douglas, was a fanatical climber and shot, as well as a gifted amateur scientist and local historian, his publications including scholarly accounts of the Romans and the Celts in the Vorarlberg and Liechtenstein areas. Through him, the family became real Vorarlberger stock, since he married a girl from a distinguished Bregenzer line, Wanda von Pöllnitz. After his death she remarried (against the wishes of her relations on both sides) the painter Jakob Jehly of Bludenz, the forbidden romance being described in a famous memoir ('*Geliebte Schatten*') by their daughter, Grete Gulbransson. Sholto Douglas founded what became the largest climbing association (*Alpenverein*) of Austria and Germany at Bludenz in 1873 and died aged only 36 by falling off the Radonatobel near Dalaas while out stalking the following year.

The epicurean Norman Douglas (1868–1952) inherited both the robust constitution and scientific curiosity of his father. His most celebrated book is *Old Calabria* (1919), which has seldom been bettered in its combination of learning and entertaining personal observation. His novel *South Wind* (1917) is a work of somewhat brittle sophistication set in Capri, and was the model for several similar efforts, notably having influence on the work of Aldous Huxley. The delightful, meditative travel book *Together* (1923) describes Douglas's return to Vorarlberg in middle age.

Beyond Thüringerberg the road winds up to the **Abbey of St Gerold**, set in a fold of the hills bordering the Große Walsertal, the valley being named after the Alemannic tribe which emigrated from Switzerland (Valais) over the (Swiss) Furka and Oberalp passes in the 13C and 14C. They were favoured by the rulers of the time, becoming free peasants who acknowledged an obligation for military service, but in return were excused from the robot and allowed autonomous administration of justice. Notable features of their culture are the Walsinger vernacular wooden houses (so-called *Blockbau*, a unit incorporating both farm and dwelling with tiny windows to preserve maximum warmth), and the women's costumes, with long pleated skirts rising above the waist and richly embroidered bodices.

The present abbey and church of St Gerold mostly date from rebuilding between 1580 and 1600, but there were earlier Gothic and Romanesque structures growing out of what was originally a 10C hermitage. For some time the settlement belonged to the ancient Swiss abbey of Einsiedeln (the Swiss Patres were expelled by the Nazis but returned in 1947). The most interesting artwork is in the former choir of the old church, which is now enclosed (**St Geroldgedenkstätte**) and consists of a vivid cycle of ten scenes from the *Life of St Gerold* painted (1684) by a monk, Fridolin Dumeisen. Nearby is the grave of the saint (d. 978), with his skull preserved in a reliquary. The modern **interior** of the church boasts a huge wall painting (1966) by Ferdinand Gehr, the theme of which is *God made flesh through Christ*. In the cemetery are some interesting modern sculptures on New Testament themes by Hugo Imfeld. The abbey is now a religiously oriented social and cultural centre.

If you return to Thüringen and continue south-east to **Ludesch**, you pass by **St Martins-Kirche** (founded 842, enlarged 1480) whose restoration is due to be completed 2000–2001. Nestling on the slopes above the village, this is a little gem of Romanesque and Gothic architecture; although two Romanesque crucifixes from the church are on permanent loan to the Landesmuseum in Bregenz, there is still plenty to see. On the north side are frescoes of *Christ on the Mount of Olives*, *St Christopher* and a bell, the latter being the symbol of the Walsinger St Theodul. The Renaissance and Gothic high altar (fragments of the two were combined in 1629) shows a crowned *Madonna and Child* in the shrine with *Sts Oswald* and *Lucius*, beyond them *Sts Emerita* and *Florian*, and above a highly decorative carved baldachin. On the predella is a striking relief of *St Martin and the Beggar*. To the right of the high altar is a **Rosary Altar** (1488) with symbolic representations of sickness and healing, to the left a **Marian Altar** (1487) showing *Sts Barbara and Catherine*. (It is possible these two winged altars will also be placed in the museum.) Other frescoes in the nave date to 1600 and show 24 scenes from the *Passion* and the *Life of the Virgin Mary*. If the church is again accessible, the key should be obtainable from no 255, St Martinstraße, in the village.

Nearby **Bludenz** is an important provincial centre with offices of local administration and some light industry. It was completely rebuilt after a fire in 1638. There is, however, little to detain the tourist although the **St Laurentius-Pfarrkirche** (1514, the tower 1670, reached by a covered stone stairway from the town centre) and the neighbouring **Schloß Gayenhofen** (seat of the Habsburg *Vögte* from 1752 to their extinction in 1806) are worth a glance. So also is the **Museum der Stadt Bludenz** (open June–Sept, Mon–Sat,

15.00–17.00) at Kirchgasse 9. Exhibits include wrought ironwork, prehistorical finds and (on the second floor) folklore and local art. In the **Schloßhotel** (then the 'Marksmen's House') John Sholto Douglas founded the mountaineer's association (see above), as a plaque records. Portraits of him and his wife and her second husband, the Bludenzer artist Jakob Jehly, together with other works by the still active Jehly dynasty of artists, may be seen in the museum.

Montafon Valley

Tourist information

Silvrettastraße 6, Schruns, open Mon–Fri, 08.00–12.00, 14.00–16.00, Sat 09.00–12.00, 16.00–18.00. ☎ 72166. Fax: 72554. Leaflets and hiking maps, as well as seven- and ten-day passes for cable-cars and timed concessionary entrance permits for other facilities, can be obtained here.

South-east of Bludenz on road 188 is the village of **Tschagguns**, with a **parish church** frescoed by a member of the Bertle painter dynasty (see p 419). The church's Gothic *pietà* is an object of veneration for pilgrims.

A few kilometres to the north, along a narrow and steeply scenic road with fabulous views over the valley and surrounding peaks, is **Bartholomäberg**, where the church (1743) has a coffered ceiling decorated with portraits of the 14 auxiliary saints or '*Holy Helpers*', so-called for their supposed efficacy in intercession for human afflictions. A typical example is St Blasius, who is said to have saved the life of a child who choked on a fishbone, and is therefore believed to be helpful to those with throat problems. The others (some of whom never existed, although apparently this does not impair their effectiveness) are St George (plague, leprosy, syphilis), Erasmus (colic), Pantaleon, Vitus (epilepsy, St Vitus's Dance, snakebites), Christopher (sea disasters, motor accidents), Denys (headaches, frenzy), Cyriacus, Acacius, Eustace, Giles, Margaret, Barbara (fire, lightning) and Catherine of Alexandria.

On the right-hand wall is a late Gothic altar (1525) dedicated by local miners of silver, copper and iron ore. The central figure is that of *St Anne*; *St Barbara* (patron saint of miners) is featured on the right-hand wing, while *St Eloi* (Eligius, a goldsmith who became the patron saint of smiths and metal workers) is on the left. Also represented is the Walser's patron, *St Theodul*, this being a very early Walser settlement. The high altar is impressive, with Salomonic columns at the centre flanked by statues of *St Joseph* and *St John Nepomuk*; the tabernacle has a delicately carved representation of the *Last Supper* (Michael Lechleitner, 1635), and the altarpiece shows the *Apotheosis of St Bartholomew* (Carl Stauder of Constance, 1737). A 12C processional cross kept in the sacristy may be viewed on application to the parish priest.

Not far to the east of Bartholomäberg is **Silbertal** (its name recalling the silvermines) with a fine neo-Gothic **church** (1893) designed by Friedrich Schmidt, the distinguished architect of Vienna's City Hall. The walls of the church are painted with floral patterns (as the 19C imagined medieval churches to have been) and the local architectural peculiarity of a double nave supported by three central columns has been imitated. Further up the valley a rather expensive cable-car runs to the

Kristberg with a fine view from the top, where there is also a restaurant.

Returning to the main road and passing the market town of **Schruns** (for tourist information, see above) you reach **St Gallenkirch** with a frescoed church, whose altarpiece (1862) by a member of the Bertle dynasty shows the Irish missionary, St Gallus, casting pagan idols into the Bodensee at *Brigantium* (Bregenz). A minor road south brings you to **Gargellen**, a small resort famous for the clemency of its climate, which has an attractive little Baroque church. However, the main road leads on to **Gaschurn**, notable for the restored *Tanzlaube* (a wooden pavilion for announcements, socialising and dancing) adjacent to the church. These pavilions were once a feature of many Vorarlberg villages, but many have disappeared. On the south-east of the village is the charming **Maria Schnee Chapel** on a mound overlooking the River Ill. It was founded by a Tyrolean who wished to build a church in thanksgiving after recovering from an illness, and announced that he would build it on the spot where it snowed in summer. The painted wooden panels of the ceiling depict the *Seven Joys of Mary*.

Road 188 continues south-east to become the exciting **Silvretta-Hochalpenstraße** (toll) leading to Tyrol, at the top of which is a huge reservoir. From here there are marvellous views of the **Piz Buin** (3312m) and surrounding peaks on or across the Swiss border.

From Bludenz along the Klostertal to the Arlberg Tunnel

On the S16 on the south-eastern outskirts of Bludenz is the hamlet of **Bings**, where the **St Leonard Chapel** is worth a visit. Over the portal is a statue of the saint (*Leonard the Hermit*), who was protector of herdsmen, horses and thus also of the guides for the mountain passes; he is shown girdled with a chain, an allusion to his further role (popularised by the crusaders) as the patron saint of prisoners. The interior contains a Baroque *Crucifixion* and a Gothic *pietà*, but access may be difficult (apply at the adjacent house). At nearby **Braz** the church has Baroque frescoes by Tyrolean masters, including a particularly vivid *Martyrdom of St John Nepomuk*. The impressive statues on the high altar (*St Nicholas* flanked by *Sts Martin and Ulrich*, 1774) are by Joseph Witwer. At **Dalaas** further east the parish church of St Oswald, strikingly situated on a hill, is worth a visit for the frescoes by the Bertle family of painters.

As you enter **Klösterle** further east you pass a picturesque water-wheel for a sawmill on the left of the road. The modern church (1973) was designed by the Tyrolean Clemens Holzmeister and was his last work, completed in his 87th year. Enthusiasts for modern architecture might consider a trip up the **Flexenpass**, the beginning of which is reached shortly on your left after **Stuben**, and which leads up to the ski resorts of Zürs and Lech, the latter a favourite with the Dutch royal family and the late Princess Diana.

At **Lech** pressure on space in the attractive but diminutive old church led to a new one being built adjacent to it in 1975, which was designed by Roland Ostertag. The impressively spare interior is relieved by a few traditional touches, such as the early 16C vestry chest on the right-hand wall and a Gothic crucifix. **Zürs** is a winter resort, but **Lech** is lively also in summer.

From here you can continue into Tyrol on road 198 via **Warth**, leaving the isolated **Kleines Walsertal** to the north, the latter being only accessible from Germany (via Oberstdorf) and for that reason is (since 1891) part of the German customs area. Its main town (**Mittelberg**) has greatly profited from this, as indeed has the whole region, which is religiously and nationally more mixed than elsewhere in Vorarlberg after German and Protestant influxes from the turn of the century. If the **Flexenpass** is not taken, the main route to Tyrol runs through the 14km long **Arlbergtunnel** (toll) between **Langen** and **St Anton am Arlberg**, which was completed in 1978 at a cost of 4 billion ATS.

Glossary of art and architectural terms

Acanthus: Mediterranean plant with thick tendril-like leaves, supposedly the original model for the ornament of Corinthian capitals. It is extremely common in Baroque ornament, especially in carving and wrought-iron screens etc. where it affords the opportunity for a display of superior craftsmanship.

Altarpiece: **1**. A painting hung at, or rising from, the rear of an altar, this type of picture being typical of Catholic Europe. Altarpieces first came into existence as a result of a liturgical change in the 13C, when priests celebrated Mass with their backs to the congregation. **2**. A large carved and painted structure, usually consisting of a shrine with flanking panels, and placed on or behind the altar (see also *retable* and *winged altar (piece)* below).

Ambulatory: The processional area behind the main altar used by clergy or medieval pilgrims, who would systematically perambulate the church visiting the votive shrines.

Art Nouveau: The name is derived from a shop in Paris (opened 1895), which sold artefacts with original designs. The new art's stress on liberating the imagination represented a reaction against the derivative artificiality of *Historicism* and conservative Academicism. *Art Nouveau* was a strong intellectual influence on the *Viennese Secession* at the turn of the century; however, the latter developed its own version of the movement (the *Secessionist* architecture of Otto Wagner, the *Wiener Werkstätte* etc., see below).

Baldachin: A canopy over an altar, tomb, throne or similar construction.

Baroque: The style in the arts generally synchronic with the Counter-Reformation and designed to impress with its grandeur (in the profane architecture of great palaces) and seduce with its didactic sensuality (in ecclesiastical architecture, as also in music, the Jesuit theatre, etc.). The heyday of the Austrian Baroque is approximately from 1690 to 1730 and the greatest exponents were at first Italian masters (Domenico Martinelli; Giovane Tencala, the Carlone dynasty), who were followed by several distinguished Austrians (for example Fischer von Erlach, father and son, Lukas von Hildebrandt and Jakob Prandtauer). The vast majority of Austrian churches were 'barockised' in the course of the Counter-Reformation, at least as regards their interiors, but often also in terms of fabric, some being completely rebuilt.

Basilica: Originally a term from ancient Rome referring to function (a law court, commercial exchange or other public hall) rather than form. However, early Christian churches evolved from this type of building; basilicas tended to have an oblong shape, a flat ceiling, a rectangular or apsidal termination in the east and a nave higher than the two side-aisles. The title of 'Basilica' ('Major' or 'Minor') is also bestowed on certain privileged churches by the Pope (there are several in Austria).

Biedermeier: The elegantly simple style of artefacts (notably furniture) made between 1815 and 1848 is known as *Biedermeier*. The simple design reflects also the politically circumscribed life-style of the bourgeoisie, treated, politically speaking, as children by its masters and devoted to a life of 'happiness in a quiet corner'. In painting, idealised family portraits and landscapes of restrained Romanticism were expressions of the Biedermeier spirit, and Austria produced the quintessential Biedermeier novel (albeit in retrospect) in Adalbert Stifter's *Der Nachsommer* (*Indian Summer*, 1857). Biedermeier furniture often shows neo-classical or Empire influence, the former also being evident in Biedermeier villa architecture.

Cartouche: Ornamental panel in the form of a scroll or sheet of paper with curling edges, often bearing an heroic or dedicatory inscription.

Caryatid: A sculptured female figure used in Classical architecture to support an entablature, but in Baroque architecture merely one of many ornamental devices. The caryatid's male equivalent (*atlantes*) is frequently encountered in Baroque palace architecture (e.g. in the *sala terrena* of Prince Eugene of Savoy's Schloss Belvedere in Vienna). The latter word appears to be derived from the mythological Atlas, who held up the heavens.

Chancel: The whole eastward continuation of the nave of a church after the *crossing*.

Choir: The part of the church where divine service is sung and usually constituting part of the chancel.

Coffered ceiling: A ceiling consisting of sunken square or polygonal ornamental panels encountered in the rooms of monasteries, *Schlösser*, etc.

Columns: A feature of Baroque townscapes in Austria are the many free-standing columns with elaborate decoration. The vast majority of these were erected in thanksgiving for deliverance from the plague, mostly after the dreadful epidemics in 1679 (e.g. the column on the Graben in Vienna) and 1713. Many of them have quite elaborate doctrinal schemes, a favourite theme being the Trinity; these are called *Dreifaltigkeitssäulen* (**Trinity Columns**), while another frequent theme is Marian devotion.

Console: Ornamental wall bracket designed to carry a projecting weight, which can be architectural or a statue etc. See also *Volutes*.

Crossing: The space where the nave, chancel and transepts of a church meet, in Austrian Baroque churches often surmounted by a cupola.

Danube School: (*Donauschule, Donaustil*) A term suggesting the romantic landscape effects seen in the work of its greatest practitioner, Albrecht Altdorfer (c 1480–1538); but other pictures included in this 'school' exhibit a grisly realism in their treatment of brutal scenes of the *Passion*, etc.

Fresco: Painting applied to wet plaster so that the colours sink into the wall. In a number of cases it has been possible to retrieve Gothic or Romanesque frescoes where they had been plastered or painted over in Baroque times.

Gallery: In descriptions of churches in the Guide, this means an intermediate storey running round the main body of the church, usually with arched openings on to the nave. In Baroque churches a gallery for the organ at the rear (organ loft) is common, and has sufficient space to accommodate a small choir.

Gesamtkunstwerk: Useful German term for which there is no satisfactory equivalent in English. It implies a unified work of art, i.e. one where all elements and genres have been symbiotically employed to create a cohesive overall effect. The interiors of many Baroque and Rococo churches are often *Gesamtkunstwerke* devoted to a particular theme, such as the celebration of the Virgin Mary.

Gothic: The Gothic style in ecclesiastical architecture was brought to

Austria from France by the Cistercian monks, whose earliest Gothic *Hall Church* (see below) may be seen at Lilienfeld (1202–30, see p 125). The chief characteristic of the style is the pointed arch, replacing the rounded arches of the Romanesque style. Another feature that reached great refinement in Austria, sometimes with local idiosyncracies, is the ribbed, net and star vault (see for instance Bartlmä Firtaler's work at Kötschach and Laas, p 351. Gothic features may still be seen not only in churches but also in *Burgen* and even burgher houses in Austrian towns, although the buildings have generally been subject to later alteration. Austria is particularly rich in **late Gothic** (c 1500–c 1540) architecture and artefacts, of which the many winged altarpieces in Upper Austria are outstanding examples. These are transitional works in that they already show individual features of the *Renaissance*, for example in the naturalistic treatment of faces and the use of perspective.

International Soft Style of Gothic. A later phase of Gothic, developed in the 1380s and lasting in Central Europe until the late 1430s. The style stresses elegance of line and soft forms, and its masters exhibited a clear preference for lyrical subject matter (e.g. *The Nativity*). It represents a significant individualisation of the more iconic Byzantium-influenced traditon of early Gothic.

Hall Church. German type of church design in which the nave and side-aisles are of equal height. The same principle applies to a **Hall Choir**.

Historicism: The 19C revival of historical styles in architecture (Historicism) was conceived in terms of religious and social allusion. The prime example of Historicism in

Austria is the Vienna Ringstraße, where each public building is designed with reference to a past ideal—the University in neo-Renaissance style symbolising Renaissance learning, the Parliament in Classical style symbolising Athenian democracy and so forth.

History Painting took inspiring historical subjects and also imitated the styles of previous eras. Although the style degenerated and provoked a fierce reaction (*Art Nouveau, Secession*) at the turn of the century, its best achievements have been re-evaluated in the 20C and have come to be seen for the magnificent works they often are.

Jugendstil: German designation for *Art Nouveau* and (partly) *Secession* (see above and below). The word means literally 'youth style'.

Keep: The principal tower of a castle (*Burg*), large enough to accommodate the inhabitants in time of siege. Also known as a **donjon**; in German 'Bergfried'.

Lunette: A semi-circular opening in an architectural construct. References in the Guide are usually to painted lunettes.

Mannerism: Generally the style current in Italy from Michelangelo to the end of the 16C. However, the term as applied to architecture has been stretched to include several different ideas (e.g. the work of Palladio or rigid Classicism). Its characteristics are said to be 'ease of manner, virtuosity, fluency or refinement', but also a tendency to use motifs in 'deliberate opposition to their original significance or context'. The great **Mausoleum** for Emperor Ferdinand II in Graz (see p 211) is said to be an example of Mannerism in the Austrian context. The application of the term in painting is less controversial.

Marmorsaal: The ceremonial hall of a Baroque palace etc. with marble clad walls.

Neo-classicism: In Austria a transition to neoclassicism appears around the time of the Enlightenment, the name of the so-called *Zopfstil* (1760–80), 'pigtail style' being a reference to its vertical ornamentation that vaguely resemble pigtails. However, the full-blooded neo-classical style in buildings comes under the Emperor Franz I (1792–1835), and is associated particularly with the work of Josef Kornhäusel. The architecture is often austere and is inspired by pure geometrical forms.

Oratory: A small chapel for private devotion, usually attached to the choir. In Austrian churches such chapels were generally for the use of the local lord or some other dignitary.

Pietà: (From the Italian for 'pity'). A representation of the weeping Virgin Mary holding in her lap the body of Christ (sometimes known as *The Lamentation of Christ*).

Pilaster: A shallow pier or rectangular column projecting only slightly from the wall and generally decorative rather than structural.

Putto: Italian for a male child, but in the context of the fine arts, one shown naked in Renaissance or (in Austria) especially in Baroque pictures, usually assisting at some transcendental scene involving saints, the Virgin Mary, etc.

Relief: Sculptural decoration embossed on a surface of stone or metal (usually bronze). **Intaglio** is an inverse form of the same, sunk into the surface, instead of standing proud of it.

Reliquary: Decorative holder for the **relics** of saints. In the Middle Ages there was a brisk trade in such relics and commissioners of churches were still acquiring them to raise the dignity of their foundations well into Baroque times.

Renaissance: Austria had an especially flourishing late Gothic art (see *Gothic* above), and the boundaries between this and Renaissance work are not very rigidly defined. In fact there is not a great deal of purely Renaissance ecclesiastical architecture in Austria, but many *Burgen* were extended or reached their most refined form in the Renaissance.

Retable: A superstructure at the rear of an altar or on its own pedestal behind the altar, usually with a carved central figure and painted wings. A decorated wall or screen rising behind an altar is known as a *reredos*. See also *Altarpiece* above.

Rococo: Florid, colourful and lush style emerging (1720–70) from Baroque, and associated with an exuberance of decoration in terms of stucco, frescoes, rocaille ornament, etc. In West Austria the influence of Bavarian Rococo can be seen, for example in Innsbruck in the work of the painter and craftsmen dynasty of the Asams, while the architecture of the Tyrolean Gumpp dynasty of architects owes more to Italian precedents in the High Baroque.

Romanesque: Austrian Romanesque shows a mixture of influences, of which the Bavarian (in construction) and the Lombardy (in decoration) are perhaps the most important. The usual basilical form with pillars, no transept and three parallel apses comes from Bavaria, while striking decorative effects (e.g. the crypt of the monastery church at Gurk, with its 100 marble columns, see p 338) are Lombardian. A special feature of the Austrian Romanesque which has survived is the large number of **charnel houses** with polygonal walls, sometimes also frescoes. Of those Romanesque frescoes that have survived, some show Byzantine influence, doubtless again absorbed via Northern Italy.

Rustication: Masonry in massive blocks (frequently undressed), almost always placed at the bottom of a building and designed to give it an imposing and formidable aspect.

Salomonic (or Solomonic) Column: A spirally fluted column in churches (supporting *baldachins* etc.), often called 'barley-sugar column' and modelled on the similar ones of St Peter's in Rome. The form is supposed to have been that of the columns of Solomon's temple.

Secession: The name alludes to a group of artists under the leadership of Gustav Klimt who 'seceded' from the officially sanctioned and very conservative Academy in Vienna in 1897. The **Vienna Secession** was influenced by *Art Nouveau* (see above) and developed a Secession style in the applied arts (*Wiener Werkstätte*, founded 1903, of which Josef Hoffmann was the leading light), and in painting, where Gustav Klimt, Carl Moll and others transformed the Viennese art scene. Notable Secession architecture includes a villa colony by Hoffmann, and the Secession exhibition hall itself, designed by Joseph Maria Olbrich. Otto Wagner made the designs for Vienna's rapid transit system that have left their mark on the city, but his most celebrated work is perhaps the Steinhof Church (see p 109).

Sgraffito: Monochrome decoration scratched on to wall plaster which is a feature of 16C burgher houses on the main squares of several Austrian towns. The design can be quite elaborate and often has a theme from Greek mythology.

Spandrel: The surface area between two adjacent arches (occasionally the surface of a vault between two adjacent ribs). The references in the Guide are to painted spandrels, typically portraits of the Fathers of the Church below a Baroque cupola. These are usually in **pendentives**, i.e. the concave spandrels leading from the angle of two walls to the base of a circular dome.

Stucco: Plasterwork used for decoration. In Austria, where stucco was brought to a high degree of refinement, the most remarkable effects are to be seen in churches (for example the stucco and plaster statuary of Johann Georg Üblher and others at Wilhering and Engelhartszell, see p 257 and p 277). Stucco was made from a mixture including lime and powdered marble.

Stucco lustro: The highly polished version used to imitate marble is sometimes called '*stucco lustro*'.

Transept: The transverse arms of a cruciform church, usually dividing the nave from the chancel.

Triumphal Arch: Originally a freestanding arch erected for commemorative purposes in antiquity. However, the form of the arch (i.e. with one large and two smaller doorways) became identified with the choir screen in medieval churches. References in the Guide are usually to choir or chancel arches painted with frescoes. A few Baroque Triumphal Arches on the Roman free-standing model were erected under Maria Theresia (e.g. in Innsbruck).

Trophy: In antiquity trophies were the memorials of victory of the Roman armies. As heaped up arms and armour trophies are a common decorative element of the Baroque.

Trompe l'oeil: Illusionist architectural effects making skilful use of perspective. *Trompe l'oeil* frescoes were often painted on church ceilings etc., and were a much favoured Baroque and Rococo form of decoration.

Tympanum: The triangular or segmental space enclosed by the mouldings of a pediment or the area between the lintel of a doorway and the arch above it. Most references in the Guide are to carved Gothic tympanums above the doorways of medieval churches. A **pediment** is a low pitched gable over a portico, door or window.

Vaulting: A masonry roof or ceiling constructed on the principle of the arch. A **groin vault** is produced by the intersection of two identical **tunnel vaults**. More commonly encountered in the churches covered by the Guide are **rib vaults** (consisting of arched diagonal ribs with lighter stone between them), **fan vaults** (fanning out from the top of a column), **net vaults** and **stellar vaults**,

whose names roughly describe their aspect, although late Gothic net vaults can look more like dense foliage. The last-named is also sometimes described as *reticulated*.

Volute: A spiral scroll, originally the main feature of an Ionic capital, but widely occurring as Baroque ornament, for example as the supports for *consoles* (see above).

Winged altar(piece): A carved and painted Gothic altarpiece usually consisting of a carved shrine at the centre and outer wings (usually painted panels) that can be opened or closed to show different cycles of scenes according to liturgical or feast day requirements. The base on which the altarpiece rests is called the *predella*, and is also painted with biblical scenes, saints, etc.

Some commonly occurring words

Bad: Bath, often occuring in place-names of spas (e.g. Bad Bleiberg, Badgastein, Bad Radkersburg etc.).

Burg: Castle, usually implying something more than a solely military function, for which the term **Festung** (fortress, citadel) may be used.

Freistadt: A city or town originally awarded its 'freedom' by the monarch (usually in the Middle Ages), i.e. the right to self-administration coupled with tax or trading privileges. Many of these privileges have survived in the context of modern administration (at least on paper). Special cases are Eisenstadt and Rust in Burgenland

(formerly Hungary), which were originally made constituents of the elective *Reichstag* (Diet) by the Hungarian king, and were recognised in 1926 (after the annexation of Burgenland to the Republic of Austria) as towns 'with their own status'.

Heuriger: tavern selling the wine of the current vintage only (see p 430).

Landtag: Provincial Parliament.

Rathaus: Town (or City) Hall.

Stift: Monastery, abbey or convent.

Tal: Valley

Turm: Tower.

Vorhof: the outer of two (or more) courtyards in a castle, monastery etc.

Index